of Hawai'i

Big Island of Hawai'i

8th Edition

The Most Complete Guide to Family Fun and Adventure!

Catherine Bridges Tarleton

Ulysses Press

Published by: Ulysses Press
P.O. Box 3440
Berkeley, CA 94703
www.ulyssespress.com

ISSN 1042-8062
ISBN 1-56975-381-4

Printed in Canada by Transcontinental Printing

10 9 8 7 6 5 4 3 2 1

Managing Editor: Claire Chun
Editor: Lily Chou
Editorial and Production: Katharine Allen, Claire Hutkins, Lisa Kester, James Meetze, Kaori Takee
Cartography: Pease Press
Cover Design: Leslie Henriques, Sarah Levin
Indexer: Sayre Van Young
Cover Photography: Ron Dahlquist (girl and father in water); Leslie Henriques (boy feeding dolphin); all other photos from photos.com

History section in Chapter 1 by John Penisten

Distributed in the United States by Publishers Group West and in Canada by Raincoast Books

Write to Us!

If in your travels you discover a spot that captures the spirit of the Big Island, or if you live in the region and have a favorite place to share, or if you just feel like expressing your views, write to us and we'll pass your note along to the author.

Ulysses Press
P.O. Box 3440
Berkeley, CA 94703
E-mail: readermail@ulyssespress.com

Acknowledgments

I am grateful to friends who shared their thoughts and experiences, and the many people who shared the stories of their enterprises islandwide. Thanks go to Christie Stilson for the opportunity/challenge, to previous author John Penisten for so thoroughly laying the groundwork and to Claire Chun and her team at Ulysses Press. Mahalo to Lona Lyons, Sue Young, Bob Nelson, Keoki Pelfrey and Dennis Michalske for their assistance and to Roxanne Pung, Claire Makahi and Aven Wright-McIntosh for their support at my "real" job. Always to Dwight, for his unflappable, almost unfathomable encouragement as befits the best traditions of Star Fleet.

It is my understanding that the ancient Hawaiians who lived here long before me did nothing without first saying a prayer to the relevant gods. No tree was cut for a canoe, no field planted, no voyage, battle or work of art begun without expressing thanks and requesting guidance. In that tradition, I would respectfully like to thank the appropriate deities for their help, and request proper guidance for this little book as its journey begins.

Catherine Bridges Tarleton
December 2003

Table of Contents

MAPS

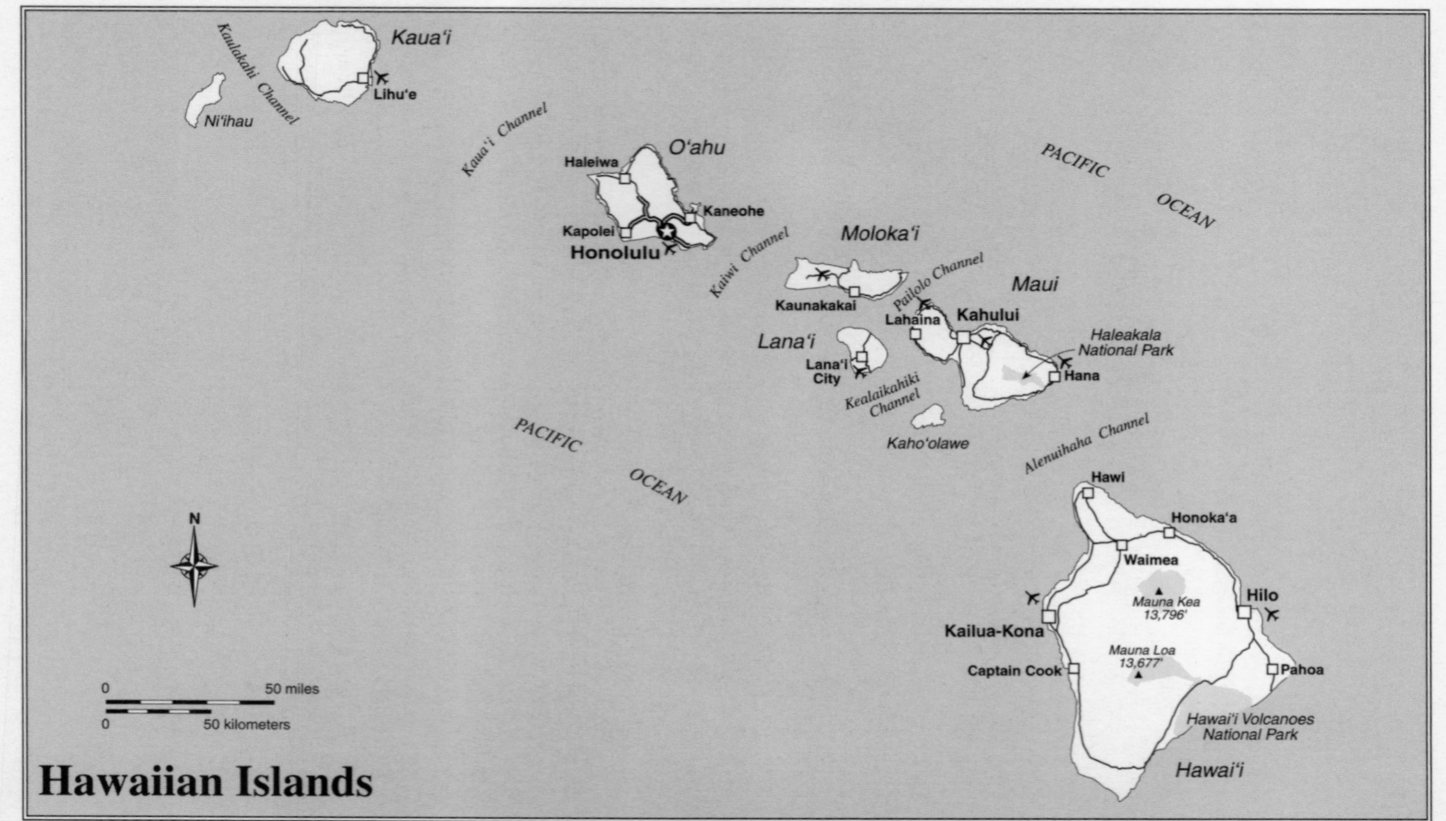

Hawaiian Islands

Preface

The eighth edition of *Paradise Family Guides: Big Island of Hawai'i* is completed during a time of conflict, where a nervous world looks at travel with more anxiety than anticipation. During times like these, the visitor industry has to ask itself some hard questions. How do we project and sell the concept of a carefree vacation in an idyllic setting when the world is such a mess? Is it right to even try?

Not only is it right, it is important. Tourism promotes peace between nations. Travel allows the traveler to see life from a different point of view, and for a time to walk a distance if not in someone else's shoes, at least along their sidewalks and trails. By engaging the senses in new and different ways, we grow as human beings. In the simple acts of seeing new country, tasting the food, listening to the music, feeling the earth beneath our feet, and smelling the regional roses as it were, we become more than we were at home. And by growing larger as individuals, we expand our boundaries to include others, perhaps even those who once were enemies.

A place like the Big Island presents unlimited opportunities for these kinds of experiences. Where else can you stand at the rim of an active volcano and in the same day walk through a rainforest, watch whales swim in the cool blue Pacific, or gaze at the stars from a mountain summit high above the atmosphere? Our island is one of dramatic contrast—from the mountains to the sea, from luxury to wilderness, lavaflow to waterfall, destruction to creation. This is the Big Island on a daily basis, and it helps make us who we are.

The Big Island is an example of peace through (not in spite of) diversity. Hawai`i is volcanic rock, the most isolated land on earth, thousands of miles from any continent, and at the mercy of lava, tsunami, storms and acts of war a world away. Our people came from many places, as Polynesian explorers, New England missionaries,

American whalers, European traders, Chinese, Japanese, Korean, Filipino and Portuguese indentured laborers, multi-cultural retirees, hoteliers, millionaires, soldiers and organic herb farmers. But they all had one thing in common: they wanted a better life. And they found a way to make it work.

They did it, and do it still, not by closing doors and building walls, but by opening up their world, embracing the people who came next, and joining together to build something greater for all. People here learned a long time ago to combine their ethnic resources like their lunch pails and make a better meal as a result. They are an example for the world. They are diversity in action.

When you visit us, see the volcano by all means. Play golf. Swim and enjoy the ocean with your kids. Eat our food and drink a toast to our sunsets. At the same time, be aware that the Big Island's people are its greatest strength, its most treasured asset. This little book is dedicated to them, with gratitude, admiration and humility.

People make war; people make peace.

Catherine Bridges Tarleton
December 2003

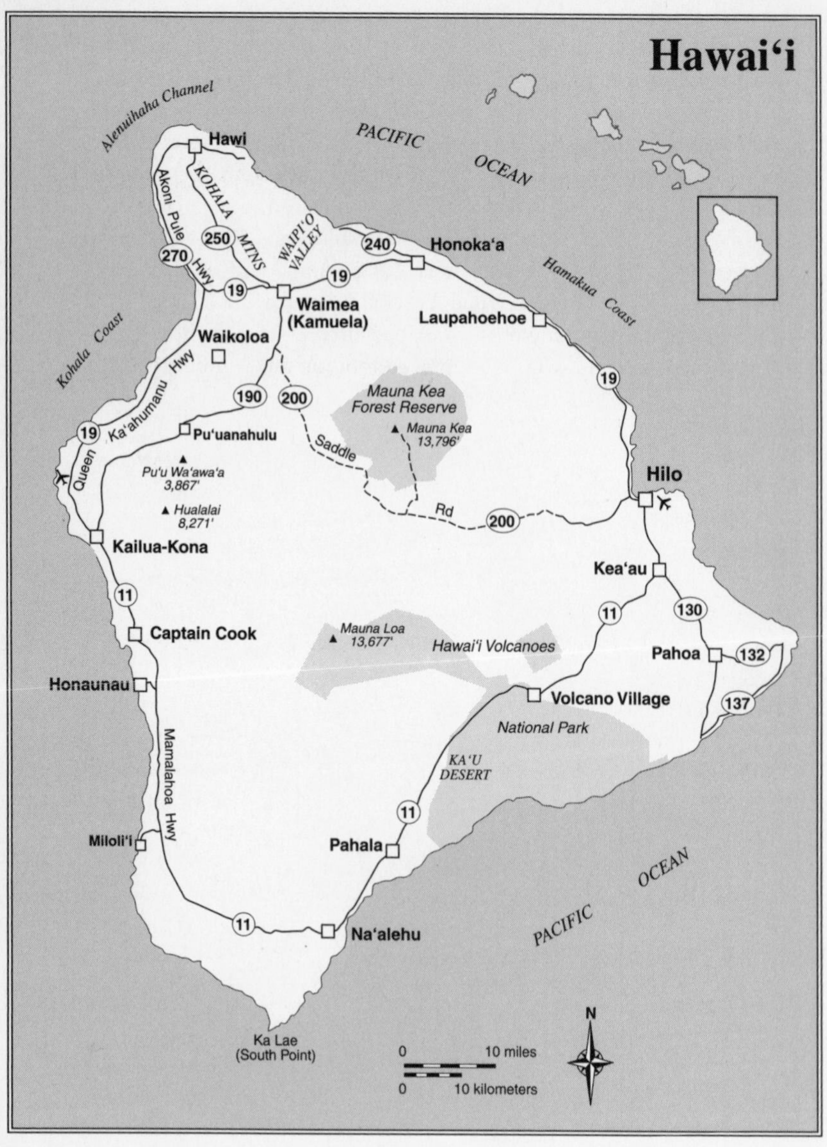

Hawai'i
Alenuihaha Channel
PACIFIC OCEAN
Hawi
KOHALA MTNS
Akoni Pule Hwy
250
270
19
WAIPI'O VALLEY
240
Honoka'a
Hamakua Coast
19
Waimea (Kamuela)
Laupahoehoe
Kohala Coast
Waikoloa
Queen Ka'ahumanu Hwy
190
200
Mauna Kea Forest Reserve
Mauna Kea 13,796'
Pu'uanahulu
Saddle Rd
Pu'u Wa'awa'a 3,867'
Hualalai 8,271'
Hilo
200
Kailua-Kona
Kea'au
11
130
Captain Cook
Mauna Loa 13,677'
Hawai'i Volcanoes National Park
Pahoa
132
Honaunau
Volcano Village
137
Mamalahoa Hwy
KA'U DESERT
Miloli'i
Pahala
PACIFIC OCEAN
Na'alehu
Ka Lae (South Point)
0 10 miles
0 10 kilometers
N

CHAPTER 1

Family Paradise

The Big Island's Best Bets

Attraction Unless of course you have an active volcano in your own back yard, Volcanoes National Park is a rare and awesome experience. In addition to the active eruption, there are exploration hikes and nature trails, a cool museum on the rim of Halema'uma'u Crater, Hawaiian cultural performances and programs at Volcano Art Center and a Junior Ranger Program for kids 5–12.

Best Way to See the Volcano on a Tight Schedule A helicopter flightseeing tour

Best Attraction #2 The Beach. Isn't this why you come to Hawai'i? For almost any kind of beach-goer, from sun worshipper to windsurfer, we recommend Hapuna Beach State Park on the Kohala Coast. Wide white sand, reliable conditions, picnic pavilions, ample parking, restrooms, showers and a snack bar make this the Best Bet for Big Island beaches.

Best Sunset Cocktails The Gazebo Bar, Mauna Kea Beach Hotel. OK, this guide certainly does not promote drinking as a pastime, especially drinking and driving and especially with kids along, *but* just in case your Hawaiian fantasy is to sip one of those fancy libations in the tall glass with a paper umbrella, while waiting for the elusive green flash on the horizon just as the sun sinks into it...you've come to the right place.

Best Ocean Activity Whale watching

Best New Ocean Activity A trip in a see-through kayak.

Best Free (or Nearly Free) Things to Do • Volcanoes National Park • Beach • Lapakahi State Park and Pu'ukohola Heiau National Historic Site • Pu'uhonua o Honaunau Place of Refuge • Petroglyph trail at

'Anaeho'omalu • Hula show at the Kings' Shops, Waikoloa • A stroll through Liliuokalani Park and along Banyan Drive in Hilo • A drive to Kapa'au to see the King Kamehameha statue and the end of the road at Pololu and/or a drive through Honoka'a to Kukuihaele and the Waipi'o Valley Overlook • Hilo Farmers' Market • Akaka Falls State Park • Amy B.H. Greenwell Ethnobotanical Garden in Kona • Ahuena Heiau, Mokuaikaua Church and Hulihe'e Palace in Kona
Most Beautiful Beach Kaunaoa Bay Beach (Mauna Kea Beach)
Scenic Views Pololu Valley Overlook at the end of the road in North Kohala, and the Waipi'o Valley Overlook at the opposite end in the Hamakua District
Place for Hikes and Explorations Volcanoes National Park
Easy Hike Across the floor of steaming Kilauea Iki Crater
Moderate Hike Kipuka Puaulu/Bird Park
Challenging Hike for Experienced Backpackers 1) Mauna Loa Summit Trail, Hawai'i Volcanoes National Park, a strenuous 36.6

VOLCANOES FROM THE SKY

It's a long drive to Volcanoes National Park, two hours from either Kona along the southern route or the Kohala Coast resorts along the northern route. Once you enter the park and make stops at the visitors center and interesting sites along the way, it's another hour before you reach the eruption itself. Don't get us wrong, this is a most worthwhile trip, but if time is limited and you want to do it all, spend the extra dollars and take the flightseeing tour. This is absolutely the best way to see the Big Island's most spectacular show.

Most "birds" take up to six passengers in comfortable, air-conditioned cabins, some with stereo headsets and music synchronized with the flight path. The ride is smooth and the view is awesome. Skilled pilots can position you just above the most current lava flow activity, where you may see red lava emerge from the earth's core and flow seaward, where its encounter with the ocean forms a giant column of steam. You'll soar over inaccessible waterfalls and Eden-like valleys, across lush tropical forests and remote rocky terrain. It's like being in a movie. Everything depends on the weather, and conditions change constantly. Several local helicopter companies offer similar trips at competitive prices. Ask your hotel concierge.

A word about photographs. If you're a fanatic or a pro, by all means, put the lens up to your face and click away. If not, put the camera down and take in everything with your own two eyes. A photograph can barely capture the dramatic experience you're about to undertake, and too much time looking through the lens could make you nauseous. Some of the companies offer multi-camera videos of your flight, starring you and your family. Take 'em up on it.

miles, 4-day hike to mountain summit; 2) Waipi'o and Waimanu Valley Trail (Muliwai), Hamakua Coast, a difficult 2-3 day wilderness backpacking trip

Adventures on Land Kohala Mountain Kayak Cruise through the canals, flumes and caves of the irrigation ditch system of North Kohala's old sugar plantations; or a trail ride through Pololu Valley on mule-back, with Hawai'i Forest & Trail Outfitters

Way to See the Stars Weekly (free!) star-gazing astronomy program at the Onizuka Center for International Astronomy at 9,200-foot level of Mauna Kea.

Must-see Cultural Tour A self-guided walking tour through Pu'uhonua o Honaunau Place of Refuge, South Kona Coast. Also Lapakahi State Park on Highway 19 in North Kohala and Pu'ukohola Heiau at Kawaihae

Cultural Events 1) The annual spring Merrie Monarch Hula Festival, Hilo (tickets are hard to get but the town is jam-packed with related cultural festivities). 2) Any of the series of Na Mea Hawai'i Hula Kahiko performances, free to the public, Volcano Art Center, Hawai'i Volcanoes National Park. Also the myriad Aloha Festivals food events, parades, concerts, hula performances and many other happenings islandwide, annually in September and the Kona Coffee Festival in November

Scenic Drives 1) Kawaihae to North Kohala (Hawi and Kapa'au), to Pololu Lookout, back via the Mountain Road to Waimea. Then, Waimea to Honoka'a, Kukuihaele and Waipi'o Valley Overlook; 2) Kona Coffee Country, including Pu'uhonua o Honaunau Place of Refuge, then back through Holualoa and the upper road; 3) Hamakua Coastline to Hilo, stopping at Laupahoehoe Beach Park, Akaka Falls and Onomea Scenic Drive

Golf Course A toss-up—the Mauna Kea Golf course, Mauna Kea Resort, ranked among "America's 100 Greatest" and "Hawai'i's Finest" by *Golf Digest*, or the Francis I'i Brown South Course at Mauna Lani Resort, equally acclaimed by the same magazine for its 17th hole, which it ranks as a "Pearl of the Pacific"

Golf Course on a Budget The Robert Trent Jones, Jr., course in Waikoloa Village

Best Resort for Kid Stuff Hilton Waikoloa Village, Kohala Coast

Chocolate Big Island Candies in Hilo or Kona; Kailua Candy Company in Kona

Family-friendly Restaurants Denny's in Kona; Don's Grill or Ken's Pancake House in Hilo; Paniolo Country Inn in Waimea; Waiakea Center Food Court in Hilo; Kings' Shops in Waikoloa Beach Resort

Macadamia Nuts and Confections Mauna Loa Macadamia Nut Farms in Hilo; Mac Pie in Kona

The Big Island

If you've ever had a cup of Kona coffee, you've tasted the Big Island. Robust, fortifying, indulgent, luxurious, warm, fragrant, complex, comforting. Once you've taken it in, your concept of coffee changes. Your expectations are greater, your tastes are more experienced and your life is a little richer.

The Big Island is all those things. The Big Island is the Big Island because it's big. Too big, too diverse to be characterized by only one name. Officially, it is "Hawai'i," the same name as the state. And despite the best efforts of PR persons and tourism bureaucrats to put a more glamorous spin on the name (the Orchid Island, the Volcano Island and, most recently, the Healing Island), "Big Island" is the one that stuck and stayed over the years—just like a lot of folks who live here.

The Big Island is home to the rainiest city in the U.S. (Hilo), its highest mountain (Mauna Kea, 13,796 feet measured from sea level) and the country's southernmost point at Ka Lae. It grows the only American coffee, has the largest non–long distance calling area, the most ethnically diverse population per capita, and the highest gas prices ($2.27 regular), and is the largest consumer of Spam. It is the largest of Hawai'i's main islands, larger than O'ahu, Maui, Kaua'i, Moloka'i, Lana'i, Kaho'olawe and Ni'ihau put together. It is also the youngest geologically, with new land still under construction thanks to ongoing volcanic activity. In fact it is the *hanai* (adopted) mother of Hawai'i's newest island, Lo'ihi Seamount, forming underwater off the southern coastline.

Historically, it was the first island sighted by Polynesian explorers, who perhaps were guided by the steam clouds from Mauna Loa's eruption at the time. It is the birthplace and the final (secret) resting place of King Kamehameha the Great, the first *ali'i* (chief) to conquer, unite and rule all the main islands as one kingdom. This is the place where Captain Cook landed in 1778 and was mistaken for the god Lono, and where he was killed. This is where missionaries built their first commissioned church in the islands, and where Queen Ka'ahumanu first broke the ancient *kapu* (taboo) system. These events forever changed the course of Hawai'i's history.

The Big Island is internationally known for Kona coffee, thanks to the caffeine wars of the 1990s, and also in the last century it was reportedly the *pakalolo* (marijuana) capitol of the state. Kilauea Volcano, Hawai'i's first big attraction, is located in a remote and desolate area, miles from anything that looks like tourism. The expensive mega-resorts for the rich and famous are set along the Kohala Coast, surrounded by inhospitably bleak lava rock. Gray, rainy Hilo hosts the world's brightest hula talents during the annual Merrie Monarch Festival. In Kona, modern athletes compete in the Ironman World Championship Triathlon and the Hawaiian International Billfish Tournament while down the coast at the restored village of Pu'uhonua o Honaunau, stone-age crafts are taught and practiced. Cowboys ride and rope on horseback in Waimea while soldiers maneuver tanks at Pohakuloa. Chefs prepare Maine lobsters from Kona and Japanese Kobe-style beef from Kohala. In hospitals, advanced medical machines treat patients side by side with "healing touch" practitioners, acupuncturists and *lomi lomi* massage therapists. On the same night, a scientist studies the constellations from the international astronomy community at Mauna Kea's summit, while far below a navigator charts the course for his canoe. The Big Island is a place that brings contradictions together, a place of amazing change.

But to truly take it in and appreciate the scope of the Big Island, you have to let go of your preconceptions. As your plane approaches Kona International Airport, close your eyes and picture Hawai'i. Palm trees, white beaches, tropical flowers, mai tais and hula dancers. Now open your eyes. Oops, what happened? There's nothing here that resembles the common vision of Hawai'i. As far as you can see, it's rock—black, empty, lifeless lava rock, like a gigantic parking lot half-bulldozed by Godzilla then abandoned. Take heart, this is just a tease, and it's just the beginning. The Big Island is good at teasing. It's never what you expect, but it always exceeds your expectations in some way. We suggest you approach your Big Island vacation with a plan, but not an itinerary, and allow some time to be swept away by your fantasy. Whatever you're looking for, whether it's beach time, great golf, ocean adventures, hiking, biking, history or just something new to eat, you'll find it.

History of the Big Island

The history of Hawai'i is generally recognized as covering four periods. The first is the prehistoric period of "The Early Hawaiians" before the Western world stumbled upon the islands in 1778, thus exposing them to influences that would change them forever. This era is marked by the discovery of the islands by the first Polynesian migrants, the establishing of their colonies in Hawai'i, their adaptation to the unique natural world of the islands, and their existence in isolation from the rest of the world.

The second period, "Hawai'i Revealed to the Western World," spans the accidental discovery of the islands by the great British explorer, Captain James Cook, in 1778. This period covers the rise to power of Kamehameha, his conquest of all the islands of Hawai'i by 1796, the founding of the Hawaiian monarchy and the coming of traders, missionaries and settlers.

The third period, "Hawai'i under the Monarchy," covers the period from 1810–1900, the Hawaiian Kingdom from Kamehameha the Great through the succeeding Kamehamehas, King Lunalilo, King Kalakaua and the last reigning Hawaiian monarch, Queen Liliuokalani. The period includes the overthrow and deposing of the monarchy, the founding of the Republic of Hawai'i and annexation by the United States in 1898, and the islands' organization as the Territory of Hawai'i in 1900.

The fourth period of Hawai'i's history, "Hawai'i in the Modern Era," covers the period from 1900 on to the present and the rise of Hawai'i's agricultural economy, its growing importance as a strategic port and trade center in the Pacific, its pivotal role in World War II, and its admission into the Union as the Fiftieth State in 1959. After statehood, there was a rapid assimilation into the American mainstream and the current age of electronics, high-tech communications, computers, jet transportation and mass tourism.

THE EARLY HAWAIIANS It's generally thought by scholars and historians that the Hawaiian Islands were first settled by Polynesian migrants several hundred years before Columbus discovered America and before the Western world embarked on its great age of discovery and world exploration. The first settlers of Hawai'i probably came from the Marquesas Islands, a group of islands near today's French Polynesia, directly south of Hawai'i over thousands of miles of open ocean. These first settlers probably arrived in Hawai'i around 500 A.D. Some of Hawai'i's oldest archaeological sites date back to that era. Later settlers probably came from the Society Islands, also part of today's French Polynesia.

These early Polynesians were master navigators and sailors in a world dominated by the Pacific Ocean. They originated in Southeast Asia and Indonesia in times past and spread across the Pacific, island-hopping in their simple double-hulled sailing canoes, settling the islands along the way. They crossed vast stretches of open ocean, using only their knowledge of ocean currents, winds and stars to navigate. That fact is undisputed by academics. What is disputed are the routes, times and other details as to when this all happened.

Some believe that the first Polynesians made landfall along the southern shore of the Big Island of Hawai'i. It's reasoned that the Big Island volcanoes, Mauna Kea and Mauna Loa, would have been the first visible landmarks from the south. The southern shore of the Big Island would have made for a natural landing site after a long sail across the ocean. Tradition has it that Ka Lae, South Point, is where those first migrants stepped ashore in Hawai'i. From there, over succeeding generations of migrants, they spread among all the islands of Hawai'i.

The first Polynesian settlers arrived in a Hawai'i that was uninhabited by humans and an undisturbed tropical ecosystem. The islands had evolved through undersea volcanic action over the eons. As the islands grew, finally reaching above the ocean's surface, they developed a unique indigenous ecosystem of flora and fauna. Thousands of species arrived by wind and ocean current to become established and adapt to the unique island environment. Everything from the tiniest insects and plants to the tallest rainforest trees had evolved in complete isolation.

These first settlers of Hawai'i learned to live in harmony with the islands' natural balance of life. These original Hawaiians lived a communal self-sufficient lifestyle, following a rigid system of beliefs in which their lives were controlled by supernatural gods of the earth, sea and sky. Their existence was regimented by a social and political system known as the *kapu* system, overseen by the ruling *ali'i* (royalty), *kahuna* (priests and sorcerers) and a warrior class that controlled the commoners. The early Hawaiian's lifestyle revolved around the daily events of fishing, hunting, farming and gathering, close-knit village and clan life, and adherence to the strict ceremonial regulations of the *kapu* system. Violations of the system carried severe penalties, often death, at the hands of the ruling *ali'i* and *kahuna*.

Each island had its ruling *ali'i* (chiefs) and their clans who ruled by fear and intimidation. There was continuous maneuvering for supremacy on each island. Civil war was common practice among ruling *ali'i* and their warrior clans. Kamehameha the Great, from Kohala on the Big Island of Hawai'i, was known as a fierce warrior and became a prominent ruling chief on the Big Island. Around 1790, Kamehameha consolidated his power on the island of Hawai'i by defeating rival chiefs in battle. He then went on to raise a large army, and over the next few years conquered the islands of Maui, Moloka'i and O'ahu. He attempted to conquer Kaua'i, but was turned back by a storm at sea. However, in 1810, Kaua'i recognized Kamehameha's rule. He was then able to unite the islands and greatly influenced the course of Hawaiian history.

CAPTAIN COOK It was Captain James Cook, the famed British explorer of the Pacific, who was the first Westerner to land in Hawai'i in January 1778. Cook was en route to the west coast of North America in search of the fabled Strait of Anian, a passage through North America that would shorten the voyage from Europe to Asia. While en route from Tahiti, Cook stumbled upon Hawai'i, sighting the islands of Kaua'i and O'ahu. He made his first landfall at Kaua'i. Cook named the group the Sandwich Islands in honor of his friend and patron, the Earl of Sandwich, then First Lord of the British Admiralty.

He spent a fortnight there but did not visit any of the other islands of the group. Cook's men traded nails and bits of iron with the Hawaiians for fresh supplies of pork, fish, fowl, sweet potato, taro, yam and water. With his ships, *Resolution* and *Discovery*, Cook sailed on to North America to continue his explorations.

After spending the next eight months exploring North America's west coast, Cook's party returned to Hawai'i with the intention of wintering there to refit and re-provision. They made the north coast of Maui in November 1778, and Cook made it a point to sail leisurely through the Hawaiian group during the next few weeks, learning what he could about the people of Hawai'i.

At the various stops along the way, Cook took several of the Hawaiian chiefs aboard his ship to exchange gifts and courtesies. One of Cook's guests was the then-obscure chief Kamehameha from the Big Island. Little did these two men know at their casual meeting then that, between them, they would bring about incredible changes upon Hawai'i that would have a lingering impact today.

On January 17, 1779, the *Resolution* and the *Discovery* anchored in Kealakekua Bay on the Kona Coast of the Big Island. When Cook landed, he was taken to a *heiau* (temple) where he underwent a religious ceremony recognizing him as the incarnation of Lono, the Hawaiian god of the *makahiki* (harvest) season. The Hawaiians believed that with Cook's arrival at such an auspicious time, he indeed was the revered god, Lono.

Having refit and resupplied their ships, Cook's party set sail along the Kona Coast on February 4. Unfortunately, a storm off the Kohala Coast damaged the mast of the *Resolution* and the group turned back to the safety of Kealakekua Bay. It was a fateful decision.

On February 13 while Cook's group was tending to repairs, various altercations arose between Cook's men and the Hawaiians. The next morning, it was discovered that a small boat from the *Discovery* had been stolen. Cook intended to get it back and landed with an armed marine guard. He planned to take the chief hostage until the boat was returned, a plan that had worked in previous such incidents with the Polynesians.

With Cook and his armed guards on the shore and a large restless crowd of Hawaiians armed with daggers, clubs and spears, the situation became quite tense. The Hawaiians were alarmed at the hostile intent of Lono and his armed guard. Word came that another chief had been killed by a shot from another boat.

The Hawaiians now became visibly angered and made threatening advances toward the Cook party. Cook ordered his men to withdraw to the small boats on the shore. In the heated exchange, a Hawaiian threw his dagger at Cook, who in turn fired one barrel of his gun, which injured no one but angered the crowd more. Cook fired his second barrel and killed a Hawaiian. At that point, Cook's guards opened fire and a general melee broke out. Cook apparently turned to run to the boats but was struck down with a club and stabbed in the back with a dagger. He fell into the water and died on the spot.

And so the world's foremost explorer of the Pacific met a tragic and untimely death in a place he introduced to the world. Today, a monument stands on the shore of Kealakekua Bay on the Kona Coast marking the exact spot where Captain James Cook met his fate.

HAWAI'I UNDER THE MONARCHY Kamehameha (The Lonely One) was born in Kohala on the Big Island of Hawai'i about 1758. Although his parents were of noble rank, he was not in a direct line of succession to an *ali'i* position. Kamehameha grew up to be a fierce warrior noted for his tenaciousness, strength and intelligence.

It is somewhat ironic that much of the history of today's Hawai'i is inextricably linked to the Big Island, the youngest and still growing member of the archipelago. And the history of early Hawai'i was affected by one man, Kamehameha the Great, a Big Island native son.

The Hawai'i of the period was marked by civil war among the individual island chiefs and kings. And even on the Big Island, there was civil war among the chiefs who vied for dominance. Some chiefs from the Kona district, fearful of losing their lands under a new leading chief, asked Kamehameha to be their leader. Kamehameha had an ambition to conquer the Big Island and all of Hawai'i and unite the islands under one rule.

The 1780s saw the Big Island embroiled in civil war between Kamehameha of Kona-Kohala, Keawemauhili of Puna, Keoua of Ka'u, and Kahekili, king of neighboring Maui Island. In 1790–1791, Kamehameha consulted a prophet from Kaua'i, Kapoukahi, who advised him that he would conquer all the islands if he built a large temple to his family war god, Ku-ka-ili-moku.

And so it came to be that Kamehameha did build his temple, Pu'ukohola Heiau (Hill of the Whale), located on a hill above Kawaihae Bay, Kohala, in 1791 and launched his rendezvous with destiny. Kamehameha's plans to conquer Hawai'i were primarily hindered at this time by his cousin, Keoua Ku'ahu'ula, his last major Big Island rival. Kamehameha invited Ku'ahu'ula to his temple dedication to make peace and Ku'ahu'ula willingly accepted. As Ku'ahu'ula and his companions landed on the beach below the *heiau*, Kamehameha's warriors swept down and killed them all. Ku'ahu'ula's body was carried up to the temple and was offered as the principal sacrifice to Kamehameha's war god.

After Keoua Ku'ahu'ula's death, virtually all opposition on the Big Island to Kamehameha ended and the prophecy began to be fulfilled. By 1794, Kamehameha had conquered Maui, Moloka'i and Lana'i, and in 1795, the island of O'ahu. It was little wonder that he became known as Kamehameha the Great and established his kingdom over most of the islands of Hawai'i. In 1796, an attempted invasion of Kaua'i was disrupted by a storm. It wasn't until 1810, through an agreement with its king, that Kaua'i came under Kamehameha's control. Thus Kaua'i and nearby Ni'ihau have the distinction of being the only Hawaiian Islands not conquered in battle by Kamehameha.

However, Kamehameha did fulfill the prophecy and united all the Hawaiian Islands under one kingdom. Kamehameha the Great ruled his realm from Kailua on the Kona Coast until his death in 1819. He strictly observed the ancient religion of the Hawaiians and served as the official guardian of the war god that had brought him success in his conquests of Hawai'i.

Prior to his death, Kamehameha the Great had little idea of the impending changes that were about to take place in his Hawai'i. Since the discovery of Hawai'i by the Western world in 1778, the islands were increasingly exposed to an influx of traders, explorers, settlers and, in 1820 just after Kamehameha's death, the arrival of the first of many New England Congregational and Presbyterian missionaries. All of these Westerners were to bring about significant changes over the coming generations as Hawai'i was forced into a world of which it knew nothing when it was "discovered" in 1778.

Soon after Kamehameha the Great's death, his son and successor, Liholiho, overthrew the *kapu* system and belief in the old Hawaiian religion. During this period in the early 1820s, the Christian missionaries, traders and other foreigners who ventured into the islands did so at an opportune time. They easily established footholds and through their various efforts gained power and influence. Contacts with the Western world increased, and by the early 1840s the Kingdom of Hawai'i was recognized by the United States, France and Great Britain.

In 1824, after just five years of rule, Kamehameha II, along with his Queen, Kamamalu, traveled to London, England. While on the trip, they both contracted measles and died within a few days of each other.

A second son of Kamehameha the Great, Kauikeaouli, was soon proclaimed King and took the title of Kamehameha III. During his 30-year reign, the kingdom of Hawai'i increased in stature and importance. Honolulu grew from a small village to an important and strategic trading and naval port, attracting interest from the world's powers.

During Kamehameha II's reign, in 1840, Hawai'i's political system was transformed from an absolute to a constitutional monarchy.

Alexander Liholiho became Kamehameha IV, succeeding Kamehameha III after his death. Alexander Liholiho was a grandson of Kamehameha the Great and ruled from 1855–1863. He and his wife, Queen Emma, were greatly concerned with the general welfare of the Hawaiian people. One of their greatest accomplishments was the founding of Queen's Hospital.

Kamehameha IV was succeeded by his brother, Lot, who became Kamehameha V. Lot reigned from 1863–1872, and was to be the last of the Kamehamehas to rule the Hawaiian Kingdom established by his grandfather, King Kamehameha the Great. During this time there were various political struggles over the constitution between those wanting to limit democracy and strengthen the monarchy's power and those wanting to increase democratic measures and limit the monarch's powers.

With the death of Kamehameha V, the line of direct descendants of Kamehameha the Great ended, and the legislature, after a popular vote was conducted, confirmed William Charles Lunalilo as king. However, Lunalilo's reign was to be the shortest of any Hawaiian monarch, only one year.

The legislature set about electing a new king and chose David Kalakaua as successor. But supporters of former Queen Emma, widow of Kamehameha IV, rose up in anger with the announcement and sparked general disorder and riot. Order was finally restored by British and American troops that came ashore from ships in the harbor. King Kalakaua was inaugurated as the seventh monarch of the Hawaiian Kingdom on February 13, 1874.

King Kalakaua ruled from 1874–1891. Kalakaua continued negotiations begun earlier with the United States and in 1875 completed a treaty of reciprocity between the two nations. The treaty assured Hawai'i a market for its sugar in the United States and upon its renewal in 1887, the U.S. secured the exclusive use of Pearl Harbor in Honolulu as a coaling station for its navy.

Kalakaua, known as the Merry Monarch for his love of the hula (which the missionaries had long sought to ban), luaus and social gatherings, had a stormy political reign. The American businessmen who controlled much of Hawai'i's commerce and trade, as well as the sugar industry, saw Kalakaua as an obstruction to their plans. With his affinity for the hula and attempts to revive Hawaiian culture and traditions, they saw him as someone who was stirring up native Hawaiians against non-Hawaiians. Among Kalakaua's major accomplishments was the construction of Iolani Palace in 1882 in Honolulu.

In 1887, through crafty political intrigue, Kalakaua was forced to accept a new constitution. It was called the Bayonet Constitution because it was imposed by force, and took many of the king's powers away. He could no longer appoint the House of Nobles and no longer had absolute veto power, and the king's cabinet became responsible to the legislature and not to the king. This effectively limited the king's powers. The new constitution also imposed new voting rights for all male residents of the Kingdom, thus giving foreigners the right to vote. At the same time, it set up a property qualification in order to vote. This stipulation effectively reduced the power of Hawaiians in the political life of the Kingdom and increased the control of resident foreign businessmen. The loss of his royal powers greatly affected Kalakaua. He died during a visit to San Francisco in 1891 and was succeeded by his sister, Liliuokalani, who became queen.

Queen Liliuokalani was to be Hawai'i's last monarch. She reigned from 1891–1893, and made great efforts to eliminate the restrictions that had been imposed on the monarchy and had reduced the participation of Hawaiians in their own government. In 1892, she attempted to proclaim another constitution to restore the monarchy's powers. This action led her opponents, mostly American businessmen, to stage a bloodless "revolution." On January 17, 1893, with the assistance of U.S. marines from the U.S.S. *Boston* anchored in Honolulu Harbor and with the support of the resident U.S. minister, Queen Liliuokalani was deposed and a provisional government was formed. The Hawaiian monarchy had effectively ended.

During the rise of the monarchy, sugar, which was first grown commercially in Hawai'i in 1835, became the kingdom's principal industry with large tracts of land developed into plantations. In the early years, the cultivation, harvesting and processing of sugar was labor-intensive and the sugar planters needed laborers. Throughout the 19th century the native Hawaiian population declined from about 85,000 in 1850 to some 40,000 in 1890. This was due in part to such things as the introduction of Western disease and the loss of many of its youth to the whaling ship industry in the 1840s. In the last half of the 19th century, the Hawaiian government began allowing the importation of foreign laborers to support the increasingly important sugar industry. Thus, the great waves of immigration began, with large numbers of Chinese, Portuguese, Japanese, Koreans and Filipinos brought in to work the plantations, often under harsh conditions and standards. Labor immigration continued into the early 1900s and to an extent still continues today. From these mixed ethnic groups came Hawai'i's label as a cosmopolitan, multi-ethnic, melting pot of diverse peoples.

HAWAI'I IN THE MODERN ERA The new provisional government, under the leadership of Sanford Ballard Dole, requested annexation by the United States, but was turned down by President Grover Cleveland. The leaders of the revolution then declared Hawai'i a

Republic and Dole was proclaimed president on July 4, 1894. After repeated efforts, the islands were formally annexed as a territory of the United States in August 1898.

The early 1900s in Hawai'i were years of relative peace and development. Hawai'i burst upon the American consciousness once again on the morning of Sunday, December 7, 1941, when Japan attacked Pearl Harbor. In one quick change of scene, Hawai'i entered the stage to play a pivotal role in the tragic drama that was World War II in the Pacific. Like the rest of post-war America, Hawai'i was on the threshold of even greater social, cultural and economic development. The post-war years have seen Hawai'i grow tremendously. Hawai'i's admission to the Union as the 50th state in 1959 was recognition of its achievements and future potential.

In 1993, on the centennial observance of Queen Liliuokalani's overthrow by American interests, the U.S. Congress officially offered an apology for the overthrow of the sovereign government of Hawai'i and recognized the act as illegal. Various native Hawaiian groups and organizations have long been pushing for such congressional action to recognize the Hawaiian sovereignty movement, a step toward reestablishing a sovereign Hawaiian nation and reclaiming native Hawaiian land rights. The next few years will no doubt be dramatic as the Hawaiians decide for themselves what directions and results are to be expected from the sovereignty movement.

Hawaiian Language

One of the more positive things the early missionaries did for Hawai'i was to standardize the ancient spoken language into an alphabet and system of writing. Until then, Hawaiian was a spoken language only. A member of the Polynesian language family, Hawaiian is very similar to Tahitian and other Pacific Island languages and dialects.

The written Hawaiian language has an alphabet of twelve letters: five vowels (a, e, i, o, u) and seven consonants (h, k, l, m, n, p, w). Syllables are made up of one, two or three letters. Every syllable in a word is pronounced. Every syllable ends in a vowel, so every word ends in a vowel. For example, look at the word "Ho/no/lu/lu." Each syllable contains two letters, a consonant and a vowel. Each syllable is pronounced and each ends with a vowel sound.

The vowels are pronounced as follows:

a—Say "ah" (aloha)
e—Hey (lei)
i—See (Waikiki)
o—Oh no (aloha)
u—Ooo la la (luau)

Some vowel combinations resemble diphthongs and are pronounced as combination sounds:

ai and *ae*—Aye aye sir—Waikiki, Kawaihae (kah-wye-high)
ao and *au*—Powwow (luau)
ei—hay (lei)
oe—boy (aloha oe)

The accent generally falls on the next to last syllable (as in "Honolulu"), although some words are evenly accented (as in "Waikiki"). The *okina* (') is used to indicate a glottal stop, or pause, between sounds. This may have been an indicator that a *k* sound found in other Polynesian dialects has disappeared in Hawaiian usage. Where this mark appears, the accent falls on the preceding vowel, as in the following: *pu'u* (poo-oo; hill), *ali'i* (ah-lee-ee; chief) or *a'a* (ah-ah; rough lava).

The consonants are pronounced as they are in English, except for *w*, which is sounded as a *v* if it introduces the last syllable of a word. Examples are the famous Polynesian ceremonial drink, *awa* (actually pronounced "ava"), and the area on O'ahu called Ewa (pronounced "Ehva").

The name "Hawai'i" is still under debate. Although it introduces the next-to-last syllable, many people insist that the *v* sound prevails. Likewise, the glottal stop is often glossed over. (Don't be concerned with perfect pronunciation on this word because someone is going to disagree with you no matter what you say. However, you can avoid sounding too much like a *malihini* (stranger) by avoiding the pronunciation "hah-wye-yah." That just doesn't work.)

It's going to be easy for you to learn and try using a few words of Hawaiian on your visit. Almost all place names are Hawaiian words, so that's a good starting point. Remember that new words, like new tastes and sights, add dimension to your travel experience and your memories afterward. Here is a very brief glossary to get you started, and we'd recommend you also purchase a pocket Hawaiian language dictionary.

GLOSSARY

a'a—(ah-ah)—rough, clinky lava
ae—(ay)—eyes
aina—(eye-nah)—land
akamai—(ah-ka-MYE)—smart
ali'i—(ah-lee-ee)—chief
aloha—(ah-loh-hah)—greetings
a'ole—(ah-OH-lay)—no
auwe—(ow-way)—oh no!
hale—(hah-lay)—house

hana—(ha-nah)—work

hana hou—(ha-nah HO)—to do it again, encore

hanai—(hah-NYE)—adopted

haole—(how-lee)—a caucasian, foreigner

hapa—(hah-pah)—half

hapai—(hah-PYE)—pregnant

hauoli—(how-OH-lee)—happy

heiau—(heh-ow)—temple

holoholo—(just like it looks)—to travel

huhu—(hoo-hoo) angry, upset

hui—(hoo-ee)—group, union, club, etc., most often referred to business groups who pool their money for investment purposes

hula—(hoo-lah)—dance

imu—(ee-moo)—underground oven to roast luau food

ipo—(ee-po)—sweetheart

kai—(kye)—ocean

kahuna—(kah-HOO-nah)—teacher, priest

kalo—(kah-loh)—taro, poi is made from its root

kama'aina—(kah-mah-AI-nuh)—native born

kane—(kah-nay)—man

kapu—(kah-poo)—keep out, forbidden

kaukau—(kow-kow)—food

keiki—(kay-kee)—child

kokua—(koh-KOO-ah)—help

kona—(koh-nah)—south, direction from which winds and rain often come

lanai—(lah-NAH-ee)—porch or patio

lei—(lay)—garland of flowers

lomi lomi—(loh-mee LOH-mee)—to rub or massage

luau—(loo-ow)—party with entertainment and *imu*-cooked food

mahalo—(mah-HA-low)—praise, thanks

makai—(mah-KYE)—toward the ocean

malihini—(mah-lee-HEE-nee)—a newcomer or visitor

mana—(mah-nah)—supernatural or divine power

mauka—(mau-*rhymes with cow*-kah)—toward the mountain

mauna—(mau-nah)—mountain

mele—(may-leh)—Hawaiian song or chant

menehune—(may-nay-HOO-nee)—Hawaiian dwarf or elf

moana—(moh-AH-nah)—ocean

nani—(nah-nee)—beautiful

okole—(oh-KOH-lay)—bottom (butt)

ono—(oh-no)—delicious

pali—(pah-lee)—cliff, precipice

A FEW WORDS ABOUT PIDGIN ENGLISH

Pidgin is one of those great, eclectic "chop suey" languages that includes a little bit of everything—perfect for the Big Island. It contains a colorful mingle mangle of Hawaiian with some English, Spanish, Portuguese, Japanese, Chinese, Korean and Filipino words thrown in for good measure. Some linguists believe it was invented by sugar cane plantation children while they were playing together. You'll hear pidgin words and phrases at the beach, the gas station, local stores and restaurants, although you might not recognize them as a separate language. Pidgin has been commonly used by enough people for enough years that it's a trend among Hawai'i's contemporary writers to use Pidgin exclusively in novels, periodicals and some non-fiction works.

Here is a short course on common pidgin phrases you may hear, with the polite suggestion that you use this to develop your skills in listening to pidgin, not speaking it.

any kine—anything
ass why—that's the reason, that's why
brah, bruddah—brother, good friend
buggah—guy, friend, also a pest or nuisance
bumbye—soon enough
chicken skin—goose bumps, when your skin gets the chills
chop suey—all mixed up
cockaroach—to steal or sneak away with something
da kine—a generally used term referring to everything, as in the right thing

paniolo—(pah-nee-O-low)—Hawaiian cowboy
pau—(pow)—finished
poi—(poy)—a paste made from the taro root
pua—(poo-ah)—flower
puka—(poo-ka)—a hole
pupus—(poo-poos)—appetizers
wahine—(wah-HEE-nay)—woman
wiki wiki—(WEE-kee WEE-kee)—hurry

BIG ISLAND PLACE NAMES

Halema'uma'u—crater, fire pit
Hilo—first night of new moon
Holualoa—long sled course
Honoka'a—rolling bay
Ka Lae—the point

fo'real—this is for real, no kidding
garans—guaranteed, for sure
get—used in place of verb "have"
hele on—get moving
Howzit!—How are you?
junk—lousy, terrible
li'dat—like that
like—to want or want to
lolo—stupid, dumb
lua—toilet
manini—stingy, cheap
mo bettah—better
nah, nah, nah—no, just kidding
ni'ele—nosy
no can—cannot
no mo—none
no mo nuff—not enough
no shame—don't be shy
not!—you must be kidding, it cannot be
or what?—phrase added to any question
pau hana—after work
stink-eye—dirty look
talk story—talk, gossip
whatevah—applied to just about anything

Kailua—two seas

Kapa'au—elevated portion of a *heiau*

Kawaihae—water of wrath; refers to people who fought over water supply in this arid area

Kealakekua—pathway of the god

Kona—leeward side

Mauna Kea—white mountain

Mauna Loa—long mountain

Na'alehu—volcanic ashes

Pahoa—dagger

Pu'ukohola—hill of the whale

Waiakea—broad water

Waikoloa—water for ducks

Waimea—red water

Waipi'o—curved water

Island Ecology

FAUNA

MONGOOSE No, it's not a rat. That sneaky brown animal with the long tail is a mongoose, brought in by farmers during the last century to eat the cane toad (which did not work since the toads are nocturnal and mongoose are not) Mongoose are harmless, ferret-like animals that populate most of the island. You'll see them hopping out of rubbish cans or patrolling empty lots.

GOATS Small families of wild goats are often seen grazing along roadsides, even in the drier areas. These are descendants of "escapees" and are very shy.

DONKEYS The "Kona nightingales" came to the island many years ago to help haul coffee beans down from the mountains. Now their great-great grandchildren range the *mauka* (mountain) areas unrestrained. You'll see the donkey-crossing signs along the highway, and you may see the donkeys themselves, particularly at dusk.

CATS Feral cats are everywhere on the island. You'll see them roaming beach parks and campsites at night, sometimes in groups. Animal activist organizations are making various efforts to control the population and care for the colonies appropriately. For the most part these cats have been living wild for generations and are not domestic animals. They are wary of humans, but if you're camping, do be sure to secure your food. And if you choose to feed them, be aware that you may draw large numbers.

GECKOS Geckos are amusingly animated little "lizards" that find homes in the most unlikely places around the island. You find them in plants and trees, on window screens and picnic tables, in trunks of cars and sometimes suitcases. They are harmless bug-eaters and there are many species, including a bright green-to-brown chameleon, a putty-colored house gecko that chirps in the evening and a recent addition, the Madagascar gecko, vivid chartreuse with blue toes and splashes of red on his back. Visiting kids will enjoy a gecko hunt, but be sure to let them go.

BIRDS The Big Island is home to many indigenous birds such as the *'elepaio, 'i'iwi,* and various species of honeycreeper that only experienced birders are likely to spot. However, birdlife is plentiful and the more common bird species are fun to watch as you make your way around the island. It might surprise you to see cardinals, English sparrows, mockingbirds and other "stowaway" species that came to the island on ships. Although seagulls are rare, you might see a Hawaiian stilt as he trips along the beach at dinnertime, or the large white frigate bird soaring overhead.

CREATURES TO WATCH OUT FOR

Campers and hikers should be aware that the Big Island hosts both centipedes and small scorpions. While neither are deadly poisonous, both have nasty stings. Scorpions hide under rocks in dry areas, and centipedes turn up almost anywhere. If you have a close encounter, treat it like a bee sting and watch for unusual swelling, redness or signs of allergic reaction. Consult a doctor if you are concerned. There are also various species of spiders, bees and wasps, including ground-dwelling bees. The good news is—no snakes!

The common mynah is a robin-size black bird with a bright yellow beak and, yes, he's related to the talking mynahs in pet stores. He loves to steal rubbish or leftover food, and his raucous cries and animated behavior are unmistakable.

Majiro are tiny green birds that have white circles around their black eyes, and are often seen in papaya trees, enjoying the fruit for breakfast.

If a loud, musical bird call or a persistent knocking on the roof wakes you up in the morning, it's a francolin. These quail-like ground birds live in family groups and patrol their neighborhood like clockwork, announcing sunrise and sunset to anyone within earshot.

If you're lucky enough to spot the Hawaiian *pu'eo,* it's said to be a good omen for your travels. This small, brown and white owl might be seen silently gliding over the fields at dusk as he hunts for dinner.

The *i'o*, or Hawaiian hawk, is a rare sight, too, but you might see one soaring over higher elevations, or patiently watching the road from a telephone line.

A distant relative of the Canadian goose, the *nene* is a protected species of ground-dwelling bird. You may see them in Volcanoes National Park or other remote areas and will recognize them by their size and distinctive black markings. Please don't approach them.

FLORA

As you cruise along Big Island roads, take a look at the veritable Garden of Eden growing all around you. Especially in rainier areas, worlds of flowers, fruit trees and tropical plants decorate the landscape with lush color and a thousand shades of green.

Banana trees grow wild in wetter areas. They are broadleafed stalks that grow in patches and a ripe bunch will hang away from the tree, "upside down" to what you may expect, with the bananas pointing upward.

Guava are small, about lemon-sized, yellow fruits that grow on scrubby trees in the gulches and along backroads.

FORAGING

Now before we go any farther, we are *not* suggesting that any visitor break the law by stealing fruit, coffee, nuts or flowers from a farmer's land just because they happen to grow close to the roadside. What we *are* saying is that the Big Island is a huge garden, and someone—especially someone from a city—hiking or casually driving along might enjoy the unique experience of picking and eating something wonderful. Here, then is a very brief guide to "free-range" foods you might find at random. As always, if you're not sure, do what your mother told you, "Don't eat that!"

Avocado Avocados fall to the ground when they are ripe. However, avocados generally turn to baby food once they hit the ground and you really need a long-handled picker to bother with them. In season they are plentiful and cheap, but if you're lucky enough to find a short enough tree, look for fruit that pulls off the stem easily, and don't take more than you can eat.

Bananas If they're completely green, don't bother; they will not ripen once picked. They'll begin to turn yellow from the top of the bunch. Take a few and leave the rest, being careful not to pull down the tree.

Coconuts Now this is fun. Find a brown, dry coconut that is lightweight. Break the stem end off, decorate it with aloha motif, and address it to a friend back home. The post office is still happy to handle these Hawaiian postcards. Perfect for anyone who thinks they have everything. If you want to eat one, find one that is golden brown in color, with no cracks. You'll need a machete to whack the outer husk off and get to the round, woody nut inside. Once you've extracted that, you should be able to punch holes through the "eyes," drain the juice out, crack the shell and scrape out the white coconut meat. Unless you happened to pack your machete, visit a local craft show for a coconut demonstration.

Coffee Do not pick coffee beans. This is a serious cash crop that should be left untouched, and there are plenty of free samples available on the Kona side. Enjoy looking at the trees.

In season, *mangoes* are abundant in the island's rainier neighborhoods. Look for a long stem hanging from the branches, and a green to gold and crimson, almond-shaped fruit.

Coffee trees are short shrubs with long sprays of white flowers that become red "cherries," which are picked, dried, husked, roasted and brewed into extraordinary coffee.

Once most of the Big Island was devoted to *sugar cane*. This beautiful crop spread tall, green tufted grass across acre after hilly acre,

Flowers Local custom says unless you're making a lei, or plucking one blossom for behind your ear, leave the flowers for everyone to enjoy. (Note: Oleanders are toxic.) It is particularly uncool to disturb the fuzzy bright red *lehua* flowers on an *ohia* tree. These are favorites of volcano goddess Pele.

Guava Don't climb the scrubby trees; the fruits fall when they're ripe. Examine the fruit and don't take any with holes as they will have bugs. Cut them in half and suck the delicious pulp off the seeds. Some people eat the skin, seeds and all.

Macadamia nuts Leave them on the trees. Trust us, you do not have anything that can crack one. And farmers take trespassers very seriously. The trees are beautiful and can be identified usually by a sign that says "Somebody's Mac Nut Farms," or something to that effect.

Mango The trees are tall, but again the fruit falls to the ground when ripe. Pick up unbruised green fruit with a yellow-pinkish tinge, check for bug holes, then peel and eat the orange flesh around the large central seed. Start slowly, as some people have an adverse reaction that produces cracks around their lips. Mangoes are so delicious it's almost worth the risk.

Papaya Growing from umbrella-like trees, the fruit is suspended from the very top, which is usually hard to reach, and the trunk is not strong enough to support a climber. If you find one with reachable fruit, select one or two with a some yellow showing. Fully yellow fruit will be too ripe and fully green fruit will not ripen off the tree. Slice the papaya in half, discard the black seeds and enjoy with a spritz of lime juice.

Sugar cane Look for the white tufted stalks, resembling pampas grass. You can peel a piece of the cane and suck the sweet pulp.

waving and singing in the tradewinds. Although the industry has gone, sugar cane plants continue to grow wild in most wet areas.

Avocados, like mangoes, grow wild in many areas. There are many species of both. Look for ripes ones in Hilo Farmers' Market, roadside stands or local grocery stores.

Papayas grow on funny-looking trees that resemble green umbrellas—long, pale trunks with fan-shaped leaves; they grow wild in many areas.

"Wild" flowers, many escapees from island gardens, bloom along roadsides and trails. Look for the tiny purple-white bamboo orchids peeking above their tall, grassy stalks; red, white and fragrant yellow ginger with their shiny oval leaves growing among shade trees; trailing vines of yellow flowers that become "wood roses" when dry; the large trumpets of belladonna, multicolored nasturtiums, impatiens; yellow, red, white or pink hibiscus; and many others in Big Island forests, roadsides and parks.

It's hard to distinguish "native" Hawaiian plants since so many varieties have been imported for agriculture and landscaping. Ancient Polynesian settlers arrived with taro plants, whose cooked root becomes the food staple poi, breadfruit *(ulu),* coconut and ti plants, and found creative ways to use the plantlife they found. If you're interested in learning more, we'd suggest a visit to the Amy B. H. Greenwell Ethnobotanical Garden in Captain Cook, or one of the other botanical gardens islandwide.

Traveling with Children

Most *keiki* (kids) will handle the stress, excitement and strangeness of travel better if they are adequately prepared ahead of time and have things available to keep them occupied. If they have never flown before, you can help them understand a little about what to expect on a plane, what happens when you take off and land, and something about what good travel manners are (e.g., no kicking the seat in front of you). Kids have a natural curiosity and some basic advance information might help increase their excitement about the trip—and decrease the possibility of a bad time. One good thing to do might be to visit a library or bookstore together for some background information and reading on Hawai'i. (Suggested reading is provided at the end of this book). Or, spend some time exploring the internet for an amazing amount of interesting information, and great geography or science report material (see "Communications: Websites" later in this chapter). Try www.gohawaii.com, the Hawai'i Visitors and Convention Bureau site; www.nps.gov/havo, Volcanoes National Park site; or www.ifa.hawaii.edu/mok/about_maunakea.htm, the Center for International Astronomy site.

ON THE PLANE WITH KIDS

A word about flying with kids. We don't want to harp on this. We know it can't be any fun for parents of crying babies and bored, fussy children on an airplane. We sympathize. We really do. And we all have stories of flights from hell caused by kids out of control. Some of this is inevitable and can be ignored. That's what headphones are for. And first class, if you can afford it. And Bloody Marys. Flights to Hawai'i, in general, are long, crowded and uncomfortable. And quite frankly, there are times we'd all love to run up and down the aisle throwing cookies and screaming like banshees. Barring that, we do have a couple of suggestions, from observation, and trust that somewhere out there in the world there must be experts on the subject who wrote books about this for parents to read.

Start with planning. If your family wants to be together, please, please advise the airline when you make reservations. Do not wait until everyone's seated then try to get the attendant to rearrange everyone (and their carry-on bags) for your convenience. Sometimes it's unavoidable, and we sympathize. On the other hand, know your kids. If they fight all day long at home, chances are good they'll fight all night on the plane. Maybe you want them separated, maybe on opposite sides of the plane.

It may help to include in your carry-on a goody bag for each child, with enough surprises to hand out at intervals throughout the trip, selected just for them. Books, crayons, stickers, favorite snacks like individual cereals or juice boxes with straw attached, and quiet, self-contained toys like dolls or small stuffed animals are good diversions. Even simple things like printed band-aids can take a *keiki*'s mind off how bored she is. (Airlines may be able to provide complimentary gift bags for the kids, but it pays to come prepared with your own personalized stuff.)

On the other hand, if your well-planned goody bags involve regular intervals of climbing over seatmates and digging into a 95-pound backpack stored in the overhead bin, you might re-think the plan. Bringing all that stuff seems to make some *keiki* want it all, right now, and when you get to the bottom of the bag, you're out of options. If you do bring a load of toys, may we ask that you not bring talking or singing ones? (Do you really want to listen to the Barney song for five and a half hours?) Books are really, really good. Start them reading young and have a nice flight. Gameboys and electronics can keep kids occupied (bring extra batteries).

Awareness is important all around. Please know if your kid is kicking the seat in front of him, or wandering around the plane, or otherwise being a nuisance. We know for a fact that the most important thing you can give a kid on a plane is *attention*, your positive attention, before things get out of hand. Oftentimes parents seem to focus more on "parenting" and less on the kids themselves. We've seen a little attention go a long, long way with even the most difficult children. Parents who talk to their boys and girls, who watch what they're doing and show interest have a lot better flight than those who just say no or ignore them. Play with them. Read to them (we'd much rather listen to a storybook than you saying "no" and them saying "I want"). We've seen kids, already bored with the Gameboy and the in-flight movie, respond to simple games like tic tac toe, hangman or Go Fish if Mommy or Daddy plays too. (Of course, the time to do this is before they're out of control.) Every kid wants attention. Give them some. You might enjoy it. (P.S. This works in restaurants too.)

You can have your Bloody Mary later, at the beach.

You know this, but go ahead and put it on your list. If you are traveling with an infant, make sure you have enough supplies of diapers, baby food, formula and other needs; don't count on the airline. Soft teething rings and toys can help an infant clear the ears and equalize the air pressure if there is a problem. (And try a gentle massage of the soft area above their ears.) Older kids can do the same with chewing gum.

TRAVELING IN THE ISLAND WITH KIDS

BABYSITTING Babysitting is available through most hotels and condos have a babysitting service or list of available babysitters and will help you with arrangements. Fees usually run from about $12 to $15 per hour and up. Certified babysitters are also available in some areas through People Attentive To Children Hawai'i (PATCH) at Malihini Keiki Care (808-331-2909, fax 808-331-2810).

CAR SEATS Car seats are required by Hawai'i state law for children age three and under at all times when riding in an automobile. Most car rental companies have child car seats available but charge a $10 to $15 daily fee. Also, during peak travel seasons, demand may be high and reservations for car seats may not be completely reliable. You may want to consider bringing your own, and possibly use it on the plane. Check with your travel agent or airline. If you check the car seat as baggage, put it in a box or use a large plastic bag and be sure to label it clearly.

CRIBS Cribs can be provided by most hotels and condos for a fee of $10 to $15 per night. Local rental shops also have them available for a few dollars per night if you opt to not bring your own portable crib.

DINING Most restaurants provide a special *keiki* (children's) menu, and you'll find McDonald's, Burger King and other familiar eateries around the island, some with a playground area. Check the menus at fast food stores for interesting local items you can't get anywhere else.

FOR EMERGENCIES See "Medical Information" later in this chapter.

Always be attentive to keiki *near the water.*

Even at the calmest of beaches, an occasional large wave can roll in by surprise. Currents can be strong and shallow water can be deceiving. A children's flotation device is strongly recommended in all cases. Apply a good sunscreen before beachtime, and don't let the kids stay out in the sun for too long. Several short periods are better in Hawai'i's strong sunshine. (The same goes for mom and dad.)

When you arrive, we suggest you pick up a copy of the free *Big Island Beach & Activity Guide* (www.beachactivityguide.com) for maps, tips and the most current information on Big Island beaches and beach parks.

On the west side of the island, **Spencer Beach Park** at Kawaihae provides one of the calmest beaches on the Big Island. Its small beach and sparkling clear water are perfect for the small ones. **Hapuna Beach State Park**, below the Hapuna Beach Prince Hotel on the Kohala Coast, is a large expanse of open sand, great for the kids to run and play. The water is shallow and the surf moderate but adults must be vigilant with youngsters in the water. **'Anaeho'omalu Beach Park**, fronting the Waikoloa Beach Marriott on the Kohala Coast, is a large sweeping crescent with fine sand, moderate surf and shallow water. In Kona, **Kamakahonu Beach**, fronting the King Kamehameha Kona Beach Hotel next to the Kailua-Kona Pier, is also a fine small beach with gentle water that seems to have been made just for *keiki*.

On the east or Hilo side of the island, one of the better beaches for kids is **Onekahaka Beach Park**, with nice sandy-bottom pools created by the large breakwater and retaining walls. **Coconut Island** is another fun place to play, just off Banyan Drive, and connected to the shore by a long footbridge. This is a good spot for picnicking, fishing and playing in the shallow, sandy pools. Conditions at **Hilo Bayfront Park** are not the best for swimming, but it's a popular fishing spot, and a good place to watch canoe races on the weekends.

Most kids (and parents too) are fascinated with exploring the beach and shores for bits of coral, seashells and the interesting creatures who live in ocean tidepools. A guidebook to Hawai'i's shells, reef fish, and marine life may help them develop a better understanding of the beach and shore ecosystems. *Hawaiian Reef Animals* by Hobson and Chave and *Hawaiian Fishwatcher's Field Guide* by Greenberg are two good references. Another excellent book especially for children is *Sand to Sea: Marine Life of Hawai'i* by Feeney and Fielding. A good place to see and feed the myriad schools of Hawai'i's colorful reef fish is at **Kahalu'u Beach Park**, in Keauhou just south of Kailua-Kona. At the beach park next to the Keauhou Beach Hotel, schools of colorful fish swarm about in the shallow calm waters. It is a perfect place to view and handfeed the fish. Children will enjoy the experience of seeing the marine life up close. If they are old enough, they can use a mask and snorkel to gain an underwater view of the colorful reef life.

Check with your hotel or condo desk, visitor publications and the local newspapers for additional children's activities around the Big Island. It's a busy, community-minded place, and almost any weekend, almost everywhere on the island you'll find an interesting cultural festival, concert, charity fun run or walk, ball game, ice cream social, food event or arts-and-crafts fair. These are well worth looking into, and can be great opportunities to experience some of the Big Island's many diverse aspects.

CHILDCARE PROGRAMS

Kohala Coast resorts have supervised kids' activity programs with swimming, shoreline explorations, Hawaiian arts and crafts like lei making and hula dancing and other fun things.

The **Fairmont Orchid Hawai'i's** Keiki Aloha program offered to kids 5-12 features Hawaiian arts and crafts, outdoor games and explorations. Full-day program is $60 including lunch, half-day or Saturday evening program is $40. 808-885-2000.

The **Four Seasons Resort Hualalai**'s "Kids for All Seasons" is for children 5-12 and is complimentary to resort guests. Fun activities include volcano building and gecko hunts. The "Tsunami" activities center for teens and families has a 54-inch surround-sound TV, Sega game centers, internet stations, pool, ping-pong and other games, plus access to off-site teen activities like hiking, surfing and horseback riding. 808-325-8000.

The **Hapuna Beach Prince Hotel**'s year-round Keiki Camp provides kids with the opportunity to make new friends, play games,

HOTEL & CONDO SWIMMING POOLS

It is essential to supervise your children at the hotel or condo swimming pool as these are generally not staffed with lifeguards. Most hotel/condo pools usually aren't more than five or six feet at the deep end and two or three feet at the shallow end. Several of the newer hotels and resorts have jacuzzi pools next to the regular pool. Be careful to read posted safety information and do not let the kids stay in the very warm water too long. Again, even at hotel/condo pools, use of a children's flotation device is highly recommended. Resort swimming pools at the **Waikoloa Beach Marriott** and **Hilton Waikoloa Village** have water features and slides (Hilton's is giant and resembles a water theme park).

explore and learn something about Hawai'i in a fun-filled day. Cost is $50 for the full day, including lunch, $25 for the half-day program. 808-880-1111.

With a nod to the other excellent Kohala Coast resorts, **Hilton Waikoloa Village** really has the most to offer active families, with the biggest variety and largest number of things for kids to see and do. The lobby and public areas are full of tropical birds and the ponds are full of swans, koi fish and waterfowl (even flamingos). Their inter-resort transportation is done by small-gauge railroad train or a mini motorboat. For kids 5-12, there's Camp Menehune, a daily program (9 a.m. to 4 p.m.) of activities with everything from arts and crafts to hula dancing and swimming. Full day is $55 per child and includes lunch; half day is $40. Babysitting and a teen program are also available. 808-886-1234.

"Na Keiki in Paradise" at the **Kona Village Resort** is a complimentary activities program for kids 6 and older, with tours and explorations, storytelling, glass-bottom boat rides and more fun things to do. There is also a kid's dinner and activities program from 5:30 p.m. to 8:30 p.m., allowing Mom and Dad some time to themselves. 808-325-5555.

At the **Mauna Kea Beach Hotel**, Keiki Camp is available for $50 full day, including lunch, and $25 half day. Kids enjoy supervised activities at the beach and around the grounds, games, Hawaiian crafts and making new friends. 808-882-7222.

For *keiki* 5-12, Camp Mauna Lani at **Mauna Lani Bay Hotel and Bungalows** offers activities, games, snacks and Hawaiian crafts year-round. The cost is $35 per day for the first child and $25 for other children in the same family, which includes T-shirts and sand pails. Lunch or dinner is additional. 808-885-6622.

Waikoloa Beach Marriott, An Outrigger Resort hosts the Cowabunga Club, a fun alternative for kids 5-13. Cost is $55 for a full day including a snack and lunch; half-day is $40 for morning or afternoon programs. Cowabunga kids receive a T-shirt and engage in activities like Hawaiian arts and crafts, kite flying and a glass-bottom boat tour. 808-886-6789.

EXCURSIONS AND ADVENTURES

KONA DISTRICT Kona offers numerous ocean activities, great for kids of all ages. Glass-bottom boat cruises over shallow reef waters along the Kailua-Kona Coast provide fascinating glimpses of marine life that will delight and enthrall youngsters, and snorkel gear is available for rent in many places islandwide. More adventurous kids might also enjoy the underwater thrill of a submarine ride with **Atlantis Submarine** (808-329-6626) for close-up underwater views of coral reefs and lots of colorful fascinating fish. Snorkel and dive cruises—and Snuba, an easy way to dive, connected to underwater breathing apparatus in a nearby boat—take in the protected marine life preserve of Kealakekua Bay and many other spots along the Kona Coast. Swimmers and snorkelers in the super-clear waters enjoy watching the schools of reef fish and coral gardens. And now there's a device called a torpedo available, which helps propel you through the water at about 2 mph. Other family options include a see-through kayak cruise with **Clear Blue Hawai'i** (808-322-2868), do-it-yourself boat rentals from **Captain Cruise** (808-329-4977) and other providers, along with myriad others: jetskis, parasailing, windsurfing, deep-sea fishing charters, surf lessons and our favorite: whale watching in season.

KOHALA COAST Resort guests here are steps away from everything you ever wanted to do in the ocean. Swim, snorkel, scuba or snuba dive; take a sunset sail or fishing cruise; windsurf, kayak, boogieboard or cruise along on glass-bottom boat. Hilton Waikoloa Village is where you go to sign up for **Dolphin Quest**, a chance to encounter bottlenose dolphins on a supervised swim with them in a saltwater pool during a dolphin-training session, a twilight camp or a family program. Much has been written about the physical and mental benefits of the experience, and it is one of the more popular and unique attractions on the island. Dolphin Quest gives priority to resort guests, but there is a system for outside reservations and education programs. Due to its popularity, participation is by lottery only. Rates: adults $115, couple $190, children $85. Reservations are required and recommended two months in advance. 808-886-2875; fax 808-886-7030; www.dolphinquest.org; e-mail: dqhawaii@dolphinquest.org.

HILO A good place to check out marine life is at the **Richardson Ocean Center** in the Keaukaha area. Here displays and aquariums explain much about the ecosystem and marine life of Hawai'i's beaches, reefs and ocean. There are also calm tidal pools in which to look for sea cucumbers, sea urchins, starfish, crabs, limpets and other interesting forms of marine life. Youngsters can swim in the calm water too. 2349 Kalanianaole Avenue; 808-961-8695.

In the general area, kids might enjoy a run across the many different kinds of bridges of **Queen Liliuokalani Gardens**, or the "wavy" bridges at **Wailoa State Park**. If you want to do something besides the beach when you visit Hilo, just outside of town is one of the Big Island's least known attractions, perfect for kids of all ages. The **Panaewa Rain Forest Zoo**, operated by the County of Hawai'i, is the only authentic rainforest zoo in the country. On display are animals from around the world representative of rainforest dwellers. Included are various species of monkeys, tapir, pygmy hippopotamus, a white tiger, land tortoise, parrots, wild Hawaiian pigs, axis deer and more. It's a pleasant place to stroll and picnic. There are no crowds and it's free! Open daily 9 a.m. to 4 p.m. The zoo is on Mamaki Street off the Volcano Highway (Highway 11) three miles south of Hilo. Watch for a sign indicating the turnoff; 808-959-7224.

MOVIES

Both Hilo and Kona and several of the small towns around the island offer movie theaters showing the latest films. In Hilo are Prince Kuhio Theaters (808-959-4595) in the Prince Kuhio Plaza and Kress Cinemas (808-961-3456) downtown. In Kona there are Makalapua Stadium Cinemas (808-327-0444) in Makalapua Center and Keauhou Cinemas (808-324-7200) in Keauhou Shopping Center. Aloha Theatre in Kainaliu, Kahilu Theatre in Waimea and the People's Theater in Honoka'a show movies on weekends. (Aloha's movies are usually classics or art films, and they have the added bonus of Aloha Angel Cafe downstairs.) Most of the hotels have cable television as well as in-house movies.

Especially for Seniors

The Big Island is big on *ohana* (family), particularly the multi-generational extended family that seems to embrace everyone. The families, from grandparents to babies, like to do things together—whether it's spending time at the beach, eating in a restaurant or touring around the island telling stories. Maybe that's why multi-generational family groups choose the Big Island as a vacation destination. There's something for everyone, and plenty of room for even the larger family to spread out in different directions, or gather together and enjoy the company. In general seniors are treated respectfully, perhaps more so than in other vacation areas.

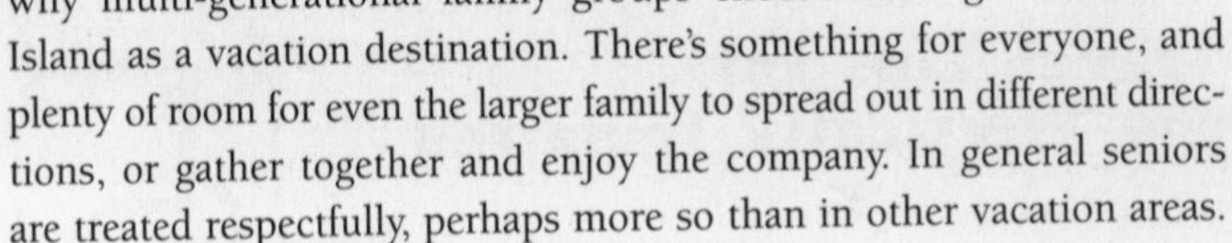

SENIOR DISCOUNTS Seniors traveling to and around the Big Island are advised to inquire with all airline, car rental firms, hotels, restaurants and paid attractions/activities as to whether any senior discounts are available. Your travel agent can be helpful on this also but don't hesitate to ask if you make your own reservations. Be ready to provide a valid driver's license or photo I.D. To help you get around if you don't drive, the County of Hawai'i offers seniors a discount of a third off the regular bus fares on its Hele On bus system. The bus system covers the entire Big Island with regularly scheduled services. For complete information and the latest fares, contact the Hele On Bus, County of Hawai'i Transit Agency, 25 Aupuni Street, Hilo, HI 96720; 808-961-8744 or 808-961-8343.

ELDERHOSTEL PROGRAMS The national Elderhostel program conducts courses, workshops, seminars and activities of various types throughout the country specifically for seniors. For details, information and costs on Hawai'i programs, contact Elderhostel, 11 Avenue de Lafayette, Boston, MA 02111; 617-426-8506; 877-426-8056; fax 877-426-2166; www.elderhostel.org. On the Big Island, the following groups/organizations host various Elderhostel courses and activities. Contact them directly for schedule and information.

The **University of Hawai'i at Hilo** participates in the Elderhostel program, offering seniors the opportunity to spend one or two weeks on campus or nearby areas in various programs such as Hawai'i-Pacific culture, history, language, astronomy, vulcanology, oceanography, marine science and more. Fees cover tuition, room and board. Inquire with Elderhostel Program Director, University of Hawai'i at Hilo, 200 West Kawili Street, Hilo, HI 96720-4091; 808-974-7555; fax 808-974-7684.

The **Lyman Museum and Mission House** also coordinates and hosts one- or two-week annual Elderhostel program seminars, workshops and cultural activities for seniors. 276 Haili Street, Hilo, HI 96720; 808-935-5021.

The **Volcano Art Center** coordinates an annual schedule of two-week Elderhostel courses and activities. These programs are geared toward active participants, including nature hikes through volcano craters and rainforests, Hawaiian culture and natural history lectures, demonstrations and snorkel excursions. Program price includes all lodging, food, field trips and instruction. P.O. Box 104, Hawai'i National Park, HI 96718; 808-967-8222; fax 808-967-8512; www.bishop.hawaii.org/vac/home.html; e-mail: vaceh@gte.net.

Travel Tips for the Physically Impaired

When making your travel plans it is best to do so well in advance and to inform the hotels and airlines that you have special needs that require specific services. A good travel agent should also be able to assist, and visitor industry facilities in Hawai'i can accommodate you. It would be wise to bring along your medical records in case of an emergency, and it is recommended that you bring your own wheelchair and inform the airlines accordingly.

ARRIVAL AND DEPARTURE Both the Hilo and Kona airports on the Big Island are accessible for mobility impaired persons. Parking stalls are available at both terminals for the disabled. Restrooms with wheelchair accessible stalls are also found in both terminals. The local airlines are very conscientious in accommodating those with special needs. Special lifts to the aircraft are provided for wheelchair passengers at Kona airport but the Hilo airport has jetway ramps available for boarding and exiting planes.

TRANSPORTATION Check with **Accessible Vans of Hawai'i** for information/rates and arrangements on renting a wheelchair-accessible van. They rent special vans throughout the Hawaiian islands. 800-303-3750; www.accessiblevans.com.

The Hawai'i County Hele On bus system provides a demand-response transportation service with lift-equipped vans within the Hilo and Kona areas only to accommodate individuals unable to utilize the standard transit buses. This curb to curb service is available 7 a.m. to 4:30 p.m. Monday through Friday except county holidays. Requests for service must be made at least a day in advance. For information, call the Transit Agency's Hele On Bus Office at 808-961-8343; for county bus schedule information call 808-961-8744.

MEDICAL SERVICES AND EQUIPMENT For a list of medical centers and hospitals, see "Medical Information" later in this chapter. Some agencies can assist in providing personal care attendants, companions and nursing aides while on your visit. Contact **Center for Independent Living-East Hawai'i** in Hilo at 808-935-3777 and in West Hawai'i/Kona at 808-323-2221; **Interim Health Care** in Hilo at 808-961-4621; and in Kona at 808-326-2722.

The following companies provide medical equipment rentals: **Big Island Medical Equipment**, Kona, 808-323-3313; **Rainbow Medical Supply**, 180 Kinoole Street, Hilo, 808-935-9393; **Orchid Isle Hospital Equipment**, Kona 808-322-2269, Hilo 808-935-6105, Waimea 808-885-9681; **Ban-Nix Home Medical Equipment**, Waimea, 808-885-1925. **Pacific Rent-All**, 1080 Kilauea Avenue, Hilo, 808-935-2974, rents everything from hospital beds to wheelchairs. **Kona Rent All**, 74-5603 Pawai Place, Kailua-Kona, 808-329-1644, has a large line of rental equipment.

ACCOMMODATIONS Big Island hotels and condominiums in general provide accessible rooms and facilities. Because these are subject to availability, request reservations well in advance and be specific about your needs. Inform the reservationist if you need an accessible bathroom, shower stall, grab bars or special toilet seat. If you have oxygen equipment in your room, it is important to inform your hotel for fire safety reasons. If you are hearing-impaired you should inform your hotel so that you can be assisted in case of emergency. Most hotel accommodations can also provide flashing-light telephones and doorbell indicator lights.

GUIDE DOGS AND SERVICE DOGS The State of Hawai'i has recently revised its strict 120-day quarantine for dogs and cats; however, bringing pets along on your Hawai'i vacation is not a recommended practice. Guide dogs for the blind and service dogs for hearing-impaired persons may be admitted into the state under a specific set of quarantine regulations. All arrivals must enter the state through Honolulu International Airport only; the Animal Quarantine Branch (808-837-8092; fax 808-483-7161) must receive notification at least 24 hours in advance, and a series of very detailed requirements must be met. Please plan well in advance. For more information contact Hawai'i Department of Agriculture, Animal Quarantine Station, 99-951 Halawa Valley Street, Aiea, HI 96701-5602; 808-483-7151; fax 808-483-7161; e-mail: eqs.rabies@gte.net.

What to Pack

It's easy to pack for a Big Island vacation. Bring your favorite, most comfortable summer clothes, walking shoes and a swimsuit. Dress is very casual here; shorts, T-shirts and sandals are perfectly acceptable almost everywhere, day and night. If you're a jeans person, that's fine too. What that doesn't cover, the following will: slacks and an aloha shirt for gentlemen, a muumuu or casual dress for the ladies. Even in the fancier restaurants ladies never need hose or heels; gentlemen never need ties. Some places recommend jackets, but it's not required generally. Other than that, pack for what you like to do. Resorts expect proper golf or tennis attire (collared shirt and appropriate shoes) and beach coverups in public areas. If you're touring, plan on dressing in light layers. A big shirt over a tank top protects you from sunburn as well as a chilly tropical breeze or air conditioning. Your swimsuit can serve double duty with a pareau wrap or coverup. (It's not customary on the Big Island for people to be "out" in swimwear.)

For the kids, bring plenty of play clothes to cut down on laundry time, and a couple of swimsuits to let one dry while the other's in use. We've noticed *keiki* (kids) tend to over-pack toys and games, then want more when they get here. For them, a lesson in focus might be helpful, but you know the stuff they absolutely cannot live without. If that rotten-looking "bankie" has to come along, it has to come along. Don't worry about what people will think; they had bankies too.

Speaking of living without, a word about electronics. We can almost guarantee that if you can live without your cell phone and laptop on vacation, you're going to have a better time (and so will the people around you). Unless you're a roving reporter on assignment, please consider leaving these symbols of the outside world behind and allow yourself the freedom to enjoy a totally detached, complete retreat. It will be good for you. (You might even take your watch off.) If you can't stand to be disconnected, you'll find most hotels have in-room internet access, some have dataports, and even in the more remote areas of the island you can find the occasional internet café or business center with computer time for rent.

If you dress comfortably for the flight, you'll be ready to go when you reach the Big Island. Your carry-on luggage should include necessary medications, toilet articles, and a change of underwear (if not a complete change of clothes) in case your luggage is misdirected or a delayed flight causes an overnight at another airport. We'd also suggest you include your swimsuit and sunglasses so you can hit the beach immediately, luggage or not. And a good book will get you through the longest wait, no matter where you are. It might be smart to equally distribute important items and even clothing in everyone's luggage so the delay of one bag won't be traumatic for one individual.

SELF-SERVICE LAUNDRIES

Most hotels and condo units have a laundry service available, either the commercial send-out type or in-house coin-operated machines. Check with your front desk. For those in need of self-service laundries, there are a few located around the island. Hours of operation may vary.

Ed's Laundromat, open daily 6 a.m. to 10 p.m. Na'alehu Shopping Center, Na'alehu, Ka'u District, just off Highway 11 in town center.

Hale Haloi, open daily 6 a.m. to 10 p.m. Kealakekua Shopping complex, Highway 11, next to Cap's Drive In.

Hele Mai Laundromat, open daily 6 a.m. to 10 p.m. Kailua-Kona, Palani Road and Kuakini Highway a block above the King Kam Hotel, North Kona Shopping Center; 808-329-3494.

Hilo Quality Washerette, open daily 6 a.m. to 10 p.m. 210 Hoku, Hilo; 808-961-6490.

KC Washerette, open daily 5 a.m. to 9 p.m. In the village of Kainaliu, Kona; 808-322-2929.

Suds n' Duds Laundromat, open daily 7:30 a.m. to 8:30 p.m., Sunday till 7:30 p.m. Kea'au Town Center, Kea'au; 808-965-2621.

The Wash Laundromat, open daily 6 a.m. to 8 p.m. Hawaiian Ranchos Center, Hawaiian Oceanview Estates, South Kona; 808-929-7072.

Tyke's Laundromat, open daily 6:30 a.m. to 9 p.m., 74-5583 Pawai Place, Kailua-Kona, 808-326-1515; and open 6 a.m. to 10 p.m. at 1454 Kilauea Avenue, Hilo; 808-935-1093.

Volcano Wash & Dry, open daily 7 a.m. to 9 p.m., 19-4084 Old Volcano Road, behind Thai Thai Restaurant in Volcano Village.

Use the buddy system to keep up with carry-ons. Before you leave on your trip, be sure to check with your pediatrician especially if your child has a cold or is subject to allergies or ear problems. Inquire about the use of antihistamines, airsickness pills or special children's medicines.

Sunscreen, shades, hats, towels, film, disposable cameras, beach toys and other necessities are readily available in shops almost everywhere. We recommend you double-check any prescription medication you take on a regular basis so you don't waste vacation time getting a refill, and pack a second pair of reading glasses in a different place from the first, just in case. (Our only other packing tip is this: Don't buy new shoes for the trip. Bring your most comfortable pair of sandals or walking shoes and sneakers as a backup. Don't let bad shoes and sore feet hold you back!)

Weddings & Honeymoons

The Big Island is very big on *aloha*. Of course, that means love, and there are very few places left on the planet where there is so much love in the air. If you dream of a Hawaiian honeymoon, you can make it come true here. Surrounded by natural beauty, blessed with nearly perfect weather every day of the year, this is the kind of place where people remember how to relax, get to know each other on a different level, and return home in some way transformed. The Big Island loves honeymooners. It also loves to welcome couples for their weddings—from grand celebrations at the best resorts to barefoot ceremonies on the beach. Here you can step across the Japanese bridges of Liliuokalani Park in Hilo, exchange vows at sea aboard a sleek catamaran, walk down the aisle of a 200-year-old stone church or a tiny country chapel overlooking the ocean. The selection of settings is limited only by your fantasy.

REGULATIONS Obtaining a marriage license is easy. Just visit www.hawaii.gov/doh/records/vr_marri.html. There is a bride-friendly list of requirements and procedures; you can even download a license application on the spot. Or call 808-586-4545 or e-mail vr-info@mail.health.state.hi.us.

Basically, this is all there is to it. You do not have to be a resident of Hawaii, or a U.S. citizen, and you don't need a blood test. Legal age to marry is 18 and proof of age is required. If you're 18, you'll need a certified copy of your birth certificate. Those over 18 may present a driver's license, passport or other valid photo I.D. When you arrive in Hawaii, you need to appear together in person before a marriage license agent. You'll need the completed application, proof of age (written consent from both parents if you're under 18) and a $60 fee. There is no waiting period and the license is valid for 30 days. Your marriage must be officiated by a licensed performer, and a copy of the marriage certificate will be mailed to you within 60 to 120 days after the ceremony. For contact information on marriage license agents, you may write to the Marriage License Section, Department of Health, State of Hawai'i, 1250 Punchbowl Street, Honolulu, HI 96813, or call 808-586-4545. On the Big Island, call the Department of Health at 808-974-6008. Resort wedding coordinators and independent wedding planners will also be able to assist with marriage license agents and officiants.

One small note about a controversial subject. At present the State of Hawai'i does not recognize same-sex marriage, nor does that appear to be on the political agenda in the near future. There are, however, special celebrations and ceremonies performed for any couple who wishes to publicly affirm their commitment to each other in a discreet fashion. Wedding planners can assist.

WEDDING SERVICES

The following wedding coordinators and planning services can provide everything you need, down to the last detail, for a flawless Hawaiian wedding from simple to spectacular. Various packages are available and may include such extras as flowers, photography, video, music, champagne, wedding cake and limousine. Once again, with the Big Island's diverse culture and mid-Pacific location, our professional wedding planners are experienced in wedding customs from just about everywhere. Priests and ministers of practically every religious persuasion are available, as are non-denominational and lay celebrants. If your perfect wedding includes a kosher menu or a Buddhist blessing, it is only necessary to ask.

Paradise Weddings Hawai'i—This full-service wedding coordinator can arrange everything on the Big Island including location, minister, music, flowers and leis, photographer, video service, champagne and wedding cake. Complete wedding packages start at $425. Custom arrangements, from intimate to outrageous, are Debbie Cravatta's specialty. Get married on a beach at sunset, in a quaint chapel by the sea, aboard a sailboat, on a cliff-top golf tee, in a quiet garden near the sacred ponds of King Kamehameha the Great, or any resort location. This is a very reputable service, highly recommended. P.O. Box 383433, Waikoloa, HI 96738; 808-883-9067; 800-428-5844; fax 808-883-8479; www.paradiseweddingshawaii.com; e-mail: wwwed@aloha.net.

Romantic Beach Weddings—These beautiful, original ceremonies are performed by Rev. Lona Lyons, a licensed, non-denominational minister. Services include wedding ceremonies, renewals of vows, partners for life ceremonies and island activities/honeymoon planning. Romantic packages are designed for both budget and luxury brides and grooms. Choose from a cowboy and cowgirl Hawai'i ranch wedding at sunset, a wedding at sea aboard a private charter sailboat, a helicopter flight to a secluded waterfall site, or many others, limited only by your imagination. Lyons specializes in creating an atmosphere with warmth, gentleness and joy that deepens the experience of love as couples say "I do" in paradise. 808-896-6666; www.romanticbeach weddings.com.

Most Big Island hotels and resorts love to host weddings, renewals of vows, honeymoons, anniversaries and other special celebrations. They may also have a full-time wedding coordinator on staff to assist with all the arrangements and fine details. If they do not, a professional wedding planner (such as Paradise Weddings Hawai'i, above) can easily work with your hotel to help sort out all the options available and arrange your wedding, reception and honeymoon requirements. This is especially helpful if you live elsewhere and are trying to make plans long-distance. A wedding planner can also be a more economical choice, but this is not always the case. The hotels and resorts have been hosting wedding couples for a long time, and it is a big part of the hospitality business. Various packages are offered to suit your needs, and many couples choose to have the resort staff take care of everything—wedding site and ceremony, reception menu and wedding cake, a block of rooms for guests, and the honeymoon suite. As always, do your homework, check with various sources, and keep in mind that this is an island. Things tend to move more slowly over here, and it may take a little extra time to bring in a particular flower, bottle of wine or other essential touch for your special day—but hardly anything is impossible. Remember: Rates are subject to change.

Fairmont Orchid Hawaii—Offers a 14,000-square-foot grand ballroom and a clutch of scenic resort settings for lovely weddings, with a reputation for fine service and first-class facilities. Its conference/catering department ably assists with arrangements for custom weddings including ceremony, reception and all the details. Site fees start at $500. Newlyweds can take advantage of the Orchid's "Luxury Romance Experience," a $500 to $595 package inclusive of accommodations, full American breakfast for two daily, and a welcome bottle of champagne and fresh flowers upon arrival. Wedding couples can then combine the wedding ceremony-reception with a basic room package. The Orchid also has special romantic "Sunset Experiences." 1 North Kaniku Drive, Kohala Coast, HI 96743; 808-885-2000; 800-845-9905; fax 808-885-8886; e-mail orchid@fairmont.com.

Four Seasons Resort Hualalai—Offers its well-known level of excellence to wedding couples who seek a particular style in a romantic Hawaiian setting. Honeymooners can choose the "Romance of Hualalai" package (from $1,625 to $1,775 seasonally), which includes three nights' deluxe accommodations, full-size Hertz rental car or full American breakfast for two daily, a welcome bottle of champagne upon arrival, waffle-cloth robes and a Hawaiian music CD. Or upgrade to the "Ultimate Honeymoon" (from $2,170 to $2,560 seasonally), including car, daily breakfast, lei for the bride and groom, Hawaiian CD, plush terry robes, a commemorative Hualalai keepsake, "Romantic Dinner for Two on the Beach" and two 50-minute massages at the spa. P.O. Box 1269, Kailua-Kona, HI 96745; 808-325-8000; fax 808-325-8100; www.fourseasons.com.

Hapuna Beach Prince Hotel—A beautiful, contemporary property designed to maximize its picturesque setting overlooking one of Hawai'i's very best beaches. With a grand ballroom to accommodate 850 guests and a selection of open-air tropical settings, Hapuna is an excellent choice. As an added benefit, Hapuna is partnered with Mauna Kea Beach Hotel next door in one elegant resort. Wedding parties have access to the entire collection of scenic ceremony sites, luxury guest rooms and reception facilities. The resort's Honeymoon/Romance Package starts at $499 per night and includes round-trip limo transportation from Kona International Airport, a chilled bottle of champagne and tropical bouquet waiting in your oceanview room, and a special departure gift. In addition, you are provided with a lavish buffet breakfast for two each day, one candlelit dinner for two on your private lanai or at the award-winning Coast Grille or Batik restaurants. A three-night minimum stay is required.

A full-time wedding coordinator is on staff to assist couples with every arrangement. Thoughtfully organized wedding packages begin with the essential Maile Package, $1,050 including your choice of wedding site, clergy and photographer. The Orchid Package, $1,375, adds to the above a bottle of house champagne, wedding cake for two, flower lei for the bride and maile lei for the groom. The Pikake Package, $2,200, enhances the ceremony with a professional solo musician, special Hawaiian wedding certificate and a videographer; and the Prince Package, $2,600, completes the day with spa treatments for the bride and groom and a manicure, shampoo and hairstyle for the bride. The resort also offers extra-mile assistance with reception menus, decor and entertainment, rooms for your guests and other personalized arrangements. 62-100 Kauna'oa Drive, Kohala Coast, HI 96743; Wedding Services 808-882-5465; fax 808-880-3200; www.hapunabeachprincehotel.com.

Hilton Waikoloa Village—Hale Aloha (house of love) is the resort's private wedding pavilion overlooking Wailua Bay. The quaint, Hawaiian-style wedding chapel has simple yet elegant *koa* wood, stained glass and custom tile interiors. Hale Aloha is constructed to maximize the natural light and scenic ocean setting for your special day. The Hilton Waikoloa has a large professional banquet and catering and special function staff that can tailor-make your wedding start to finish. Or you may select from their varying levels of prix-fixe wedding packages, named for exotic Hawaiian flowers. Start with Ginger, $900, for use of grounds, non-denominational minister, two leis and roses, bottle of champagne, wedding cake for two and a resort "Just Married" boat ride. Jadeflower, $1,150, adds to the above package a bridal bouquet, groom's boutonniere, photography package, a solo guitarist, dinner at one of four restaurants, *lomi lomi* massage for bride and groom, and salon services for the bride. Orchid, $1,400, takes the next step, with the addition of one-night accommodations in the Bay Suite and chocolate strawberries at evening turndown. Maile, $1,800, includes a video, and Pikake completes the day with round-trip airport transfers, choice of pianist or violinist (in lieu of guitarist) and one-night accommodations in Palace Suite (as opposed to Bay Suite.)

For honeymooners, the Hilton's "Romance Package" is $639 per night and includes oceanview guest room, welcome amenity, Seaside Cabana massage for two, one dinner for two at Kamuela Provision Company or Donatoni's, complimentary yukata robes, sunset catamaran sail for two and full American breakfast for two each day (three-night minimum stay required). For the active health-minded couple that wants some of everything, check out the "Pleasures in Paradise Package," a seven-night super-spa package priced at $6,100, which includes oceanview room accommodations, two spa cuisine meals per day, unlimited fitness classes, nutritional evaluation, computerized fitness evaluation, Red Sail Sports Snorkel Adventure, a personal training session, two massages, two facials, two herbal wraps, two specialty baths, a waterfall hike, round-trip airport transfers from Kona International Airport and welcome amenities. 425 Waikoloa Beach Resort, Kohala Coast, HI 96743; 808-886-1234; 800-HILTONS; fax 808-886-2901; www.hilton.com/hawaii/waikoloa.

Kona Village Resort—If you want a big fancy wedding to out-do your best friend's, don't get married at Kona Village. If you want a simple, elegant ceremony that focuses on the most essential aspect of marriage (the two of you), this is the place. Kona Village's on-site coordinator sees to music, ministers, marriage licenses and a generous portion of aloha for special weddings at the beach, on a private island in a tropical fishpond or other romantic settings under the rustling palms. For newlyweds, romance is in the air, and everywhere else, here. Guest rooms are secluded individual *hale* (thatched-roof huts), some with a beachside hammock or private jacuzzi, and none with telephone, TV, radio or alarm clock to distract you from each other.

There is a weekly sunset reception at the Bora Bora Bar just for honeymooners, and as a special enticement for couples during the months of May and September, children's programs are not offered.

The three-night "Celebration Package" ($1,515 to $2,685) includes accommodations, full American plan (breakfast, lunch and dinner for two daily), beach activities, tennis, fitness center, glass-bottom boat, a bottle of champagne, line art drawing of your *hale*, and a gift basket. The five-night Celebration, $2,525 to $4,475, adds two pareaus (Hawaiian beach wraps) and the seven-night Celebration adds your choice of massage, tennis lesson or sunset catamaran sail for two. P.O. Box 1299, Kaupulehu-Kona, HI 96745; 808-325-5555; 800-367-5290; fax 808-325-5124; www.konavillage.com; e-mail: kvr@aloha.net.

Mauna Kea Beach Hotel—A classic, timeless setting for all manner of celebrations. With its idyllic location along the crescent sands of Kauna'oa Bay and long history of gracious hospitality, Mauna Kea has, since 1965, been the place where traditions begin for happy couples. As an added benefit, Mauna Kea is partnered with Hapuna Beach Prince Hotel next door in one elegant resort. Wedding parties have access to the entire collection of scenic ceremony sites, luxury guest rooms and reception facilities. The resort's Honeymoon/Romance Package starts at $499 per night and includes round-trip limo transportation from Kona International Airport, a chilled bottle of champagne and tropical bouquet waiting in your oceanview room, and a special departure gift. In addition, you are provided with a lavish buffet breakfast for two each day, one candlelit dinner for two on your private lanai or at the award-winning Coast Grille or Batik restaurants. Three-night minimum stay required.

A full-time wedding coordinator assists couples with every arrangement. Thoughtfully organized wedding packages begin with the essential Maile Package, $1,050 including your choice of wedding site, clergy and photographer. The Orchid Package, $1,375, adds to the above a bottle of house champagne, wedding cake for two, flower lei for the bride and maile lei for the groom. The Pikake Package, $2,200, enhances the ceremony with a professional solo musician, special Hawaiian wedding certificate and a videographer; and the Prince Package, $2,600, completes the day with spa treatments for the bride and groom and a manicure, shampoo and hairstyle for the bride. The resort also offers extra-mile assistance with reception menus, decor and entertainment, rooms for your guests and other personalized arrangements. 62-100 Mauna Kea Beach Drive, Kamuela, HI 96743; Wedding Services 808-882-5465; fax 808-880-3200; e-mail: mkrres@maunakeabeachhotel.com; www.maunakeabeachhotel.com.

Mauna Lani Bay Hotel and Bungalows—Mauna Lani has something nobody else has: a gracious, talented director of weddings and

RELIGIOUS SERVICES

Respect for Hawaiian mythology and the traditional deities is very much alive here, though subtle and not easy to explain or fully understand. The Big Island contains Pele's home at Halema'uma'u in Kilauea Caldera. She is the goddess of fire, said to take on the aspect of an old woman with a white dog or other forms as she walks through everyday life. People speak of encounters with her, of visions in the glowing lava, a whispery voice, a sense of presence. Pele's story is old; it comes from a time when the world was much simpler, where people lived in partnership with nature in order to survive. To love, respect and actually deify that which gives you life is not that hard to understand. In a way, we are all guests of nature, all guests in Pele's home. It is not a bad idea to be mindful of that, and to behave with courtesy and respect.

Everybody comes to Hawai'i to have a better life—whether traveling by voyaging canoe, American missionary ship, sugar cane or whaling trader, wartime troop carrier, luxury liner or Boeing 747. And almost everyone who comes here feels a special, at least somewhat mystic, connection at some point during their stay. These experiences are commonplace; it is far and away the exceptional person who does not feel "chicken skin," or goosebumps, when he first sees the *pu'eo* (owl) just at dusk, or watches a whale breach and crash back into the ocean surface, or feels primeval steam from deep-earth volcanic vents, or hears the pure and powerful force of Hawaiian chant and drums. Some people, like us, are compelled to come back and stay. Your experience will be uniquely your own, and we invite you to pay attention to that sort of thing without working at it too hard. At the very least, you'll have a great story to tell.

All that being said, the Big Island is a very special place for the spiritually minded with many different disciplines, from established churches to aesthetic retreats, spas and sweat lodges, swims with

romance, with many years of experience building wonderful weddings. Mrs. Pinkie Crowe and her staff preside over the comprehensive details of elaborate-to-barefoot ceremonies and receptions, with music, flowers and lei, photography, video and other special touches. The resort offers "storybook" sites such as the historic Eva Parker Woods Cottage on the beach, and the reflective Hawaiian fishponds and coconut groves of Kalahuipua'a. Mrs. Crowe is an authorized marriage license agent; advance appointments for licenses required.

For your honeymoon stay, consider Mauna Lani's special "Romantic Interludes" package. From $575 to $680, depending on room cat-

dolphins, readers of tarot, aura, past-life, astrology and other things, and whole realms of intriguing activities to nurture body and soul. These services are not detailed in this guidebook, but we'd like to direct you to the Yellow Pages or local newspapers and visitor publications for more information, with the following advice: If you are looking for a spiritual experience here, you're likely to find it with or without the help of a hired guide. We can also say from experience that most people are more likely to find spirituality in the most unlikely places.

For those who like to include church as part of their vacation, many resorts offer Sunday service on-property, but if yours does not, there is a place for you to go. Visitors are always welcome in local churches, and in resort areas they make up a regular part of the church family. Like everything else on the island, the diverse ethnic makeup and wide range of different lifestyles is reflected in the places of worship. There are Korean, Chinese and Japanese-style Buddhist temples, synagogues, Catholic and Protestant churches of many denominations, Mormon temples, gathering places for Bahai, Jehovah's Witness, Seventh-Day Adventist, Christian Science and many others.

In Kailua-Kona, you can attend Sunday services at Mokuaikaua Church, Hawai'i's first Christian church built by missionaries in 1820. Or visit the remarkable painted churches in Captain Cook or Puna, with vivid, floor-to-ceiling murals of Bible stories. Imiola Congregational Church, the cornerstone of "church row" in Waimea, is a tiny place bursting with aloha (visit them at www.imiola.com). In Puako, the Catholic Church of the Ascension is a beautiful, circular sanctuary decorated with bright tropical flowers from people's yards. A look in the Yellow Pages (between Chocolate and Cigars) will probably tell you everything you need to know, or check with your hotel or condo concierge desk.

egory, your Interlude includes accommodations, rose petal turndown with champagne and chocolate-dipped strawberries on arrival night, breakfast for two daily, one elegant dinner for two in resort restaurants, your choice of a romantic picnic basket or lunch at The Gallery and a special keepsake amenity. The rate is based on a three-night stay and additional nights are priced separately. For couples with the means to enjoy it, indulge in a "$25,000 Weekend Bungalow Package." This extravagance provides three nights in your private 4,000-square-foot bungalow with pool and whirlpool spa, full gourmet kitchen, fully stocked premium bar, and daily hors d'oeuvres served by attendant butler and maid. Also included are breakfast, lunch and dinner daily composed to your liking by the hotel chef de cuisine or in resort restaurants, a privately chartered sunset cruise aboard a sailing catamaran, golf, tennis, scuba, helicopter tours and other activities, round-trip airport transfers and a gift from the general manager. 68-1400 Mauna Lani Drive, Kohala Coast, HI 96743; 808-885-6622; 800-367-2323; fax 808-885-1484; www.maunalani.com; e-mail: maunalani@maunalani.com.

Royal Kona Resort—The Royal Kona has two basic wedding packages. The Orchid Wedding is from $400 and includes a marriage license appointment, minister for an oceanfront ceremony, special bridal party flowers, champagne and keepsake glasses, and Hawaiian wedding certificate. The Maile Wedding is from $900 and includes all Orchid package items plus maile leis, deluxe wedding cake, and a photography package. Special honeymoon room packages are also available with the wedding packages. 75-5852 Ali'i Drive, Kailua-Kona, HI 96740; 808-329-3111; 800-22-ALOHA; fax 808-329-7230; www.royalkona.com.

Waikoloa Beach Marriott, Outrigger Resort—With its lovely proximity to 'Anaeho'omalu Bay as well as the excellent array of Waikoloa resort amenities, a wedding coordinator on staff and flexible, reasonably priced packages, this property is an excellent choice. Location-only site fees are $275 when the wedding couple provides their own minister, flowers and additional accoutrements. The simplest package, however, is priced at only $485, which includes the site fee, minister, solo guitarist and leis for the bride and groom. Package II, at $595, adds to the above a bottle of house champagne and wedding cake for two. For $950, Package III upgrades the champagne to Moet et Chandon White Star, adds a select tray of hors d'oeuvres for two, provides a larger, two-tier wedding cake and a large ivory and white floral basket at the site. Hawai'i Calls restaurant offers intimate private dining rooms for wedding parties or elegant banquet facilities for grander receptions. The hotel welcomes your private wedding coordinator, or will assist personally with details for your special day. 69-275 Waikoloa Beach Drive, Waikoloa, HI 96738-5711; 808-886-6789; 800-922-5533; fax 808-886-1832; www.waikoloabeachmarriott.com.

Helpful Information

INFORMATION BOOTHS Booths located in the shopping areas of the bigger towns and along the main drags can provide helpful information and lots of brochures.

Big Island Visitors Bureau: 250 Keawe Street, Hilo; 808-961-5797; fax 808-961-2126; www.bigisland.org.

BANKS Basic hours are 8:30 a.m. to 3 p.m., but some are open until 4 or 5 p.m. Most will cash U.S. traveler's checks with a picture ID.

CREDIT CARDS A few small condominiums still do not accept any form of credit card payment, but stores and hotels almost always do. For lost or stolen credit cards phone: American Express 800-992-3404; VISA 800-847-2911.

SALES TAX A sales tax of 4.167 is added to all purchases made in Hawai'i. There is an additional room-use tax added to your hotel or condominium bill.

HOLIDAYS Holidays unique to the state of Hawai'i: March 26 is Prince Kuhio Day, June 11 is Kamehameha Day and August 21 is Admissions Day.

Communications

Television Most hotels and condominiumss have in-room televisions with cable service and pay-per-view movies. The major broadcast networks have Honolulu stations that telecast to the Big Island. They are KHON-FOX, KGMB-CBS, KHNL-NBC, KHET-PBS and KITV-ABC. Other major TV channels are carried by cable TV companies, and generally most programming is current with what you're used to watching on the mainland. (In some cases, episodes run about a week late.) Sports enthusiasts, please remember the time difference—you may have to get up early to watch your favorite game. Or, some sports events may be shown pre-recorded. Channel numbers can vary from district to district depending on the cable company and from hotel to hotel depending on their arrangements with same. *Big Island Visitor Magazine* does a pretty good job of sorting out the channel numbers, and there's always the TV guide channel on your television. Big Island Television broadcasts on Channel 9 and provides insider tips and special programs about the Big Island 24 hours a day.

RADIO Because of the massive mountains Mauna Kea and Mauna Loa, radio reception on the Big Island can be tricky when you're on the road. Some of the larger stations are: KANO, 91.1 FM Hilo, National Public Radio; KAPA, 99.1 FM Kona, 100.3 FM Hilo, "all Hawaiian all the time"; KAOY "K-Hawai'i," 101.5 FM Kona, 92.7 FM Hilo, rock from around the world; K-BIG, 106.1 FM Kona, 97.9 FM Hilo, Hawaiian music and current hits; KIPA, 790 AM Kona, 620 AM Hilo, oldies; KISS, 93.9 FM Kona, 95.9 FM Hilo contemporary Top 40 KWYI, 106.9 FM Kona, light contemporary and oldies.

PERIODICALS If you're planning your visit far enough in advance, or if you love the island and want to keep informed, you may want to subscribe to one of the daily newspapers. Because the papers will be sent via third-class mail, it can take a week or more to receive your paper, therefore it's practical to only subscribe to the Sunday edition. *Hawai'i Tribune-Herald* is a daily paper published in Hilo, with island, state, national and international news; 355 Kinoole Street, Hilo, HI 96720; 808-935-6621; www.hilohawaiitribune.com. *West Hawai'i Today* is a similar paper published in Kona and includes the weekly *North Hawai'i News* insert; 75-5580 Kuakini Highway, Kailua-Kona, HI 96740; 808-329-9311; www.westhawaiitoday.com. There are also a couple of small press publications with specialized emphasis and coverage. The monthly *Coffee Times* is a magazine format with focus on Kona coffee country and culture; P.O. Box 1092, Captain Cook, HI 96704; 800-750-5662; www.coffeetimes.com. *Hawai'i Island Journal* is a bimonthly paper that provides an energetic, fresh perspective on island news and events; P.O. Box 227, Captain Cook, HI 96704; 808-328-1880; www.hawaiiislandjournal.com.

VISITOR PUBLICATIONS Many free publications are available at hotel and condo concierge desks, visitor kiosks, the airport, shopping centers and many other spots islandwide. Most of these are very good, targeted to the Big Island visitor and focused on their needs. They make their money by selling advertising so naturally the pages are full of tourist-related ads; however, the information between those pages can be very interesting and helpful, and is updated on a quarterly or monthly basis. Plus, these publications often have discount coupons on everything from meals to island tours, souvenirs, clothing and film processing.

Some of the best to look for are *Big Island Beach & Activity Guide* (www.beachactivityguide.com), a good quick reference to beaches islandwide; *101 Things to Do on Hawai'i the Big Island* (www.101things.com); *Kona Views* (www.konaviews.com); *Big Island Visitor Magazine,* a complete cable TV guide (www.bigislandvisitor.com); *This Week Big Island* (www.thisweek.com); and *Spotlight's Big Island Gold* (www.spotlighthawaii.com). Believe it or not, there's also a wealth of information in Big Island phone books.

WEBSITES If you're a net-surfer you already know there is a limitless world of information on the web. There are thousands of Hawai'i-based websites available, some, of course, better than others. Most provide active, clickable links to other sites that will lead you on a virtual journey through any aspect of travel that suits your fancy.

For travel arrangements, you may already be familiar with the bigger travel sites: www.expedia.com, www.travelocity.com and www.priceline.com. These offer bargain airfares, cruises, car rentals, hotel accommodations and activities. Expedia and travelocity book specific airlines, hotels and other products. Priceline is strictly a price-driven, "blind" service. You plug in a price you want to pay along with your credit card, and if any provider is willing to sell to you at that price, you're booked. That's when you find out which airline you'll be flying or hotel you'll be staying in. If your schedule is flexible and you're a bit of a gambler, you may find excellent bargains on the internet. Rates, restrictions and availability change rapidly on the web. Be sure of what you want before you commit since changes cost money, presently a $100 re-ticketing fee on major air carriers. If you're putting your own itinerary together, it's usually best to book your airfare first, then go to work on hotel rooms. Check your family's priorities first. If you want particular rooms at a particular place, start with that and work your airfare around it.

For island information, please be aware that posted data on Hawai'i and the Big Island is subject to frequent, rapid and unannounced change. Nearly every business related to the visitor industry now hosts its own website. Hotels, condos, B&Bs, airlines, cruise ships, restaurants, attractions, activities and shops are available on-line in infinite numbers. A little surfing can yield a huge, maybe overwhelming, amount of information.

We suggest you start with the following sites, and we encourage the whole family to get involved.

www.gohawaii.com, the Hawai'i Visitors and Convention Bureau site, with many live links to its members and associates, a good calendar of events, island-by-island guide, historical information and more.

www.alternative-hawaii.com, one of the best calendar sites, with easy-to-use and attractive presentations for all types of island events, things to see and do, and absolutely gorgeous photography.

From there, visit the Big Island's biggest attraction, Volcanoes National Park, www.nps.gov/havo, an excellent site with a world of information, maps, tips and suggestions. Then go to the stars and see the Center for International Astronomy site at www.ifa.hawaii.edu/mok/about_maunakea.htm.

There are thousands of sites about accommodations. If you're looking for a bed and breakfast, start with Hawai'i Island Bed & Breakfast Association, www.stayhawaii.com/index.html. For a condo vacation in Kona, try Kona Hawai'i Vacation Rentals, www.konahawaii.com.

Kona Web: www.konaweb.com is a fun, independent site with lots of active links to other pages and all sorts of information on island attractions, restaurants, activities and a calendar of events. It features personal reviews of all kinds of things from visitors and residents as well.

Medical Information

Hospitals

Kona Hospital, Kealakekua (808-322-9311)

Hilo Medical Center, 1190 Waianuenue Avenue (808-974-4700)

Ka'u Hospital (808-928-8331)

Kohala Hospital (808-889-6211)

Honoka'a, Hale Ho'ola (808-775-7211)

North Hawai'i Community Hospital, 67-1125 Mamalahoa Highway, Waimea (808-885-4444).

There are also several clinics around the Big Island to handle emergencies or walk-in patients needing urgent care. Your condominium or hotel desk can provide you with suggestions or check the Yellow Pages.

Kona District Kaiser Permanente Medical Care Clinic, 75-184 Hualalai Road (808-327-2900); Keauhou-Kona Medical Clinic, 78-6740 Ali'i Drive, Suite 102, Keauhou (808-322-2750); Kona-Kohala Medical Associates, 75-137 Hualalai Road, Kailua-Kona (808-329-1346); Hualalai Urgent Care, Crossroads Medical Centre, Henry Street (808-327-4357)

Kohala Coast Hawai'i Family Medical Center (808-883-8877)

Waimea Kaiser Permanente Medical Care Clinic, 67-1190 Lindsey Road (808-881-4500); Lucy Henriques Medical Center, on Highway 19 near Parker Ranch Center (808-885-7297)

Hamakua Coast Hamakua Health Center (808-775-7204)

Hilo Kaiser Permanente Medical Care Clinic, 1292 Waianuenue Avenue (808-934-4000); Hilo Medical Associates, 73 Pu'uhonu Place (808-934-2000)

See "Helpful Phone Numbers" at the end of the chapter for more numbers. Calling 911 will put you in contact with local police, fire and ambulances.

Hazards

SUN SAFETY The sunshine is stronger in Hawai'i than on the mainland, so a few basic guidelines will ensure that you return home with a tan, not a burn. Use a good lotion with a sunscreen, reapply after swimming and don't forget the lips. Be sure to moisturize after a day in the sun and wear a hat to protect your face. Exercise self-control and stay out a limited time the first few days, remembering that a gradual tan will last longer. It is best to avoid being out between the hours of noon and three when it is the hottest. Be cautious of overcast days when it is very easy to become burned unknowingly. Don't forget that the ocean acts as a reflector and time spent in it equals time spent on the beach.

Getting There

Arrival and Departure Tips: We confidently recommend professional travel agents to help plan your Big Island vacation. Even though new worlds of information and almost-unbelievable bargains open up daily on the internet, a travel professional can work with you and your family to provide the very best options regarding price and priorities. That being said, following are suggestions to help you do your homework well in advance, before you visit your travel planner.

AIRLINE INFORMATION

Air travel has changed since September 11, 2001. Added restrictions and fewer travelers can drive rates up and cut flight schedules. Recent years have seen the disappearance of TWA and Pan Am, and in 2002, United Airlines, Hawai'i's largest air travel provider, filed for Chapter 11 bankruptcy, making the picture even more uncertain.

Uncertainty, however, can make for some interesting times. The Big Island is seeing an increase in Midwestern and East Coast travelers who might otherwise have vacationed in Europe. There's also a closer-in booking "window," with visitors making their reservations within 30 days (or less) of travel. These changes make for more flexible rates, deposit policies and cancellation policies on travel services and accommodations—which translate into benefits for the visitor. Additionally, there are more ways to plan travel than ever before. Competition is fierce and services are interconnected. You can book room and car packages through your air carrier, earn airline miles from your rental car company, and pay part of your hotel room with your airline miles. Travel planning by internet opens even more options, worlds of information and bargain basement prices at the touch of a button.

Because of the complexities of today's travel universe, again recommend a professional travel agent to help you with your Hawai'i vacation. Travel agents do not charge their traveling clients; they earn commissions from travel providers based on a percentage of the rates (10 to 15 percent in the case of most hotels) or a flat rate (currently $50 per booking from the airlines). Travel agents have access to an enormous amount of information, information that changes constantly. More and more, they are networking with wholesale companies, allying with travel consortia and otherwise working very hard to keep up with the times and provide their clients with the very best possible rates. You can do it yourself; it's easy. However, travel agents book trips for a living and they can almost always save you money. More importantly, they can save you a great deal of time and aggravation. Remember, time is the most valuable commodity you have to spend, particularly on vacation.

This is particularly true if your family is coming together from different cities for a reunion, wedding or other special occasion. Either one lucky person usually gets charged with making the travel arrangements for everybody, or it's every man for himself. Either way, it's difficult to avoid wasted time, hard feelings or inevitable frustrations. Visit a professional, give them your complete itinerary and let them handle it for you.

FLIGHTS TO THE ISLANDS

At present, several airlines fly directly into Kona International Airport from mainland cities, the most convenient way to go, but currently there are no direct mainland flights into Hilo. Both Kona International Airport and Hilo International Airport are modern terminal facilities. Kona airport's runway was recently expanded to accommodate international jumbo jet flights and the terminal got a major facelift. Hilo's runway can also handle large aircraft, but it remains under-utilized, not the second gateway to the Big Island as its designers planned. Kona is increasingly busy with more and more flights as the visitor industry develops on the island's sunny west side. In fact, you can start sightseeing right at Kona airport with a visit to the Ellison S. Onizuka Space Center (see Chapter 2 for more information).

Many of the major U.S. and international airlines fly into Honolulu, from where you can take a 35-minute interisland flight on Hawaiian or Aloha Airlines, which also provides connections through Kahului Airport on Maui to Hilo or Kona. In spite of United Airlines' financial struggles, it is still the dominant air carrier to Hawai'i with about half of all traffic to and from the islands. United provides direct mainland to Kona service (without the Honolulu stopover) from Los Angeles and San Francisco daily, and Denver weekly. Their schedule may shift according to seasonal demand (Christmas–New Year's, for example), when they may add flights. If your schedule allows you to book these direct flights, especially traveling with kids, you'll appreciate the savings of time and trouble.

Please be aware that if your mainland-based carrier does not fly directly into Hilo or Kona, they will book your connecting flight from Honolulu at a substantially discounted rate. It is no longer necessary or advisable to book only as far as Honolulu and count on a less expensive interisland flight when you arrive. When you check in at the airport, have your luggage checked to your final destination, Hilo or Kona. At the Honolulu International Airport, the mainland terminal is a separate building, about a quarter-mile walk or shuttle ride from the interisland terminal, so it's impractical and unnecessary to retrieve luggage in Honolulu and re-check it on your interisland flight.

The following airlines have direct flights into Kona International Airport (as always, subject to change).

Hawai'i-based Carriers

Aloha Airlines—Aloha Airlines flies directly into Kona from Oakland, CA (with connection from Las Vegas), and Vancouver, Canada. In addition to these cities, Aloha also has flights from Burbank and Orange County, CA (with connection from Phoenix), through Honolulu. 800-367-5250; www.alohaairlines.com.

Hawaiian Airlines—Hawaiian Airlines flies into Kona from Los Angeles, Phoenix and San Diego, with stops in Honolulu. At this time, Hilo International Airport only has interisland flights from Hawaiian and Aloha Airlines. 800-882-8811; www.hawaiianair.com.

U.S./International Carriers

American Airlines—800-433-7300; www.aa.com
Japan Airlines—800-525-3663
United Airlines—800-241-6522; www.ual.com

The following American and international airlines have flights into Honolulu International Airport and can arrange your interisland reservations to Kona or Hilo.

Air Canada—888-247-2262; www.aircanada.ca
Air New Zealand—800-262-1234
Air Pacific—800-227-4446
All Nippon Airways—800-235-9262
Aloha Airlines—800-367-5250; www.alohaairlines.com
American Airlines—800-433-7300; www.aa.com
American Trans Air/Pleasant Hawaiian Holidays—800-435-9282
China Airlines—800-227-5118
Continental Airlines—800-523-3273; www.continental.com
Delta Airlines—800-221-1212; www.delta-air.com
Hawaiian Airlines—800-367-5320; www.hawaiianair.com
Japan Airlines/Jalways—800-521-1441
JTB/Oli Oli—800-839-6636
Korean Air—800-438-5000
Northwest Airlines—800-225-2525; www.nwa.com
Philippines Airlines—800-435-7725
Polynesian Airlines—800-842-7659
Quantas Airways—800-227-4500
United Airlines—800-241-6522; www.ual.com

INTERISLAND FLIGHTS

Hawaiian and Aloha Airlines are the primary interisland air carriers and offer generally competitive fares. Advance reservations are required and you'll need to check in through several security points, so arrival 90 minutes before your scheduled flight is recommended. It's possible to purchase seven-day passes from both Aloha Airlines and Hawaiian Airlines, providing unlimited travel for a week, for approximately $350 to $400. Both airlines also offer promotional discounts, group rates, wedding party specials, internet-only discount rates, and air-room-car packages.

Aloha Airlines—In the U.S. & Canada 800-367-5250, 877-879-2564; in Honolulu 808-484-1111; on the Big Island 808-935-5771; e-mail: aloha@alohaair.com; www.alohaairlines.com.

Hawaiian Airlines—In the U.S. & Canada 800-367-5320; in Honolulu 808-838-1555; on the Big Island 800-882-8811; www.hawaiianair.com.

Island Air—Flights are limited between Kona on the Big Island and Honolulu via Lanai or Kapalua on Maui. In the U.S. 800-323-3345; in Honolulu 808-484-2222; from the Neighbor Islands 800-652-6541; www.islandair.com.

Mokulele Flight Service—This Hawaiian family–owned independent air service offers interisland flights on a regular schedule between Kona and Honolulu, and Kona and Kahului Airport on Maui. 808-326-7070

Pacific Wings—Pacific Wings is a small commuter air service based on Maui and connects several Hawai'i destinations with Kamuela Airport on the Big Island. The airline provides scheduled air service in and out of Kamuela Airport to Kahului on Maui and to Honolulu with connecting services to other points. The airline provides service to those smaller island airports not as readily serviced by Hawaiian and Aloha Air lines. Pacific Wings operates twin-engine Cessna 402C aircraft and offers competitive fares with Hawaiian and Aloha. Pacific Wings also offers special air tour packages to specific island destinations/attractions. 808-873-0877, 888-575-4546, fax 808-873-7920; e-mail: info@pacificwings.com.

Cruise Lines

Before the advent of modern jet airlines, most visitors to Hawai'i traveled by elegant ocean liner for a "Titanic" luxury experience (minus the sinking, of course). Today, cruise ships have added a whole new dimension to Hawai'i vacation options. Like self-contained floating resorts, cruise ships now offer indulgent spas and fitness centers with shipboard exercise programs in addition to (perhaps) over-indulgent food service, casinos, professional entertainment and overall party atmosphere. Cruising can be a great way for families to go, with a wide range of kid's games and organized activities, special menus and over-the-top treats (like 24-hour pizza by the slice and endless soda refills with the ship's logo cups). Special programs allow mom and dad to enjoy dinner and a show by themselves while the kids do their own things with friends (and remember, they can't get off the boat). Several ships call regularly at Hilo and Kona harbors. Some schedule interisland cruises, which can be a great way to see more than one island without making separate arrangements for flights, hotels and cars. It does take longer to cruise than to fly, but the convenience may be a good trade-off, depending on how much time you have. Plus, prices are generally inclusive of meals and shipboard activities.

As with every other aspect of planning your Big Island vacation, there are a lot of options to choose from. Once again, we recommend an experienced travel agent (there are cruise specialists) and a little homework. A good site to start with on the internet is www.cruiseweb.com. Another benefit of cruising is the warm welcome you receive when the ship docks. With the dramatic increase in cruise ship arrivals into Hilo and Kona, the old "boat days" festivities are making a comeback. Often local visitor industry groups, civic and cultural clubs and craft vendors are on hand to meet and greet arriving passengers at the docks. This is a resurgent and rapidly growing segment of the travel industry, one which we expect to hear more good things about as more ships choose the Big Island for a destination.

Following are cruise lines whose ships presently call at Hilo or Kona ports:

Norwegian Cruise Lines—800-327-7030; www.ncl.com
Holland America—877-SAIL-HAL; www.hollandamerica.com
Royal Caribbean—800-398-9819; www.royalcaribbean.com
Carnival Cruise Lines—888-CARNIVAL; www.carnival.com

Driving on the Big Island

STOP

Driving on the Big Island is really no different from anywhere else, with one small exception: People are nice. Big Island drivers are generally the most courteous and congenial you're likely to find. The majority drive with aloha, which may catch you off guard when they yield to let you make a left turn in front of them, wave you through an intersection and even smile. Unfortunately like anywhere else too, there are, of course, some who don't, so it pays to drive with aloha *and* awareness at the same time.

The speed limit is 55, despite long, tempting stretches of nearly empty road on the Kona side. Police do enforce the speed limits; they also enforce the seatbelt law. Don't let a ticket mar your vacation.

Directions are easy. (Remember the *shaka* map in your hand? Make a fist with your right hand. Extend your thumb, north and pinkie, south.) There's basically only one road. Queen Ka'ahumanu Highway, Route 19, covers the northern half of the island from Kailua-Kona to Hilo (from your middle finger, under your thumb and over to your wrist). And Hawai'i Belt Road, Route 11, covers the southern half (from your wrist around the top of your pinkie back to your middle finger).

Small, green, numbered signs on the shoulders are mile markers between towns and very often used to give directions. It's also a good idea to use the practical Hawaiian words *mauka* toward the mountains and *makai* toward the ocean. In other words, if somebody tells you the gas station is just past 113-mile marker on the Queen K *mauka* side, you should know exactly where to go. Also keep your eyes open for the bright red and yellow Hawaiian warrior markers, which indicate historic sites.

An excellent road map of the Big Island, *Hawai'i, The Big Island* by cartographer James A. Bier, is highly recommended. It's available at local bookstores or can be ordered from Catalog Order Desk, The University of Hawai'i Press, Honolulu, HI 96822.

Getting Around

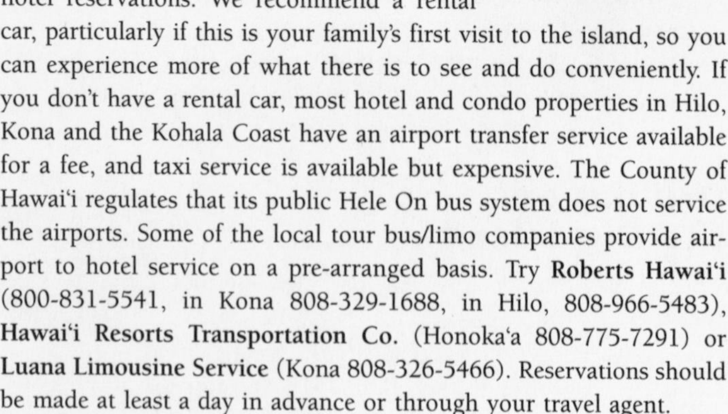

FROM THE AIRPORT It's best to arrange your ground transportation at the same time you book airline and hotel reservations. We recommend a rental car, particularly if this is your family's first visit to the island, so you can experience more of what there is to see and do conveniently. If you don't have a rental car, most hotel and condo properties in Hilo, Kona and the Kohala Coast have an airport transfer service available for a fee, and taxi service is available but expensive. The County of Hawai'i regulates that its public Hele On bus system does not service the airports. Some of the local tour bus/limo companies provide airport to hotel service on a pre-arranged basis. Try **Roberts Hawai'i** (800-831-5541, in Kona 808-329-1688, in Hilo, 808-966-5483), **Hawai'i Resorts Transportation Co.** (Honoka'a 808-775-7291) or **Luana Limousine Service** (Kona 808-326-5466). Reservations should be made at least a day in advance or through your travel agent.

PUBLIC TRANSPORTATION In the Kailua-Kona and Keauhou areas, you can catch the **Ali'i Shuttle**, which serves the entire length of Ali'i Drive from Kailua-Kona to Keauhou. The shuttle runs Monday

CIRCLE ISLAND DRIVE

You can drive completely around the Big Island from Hilo to Kona in a day. It's only 225 miles, but it is a long and tiring drive, not really conducive to sightseeing and leisurely exploring. We'd suggest you make a two-day tour of it and give yourself time to see everything. Drive the 100 miles on the northern route from Kona to Hilo through Waimea, spend the night, see the volcano the next day and return along the southern route.

From Kailua-Kona, drive north on Route 19 along the hot, black lava coastline on your right and the sparkling Pacific on your left. About 30 miles pass, then you reach the stop sign at Kawaihae. Turn right and head inland and uphill along a winding road through gradually greener countryside, and be on the lookout for rainbows. In Waimea, it's suddenly cooler and misty. Turn left at the stoplight and continue through a Western-style town surrounded by rolling hills that make you think of Ireland instead of islands. When you leave town, the scene opens up into a vast panoramic pasture land, and you pass between flanks of tall forest.

A few more miles later, past Honoka'a, the sun comes out again and you're back to the ocean on the other side of the island. The road swings southward along beautiful stretches of farmland. If you look closely, you can still see sugar cane waving in the breeze, or spot banana trees along the roadside, or gardens of tropical flowers. The road winds through three V-shaped gulches into deep, almost-secret valleys and crosses a series of bridges where a quick look to the right might show you a waterfall. If not, you might visit Akaka Falls State Park or the World Botanical Gardens at Umauma before you continue to Hilo. Just outside of town, at the village of Peepeekeo, look straight ahead at the horizon. If it's a fairly clear day, you might be able to make out the steam cloud from Kilauea for a moment. Cross the "singing bridge" over the Wailoa River into Hilo and cruise along the shoreline of tranquil Hilo Bay.

Enjoy your time in Hilo, then head to Volcanoes National Park, south on what is now Highway 11, past farm communities and misty *ohia* forest, gradually climbing up to Kilauea.

After your experience in the park, head south on Hawai'i Belt Road, Route 11, towards the southern tip of the island. Cruise along uncluttered highway, through farmland and colorful little towns worth a stop, and long stretches of empty, rainy lava fields before the road reaches the ocean again on the Kona side and turns north. If you're not worn out, take time to explore Pu'uhonua o Honaunau, a "place of refuge" where fugitives found sanctuary and forgiveness. From here the road winds through the upper elevations of Kona coffee country before dropping back down into familiar territory and the flat black lava land of Kona.

through Saturday and takes 45 minutes in each direction. Its turnaround points are the Lanihau Shopping Center in Kailua-Kona and the Kona Surf Resort in Keauhou. The shuttle makes stops along Ali'i Drive at all major hotels and shopping centers. The fare is $2 each way; hours of operation are (northbound) from Kona Surf every 90 minutes 8:30 a.m. to 7 p.m. and (southbound) from Lanihau Center 9:20 a.m. to 6:20 p.m. Look for the white bus and just flag it down. 808-938-1112, 808-775-7121.

The other general transportation alternative is the **Hele On bus system** operated by the County of Hawai'i. The public buses operate in both Hilo and Kailua-Kona as well as offer islandwide service. Standard fare for short distances is 75¢ within Hilo or Kailua-Kona, and gradually increases depending on how far you are going around the island. The around-the-island fare, Hilo to Kona, is a reasonable $6 one way/$12 round trip.

Hele On bus tickets are sold by the sheet at a 10 percent discount from the regular per ticket fare. Ten tickets per sheet cost $6.75. Seniors (60+), the disabled and students can buy ticket sheets for $5. As an example, a one way trip from Hilo to Kona would cost seven tickets. Bus tickets are available at various stores, shops and businesses around the island displaying the Hele On bus poster. There is a $1 per piece charge for luggage and backpacks. For bus schedules and ticket information, contact County of Hawai'i, Mass Transportation Agency, 630 East Lanikaula Street, Hilo, HI 96720; 808-961-8744.

LIMOUSINE SERVICES If you want to splurge on transportation for that special occasion, wedding, honeymoon or for whatever reason, you can arrange for a personalized limousine for everything from airport-hotel service to a complete private around-the-island tour

BIG ISLAND DISTANCES

Distances from Kona Airport: to Hilo via the north route Highway 19 is 97.5 miles; to Kamuela via Highway 19 is 34 miles; to Volcano via Highway 11 is 100 miles; to South Point via Highway 11 is 60 miles; to Honoka'a via Highway 19 is 49 miles; and to Hawi in North Kohala via Highways 19/270 is 44 miles. Distances from the Hilo Airport to other areas: to Kailua-Kona via Highway 19 is 97.5 miles; to Honoka'a via Highway 19 is 42 miles; to Hawi in North Kohala via Highways 19/250 is 76 miles; to Kamuela via Highway 19 is 54.6 miles; to Volcano via Highway 11 is 28 miles; and to South Point via Highway 11 is 73 miles. The distance between Hilo and Kailua-Kona via the south route Highway 11 is 125 miles.

complete with champagne and catered lunch. The cost is obviously expensive but first-class for those who can afford it. Here's a listing of limousine service operators:

Carey Town & Country Limousine (888-563-2888) provides chauffeur-driven luxury sedans, limousines, vans, etc., plus airport/hotel transfer service on all the Hawaiian islands.

Island Luxury Service (808-883-0198) provides fine touring vehicles, luxury vans and airport/hotel transfer services on the Kona and Kohala coasts.

Luana Limousine Service (808-326-LIMO; 800-999-4001) provides full-service limousine service on the Big Island.

Meridian Hawaiian Resorts Transport (808-885-7484) operates out of Mauna Lani Bay Hotel and Bungalows, Kohala Coast.

Resorts Limousines (808-327-9742; fax 808-327-0023; e-mail: resortslimos@aol.com) offers transportation by limo, SUV and multi-passenger vans or airport transfers, hotel pickups, customized tours and more. Special wedding/honeymoon touches available by request include fun things like magnetic "just married" signs, champagne and a red carpet.

Taxis Big Island taxi service is expensive. Metered fares are standard between companies islandwide, currently $2 for pickup plus $2 per mile, but miles add up fast in the long distances between airports and hotels, or hotels and island attractions. For example, from Kona International to King Kamehameha's Kona Beach Hotel downtown is $19.50. Going the other direction, to Hapuna Beach Prince Hotel on the Kohala Coast, is $55. From Hilo International Airport to Banyan Drive hotels is $10. If you do choose to use taxi service, it's best to pre-arrange transportation and to clarify hours of operation. Unlike mainland taxicabs, some companies in some locations close at night unless a pickup time is pre-arranged. On the other hand, many taxi companies offer sightseeing tours and special service 24 hours a day.

Hilo's taxi services include **A-1 Bob's Taxi** (808-959-4800, 808-963-5470), **AA Marshall's Taxi** (808-936-2654), **Ace One Taxi** (808-935-8303), **Percy's Taxi** (808-969-7060), **Hilo Harry's Taxi** (808-935-7091) and **Anuenue/Rainbow Taxi** (808-896-8294). Kona/Kohala/Waimea taxi services include **Air Taxi & Tours** (808-883-8262), **Aloha Taxi** (808-325-5448, 808-329-7779), **Alpha Star Taxi** (808-885-4771), **C & C Taxi** (808-329-6388, 808-325-5121), **D & E Taxi** (808-329-4279), **Elsa Taxi** (808-937-8888), **Kona Airport Taxi** (808-329-7779), **Paradise Taxi** (808-329-1234) and **Triple A-1 Taxi** (808-325-3818).

RENTAL CARS, VANS AND FOUR-WHEEL DRIVES The Big Island has some 1,500 miles of paved county and state roads and highways. And those roads and highways pass through some of the loveliest and most diverse scenery in Hawai'i. The best way to see it all is by hiring your own car. Most standard rental car companies have outlets at Hilo and Kona airports and a few have desks at major hotels and resorts. They offer a variety of cars at a variety of rates, with special low-season, weekly discount, and holiday package deals. You can check out the following list and contact them yourself (most have toll-free numbers and websites) or you can have your travel agent do it. Do inquire about room and car or air, room and car packages.

Rental cars are your best bargain for transportation since they give you the independence and mobility to come and go as you please and to see and do what you want. Rates vary greatly among the car rental agencies as well as by season so it's wise to shop around. A survey of Big Island car rental agencies revealed the following rates, all with no mileage charges. The daily rate for an economy/compact ranges from $30 to $50. For a mid-size car, the daily rate ranges from $35 to $55. Full-size cars range from $40 to $60. Mini-vans range from $55 to $85. Keep in mind that these figures are only approximate.

Special rates may apply during the "low" season in Hawai'i, usually from Labor Day until about Thanksgiving and again from Easter until about June 1. Hawai'i's peak season from Thanksgiving to Easter or spring break finds demand and prices high on rental cars. The summer season, although not as strong as winter, generates a fair amount of demand and rates seem to fluctuate. Some local events, such as the Merrie Monarch hula competition in Hilo and the Ironman Triathlon in Kona, can deplete the rental car supply and drive the prices up.

One thing that affects car rental rates is the extra charge for insurance coverage. This rate can run anywhere from $15 and up per day. This increases the daily rate drastically and most agencies strongly encourage you to buy the coverage. However, it is suggested that you check with your own insurance company at home to verify exactly what your policy covers. In fact, bring along your insurance company's address and telephone number just in case. Hawai'i is a no-fault state and without the insurance, if there is an accident, you are required to take care of all the damages before leaving the island.

Most of the car rental agencies have similar policies. They require a minimum age of 25 and a major credit card for a deposit to hold your reservation. Most feature no mileage charges, with you paying for the gas (from $1.85 to $2.25 or more per gallon). There is also a 4 percent sales tax and other fees like an airport concession tax and vehicle surtax, which add on another $3 to $5 or more.

The Saddle Road is off limits to regular rental cars. Driving on it violates the rental car agreement. You'd need a four-wheel-drive vehicle to reach such places as the summit of 14,000-foot Mauna Kea and other inaccessible backcountry or off-road locations, which are also off limits to regular rental cars.

One final note on renting a car on the Big Island. If you pick up your car at one airport, say at Kona, and drop it off at Hilo, most car rental agencies will charge you what is called a "drop" charge. This can run as high as $30 to $40. That's why it is usually best to pick up and return a rental car at the same location.

Warning: Even paradise has its share of thieves so *never* leave your automobile unlocked at the beach, park, scenic site or parking lot. Also, take personal valuables with you. Secure your car and your valuables. And don't leave the keys in your car.

RENTAL CAR LISTINGS **AA Aloha Cars-R-Us**, 800-655-7989 or 800-852-9993; Kona 808-879-7989; Hilo 808-969-1478; www.hawaiicarrental.com

Alamo Rent A Car, 800-327-9633; Kona 808-329-8896; Hilo 808-961-3353

Avis Rent A Car, 800-321-3712; Kona 808-327-3000; Hilo 808-935-1290

Budget Rent A Car, all locations, 800-527-0700

Dollar Rent A Car, 800-800-4000; Kona 808-329-2744; Hilo 808-961-6059

Enterprise, 800-800-4000; Kona 808-331-2509

Hertz Rent a Car, 877-603-0615; Kona 329-3566; Hilo 808-935-2896; www.hertz.com

National Car Rental, 800-321-3712; Kona 808-329-1674; Hilo 808-935-0891; www.nationalcar.com

Thrifty Car Rental, all locations 800-527-0700; 800-367-5238; Kona 808-329-1339; Hilo 808-961-6698; www.thrifty.com

Big Island Exotic Cars has something different. Contact owner/"Director of Fun" Tim Kuglin for a stylish ride in one of their 1957 Porsche Speedster replicas. The perfect island cruiser, this four-speed sportscar is a brand-new car rental option at time of publication so inquire about other vehicles. Drivers must be at least 30 years old with valid credit card, driver's license and active insurance. Rates: from $299. Kona; 808-331-1997; www.bigislandexoticcars.com.

CAMPER/RV RENTALS In recent years, two companies started offering modern, self-contained RVs for rent, in part due to the increasing demand for alternative vacation experiences. While this is a great opportunity for those who enjoy RV camping, a word of caution is in order. Most of the Big Island campgrounds and state/county parks that allow camping are not really as equipped for RV motorhomes as those on the mainland. Electrical, water and disposal hook-ups for RVs may be hard to find, and we suggest you talk at length with the rental company you choose. However, since the RVs are rented as fully self-contained, including their own water supply, etc., finding a place to park and set up camp for a night shouldn't be much of a problem. As with any other situation on your trip, use common sense, lock up valuables and be aware of what might be private property or otherwise questionable surroundings.

Harper Car and Truck Rentals arranges pick-ups and returns for either Hilo or Kona. They have two- and four-wheel-drive Winnebago motor homes available that sleep up to five people. The campers have stove, oven, shower, refrigerator, a/c, microwave, sink, generator, propane tank and shade awning. Water tanks hold a two- to three-day supply. Two-day rental minimum. Rates: 2-wheel-drive motorhome $135.95 per day; 4-wheel-drive motorhome, $149.95 per day. 456 Kalanianaole Street, Hilo, HI 96720; 808-969-1478; 800-852-9993; fax 808-961-0423.

Island RV/Safari Activities rents self-contained Tioga motorcoaches. These vehicles are top-of-the-line and comfortable, with all the conveniences including linens, grill, lounge chairs, galley, utensils, cookery equipment, etc., and sleep up to four people. The company also has snorkel gear and beach equipment available for rent, and offers shuttle service and island tours. Rates: Motorhomes begin at $250 per day. 75-5785 Kuakini Highway, Kailua-Kona, HI 96740-3137; 808-334-04640; 800-406-4555; e-mail: info@islandrv.com; www.islandrv.com.

MOTORCYCLE, MOPED, MOTORSCOOTER RENTALS The Big Island is a great place to ride motorcycles—from long stretches of sunny coastline with stark black lava on the one side and the sparkling blue Pacific on the other, to winding mountain lanes under a canopy of trees, through green pastureland, forested highway and breathtaking V-shaped cutaways over forested gulches with distant waterfalls. The list goes on. Unfortunately, the weather can vary as widely as the scenery, and bikers need to be prepared for rain and be aware of wind. There is presently no helmet law in Hawaii, but caution is always advised.

DJ's Rentals rents scooters, mopeds, small bikes and large Harley-Davidsons. Rates: from $150 for 24 hours. 75-5663A Palani Road, Kailua-Kona, across from King Kamehameha's Kona Beach Hotel; 808-329-1700; 800-993-HOGS; e-mail: rent@harleys.com; www.harleys.com.

Kona Harley-Davidson rents and specializes strictly in Harley-Davidson motorcycles. Rates: $120-$150 per day. 74-5615 Luhia Street, Kailua-Kona; 808-326-9887; e-mail: konahd@kona.net; www.konaharleydavidson.com.

BICYCLE RENTALS **B & L Bike & Sports**, 75-5699 Kopiko Place, Kailua-Kona; 808-329-3309.

Banyan Bicycle Adventures, 111 Banyan Drive, Hilo; 808-933-1228.

C&S Outfitters, 64-1066 Mamalahoa Highway on east side of Kamuela; 808-885-5005; fax 808-885-5683.

Dave's Bike & Triathlon Shop, 75-5669 Ali'i Drive, Kailua-Kona, behind Atlantis Submarine and Kona Pier; 808-329-4522.

H P Bike Works, 74-5599 Luhia, Kailua-Kona; 808-326-2453.

Hawaiian Pedals, Kona Inn Shopping Village, Ali'i Drive, Kailua-Kona; 808-329-2294.

Hilo Bike Hub, 318 East Kawili Street, Hilo; 808-961-4452.

Mauna Kea Mountain Bikes Inc., P.O. Box 44672, Kamuela, 96743; 808-883-1030.

Mid Pacific Wheels, 1133C Manono Street, Hilo; 808-935-6211.

AIRPLANE RENTALS For those who prefer wings to wheels, **Big Island Air Service Hawai'i** can help. This company rents Cessna 150 and 172 airplanes for your airborne photo safari, personal circle-island tours and adventures in Big Island skies. Rentals to qualified pilots only; dual-rentals available. Kona International Airport; 808-326-2288.

Grocery Shopping

You can expect to pay quite a bit more on average for groceries on the Big Island compared to what you pay in most areas of the U.S. mainland. Like on the mainland, however, island markets vary in price so it pays to shop around. You'll find a range of grocery stores on the Big Island, from simple mom-and-pop country stores to modern convenient supermarkets like Safeway. Grocery store chains you might not be familiar with are KTA, Sack n' Save, Suresave and Foodland. Most of them advertise in the local newspapers, offering weekly specials and coupons.

On your trips around the island and through the towns, don't hesitate to visit one of the nondescript mom-and-pop stores. These are old-fashioned, small town general stores, usually with grandma or grandpa still tending the register, maybe with the help of a younger family member who's returned to take over the family enterprise. With their homey country atmosphere, simple furnishings and fixtures and ancient coolers that keep beer and soda chilled, these old town stores allow you to step back into an earlier era of Hawaiian history. You might luck out and get there just as the homemade cookies, fresh sushi, or other country goodies are coming out of the kitchen, or somebody's cranking up the shave ice machine.

Calendar of Annual Events

Following are some of the best cultural, community and sporting events that take place around the Big Island each year. For detailed information and specific dates (which vary annually) see www.gohawaii.com, the Hawai'i Visitors & Convention Bureau site, and While you're here, check out the local Big Island newspapers and visitor periodicals where you are staying.

January

Hauoli Makahiki Hou!—New Year celebrations islandwide

USTA Challenger Tennis Tournament—Hilton Waikoloa Village, Kohala Coast

Senior PGA Mastercard Championship Golf Tournament—Four Seasons Resort Hualalai, Kona

February

Kung Hee Fat Choy!—Chinese New Year celebrations islandwide

Heiva—Tahiti Fete of Hilo Tahitian Dance Extravaganza, Hilo

Waimea Cherry Blossom Heritage Festival—Waimea

March

Kona Stampede Rodeo—Honaunau

Prince Kuhio Day (March 26)—State holiday

Haili Men's Invitational Volleyball Tournament—Hilo

Kona International Brewer's Festival—Kailua-Kona

Kona Chocolate Festival—Kailua-Kona

Annual Dance & Music Concert—Volcano Art Center, Volcano

April

Hilo Rain Festival

Ka Ulu Lauhala O Kona Festival—Kona–Kohala Coast

Lava Man Triathlon—Kohala Coast

Merrie Monarch Hula Festival—and related activities, Hilo

Merrie Monarch Parade—Hilo

Merrie Monarch Quilt Show—Hilo

May

May Day–Lei Day Observances—islandwide

Na Mea Hawai'i Hula Kahiko Series—Hawai'i Volcanoes National Park

Keauhou Kona Triathlon

Visitor Industry Charity Walk—Kona

Memorial Day Observances—islandwide

June

King Kamehameha Day—(June 11) Floral Parade, Kailua-Kona

King Kamehameha Day Celebration—Coconut Island, Hilo Bay

Lei-draping of King Kamehameha statues—(June 11) at the old Kapa'au Courthouse, North Kohala and at Wailoa State Park, Hilo

Annual Forage Field Day Taste of Hawaiian Range—Kamuela

Kona Marathon & Family Fun Runs—Kailua-Kona

Waiki'i Music Festival—Waiki'i Ranch, Kohala

Dolphin Days—Hilton Waikoloa Village, Kohala Coast

The Great Waikoloa Food, Wine & Music Fest—Hilton Waikoloa Village, Kohala Coast

Pu'uhonua o Honaunau Cultural Festival—Honaunau

Na Mea Hawai'i Hula Kahiko Series—Hawai'i Volcanoes National Park

Kona Classic fishing tournament—Kona

July

Fourth of July—celebrations islandwide

Parker Ranch Fourth of July Rodeo—Waimea

Turtle Independence Day Celebration—Mauna Lani Bay Hotel & Bungalows

Rubber Duckie Race—Kings' Shops at Waikoloa Beach Resort, Kohala Coast

Annual Big Island Slack Key Guitar Festival—Hilo

Firecracker Fishing Tournament—Kailua-Kona

Obon Festivals—islandwide Buddhist temples

Annual Big Island Bonsai Show—Hilo

Annual Hilo Orchid Society Show—Hilo

Big Island Slack Key Guitar Festival—Hilo

Annual Skins Marlin Derby—Kailua-Kona

Kilauea Volcano Wilderness Run—Hawai'i Volcanoes National Park

Na Mea Hawai'i Hula Kahiko Series—Hawai'i Volcanoes National Park

Kilauea Cultural Festival—Kilauea Military Camp, Volcano

Mango Festival—Pahala, Ka'u District

King's Swim—Kona

August

Aloha Festival Royal Court Investiture—Hawai'i Volcanoes National Park

Pu'ukohola Heiau National Historic Site Hawaiian Cultural Festival—Kawaihae

International Festival of the Pacific—Hilo

Admissions Day Holiday Celebrations—islandwide

Na Mea Hawai'i Hula Kahiko Series—Hawai'i Volcanoes National Park

Queen Liliuokalani Outrigger Canoe Races—Kona

Hawaiian International Billfish Tournament—Kailua-Kona

September

Big Island Aloha Festivals—numerous interesting and fun activities islandwide including the **Falsetto and Storytelling Contest** (at the Waikoloa Beach Marriott, An Outrigger Resort), **Miss Aloha Nui Contest** (on the Kohala Coast) and the **Kupuna Hula Festival**

Terry Fox Weekend—Four Seasons Resort Hualalai

Parker Ranch Round-Up Rodeo—Waimea

Kona Marathon—Kona

Waikoloa Open Golf Championship—Waikoloa Village

Queen Liliuokalani Birthday Celebration—Hilo

October

Hamakua Music Festival—Honoka'a, Hamakua Coast

Annual Waimea Powwow–Native American Culture Fest—Waimea

Mauna Loa Macadamia Nut Festival & Parade—Hilo

Ironman World Championship Triathlon—Kailua-Kona

November

Hawai'i International Film Festival—islandwide theaters

Big Island Festival of Fine Food, Wine, Culture and Relaxation—Kohala Coast (www.bigislandfestival.com)

KONA COFFEE FARMS

The Big Island is big on coffee. Kona coffee is about the best in the world. If you don't believe us, ask Starbucks, or just look at the price tag: $13 to $15 a pound for 100 percent Kona coffee beans. The Kona district has the perfect combination of altitude, sunshine, rainfall and volcanic soil to produce excellent coffee beans, internationally recognized for quality and taste. The first coffee tree was brought to the island in 1813 by King Kamehameha the Great's consultant Don Francisco de Paula y Marin (who is responsible for bringing in many of the plants, trees and flowers we take for granted as "Hawaiian"). In 1828, an American missionary transplanted a *coffee arabica* tree to Kona, and the rest is history. Today there are over 600 private, largely family-run coffee farms on the island. Coffee is also grown on Oahu, Kauai, Maui and even Molokai, but Kona still dominates the market.

A word about buying Kona coffee. The best and most expensive is 100 percent Kona. Regulations permit coffee companies to use the words "Kona Blend" on their packaging if their blend of coffee beans includes at least 10 percent Kona beans. Most flavored coffees will be blends and can be very good. But if you want the real deal, read the label. Kona blends and 100 percent Kona coffees are available at most island grocery stores (hint: look for discount coupons in tourist publications), Hilo Hattie's, K-Mart, Costco and elsewhere. However, genuine coffee lovers will appreciate the chance to visit coffee farms, roasteries and museums for a closer look at their favorite beverage and spend a pleasant day touring the "Napa" of coffee. See "Coffee Farms" in Chapter 6 for more details.

Christmas in the Country—Volcano Art Center, Volcano

Christmas Arts and Crafts Fairs—Hilo, Kona and Kamuela

Kona Coffee Cultural Festival & Parade—and related activities, Kailua-Kona

December

Annual Waimea Christmas Parade—Waimea

Christmas Parades and Holiday Craft Fairs—islandwide

Christmas at Hulihe'e Palace—Kailua-Kona

Christmas Concerts—UH-Hilo Theater, Hilo

Lyman House Museum's "A Christmas Tradition"—Hilo

Christmas Concert in the Park—Hilo

Passport to International Cultures Culinary Show—Waikoloa Beach Resort

Traditional Mochi Rice Pounding—islandwide (808-963-6422)

Mele Kalikimaka!

Island Geology

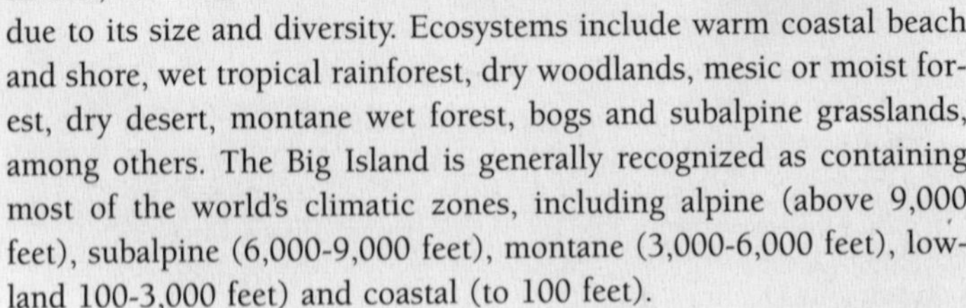

The Big Island has a diverse environmental landscape of varied climatic zones and ecosystems. In fact, some think of it as a "mini-continent" due to its size and diversity. Ecosystems include warm coastal beach and shore, wet tropical rainforest, dry woodlands, mesic or moist forest, dry desert, montane wet forest, bogs and subalpine grasslands, among others. The Big Island is generally recognized as containing most of the world's climatic zones, including alpine (above 9,000 feet), subalpine (6,000-9,000 feet), montane (3,000-6,000 feet), lowland 100-3,000 feet) and coastal (to 100 feet).

The prevailing northeast trade winds that blow regularly during summer (May through October) bring rainfall to windward coasts, slopes and summits. In winter (November through April) the northeast trades blow less steadily, competing with weather fronts, storms, etc. But while the windward sides of the Big Island facing the east and northeast get abundant rainfall, the leeward sides facing south and west are considerably drier. This is determined largely by the relative height of the Big Island's volcanic peaks.

The alpine desert of the high volcano summits of Mauna Loa and Mauna Kea are above 9,000-feet elevation. These areas are above the treeline and have very sparse vegetation and less than 20 inches of annual rainfall. It snows on the summits in winter and freezing conditions can exist year-round. The mountain subalpine forest of woodlands and shrublands are above the 6,000-feet elevation and usually get 20 to 50 inches of rainfall annually.

The montane dry and mesic forest and woodlands of Big Island leeward slopes, from 3,000- to 6,000-feet elevation, have a high canopy of larger trees and get under 100 inches of rain yearly. The wet forest or tropical rainforest of the windward slopes of the Big Island get 80 to over 300 inches of rainfall annually. The tropical rainforest has a high canopy of dense trees and some bog areas.

The lowland dry and mesic forest of the lower leeward slopes up to the 3,000-foot elevation get only about 20 to 80 inches of rainfall annually and have mostly grasses and shrubs with some smaller tree species. The lowland sparse shrublands and grasslands of the lower leeward slopes are very hot and dry and get less than 20 inches of rainfall annually.

The coastal ecosystem and zone covers the seashores and beaches of the Big Island. These warm leeward coastal shores get less than 30 inches of annual rainfall. Some windward shores get up to 120 inches of annual rainfall.

Weather

The Big Island's weather is a study in variety and extremes. Claiming both the driest locality in the state as well as the wettest population center in the islands, the Big Island lies well within the belt of northeasterly trade winds generated by the semi-permanent Pacific high pressure cell to the northeast. The climate of the island is greatly influenced by terrain. Its outstanding weather features are the marked variations in rainfall by elevation, the persistent northeasterly trade winds and the equable year-round temperatures in localities near sea level.

Over the island's east windward slopes, rainfall occurs principally in the form of showers within the ascending moist trade winds. Mean annual rainfall, except for the semi-sheltered Hamakua district, increases from 100 inches or more along the coasts to a maximum of over 300 inches at elevations of 2,000 to 3,000 feet and declines to about 15 inches at the summits of Mauna Kea and Mauna Loa. In general, the southern and western leeward areas are sheltered from the trades by the high mountains and are therefore drier. Mean annual rainfall may range from 10 to 30 inches along the coasts to 120 inches at elevations of 2,500 to 3,000 feet.

Kohala and Kona: The driest area on the Big Island and the state with an average annual rainfall of less than 10 inches, is the coastal strip just leeward of the southern portion of the Kohala Mountains and of the saddle between the Kohalas and Mauna Kea. This is the area surrounding Kawaihae Bay on the Kohala Coast. Not long ago, the Hawai'i State Planning and Economic Development Department did a "Sunshine Map" study and found that the Kohala Coast has the highest sunshine rating in the state—even higher than such noted resorts as Ka'anapali on Maui and Waikiki on O'ahu. Kohala also maintains a near-constant 78°F year-round. The Kailua-Kona and Keauhou resort areas average about 20 inches of rainfall annually. With such consistent sunny dry weather it is easy to see why the Kona and Kohala areas have become such popular destinations.

Hilo: And then we have Hilo. Poor Hilo! It has been the butt of more jokes about its rain than there are umbrellas to sell. It seems that through the years, people have taken a special delight in maligning Hilo for its rather damp atmosphere. They make up stories about how you don't tan in Hilo, you rust!

All kidding aside, it does rain an awful lot in Hilo, more than any other population center in the Hawaiian archipelago. Within the city of Hilo average rainfall varies from about 130 inches a year near the shore to as much as 200 inches in mountain sections. The wettest part of the island, with a mean annual rainfall exceeding 300 inches, lies about 6 miles up-slope from the city limits. Rain falls about 280 days a year in the Hilo area.

In fact, Hilo is recognized as the rainiest city in the United States by the U.S. Census Bureau's County and City Data Book. Hilo has the highest average annual rainfall, 128.15 inches, of any of the nation's cities with a population of 25,000 or more. Interestingly, Hilo's total rainfall in 1990 surpassed all previous records when 211.22 inches of rain were recorded.

Needless to say, even Hiloans were in awe of nature's abundance that year. With such a soggy reputation, Hilo certainly doesn't need any more detractors. In fact, it really isn't as bad as one would think. Many of the showers are brief passing ones and, according to statistics, three-quarters of Hilo's rain falls at night. Thus it doesn't spoil most daytime visitor activities. Also, the number of clear to partly sunny days far surpasses the number of totally cloudy/rainy days annually. Another thing about Hilo's infamous rain is that it is equally distributed throughout the year. There is no distinct wet or dry season. Hilo's temperatures remain fairly constant also, averaging a high of 81°F and a low of 66°F year-round. And although the relative humidity in Hilo is in the moderate to high range, as would be expected, the weather is seldom oppressive and uncomfortable due to the natural ventilation and cooling provided by the prevailing northeast trade winds.

And like the Kona-Kohala climate that has provided such marvelous conditions for resorts and the visitor industry, Hilo's climate has created special conditions also. Only in Hilo and the surrounding area will you find the lush tropical beauty of the rain forest jungle, breathtaking waterfalls cascading down green gulches, and acres of

DRESSING FOR THE WEATHER

Comfortable summer-type wear is suitable all year-round on the Big Island. Dress is casual. However, a warm sweater or jacket would be useful for cool evening breezes or for visits to cool areas like Volcanoes National Park or Waimea ranch country. And if you plan hiking excursions, you may find light rain gear useful. For treks to Mauna Kea or Mauna Loa, resort wear is definitely out. It can snow at any time of the year on either mountain and very cold weather can be experienced at any time at high elevations.

gorgeous tropical flowers like anthuriums, orchids, birds-of-paradise and ginger. The ample tropical rain makes Hilo and the windward side of the Big Island a real paradise. Even with its sodden reputation as a rainy old town, Hilo indeed is a special place for many people.

Trade Winds Trade winds are an almost constant wind blowing from the northeast through the east, averaging 5 to 5 mph, and caused by the Pacific anti-cyclone, a high pressure area. The cell remains fairly stationary in the summer (May through October), causing the trades to blow steadily 90 percent of the time, bringing cooling relief for the generally warmer temperatures. In winter (November through April), interruptions diminish the winds' constancy and they blow 40 to 60 percent of the time with competing weather fronts and storms.

Kona Weather Hot, humid and muggy weather is called Kona weather and is often due to an interruption of the trade winds. The trades are replaced by light variable winds and are most noticeable during the warmer summer months. Kona winds may also bring storm fronts and rain from the southwest, the opposite direction from which storms generally approach the islands. Kona storms are noted for their ferocity, bringing high winds, surf and rain, and have occasionally caused property damage.

Hurricanes Hawai'i lies in the hurricane belt and is susceptible to these tropical cyclones from June through December. These storms carry severe winds of between 75 and 150 mph and are often marked by rain, thunder and lightning. Most are spawned along the coast of Mexico and follow the trade winds in a westerly direction across the Pacific. Some are born close to the equator and move north. Since 1950, over a hundred hurricanes have been recorded in Hawaiian waters. Of these, only a few have passed nearby or directly struck parts of the Hawaiian islands. Hurricane Iwa in 1982 and Hurricane Iniki in 1992 did extensive damage and that was mostly confined to the island of Kaua'i and to a lesser extent O'ahu. The Big Island has luckily been to be avoided by hurricanes most of the time, due to its large mountain masses.

Tsunami Hawai'i is susceptible to tsunamis or tidal waves. Over the last century and a half, nine major tsunamis have caused moderate to severe damage and numerous deaths along affected coastlines. Although some tidal waves are locally generated from earthquakes, most of Hawai'i's tidal wave threats originate in South America or Alaska's Aleutian Islands. On the Big Island, Hilo is particularly vulnerable to tsunamis due to the funnel shape of Hilo Bay, allowing an already speeding tidal wave to concentrate its force upon reaching land. An Aleutian Islands tsunami in 1946 rolled into Hilo, pushing the water to 10 meters above sea level in some places. The death toll reached 83 and property damage was extensive. In 1960, a Chilean-generated tsunami struck Hilo at a speed of 65 kilometers per hour and wreaked havoc along Hilo's bayfront, destroying a major residential and business section. The water rolled in 11 meters high and 61 people were killed. There have been a few tidal waves generated by Big Island earthquakes as well. There is a statewide Tsunami Warning System in place and the Hawai'i Civil Defense System also coordinates disaster programs. Warning sirens and TV-radio broadcasts indicate approaching danger around all the islands. If you are on a beach or low-lying coastal area when you receive such a warning, you must immediately seek higher ground as far away from the coast as possible. (Note: The tsunami warning system is tested at 12 noon on the first Monday of every month.)

Earthquakes Because of its volcanic origins and ongoing activity, earthquakes are part of Hawai'i's geosystem. Volcanic eruptions on the Big Island are often preceded and accompanied by earthquakes. Few of these are generally strong enough to be felt or cause any damage. Major earthquakes are the result of fault action. Some of these faults are on the ocean floor while others are volcano related. Volcanic earthquakes are caused when sections of a volcano's inner works shift prior to erupting. It is usually associated with the inflation or deflation of a lava reservoir beneath the mountain as the lava swells or drains away.

Helpful Phone Numbers

The area code for the entire state is (808). Calls anywhere on the Big Island are considered local calls, and do not require the area code when dialing. If calling off-island from one island to another, it is necessary to dial 1-808 and the number.

EMERGENCY: Police, Ambulance, Fire, **911**

Police Non-emergency:
Hilo 808-935-3311
Kailua-Kona 808-326-4646
Waimea 808-887-3080
Otherwise dial "0" for operator who will assist you

Crime Stoppers:
Hilo 808-961-8300
Kona 808-329-8181

Poison Control Center (on O'ahu): 800-362-3585

Crisis/Help Line:
Hilo 808-935-3393
Kona 808-322-7444

Sexual Assault Crisis Line: 808-935-0677

Spouse Abuse/Family Crisis Shelter:
Hilo 808-959-8864
Kona 808-322-7233

Missing Child Center Hawai'i Hotline: 800-753-9797

American Red Cross:
Hilo 808-935-8305
Kona 808-326-9488

Hawai'i Island Chamber of Commerce: 808-935-7178

Kona-Kohala Chamber of Commerce: 808-329-1758

Hospitals:
Hilo Medical Center 808-974-4700
Kona Hospital 808-322-9311

Hawai'i Volcanoes National Park Headquarters: 808-985-6000

Volcano Eruption Message/Information: 808-985-6000

Hawai'i State Parks Division: 808-974-6200

Hawai'i County:
Parks & Recreation 808-961-8311
Office of Complaints & Information 808-961-8223
Research & Development 808-961-8366

U.S. Coast Guard: 808-933-6943

Search & Rescue: 800-552-6458

Weather Forecast:
Island of Hawai'i 808-961-5582
Hawaiian Waters 808-935-9883
NOA weather radio broadcast 808-935-5055

CHAPTER 2

What to See, Where to Shop

To understand the lay of the Big Island, just take a look at a map and keep the weather in mind. The island is roughly shaped like a hand in the "shaka" gesture. (Make a fist with your right hand. Extend your thumb and pinkie. That's a *shaka*, a gesture of greeting and a friendly wave.) Your folded fingers are the west side of the island (Kona side), where it's reliably dry and sunny. Your wrist is the east side (Hilo side), where it's rainy most of the time. Most tourist action is in the west; most government and "real" business takes place in Hilo. The volcano is on the Hilo side; the best beaches are on the Kona side. Your thumb and pinkie are the North Kohala and Ka'u districts, respectively. North Kohala is a lush, green former sugarcane plantation; Ka'u is dry and secluded, the southernmost point in the U.S.

On a real map, the Big Island is divided into districts, each with their own personality. Starting with the North Kona District, at about your middle finger, is Kailua-Kona town. This is a busy tourist area, full of restaurants and shops and a world of ocean activities. It's a great place for active families to rent a car and take it from there. Most accommodations are condominiums.

About 30 miles north of Kailua-Kona is the South Kohala District, containing the sunny stretch of shoreline called the Kohala Coast, where the most expensive luxury resorts live, along the very best beaches. The Kohala Coast resorts are great places for just about everything—golf, tennis, dining, shopping, spas, ocean activities, luxury accommodations, lush tropical landscaping and, again, truly excellent beaches.

The farther you go from the Kohala Coast, the prices go down, accommodations vary, the weather is less dependable and the beaches less perfect. But that doesn't mean you shouldn't do it. The Big Island is overall a magnificent place to drive, with a huge variety of scenery, climate (23 of the planet's 25 microclimates), elevation and adventure. If you don't like the weather where you are, get in the car and a short drive will put you in a completely different environment—and remember, you can't get more than 26 miles away from the ocean. If you're lucky enough to rent a convertible or a motorcycle, take advantage of it.

Driving up your thumb to North Kohala takes you to an area that is not as rural as it used to be, with new luxury subdivisions developing along the coast. The little towns of Hawi and Kapa'au are growing into interesting art communities surrounded by tropical foliage in the old-fashioned plantation area until you reach the end of the road at Pololu Valley Overlook. North Kohala is a great scenic drive, and a great place to shop, stroll around and enjoy. Uncommon historical sites, nearly inaccessible valleys, rugged beaches and remote forests make it a great place to explore on foot, mule, horseback or ATV.

At the crossroads of your thumb and first finger (the intersection of North and South Kohala districts) is the *paniolo* (cowboy) town of Waimea/Kamuela (both names apply). A cool, green, upcountry community once home to the largest privately owned cattle ranch in the world, Waimea is now an up-and-coming residential community, rapidly expanding to meet demand. Waimea is a great place to shop and eat, to catch a colorful cultural festival and to experience the countryside on horseback.

Heading east you reach the Hamakua Coast, an absolutely stunning stretch of agricultural property along the ocean *pali* (cliffs) including the idyllic Waipi'o Valley. The Hamakua District also reaches up *mauka* (toward the mountain) to include Pohakuloa Training Area military base and the summits of both Mauna Kea and Mauna Loa. Hamakua is a great scenic drive, and Waipi'o is a great place to backpack and escape from the rest of the world. To the south is the small, wedge-shaped North Hilo district, then the much larger South Hilo District, where Hilo town is located. Hilo is rainy but full of charm, surprises and things to see and do. A place where "real" people live and work, Hilo has its own brand of aloha.

South of Hilo, past your wrist and heading for your pinkie, is the Puna District then the Ka'u District. These two districts share Volcanoes National Park, along with its benefits and dangers. Puna, once a relatively undeveloped area for alternative lifestyles and escapists, is well on its way to becoming a prosperous agricultural community. Ka'u is remote and still fairly empty, holding its own as a rural Big Island retreat. Volcanoes National Park is a great place to hike and to learn about the island's culture as well as its geography.

From your pinkie heading back north to the airport (at about your ring finger) is the South Kona District, home of Kona coffee country and important historical sites at Captain Cook and Pu'uhonua o Honaunau. South Kona is a great place to kayak, snorkel and play in the water, hike, bike and explore on land.

Now that you have the island "well in hand," we hope you enjoy planning your Big Island vacation, that the information provided here is useful, and that your Big Island visit is more than you hope for. We encourage you to engage all of your senses and take in the Big Island like a cup of Kona coffee, a delicious experience to be tasted and savored, enjoyed and remembered again and again

Kona District

As your plane approaches Kona International Airport, you may be in for a shock. "This is Hawai'i? It looks like the moon!" Nothing but flat, black rock as far as you can see. That's Kona. Lava flows from Mauna Kea, Mauna Loa and Hualalai over the last 300 years have created what looks like a gigantic parking lot for rugged SUVs. Don't be alarmed. A short drive north or south brings you to the Hawai'i you're looking for, complete with sandy beaches, coconut trees, rainbows over mountain slopes and tropical flowers arrayed along forested country roads.

The Kona Coast has a reputation for fine sunny weather, with daytime temperatures averaging in the high 70s and low 80s year-round. Rainfall varies by elevation but averages from 10 to 40 inches per year, making it the perfect habitat for sun worshippers. Most Kona accommodations are in condominium properties, with a wide range of prices and amenities to choose from. There are also several good hotels and a selection of bed and breakfasts in interesting locations. The full spectrum of restaurant options is available within a few miles, and there is unlimited variety in shopping, unless you're shopping for snowshoes.

Heading south from the airport along Highway 11 (the only road) takes you to Kailua-Kona town (just "Kona" locally), a rapidly growing visitor and *kama'aina* community and active tourist location. One of the most active and energetic locations on the island, Kona is where you go to *do* things, especially things in the ocean, like snorkel and sightseeing cruises, fishing charters, submarine rides, parasailing, and much, much more. (See Chapter 6 for details.) It's also a good place to shop, eat and stroll, with fascinating historical sites within easy walking distance from downtown hotels and condos.

Above Kailua-Kona, a short stretch of Highway 180 takes you through the interesting art community of Holualoa, then reconnects with Highway 11 heading south as it passes through the greener, cooler Kona coffee country communities Kainaliu, Kealakekua, Captain Cook, Keei and Honaunau. An excellent guide, the *Kona Coffee Country Driving Tour* (available from concierge desks, visitor kiosks or www.konacoffeefest.com) takes aficionados through the "Napa of coffee" for an excellent day of sightseeing, education and tastings.

The South Kona district is an important area in Hawai'i's history. Captain Cook is named after Captain James Cook, who "discovered" Hawai'i in 1775. A memorial just off Kealakekua Bay marks the site of his death some years later. Further south, Pu'uhonua o Honaunau is a painstakingly restored Hawaiian village and *heiau* (temple) where ancient tradition permitted sanctuary to fugitives.

From there, the drive south becomes longer and less populated, with stretches of barren black lava or dry hill country for miles until you cross into the Ka'u District, which contains Ka Lae (South Point), the southernmost point in the U.S.

North and South Kona are vast, diverse and alluring, containing a taste of Hawai'i's favorite things from the mountains to the sea: verdant tropical landscape, quaint little towns with a sense of history, the sparkling blue Pacific and a world of ways to explore it, good accommodations, fine restaurants and a welcoming attitude. When you think about it, where else in the world can you sit at a restaurant and look out at the ocean where your dinner was fished up, and at the same time see the mountains where your coffee came from? There's a lot to like about Kona.

KAILUA-KONA TOWN

Kona is a town that loves change. Over the years it has been the site of Hawai'i's very first commissioned Christian church, and one of the last homes of its reigning monarchy. It has grown from a quiet fishing village to a remote destination for the more adventurous 1930s tourist, and has now earned global recognition for the Hawaiian International Billfish Tournament and the Ironman Triathlon, not to mention the world's greatest cup of coffee (in a town that only got its first Starbucks a couple years ago).

While everything in Kona used to be concentrated along Ali'i Drive, now shops, restaurants and businesses stretch *mauka* to include new shopping centers with mainland chains like K-Mart and Wal-Mart, Border's Books & Music, Safeway, Costco, Macy's, Home Depot and many others. Kona now looks more like a modern suburb than a fishing village, with a lot more to offer visiting families.

You're going to want a rental car, but right in town are three of the Big Island's most interesting and important historical sites, Ahuena Heiau, Mokuaikaua Church and Hulihe'e Palace, all located within

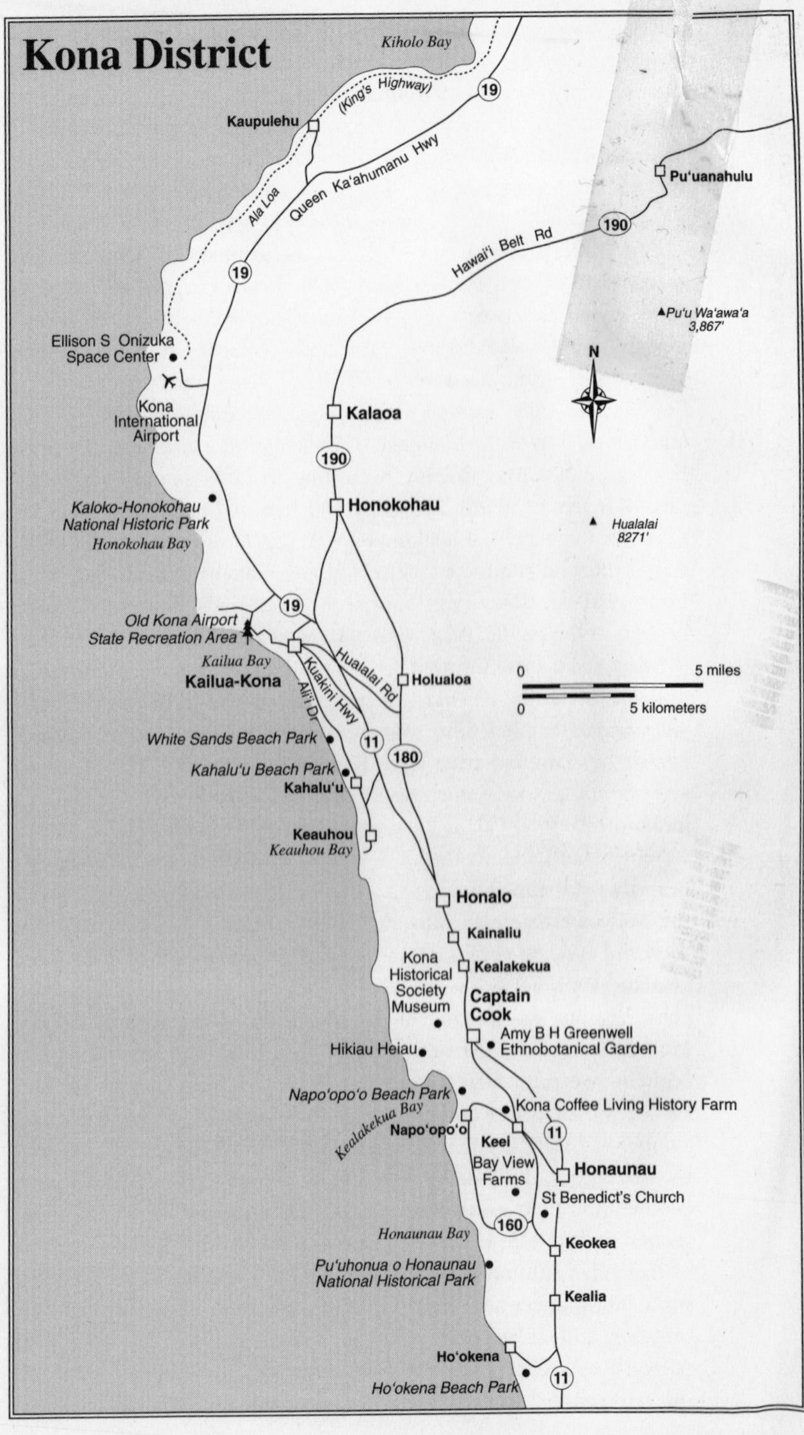
Kona District
Kiholo Bay
(King's Highway)
19
Kaupulehu
Queen Ka'ahumanu Hwy
Ala Loa
Pu'uanahulu
190
Hawai'i Belt Rd
Pu'u Wa'awa'a
3,867'
Ellison S Onizuka
Space Center
Kona
International
Airport
N
Kalaoa
Honokohau
Kaloko-Honokohau
National Historic Park
Honokohau Bay
Hualalai
8271'
Old Kona Airport
State Recreation Area
Kailua Bay
Kailua-Kona
Hualalai Rd
Kuakini Hwy
Ali'i Dr
Holualoa
0
5 miles
5 kilometers
White Sands Beach Park
11
180
Kahalu'u Beach Park
Kahalu'u
Keauhou
Keauhou Bay
Honalo
Kainaliu
Kealakekua
Kona
Historical
Society
Museum
Captain
Cook
Amy B H Greenwell
Ethnobotanical Garden
Hikiau Heiau
Napo'opo'o Beach Park
Kona Coffee Living History Farm
Kealakekua Bay
Napo'opo'o
Keei
Bay View
Farms
Honaunau
St Benedict's Church
160
Honaunau Bay
Keokea
Pu'uhonua o Honaunau
National Historical Park
Kealia
Ho'okena
Ho'okena Beach Park

walking distance of each other along Ali'i Drive. These three structures may look like simple buildings—a Hawaiian *heiau*, a rustic stone church and a European mansion—but together they represent an amazing timeline for the Big Island, each marking endings and beginnings to an era. Ahuena was King Kamehameha's final residence. Mokuaikaua was the first commissioned Christian church in Hawai'i. Hulihe'e Palace was one of the last homes of Hawai'i's reigning monarchy.

★ **Ahuena Heiau** is located on the grounds of King Kamehameha's Kona Beach Hotel. The ancient *heiau* was reconstructed by Kamehameha I between 1812–1813 after he had achieved his goal or destiny to unite all the Hawaiian islands under his rule. The *heiau* is dedicated to Lono, god of peace, agriculture and prosperity. The buildings are fully restored with wood-frame and grass-thatched huts and carved tikis with the image of Kalaemoku, a chief deified for his healing powers over disease, according to hotel sources. Other tiki images represent deities respected and honored by Kamehameha the Great for the benefit of his kingdom. In this area Kamehameha I lived out his life and conducted matters of government until his demise on May 8, 1819. A walkway in front of the hotel leads directly to it, and it is open to the public. After your visit, you may enjoy an escape from the heat and a stroll through the hotel lobby to see its many Hawaiian artifacts, including *ahu'ula* (feather cape), *mahi'ole* (feather helmet), *pahu heiau* (temple drum), war weapons, hula implements, dramatic murals by Hawaiian artist Herb Kane and portraits of Hawaiian royalty including King Kamehameha I and his favorite wife Queen Ka'ahumanu. 75-5660 Palani Road. 808-329-2911.

Just south and across Ali'i Drive is ★ **Mokuaikaua Church**. This beautiful old stone edifice was built by missionaries in 1837 and is the first commissioned Christian church in Hawai'i. Constructed of lava rock and crushed-coral mortar, its interiors are fashioned from native *ohia* and *koa* woods. It is open to the public and Sunday services welcome visitors. As Ahuena stands for the end of Kamehameha's rule, Mokuaikaua marks the beginning of the missionary era and its subsequent sweep through Hawaiian culture. One year later, ★ **Hulihe'e Palace** was built as a summer home for Hawaiian royalty, a dramatic symbol of drastic change in less than 50 years. The palace was built by Governor John Adams Kuakini, who was Queen Ka'ahumanu's brother, and used as a vacation residence until the overthrow of the monarchy in 1893. Hulihe'e Palace was purchased by the Daughters of Hawai'i, a cultural preservation and civic society, in 1925 to save it from being auctioned. Their docents maintain stewardship of the building and its manicured grounds, museum and gift shop. The palace boasts fascinating Hawaiian antiques, including a formal dining table carved from a single tree, a steamer trunk used by Queen

Kapiolani on her 1887 voyage to England, priceless pre-contact artifacts, tools and jewelry and handmade Hawaiian quilts. Free concerts are performed on the grounds on the last Sunday of each month in honor of Hawaiian monarchy. Open daily 9 a.m. to 4 p.m. Admission $4. 808-329-1877.

Right next door is one of Kona's original hotels, the old **Kona Inn**, originally built in 1929. Now restored as **Kona Inn Shopping Village**, it stretches along the ocean with a variety of shops and eateries. At the far south end is the **Kona Inn Restaurant**, worth stopping by for a look at its collection of "granders" (1,000-pound marlin and other trophy fish) mounted on the walls. You should be thirsty by now, so sit down for a cold one. You'll get a kick out of the old-fashioned belt-driven ceiling fans, and the ocean view

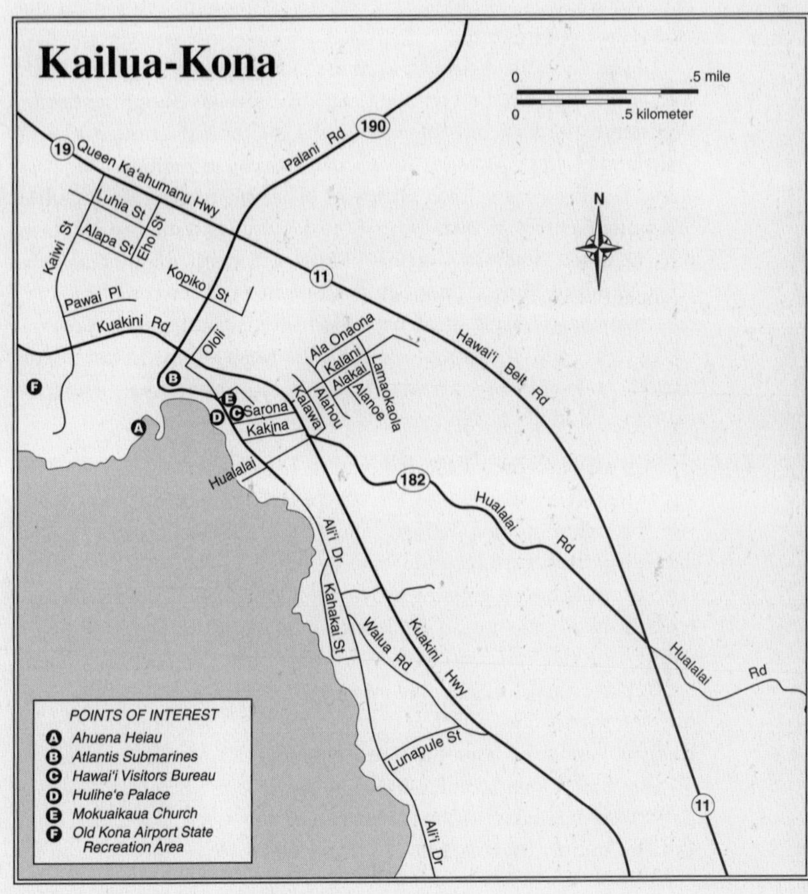

is lovely. If your visit occurs when the Kona Symphony plays one of its concerts here on the lawn, you're in for a very special treat.

Kona Inn is a marvelous place to stroll, shop, snack and people-watch (for that matter, so is the entire length of Ali'i Drive from King Kamehameha's Kona Beach Hotel south to the Royal Kona Resort, about 1 mile). Browse through a remarkable collection of funky, fun, fine, functional, fashionable, fabulous shops, galleries and restaurants in the various small, colorful shopping centers: **Seaside Mall**, **Kona Banyan Court**, **Kim Chong Complex**, **Kona Marketplace**, **Ali'i Sunset Plaza**, **Coconut Grove Marketplace**, **Waterfront Row** and back to Kona Inn Shopping Village. But wait—there's more (you may want to get the car): 200 yards up Palani Road is **Kona Coast Shopping Center**, **Lanihau Center** and **Kopiko Plaza**. And you really owe yourself a stop into **Hilo Hattie's** for a shell lei, a taste of Kona coffee, a video or craft demonstration and the ultimate selection of Hawai'i souvenirs and aloha attire. (If you don't feel like walking there's a free shuttle from most Kona hotels.) Do look for freebies and discount coupons in current visitor publications.

If you continue *mauka* (toward the mountain), turn right on Highway 11 and take the first left, you reach **Crossroads Shopping Center** (Wal-Mart, Border's and Safeway). Look for the cut-through road to **Makalapua Center** (K-Mart, Macy's and Makalapua Stadium Cinemas). About 6 miles south down Highway 11 is the turn-off for **Keauhou Shopping Center**, with its group of restaurants and interesting stores plus Keauhou Stadium Cinemas. Most of the shopping areas offer scheduled hula shows, craft demonstrations or other complimentary entertainment. Check local newspapers or your hotel/condo concierge desk. Your shopping tour of Kailua-Kona will be full of opportunities (sales pitches) to sign up for island tours, ocean activities, luau and all kinds of fun events.

Up *mauka* (toward the mountain), between Kailua-Kona on the upper road (Highway 11) is a short bypass road, Route 180, that takes you through **Holualoa Village**. Route 180 is a twisty country lane, flanked by trees, pastures and tropical greenery. Holualoa, once a sleepy farm town, is now a growing artist community full of interesting galleries, studios and shops. Check out **Kimura Lauhala Shop** (808-324-0053) for a fine selection of woven *lauhala* hats (as good as Panama hats), purses and baskets plus other local authentic handicrafts. This tiny, family-run business has been around for a long time. They are happy to answer your questions and help find the perfect remembrance of your visit. Open Monday-Friday 9 a.m.-5 p.m., Saturday 9 a.m.-4 p.m., closed Sunday. Holualoa is one of the stops along the **Kona Coffee Country Driving Tour**, a tour guide brochure published by the

As a word of advice, remember that your time on vacation is the most important thing. Don't overcommit yourself or feel that you absolutely must do everything there is to do or your trip is ruined. Also be aware that kiosks sell deeply discounted activities in exchange for your attendance at a timeshare presentation. This can be a good savings if you want to spend the time and happen to be in the market for real estate. It might work for your family to hold a little meeting in advance, decide on a few "must-do" things, like a luau, a helicopter ride and a snorkel trip. Divide up into two groups if somebody gets seasick and somebody else is allergic to hula. The more time you spend planning in advance, the less time you spend decision-making on the island. The main thing is: remember, it's *your* vacation. Relax; don't be pressured; do what you want to do. We're all here to help you have fun in different ways.

County of Hawai`i and the Kona Coffee Cultural Festival (808-326-7820; www.konacoffeefest.com), and is home to several good roasteries.

Hawaiian Gardens, about three miles above Kailua-Kona town, is a full-service tropical garden center and also has beautifully landscaped tropical gardens and grounds. The garden center is noted for its towering trees, lush landscaped grounds and numerous displays of exotic flowers. A full-service gift shop features cut tropical flowers, potted orchids, bromeliads and bonzai trees plus other Hawaiiana gifts. At the junction of Palani Road and the Mamalahoa Highway (old Route 180); 808-329-5702.

SOUTH KONA DISTRICT

Continuing south on Highway 11, you can explore **Kainaliu** town, home of the restored Aloha Theatre, a main street full of interesting shops old and new and, if you're lucky, some of the best *huli huli* chicken anywhere. Follow your nose—on the weekends there's usually a truck-pulled rotisserie set up on the *makai* side of the road, selling whole or half *kiawe*-roasted chickens for local charities.

Next stop is just outside of Kealakekua at the ★ **Little Grass Shack** right on the highway. Even if you don't remember the old song, this is a perfect photo-op and the shop has a good collection of Hawaiiana, gifts, a few antiques and local arts and crafts. Open Monday-Saturday 9:30 a.m.-5 p.m., Sunday 10:30 a.m.-5 p.m. 808-323-2877.

Nearby, the ★ **Kona Historical Society Museum** is housed in the historic Greenwell Store located on Highway 11, a half mile south of Kealakekua. The museum has fascinating historic displays featuring early Kona history; it also maintains a growing reference library and archives. The historical society also conducts guided walking tours of historic Kailua Village. The ★ **Greenwell Coffee Farms** (808-323-2275; www.greenwellfarms.com) is next door to the Kona Historical Society Museum. Tour coffee groves and learn about the famed Kona coffee industry while you taste the finished product for yourself. Also operated by the Kona Historical Society is the ★ **D. Uchida Farm** (808-323-2006), Hawai'i's first living history farm. The seven-acre working coffee and macadamia nut farm is listed on both the State and National Registers for Historic Places. The farm was homesteaded in 1900 by a Japanese immigrant family, and its present tours and programs help keep the history of Kona's coffee farming community alive. Historic buildings, authentic artifacts, costumed interpreters and guides, live animals, working machinery and producing orchards give a true sense of place. See "Museums" in Chapter 6 for more information. Kona Historical Society Museum: Open 9 a.m. to 3 p.m. weekdays, closed holidays. P.O. Box 398, 81-6551 Mamalahoa Highway, Captain Cook, HI 96704; 808-323-3222 or 808-323-2005.

In the village of Captain Cook, look for the famous old landmark, **Manago Hotel**, where room rates are reasonable and local-style family meals are still served in the dining room. Captain Cook has its own collection of shops and eateries to explore for gifts, antiques and souvenirs. There are also several coffee farms listed on the Kona Coffee Country Driving Tour and two important historical sites: **Kealakekua Bay** and Hikiau Heiau, relevant to British explorer and navigator Captain James Cook, who "discovered" Hawai'i late in the 18th century.

★ **Hikiau Heiau** is a restored temple site located near the bay in the village of Napo'opo'o. It was here in late 1778 and early 1779 that Captain Cook was initially received with great respect and reverence by the Hawaiians who thought him to be their god, Lono. A monument across the bay, accessible by boat or kayak, marks the exact spot where Captain Cook later fell, mortally wounded in a confrontation with the Hawaiians. Many of the snorkel/dive cruise boats come here to let guests dive in the clear waters of the **Kealakekua Bay Marine Reserve** sanctuary. The Captain

The **Ellison S. Onizuka Space Center**, located at the Kona airport, is a memorial to the Big Island's own native son and astronaut. Born and raised on a Kona coffee farm, he was lost aboard the Challenger space shuttle in 1986. The museum features memorabilia from Ellison's career in space exploration and includes hands-on displays and a piece of "moon rock" on loan from NASA. Open daily 8:30 a.m. to 4:30 p.m.; adults $3, children $1. For information, contact Onizuka Space Center, P.O. Box 833, Kailua-Kona, HI 96745; 808-329-3441.

Cook monument is also reached by a moderately difficult hiking trail from Highway 11 at Captain Cook town (see "Hiking" in Chapter 6 for more information). The waters of Kealakekua Bay are designated as the Kealakekua Bay State Historical & Underwater Parks and are a wonderful snorkel and dive zone.

★ **Amy B. H. Greenwell Ethnobotanical Garden** is about 12 miles south of Captain Cook. One of the best attractions on the island, this 15-acre botanical garden is a trip back through time, giving visitors a look at Hawaiian plant life before foreign contact. A living museum of Hawaiian ethnobotany (the study of plants and human culture that support each other), the garden hosts 45 kinds of *kalo* (taro), 35 varieties of sugarcane, 23 banana species and many other endemic plants, medicinal herbs and more. Open 8:30 a.m. to 5 p.m. daily, except Sundays and holidays, for self-guided tours. Docent guided tours given on second Saturday of each month. Located at 10-mile marker on Highway 11; 808-323-3318.

★ **St. Benedict's Church**, just off Highway 160, which branches off from Highway 11, is well worth a visit. The church's interior is elaborately painted in colorful, dramatic religious scenes and Bible stories. 84-5140 Painted Church Road.

Highway 160 leads on down to Honaunau Bay and to the ★ **Pu'uhonua o Honaunau National Historical Park**. This very special place is the best-preserved *heiau* in the islands. The "City of Refuge" was a designated sanctuary for fugitives who could be taken in with permission of the *kahuna* (priests) if they were able to reach its remote location. It is a must-see for vacationers because it clearly gives a picture of Hawai'i's ancient history and culture, as well as the simple pleasures and challenges of everyday life in a difficult environment. Knowledgeable park rangers provide information and maps for the easy, self-guided walking tour through the complex. The site has a restored village and ancient temple with carved wooden tiki images, thatch-roofed *hale* lining an ancient cultivated fishpond, and canoe and tapa houses, each of which has a story to tell. At various times of the year, local Hawaiian cultural groups put on authentic arts-and-crafts demonstrations, cultural festivals and other educational events. There is ample parking, restrooms, a shop, and a nice beach nearby for a picnic. 808-328-2288.

Kohala Coast

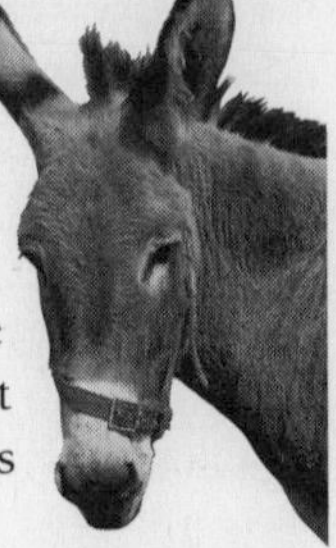

The northwestern edge of the Big Island is divided into two districts, the South Kohala and North Kohala districts. Most of the South Kohala District is a long stretch of rugged black lava coastline on the western side of the Big Island and it is in this district that the Kohala Coast proper, home to the best beaches and fancy resorts, lies. One of the most reliably sunny spots in the state with less than nine inches of rain annually, its dry, scrubby landscape has been made beautiful by expensive resort and residential developments over the last 40 years. The South Kohala District is the "high-rent neighborhood" of the Big Island because it includes the four mega-resorts along the Kohala Coast: Hualalai Resort (Kona Village Resort and Four Seasons Hualalai), Waikoloa Beach Resort (Hilton Waikoloa Village and Waikoloa Beach Marriott), Mauna Lani Resort (Mauna Lani Bay Hotel & Bungalows and the Fairmont Orchid) and Mauna Kea Resort (Mauna Kea Beach Hotel and Hapuna Beach Prince Hotel). (Hualalai is technically in the North Kona District, but the resort is included here for your convenience). While this acclaimed resort area is a world unto itself, the island's South Kohala District also includes the small harbor town at Kawaihae, the uphill subdivision of Waikoloa Village and the cooler, greener pastures of the town with two names: Waimea/Kamuela (same place), 12 miles east of the coastline, inland.

The rest of the district, downslope from Waimea and along the coast to the higher elevations in North Kohala (a separate district about 20 miles away), is virtually desert. Only the resort areas, where irrigation and technology permit the lush tropical landscaping we expect, are green. It's hard to imagine what life was like for early Hawaiian villagers, with very little fresh water and almost no rain or no edible vegetation. A look at the windblown brown coast, carved with old lava flows and studded with stubborn *kiawe* (mesquite) takes a lot of romance out of the image of tropical island living. Dry areas like this had the reputation for producing strong people and fierce warriors. It's easy to see why.

For travelers, however, so much sunshine is a blessing. A few years ago, the State of Hawai'i produced a statewide sunshine map that confirmed what Hawaiians knew long ago: the Kohala Coast has the highest sunshine rating in the islands—even higher than such sun resorts as Ka'anapali on Maui and Waikiki on O'ahu. Kohala Coast weather is consistent: average annual rainfall was 8.7 inches over the last 35 years or so that records have been kept. Temperatures average in the mid-60s for lows and mid- to upper 80s for highs, with 78 degrees the average year-round. Once the site of small fishing villages and canoe harbors, the "sunniest coast in Hawai'i" is now an international destination for golfers and beach-lovers, thanks to the weather.

SOUTH KOHALA DISTRICT

The road system through South Kohala is easy to follow because there's basically only one road. The Kohala Coast Highway 19, Queen Ka'ahumanu Highway, connects Waimea, Kawaihae and Kailua-Kona.

It was completed in the mid-1970s by the County of Hawai'i, with the aid of resort developers like Laurance S. Rockefeller (Mauna Kea Beach Hotel), to give hotel guests access to and from the Kona Airport, who otherwise traveled the 90-some miles from Hilo Airport. Highway 19 in this area is generally straight, with fairly unobstructed views of the sloping uplands of Kohala and many vast old lava flows on the *mauka* side, and the amazing Pacific ocean on the *makai* side.

In the area just above the Kona Village Resort, about 14 to 15 miles north of Kailua-Kona, be on the lookout for yellow road signs with the silhouette of a donkey along Highway 19. This area is frequented by the small herds of "Kona Nightingales," the descendants

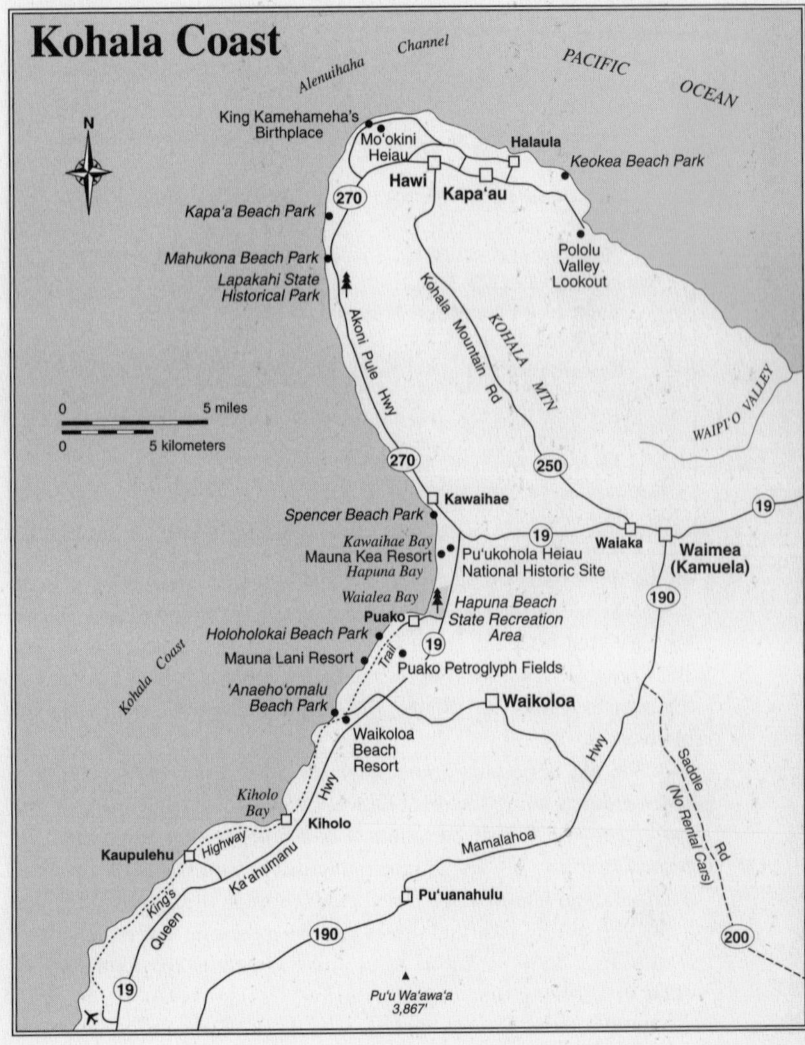

SHOPPING FOR ANTIQUES

If you are an antique buff, you'll find all sorts of antiques, collectibles and old attic items like vintage aloha shirts and muumuus, old soda and milk bottles from now-defunct Big Island bottle works, plantation-era items, books, interesting ethnic treasures, Hawaiian implements and artifacts of all manners of eclectic things. The following is a list of antique shops worth browsing. If you're planning a stop at a particular shop, you might want to call ahead to check on their hours, as those can vary. We'd like to suggest a stroll down Honoka'a town's Main Street, which offers several of the better, funkier and more interesting shops for antiques.

Kona District

Antiques-Art-And—in Kealakekua, across from Chris' Bakery; 808-323-2239

Cinderella's—in Holualoa, next to Kona Arts Center; 808-322-2474

Hula Heaven—Kona Inn Shopping Village, 75-5744 Ali'i Drive, Kailua-Kona; 808-329-7885

Once in a Blue Moon Antiques—74-5598 Luhia, Kailua-Kona; 808-334-0022

Statements—73-5564 Owalu Street, Kailua-Kona; 808-326-7760

North Kohala District

Mother's Antiques & Fine Cigars—55-3419 Akoni Pule Highway, Hawi; 808-889-0496

of the donkeys used years ago to pack supplies and goods up and down the old coastal trail. They were also used to carry bags of coffee harvested from the coffee farms on Kona's steep mountain slopes. They now roam wild in this area and can sometimes be seen near the highway, especially at twilight when they are more likely to cross the highway.

The old upcountry route, Highway 190, passes through rolling ranch country along the drive between Kailua-Kona and Waimea. Because it is at a higher elevation, it is a much cooler drive than the coastal Highway 19. It's an interesting drive, with beautiful coastline overlooks and winding, tree-lined roads through the country. If you're lucky, the purple jacaranda trees will be in bloom. On either route, the distance between Kailua-Kona and Kamuela is approximately 40 miles or a driving time of one hour.

Waimea

Silk Road Gallery—Parker Square Center, Highway 19, Kawaihae Road in Waimea; 808-885-7474

Upcountry Connection Gallery—in Waimea; 808-885-0623

Hamakua Coast

Honoka'a Market Place—45-3586 Mamane Street, Honoka'a; 808-775-8255

Honoka'a Trading Co.—Mamane Street, Honoka'a; 808-775-0808

Seconds to Go Inc.—in Honoka'a; 808-775-9212

Hilo

Coins & Collectibles—191 Kilauea Avenue, Hilo; 808-969-1881

Dragon Mama Futon Shop—266 Kamehameha Avenue, Hilo, 808-934-9081, and also 159 Kalanikoa, Hilo, 808-933-9816; www.dragonmama.com

Ets'ko—35 Waianuenue Avenue, Hilo; 808-961-3778

Home Place—197 Kilauea Avenue, Hilo, below Spencer's Gym; 808-935-7494

Mauna Kea Galleries—276 Keawe Street, Hilo; 808-969-1184

Mid Pacific Store—76 Kapiolani Street, Hilo, opposite Lyman Museum; 808-935-3822

Oshima's Art & Collectibles—202 Kamehameha Avenue, Hilo; 808-969-1554

Puna District

Tinny Fisher's Antique Shop—Highway 19, Mountain View; 808-968-6011

Along the Big Island's noted Kohala Coast is a string of luxury resorts, golf courses and some of Hawai'i's best beaches. The turnoff at **Waikoloa Beach Resort** leads to ★ **'Anaeho'omalu Beach Park**, the Waikoloa Beach Marriott, Outrigger Resort the Hilton Waikoloa Village, golf courses, and the condo complexes The Shores at Waikoloa and Vista Waikoloa. 'Anaeho'omalu Beach is a lovely wide, sweeping crescent of golden sand fronting a fishpond. The Waikoloa Beach Marriott, An Outrigger Resort sits behind the beach and fishpond areas with easy access to the beach.

King's Highway is the centuries old footpath that winds along the Kohala Coast and through the Waikoloa Beach Resort. Portions of the old coastal trail wind through the lava fields and golf courses and hiking is allowed. Hawaiian petroglyph fields lie scattered throughout the area.

South Kohala shopping is concentrated in the Kohala Coast resort areas and up in Waimea town. Naturally, the resort-area outlets are more pricey, but the atmosphere is festive and if this is your passion, resort shopping is a perfect way to spend the day. Mauna Kea Resort and Mauna Lani Resort hotels offer their own collections of shops featuring fine art and jewelry, resort wear, gifts and sundries, but Waikoloa Resort is the best bet for a shopping day.

The **Kings' Shops** at Waikoloa Beach Resort is a great way to spend the day and satisfy your need to shop (for all budgets). Indulge in some fast or fine food, absorb a little culture at complimentary afternoon hula shows and sign up for island activities. Among the tenants are Endangered Species, Noa Noa, Under the Koa Tree, Island Shells, Indochine, Sgt. Leisure, Crazy Shirts, The Gecko Store, Blue Ginger, DFS Galleria (duty-free), Pacific Rim Collections, Genesis Galleries, Dolphin Galleries, Malia Waikoloa, Kane By Malia, Making Waves, Paradise Walking Co., Maui Divers, Whalers General Store, Giggles, Haimoff & Haimoff Creations in Gold, Louis Vuitton, Macy's, Royal Gold, Sunglass Hut, Zac's Photo and the Ukulele House. There's a Starbucks and a nice food court with a lovely outdoor gazebo overlooking the lake.

Hilton Waikoloa Village also offers options for die-hard shoppers in its a complex of 18 shops and boutiques. **Waikoloa Village** is located on the mountain slopes above the resort about five miles. Waikoloa Road, which leads to the village, intersects Highway 19 (Queen Ka'ahumanu Highway on the Kohala Coast) and connects the old Waimea to Kailua-Kona upcountry road, Highway 190. At Waikoloa Village, there is the **Waikoloa Highlands Center**, a small full-service shopping center with a grocery, **Waikoloa Village Market**, **B Natural** healthfoods store, **Exclusive Designs** aloha wear, **Elegant Flowers & Gifts**, a pharmacy, gas station, health care clinic, post office and a golf course, as well as several eateries. Although there are no tourist attractions as such, the village's convenient location near the Kohala Coast resorts makes it a good option for condominium vacation rentals.

Kawaihae Shopping Center is worth a stop to browse through its galleries and gift shops and enjoy an ice cream treat before you head uphill to Waimea. **Kawaihae Village**, just north of the intersection of Highways 270 and 19 is a worthwhile short stop. Kawaihae is most noted as a fishing and commercial boating harbor port facility, but **Kawaihae Center**, a small shopping complex, houses a number of shops and eateries including the classic Harbor Gallery.

Back on Highway 19, **Mauna Lani Resort** has Fairmont Orchid, Mauna Lani Bay Hotel and Bungalows, and The Islands, Mauna Lani

Point and Mauna Lani Terrace condos. The ancient fishponds at **Kalahuipua'a** next to the Mauna Lani Bay Hotel have been restored and can be seen on a walk through the hotel grounds. This beautiful site is now operated as a working aquaculture preserve stocked with mullet fish.

★ **Holoholokai Beach Park** is just north of the Fairmont Orchid, where a trail leads to the nearby ★ **Puako Petroglyph Fields**. Petroglyphs are images hand-carved into the rock, as a system of language, historical record or storytelling. The fields at Puako offer some of the best examples of human and mythical figures, easily accessible and fascinating to see.

A mile south of Hapuna Beach on Highway 19 is the Puako Road turnoff, where there is public access to the beach areas of **Puako**. Puako is a very small town, consisting of one road, one store, one apartment-condo building and interesting houses from luxury oceanside mini-resorts to ramshackle shacks. The Catholic Ascension Church is a beautiful, island-style church that welcomes visitors to Sunday mass.

★ **Hapuna Beach State Recreation Area** is one of the best, with good facilities for swimming as well as picnicking and photo-ops.

Mauna Kea Resort comprises the Mauna Kea Beach Hotel and the Hapuna Beach Prince Hotel and surrounding golf courses. The resort covers a large tract of land between and above Kauna'oa Bay and Hapuna Beach and the rolling hills above. Mauna Kea was built by Laurance S. Rockefeller in 1965 and was the first hotel in the area.

NORTH KOHALA DISTRICT

North Kohala has changed. Hawi, 18 miles north of Kawaihae on Route 270, used to be an undiscovered treasure, pleasantly distanced from the resorts. Now this former sugar cane plantation town has met the demand of returning visitors for a more genuine Hawai'i experience. Run-down streets with abandoned storefronts have transformed into eclectic little galleries, shops and restaurants—delightfully and colorfully presented in a cozy, funky array, well worth the trip. Or, make a day of it by also taking in often-overlooked historical sites, excellent photo opportunities and a couple of lovely, smaller beach parks. The coastal drive along Route 270 is spectacular, as is the mountain Route 250 in a completely different way.

From the Kohala Coast resorts, head north on Highway 19. Turn left at the stop sign and head up the coast. Start off early in the day because the first two stops get very hot before noon. Almost immediately on the left is a sign for ★ **Pu'ukohola Heiau National Historic Site**. Stop by the visitors center, then take the relatively easy hike around this important Hawaiian landmark. If your visit brings you to the island in August, you might be lucky enough to catch part of the annual re-enactment (minus the sacrificial part), when hundreds of islanders dress in authentic *malo*, feather headgear and ti-leaf capes and walk in the footsteps of the ancestors for a day. Pu'ukohola Heiau National Historic Site is on the Kohala Coast at Kawaihae Bay and is well worth a visit. This massive *heiau* was built by Kamehameha the Great in 1791 upon the advice of a priest who told Kamehameha that he would conquer all the islands of Hawai'i if he did so. By 1795, Kamehameha did conquer in battle all the islands of Hawai'i except Kaua'i, which later acceded to and recognized him as the ruler of all Hawai'i. At the time Kamehameha built his *heiau*, his main rival was his cousin Keoua Ku'ahu'ula, also a chief. Kamehameha invited Ku'ahu'ula to his temple dedication to make peace and Ku'ahu'ula fatefully accepted. As Ku'ahu'ula and his party landed at the beach below the *heiau*, Kamehameha's warriors swept down and killed them all. Ku'ahu'ula's body was carried up to the temple and offered as the principal sacrifice to Kamehameha's war god. Thus the *heiau* was dedicated according to ancient Hawaiian religious custom.

Continuing north, on the *makai* (ocean) side of the road, look for the sign for **Lapakahi State Historical Park.** On this site is a restored Hawaiian village, and a fairly easy hike along its rocky paths may change your mind dramatically about the romantic life of a tropical native. As you look around and realize very little has changed in the 200 or so years since Hawaiians populated the spot where you stand, notice that fresh water was a precious commodity, that everything you needed had to come from the land or the ocean. Fish were traded to upcountry farmers for sweet potatoes or taro. Salt was "mined" from sea water in handcarved pockets in the stones near shore. Cloth was made by beating plant fiber into pulp. Coconut trees were the general store of the time, providing food, dishes and utensils, roofing supplies, musical instruments and toys. It was a difficult, physically demanding life, yet one which produced one of the most poetic, spiritual, ecologically sensible, good-humored cultures to evolve on the planet—one which was apparently successful, by standards of population and artistry, until the outside world "discovered" it in the 19th century.

As you continue north, you'll see signs for **Mahukona Beach Park** and **Kapa'a Beach Park**, both of which have parking, restrooms, picnic pavilions and a small stretch of beach for swimming and sunning. At Mahukona, you may see signs of the old railroad that used to serve the sugar cane plantations. After the Japanese attack on Pearl Harbor, the railroad was destroyed and most of the equipment dumped into the ocean, but there are places where you can see the old ties and platforms.

If you're feeling adventurous, you may want to explore King Kamehameha's Birthplace and Mo'okini Heiau, a bit of a drive down a dusty dirt lane just before Upolu Airport at the very north tip of the island. This ancient, remote area is maintained as an important historic site for visitors and residents, featuring a large original *heiau* complex and *kahuna*'s (priest's) house arranged on a wide green lawn overlooking the vast ocean, where whales are commonly seen in season. To find them, look for Upolu Airport Road two miles west of Hawi on Route 270. The turn-off leads down two miles to the coast and the tiny airstrip at Upolu Point, the northernmost point on the Big Island. The airport road is a bumpy narrow asphalt single-lane strip through cattle pastures.

King Kamehameha's Birthplace and the adjacent Mo'okini Heiau are just west of the airstrip. A sign points the direction along the coast to the old settlement. The 1.5-mile bumpy, rutted and very dusty road from the airstrip along the coast to the restored birthplace site is unimproved dirt and driving it can be hazardous. There can be several deep ruts and mud bogs that may or may not be passable. Drive at your own risk! If you can't get through, you can always park the car and walk the rest of the way. Kamehameha's birthplace is a large square-shaped rock wall enclosure about 75 yards per side, and encloses various other foundations and structures. It sits about 50 yards from the beach in an open, sloping area. The wind and sun are both strong here.

★ **Mo'okini Heiau** is located just off the same road as the birthplace site. It occupies the summit of a hill and as such dominates the immediate area. The temple is where the *ali'i nui*, the kings and ruling chiefs, fasted, prayed and offered human sacrifices to their gods. The temple was built about 480 A.D. and is one of the largest on the Big Island, measuring 267 feet by 250 feet on the west and east walls, and 135 feet and 112 feet on the north and south walls. The walls are 30 feet high and 15 feet wide. The structure is in the shape of an irregular parallelogram.

The stones used in constructing the temple are of smooth, waterworn basalt. Legend has it that the stones come from Pololu Valley on the east side of the Kohala peninsula, a distance of some 10 to 14 miles. It is said that each stone was passed by hand from man to man the entire distance, a feat requiring from 15,000 to 18,000 men. By this method, so says the legend, the temple was built in a single night, from sunset to sunrise. Mo'okini was constructed under the direction of High Priest Kuamo'o Mo'okini and was dedicated to the battle god, Ku. The priestly order of Ku, through the Kahuna Nui, provides the guidance and direction of the temple. Throughout its 1,500-year history, members of the Mo'okini family have served as *kahu* (guardian) of the Mo'okini. The latest member of the family to inherit the title of Kahuna Nui (high priestess and councilor to a high chief) is Leimomi Mo'okini Lum, a direct descendant of High Priest Kuamo'o Mo'okini.

Today, the *heiau* and adjoining Kamehameha birthplace are open to visitors to stroll the grounds and learn about the history and culture of old Hawai'i. Various celebrations and cultural days are held here on special occasions such as King Kamehameha Day (June 11).

Just up the road is the former sugar cane town of **Hawi**. There's only one street, so park on the right and enjoy the short walk around. Starting on the right is **Aunty's Place**, a local eatery with a tiny bar (see Chapter 4). Next door is **Sandwich Isle Designs**, an interesting jewelry shop made even more so by floor-to-ceiling murals of oceanscape. Step in the front door and say hello to the mermaid at your feet, dolphins and *honu* (turtles) just under the surface. Fluffy white clouds hang overhead and the horizon traces the circumference of the room.

Other great stops are **Mother's Antiques, Imports & Fine Cigars** for Hawai'i-made smokes, **L. Zeidman Gallery** for finely crafted wooden bowls and sculptures, **Star Light Crystals, Kohala Healthfoods** or **Kohala Coffee Mill** for a great selection of snacks, *omiyage* (gifts) and ice cream. **As Hawi Turns** is famous for fantastic and funky gifts (check out the "fat mermaid" ornaments) and **Na Pua O Kohala** offers fresh-flower leis and lei-making kits, tropical bouquets and a creative "Frequent Flowers" program to enjoy year-round.

Ahead is the smaller town of **Kapa'au**, with its own interesting selection of arts, eats and history. You can't miss the grand ★ **statue of King Kamehameha I**, as he gestures in welcome from his lofty vantage point in front of the old North Kohala Civic Center. Park here and stroll around the quiet grounds, read some interesting history of plantation days, war days and present days posted on the building's aging walls, and take advantage of the photo-op with His Royal Highness.

The statue was originally commissioned as a monument for Honolulu. It was cast in bronze in the 1880s in Paris and, after a rather turbulent history, including being sunk in the South Atlantic Ocean near Cape Horn at Port Stanley in the Falkland Islands, it ended up here at the Kapa'au Courthouse in 1912. Before this statue was salvaged from the icy waters of the Atlantic, a duplicate model was cast and that one now stands in front of the Judiciary Building, Ali'iolani Hale, across from Iolani Palace in Honolulu. Since the original statue was no longer needed in Honolulu, it was placed in North Kohala. Each June 11, Kamehameha Day, local residents drape the statue with beautiful flowing flower leis.

Several years ago the statue was restored by art conservators who painstakingly removed more than 20 coats of paint. When they reached the base bronze, a community meeting was held to see if it should be left "naked," as the original sculptor intended, or to re-apply the paint. After much deliberation, elders elected to give the statue its bright colors back, and the art experts agreed. Since it had never stood as a bronze statue, it was now more of a folk art work, and a part of community tradition. The town fathers found a small piece of an authentic feather cape and showed it to conservators so they could match the exact yellow, and a special high-tech automotive paint was tinted and applied.

There's also a story about Kamehameha's eyes. We're told that most sculptors make eyes by carving deep holes into the metal, where the pupils would be, to give depth to the expression. However, when Kamehameha was first brought to town, one of the townsmen thought he needed actual eyeballs. He found a couple of ball bearings, just the right size, and hammered them in place. This local legend has yet to be verified.

Across the street is **Jen's Kohala Cafe** if you need refreshment before strolling through Kapa'au, with its own special collection of interesting places and things.

Visit **Sue Swerdlow Gallery** to enjoy her vivid Hawaiian tropicals. One of the Big Island's most popular artists, Sue owns and operates her spacious gallery in the growing art community of Kapa'au, which she calls "a gem in the jungle." Fine art and smaller gift items feature the vivid, energetic style of an artist in love with Hawai'i. Hours can vary, but appointments can be arranged any time. Kapa'au; 808-889-0002, 808-883-9543, www.sueswerdlowart.com. **Victoria Fine Art** has art gifts and conversation.

Gary Ackerman established his **Ackerman Galleries** over 25 years ago. Today it still offers work by him and other outstanding island artists, and a Gift Gallery featuring fine jewelry including the signature gold plumeria collection. Open daily 9:30 a.m.-6 p.m. Kapa'au; 808-889-5971; e-mail: ack4art@hialoha.net; www.ackermangalleries.com.

Take time to browse through **Kohala Book Shop**, the "largest used bookstore in Hawai'i," for hard-to-find titles, beach reads or antique Hawaiiana (see "Browsing for Books" in this chapter). Enjoy a coffee break at **Nanbu Gallery Espresso Deli** before continuing your drive tour.

From here the road gets more interesting, winding through jungly gulches past an occasional house or fruit stand, climbing up to higher

BROWSING FOR BOOKS

Big Island bookstores make up in quality what they might lack in quantity of shops. Each area has at least one good choice for booklovers seeking the latest in contemporary fiction, antique Hawaiiana, a comfortable beach read or island-style children's story. Books are valued *omiyage* (gifts) and make wonderful souvenirs, allowing you to enjoy your vacation again and again. Although you can pick up books at K-Mart, Wal-Mart and Costco, these shops are the kinds of places to take your time, ask questions and enjoy browsing.

Kona District

The sole proprietor of **Island Books**, a classic, jam-packed bookshop, has 30 years in the book business, and the reputation as "the oldest used bookstore in the state." An impressive collection of Hawaiiana from 50 cents to $1,000 includes rare and out-of-print titles on every imaginable island topic. Located one block south of the Aloha Theatre in Kainaliu town, mailing address: 79-7430 Mamalahoa Highway, Kealakekua, HI 96750; 808-322-2006.

Tucked away, behind Kona Marketplace, **Middle Earth Bookshoppe** is a cozy, meandering bookshop that offers way more than the Tolkien classic. Open Monday-Friday 9 a.m.-9 p.m., Sun 9 a.m.-6 p.m., closed Saturday. 75-5719 Ali'i Drive, Kona Plaza Building, Kailua-Kona; 808-329-2123.

Kohala Coast

A must-stop on your visit to Kapa'au, **Kohala Book Shop** is a booklover's paradise—with rooms full of floor-to-ceiling shelves crammed with new, used and out-of-print books, classic Hawaiiana, bestselling fiction and more. Lots of comfortable niches to curl up in, and friendly folks to answer questions or let you browse at leisure. A coffee shop next door completes a perfect rainy-day experience. Open Tuesday-Saturday 11 a.m.-5 p.m. 35-4522 Akoni Pule Highway, Kapa'au town; 808-889-6400.

Waimea

More of a Hawai'i treasure shop than a bookstore, **Cook's Discoveries** is still an excellent source for books, from Hawaiian history to contemporary cookbooks, artistic coffee-table books, chil-

elevations where wild fields and wind-bent trees live. Near the end of the road, you come around one final curve and confront a dramatic view of ★ **Pololu Valley** that will take your breath away. Park in the circle, but watch out for the yellow cats that usually monitor the parking lot. Look down onto a rugged gray-sand beach and watch waves

dren's books by Hawaiian authors, creative fiction works and more. P.O. Box 6960, Kamuela, HI 96743-6960, e-mail: cookshi@aol.com, www.hawaii-island.com/cooks.htm; 808-885-3633, 808-937-2833.

Hilo

Basically Books is something special. If you have a question about Hawai'i, the answer is here somewhere, in one of their hundreds of books and maps. Named 2002 Retailer of the Year by the Retail Merchants of Hawai'i, Basically Books is one of the best stops you can make in Hilo town before you begin your special Big Island pursuits. They have books, maps and guides for paddlers, divers, surfers, snorkelers, hikers, campers, bikers and backpackers (and those of us who like to lay on the beach and read). New, used, out-of-print, reference, contemporary fiction, spirituality, children's books and gifts are available along with any kind of map you can think of, nautical charts, globes, compasses and flags. Always-friendly, knowledgeable staff can answer your questions. (See "Suggested Reading" at the end of this book.) Open Monday-Friday 9 a.m.-5 p.m., Saturday 9 a.m.-3 p.m. 160 Kamehameha Avenue, Hilo, HI 96720, e-mail: bbinfo@basicallybooks.com, www.basicallybooks.com; 808-961-0144, 800-903-6277.

Book Gallery is a good source for a wide variety of books about everything to do with Hawai'i, including fiction, nonfiction, spirituality, crafts, cookery, kids' books, maps and gift items. Prince Kuhio Plaza, Hilo; 808-935-4943.

The Big Island version of the national franchise **Waldenbooks** has plenty of Hawai'i-based books to choose from. Open Monday-Friday 10 a.m.-9 p.m., Saturday 9:30 a.m.-7 p.m., Sunday 10 a.m.-6 p.m. Prince Kuhio Plaza, 111 East Puainako, Hilo; 808-959-6468.

The bookstore franchise and coffee shop operation **Borders Books & Music** has an extensive selection of Hawai'i-based books, videos, CDs and gift items. Same great Borders service. Check local newspapers for visiting authors and special community activities. Open 10 a.m.-6 p.m. daily. 301 Maka'ala Street, Hilo (across from Prince Kuhio Plaza on Kanoelehua Avenue/Highway 11); 808-933-1410. There's also a location in Kailua-Kona at 75-1000 Henry Street, Kailua-Kona, at the corner of Henry and Highway 11 just below Wal-Mart; 808-331-1668.

progress from miles out, to boom onshore at the foot of misty green, unspoiled hills. If the weather is clear, you may see entries to the other valleys between here and Waipi'o, where the road picks up again.

Pololu Valley is at the end of Highway 270, which continues east of Kapa'au about nine miles. From the parking area and overlook there is a majestic view of the valley walls and floor as it reaches back toward the Kohala Mountains. Perhaps most dramatic are the rock islets that stand just off the mouth and beach of the valley. These islets are actually chunks of the Big Island that were separated at some time in the far past, probably by volcanic activity. They present interesting subjects for photography buffs.

The beach of Pololu Valley is composed of fine black lava sand. However, the surf here is quite dangerous as the undertow is very strong and swimming is not advised. The trail leading down to the valley floor and the beach is a nice hike but can be hazardous in or just after rain and caution is advised. It's only a 15-minute hike down, quite a bit longer back up, and the trail is often wet and muddy in places. Some parts are quite rocky as well, so good footwear and hiking attire is recommended. The beach is piled high with lava rocks but there is some black-sand beach area as well. It's a beautiful view from beachside, looking at the *pali* leading off along the coast in either direction. A stream flows down from the valley and there are nice views back into its far reaches. It's posted "No Trespassing" so it's not advisable to go back into the valley.

For a different, equally spectacular route home, turn left in Hawi town on Highway 250 and head uphill. This road will lead to Waimea in 21 miles, through gorgeous upcountry ranchland, tree-lined winding roads and vistas from the top of the world. Do stop at the overlook point and look down upon the coastline and tiny beaches in the distance, taking a moment to let it sink in how big the Big Island really is.

If you've started out early enough, you may want to close the loop on this tour by continuing on to Honoka'a and **Waipi'o Valley overlook**, 13 miles east. Turn left at the intersection of Highways 250 and 19, go into town and left again at the stoplight in Honoka'a and turn left into town. (There are three streets going down toward the ocean from the highway and it doesn't matter which one you take.) At the bottom of the hill, turn left on Highway 240 and head down the woodsy road, through old plantation subdivisions vividly planted with tropical flowers, to the end of the road at the entry to Waipi'o Valley.

Park and walk to the railing. Now you are looking at the opposite end of the series of valleys that began at Pololu. It always strikes us how gray and misty Pololu is compared to green Waipi'o with its turquoise water and white-sand beach. Waipi'o is home to many Big Islanders who make a living with a remote tourist trade, or by farming. Some make the steep 4WD-only commute out every day for hotel jobs or other work. In the old days, it was a busy farm community, and over the years it has been an area for "alternative" lifestyles, a training ground for the Peace Corps (complete with water buffalo) and a beautiful, relatively untouched and timeless place to explore.

Don't take the rental car down. Tours by van, horse-drawn wagon or horseback, ATV, mountain bike and foot are available in nearby Kukuihaele, all of which give you safe transportation, refreshments, a chance to experience the beach and provide a sense of place.

Waimea Town

Waimea is an interesting place for a lot of reasons, and is not what you expect to find in Hawai'i. Although part of the South Kohala District, Waimea is home to one of the largest privately owned cattle ranches in the country, Parker Ranch, and has always been a *paniolo* town. Its Western theme is everywhere; even the stop signs at Parker Ranch Center say "Whoa." *Waimea* means "red water," and the town was originally named after seasonal mountain streams with their reddish hue. When the post office was built, it was named after Samuel ("Kamuela") Parker of Parker Ranch, and that's where the confusion began. To make matters even more confusing, there is a Waimea town on each of the other major Hawaiian islands, which may be why the postmaster at the time preferred the name Kamuela for the Big Island's Waimea. Many Big Islanders use the two names interchangeably when talking of the same place, but we're not trying to throw you off, honest.

Waimea town lies at the foot of the Kohala Mountains, on the edge of a vast plateau that stretches to the base of towering Mauna Kea. The plateau slopes gradually to both the east and west, forming a perfect valley for pasture and farmland. Many of the vegetables, herbs, edible flowers and other specialty produce served in island restaurants is grown right here in Waimea.

★ **Parker Ranch Visitor Center** is located in the back of Parker Ranch Center on Highway 19 in the heart of Waimea town. This is where you sign up for Parker Ranch Tours and the tours of historic homes in Waimea. Those who take the time off from the beach to experience "Old Hawai'i" from the Parker Ranch point of view find it fascinating, time well spent. At this museum visitors learn the interesting history and operations of Parker Ranch and the Hawaiian *paniolo* lifestyle. Then stop in the Parker Ranch Store for great Western-style clothing, hats, belts, boots, T-shirts, cowboy and cowgirl outfits, great *omiyage* (gifts) and much more. Open daily except Sunday, 9 a.m. to 4 p.m. Admission: $6.50 adults, $5.50 seniors, $5 children 4 to 11. P.O. Box 458, Kamuela, HI 96743; 808-885-7655; www.parkerranch.com.

Another Parker Ranch Visitor Center attraction, ★ **Parker Ranch Historic Homes** is the historic Parker Ranch home complex one mile west of Waimea on Highway 190. Here is an 1847 New England–style house as well as the 1862 main ranch residence, *Pu'uopelu*, featuring an art gallery with an impressive collection of original paintings. Pu'uopelu is open daily except Sunday, 9 a.m. to 5 p.m. Admission: $8.50 adults, $7.50 seniors, $6 children 4 to 11. 808-885-5433.

Camp Tarawa Monument is of interest to World War II/Pacific War vets and history buffs. This is a large stone marker and plaque on Highway 190 near the entrance of Pu'uopelu. The marker notes the surrounding grounds of Parker Ranch that were used as "Camp Tarawa" from 1943–45 by the 2nd and 5th U.S. Marine Divisions that trained here prior to the invasion of Iwo Jima, Okinawa and other islands in the far west Pacific leading to the end of the war.

Kamuela Museum in Waimea is at the intersection of Routes 19 and 250 (Kohala Mountain Road). It is the largest privately owned museum in Hawai'i with interesting collections of ancient Hawaiian weapons, World War II relics, furniture of Hawaiian royalty, and other antiques and art objects. Open daily 9 a.m. to 5 p.m. Adults $5, children under age 12 $2. 808-885-4724.

As you drive into town up Kawaihae Road, stop at **Parker Square** on your right. This nice, U-shaped building offers a pleasant stroll through various shops on an old-fashioned wooden plankway that just sounds good as you go. Start at the **Gallery of Great Things** on one end and dig through a collection of Asian and Pacific treasures in all shapes, sizes and budgets, including museum-quality art, Hawai'i-made jewelry, quilts, paintings and sculptures. Do at least pick up and hold one of Jesus Sanchez's hand-bound, *koa*-covered blank books (painstakingly crafted in Hilo) and look at the *netsuke* collectibles right beside the front door. Open Monday-Saturday 9 a.m.-5:30 pm, Sunday 10 a.m.-4 p.m. P.O. Box 6209, Kamuela, HI 96743; 808-885-7706; fax 808-885-0098; e-mail: ggt@ilhawaii.net. Wander through the other shops and end up in Waimea General Store, or the coffee shop next door, before continuing on your way into town.

On the right is the **Quilted Horse** in the High Country Traders building. This is a source for Hawaiian quilts and quilting supplies, gift items and usually friendly conversation. Hawaiian quilts are deceptively expensive, but a real quilter will attest to their value. This folk-art form has been practiced by Hawai'i's women since the late 19th century, when missionary women taught sewing outdoors, under the trees. The bright sunlight made crisp shadows of leaves on the plain white cloth, which inspired cut-work patterns, each cut from one piece of contrasting, bright-colored fabric. It's assumed that Hawaiian women, who made cloth by an arduous process of tapa beating, thought the missionary ladies were nuts to cut up beautiful whole cloth, then sew it back together. However, they excelled at it and passed the tradition on to the present, with its share of *kapu*, taboo and legend. Traditionally, each quilt has a name and a secret name, known only to the quilter. A quilt can decorate the bed, but is never sat upon. And if they become worn or faded, they must be burned. (Please note that some machine-made knock-offs are available at much lower prices, but if you want an authentic quilt, ask questions and be sure of what you're buying.)

Leaving the Quilted Horse and Parker Square, turn right onto the main road, which curves to the right just before a stoplight. Go straight through the intersection and you will see **Parker Ranch Center** on the left. Take a look at the **Ikua Purdy Statue**, a life-sized bronze sculpture of horse and rider working a steer. There is ample parking in the complex, large restrooms, a variety of eateries and plenty of stores to explore. On the west end is **Healthways II**, a nice, big health food store jammed with fresh organic fruits and vegetables, canned and frozen vegetarian meals, vitamins, aromatherapy products and natural cosmetics. In the back is a deli counter, offering veggie sandwiches, smoothies and other fare for the conscientious.

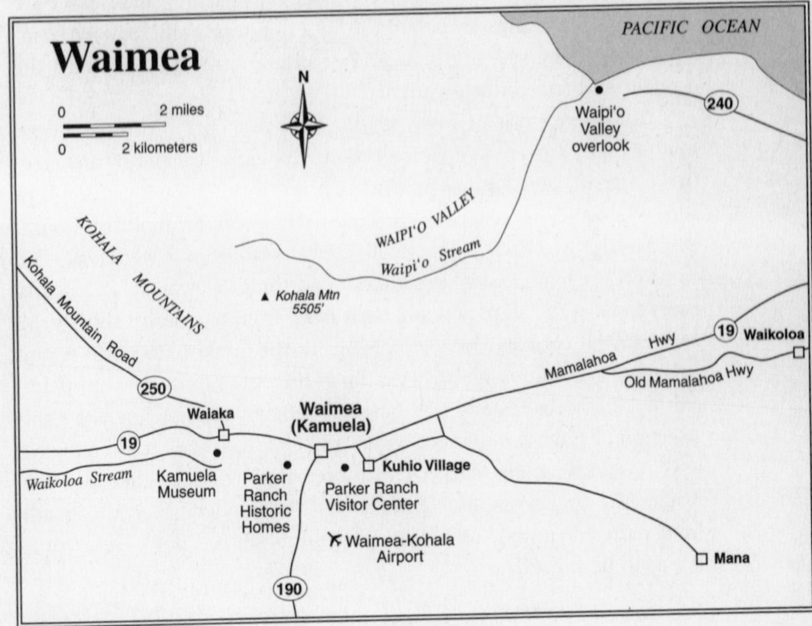

The **Parker Ranch Store**, full of *paniolo* souvenirs, cowboy and cowgirl attire and a funky combination of Western-Hawaiian gift items, leads into a central food court. A huge stone fireplace is surrounded by handpainted murals of Waimea countryside. There is a Starbucks on the opposite corner, that offers a selection of Kona coffees along with its usual menu, and comfortable areas to sit and "talk story." Beyond that is the Foodland grocery store and a Blockbuster Video.

Note that both Foodland and KTA (across the street) have competitive prices on popular *omiyage* items like Kona coffee and macadamia nuts. We'd encourage you to read labels and be sure of what you are buying. To be labeled "Kona Coffee," a blend is only required to have 10 percent Kona coffee beans. Most flavored varieties and decafs contain very little actual Kona beans. There are also blends of "Hawai'i Coffee," which include beans from Kaua'i, Maui and Moloka'i farms. These are fine coffees, but if you want 100 percent Kona, it's expensive. And, if you're planning to tour the coffee region, you'll have numerous opportunities to taste some of the best on the planet.

Across the street from Parker Ranch Visitor Center is **Waimea Center**, smaller and funkier, but worth the stop, if just to wander down the sidewalk once and smell the different eateries. Say hello to the cowboy statue and take a look at the beautiful stained-glass landscape in the central courtyard. For fresh flowers or to treat yourself to a lei, stop in **C&K Flowers**, and feel free to ask questions. There's a lot of aloha spoken here. Please note that parking here can be a challenge. The entire lot is laid out in a one-way traffic pattern, usually enforced by security guards. Pay attention to the arrows on the asphalt, and have a little patience.

Continuing out of town to the east, you pass historic "church row," a pretty strip of five various church buildings fronted by a cherry-tree-covered lawn—a real picture-postcard if you're lucky enough to visit when they're in bloom. Just past the stoplight, look for **Cook's Discoveries** (808-885-3633; e-mail: cookshi@aol.com; www.hawaiinow.com) on the left. Cook's specializes in all things Hawaiian, and nearly every item in the shop is made right here, from wonderful shortbread and oatmeal cookies (free samples from the cookie jars), *lilikoi* and *poha* jams, fabulous aloha wear including muumuus, beautiful lei-painted Ts for ladies and *koa* baseball caps for men. There is a good selection of Hawai'i books for adults and children. Look at the unusual jewelry and seed and feather lei for lifetime souvenirs. There are hair ornaments, art, cards, music and toys (like handcrafted rattles made from baby coconuts). As much museum as shop, Cook's Discoveries is not to be missed.

You can do Waimea in half a day. One strategy is to save it for your day-after-sunburn, when you'd most appreciate cooler temperatures. Another is to check the *Waimea Gazette*, *West Hawai'i Today* or *North Hawai'i News* for festivals, parades and other events happening in town. Waimea is a busy community and takes its holidays and special occasions very seriously. The Cherry Blossom Festival, Aloha Week festivities, Christmas parade, Pow Wow and many others make great excuses to drive into town, do a little shopping and stay for a meal.

Saddle Road

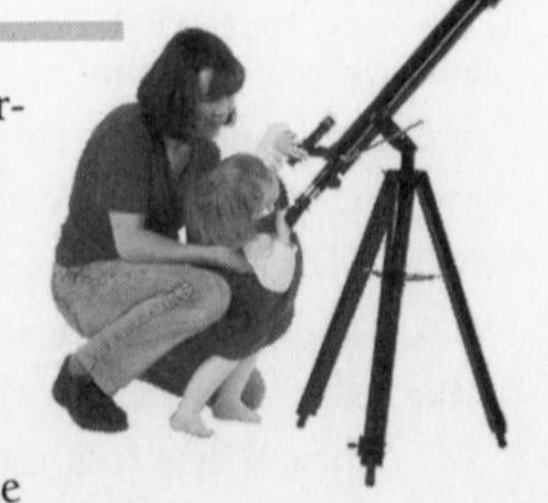

This section is added for informational purposes even though there are no towns or villages and no stores or services of any kind along the Saddle Road. It is included because the road winds through some surreal-looking landscape with stark lava flows, cinder cones and volcanic peaks. This is the route to one of the island's primary attractions: the world-renowned telescope observatories at the summit of Mauna Kea mountain and the weather observatory on Mauna Loa.

Caution: Driving on Saddle Road, Highway 200, is prohibited in rental cars due to hazardous driving conditions. It is a violation of car rental contracts.

The Saddle Road is so-called because it passes through the plateau adjoining the massive Mauna Kea and Mauna Loa mountains, like a saddle in between. From Waimea to Hilo via the Saddle Road is a distance of 60 miles and from Kailua-Kona to Hilo it is 87 miles. However, because of the narrow winding road conditions (especially near the Hilo side) and the extreme caution needed when driving it, this route often takes longer to drive than other routes around the island.

The drive does present some different scenery, however. The towering peaks of Mauna Kea and Mauna Loa are seen from a closer perspective along the road in between them. The early-morning hours are generally clear while from midday on into the afternoon, clouds roll upslope from the eastern Hilo and Hamakua districts and tend to fill up the plateau area between the mountains, obscuring the views. Traveling from west to east, the road passes through vast tracts of green ranch pastures, extending down from Mauna Kea's lower slopes. This is generally dry, windy and wide-open countryside. On the Hilo side, the road passes through several miles of heavy rainforest vegetation above the town that gives way to extensive fern and *ohia lehua* forest of the mountain's mid-elevation slopes. Interspersed here and there are rough and rugged lava flows until at the 3,000-foot level on the central plateau, where it appears to be one huge lava flow.

Midway on the Saddle Road is the turn-off for the Mauna Kea Summit Road, which leads up to the summit of the 13,796-foot mountain (about 1 hour from Hilo, Waikoloa or Waimea and 2 hours from Kailua-Kona).

Caution: Youngsters under 12, pregnant women and anyone with respiratory or cardiac problems are advised *not* to go to Mauna Kea's summit. The very thin air (60 percent of normal oxygen) can cause altitude sickness and nausea. Even scientists working at this elevation experience difficulties. Mauna Kea's weather can change suddenly and dramatically, especially in winter months. From November to March, it can snow anytime and blizzard conditions are possible. Even the summer months can bring strong winds and below-freezing temperatures at the summit. Warm clothing is essential year-round and warm drinks, food and emergency supplies are essential. There are no services at the summit. We strongly advise you limit your visit to the Onizuka Center and enjoy the stars safely.

At the 9,200-foot elevation level (6.5 miles up the summit road) is the **Onizuka Center for International Astronomy**, named in honor of Astronaut Ellison Onizuka, a native son of the Big Island who died aboard the *Challenger* space shuttle in 1986. The visitors center is open daily 9 a.m. to 10 p.m. with free lectures and star-gazing programs. This is truly cool. Pack a picnic, all your warm clothes and plenty of water and hot beverages. Go up in time for sunset, genuinely awesome at this elevation. On a clear night, you can even see the glow of red lava from the flow many miles away. At twilight, watch for satellites and the space station, then at dark, get a glimpse of the rest of the galaxy, up close and personal, through 14-inch Celestron telescopes. See the rings of Saturn, canals on Mars and other wonders from the best vantage point on Earth. Programs are conducted every evening from 6 p.m. to 10 p.m., weather permitting. And they're free. For more information, call the center at 808-961-2180 or 808-974-4273 for a recorded message. For weather updates and snow and road conditions on Mauna Kea: 808-961-5582; e-mail: mkvisa@ifa.hawaii.edu; www.ifa.hawaii.edu/mok/about_maunakea.htm. (Commercial tours are also available from various providers.)

The Onizuka Center also serves as the base camp for scientists and astronomers engaged in research projects using the telescopes up at the summit. The center, at 9,200 feet, is a safer and more comfortable elevation for researchers than the extremely thin air at the nearly 14,000-foot peak. Above the Onizuka Center, the John A. Burns Way extends another 6.6 miles to the very top. There are no facilities for the public above the center; 4WD transportation is required, with adequate fuel for the return to Hilo or Waimea. There are no opportunities to look through the telescopes during the day and visitors are not permitted after dark. The road to the summit can be dangerous and is subject to severe weather. The high altitude carries serious health risks.

Mauna Kea's extremely dry climate, high altitude and remote location far away from lighted areas offer some of the consistently best conditions for optical, infrared and radio astronomy of any site on the planet. Here at the summit, above 40 percent of the earth's atmosphere, water vapor in the air is minimal, and the number of cloud-free nights is greater than anywhere else in the world.

There are 13 working telescopes here, 9 for optical and infrared astronomy, 3 for submillimeter wavelength astronomy and 1 for radio astronomy. These amazing instruments represent the leaders of the astronomy community, including the twin W. M. Keck Telescopes, the largest optical/infrared instruments in the world, and the James Clerk Maxwell Telescope, the largest submillimeter instrument. The 82-foot wide, 100-foot tall antenna dish of the Very Long Baseline Array is part of the 5,000-mile-wide radio telescope that stretches from the Virgin Islands to Hawai'i, with dish sites across the mainland.

The **Mauna Loa Access Road** leads off the Saddle Road in the opposite direction of the Mauna Kea Summit Road. This drive of just over 17 miles to the 11,000-foot level of Mauna Loa passes through nothing but stark barren lava flow country. There are sweeping views back across the Saddle Road plateau and to Mauna Kea on cloudless days. But other than that, the 34-mile round trip on this road is a drive across a moonscape rock desert.

At the end of the Mauna Loa Access Road is the **National Oceanic and Atmospheric Administration (NOAA) Mauna Loa Weather Observatory**, which keeps track of developing weather over Hawai'i using sophisticated instruments and satellite communications. A hiking trail from the end of the road here continues on up to Mauna Loa's summit and to a hiker's cabin. Hikers can connect to a trail system leading downslope on the other side to Hawai'i Volcanoes National Park headquarters, but it is not a hike for novices or unprepared casual hikers. It is a very strenuous hike over very rugged terrain. Only experienced backpackers with full supplies should attempt the route. Check "Hiking" in Chapter 6 for details.

Along the Saddle Road is **Pohakuloa Training Area**, a large military base used by the Army for live firing exercises and military maneuvers. Be on the alert for large, slow-moving military trucks on the Saddle Road and an occasional convoy of military vehicles or even a tank! A road improvement project began in 2003.

Mauna Kea State Recreation Area is also located on the Saddle Road, with picnic areas, restrooms and phone available. The park is on the plateau at the foot of Mauna Kea and the area abounds with introduced wild game birds like pheasant, quail and partridge as well as many species of native Hawaiian bird life. Visitors can enjoy the peace and solitude of this remote area and stroll through the trails and backroads of the park area to gain a perspective of this most unusual part of Hawai'i.

Hamakua Coast

Just north of Hilo, and running the length of the Big Island's east side some 40 miles to Honoka'a and another 10 miles beyond to Waipi'o Valley, is the Hamakua Coast. Up until the early '90s, when the sugar industry finally closed down completely after a long decline, this region's vast sugar plantations annually produced thousands of tons of raw cane to feed the several sugar mills located along the coast. And while there are still thousands of acres of once-productive sugar cane fields lying dormant, there is a growing diversified agriculture economy being developed in macadamia nut orchards, ginger, papaya, bananas, dryland taro and other crops and timber throughout the region. Farmers are branching out into other crops and taking advantage of the large tracts of good productive agriculture land available.

Along the Hamakua Coast are numerous gulches and ravines filled with gushing streams and waterfalls, verdant tropical rainforest vegetation, and scattered stands of forest. Weathered old sugar plantation villages appear amid the fields, presenting a vestige of Hawai'i's past. A generation or two ago, most of the Big Island's population lived in such plantation camps.

Driving the length of the Hamakua Coast can be a most enjoyable experience. The route passes through a number of small towns and settlements along the way, each with a melodious Hawaiian name: Papa'ikou, Pepe'ekeo, Honomu, Hakalau, Laupahoehoe, O'okala, Pa'auilo and Pa'auhau.

As is the immediate Hilo area, the Hamakua Coast is generally quite wet, receiving well over 100 inches of rainfall annually. This accounts for the rainforest and lush fields of greenery everywhere. However, rainfall varies by elevation and you will notice changes in vegetation and terrain as you travel north towards Honoka'a. It does become somewhat drier.

After the demise of the sugar industry in the early '90s, local community groups along with county and state governments organized the **Hilo-Hamakua Heritage Coast** program in an attempt to help rebuild the area's economy and preserve its historic, cultural and naturally scenic assets. The published driver's guide to the Hilo-Hamakua Heritage Coast covers important points of interest along the 45-mile route from Hilo to Honoka'a and the Waipi'o Valley, and Highway 19 is marked with numerous brown and white "heritage" signs. The guides are available at visitor information desks at the Hilo and Kona airports, through the Hawai'i Visitors Bureau Big Island offices and other visitor information outlets.

Most of the coastline on this eastern side of the island is quite rugged, marked by high cliffs, sometimes several hundred feet high, that drop straight to the pounding ocean surf. There are very few safe beach areas along this entire coast due to the rocky nature of the coastline. However, the parks and overlooks along the way provide wonderful scenic vistas, often with cascading streams and waterfalls dropping into the ocean. Compared to the Big Island's dry west side, the east side is indeed a paradise and a garden of Eden, it is so lush and green.

★ **Old Mamalahoa Highway Scenic Drive** is just five miles north of Hilo at the intersection with Kalanianaole School. Old Highway 19 follows the rugged rainforested Hamakua Coast for four miles before linking back with the newer Highway 19. The scenic route takes in numerous gulches and coves as it winds through lovely coastal country with scenic views of the rugged Hamakua Coast and lush rainforest jungles. Shower trees, royal poinciana, breadfruit, coconut, African tulip, and royal palms line the route much of the way. The old route

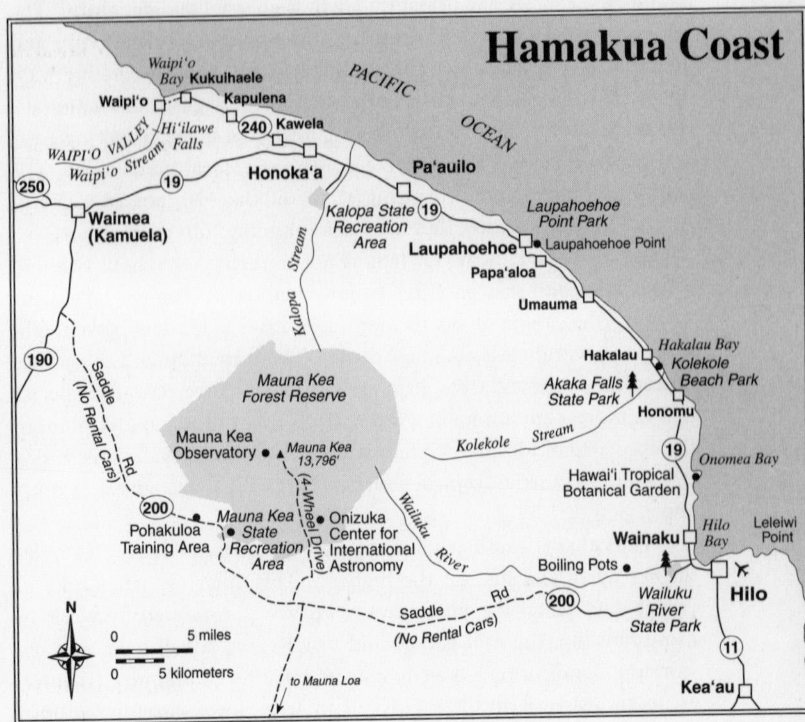

passes through aged sugar plantation villages with melodious names such as Papaikou, Onomea, Peepeekeo, and Kawai Nui. It's definitely an easy and scenic drive well worth taking; this was the only route around the island in the pre–World War II days.

★ **Hawai'i Tropical Botanical Garden** is located along this scenic route just north of Papa`ikou at Onomea Bay. Nature trails meander through tropical rainforest, cross streams and waterfalls, and follow the rugged coast. There are extensive collections of palms, bromeliads, gingers, exotic ornamentals, and rare plants. Well worth the ticket price when you see what they have created out of former overgrown wild jungle. A garden of joy for nature photographers. Open daily 8 a.m. through 5 p.m. Adults $15, children under 16 $5, group/family one-year pass $35. 808-954-5233.

Honomu is about 11 miles north of Hilo and is a typical old sugar plantation country town whose two-block main street hosts a small group of interesting shops, galleries, diners and churches on the route up to Akaka Falls.

★ **Akaka Falls State Park** is located above Honomu town. Take Route 22 on out and above town. The paved road rises sharply through the hilly fields above town on its 3.6-mile route to the park. Here under a rainforest canopy, the ocean tradewinds are cool and delightful. The 66-acre park is a refreshing stop after the uphill drive. Restrooms and picnic tables are available. The main attraction is the fascinating walk down into the ravines where mountain streams gush and waterfalls splash. Beautiful stands of bamboo, ginger, and many flowering trees and plants delight walkers. It's a gorgeous tropical greenhouse. The walk is highlighted by inspiring views of the 420-foot cascades of Akaka Falls and nearby Kahuna Falls tumbling into deep gorges.

★ **World Botanical Gardens** is north of Honomu about two and a half miles and just past the 16-mile marker on Highway 19. This 300-acre development on former sugar cane fields has been established as a world-class botanical garden. There are thousands of species of tropical plants and trees, fruit orchards, and native Hawaiian species in a rainforest environment. Nature trails lead to the lookout point of the spectacular 300-foot triple cascades of Umauma Waterfalls. Enjoy free samples of fresh tropical fruit like banana, papaya, guava or pineapple. 808-963-5427.

Papa'aloa is another old plantation village located some 11 miles further north and just off the highway. This village is a reminder of earlier days when the plantation town was surrounded by workers' camp housing, the mill garage and warehouses, a ball field, and old storefronts indicating a once lively and bustling community. It's interesting to just turn off the highway and drive down through the quiet little village. Today, Papa'aloa, still a resident community, basks in quiet obscurity along a quiet coast. The **Papa'aloa Store** is a good place for a cool drink or to sample some of the local goodies like daily special plate lunches. While in the store, stroll the aisles, look at the old photographs on the walls, and get the feel for an old plantation town mom-and-pop store. It's almost like a museum visit.

★ **Laupahoehoe** and **Laupahoehoe Point** are another mile or so north. The old town area has a school, bakery, post office, a police station and the former jail. There is also the old **M. Sakado Store**, another real classic mom-and-pop store survivor from an earlier era.

The ★ **Laupahoehoe Train Museum** is located in town at the intersection of main street and the highway. Displays and exhibits keep the Hamakua Coast's railroad heritage alive. The museum serves as an official visitors center for the Hilo-Hamakua Heritage Coast Trail. Check the museum website: www.cs.uhh.hawaii.edu/~train.

Just on the north edge of town, there is a scenic overlook alongside the highway before you get to the gulch leading down to Laupahoehoe Point. The point itself is a lava peninsula extending into the ocean. There is a grassy park area with picnic tables, restrooms and shelters. Small boat-launching facilities are available and from the point there are scenic views of the Hamakua Coast. A monument stands on the point in memory of the 24 teachers and school children who were swept to sea in a 1946 tidal wave that devastated a school that occupied the site.

Pa'auilo is located some 10 miles or so north along Highway 19 and is another fading sugar plantation village. There's a view of the former plantation manager's residence set back on the hill next to **Earl's Snack Shop** in town. The workers' camp housing stretches out below the highway and the manager's house is up on the hill. The town has changed little since its heyday as a plantation center. Be sure to stop just south of Pa'auilo at Donna's Cookies for the some of the best homemade cookies on the Big Island.

★ **Kalopa State Recreation Area** turn-off is about five miles north of Pa'auilo and a couple of miles south of Honoka'a town. The park has camping cabins and picnic tables, as well as a nature trail system through stands of reforested lands as well as native rainforest.

★ **Honoka'a** is only seven miles north of Pa'auilo. Honoka'a is the largest country town on the Hamakua Coast. Since the sugar industry soured, it's started to branch out in different directions, as an art community and a diverse, growing residential neighborhood. You may enjoy a one-street walking tour for a chance to nose through overstuffed antique stores and junk shops, visit the macadamia nut factory, take in the galleries and wonderful smells of fresh coffee, pizza and other good things. Walk by the **People Theatre**, and appreciate the restoration efforts that went into making a retro classic from a falling-down movie theater, now home of the successful annual Hamakua Music Festival in October. 808-775-FEST.

★ **Tex's Drive In** is on Highway 19 above Honoka'a town. Don't miss this Honoka'a institution, famous for fresh hot *malasadas* (deep-fried Portuguese doughnuts, a sheer delight anytime) and other local fast-food items. Just across the road from Tex's is the **Honoka'a Visitors Center**. Here there are public restrooms and information on local area attractions and activities.

★ **Waipi'o Valley** is located at the end of Route 240, about nine miles north of Honoka'a. The road passes through the tiny villages of **Kawela**, **Kapulena** and **Kukuihaele**. You can visit **The Last Chance Store** for cold sodas and snacks and see what a small country village general store is like. **Waipi'o Wood Works Art Gallery** is a great place for handcrafted Hawaiian wood products, paintings, prints, photos, glasswork, pottery, jewelry, baskets, batik art, and general Hawaiiana created by island artists. Also, in this shop you can book a tour with **Waipi'o Valley Shuttle** to take a narrated one-and-a-half-hour 4x4 drive down into the magnificent Waipi'o Valley, just a half mile further on. The tour details the history and culture of the valley from past to present, and includes information on taro growing, the main economic activity at present. The shuttle tour is $37 per person, children under 12 are $15. Shuttles operate daily except Sunday, 9 a.m., 11 a.m., 1 p.m. and 3 p.m. 808-775-7121.

You can also see the Waipi'o Valley via horseback rides booked through **Waipi'o Na'alapa Trail Rides** (808-775-0419) or **Hawaii Resorts Transportation** (808-775-7291). These are two-and-a-half-hour horseback tours on the floor of Waipi'o Valley.

★ **Waipi'o Valley State Park** and the overlook at the top of the valley is the starting point for the steep winding road leading into the valley. *Caution*: Under no circumstances should you attempt to drive your rental car down the dangerously steep valley road. Only 4x4 vehicles are allowed. In addition to the steep road, there are numerous streams on the valley floor that must be crossed and regular rental cars will not make it.

Waipi'o Valley Park provides a covered picnic pavilion and restrooms at the top of the valley and spectacular views from an overlook of the six-mile-long valley interior with its almost vertical 2,000-foot walls, and also of the northern coastline of the Big Island. The valley fronts the ocean with a wide black-sand beach and heavy pounding surf. This beach is not safe for swimming due to hazardous undercurrents.

Hilo

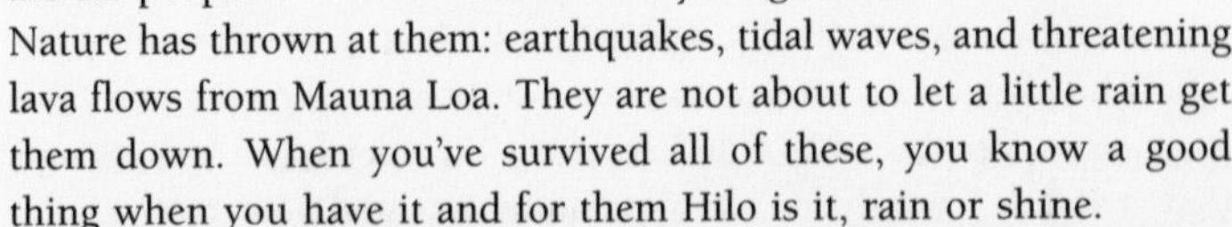

Mention has already been made of Hilo and its notorious rainy reputation. Granted, it's probably Hawai'i's most underrated and least glamorous place. It has what public relations experts call "an image problem." Even though it does rain a lot—some 130 inches annually—Hilo folks remain decidedly cheerful, open, friendly and optimistic. After all, these are the people who have endured everything Mother Nature has thrown at them: earthquakes, tidal waves, and threatening lava flows from Mauna Loa. They are not about to let a little rain get them down. When you've survived all of these, you know a good thing when you have it and for them Hilo is it, rain or shine.

What we love about visiting Hilo is its special sense of being a "real" place, where real people live and work. Hilo was not invented for the visitor industry; it was an industrial blue-collar town that grew up on its own and is now the seat of county government, and the second largest city in Hawai'i (believe it or not).

Hilo was the government and commercial trade center for the sugar plantations that dominated island industry until its decline. The abundant rains still produce a lush green tropical landscape and former cane lands are being planted in macadamia nuts, papayas, bananas, tropical flowers and garden crops that hold more economic promise and are more environmentally sound. With its distinctly tropical climate, Hilo has become the center for the world's largest tropical flower industry. Anthuriums, those heart-shaped long-lasting blooms that fetch \$3-\$5 each in winter, are marketed by the thousands by numerous farmer co-ops and flower farm exporters. The orchid industry features countless varieties of award-winning flowering plants that are exported worldwide.

Hilo is also gaining recognition as a residential small college town with the growth and expansion of the state-supported *University of Hawai'i at Hilo* and adjoining *Hawai'i Community College*. The schools share a lovely campus and a cosmopolitan enrollment of some 4,000 to 5,000 students from around the islands of Hawai'i, the U.S. mainland and all over the Pacific Rim. The University of Hawaii at Hilo's University Research Park is home to the Joint Astronomy Center, which operates two observatories on Mauna Kea and the headquarters of the Caltech Submillimeter Observatory, also on Mauna Kea, operated by the California Institute of Technology.

The last few years have seen much improvement in downtown Hilo, particularly along the bayfront, as new businesses have renovated old shop buildings. Restaurants, gift shops, art galleries, boutiques and other interesting places add new life to the old-fashioned downtown area without taking away from its charm.

As John Penisten says, "After experiencing the real Hilo and its notorious rain, perhaps you'll come to see that Hilo does indeed have its place in the sun. Some see Hilo as a salve to soothe and comfort those with tortured soul and psyche who seek relief in a definitely slower and perhaps saner pace of life. With its warm showers, lush tropical splendor, and friendly caring folks, Hilo is indeed a balm for troubled souls and aching hearts. You see, the old line about Hilo's rain is really relative. It's all in how you look at it. Hilo's rainy reputation has kept the visitor counts to a minimum, which some folks don't mind. Because of it, Hilo has been slow to change. And perhaps that's good. It has helped Hilo to retain its essential hometown charm and personality, a valuable asset these days. Yes, there is a bright side to Hilo. And you really need to discover it for yourself. Oh, and when you come, bring your umbrella. It looks like a shower today!"

Hilo and vicinity receive little attention from the visitor industry as a destination. But partly because of Hilo's anonymity, it has something of an "unspoiled paradise" image, if there is such a thing. There is so much to see, experience, and enjoy in this perennial Hawaiian hometown that you'll need more than a day or two to see it all. A locally organized group, **Destination Hilo**, is working to publicize the area's attractions. 2109F Kaiwiki Road, Hilo, HI 96720; 808-935-5294; fax 808-969-1984.

★ **Liliuokalani Park** is located on Banyan Drive on the Waiakea Peninsula, adjacent to the hotels and on the shore of Hilo Bay. This authentic Japanese garden park was named in honor of Hawai'i's last reigning monarch, Queen Liliuokalani. It was built in the early 1900s as a memorial to the immigrant Japanese who developed the old Waiakea Sugar Plantation. The park features several magnificent Japanese stone lanterns, pavilions, an arching footbridge, a tea house, and reflecting lagoons. It is one of Hawai'i's loveliest cultural parks. Free. This is a must-see place in Hilo.

Banyan trees line Hilo's hotel row and give it the name ★ **Banyan Drive**. Most of these handsome spreading trees were planted over a 40-year period beginning in 1933 by such VIPs as President Franklin D. Roosevelt, Amelia Earhart, Babe Ruth, Fannie Hurst and other notables of the era. There's even one planted by a then-aspiring politician named Richard Nixon. Each tree is marked accordingly.

★ **Coconut Island** in Hilo Bay is a small island just offshore from Liliuokalani Park. A footbridge just opposite the Hilo Hawaiian Hotel leads to it. It is a great place for watching local fishermen angling and kids swimming and diving from an old bridge platform. There are pic-

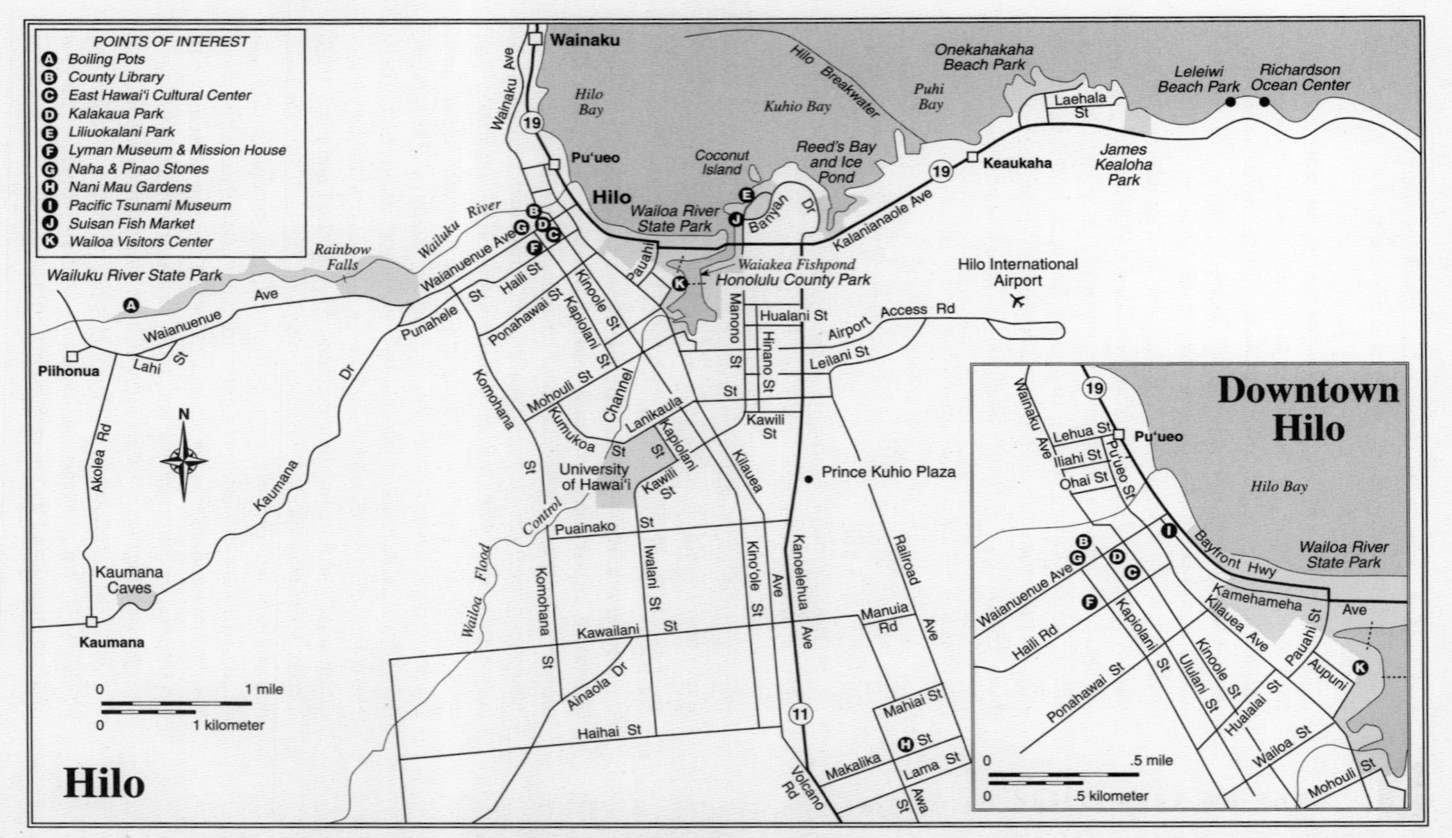
Hilo
POINTS OF INTEREST
A Boiling Pots
B County Library
C East Hawai'i Cultural Center
D Kalakaua Park
E Liliuokalani Park
F Lyman Museum & Mission House
G Naha & Pinao Stones
H Nani Mau Gardens
I Pacific Tsunami Museum
J Suisan Fish Market
K Wailoa Visitors Center
Wainaku
Hilo Bay
Kuhio Bay
Hilo Breakwater
Puhi Bay
Onekahakaha Beach Park
Leleiwi Beach Park
Richardson Ocean Center
Laehala St
James Kealoha Park
Keaukaha
Pu'ueo
Hilo
Coconut Island
Reed's Bay and Ice Pond
Banyan Dr
Wailoa River State Park
Kalanianaole Ave
Waiakea Fishpond
Honolulu County Park
Hilo International Airport
Airport Access Rd
Leilani St
Hualani St
Hinano St
Manono St
Kawili St
Prince Kuhio Plaza
Kanoelehua Ave
Railroad Ave
Manuia Rd
Mahiai St
H St
Lama St
Makalika
Awa St
Volcano Rd
Kilauea Ave
Kino'ole St
Iwalani St
Puainako St
Kawailani St
Haihai St
Ainaola Dr
Komohana St
University of Hawai'i
Kapiolani St
Lanikaula St
Kumukoa St
Channel
Wailoa Flood Control
Mohouli St
Kinoole St
Kapiolani St
Ponahawai St
Haili St
Pauahi
Waianuenue Ave
Punahele St
Wailuku River
Rainbow Falls
Wailuku River State Park
Waianuenue Ave
Lahi St
Piihonua
Akolea Rd
Kaumana Dr
Kaumana Caves
Kaumana
Wainaku Ave
N
0 1 mile
0 1 kilometer
Downtown Hilo
Hilo Bay
Wailoa River State Park
Bayfront Hwy
Kamehameha Ave
Pu'ueo
Pu'ueo St
Lehua St
Iliahi St
Ohai St
Wainaku Ave
Waianuenue Ave
Haili Rd
Ponahawai St
Kapiolani St
Ululani St
Kinoole St
Kilauea Ave
Hualalai St
Wailoa St
Pauahi St
Aupuni
Mohouli St
0 .5 mile
0 .5 kilometer

nic tables and shelters available. Coconut Island is often used for cultural events by local groups. Worth a stroll at sunset if you are staying at a nearby hotel.

Rainbow Falls and Boiling Pots are above old downtown Hilo and just off Waianuenue Avenue on Rainbow Drive at **Wailuku River State Park**. This small park features walking trails, restrooms and magnificent views of **Rainbow Falls**, best viewed early in the morning when the sun strikes the falls, sending rainbows over the spray and pool. A little further up the road, above Hilo Hospital, the Wailuku River is marked by giant holes and recesses, called **Boiling Pots**, in the lava-rock gorge. The Pots create a series of deep swirling pools, falls and rapids during heavy rain periods. There is no safe swimming in this treacherous and deep gorge. There are restroom facilities, picnic tables, and a scenic overlook of the Wailuku River Gorge.

Suisan Fish Market is located on Hilo Bay at the mouth of the Wailoa River and within walking distance of the Banyan Drive hotels. 85 Lihiwai Street; 808-935-8051.

★ **Hilo Farmers' Market** is a general fruit-vegetable produce, tropical flower and flea-market operation on Wednesday, Saturday and Sunday mornings from early until noon or so at the corner of Mamo Street and Kamehameha Avenue, across from Mo'oheau Park. Bargains galore and wonderful fresh local produce!

University of Hawai'i at Hilo and Hawai'i Community College Campus is located between Lanikaula and Kawili streets in Hilo. The university and community college, which share a common campus and have a combined enrollment of some 5,000, offer two- and four-year degree programs. The university utilizes its special geography and resources to offer programs of study in such unique fields as Hawaiian Studies, Pacific Islands Anthropology, Marine Science, Oceanography, Aquaculture, Volcanology, Geothermal Energy, Astronomy and others. The community college specializes in the Liberal Arts, Business Education and vocational-technical trades. The serene campus is landscaped with many species of tropical trees and plants. Its theater hosts numerous public performances, concerts, shows and plays throughout the year and the Campus Center art gallery has ongoing displays. The campus annually hosts several Elderhostel Program senior citizen courses for U.S. mainland visitors as well as a broad range of summer session offerings. Visitors are welcome. For information, contact the Office of University Relations, 200 West Kawili Street, Hilo, HI 96720-4091 (both colleges at the same address); UH-Hilo 808-933-3567 or HCC Provost's Office 808-933-3611.

★ **Lyman Museum & Mission House** is an old New England–style missionary home built in 1839 for Rev. David and Sarah Lyman, the first Christian missionaries to arrive in Hilo. In addition to the original Lyman House, the museum next door holds a unique collection of memorabilia of early Hilo and Big Island life. Numerous artifacts from the different cultures that populated Hawai'i are also on display. Museum hours are Monday through Saturday, 9:30 a.m. to 4:30 p.m. Admission $7 adults, $5 seniors, $3 children under 18. Mission House tours are given several times daily beginning at 9:30 a.m. 276 Haili Street; 808-935-5021.

★ **Pacific Tsunami Museum** is one of Hilo's most unique museums. It's located in the old First Hawaiian Bank along Kamehameha Avenue. The museum serves as a repository of information and research for scholars on global tsunami and tidal wave phenomena and as an educational museum for the public. Displays and exhibits preserve the history of the local community and serve as a living memorial to those who lost their lives in past tsunami events in Hawai'i. There are guided tours, movies of tsunami events, interactive computer terminals, and a gift shop. Admission: $5 per person. Corner of Kalakaua and Kamehameha Avenues, downtown Hilo, P.O. Box 806, Hilo, HI 96721; 808-935-0926; www.tsunami.org.

The **Naha Stone** is at the Hilo Public Library, three blocks uphill from the Hilo Bay waterfront. There are two large stones on the front lawn. The long horizontal one is called the Naha Stone, which, according to Hawaiian legend, was used in ancient times to sever the umbilical cords of royal children. It was also used to test the claims of royal blood in newborn males. During a ceremony, those who remained silent were recognized as future mighty warriors, while those who cried out were said to lack courage. As a young man, Kamehameha the Great was said to have lifted and overturned the large stone, proving his strength and courage. King Kamehameha went on to conquer and unite the Hawaiian Islands under one kingdom in 1810. The Naha Stone is estimated to weigh three and a half tons and was brought from the island of Kaua'i in a high chief's canoe. The small upright stone is said to be the entrance pillar to the Pinao Temple, an ancient sacred temple on the Big Island, where the Naha Stone was originally located. 300 Waianuenue Avenue.

★ **Downtown Hilo Walking Tours** are scheduled for the third Saturday of each month at 9 a.m. Sites include **Kalakaua Park**, in the center of downtown Hilo, originally conceived as a civic center by King Kalakaua. The park has roots to one of the first missionary stations as early as 1825. Other nearby places of historical interest included in the walking tour are Niolopa (once the Hilo Hotel), the old and new library buildings, the old federal building, Lyman Museum and others.

Reservations can be made through Lyman Museum. The tours are free and begin at the museum. 276 Haili Street, Hilo; 808-935-5021.

East Hawai'i Cultural Center is located in downtown Hilo, opposite Kalakaua Park and the post office. The center is housed in the old police station, a historic building constructed in 1932 and placed on the National Register of Historic Buildings and Places. It resembles a Hawaiian *hale* (house) of the 1800s with its hipped roof. The center is dedicated to culture and the arts in East Hawai'i. Ongoing art gallery shows and exhibits are free and open to the public. Community theater performances are sponsored by the center throughout the year as well as special events and activities. Open daily except Sunday, 10 a.m. to 4 p.m. 141 Kalakaua Street; 808-951-5711.

FACTORY TOURS

★ **Mauna Loa Macadamia Nut Factory** is located three miles south of Hilo on the east side of Volcano Highway 11 and back in through the orchards a couple of miles. Look for road signs marking the entrance. A visitors center provides free samples of Hawai'i's popular gourmet nut and a wide variety of macadamia nut products are available for purchase. There is also a free narrated factory tour. Open daily 9 a.m. to 5 p.m. 808-955-8612.

★ **Big Island Candies** is straight ahead as you exit the Hilo Airport Road at the main intersection of Kanoelehua Avenue. Go straight through the intersection onto Kekuanaoa Street and go three blocks, turn right on Hinano Street and the factory is on the immediate right. This must-see candy factory is famous for its delectable hand-dipped dark and white chocolate shortbread cookies, macadamia nut shortbread, coffee shortbread and peanut butter shortbread. They also make fine macadamia nut chocolates, chocolate brownies, biscotti, macadamia nut crunchies, rocky road chocolate, caramel clusters, and many other tempting, tasty treats. Browse the gift shop, watch the factory operations through large windows, and sample fresh Kona coffee and chocolates. This will be one stop you won't regret. 585 Hinano Street; 808-935-8890; e-mail: bic@bigislandcandies.com; www.bigislandcandies.com.

Mehana Brewing Company welcomes visitors who stop by the tasting room with free samples of its various microbrews. Sample from Mehana Beer, Volcano Red Ale (won bronze medal in 1998 World Beer Championships) and Mehana Mauna Kea Pale Ale, among others. Mehana's smooth taste is from the pure Hawaiian water and fresh ingredients used. They also have a gift shop with logo-wear, caps, glasses and gift items. Open Monday through Friday 9 a.m. to 5:30 p.m., Saturday 10 a.m. to 4 p.m. 275 East Kawili Street; 808-934-8211; e-mail: karen@mehana.com; www.mehana.com.

★ **Panaewa Rain Forest Zoo** is one of Hilo's least known and most delightful free attractions. It is one of the few natural tropical rainforest zoos in the United States. The small facility is operated by the County of Hawai'i and features several rainforest species in natural environment enclosures. Among the animals on display are a white tiger, African pygmy hippopotamus, water buffalo, rainforest monkeys, a tapir, various jungle parrots, and endangered Hawaiian birds like the nene goose, Hawaiian *i'o* (hawk), *pu'eo* (owl) and Hawaiian stilt. The zoo is a pleasant walk through natural Hawaiian rainforest with numerous flowering trees and shrubs. Colorful peacocks strut openly. The zoo is adjacent to the Panaewa Equestrian Center. Open daily 9 a.m. to 4 p.m. Located a couple of miles south of Hilo just off the Volcano Highway 11 on Mamaki Street; 808-959-7224.

★ **Wailoa State Park–Wailoa Center** is adjacent to Suisan Fish Market on the Wailoa River and behind Kamehameha Avenue and the Hilo bayfront. Wailoa State Park comprises the lands surrounding the Wailoa River and Waiakea Fish Pond. There are lots of picnic tables and several covered pavilions; it's a good place for a pleasant picnic lunch or a stroll over the arching bridges. Fishermen in rowboats are often seen floating around the pond, angling for the abundant mullet fish. There are also a Vietnam Veterans War Memorial and a Tsunami Memorial in the park. The Wailoa Center on Piopio Street in the park features various free art exhibits, seasonal showings, and cultural displays by local artisans. Check the schedule at the center for current show. Center hours Monday, Tuesday, Thursday and Friday 8 a.m. to 4:30 p.m., Wednesday 12 p.m. to 4:30 p.m., Saturday 9:30 a.m. to 3 p.m., closed Sunday and holidays. 808-933-0416.

★ **Nani Mau Gardens** is just south of town off Volcano Highway. You can't miss the turn off the highway, just look for beautiful floral beds and displays on both sides of Makalika Street. From the highway, it's a half-mile to the gardens. There are some 20 acres of tropical foliage, flowers, trees and plants along with a waterfall, pond and Japanese garden. Visitors can stroll on their own or opt for a tram tour through the grounds. The orchid greenhouse is spectacular, with many varieties of orchids in bloom. There is a large gift shop also. Open daily 8 a.m. to 5 p.m. Adults $10 and children ages 5 to 12 $5. 421 Makalika Street, Hilo; 808-959-3500.

Hilo can be a great place to shop. It has everything from modern shopping centers with the latest boutiques, fashion shops, and department stores, to unassuming little arts-and-crafts and antique shops in old downtown Hilo. Some of the shopping centers and specialty shops worth checking are listed below.

Shopping centers in Hilo have everything from major department stores (Sears, Macy's) to discount stores (Longs Drugs, Payless, Wal-

Mart) to fashion stores, shoe stores, bookstores, jewelry stores, etc. Many fashion and department stores carry Hawai'i-made aloha clothing for those who want to get into colorful shirts and muumuus. Shopping centers include our one actual mall, **Prince Kuhio Plaza,** at the intersection of Kanoelehua (Volcano Highway) and Puainako streets, **Hilo Shopping Center** at corner of Kekuanaoa and Kilauea Avenue, and **Puainako Town Center** on Kanoelehua opposite Prince Kuhio Plaza.

Sugawara Lauhala & Gift Shop is the place to visit if you are looking for authentic Hawaiian handicraft items. Look for genuine locally made Hawaiian *lauhala* woven slippers, hats, baskets, handbags, mats and related goods. 59 Kalakaua Street; 808-935-8071. **Sig Zane Designs** carries a variety of beautiful, locally designed and Hawaiian-motif alohawear for men and women. And do check out the craft village at **Hilo Farmers' Market** on Saturdays. 122 Kamehameha Avenue; 808-935-7077.

★ **Hilo Hattie's** is the original alohawear factory. A wonderfully tourist-geared all-in-one-store, Hilo Hattie's features Hawaiian shirts, shorts, dresses and muumuus plus other gift items like jewelry, macadamia nuts, chocolates, souvenirs, books and videos, toys and more. Free samples of Kona coffee, tropical juice, a shell lei and people who go out of their way to make you feel welcome. This is really a must-stop. Open daily 8:30 a.m. to 6 p.m. 111 East Puainako in the Prince Kuhio Plaza; 808-961-3077; www.hilohattie.com.

Other than these, take time to explore Hilo's shops, antique stores, boutiques and galleries and discover its many surprises and treasures. Don't miss **Basically Books** for maps, globes and books on everything you ever wanted to know about Hawai'i, from the stars above the mountains to the secrets under the sea. (See "Browsing for Books" in this chapter for more information.) 160 Kamehameha Avenue; www.basicallybooks.com. Check out the beautiful little stores in the restored S. **Hata Building**, with its handsome bell tower out front, and drop by **Two Ladies Kitchen** for a fresh strawberry mochi. 274 Kilauea Avenue; 800-903-6277.

Puna District

The Puna District comprises the area immediately south and southeast of Hilo town. It is a wide open area of lava lands, rugged coasts, and rainforest slopes leading up to Hawai'i Volcanoes National Park, which straddles the Puna–Ka'u border. Within Puna are the country towns of

Kea'au, Kurtistown, Mountain View, Pahoa, Volcano and a few other residential subdivisions. The district is noted for orchid, anthurium, papaya, banana, macadamia nut, and other tropical farm products. The combination of adequate rainfall and warm sunny conditions make it ideal for cultivating tropical fruits and flowers. Puna has experienced a lot of growth in recent years. A new highway bypass, agricultural development, construction of a Kamehameha Schools satellite and other additions have made what was once a sleepy community for those seeking an alternative lifestyle into a busier, more prosperous community. If you haven't visited for a while, you're going to be surprised.

About one-third of Hawai'i Volcanoes National Park is located within the Puna District (and two-thirds in the Ka'u District). Since 1983, Puna, in the "east rift zone," has been the site of ongoing volcanic eruptions and spectacular lava flows from Kilauea Volcano's vents, Pu'u O'o and Kupaianaha. The first three years of the eruption

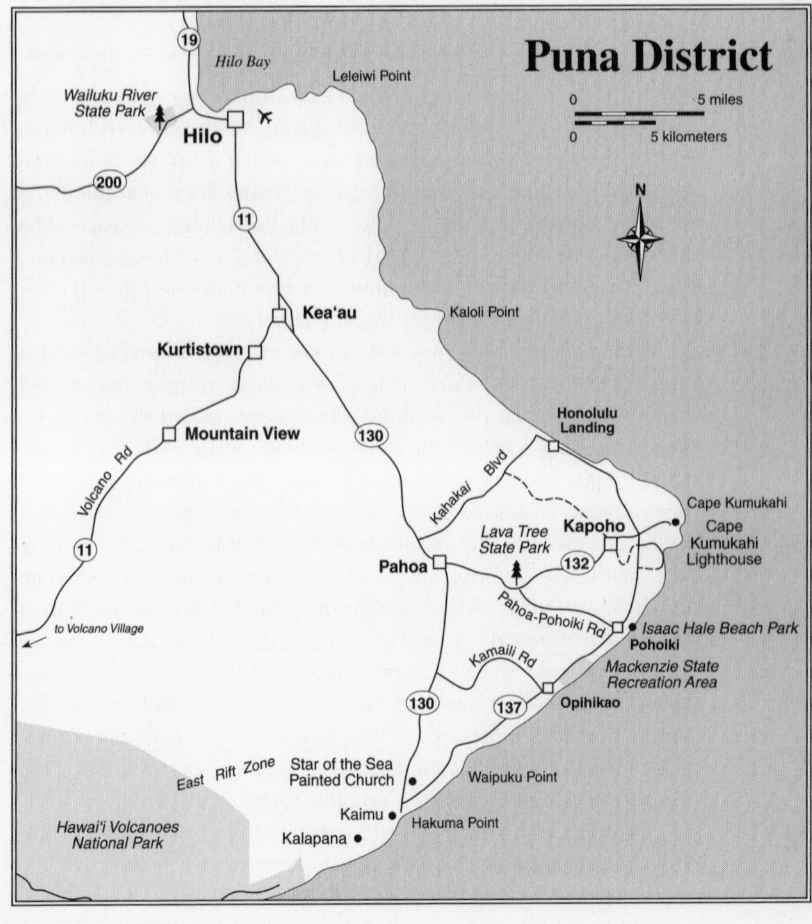

FLOWER FARMS

For tropical flower aficionados, there are numerous orchid and anthurium farms and nurseries throughout the Puna District, most of which welcome visitors. On the main Highway 11, at the 22.5-mile marker in the Glenwood area, is **Akatsuka Orchid Gardens** (808-967-8234), one of the largest orchid farms in Hawai'i with many varieties of orchids on display and for sale. **Yamamoto Dendrobiums Hawai'i** (808-968-6955) and **Bergstrom Orchids** (808-982-6047) are but a few of the orchid and anthurium farms in the Kea'au–Mountain View area that welcome visitors. In Pahoa, try **Hawaiian Greenhouse Inc.** (808-965-8351), **Puna Flowers & Foliage** (808-965-8444), or **Puna Ohana Flowers** (808-965-8456), and in Kurtistown stop at **Hata Farm** (808-966-9240) for all types of tropical flowers and plants. In addition, as you drive along be on the lookout for farm and nursery signs welcoming visitors to stroll the gardens.

were episodic outbreaks of dramatic lava fountaining and bursts from Pu'u O'o vent, which gradually formed a cinder cone several hundred feet high. The eruptive activity of more recent years has come from the large lava pond and vent called Kupaianaha, located at the 2,200-foot elevation level. Both of these vents are in remote, inaccessible areas. Viewing of eruption activity is best done by plane or helicopter. (See "Air Tours" for information; there's also more information about Volcanoes National Park later in the chapter.)

This almost continuous volcanic eruption is unprecedented in modern history. For more than 20 years the volcano has steadily erupted, sending lava flows rolling downslope toward the sea, in the process causing considerable damage to man-made structures as well as thousands of acres of Hawaiian forests. The entire village and residential areas of Kalapana on the island's southeast coast have been totally destroyed by the various lava flows, forcing residents to evacuate their homes and relocate elsewhere. Altogether, almost 200 homes and 25 square miles of land have been covered by lava up to 50 to 70 feet deep. However the destructive force of the volcano is also creative, adding hundreds of acres of new land to the Big Island coastline since 1983. As the molten lava enters the sea it explodes and shatters into fine pumice and cinders, which are carried by the surf along the coast. This volcanic residue accumulates in such great quantities that it creates new black-sand beaches along this rocky shore.

Highway 130, which passed through the Kalapana area and continued around the island, ends here. It is no longer possible to drive through Kalapana and on out the coast to the south entrance of Hawai'i Volcanoes National Park. The black-sand beaches, for which the area was famous, have been covered with lava and no longer exist. Visitors can travel Highway 130, the Chain of Craters Road, from inside Volcanoes National Park, but it dead-ends now just west of the Kalapana area.

In the past, the biggest attraction in Puna was the volcanic activity. However, National Park rangers now operate a mobile visitors center van at the end of the road here. The rangers provide maps and information on hiking trails to the current eruption site and lava flows. Check first to be sure conditions are safe for hiking the area, as the east rift zone changes constantly.

To reach the other side of the lava flows, you have to backtrack through Pahoa and go through the main entrance of Hawai'i Volcanoes National Park and follow Highway 130, the Chain of Craters Road to the Kamoamoa area (minimum 2-hour drive from Kalapana). If the eruption is still current, you will likely see a vast steam plume rising from the water, glowing cracks in the palisades, and perhaps red lava pouring over the *pali*. There may be monitored trails of varying lengths leading to viewing sites.

Caution: Conditions changes frequently. Check with the visitors center at the park entry first. Listen to and take their advice. There are no restrooms, water, phones or facilities of any kind along the coast and no shade. Volcanic fumes can present health dangers to children, pregnant women, or those with cardiac or respiratory difficulties. If you do any hiking, prepare for a long, hot walk in the sun with adequate water, a hat, sunscreen and good-quality covered shoes for the sharp jagged lava rock trails.

★ **Star of the Sea Painted Church** is one of the Kalapana area's more famous attractions. The historic church was rescued from lava flow destruction in 1990 and moved to a new location alongside Highway 130 just above the Kalapana area. This wooden frame structure dates from the early 1900s and was built by an early Belgian Catholic missionary priest who also did the intricate paintings of religious scenes on the walls and ceiling. It is now a community center.

Highway 132 (Kapoho Road) passes through papaya and orchid fields to the site of the former **Kapoho Village**, which was completely covered by a fiery lava flow in 1960. A historic plaque marks the site. At the end of Kapoho Road you can drive right up to the **Cape Kumukahi Lighthouse**, which, according to local lore, was spared by Madame Pele to protect Hawaiian fishermen at sea. The lava flowed around and past the lighthouse grounds but did not touch the lighthouse itself.

Text continued on page 118.

SHOPPING FOR ART AND HANDICRAFTS

You can bring a part of your Big Island vacation home to enjoy year-round, with a piece of fine art or expertly crafted work by local artisans. Friends and family will also appreciate hand-made gifts from authentic Hawai'i sources. Although souvenirs are available everywhere you go, for genuine made-in-Hawai'i arts and crafts, please be selective. Many souvenir and gift items in the shops are imported from the Philippines or elsewhere. If you have questions about a product's origin, ask the shop clerks, and be sure you're buying what you think you're buying. Following are some of the galleries and shops not mentioned elsewhere in this chapter.

Kona District

Blue Ginger Gallery Closed Sunday. Kainaliu; 808-322-3898.

Eclectic Craftsman Kona Marketplace, Ali'i Drive, Kailua-Kona; 808-334-0562.

Hale O Kula Goldsmith Gallery Closed Sunday-Monday. Holualoa; 808-324-1688.

Holualoa Gallery Closed Sunday-Monday. 76-5921 Mamalahoa Highway, Holualoa; 808-322-8484.

Hulihe'e Palace Gift Shop Hulihe'e Palace, 75-5718 Ali'i Drive, Kailua-Kona; 808-329-6558.

Kailua Village Artists Inc. Big Island artists' co-op featuring a broad range of artworks, handicrafts and gift items. 75-5660 Palani Road, King Kamehameha's Kona Beach Hotel, Kailua-Kona, 808-329-6653; also in the Keauhou Beach Hotel, 78-6740 Ali'i Drive, Keauhou-Kona, 808-324-7060; www.kailuavillageartists.com.

Neptune's Garden 75-5663 Palani Road, across from the pier, Kailua-Kona; 808-326-7490.

Rapozo Art Studio Retro-style gallery of art and nostalgic collectibles reminiscent of 1940s Hawai`i. Closed Sunday. Seaside Mall, 75-5663 Palani Road, Kailua-Kona; 808-326-1359; www.rapozo-studio.com.

Riftzone Gallery Coconut Grove Marketplace, 75-5801 Ali'i Drive, Kailua-Kona; 888-596-1100, 808-331-1100.

Showcase Gallery Keauhou Shopping Center, Keauhou-Kona; 808-322-9711.

Thomas Kinkade Gallery/Showcase by the Sea Kona Inn Shopping Village, 75-5744 Ali'i Drive, Kailua-Kona; 888-773-9424.

White Garden Gallery Closed Sunday-Monday. Holualoa; 808-322-7733.

Wyland Galleries Famous paintings of whales, dolphins and other sealife that decorate offices and walls throughout Hawai'i. Waterfront Row, 75-5770 Ali'i Drive, Kailua-Kona, 808-334-0037; Hilton Waikoloa Village, Kohala Coast, 808-886-5258; Kings Shops, Kohala Coast, 808-885-8882; www.wyland.com.

Kohala

Genesis Galleries Kings' Shops, 69-250 Waikoloa Beach Drive, Kohala Coast; 808-886-7770.

Harbor Gallery Bright tropical landscapes, exquisite wood carvings and other works of island art. Kawaihae Shopping Center, just north of Kohala Coast resorts; 808-882-1510; www.pacificart.com.

Nanbu Gallery 54-3885A Akoni Pule Highway, North Kohala; 808-889-0997.

Rankin Fine Art Gallery Closed Monday. 53-4380 Akoni Pule Highway, North Kohala; 808-889-6849.

Sugar Moon Clay Works and Kalia Tile Design Tiles, pottery, custom mirrors and other beautiful things from two longtime Kohala artisans. 55-3435 Akoni Pule Highway, Hawi, North Kohala; 808-889-0994.

Waimea

Dan DeLuz Woods Inc. Elegant, hand-carved bowls, boxes, frames, figures and other beautiful things by master woodworker Dan DeLuz. Artist's workshop in back. 64-1013 Mamalahoa Highway, Waimea town, 808-885-5856; another location at the 12-mile marker near Mountain View village on Highway 11, Puna District; 808-968-6607.

Hamakua Coast

Kama'aina Woods Closed Sunday. Lehua Street, Honoka'a, down the hill from the post office; 808-775-7722.

Panua Collections Main Street, Honomu; 808-963-5421.

Waipi'o Valley Artworks Kukuihaele; 808-775-0958.

Woodshop Gallery & Cafe Main Street, Honomu; 808-963-6363.

Hilo

Avi Kiriaty's Art Closed Saturday-Sunday. 106 Kamehameha Avenue, Hilo; 808-933-6659.

Big Island Woodworks Closed Sunday. S. Hata Building, 206 Kamehameha Avenue, Hilo, 808-982-8101.

Creative Arts Hawai'i 500 Kalanianaole, Hilo; 808-935-7393

Cunningham Gallery Closed Sunday. 794 Pi'ilani Street, Hilo; 808-935-7223

Dreams of Paradise S. Hata Building, 308 Kamehameha Avenue, Hilo; 808-935-5670.

Hana Hou 164 Kamehameha Avenue, Hilo; 808-935-4555.

Mauna Kea Gallerie Closed Thursday and Sunday. 276 Keawe Street, Hilo; 808-969-1184.

Ohana Gallery O Hawaii 46 Wainuenue Avenue, Hilo; 808-935-8494.

Also on Kapoho Road is ★ **Lava Tree State Park**, where hollow lava impressions of tree stumps are visible. The lava flowed around the living trees and baked them, leaving a hollow lava shell. Tall, ancient trees in the *kipuka* (area untouched by lava) seem to talk to each other as the wind rustles their high canopy. A multitude of birds make their home in the forest, including several protected Hawaiian species.

The end of Kapoho Road near the Cape Kumukahi Lighthouse intersects with Highway 137, known as the Opihikao Road. Highway 137 follows the coast south toward Kalapana. While driving on this road, be aware that it is very narrow and winding in places. There are large orchards of papaya and macadamia nut trees in the area as well as some magnificent views of rugged coastline.

The 32-mile drive from Hilo to Volcano Village near Hawai'i Volcanoes National Park is all uphill. The drive on Highway 11 goes from sea level in Hilo to 4,000 feet at Volcano. Along the way, the route passes through the abandoned cane fields of the former Puna Sugar Company and its old mill near **Kea'au.** Further on upslope, the cane fields give way to groves of eucalyptus trees and vegetation of the tropical rainforest. Fields of wild ginger, orchids and other exotic plants fill the roadsides and meadows of the scattered country homesites and small ranches of the area. Finally, stands of rugged and hearty *ohia* trees with their deep red *lehua* blossoms become apparent nearer the Volcano area.

The small towns and villages of the Puna District don't offer much in the way of shopping opportunities. The towns of Kea'au and Pahoa, the largest of the district, have more shops and stores than the rest but most cater to the needs of residents rather than visitors. Each town and village has a mom-and-pop general store that can always provide sodas, snacks and local favorites. For something quite different, stop in Mountain View at **Mountain View Bakery** (808-968-6353) for some of their famous "stone cookies," perfectly made for coffee-dunking. In the Glenwood area at the 20-mile marker is **Hirano Store** (808-968-6522), where you can buy cold drinks, sandwiches, snacks, gas and general store supplies.

★ **Volcano Village** is along the old Volcano Highway, which is just a mile from the national park entrance. In the village there are several shops and eateries offering an interesting variety for visitors. A mile and a half past the National Park entrance, on the Ka'u side, turn onto Pi'i Mauna Drive to the Volcano Country Club Golf Course and drive to the ★ **Volcano Vineyards and Winery** (808-967-7772), a must-stop for samples of the delightful Symphony wine, honey wine and tropical fruit wines produced here.

Hawai'i Volcanoes National Park

★ **Hawai'i Volcanoes National Park** is the star of the show, as far as Big Island tourist attractions. Where else in the world can you safely get close to an active volcano? On any given day, thousands of visitors pass through the park gates to experience what must be one of the last great wonders of the natural world. In 1982, the United Nations Educational, Scientific and Cultural Organization (UNESCO) declared the Park a World Heritage Site for its natural, historical and cultural importance, having "universal value" for all people. If you've come this far, please don't leave without a visit to Madame Pele's home.

The park is full of otherworldly wonders. There's a "drive-in" steam vent to peer into, a drizzly lava tube cave to walk through, a museum to explore and make your own earthquake, trails to hike

Park regulations are simple and enforced for your safety and the protection of this fragile, valuable natural area. Backcountry permits are required for overnight stays. They are available at the visitors center at no charge. Climbing on or removing rocks from any archaeological feature is prohibited. No firearms are permitted. Wildfires are a serious threat to the park, so no fires are permitted except in designated pavilion areas. Parking is restricted to parking lots only. Bicycles are only allowed on paved roads and some designated park trails. Pets must be leashed at all times and are only permitted on primary roads and developed sites. Do not feed or disturb the wildlife or exceed the posted speed limit.

What about the rocks? Don't take them with you. Leave them in the park. We remember years ago listening to a local man reassure a curious tourist that the rock thing was an old wives' tale. The hapless *malihini* (stranger) pocketed the stone and walked away, and the local guy laughed like crazy. The park receives hundreds of lava rocks in the mail every year, returned by unfortunate visitors who took them home and experienced extremely hard luck. It may be a coincidence, superstition or something else we don't understand, but it doesn't matter to us. Be respectful; leave the rocks on the island. There are plenty of nice souvenirs in the shops.

past barren wasteland or ancient forests. Then, drive (check with rangers for current conditions) down the long road back to the sunny ocean coastline towards the current eruption site. A towering plume of steam marks the spot where red lava enters the sea. If you're prepared to hike, you can get closer.

For a wealth of fascinating advance information (and great science report material) visit their website. The site is excellent and well-organized, with multiple links to other informative pages. Printed brochures, which are also excellent, should be requested by sending a postcard with your name, address and area of interest to: P.O. Box 52, Hawai'i Volcanoes National Park, Volcano, HI 96718; 808-985-6000; www.nps.gov/havo.

Entry fees are $10 per car for a 7-day pass; $20 for a yearly pass; $5 for visitors on bicycle, moped, mule or their own two feet. The 12-month Golden Eagle Passport, Golden Access Passport and Golden Age Passport is valid here. The park is open 24 hours a day year-round.

The ★ **Kilauea Visitor Center** is located a mile west of Volcano Village just inside the main entrance. Here visitors will find a natural history museum, current eruption information, and a free 20-minute movie shown on the hour from 9 a.m. to 4 p.m. daily. Park rangers are on duty to answer your questions and give instructions on viewing the eruption site, which you should listen to. Guided walks are offered daily. Open 7:45 a.m. to 5 p.m. daily.

The ★ **Thomas A. Jaggar Museum** is 3 miles inside the park, perched on the very edge of Kilauea and Halema'uma'u craters. The museum displays lava samples, seismic equipment showing island-wide mini-earthquakes (including make-your-own) and Hawaiian volcano lore. Open daily 8:30 a.m. to 5 p.m. 808-985-6049.

The ★ **Volcano Art Center**, located adjacent to the visitors center, occupies the original Big Island tourist lodging, Volcano House, constructed in 1877 to replace a thatched-roof hut that had accommodated visitors for 31 years. The art center, established in 1977, provides historic information on the park as well as works produced by local potters, painters, wood-carvers and other creative artisans. Artwork can be purchased here. The art center also stages and conducts art shows, performances, and art, writing and photography workshops year-round. Some of the programs allow visitors and residents a chance to interact with artists who receive their inspiration from the volcano. Occasionally, a resource artist will lead a walk through some spectacular area of the park to describe and demonstrate the use of natural materials and/or atmosphere of the park environment in creating artwork. The walks focus on protecting and enhancing the fragile national park environment. Open 9 a.m. to 5 p.m. P.O. Box 104, Hawai'i Volcanoes National Park, HI 96718; 808-967-8222; www.volcanoartcenter.org.

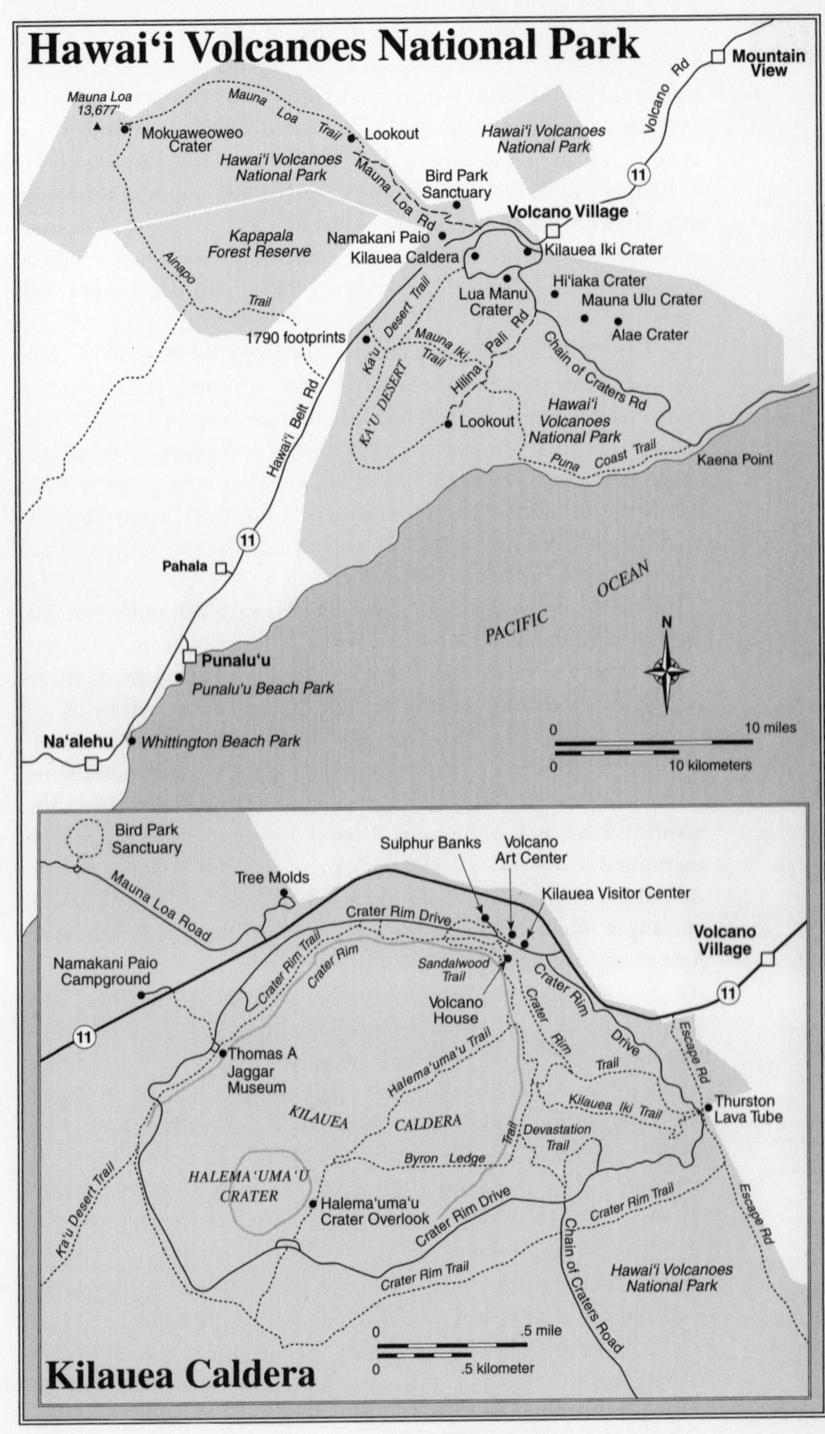

Hawai'i Volcanoes National Park
Mountain View
Volcano Rd
Mauna Loa 13,677'
Mauna Loa Trail
Mokuaweoweo Crater
Lookout
Hawai'i Volcanoes National Park
Hawai'i Volcanoes National Park
11
Mauna Loa Rd
Bird Park Sanctuary
Volcano Village
Kapapala Forest Reserve
Namakani Paio
Kilauea Caldera
Kilauea Iki Crater
Ainapo Trail
Desert Trail
Hi'iaka Crater
Lua Manu Crater
Mauna Ulu Crater
1790 footprints
Mauna Iki Trail
Pali Rd
Alae Crater
Ka'u
KA'U DESERT
Hilina
Chain of Craters Rd
Hawai'i Belt Rd
Lookout
Hawai'i Volcanoes National Park
Puna Coast Trail
Kaena Point
11
Pahala
PACIFIC OCEAN
N
Punalu'u
Punalu'u Beach Park
Na'alehu
Whittington Beach Park
0
10 miles
0
10 kilometers
Bird Park Sanctuary
Sulphur Banks
Volcano Art Center
Tree Molds
Mauna Loa Road
Kilauea Visitor Center
Crater Rim Drive
Volcano Village
Namakani Paio Campground
Crater Rim Trail
Crater Rim
Sandalwood Trail
Crater Rim Drive
11
Volcano House
Crater Rim Trail
11
Escape Rd
Thomas A Jaggar Museum
Halema'uma'u Trail
Kilauea Iki Trail
Thurston Lava Tube
KILAUEA
CALDERA
Devastation Trail
Byron Ledge
Trail
HALEMA'UMA'U CRATER
Halema'uma'u Crater Overlook
Crater Rim Drive
Crater Rim Trail
Ka'u Desert Trail
Chain of Craters Road
Escape Rd
Crater Rim Trail
Hawai'i Volcanoes National Park
0
.5 mile
0
.5 kilometer
Kilauea Caldera

The gigantic and still-steaming fire pit **Halema'uma'u**, a 3,000-foot diameter, 1,300-foot-deep lava vent, lies on the floor of **Kilauea Caldera**. **Kilauea Iki** is a huge cinder cone vent that last erupted in 1959. Both of these vents are easily viewed from **Crater Rim Drive** and can be reached on foot by easy hiking trails. There are vast fields of lava, once-molten rivers of liquid rock spewed out from the earth's center. Two types of lava emerge from Hawai'i's volcanoes: *pahoehoe*, with its black and relatively smooth surface, and *'a'a*, which solidifies in a jumble of small clinker-like rocks with sharp edges and rough surfaces.

Kilauea is the legendary home of the Hawaiian fire goddess Pele 'ai-honua (Pele who eats the land), who is both creator and destroyer. Native Hawaiians have long had a healthy respect for her, and even today ceremonial offerings are cast into Halema'uma'u while chants, songs and dances are performed in her honor. It is said that Pele has a fondness for gin. During the final days of Kalapana, before lava covered what was left of the quiet, coastal community, gin bottles, lei and other gifts lined the edge of the flow.

One of the outstanding features of Hawai'i Volcanoes National Park is its fine system of hiking trails. The trails begin at various points along the Crater Rim Drive and Chain of Craters Road. Hikers can choose from trails that offer outstanding close-up views of volcanic craters, steaming lava vents and colorful sulfur banks, to sweeping vistas of Kilauea's lava flows and sloping flanks, to a cool pastoral trail leading through a rare bird sanctuary. For your own safety, use common-sense precautions and listen to ranger advisements. Stay on the trails.

Along other trails of the park, hikers may see some rare and endangered flora and fauna. Among these are the sacred *ohelo* berry, held in high regard as an offering of appeasement to Madame Pele, or the *pukiawe*, used in making leis, and the rare sandalwood tree. Birds likely to be seen are the Hawaiian honeycreeper and the wren-like *'elepaio* that inhabit the **Bird Park Sanctuary**. Visible along some trails are petroglyphs, ancient Hawaiian rock carvings.

Devastation Trail, a raised boardwalk path located behind the cinder cone of Kilauea Iki, winds through the vast fields of lava cinders and pumice that buried and burned off most of the living vegetation. All that is left is a myriad of picturesque tree stumps and stark cinder landscape. ★ **Thurston Lava Tube Trail** is located just off the Crater Rim Drive, two miles from the visitors center. Here one can walk through a giant lava tube much like a cave. The short trail leading to it passes through a pleasantly cool fern forest. Please see "Hiking" in Chapter 6 for more details on these and other trails.

★ **Volcano House** (808-967-7321) is the national park's premiere place to stay. The original historic structure now houses the Volcano Art Center near the main entrance. The first Volcano House, now in existence across three different centuries, was built in 1846 as an overnight waystation for visitors who rode on horseback all the way from Hilo to see the splendors of the volcano. It's had a number of distinguished guests down through the years including Mark Twain, Franklin D. Roosevelt and many other celebrities. (See Chapter 3 for more lodging information.)

Ka'u District

The southern Ka'u District comprises one of the largest geographic districts on the Big Island and, at the same time, one of the more remote and least populated. It contains about one-fifth of the island's land, which represents some 800-plus square miles. The district includes most of the massive Mauna Loa (13,680 foot) and the western two-thirds of Hawai'i Volcanoes National Park. Ka Lae, South Point, on this coast of the Big Island is the southernmost point in the United States. The district is mostly dry lava desert, windblown grasslands and rugged rocky coastline. Inland, there are cattle pastures and macadamia nut orchards. Ka'u is serviced by the main around-the-island road, Highway 11, which connects it to Volcano and Hilo to the east and Kona to the west. Sparsely populated, Ka'u has only three small towns: Pahala, Na'alehu and Waiohinu.

★ **Hawai'i Volcanoes National Park** is the Ka'u District's biggest attraction. The bulk of the park lies within the district's boundaries (with a small portion in the Puna District to the east). For visitors, the national park headquarters, visitors center, volcano observatory, campgrounds, Volcano House inn, and related sites are centrally located around Kilauea Caldera in the Ka'u District near Volcano Village.

Visitors from Hilo will drive to the park via Highway 11, a distance of 35 miles, through the Puna District described in the previous section. Visitors from the Kailua-Kona area travel 96 miles via Highway 11 around the South Point area. This is a rather long drive through some pretty desolate stretches of open lava lands, dry scrub land, and the Ka'u Desert. The road has some short stretches in the South Kona area where it is winding and narrow, but otherwise the road is excellent. If you have a rental car you should plan at least a day trip to Volcano. An overnight visit is even better, which will allow you to explore the area in more depth.

Allow a minimum of two and a half hours for the drive from Kailua-Kona to the national park. It's best to get an early start. The drive up to the park passes through South Kona's coffee farms, fruit orchards and flower farm country, gradually turning away from the coast and heading further inland as it turns around Mauna Loa's southernmost slopes. The land here, some 8 to 10 miles inland from the coast and at 2,000-foot elevation, is damp and cool, a contrast to the drier resort areas of Kona and the lands traversed along the way. The terrain is marked by lush vegetation and stands of tropical forest. Ranch grazing lands appear intermittently along with macadamia nut orchards in an otherwise sparsely populated area.

Manuka State Wayside is along this route. This is a lovely and well-maintained arboretum with a variety of dry upland forest plants and trees. Picnic tables and restrooms are provided and there is a nature trail as well.

Ka Lae, South Point, is reached via South Point Road, which branches off from Highway 11 at the extreme southern tip of the Ka'u District. The narrow road continues 12 miles to the South Point Peninsula, where it terminates. It passes by the **Kamao'a Wind Farm**, a wind-powered electricity-generation facility utilizing huge wind turbines. This stark, windswept, hot, dry and grassy area is the southernmost point geographically in the United States. The first Hawaiians are believed to have landed here and settled the area around 400 A.D. There are old canoe mooring holes and the ruins of a fishermen's *heiau*. Fishermen still use South Point to moor their boats but they must hoist them up and down the high cliffs to the relatively calm waters below. The foundations of an old World War II military camp are also found in the area.

Green Sand Beach, composed of green olivine crystals giving it an "Emerald City" hue, is located five miles east of South Point. Mahana Bay, site of the beach, is accessible only by hiking. The coastal road and trail is extremely rough and rugged over rocky terrain. From the end of the road where a boat launch ramp and a parking area are located, it's a two-mile hike to the beach, located at the bottom of a steep cliff. The trail down can be hazardous, and there are no facilities of any kind at the beach. The bay is not safe for swimming due to rough surf and strong currents. It is a beautiful and unique sight, but not an easy one to reach (and harder to leave). Hiking permits to Green Sand Beach are required because you must cross private lands under control of the Department of Hawaiian Home Lands. There is no charge for the permit, which can be faxed to your hotel or condominium. Varying procedures may cause padlocks to appear on the gates, but these are usually circumventable. Vehicles are presently restricted from using the coast road. For permit information, contact: Department of Hawaiian Home Lands, 160 Baker Avenue, Hilo, HI 96720; 808-974-4250.

Na'alehu proudly proclaims itself to be "the southernmost town in the USA" and has a large sign stating the fact alongside the town shopping center. At the shopping center, located right on the highway mid-town, there is a coffee shop, grocery store, and snack shop for refreshments.

Punalu'u Sweetbread Visitor Center is across the road from the shopping center. This is a bakery and snack shop that produces thousands of loaves weekly of its popular Portuguese sweetbread plus other baked goodies.

The **Mark Twain Monkeypod Tree** is in the neighboring town of **Waiohinu**. It was planted by the famous author during his 1866 visit to this area. The original tree toppled in a storm several years ago but the roots have sprouted new saplings and the tree lives, sort of like Twain's yarns. Passing through these very small Hawaiian country towns will give you a sense of having stepped back into an earlier time, where the fast-paced modern world hasn't quite made inroads yet. It's all a very pleasant and refreshing experience to know that places like these tiny quiet villages still exist.

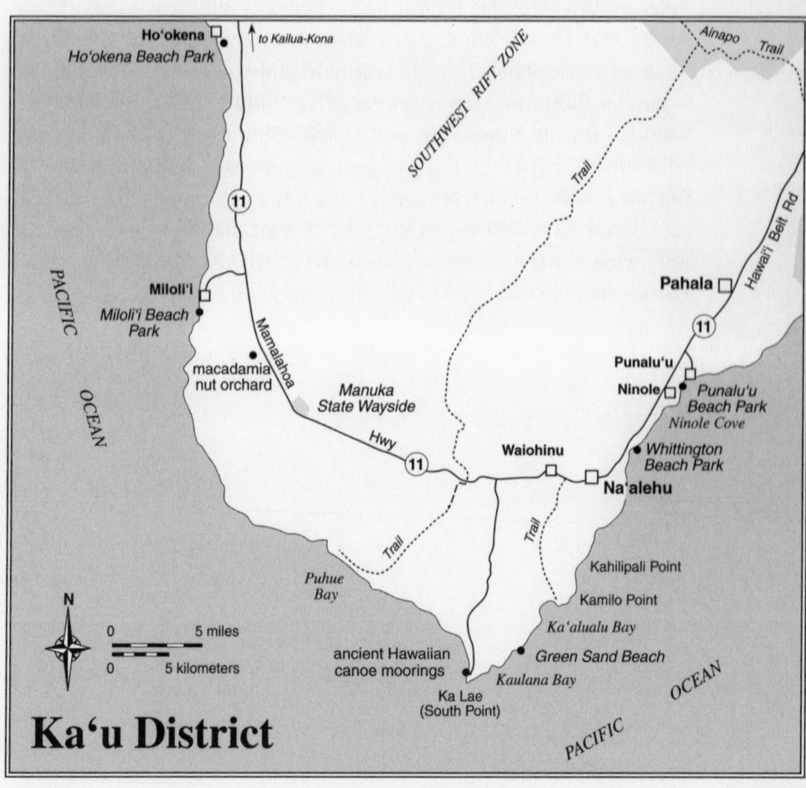

Punalu'u is about eight miles further on toward the national park. This is the location of **Punalu'u Beach Park** and Seamountain Golf Course. At Punalu'u Beach Park, spend a few minutes to watch the shoreline along the black-sand beach for sea turtles, which are often seen feeding on seaweed on the rocks and coral.

Pahala is five miles further on from here. The Ka'u Sugar Mill just off the main center of town was the last operating mill on the Big Island until it too closed in 1996. The plantation's closing was a hardship for the residents of this quiet, remote region. Where vast green fields of sugar cane once formed a beautiful background along Highway 11, macadamia nuts and other crops are planted, along with high hopes for a brighter future as a more diversified agriculture center. From Pahala it is 25 miles on to the national park through generally dry desert and lava rock country.

Near the national park entrance and leading off from Highway 11 on Pi'i Mauna Drive is the Volcano Country Club Golf Course. One mile past the golf clubhouse a mile to the end of the road is the southernmost winery in the U.S., ★ **Volcano Winery**. The winery produces delightful tropical fruit wines such as Guava Chablis, Volcano Blush, Volcano Red and the refreshing, deliciously different mead: Macadamia Nut Honey Wine. Their main attractions are the Symphony Mele and Symphony Dry, from a new grape developed by the University of California–Davis School of Viticulture. All of the wines are sound, with their own intriguing personalities, and make appreciated, unique *omiyage* (gifts) for your friends back home. The winery operates a tasting room and gift shop on site and is open daily, 10 a.m. to 5:30 p.m. It's well worth the time to visit the Big Island's best and only winery. P.O. Box 843, Volcano, HI 96785; 808-967-7479; e-mail: volcanowin@aol.com; www.volcanowinery.com.

CHAPTER 3

Where to Stay

The Big Island has a wide range of choices and prices in every category, anything from a bare-bones camper cabin in the mountains to a $7,000-a-night private suite with butler. The most expensive, high-end resorts are concentrated along the Kohala Coast on the sunny west coast, and average room rates decrease the farther you travel from this area. The rapidly growing town of Kailua-Kona has numerous vacation rentals and hotel properties. Further south, the Ka'u District offers accommodations at B&Bs; Volcano, where the Hawai'i tourist industry began, has only a handful of B&Bs, from rustic to romantically luxurious. Hilo, a wonderful place to visit with the unfortunate nickname of the rainiest city in the U.S., offers lodging in standard hotels and a variety of B&Bs, condos and private homes. There is also an interesting selection of B&Bs along the Hamakua Coast to Waipi'o Valley, upcountry in the North Kohala District and in the *paniolo* (cowboy) town of Waimea. This chapter contains separate listings for hotels, bed and breakfasts and resorts, along with condominiums that have units in rental programs and a smattering of hostels and vacation homes.

THINGS TO KNOW ABOUT USING THIS CHAPTER

Lodgings are organized geographically by district, beginning with the Kona District, followed by the Kohala Coast and continuing around the island to Waimea (Kamuela), the Hamakua Coast, Hilo, the Puna District and the Ka'u District (these last two sections both include the Volcano area).

Rates quoted for the hotels are the most current standard industry rack rates available at the time of publication and are, of course, subject to change without notice. However, hotel rack rates have become more of a goal than a reality, since most reservations are booked at various discounted rates in order to compete for your business. (The same may not be true of bed and breakfasts or other smaller, privately owned lodgings.) Accommodation rates listed in this section are for double occupancy (2 people) unless otherwise specified. There is generally an extra charge for additional adults, but usually not for children staying in their parents' room and extra bedding is not required. All lodging in Hawai'i will add on an 11.167 percent tax on all accommodation charges. This includes a 4.167 percent sales tax and 7 percent hotel room tax. Gratuities for room maids, restaurant servers, bell and valet parking staff, recreation staff and other personnel are additional at your discretion. Because of the extreme diversity of accommodations, ratings have not been given to individual properties. However, we have used a ★ to indicate a B&B, hotel, condo or other lodging with a consistent quality in its "niche." Starred properties will offer something special in price value, location, facilities or services, based on personal experience, reputation, longevity, previous editions of this guide and other travel sources. If you see the girl in a bathing suit, you've found an establishment that offers a childcare program. Please see "Traveling with Children: Childcare Programs" in Chapter 1 for more details.

Depending on how and when and where vacationers make reservations, rates can vary as much as 50 percent off the published or rack rates. The most expensive Kohala Coast resorts are traditionally booked solid from Christmas through New Year's Day, with no discounted rates available. Between Thanksgiving and Easter is generally considered "in-season," when rates are higher. The months of May and September and the first two weeks of December are usually the lowest-occupancy times of any year. Rates are much more flexible during these times, with bargains to be had for those who persevere. On the other hand, Kona hotels and condominiums will have availability at Christmas, but will be booked in October during the Ironman Triathlon. For money-saving tips, see "How to Save Money" below. However, the most important thing about your Big Island vacation is *you* and your vacation time. Determine what you and your family's priorities are and go for it. For example, if you want to sightsee, shop and sign up for activities you can stay at a Kona condominium for a week for the about same price as one or two nights in a Kohala Coast resort. If you want to spend your days lying in the sun, pay a higher room rate, forego the rental car and enjoy the island's best beaches. It's up to you!

BED AND BREAKFAST LODGING

B&Bs have proven to be the accommodation of choice for an increasing number of visitors as an alternative to the usual resort condominiums and hotels. They are often less costly and provide a range of interesting accommodations from clean simple rooms to luxurious, well-appointed, fully equipped suites, cottages and vacation homes. On the Big Island, B&Bs offer the chance to experience an overnight in a renovated 1930s sugar plantation estate, a historic missionary home, a log cabin, a ranch house, a beachside cottage and even a treehouse. In most cases, B&Bs provide a more homey atmosphere and opportunity to get to know the *kama'aina* (residents) more personally. They usually include a continental-style breakfast that varies with each operation, from a pre-stocked kitchen to a sit-down hot gourmet breakfast every morning. A B&B vacation can be a very special way to experience the Big Island up close and personal, from a unique, less commercial perspective. Visitors considering staying at B&B operations should keep in mind that there can be great variance between individual operations, regardless of the rates charged. There can be differences in accommodation level, room decor, furnishings, bathrooms, leisure facilities, breakfast provided, and overall quality. Visitors should expect differences between operations charging $50 nightly with those charging $100 and more.

B&B QUALITY AND SERVICE The B&B industry has grown significantly enough that the County of Hawai'i and industry representatives have cooperated in establishing standards and guidelines for the operation of B&Bs via the **Hawai'i Island Bed & Breakfast Association**. HIBBA as an industry organization attempts to ensure that members adhere to quality B&B operating standards of cleanliness, service and maintenance of their operation and value for lodging dollars. Member B&B operators are identified in listings by: **Member-HIBBA**.

Hawai'i's Best B&B is a booking service that handles exclusive upscale B&B operations around the Big Island. Member B&Bs are guaranteed to provide a high-quality B&B experience with overall excellent facilities, amenities and service. Member B&B operators are identified in listings by: **Member-Hawai'i's Best**.

The rest of the B&B operations listed are independently owned and operated and not subject to booking service or association standards and are included here for the information and convenience of visitors. In addition to individual B&B listings, you'll find a list of B&B reservation agencies at the end of the chapter.

WHERE TO STAY?

Kailua-Kona (just "Kona" locally) is a bustling, active tourist center, perfect for people who like to go places and do things; it's home to most of the island's more energetic, commercial activities. And, since most of Kona's visitors are on the go, it's the perfect setting for condominium vacation rentals; there are only a handful of actual hotels between Kailua-Kona town and five miles down Ali'i Drive in Keauhou. Although most of Kailua-Kona's accommodations are set along the coastline close to the ocean, few have actual sandy beaches onsite. However, a number of smaller public beaches are close by, and the views from the rugged, rocky shoreline are spectacular from almost anywhere in town.

The Kohala Coast in the South Kohala District is a 30-mile stretch of black lava and dry, *kiawe*-studded hills, from Kawaihae Harbor to Kaupulehu, just north of Kona International Airport. It is dominated by four major resort properties containing luxury hotels, condos and vacation residences, golf, tennis, restaurants and a wide variety of shops and recreation activities. This is the "high-class neighborhood" on the island, and the resorts are excellent and expensive. Condominium properties, too, are excellent here, with access to the fine facilities of the resorts. Just like in Kona, the condo buildings consist of individually owned vacation rental units, which are handled by various agents on behalf of their owners. For reservations at a particular property, contact one of the agents listed under the property name; they can describe their units at various properties in the Kohala Coast and other island areas. South Kohala's accommodations are easy to distinguish. Basically, the closer you are to the ocean, the sunnier the weather, the better the accommodations and the higher the price. Accommodations are limited in the North Kohala District, but there's a selection of unique properties in this quiet, rural area. The closest other accommodations would be in Waimea about 20 miles south or further south at the Kohala Coast resorts.

Moving away from the ocean decreases the price and increases the range of lodgings. Waimea (also Kamuela) has comfortable accommodations at reasonable rates, as well as a growing network of good quality B&B operations offering unique settings and a more personal look at the island. Waikoloa Village has a variety of vacation condo rentals only a few minutes' drive from the Kohala Coast resorts.

There is a variety of good bed-and-breakfast operations in unique locations, from restored plantation houses to lofts in the trees. Particularly for hikers, campers and off-road wanderers, the Hamakua Coast can deliver some wonderfully quiet, naturally beautiful and peaceful vacation experiences and memories.

Most of Hilo's hotels are located along Banyan Drive on the Waiakea Peninsula, which extends out into Hilo Bay. There are no sandy beaches as the lava-rock coastline is too rough and rugged, although the views are lovely. The Banyan Drive hotels offer the best views of Hilo town, Hilo Bay and, if the weather permits, the peaks of Mauna Kea and Mauna Loa. They also offer the best values in accommodations for visitors considering their amenities, facilities and location. Several good B&Bs reside in the Hilo area, as well as condominium properties and private homes for vacation rentals.

HOW TO SAVE MONEY

The Big Island's tourist business fluctuates seasonally. The peak season, with its consequent highest prices, is generally from mid-December to after Easter. Slower, shoulder periods, where promotional rates and specials are offered, are usually from after Easter to Thanksgiving. The real bargain time to visit tends to be from Labor Day through the month of September and then the first two weeks in December each year. Hilo hotels are not as prone to price fluctuations (except during Merrie Monarch week or other local events). Kohala Coast resorts are booked out over the Christmas–New Year holidays, when Kailua-Kona usually has space. And Kona hotels are jammed in October for the Ironman, when other areas are offering discounts. Travel agents are experts in finding the best accommodations at the best rate for you and your family. It pays to do a little homework in advance. If you're doing your own booking, be sure to check the internet, or take the time question the reservations staff once your priorities are in order. Internet-only rates, special packages, return-guest specials, senior citizen discounts and many other options exist to help you make the most of your vacation dollars (and airline mileage points).

The rule is simple: to find the better (and more expensive) accommodations, follow the sun, as the sunniest areas also have the best beaches and the best hotels. The price goes down as the weather gets cloudier. In a nutshell, this is how it works: Kohala Coast = luxury resorts, Kailua-Kona = mid-range hotels and lots of condos, South Kona = B&Bs and 1 condo resort, Ka'u and Puna = B&Bs and a cluster of different accommodations at Volcano Village, Hilo and Hamakua = mid- to lower-end hotels and B&Bs.

B&Bs have some of the most interesting locations, from tree houses to log cabins, coffee farms to rainforest retreats. The prices range generally from about $75-$150 a night. A condo vacation can be a real budget-stretcher, offering the most space for your dollar, from simple studio apartments to luxurious hotel-like suites in resort locations, about $100-$200 average (but the price can go much higher depending on location). Keep in mind that a little distance from the ocean is not necessarily a bad thing. The Big Island is a great place to drive—and in fact you're never more than 26 miles from the ocean. Kailua-Kona's hotels are nicely tourist-geared, set close to the ocean and within walking distance of a lot of fun, from about $150-$250. Hilo's hotels are a good value, about $100-$150, and Kohala Coast resorts are pricey, but have all the deluxe amenities, from about $300 to thousands.

A condominium vacation can be perfect for families that need room to spread out and prefer to make most of their own meals and snacks. There can be more freedom and less fuss in a condo and most are far less expensive than hotel accommodations.

GENERAL POLICIES Condominiums usually require a reservation deposit equal to one or two nights' rental to secure a confirmed reservation and some also require a security deposit. Some charge higher deposits during winter or peak season holidays like Christmas–New Year's. Generally a 30-day notice of cancellation is needed to receive a full refund, although a cancellation fee may apply at any time. Most condos and agents require payment in full either 30 days prior to or upon arrival. Most condos also require a minimum stay of three to five nights or longer in the winter and during peak holiday seasons. The peak winter season brings heavy demand for condo units, and the restrictions, cancellation policies, and payment policies are much more stringent. It is not uncommon to book as much as two years in advance for the Christmas–New Year's season. Most resident managers do not handle reservations and thus you should contact the rental agents listed for those properties.

Condos may be reserved on-line or by phone from various reputable management companies. These companies handle different units at properties for different owners. One property may deal with five or six management companies for their vacation rentals. It's a bit of a maze, but not impossible to manage. Our best suggestion is this: if you'd like to reserve a condominium (particularly in Kona, but elsewhere on the island as well) contact one of the agencies listed at the end of the chapter by phone or internet. Advise them of your priorities regarding size, location, amenities and price range. They can then recommend a selection of condos available for the dates you request. If you are looking for a particular property, let them know up front.

To further complicate the process, prices vary widely according to the season. The highest rates will be charged during the peak season between Thanksgiving and New Year's; mid-level rates are in effect during spring and fall shoulder seasons and lower rates will likely be available in the summer. In addition, various rental companies offer room and car packages and other special deals, and last-minute internet rates to boost business. Rates will also vary according to view, size, property location, facilities and the number of people in your party. Weekly and monthly rates are also available at some properties. A description and location is provided, with the recommendation to again, contact the rental agencies, let them know your needs and let them find the perfect place for you and your family. To give you an idea of the rate range, expect 1-bedroom units to average $75-$150 per night; 2-bedrooms $100-$250. As we've said, the high-end properties and vacation homes will be much higher.

Lodging Best Bets

Kona Families on a budget would do well to consider a Kona condominium vacation; condos are less expensive and usually larger than hotel rooms, with at least some cooking facilities to better accommodate family needs. For a hotel stay, King Kamehameha's Kona Beach Hotel presents a little bit of history, an accessible beach, downtown location and reasonable rates. Just outside town, Ohana Keauhou Beach Resort is a lovely, lushly landscaped property.

Kohala Coast **Kona Village** is the ultimate tropical retreat for honeymooners and others for whom privacy is paramount. **Four Seasons** is, well, Four Seasons, ultra-plush and pricey, prized for perfect service. The **Hilton Waikoloa Village** is outstanding for active families, with everything you can dream of and more. The **Waikoloa Beach Marriott** is a longstanding favorite of visitors and *kama'aina*. **Mauna Lani Bay Hotel** is known for its beach, fine dining, quality golf, beautiful rooms and a fine spa. The **Fairmont Orchid** is an elegant, elite resort at the top of its game. The **Mauna Kea Beach Hotel** is the traditional landmark, built by Laurance S. Rockefeller in 1965, and still holding its own as the preferred choice of beach and golf lovers. **Hapuna Beach Prince Hotel** is good for golfers who have the choice of two great designer golf courses and two of Hawai'i's best beaches. Waikoloa hosts several fine condominium properties, including **Waikoloa Villas**.

Waimea **Cook's Discoveries Waimea Suite**, among many others.

Hamakua Coast **Paauhau Plantation** is something special, as is **Waianuhea**. To really experience a tropical retreat, there's **Waipi'o Wayside** and others in the remote, idyllic Waipi'o Valley.

Hilo **Hilo Hawaiian** is our favorite of the hotels along Banyan Drive in Hilo town. **The Shipman House** is something special, a Victorian home in a jungly setting with a lot of class. More adventurous travellers might enjoy **Arnott's Lodge**.

Volcano Kilauea Lodge is classic part of Big Island history, with excellent dining and a perfect location for visitors to Volcanoes National Park. For romantics, the **Chalet Kilauea Collection's Inn at Volcano** has theme-decorated suites to suit your fantasy.

Kona District

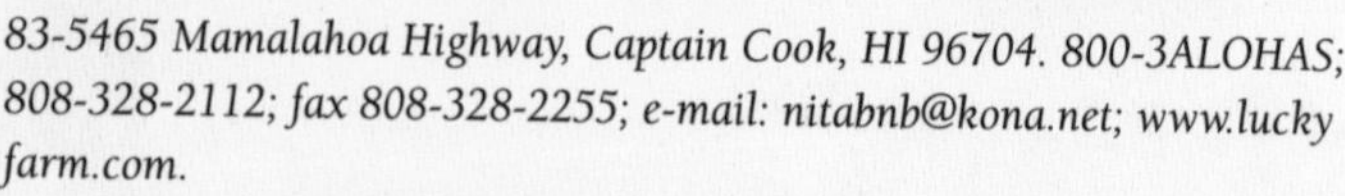

BED AND BREAKFASTS

Affordable Hawai'i at Pomaika'i (Lucky) Farm

83-5465 Mamalahoa Highway, Captain Cook, HI 96704. 800-3ALOHAS; 808-328-2112; fax 808-328-2255; e-mail: nitabnb@kona.net; www.luckyfarm.com.

This is a working four-acre coffee farm in Captain Cook overlooking Keei Bay from the 1,000-foot level, about 12 miles south of Kailua-Kona. There is one bedroom in this historic 1935 farmhouse with private bath. The Greenhouse has two large rooms with private baths and entrances and is surrounded by tropical plants. These rooms sleep 2-4. The Coffee Barn sleeps up to 5 people and also has a tropical garden setting with a queen bed, couch, half bath and an outdoor shower. Shared lanai with bay view, TV room, library and shared kitchen. Easy access to local beaches, dining, shopping, activities and attractions. French spoken here. Member-HIBBA.

Rates: $60-$75; $10 extra person

Aloha Farms B&B

93-5440 Painted Church Road, Captain Cook, HI 96704. 808-328-0604; fax 808-328-0704; e-mail: rdilts@alohafarms.com; www.alohafarms.com.

This is a farm located south of Kailua-Kona town and about two miles from Kealakekua Bay on five acres. It's a peaceful area with nice panoramic ocean and sunset views from a covered lanai. Guest rooms have queen beds and private baths. Traditional farm breakfast with the farm's own Kona coffee and tropical fruits. Snorkel, swim and scuba dive in nearby bays. Member-HIBBA.

Rates: $65-$100

Aloha Guest House

84-4780 Mamalahoa Highway, Captain Cook, HI 96704. 800-897-3188; 808-328-8955; e-mail: vacation@alohaguesthouse.com; www.alohaguesthouse.com.

This home is at the end of a private road, at the 1,500-foot elevation level, and set amid a citrus and macadamia nut plantation alongside a state forest preserve area. It's a very secluded, country atmosphere. The home provides sweeping ocean views of the Kona Coast. Free use of snorkel gear, mountain bikes and boogie boards is included. All rooms have private baths. Traditional island-style breakfast. German and French spoken here. Member-HIBBA.

Rates: from $80

Areca Palms Estate B&B

P.O. Box 489, Captain Cook, HI 96704. 800-545-4390; 808-323-2276; fax 808-323-3749; e-mail: merryman@ilhawaii.net; www.konabedand breakfast.com.

This is a comfortable cedar home located in the rural area of Kealakekua, Kona. The four spacious guest rooms are beautifully and comfortably furnished with private bath, cable TV, refrigerators and either ocean or garden view. Large open living room and front-back lanais provide lots of room. Large open yard has lots of tropical fruit trees, plants and greenery plus a garden spa. Member-HIBBA.

Rates: $85-$125; $25 extra person

★ Beautiful Edge of the World B&B

P.O. Box 888, Captain Cook, HI 96704. 800-660-8491; 808-328-7424; e-mail: weigelt@aloha.net; www.stayhawaii.com/edge.

This custom-built home features local *koa* woodwork throughout. Long, encircling lanais provide lots of room to watch Kona's famous sunsets and meet with new travel friends. Breakfast includes traditional savory or vegan specials along with the farm's own fresh Kona coffee and tropical fruits. Easy access to Kona area attractions. German, Spanish, Japanese and Korean spoken here. Member-HIBBA.

Rates: $60-$90

Cedar House B&B AND Coffee Farm

P.O. Box 823, Captain Cook, HI 96704. Phone/fax 808-328-8829; e-mail: cedarhouse@hawaii.rr.com; www.cedarhouse-hawaii.com.

This is a lovely cedar and redwood home located on 4.5 acres of beautifully landscaped tropical grounds. It's located in Captain Cook town above historic Kealakekua Bay and is 12 miles south of Kailua-Kona. Guest rooms have tasteful contemporary decor and garden or ocean view, private entrance, TV, queen/king beds and private or shared baths. Member-HIBBA.

Rates: $70-$110 per night, $660 per week

Dolores's 1st. Class B&B

77-6504 Kilohana Street, Kailua-Kona, HI 96740. 888-769-1110; 808-329-8778; fax 808-331-1974; e-mail: dolorsbb@kona.net; www.dolbandb.com.

This comfortable home is located on the slopes above Kailua-Kona overlooking Kailua Bay and the Kona Coast. It's 11 miles from Kona International Airport and 4 miles from Kailua-Kona, town yet near good snorkeling beaches. The separate and private guest cottage is set in a lush tropical garden with lanai views of Kailua Bay and the ocean. The studio and cottage both have private bath and entry, custom contemporary decor and furnishing and TV/VCR. Beach gear is provided along with visitor information from long-term resident-owner.

Rates: Studio (sleeps two) $125, Cottage (sleeps two) $135

Dragonfly Ranch: A Healing Arts Retreat

P.O. Box 675, Honaunau, HI 96726. 800-487-2159; 808-328-9570; e-mail: dfly@dragonflyranch.com; www.dragonflyranch.com.

This private country estate is only three minutes from Honaunau Bay on Highway 160, about 20 miles south of Keahole Airport, Kona. The ranch is situated just above Pu'uhonua o Honaunau and provides an alternative B&B experience. All guest rooms have private entrances, indoor bath and private outdoor shower. Choose from Honeymoon Suite, Writer's Studio, Lomilomi Suite, the Pele Room or Dolphin room. Features include fireplace, sauna, TV/VCR, kitchenette, sundeck and "spa pamperings." Luxuriously rustic, with beautiful views of the Kona Coast.

Rates: Honeymoon Suite $200; Writer's Studio $150; Lomilomi Suite $150; Pele Room $100; Dolphin room $100

Fragrant Tree Farm

P.O. Box 1051, Captain Cook, HI 96704. 800-330-6255; 808-328-9595; fax 808-328-8749; e-mail: info@fragranttree.com; www.fragranttree.com.

Located 13 miles south of Kailua-Kona, this is an attractive luxury home as well as separate guest cottages. The main house sleeps 2-6 guests in three bedrooms and has two baths plus two spacious dining rooms with ocean views. There are also spectacular coastal views, a large lanai and swimming pool, full kitchen, hot tub and tennis court. The three cottages each sleep 2-4 people and have full kitchens, separate entrances, private baths and lots of room. Cottages have garden or ocean views. In addition, there is a barbecue grill, washer/dryer and much more to make a vacation stay complete. Families welcome, crib and high chair available.

Rates: from $95

Hale Ho'ola B&B

85-4577 Mamalahoa Highway, Captain Cook, HI 96704. 877-628-9117; 808-328-9117; e-mail: tlc@hale-hoola.com; www.hale-hoola.com.

This is a nice two-story plantation-style home overlooking Honaunau Bay from the 800-foot elevation level. There are great ocean views and cool relaxing ocean breezes. Guest rooms have private entrances, baths and lanais. Welcoming hosts serve up island-style breakfast and lots of local lore and information. Member-HIBBA.

Rates: $75-$95

Hale Maluhia

76-770 Hualalai Road, Kailua-Kona, HI 96740. 800-559-6627; 808-329-5773; e-mail: ken@hawaii-inns.com; www.hawaii-inns.com.

Located just three miles upslope from Kailua-Kona village, this is a large rambling home on one acre with outdoor spa, lanai, rec room, VCR and library. The "House of Peace" is wheelchair friendly.

Rates: $90-$125, Cottage from $150; $25 extra person

Holualoa Inn B&B

P.O. Box 222, 76-5932 Mamalahoa Highway, Holualoa, HI 96725. 800-262-9912; 808-885-4550; fax 808-885-0559; e-mail: inn@aloha.net; www.holualoainn.com.

This attractive cedar home is on a 40-acre estate in the small quiet village of Holualoa on the cool slopes of Mt. Hualalai in Kona. The estate is a former cattle ranch and coffee farm. The house features a rooftop gazebo providing magnificent views of the surrounding countryside, the Kona Coast and incredible sunsets. This provides a very quiet, relaxing atmosphere. There are six spacious and well-appointed guest rooms available, all with private bath.

Rates: $75-$225; $30 extra person

Horizon Guest House

Hawai'i's Best B&Bs, P.O. Box 563, Kamuela, HI 96704. 800-262-9912; 808-885-4550; fax 808-885-0559; e-mail: reservations@bestbnb.com; www.bestbnb.com

This luxury retreat is located on 40 acres overlooking the Kona Coast, 40 minutes south of Kailua-Kona town and away from the hustle and bustle. Four guest rooms are well-kept and furnished with refrigerator, lanai and antique decor. Colorful Hawaiian quilts cover each bed. Great coast views from the spreading deck where guests enjoy pool, jacuzzi and barbecue. Member-Hawaii's Best.

Rates: $175-$250

Island Oasis

800-262-9912; 808-885-4550; fax 808-885-0559. Reservations through Hawai'i's Best B&Bs, P.O. Box 520, Kamuela, HI 96743. e-mail: reservations@bestbnb.com; www.bestbnb.com.

This contemporary home features lovely landscaped gardens and two guest suites (sleep three), which open to a garden lanai, swimming pool, cabana and barbecue area. A private 1BR cottage with full kitchen is also available. There are great views of Kona Coast sunsets. Three-night minimum stay. Member-Hawaii's Best.

Rates: $110-$165; $15 extra person

Kealakekua Bay B&B

82-6002 Napo'opo'o Road, P.O. Box 1412, Kealakekua, HI 96750. 800-328-8150; 808-328-8150; fax 808-328-8866; e-mail: kbaybb@aloha.net; www.keala.com.

This is a private cottage on five landscaped acres a short walk from Kealakekua Bay. It has two bedrooms (sleeps up to 6), 2.5 baths, full kitchen and great view of the bay from the covered porch. Great for families or couples traveling together. The nearby host home also has a master bedroom with private entry, jacuzzi and nice view of the bay. A garden-level wing has two guest bedrooms, living area and private patio. Two-night minimum stay.

Rates: Pali Room $95; Lehua Room $95; Ali'i Suite $150; Ohana Kai Guest House $200; $25 extra person

Kokoke Lani B&B Inn

74-4969 Kealakaa Street, P.O. Box 2728, Kailua-Kona, HI 96704. Phone/ fax 808-329-2226; e-mail: kokelanibnb@hawaii.rr.com; www.kokoke lani.com.

This home offers a nice oceanview setting on the slopes above Kailua-Kona. Nicely landscaped grounds with tropical gardens and forest. Comfortable guest rooms have phones, TV/cable, refrigerators, king/queen beds, antique decor and artwork, fresh flowers and private baths. Glass doors open to lanai, gardens and private sitting areas; guests enjoy pool and spa. Includes traditional island-style breakfast. Member-HIBBA.

Rates: $135-$165

Lions' Gate B&B

P.O. Box 761, Honaunau, HI 96726. 800-955-2332; phone/fax 808-328-2335; e-mail: liongte@aloha.net; www.konabnb.com.

This country home is in the Kona Coast's macadamia nut and coffee farm region with a very quiet, private setting. There is a jacuzzi, refrigerator, microwave, gazebo and TV room available for guest use. Just minutes away from Pu'uhonua o Honaunau and great snorkeling on the beach. Member-HIBBA.

Rates: $110

Pu'ukala Lodge

72-3998E Mamalahoa Highway, P.O. Box 2967, Kailua-Kona, HI 96745. 888-325-1729; 808-325-1729; e-mail: puukala1@aol.com; www.puukala-lodge.com.

This modern expansive home is located at 1,500 feet on the slopes of Mt. Hualalai above the Kona Coast. There are great 180-degree views of the Kona and Kohala coasts. The 1,400-square-foot lanai also provides ample room to enjoy those famous Kona sunsets. Located just five minutes from Kona Airport and seven miles from Kailua-Kona town. Guests choose from well-appointed suites or guest rooms. Makai Suite is spacious with two queen beds, bath, lanai. Ohana Suite has two bedrooms, two baths for four people. Pu'ukala Ohana Rooms have queen beds, private baths and lanai. All amenities, kitchen, breakfast included.

Rates: Ohana Suite $165, Makai Suite $110, Pu'ukala Ohana Rooms $85-$95

Rainbow Plantation B&B

P.O. Box 122, 81-6327B Mamalahoa Highway, Captain Cook, HI 96704. 800-494-2829; 808-323-2393; fax 808-323-9445; e-mail: sunshine@ aloha.net; www.rainbowplantation.com.

This country home is located on seven acres of organic coffee and macadamia nut orchards and forest land. Nature lovers will enjoy watching the birds in the lush gardens and the koi carp in the ponds. The large guest rooms have private entrances and baths, TV and refrigerator. Breakfast is enjoyed on the open oceanview lanai. There's an open gazebo with barbecue for guest use. Located at the 1,200-foot elevation level above Kealakekua Bay and 11 miles from Kailua-Kona town. It's just minutes to beach snorkeling, restaurants, shopping and area attractions. French and German spoken here. Member-HIBBA.

Rates: $75-$95

Silver Oaks Ranch B&B

75-1027 Henry Street #310, Kailua-Kona, HI 96740. 877-325-2300; 808-325-2000; fax 808-325-2200; e-mail: rsvp@silveroaksranch.com; www.stayhawaii.com/silveroaks.

This is a large home on a 10-acre horse ranch five miles from Kailua-Kona town and just five miles from Kona airport. There is a spectacular 40-mile panorama view of the Kona Coast. Guests enjoy pool and jacuzzi, traditional breakfast. Easy access to Kailua-Kona town activities, shopping, dining and attractions. Member-HIBBA.

Rates: $160

Sleepy Hollow B&B

73-1530 Apela Place, Kailua-Kona, HI 96740. 808-325-5043; fax 808-325-0653; e-mail: vidal@aloha.net; www.konaweb.com/shbb.

This beautiful home overlooks the Kona Coast from a three-acre estate. The home features local *koa* woodwork, wraparound lanais and wonderful panoramic ocean views. Guest rooms are spacious and well kept with Hawaiian artwork decor accents. Guests have laundry and refrigerator privileges. Hearty traditional island-style breakfast served. Just minutes from the Kona airport, fishing harbor, golf, beach and all the shopping, dining and activities of Kailua-Kona town. Children are welcome. Member-HIBBA.

Rates: $95-$150

Tara Cottage

Reservations through Hawai'i's Best B&Bs, P.O. Box 520, Kamuela, HI 96743. 800-262-9912; 808-885-455; fax 808-885-0559; e-mail: reserva tions@bestbnb.com; www.bestbnb.com.

This is a unique octagon-shaped studio cottage, rare to find in the islands. Located on 10 rural acres above Kona's Kealakekua Bay with nice ocean views. It's a peaceful, unhurried setting, ideal for those seeking to just relax or while away days snorkeling, kayaking, sunning, etc. The cottage can sleep three and has southeast Asian decor, kitchenette, barbecue, laundry facilities, phone, TV/VCR, stereo and an outdoor garden shower. Owner lives in separate cottage on property.

Rates: $175-$200; $25 extra person

CONDOMINIUMS

Ali'i Villas

75-6016 Ali'i Drive, Kailua-Kona, HI 96740. 808-329-1288. Agents: Sunquest Vacations 800-367-5168; Hawai'i Resort Management 800-622-5348; Knutson & Associates 800-800-6202.

This condo has only ten units in rental programs. It is a beachfront location with palm trees, flowers and a garden setting less than a mile from town. Units are generally clean and well kept, although this is strictly a budget-class operation.

Rates: $76-$134

Casa De Emdeko

75-6082 Ali'i Drive, Kailua-Kona, HI 96740. 808-329-6488. Agents: Sunquest Vacations 800-367-5168; Condo in Hawai'i 888-292-3307; Century 21 800-546-5662; Knutson & Associates 800-800-6202.

This lovely three-story white-washed building is located on the water, although there is no sand beach here. The 40 available units are spacious, comfortable and well-appointed. The central garden courtyard is well maintained with tropical plants. The oceanside swimming pool features a "sandy beach" surrounding the pool.

Rates: $68-$190

Country Club Villas

78-6920 Ali'i Drive, Kailua-Kona, HI 96740. 808-322-9154. Agents: Sunquest Vacations 800-367-5168; Hawai'i Resort Management 800-553-5035, 808-329-9393; Keauhou Property Management 800-745-KONA; Property Network 800-358-7977; Triad Management 800-345-2823; Century 21 800-546-5662.

This condominium is located on the Kona Country Club golf course with easy access to other Keauhou resorts, dining, shopping, etc. Amenities include TV, private lanai on each unit, two tennis courts, and on-request maid service. Available units are 2BR/3BR and have golf course views with Kona Coast beyond. Five-night minimum stay.

Rates: $120-$165

Hale Kona Kai

75-5870 Kahakai Road, Kailua-Kona, HI 96740. 800-421-3696; 808-329-2155. Agents: Sunquest Vacations 800-367-5168; Triad Management 800-345-2823.

Within walking distance to the village, this 39-unit air-conditioned condo has on-request maid service, TV, barbecue facility. No room telephones. Corner units are larger with bigger lanai area but all units are very nicely furnished. Located right on the water and immediately next door to the Royal Kona Resort, but there is no sand beach. Three-night minimum stay.

Rates: $90-$145

Kahaluu Bay Villas

78-6715A Ali'i Drive, Kailua-Kona, HI 96740. 808-322-0013. Agent: Sunquest Vacations 800-367-5168.

This luxury complex is a short walk along Ali'i Drive to Kahalu'u Beach Park, where there is good snorkeling. Spacious units have separate master bedrooms, full kitchens, ceiling fans, private lanais, pool, gazebo, parking and barbecue area.

Rates: $76-$154

Kailua Village

At the intersection of Hualalai Road and Kuakini Highway near the town center. Agent: Property Network 800-358-7977.

This multi-story complex is one block from the ocean and within easy walking distance of the town center, restaurants, shopping, attractions, Kailua Pier, etc. The 1BR units have ceiling fans, laundry facilities, parking, elevators and access to swimming pool.

Rates: $126-$155

Kalanikai Condominiums

75-5681 Kuakini Highway, Kailua-Kona, HI 96740. 808-329-5241. Agents: Century 21 800-546-5662; Property Network 800-358-7977.

This condominium is located in the heart of the village and within walking distance of resort activities, shopping and restaurants. Amenities include air conditioning and barbecue facilities. Units have mountain views.

Rates: $85-$195

Kanaloa at Kona

78-261 Manukai Street, Kailua-Kona, HI 96740. 800-688-7444; 808-322-9625; fax 808-322-3818. Agents: Sunquest Vacations 800-367-5168; Property Network 800-358-7977; Keauhou Property Management 800-745-KONA; West Hawai'i Property Services 800-799-KONA; Outrigger Hotels Hawai'i 800-OUTRIGGER, e-mail: reservations@outrigger.com, www.outrigger.com; Royal Hawai'i Condos 888-722-6284; Hawai'i Condo Exchange 800-442-0404; Maui & All Islands 800-663-6962.

This 120-unit condo is located oceanfront in Keauhou but there is no sandy beach. The luxurious units are spacious and fully equipped including lanai wet bar, *koa* wood interiors, ceiling fans and TV.

Kanaloa is bordered on one side by the sparkling blue Pacific with a secluded bay for snorkeling and sunning and on the other by the Kona Country Club golf course. Tennis courts, restaurant, cocktail lounge, barbecue facilities and recreation-meeting room are on the property.

Rates: $122-$250

Keauhou Akahi

78-7030 Ali'i Drive, Kailua-Kona, HI 96740. 808-322-2590. Agents: Triad Management 800-345-2823; Property Network 800-358-7977.

This 48-unit complex is located on the Kona Country Club golf course with ocean views. There are laundry facilities in each unit, full kitchens and an on-property swimming pool. It is 7 miles from Kailua-Kona village but shopping and dining are nearby.

Rates: $85-$135

Keauhou Palena Condominiums

78-7054 Kamehameha III Road, Kailua-Kona, HI 96740. 808-322-3620. Agents: Keauhou Property Management 800-745-KONA; Century 21 800-546-5662; Sunquest Vacations 800-367-5168; West Hawai'i Property Services 800-799-KONA.

This condo is on the eleventh fairway of the Kona Country Club golf course with easy access for golfing visitors. Units are fully equipped including ceiling fans and TV. The den can be made into an extra bedroom, enabling these units to sleep four comfortably. It's located near the end of Ali'i Drive.

Rates: $85-$135

Keauhou Punahele Condominiums

78-7070 Ali'i Drive, Kailua-Kona, HI 96740. 808-322-6585, reservations 206-742-2440. Agents: Century 21 800-546-5662; West Hawai'i Property Services 800-799-KONA; Sunquest Vacations 800-367-5168; Triad Management 800-345-2823.

This large complex (93 units) has only 2BR/3BR units available in rental programs. It is the last complex at the end of Ali'i Drive in the Keauhou area and on the Kona Country Club golf course with ocean views across golf course. Units are not air-conditioned but are roomy and generally well-appointed, with high ceilings and fans keeping units cool and breezy. The units are clean and well-kept and the grounds are well-groomed. Located 7.25 miles from the village but Keauhou Shopping Center is only half a mile away.

Rates: $83-$165

Keauhou Resort Condominiums

78-7039 Kamehameha III Road, Kailua-Kona, HI 96740. 800-367-5286; 808-322-9122; fax 322-9410; e-mail: english@aloha.net; www.tropweb.com/keauhou.htm. Agents: Sunquest Vacations 800-367-5168; Property Network 800-358-7977; West Hawai'i Property Services 800-799-KONA.

This condo has 48 townhouse units available with TV, two swimming pools and is on the golf course; maid service included. Five-night minimum stay.

Rates: $95-$160

Kona Ali'i Condominiums

75-5782 Kuakini Highway, Kailua-Kona, HI 96740. 808-329-2000. Agents: Hawai'i Resort Management 800-622-5348; Sunquest Vacations 800-367-5168.

Units are fully furnished with private lanai and major appliances. Bedding for up to 4 persons. Tennis court, top-floor sun deck, private sandy beach, barbecue area. Short two-minute walk into Kailua village for shopping, restaurants and resort activities.

Rates: $62-$90

Kona Bali Kai

76-6246 Ali'i Drive, Kailua-Kona, HI 96740. 808-329-9381. Agents: Sunquest Vacations 800-367-5168; Always Sunny Condos 800-479-2173, 360-698-7007; Property Network 800-358-7977; Century 21 800-546-5662; West Hawai'i Property Services 800-799-KONA; Hawai'i Condo Exchange 800-442-0404; Marc Resorts 800-436-1304.

This condo has 86 units available on Holualoa Bay, Kona, located three miles from town. All units have full kitchen and TV, some with air conditioning; sauna, jacuzzi, pool, health club, barbecue facilities, convenience store/deli are available.

Rates: $64-$90

Kona Billfisher Condominium

75-5841 Ali'i Drive, Kailua-Kona, HI 96740. 808-329-9277. Agents: Sunquest Vacations 800-367-5168; Hawai'i Resort Management 800-553-5035, 808-329-9393; Triad Management 800-345-2823.

This condo has 20 units in rental programs, all air-conditioned with TV and barbecue area. It is located across the street from the Royal Kona Resort and is also within easy walking distance of the town center, shopping and several restaurants.

Rates: $64-$150

★ Kona by the Sea

75-6106 Ali'i Drive, Kailua-Kona, HI 96740. 808-327-2300. Agents: Aston Hotels & Resorts 800-922-7866, 800-321-2558; Royal Hawai'i Condos 888-722-6284; Pleasant Hawaiian Holidays 800-672-4587; Maui & All Islands 800-663-6962.

This is a well-maintained, quiet, four-story condominium complex with 56 units available for vacation rentals. The bright, nicely appointed and very spacious rooms are air-conditioned with TV and fully equipped kitchen. While the complex is located on a rocky beach, there is a swimming pool, jacuzzi, adjoining grass yard for small children, sandy area with barbecue grills and lounge chairs. The shore area attracts lots of surfers because the surf builds and breaks directly in front of the complex, a great place to watch the surfers if you don't take to the board yourself. There is also a public saltwater pool beyond the rock wall at the end of the property, accessed by a public walkway. However, the heavy surf can break up and over the pool's edge so caution is required.

Rates: $107-$207

Kona Coast Resort/Keauhou Gardens

78-6842 Ali'i Drive, Keauhou-Kona, HI 96740. 808-324-1721; fax 808-322-8217. Agents: Sunquest Vacations 800-367-5168; Property Network 800-358-7977; West Hawai'i Property Services 800-799-KONA; Keauhou Property Management 800-745-KONA.

This lushly landscaped development has a number of rental units available. They are spread out among the complex on a lovely slope surrounded by the fairways of the Kona Country Club, with the ocean just beyond. The units are luxuriously furnished with plush furniture and bedding, and overall are very tastefully appointed. There is a recreation area with tennis, two pools, jacuzzi, gas barbecue area, and wet bar.

Rates: $140-$175

Kona Islander Inn

75-5776 Kuakini Highway, Kailua-Kona, HI 96740. 808-329-3181. Agents: Property Network 800-358-7977; Maui & All Islands 800-663-6962.

This condo/hotel has just 51 rental units available. Rooms have air conditioning, refrigerator and TV, and there is a pool and jacuzzi. There is a convenience shop with beverages and snacks in the lobby. While this is an older complex in Kailua-Kona (dating from 1969), it is clean and quiet and is conveniently located to the village and within easy walking distance of most things. The complex occupies a narrow strip between other buildings and stretches from Kuakini Highway to Ali'i Drive with the lower end just across Ali'i Drive from Kailua Bay. This is a good location if you don't have a rental car and want to explore Kona on foot.

Rates: $71-$151

Kona Isle Condominium

75-6100 Ali'i Drive, Kailua-Kona, HI 96740. 808-329-2241; fax 808-326-2401. Agents: Sunquest Vacations 800-367-5168; Hawai'i Resort Management 800-622-5348; Knutson & Associates 800-800-6202; Triad Management 800-345-2823; Property Network 800-358-7977; West Hawai'i Property Services 800-799-KONA.

This is an oceanfront complex, some units with oceanview. The beautifully manicured grounds are very spacious and pleasant. There are barbecue facilities and tables poolside and lounge chairs near the oceanfront seawall. There is no sand beach here, it is too rocky. Laundry facilities are in each unit. Located 2.5 miles from the village. One-week minimum stay.

Rates: $104-$115

Kona Luana

75-5958 Ali'i Drive, Kailua-Kona, HI 96740. 808-329-6488. Agent: Sunquest Vacations 800-367-5168.

This small complex less than a mile from Kailua town offers full ocean views over the Pacific with full furnishings, laundry facilities, lanai and wet bar.

Rates: $112-$138

Kona Magic Sands

77-6452 Ali'i Drive, Kailua-Kona, HI 96740. 808-329-6488. Agents: Sunquest Vacations 800-367-5168; Hawai'i Resort Management 800-553-5035, Hawai'i 808-329-9393; Maui & All Islands 800-663-6962.

Located next to famous Magic Sands Beach Park with swimming and body surfing. There are just 10 studio units. Features TV, Jameson's by the Sea restaurant, cocktail lounge, and on-request maid service. Some rooms have telephones. Three-night minimum stay.

Rates: $68-$115

Kona Makai

75-6026 Ali'i Drive, Kailua-Kona, HI 96740. 808-329-6488. Agents: Property Network 800-358-7977; Sunquest Vacations 800-367-5168; West Hawai'i Property Services 800-799-KONA.

This complex has just 15 units in rental programs. Amenities include jacuzzi, barbecue, tennis courts, sauna and exercise room. Oceanfront but no sandy beach. Three-night minimum stay.

Rates: $72-$190

Kona Nalu

76-6212 Ali'i Drive, Kailua-Kona, HI 96740. 808-329-6488. Agents: Sunquest Vacations 800-367-5168.

This small complex is located on the waterfront two miles from Kailua town. Units are completely furnished and well maintained; large lanais, laundry facilities, pool, covered parking, air conditioning.

Rates: $169-$235

Kona Pacific

75-5865 Walua Road, Kailua-Kona, HI 96740. 808-329-6140. Agents: Property Network 800-358-7977; Hawai'i Resort Management 800-622-5348, 808-329-9393; Sunquest Vacations 800-367-5168.

These 1BR and 2BR units provide all the comfort needed for a relaxing vacation experience. They are air-conditioned, have in-unit laundry facilities and a lanai with beautiful ocean view. Complex has elevator and pool. Very close to Royal Kona Resort and within easy walking of the village.

Rates: $97-$135

Kona Palms

77-6311 Ali'i Drive, Kailua-Kona, HI 96740. Agent: Knutson & Associates 800-800-6202.

This complex features 2BR units in vacation rental programs. There are in-unit laundry facilities, large lanais and guest access to barbecue, pool and jacuzzi. Building has elevators. Located about three miles from the village and across from the ocean but units have nice sunset views from lanais.

Rates: $85-$105

Kona Plaza Condominiums

75-5719 Ali'i Drive, Kailua-Kona, HI 96740. 808-329-1132. Agents: Century 21 800-546-5662; Sunquest Vacations 800-367-5168.

This complex has 75 air-conditioned units in the heart of the village on Ali'i Drive across from the Kona Inn Shopping Village. Restaurants, shopping, Kona Pier, hotels are all within walking distance. Guests have access to a rooftop sundeck.

Rates: $130-$175

Kona Reef

75-5888 Ali'i Drive, Kailua-Kona, HI 96740. 808-329-6488. Agents: Castle Resorts & Hotels 800-367-5004; Knutson & Associates 800-800-6202; West Hawai'i Property Services 800-799-KONA; Century 21 800-546-5662; Sunquest Vacations 800-367-5168; Maui & All Islands 800-663-6962.

This condo has 51 units available as vacation rentals. All rooms are air-conditioned with TV. Facilities include pool, jacuzzi, party pavilion and barbecue. The complex is near shopping and restaurants. Oceanfront location but no sandy beach. Two-night minimum stay.

Rates: $97-$235

Kona Riviera Villa Condominiums

75-6124 Ali'i Drive, Kailua-Kona, HI 96740. 808-329-1996; fax 326-2178. Agent: Knutson & Associates 800-800-6202.

This condo is located on the beach with private lanai on each unit, near tennis courts, golf and snorkeling, plus village shopping and restaurants. There are about 10 units available, accommodating up to four persons. Three-night minimum stay.

Rates: $109-$129

Kona White Sands Resort

P.O. Box 594, 77-6467 Ali'i Drive, Kailua-Kona, HI 96745. 808-329-3210; fax 808-326-4137. Agent: Hawai'i Resort Management 800-622-5348, 808-329-9393.

This small 10-unit apartment-hotel has just 5 units available in rental programs. Units have kitchenettes, TV, ceiling fans and private lanais, but no room telephones. This complex is directly across from White Sands Beach. Strictly a no-frills, budget-class lodging. Three-night minimum stay.

Rates: $105-$175

Malia Kai

75-5855 Walua Road, Kailua-Kona, HI 96740. 808-329-1897. Agent: Keauhou Property Management 800-745-KONA; Triad Management 800-345-2823.

This complex is very conveniently located, about two blocks from the center of the village and across the street from the Royal Kona Resort. The central courtyard is a profusion of tropical plants and flowers with a small relaxing swimming pool. It is a very quiet comfortable location. Units are simply furnished with ceiling and table fans, no air conditioning. The only negatives of this property are the narrow stairway leading up to each unit's split-levels and kitchens that show some age and wear.

Rates: $85-$105

Mauna Loa Village

78-7190 Kaleiopapa Road, Keauhou-Kona, HI 96740. 800-365-9190; 808-322-7999; fax 808-322-5165. Agents: Sunquest Vacations 800-367-5168; Trading Places International 800-365-1048.

This complex is in the Keauhou area, located just above Keauhou Bay. The complex is arranged in hexagonal pod-like cluster units. Lovely tropical color schemes accent the tasteful decor and contemporary furnishings of each unit. The grounds are well landscaped with numerous bubbling streams and pools, fountains, gardens and a swimming pool for every 18 units. Ten tennis courts on grounds, golf available next door at the Kona Country Club, and easy access to other resort activities and attractions, shopping and dining.

Rates: $90-$225

Royal Kahili Condominium

78-6283 Ali'i Drive, Kailua-Kona, HI 96740. 808-329-2626. Agents: Property Network 800-358-7977; Sunquest Vacations 800-367-5168; West Hawai'i Property Services 800-799-KONA.

This complex is across the street from the ocean but has a private oceanfront picnic area and barbecue area. Laundry facilities are in each unit. It is located three miles from the village.

Rates: $95-$135

Royal Kailuan

75-5863 Kuakini Highway, Kailua-Kona, HI 96740. 808-329-3318. Agent: Property Network 800-358-7977.

This condo complex is located within walking distance of Kailua-Kona village. Some units have ocean views, ceiling fans or air conditioning, and enclosed lanai. The complex has a swimming pool and laundry facilities.

Rates: $100-$210

Sea Village

75-6002 Ali'i Drive, Kailua-Kona, HI 96740. 808-329-6488. Agents: Knutson & Associates 800-800-6202; Property Network 800-358-7977; West Hawai'i Property Services 800-799-KONA; Sunquest Vacations 800-367-5168; Maui & All Islands 800-663-6962.

These large spacious units are clean and comfortable and include TV, full kitchen and dishwasher. The central grounds are beautifully maintained and landscaped. Pool area with barbecue facilities is right on water's edge but there is no beach here as it is too rocky. Nice views of Kailua Bay and the village. Three-night minimum stay.

Rates: $79-$171

White Sands Village

74-6469 Ali'i Drive, Kailua-Kona, HI 96740. Agents: Knutson & Associates 800-800-6202; Sunquest Vacations 800-367-5168; Triad Management 800-345-2823; West Hawai'i Property Services 800-799-KONA.

This 108-unit condo complex has just a few units available in rental programs. The units are air-conditioned with nicely coordinated furnishings and color schemes. Tennis courts, TV and on-request maid service are available. The central courtyard has a complete kitchen and barbecue area near the pool. The complex is across the street from White Sands Beach Park. Three-night minimum stay.

Rates: $64-$155

HOTELS, HOSTELS AND HOMES

★ King Kamehameha's Kona Beach Hotel

75-5660 Palani Road, Kailua-Kona, HI 96740. 808-329-2911; 800-367-6060; fax 808-329-4602; e-mail: reservations@hthcorp.com; www.kona beachhotel.com.

This 458-room hotel is a Kailua-Kona landmark and important historical site. King Kamehameha the Great kept his royal residence here until his death in 1819. During this time he rebuilt the ancient Ahuena Heiau, a temple dedicated to the god Lono, which still stands on the grounds, protected as a National Historic Landmark. The interior spaces of the hotel building are dramatically decorated with Hawaiian artifacts, portraits of Hawaiian royalty and contemporary murals. Cultural tours are provided complimentary to guests. Located on small, sandy Kamakahonu Beach at the head of Ali'i Drive, the hotel offers two restaurants, the popular Billfish Bar by the pool, and the colorful outdoor "Island Breeze" luau. All guest rooms are air-conditioned with TV, lanai, fridge, phone and standard hotel amenities. A variety of facilities includes tennis courts, pool and whirlpool spa, beauty salon, therapeutic massage, lobby shopping mall, Hawaiian Cultural Activity Center and meeting and banquet space. Guest parking $3 per day. Packages are available. No charge for children 18 years and younger occupying room with parents, unless additional bedding is required.

Rates: Standard $135, Mountain $145, Garden $155, Partial Oceanview $180, Oceanfront $225, 1BR Suite $500, 2BR Suite $750, 3BR Suite $950; $25 extra person

Kohala Country Adventures

P.O. Box 703, Kapa'au, HI 96755. 866-892-2484; cell 808-987-7173; 808-889-5663; fax 808-889-6133; e-mail: getaway@pixi.com; www.kcadventures.com.

This country guesthouse is set in lovely tropical gardens on a ten-acre farm in the Big Island's North Kohala District. Guest rooms have private baths and entrances. The area is noted for a cool, comfortable and breezy climate. Enjoy sunset views of neighboring Maui and easy access to Kohala Coast attractions. Member-HIBBA.

Rates: $70-$150

Kona Akua House

Reservations through Hawai'i's Best B&Bs, P.O. Box 520, Kamuela, HI 96743. 800-262-9912; 808-885-4550; fax 808-885-0559; e-mail: reservations@bestbnb.com; www.bestbnb.com.

This is a nice 1BR private home with 3BR annex and a studio and occupies an acre of lush grounds amid a macadamia nut orchard. It has a fully equipped kitchen and dining area, TV, barbecue and ceiling fans. Each room offers panoramic ocean views and super sunsets. Just ten minutes from Kailua-Kona shopping, dining, activities and near to area attractions. Great for groups.

Rates: $125-$155

Kona Hotel

P.O. Box 342, Holualoa Road, Holualoa, HI 96725. 808-324-1155.

Located approximately seven miles from Kailua-Kona town in a prime coffee farming area on the slopes of Mount Hualalai, this rustic 11-room upcountry hotel has been run by the Inaba family for many years. It is one of Kona's original lodgings and is still run with an old-fashioned family atmosphere. Nothing fancy but basic rooming house–style accommodations for guests wanting the bare necessities. Guests share a community bathroom and entertain themselves in the small lobby-TV room. This hotel has a quiet and sedate old-fashioned Hawaiian country ambience.

Rates: $25-$30

Kona Seaside Hotel

75-5646 Palani Road, Kailua-Kona, HI 96740. 808-329-2455. Reservations: Sands & Seaside Hotels 800-560-5558; fax 808-320-6157; e-mail: info@sand-seaside.com; www.sand-seaside.com.

This 200-room property partially fronts Kailua Bay. Most rooms are air-conditioned and all have TV. Restaurant, cocktail lounge, and meeting rooms available. This is in the heart of the village with shopping and restaurants all within walking distance. Kailua Pier is one block away. This is a good budget hotel with clean rooms and simple decor.

Rates: Standard $98, Deluxe $115, Studio Kitchenette $125; $12 extra person

Manago Hotel

P.O. Box 145, 82-6155 Mamalahoa Highway, Captain Cook, HI 96704. 808-323-2642; fax 323-3451.

This is another old-fashioned family hotel operated by the Manago family since its founding in 1917. There are 64 rooms, some with shared bathroom facilities. The hotel features a homey family-type environment and the restaurant serves local family-style meals. Cocktail lounge on grounds. No room telephones. Located right on Highway 11, eight miles from Kailua-Kona in the busy town of Captain Cook at 1,400-foot elevation above the Kona Coast, overlooking Kealakekua Bay and Pu'uhonua o Honaunau. The Manago Hotel enjoys sunny days and cool, quiet evenings.

Rates: Single 1BR $23, Standard $36-$41, Deluxe $55-60; $3 extra person

★ *Ohana Keauhou Beach Resort*

78-6740 Ali'i Drive, Keauhou-Kona, HI 96740. 808-322-7987; fax 808-322-3117. Agents: Aston Hotels & Resorts 800-922-7866.

The 311-room hotel is located right at the water's edge with shallow lagoons filled with marinelife, mature tropical gardens and flowering trees. The bar terrace has nice open-ocean views, great for watching the surf roll in and whales at play. Laulea Restaurant is a good place to sample island-style cuisine. Next door is Kahalu'u Beach Park, where snorkeling and swimming is good. The grounds have numerous historic and cultural connections including a summer home used by King Kalakaua in the late 1800s. There is easy access to Kona Coast attractions, dining and activities, plus the hotel has a pool and tennis complex. The hotel is located four miles south of Kailua-Kona town; free parking. When booking, ask about any Aston deals and discounts.

Rates: Garden View $115, Partial Ocean View $125, Ocean View $160, Ocean Front $175

Outrigger Royal Sea Cliff Resort

75-6040 Ali'i Drive, Kailua-Kona, HI 96740. 808-329-8021.

This is a 148-unit condo-hotel about a mile and a half south of Kailua-Kona town. The air-conditioned spacious units are excellent for families and are fully furnished, including kitchen with microwave, small appliances and full in-unit laundry facilities. Guest facilities also include parking, both fresh- and saltwater pools, tennis court and barbecues. The complex is a terrace arrangement, making the lower units closer to the shoreline and very private and quiet. Ask about special deals and discounts for extra nights.

Rates: Studio from $139, 1BR from $161, 2BR from $188; $18 extra person

Patey's Place Hostel

75-195 Ona Ona, Kailua-Kona, HI 96740. 808-326-7018; fax 808-326-7640; e-mail: ipatey@gte.net; www.hawaiian-hostels.com.

This budget accommodation is just two blocks from the ocean and near shops, restaurants and entertainment in the heart of Kailua-Kona town. Convenient to day tours to Volcano, coffee plantations, historic sites, etc.

Rates: Shared Room $19.50; Single Private $36.50; Double Private $46.50-$50.00; 2BR $125

Royal Kona Resort

75-5852 Ali'i Drive, Kailua-Kona, HI 96740. Reservations: 800-22-ALOHA; 808-329-3111; fax 808-329-7230; e-mail: info@royalkona.com; www.royalkona.com.

This 450-room hotel is a well-known Kona landmark and one of Kona's original modern tourist hotels. It sits on a rocky precipice jutting into Kailua Bay and affords a commanding view of the town and bay area. The rooms are very neat, clean and air-conditioned with TV, refrigerators, and complimentary coffee/tea making facility. Amenities include Tropics Cafe, cocktail lounge, swimming pool, tennis courts, shops and meeting rooms. The most quiet rooms are in either the village or beach buildings, away from the main building with its noisy-at-night lounge music. Check on their special room-car packages, often cheaper than buying both separately.

Rates: Garden View $140, Part Oceanview $170, Oceanview $190, Oceanfront $210, Oceanfront Corner King $250, Suites $500; $15 extra person

Sheraton Keauhou Bay Resort & Spa

78-128 Ehukai Street, Kailua-Kona, HI 96740. www.sheratonkeauhou.com. Starwood reservations 800-325-3589.

The former Kona Surf has been closed since 2000 and in late 2004 will reopen as the Sheraton Keauhou Bay Resort. Among the facilities will be 530 rooms and suites, a spa and fitness center, Kona's largest conference facility, a wedding chapel, luau garden and two restaurants: The Bayview and Manta Ray's. Geared toward family vacationers, the hotel will feature "Ohana Suites" for families of up to six, a children's play center, biking and jogging trails, game and entertainment room and a multilevel fantasy pool with meandering streams, waterfalls, interactive children's fountains and a 200-foot lava tube waterslide.

Rates: Room rates will be in the $200-$300 range

Uncle Billy's Kona Bay Hotel

75-5739 Ali'i Drive, Kailua-Kona, HI 96740. 808-329-1393; 800-367-5102; fax 808-935-7903; e-mail: resv@unclebilly.com; www.unclebilly.com.

This older hotel has 145 guest rooms available, all air-conditioned. In-room TV, swimming pool, restaurant, cocktail lounge and shops all available. Located across from the Kona Inn Shopping Village only one block from Kailua Bay, centrally located in town.

Rates: Standard $84-$92, Superior $94-$102, Superior/kitchen $104-$112; $10 extra person

Kohala Coast

BED AND BREAKFASTS

Hale Ho'onanea

P.O. Box 6568, Kamuela, HI 96743. 877-882-1653; phone/fax 808-882-1653; e-mail: jroppolo@houseofrelaxation.com; www.houseofrelaxation.com.

Three detached B&B suites located in an exclusive residence at the top of Kohala Estates two miles north of Kawaihae Harbor, Hale Suite, Tranquility Suite and Garden Suite all feature private entrance and bath, kitchenette and lanai. Each suite also includes TV/VCR, library, microwave, coffeemaker, toaster oven and refrigerator. There is lots of privacy in this country neighborhood on the famed Kohala Coast of West Hawai'i. The site offers panoramic ocean views, pleasing sunsets and mountain vistas. The hotels, fine dining restaurants, shopping, beaches, activities, golf, historic sites, etc., of the world-class Kohala Coast resorts and Waimea town are just minutes away. Member-HIBBA.

Rates: $90

Makai Hale

Reservations through Hawai'i's Best B&Bs, P.O. Box 520, Kamuela, HI 96743. U.S. 800-262-9912; 808-885-4550; fax 808-885-0559; e-mail: reservations@bestbnb.com; www.bestbnb.com.

This is a very nice private home just four miles from the best beaches on the Kohala Coast. Noted for consistently fine weather, expansive ocean views from its 500-foot elevation, and pool/jacuzzi deck. Guest wing opens directly to the swimming pool and deck. Whale watching in season (December–May) is excellent.

Rates: $135; $75 extra person

CONDOMINIUMS

★ *The Islands at Mauna Lani*

68-1050 Mauna Lani Point Drive, Mauna Lani Resort, Kohala Coast, HI 96743-9704. 808-885-5022. Agents: Classic Resorts 800-642-6284, fax 808-661-1025, e-mail: info@classicresorts.com, www.classicresorts.com; South Kohala Management 800-822-4254, 808-883-8500, fax 808-883-9818, www.southkohala.com, e-mail: info@southkohala.com.

This 46-unit super-luxury townhouse complex is surrounded by the lush fairways of the championship Francis I'i Brown Golf Course and five acres of saltwater ponds, streams and waterfalls filled with fish and marine life. The 2BR and 3BR units are incredibly spacious with full kitchen, living room, dining room, bathrooms and private lanais and carports, plus laundry room. They are tastefully furnished with contemporary island-style decor and furniture. These are excellent vacation units for large families or groups wanting lots of space. Amenities include jacuzzi, swimming pool and barbecue areas. Guests have access to Mauna Lani Resort beaches, golf, the Mauna Lani Racquet Club tennis facilities and award-winning restaurants. This condo provides the ultimate in a VIP condo vacation experience; three-night minimum stay. Rates include a full-size car picked up at Kona Airport and a grocery starter package with breakfast items.

Rates: $490-$560

Mauna Lani Point Condominiums

68-1050 Mauna Lani Point Drive, Mauna Lani Resort, Kohala Coast, HI 96743-9704. Reservations: Classic Resorts 800-642-6284, 808-885-5022, fax 808-661-0125, e-mail: info@classicresorts.com, www.classic resorts.com; Pleasant Hawaiian Holidays 800-672-4587.

This 116-unit complex sits next to the ocean amid the fairways of Mauna Lani's renowned Francis I'i Brown South Golf Course. It is perhaps one of the Big Island's best-kept secrets among luxury vacation rentals. The units have either garden fairway or ocean fairway views. The extra-large units are very well appointed and include large private lanais, living and dining areas, full kitchens, microwave, TV, laundry facilities, air conditioning, double soaking tubs and many other amenities. Each unit has carport parking. These are excellent units for families and groups, plenty of space to spread out; great for youngsters. Easy access to the resort's fine golf, tennis and award-

★ **Mauna Kea Resort Vacation Residences** boasts exclusive, private condominiums, villas and private homes available for discriminating travelers who appreciate the luxury of a quality resort destination. Two of Hawai'i's best beaches, two world-class golf courses, oceanfront tennis, fine dining, shopping and a multitude of recreation options are available to guests of the resort. Select from three different models of the Condominiums at Kumulani, all with full kitchen, two bedrooms and a 375-square-foot private lanai. Or opt for the 2,700-square-foot Villas at Mauna Kea, each with two master suites with spa-like baths, private lanai, gourmet kitchen, elegant furnishings and panoramic views. Larger families on retreat might prefer one of the Fairways homes, four to six bedroom for spacious living and gracious entertaining. Rates: Kumulani from $450-$650, The Villas from $1,200, Fairways homes from $1,200-$1,400. 62-100 Kauna'oa Drive, Kohala Coast, HI 96743. Reservations: 808-880-3490, www.maunakearesortrentals.com.

winning restaurants. Guests get preferred tee times at either of the North or South golf courses and reserved court time at the Racquet Club for tennis on hard or grass courts. There is also a private beach club with restaurant at Makaiwa Bay's lovely white-sand beach. Guests have access to a whirlpool, sauna, swimming pool and barbecue pavilion. Three-night minimum stay in high season, none in low season.

Rates: 1BR $260-$370; 2BR $325-$475; 3BR $550-$600

Mauna Lani Terrace Condominium

Mauna Lani Resort, Kohala Coast, HI 96743. Agent: South Kohala Management 800-822-4252, 808-883-8500, fax 808-883-9818, www.southkohala.com, e-mail: info@southkohala.com.

These luxury condos are located adjacent to the Mauna Lani Bay Hotel & Bungalows at Mauna Lani Resort. The spacious units are sparkling and well maintained throughout with the tasteful decor and furnishings expected of a luxury unit. There is lots of space to move around in; relax and enjoy the special luxurious ambiance of Mauna Lani. All units are air-conditioned with ceiling fan in living room, private lanais, wet bars, and complete laundry facilities. There is easy access to the resort's world-class golf and tennis, health club and water sports. Five-night minimum stay in high season, three nights in low season.

Rates: $329-$417

Puako Beach Condos

3 Puako Beach Drive, Kamuela, HI 96743. Agent: Hawai'i Vacation Rentals 808-882-7000, e-mail: seaside@aloha.net, www.vacationbigisland.com.

This 40-unit condo has only a few units available for vacation rentals. The complex is located in the quiet Puako Beach area near Hapuna Beach State Park on the Kohala Coast. Fully furnished, fully equipped 3-bedroom/2-bath units have TV and kitchen, with great ocean views.

Rates: $135

★ The Shores at Waikoloa

HC02 Box 5460, Waikoloa, HI 96743. 808-885-5001. Agents: South Kohala Management 800-822-4252, 808-883-8500, fax 808-883-9818, www.southkohala.com, e-mail: info@southkohala.com.

There are 64 units available in rental programs. These are 1-2-3 BR, all fully air-conditioned, with full kitchen, TV, washer/dryer, private lanai and wet bar as standard features. The units are very spacious and well furnished with lots of extra room and large bathrooms. Perfect for families. Guests have easy access to pool, barbecue facilities, tennis courts and adjacent Waikoloa Beach and King's Golf Courses. Guests can enjoy dining at any of several resort restaurants at the Waikoloa Beach Marriott or Hilton Waikoloa Village. Golf course fairway location in Waikoloa Beach Resort.

Rates: $153-$195

The Vista Waikoloa

69-1010 Keana Place, Waikoloa Beach Resort, Waikoloa, HI 96743. Agent: South Kohala Management 800-822-4252, 808-883-8500, fax 808-883-9818, www.southkohala.com, e-mail: info@southkohala.com.

This luxurious development has 122 units, some in vacation rental programs. The multi-building complex is located right on Waikoloa Beach Drive between the Waikoloa Beach Marriott and Hilton Waikoloa Village and next to the golf course fairways. The spacious units are very nicely furnished with full kitchens, fully air-conditioned with access to pool, spa and all resort recreational facilities. Daily maid service is included.

Rates: $165-$417

★ Waikoloa Villas

P.O. Box 385134, Lua Kula Drive, Waikoloa, HI 96743. 808-883-9144. Agents: Hawai'i Vacation Rentals 808-882-7000; Hawai'i Condo Exchange 800-442-0404, South Kohala Management 800-822-4252, 808-883-8500, fax 808-883-9818, www.southkohala.com, e-mail: info@southkohala.com.

This condo has several vacation rental units available. The units have full kitchens, telephones, ceiling fans, TV, meeting room, in-unit laundry facilities, pool, spa, barbecue facilities and weekly maid service. Golf course is nearby. Two-night minimum stay.

Rates : 1BR $125-$179, 2BR $175-$199, 3BR $259

★ ***Fairmont Orchid Hawai'i***

1 North Kaniku Drive, Kohala Coast, HI 96743. 800-845-9905; 808-885-2000; fax 808-885-1064; e-mail: orchid@fairmont.com; www.fairmont.com/orchid.

This lovely 539-room beachside hotel, located at the world-class Mauna Lani Resort, has recently been acquired by Fairmont Hotels and is undergoing an extensive renovation, bringing a new dimension to an already-excellent property. Championship golf and tennis courts, professional conference facilities, fine dining and the acclaimed, expanded Spa Without Walls add up to a rewarding resort experience for individuals, families or groups. The guest rooms and suites (54, including 2 presidential suites) are tastefully decorated and feature mini bar, marble bathrooms, TV with movies and video games, bathrobes, iron and ironing board and other amenities. A daily "resort fee" provides for additional amenities and complimentary use of resort facilities, daily newspaper, spa admission, fitness classes and other special offerings, not the least of which is a complimentary "Kids Eat Free" program.

Restaurants include the well-known Brown's Beach House, the Orchid Court, The Grill and soon-to-open Norio's Sushi Bar and Restaurant for excellent Japanese cuisine. There are also several lounges and bars, including the Kahakai Bar with unbeatable views. The hotel emphasizes recreation, with focus on the attractive white-sand beach and swimming lagoon. A beach equipment and water sports concession provides snorkel, scuba and seasonal whale-watching cruises, sunset sails and many other ocean options. A staff of "beachboys" is on hand to make you feel at home at the ocean, with activities and cultural talk-story sessions and a 35-foot voyaging canoe. There is also a large freshwater pool and jacuzzi, an excellent 10-court tennis pavilion including lighted exhibition courts, and a health and fitness center. Golfers can indulge their passion for the game at the Francis I'i Brown North and South Courses. In addition, you'll find a ballroom, meeting rooms and an outdoor amphitheater. Full-service staff, business center, and theme parties are available, as are settings for picture-perfect weddings and dreamy receptions. Babysitting can be arranged through the concierge. The hotel has received wide acclaim from the media, including Gold Key and Gold Platter Awards from *Meetings and Conventions Magazine*, among others. Value-added packages or "experiences" are offered seasonally. Please inquire when you call for reservations.

Rates: Fairmont Rooms $399-$549, Partial Ocean View $449-$599, Ocean View $559-$709, Deluxe Ocean View $669-$819, Suites $729-$2,999

★ *Four Seasons Resort Hualalai*

100 Kaupulehu Drive, Kaupulehu-Kona, HI 96740. 888-332-3442; 808-325-8000; fax 808-325-8053; www.fourseasons.com/locations/hualalai.

Since its opening in 1996, this luxury property has added an element of quality to the Kohala Coast, earning the AAA five-diamond award for excellence in 1999 and every year since. Located on a remote stretch of beachfront land just north of Kona International Airport right next door to Kona Village, the Four Seasons offers 243 rooms and suites arranged in low-rise bungalows along the beachfront or golf course. There are one-, two- and three-bedroom suites, some with private plunge pools. Guests are greeted with welcome lei, tropical juice and cold *oshibori* towels. The large guest rooms (over 600 square feet) are provided with private lanai or garden, TV, fax, refrigerator, large bathrooms with aromatherapy candles and bath salts, and many more high-caliber amenities. Its restaurants are notable for fine food and service, and there are also lounges and more casual eateries. Complimentary beach and ocean recreation includes snorkeling, kayaking, sailing, outrigger canoes and glass-bottom boat rides. Deep-sea fishing and scuba dive room packages are available seasonally. Babysitting can be arranged, and a long list of baby needs like strollers and "child-proofed" rooms are available. Meetings and group events are accommodated in flexible indoor and outdoor function spaces for up to 500 people; the creative staff and wealth of on-site facilities make it easy for planners. There are romantic wedding sites from intimate to grand, with special touches for your special day. Other packages are available except during the "Festive Season" December 19–January 3.

Rates: Golf Oceanview $540, Oceanview $675, Oceanview Prime $700, Oceanfront $750. 1BR and 2BR Suites $900-$4,050, Presidential Villa Suite $5,200-$5,950, 3BR Villa Suite, $6,700; $120 third adult in room

★ *Hapuna Beach Prince Hotel*

62-100 Kauna'oa Drive, Kohala Coast, HI 96743. 866-PRINCE-6; 808-880-1111; fax 808-880-3142; e-mail: mkrres@hapunabeachprincehotel.com; www.hapunabeachprincehotel.com.

This contemporary luxury hotel is named after its breathtaking view—Hapuna Beach, a long strand of beautiful white sand that's one of the best in the state. Hapuna is part of the legendary Mauna Kea Resort (with neighboring Mauna Kea Beach Hotel), offering two championship golf courses, two picture-perfect natural beaches, thirteen oceanside tennis courts, ten restaurants and unlimited recreation options. Hapuna's 350 ocean-facing guest rooms and suites have private lanai, TV/VCR (with video games), dataports, coffeemaker, refrigerator, bathrobes, slippers and other deluxe amenities. Guests are greeted with tropical juice and chilled *oshibori* towels. The 4,000-square-foot Hapuna Suite is an exclusive private villa with three bedrooms, kitchen, living room, dining room, den and private swimming pool, jacuzzi and large lanai overlooking the ocean. Attendants serve morning breakfast and evening *pupus*, and see to your special requests.

The hotel has a large whale-shaped swimming pool, health and fitness center, salon and day spa, resort shops and on-site services such as rental cars, helicopter flight seeing, and ocean activities. There are several restaurants and lounges. Babysitting can be arranged through the concierge. The scenic Hapuna Golf Course was designed by Arnold Palmer and Ed Seay, offering challenging links-style play from sea level to 700-foot elevation. Guests also have access to the famed Mauna Kea Golf Course designed by Robert Trent Jones, Sr., in 1965, and tennis buffs are welcome at the Mauna Kea Tennis Park. Hapuna Ballroom accommodates up to 900 guests for banquets, weddings and other special functions. Excellent conference facilities are available with full-service staff, business center, and dramatic indoor and outdoor locations. Value-added packages and promotional rates are available throughout the year, as well as internet deals. Please inquire when making reservations. Luxurious Vacation Residences are also available, 808-880-3490.

Rates: Terrace View $360, Partial Oceanview $410, Oceanview $460, Premium Oceanview $510, Oceanfront $610, Oceanfront Suite $1,250; Hapuna Suite $7,000

★ *Hilton Waikoloa Village*

425 Waikoloa Beach Drive, Kohala Coast, HI 96743-9791. 800-HILTONS; 808-886-1234; fax 808-886-2900; e-mail: waikoloa_rooms@hilton.com; www.hiltonwaikoloavillage.com.

At 1,240 rooms (57 are suites), this is the Kohala Coast's largest resort hotel. And, appropriate to the Big Island, everything here is done on a grand scale. The hotel occupies 62 acres lavishly landscaped $120 like a huge oasis in the black lava desert. Water is the theme here, and water features are everywhere. The lush gardens are accented with meandering streams and waterfalls, pools and ponds. Guests travel through the resort via canal boats that cruise over a mile of waterways, or quiet tram trains that shuttle from one end of the resort to the other. Water babies of all ages can indulge in the Ocean Tower pool, the Kohala River Pool with a series of waterslides, or the Kona Pool, complete with waterfalls, whirlpools and a giant 175-foot waterslide. The four-acre ocean-fed lagoon is a giant living aquarium with a rainbow of tropical reef fish and marine life. The famed Dolphin Quest program provides hands-on educational experiences for hotel guests, working and playing with Atlantic bottlenose dolphins. Guests can also stroll the mile-long open-air museum walkway filled with a vast collection of Pacific and Asian artworks. The Hilton hosts 18 boutique and resort shops with everything from sundry items to fine jewelry, original art, handcrafts and fashion resort wear. Additional amenities include several restaurants, a gym and spa, two golf courses and tennis courts.

Other activities that can be arranged by the activities desk include varied in-hotel tours, horseback riding, catamaran sails, snorkel-dive cruises, deep-sea fishing, petroglyph tours, scenic flights and much more. "Legends of the Pacific" luau feast and hula show is presented weekly. With so many guest rooms, Hilton naturally caters to large groups. Meeting facilities include 21 meeting rooms and full-service banquet and convention services staff who specialize in creative theme events. The Hilton is also the only hotel on the island with tele-conference capability. The Hilton's emphasis on attentive aloha-style service in all areas, plus their incredible variety of energetic activities, makes this a family-friendly resort, offering a lot of fun without ever leaving the property. Inquire about value-added packages.

Rates: Garden View/Mountain View $400, Part Oceanview $460, Ocean Accommodations $530, Hilton Executive Floor Accommodations $580, 1BR Bay Suite $875, 2BR Bay Suite $1,200, 1BR Royal Suite $1,545, 2BR Royal Suite $1,945, 2BR Presidential Suite $4,920; $35 extra person

Kohala Village Inn

19.55-514 Hawi Road, intersection of Highways 270 and 250, Hawi, HI 96719. 808-889-0419.

The affordable plantation/island-style rooms in this North Kohala Coast inn are clean and simple, all with private bath and TV. There are 17 guest rooms, which can accommodate up to four people. Easy access to Hawi and Kapa'au towns, which are both growing into colorful art communities with a variety of interesting shops and restaurants. Nearby activities include beautiful Pololu Valley for hiking or horseback riding, explorations of Mo'okini Heiau and King Kamehameha's Birthplace and seasonal whale watching. The inn has all the country charm of a very small town and friendly folks. There's also good quality food in the dining room.

Rates: $55

★ *Kona Village Resort*

P.O. Box 1299, Kailua-Kona, HI 96745. 800-367-5290; 808-325-5555; fax 808-325-5124; e-mail: kvr@aloha.net; www.konavillage.com.

Kona Village is something special. The first resort to occupy the coast and the only one to remain virtually unchanged since its creation almost 40 years ago, this is the Big Island's most thoughtfully authentic, truly unique resort experience. Situated on the beach at Kahuwai Bay, Kona Village stretches along the coastline in a leisurely fashion. There is no central hotel building; 125 separate thatch-roofed *hale* (houses) are the guest rooms. The *hale* reflect the traditional design and decor of the South Pacific Islands including Hawai'i, Tahiti, Fiji and the Marquesas. All guest *hale* have modern conveniences like a large bathroom, ceiling fan, comfortable, quality tropical furniture, coffeemaker and refrigerator, and lanai with lounges or beach hammocks. What it doesn't have are room phones, TVs or radios to disturb the peace and quiet. The only clock in your *hale* is on the coffeemaker. We suggest you ignore it, remove your watch and experience what it feels like to live on your own personal schedule. This is a magical, escapist's retreat. Appreciate it.

Excellent food and personable service are offered in the dining rooms. The resort also has cocktails and nightly entertainment. A selection of Honeymoon/Celebration packages are available seasonally and romance is encouraged during May and September, when children's programs and rates are temporarily on hold. A professional wedding coordinator on staff assists with heavenly weddings in a variety of stunning tropical settings. Kona Village has received wide acclaim and recognition from international travel guides and publications such as *Fortune*, *Travel & Leisure*, *Condé Nast Traveler*, *Gourmet Magazine* and many others. It is also winner of the prestigious Kahili Award for historic preservation from the Hawaii Visitors and Convention Bureau. Three generations of returning guests are testimony to Kona Village's success as a truly unique and valuable destination. Guest room rates include breakfast, lunch and dinner for two.

Rates: One-room *hale*: Standard $515, Moderate $650, Superior $725, Deluxe $805, Royal $910; Two-room *hale*: Garden $850, Superior $935, Deluxe $1,025, Royal $1,125; additional guests infant to two years free, 3 to 5 $38, 6 to 12 $143, 13 and up $193

★ Mauna Kea Beach Hotel

62-100 Mauna Kea Beach Drive, Kohala Coast, HI 96743. 866-PRINCE-6; 808-882-7222; fax 808-882-5700; e-mail: mkrres@maunakeabeachhotel.com; www.maunakeabeachhotel.com.

This is the property that started it all and set the bar very high for Big Island hospitality. Created by American conservationist Laurance S. Rockefeller in 1965, its $15 million price tag was the highest ever paid to build a hotel. Today, the Mauna Kea is still one of the best destinations in the world.

Guests are still welcomed with a plumeria lei, in the timeless tradition of aloha. Together with its sister property, Hapuna Beach Prince Hotel, Mauna Kea offers two of Hawaii's best beaches, two golf courses, thirteen tennis courts, ten restaurants and unlimited options for recreation, accessible to guests via complimentary inter-resort shuttle.

The 310 guest rooms and suites have ocean, mountain or beachfront views and feature large private lanais, generous closet space, comfortable island furnishings and appointments, coffeemaker, chill box, bottled water, in-room safe, robes and slippers. You can have your TV removed by request and we'd like to suggest that you take a vacation from the TV, too, and rediscover the pleasures of conversation, quiet and the sounds of nature in this very special setting. The Mauna Kea tradition of fine dining is expressed in its restaurants. The Mauna Kea food and beverage staff is room service specialists. Particularly in the mornings, extra care is taken to provide a pleasant dining experience on your private lanai, with fresh flowers and a tablecloth, iced juice, hot coffee and warm smiles. They even provide a toaster.

The hotel also houses a remarkable collection of museum-quality Pacific and Asian arts and artifacts, which includes 30 handmade Hawaiian quilts, the largest collection in Hawai'i. Complimentary tours are offered weekly, as are tours of the hotel's gardens, mature specimen trees and lush tropical landscaping. Other resort features include elegant locations for celebrations, a full range of salon services and spa therapies, artfully designed freshwater pool with jacuzzi, fitness center, yoga and other exercise classes, a program of Hawaiian arts and crafts, and boutique shops. Babysitting can be arranged with the concierge. The main event is the beach. Proclaimed the nation's #1 beach in 2000 by the "Dr. Beach" annual ratings, Kauna'oa Beach is a crescent of white sand with generally tranquil waters. Packages are available seasonally, as well as internet "hot deals." The holiday period between Christmas and New Year's is traditionally sold out a year in advance. The Mauna Kea is consistently rated among top U.S. resorts in *Condé Nast Traveler, Travel & Leisure* and *Andrew Harper's Hideaway Report.* They enjoy a loyal population of returning guests, who, combined with the genuinely hospitable nature of the staff, create a sense of family, tradition and care. It makes a difference. Luxurious Vacation Residences are also available, 808-880-3490.

Rates: Mountain View $360, Premier Mountain View $380, Beachfront floors two through four $565, Beachfront first floor $600, Deluxe Oceanview $590, Premier Oceanview $650

★ *Mauna Lani Bay Hotel and Bungalows*

68-1400 Mauna Lani Drive, Kohala Coast, HI 96743-9796. 808-885-6622; 800-367-2323; fax 808-885-1484; e-mail: reservations@maunalani.com; www.maunalani.com.

This sleek, elegant 350-room property sits on 29 lush, oceanfront acres with 36 holes of championship golf, tennis courts, beach activities, luxury spa and fitness center, excellent dining and Hawaiian cultural and archaeological sites. Built in 1983, the Mauna Lani has earned accolades from *Condé Nast Traveler*, *Travel & Leisure* and other national travel publications. The hotel fronts beautiful Makaiwa Bay Beach at Kalahuipua'a, and all but 27 guest rooms have ocean views thanks to the building's unique shape. The remainder face tropical gardens and Hawaiian fishponds. Guest rooms are very spacious at 550-plus square feet and elegantly appointed with private lanai, TV and VCR, refrigerator, air conditioning, mini-bar, dataports, robes, slippers, coffee, daily newspaper and many other high-end amenities. Fully equipped 1BR, 2BR and 3BR villas are available at Mauna Lani Terrace within the resort, ideal for families. Guests of the villas enjoy full hotel privileges with the exception of room service. Mauna Lani also offers five individual bungalows. These are private, 4,000-square-foot accommodations, each with two master bedroom suites and three baths, attended by round-the-clock butlers who tailor personal service to suit the most discriminating tastes. Babysitting can be arranged through the concierge.

Rates: Mountain View $418, Garden View $488, Oceanview $622, Deluxe Oceanview $672, Oceanfront $736, Deluxe Oceanfront $768, Corner Oceanfront $812, Suites $1,298, Oceanview Bungalow $4,900, Oceanfront Bungalow $5,600; The Villas: 1BR $550, 2BR $715, 3BR $910

★ *Waikoloa Beach Marriott, An Outrigger Resort*

69-275 Waikoloa Beach Drive, Kohala Coast, HI 96743. Reservations: Outrigger Hotels Hawaii 800-688-7444; 808-886-6789; fax 800-622-4852 or 808-886-7852; www.waikoloabeachmarriott.com.

This elegant 547-room hotel is located just off the beautiful half-mile crescent-shaped 'Anaeho'omalu Bay Beach and lagoon. A dramatic 40-foot mural by noted island artist Herb Kane graces one side of the lobby. The painting shows Captain George Vancouver's ship, *Discovery*, being escorted into 'Anaeho'omalu Bay by a Hawaiian sailing canoe with the imposing Mauna Kea and Kohala Mountains in the background. The mural sits behind the hotel's century-old Hawaiian outrigger canoe, *Kaimalino*. Guest rooms have garden, mountain or ocean views and come with TV, radio, refrigerator, robes, coffee and tea service, dataports and daily maid service. There is also a separate "Voyagers Club," located on the top floor of the Ka'ahumanu Wing, operated as a special concierge section of the hotel with a separate staff and first-class services such as complimentary continental breakfast and sunset cocktails. Other amenities include restaurants and lounges, a ballroom, a salon and spa, and beach activities. With ‘Anaeho‘omalu Beach and its historic fishponds fronting the hotel, this is one of the loveliest settings along the Kohala Coast. Guests have access to the excellent Waikoloa Beach Resort golf at the Kings' Course, designed by Tom Weiskopf and Jay Morris, and the Beach Course, designed by Robert Trent Jones, Jr. There are six tennis courts and an "action pool" with a 90-foot water slide. Guests of the hotel also have charging privileges at restaurants across the street in the Kings' Shops complex. Complimentary shuttle service is provided. Babysitting can be arranged through the concierge.

Rates: Garden/Mountain View $325, Partial Oceanview $350, Oceanview $400, Garden/Mountain State Room $385, Oceanview $400, Oceanview State Room $465, Oceanfront $485, Cabana $535. 1BR Suite $965, 1BR Cabana $1,065, Royal Suite $3,100

Waimea Town

BED AND BREAKFASTS

aaah The Views B&B

66-1773 Alaneo Street, P.O. Box 6593, Kamuela, HI 96743. 800-885-3455; 808-885-3455; fax 808-885-4031; e-mail: tommare@aloha.net; www.beingsintouch.com.

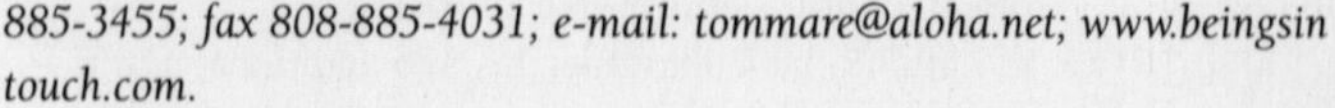

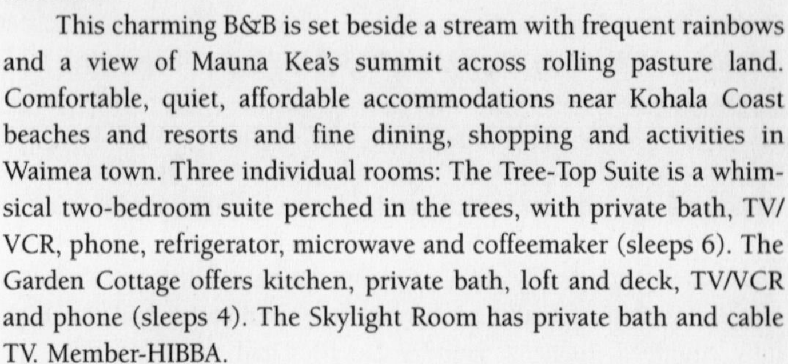

This charming B&B is set beside a stream with frequent rainbows and a view of Mauna Kea's summit across rolling pasture land. Comfortable, quiet, affordable accommodations near Kohala Coast beaches and resorts and fine dining, shopping and activities in Waimea town. Three individual rooms: The Tree-Top Suite is a whimsical two-bedroom suite perched in the trees, with private bath, TV/VCR, phone, refrigerator, microwave and coffeemaker (sleeps 6). The Garden Cottage offers kitchen, private bath, loft and deck, TV/VCR and phone (sleeps 4). The Skylight Room has private bath and cable TV. Member-HIBBA.

Rates: $75-$110

Belle Vue B&B

1351 Konokohau Road, P.O. Box 1295, Kamuela, HI 96743. 800-772-5044; phone/fax 808-885-7732; e-mail: bellvue@aloha.net; www.kona-bed-breakfast.com. Reservations also through Hawai‘i's Best B&Bs, P.O. Box 520, Kamuela, HI 96743; 800-262-9912; 808-885-4550; fax 808-885-0559; e-mail: reservations@bestbnb.com; www.bestbnb.com.

This is a spacious two-story cottage bordering the open pasturelands of famous Parker Ranch in Waimea. There is a kitchen and cozy fireplace. There are upstairs and downstairs units (each sleeps four).

Walking distance to restaurants and shopping. German, French and Italian spoken here. Member-Hawai'i's Best, HIBBA.

Rates: $85-$165; $25 extra person

★ *Cook's Discoveries' Waimea Suite*

P.O. Box 6960, Kamuela, HI 96743-6960. 808-885-3633; 808-937-2833; e-mail: cookshi@aol.com; www.hawaii-island.com/cooks.htm.

This is something special. Stop in Cook's Discoveries everything-Hawai'i shop for the key to this spacious, secluded hideaway in the green-on-green foothills of Waimea, surrounded by wide lawns and towering specimen trees of *ohia*, *koa*, jacaranda, magnolia, cypress and avocado. You won't find a more accommodating, island-worldly and gracious hostess than owner Patti Cook, and her Waimea Suite has all the comforts of a Big Island home filled with aloha and a delightful mix of old and new Hawai'i. The Suite comfortably accommodates four guests with two bedrooms, private bath, fully equipped kitchen, living room with fireplace and outdoor dining lanai. Old-fashioned Hawaiiana, all-*koa* living room, fine art, library and other nostalgic appointments blend well with more modern comforts such as cable TV/VCR, phone, microwave and CD player. Rates include breakfast provisions and milk and cookies for a bedtime snack, plus a $20 gift certificate (for direct bookings only) for treasures and *omiyage* (gifts) from the shop. Smoke-free property.

Rates: $135; $15 additional *keiki* under 12, $25 additional adults

Ekolu K Ohana Farm

P.O. Box 1621, Kamuela, HI 96743. 808-885-0525; e-mail: ekofarm@gte.net; www.localaccess.com/ekofarm.

We give credit to Ekolu K Ohana Farm for having one of the cuter websites around, with "translations" in English and pidgin. The accommodations are large and comfortable, located on the *mauka* (mountain) side of Waimea town among the fields of a working protea flower farm, with lovely views of Mauna Kea on clear days. A studio, 1BR and 2BR cottage all have private entry and bath (2 in the 2BR), fully equipped kitchens, laundry facilities and welcome basket of baked goods, coffee, fruit and juice and the farm's own *poha* jams and other goodies.

Rates: $60-$170

★ *Jacaranda Inn*

808-885-8813. Reservations through: Hawai'i's Best B&B, P.O. Box 520, Kamuela, HI 96743. 800-262-9912; 808-885-4550; fax 808-885-0559; e-mail: reservations@bestbnb.com; www.bestbnb.com.

The Jacaranda Inn is one of Waimea's most historic homes and is prominent in the history of Big Island ranching. Built in 1897 as the private residence of an early Parker Ranch manager, the home was purchased by Laurence Rockefeller in 1961 while he built the Mauna Kea Beach Hotel down on the coast. Over the years, the inn welcomed numerous VIPs and celebrities, and was used as the general manager's residence. There are eight spacious and luxurious guest suites in the main house and a separate three-bedroom and three-bathroom cottage for families or groups. Guests have access to a breakfast room, formal dining room, library/billiard room and lounge. Six of the guest suites feature a sitting room and large bath with whirlpool tub. One room is ADA compliant. The 11-acre site is next to a seasonal stream and waterfall on the west edge of Waimea on Kawaihae Road just minutes away from Kohala Coast resorts, beaches, golf and recreation. Nearby Waimea town offers several fine restaurants, shopping, activities and more. Member-Hawai'i's Best.

Rates: $95-$225

Kamuela's Mauna Kea View Suite and Cottage

P.O. Box 6375, Kamuela, HI 96743. 808-885-8425; e-mail: maunakea view1@webtv.net; www.hawaii-inns.com/bigisle/kohala/maunakea.

This home offers wide open pastoral ranchland views backdropped with Mauna Kea. There is a private suite with 2BRs, living room and kitchen. There is also an attached cottage with chalet-design living room, kitchenette, fireplace, etc. All have queen beds, color TV and phone. Convenient to area attractions and Kohala Coast resorts.

Rates: $70-$85; $15 extra person

Merry's Herb Garden

Reservations through Hawai'i's Best B&Bs, P.O. Box 520, Kamuela, HI 96743. 800-262-9912; 808-885-4550; fax 808-885-0559; e-mail: reserva tions@bestbnb.com; www.bestbnb.com.

This attractive country home reflects the ranching history of Waimea and old Hawai'i. There's an attached 2BR wing with private entrance. It opens to lush green pastures and a distant view of rising Mauna Kea Mountain. The open-beamed ceilings and walls of pane-glass windows accent a spacious living room highlighted by ranch-style furniture and decor. The living room has a dining table plus small refrigerator, microwave, TV/VCR and phone.

Rates: $110; $15 extra person

Papa Iki

Reservations through Hawai'i's Best B&Bs, P.O. Box 520, Kamuela, HI 96743. 800-262-9912; 808-885-4550; fax 808-885-0559; e-mail: reserva tions@bestbnb.com; www.bestbnb.com.

This island-style home is located just two miles from the best beaches on the Kohala Coast in the Puako residential community. It's a nicely kept 2BR/2bath cottage with full kitchen, oceanfront deck, barbecue, TV/VCR, stereo and phone. Nicely furnished throughout;

ceiling fans keep the breeze circulating. There is one king bed and a pair of twins.

Rates: $250

Waimea Gardens Cottage

Reservations through Hawai'i's Best B&Bs, P.O. Box 520, Kamuela, HI 96743. 800-262-9912; 808-885-4550; fax 808-885-0559; e-mail: reservations@bestbnb.com; www.bestbnb.com.

This streamside cottage has three private units on 1.5 acres. The cottage's Kohala and Waimea wings have antique furnishings, patio French doors and decor that lend a pleasant country atmosphere. Three-night minimum stay. Member-Hawai'i's Best.

Rates: $135-$155; $15 extra person

HOTELS, HOSTELS AND HOMES

Kamuela Inn

P.O. Box 1994, Kamuela, HI 96743. 800-555-8968; 808-885-4243; fax 808-885-8857; e-mail: kaminn@aloha.net; www.kamuelainn.com.

This country inn features 31 comfortable standard and kitchenette rooms with TV. The newer Mauna Kea Wing has several comfortable, spacious, well-decorated rooms, two executive suites and a bright cozy coffee lanai where daily continental breakfast is provided. The original wing's rooms are smaller and simpler but very well kept and clean. Located in a quiet, cool setting across from Edelweiss Restaurant off Highway 19 in Kamuela town, only 15 miles from Kohala Coast resorts and beaches. Reservations should be made well in advance.

Rates: Standard Single/Double $59, Deluxe $72; Suite (max 3) with kitchen $89, Suite (max 4) with kitchen $99, Penthouse Suite (max 5) $99; Mauna Kea Wing: King Beds $85, Two Twins $79, Executive Suites $185

Waimea Country Lodge

65-1210 Lindsey Road, Kamuela, HI 96743. 808-885-4100; fax 808-885-6711. Agents: Castle Resorts & Hotels 800-367-5004, fax 808-596-0158, www.castleresorts.com; Maui & All Islands 800-663-6962.

This small 21-unit country motel features spacious rooms all with TV and two king or queen beds. Clean pleasant furnishings, TV and phone with nice meadow and mountain views of Waimea ranch country. Adjacent to Paniolo Country Inn restaurant and nearby shopping, other restaurants and area attractions. It's only a 15-mile drive to the Kohala Coast resorts and beaches.

Rates: Standard $95, Superior $100, Studio Kitchenette $110, Deluxe $120; $1 extra person

Hamakua Coast

BED AND BREAKFASTS

★ *Akiko's Buddhist Bed & Breakfast*

P.O. Box 272, Wailea/Hakalau, HI 96710. 808-963-6422; e-mail: msakiko@aloha.net; www.alternative-hawaii.com/akiko.

Located 15 miles north of Hilo, this peaceful, simple and quiet retreat is hosted by island-born Akiko Masuda. Enjoy walks down main street Wailea town, past green plantation houses with weathered tin roofs, yards bursting in a jubilee of trees, shrubs and flowers of infinite variety in a once-thriving plantation community. Akiko invites her guests to return home to a time when life was simple and gracious. Weekly/monthly rates available.

Rates: $40 single, $55 double; $5 extra person

Hale Kukui

P.O. Box 5044, Kukuihaele, HI 96727. 800-444-7130; 808-775-7130; e-mail: retreat@halekukui.com; halekukui.com.

There are a private studio and 2BR and luxury cottage units on four acres of high cliff overlooking the Waipi'o Valley and towering coastline bluffs. Waipi'o Valley activities available include hiking in tropical rainforest, biking, swimming, surfing, horseback rides, mule wagon rides and 4x4 vehicle tours. Located in lush, landscaped grounds with a tropical setting. Units have private bath, kitchen and outdoor tubs.

Rates: Studio $125, 2BR $160, luxury cottage $175

The Log Cabin

P.O. Box 1994, Kamuela, HI 96743. 800-555-9868; 808-885-4243; fax 808-885-8857; e-mail: kaminn@aloha.net; www.kamuelainn.com.

This country log house is operated as the Kamuela Inn's guesthouse and is located a few miles east of Waimea in the upcountry Ahualoa area. The house is at the 2,500-foot elevation level in a cool, lush forest, minutes from Waimea and Honoka'a towns, Waipi'o Valley and other attractions and activities. The lodge-style house has five comfortable and well-appointed guest rooms. The Ekahi and Elima Rooms have private baths; the Elua, Ekolu and Eha Rooms have a shared bath. There is a spacious open-beam-ceiling living room with stone fireplace, library and TV and a large bright kitchen and dining room. Guests share access to an oriental-style gazebo hot tub. Two-night minimum stay.

Rates: Room/shared bath $59, Room/private bath $99, entire log cabin $375

Mountain Meadow Ranch B&B

46-3895 Kapuna Road, Ahualoa, HI 96727. Phone/fax 808-775-9376; e-mail: bill@mountainmeadowranch.com; www.mountainmeadowranch.com.

Located halfway between Kona and Hilo in romantic Ahualoa, high above the Hamakua Coast, Mountain Meadow is comprised of two separate units, each with its own charm and personality. The Main House B&B is the lower level of a large redwood ranch home, with two bedrooms and a common area with TV/VCR, book and video library, sauna, microwave and refrigerator. The Vacation Home is tucked away in a private part of the Mountain Meadow, with two bedrooms, full kitchen, laundry, TV/VCR and a wood stove. Scenic pastures and majestic trees provide lots of country charm and atmosphere on this seven-acre estate. Enjoy scenic areas like Waipi'o Valley, Parker Ranch, Mauna Kea and Waimea.

Rates: B&B $70-$80, Cottage $125

Our Place B&B

P.O. Box 469, 3 Mamalahoa Highway, Papaikou, HI 96781. 808-964-5250; e-mail: rplace@aloha.net; www.ourplacebandb.com.

Located four miles north of Hilo off Highway 19, this is a large cedar home with three guest rooms with cable TV. A common lanai, open to each bedroom, overlooks a stream and tropical vegetation; Great Room features a library, fireplace and grand piano. No smoking indoors. Easy access to snorkeling and surfing, botanical gardens, Hawai'i Volcanoes National Park, and shopping and dining in Hilo. Two-night minimum stay. Member-HIBBA.

Rates: $50-$90

★ Paauhau Plantation House

1 Kalopa Road, P.O. Box 1375, Honoka'a, HI 96727. 808-775-7222; fax 808-775-7223; e-mail: lars@deike.de; www.bbhost.com/bbpaauhauplantation.

This is a special place, although its grander days are in the past. When most of the Hamakua Coast was occupied by sugar cane plantations, this was the manager's estate. The main house on the hill overlooks a rolling green lawn, old-fashioned gardens, tall specimen trees and tropical flowers, with the sparkling ocean beyond. There are four self-contained cottages at the back of the property; each sleep four or more. The once-elegant (and still lovely), rambling main house has a Master Suite with private bath, and a second bedroom, the Yellow Room, to accommodate six guests comfortably. The house was designed for plantation entertaining, with a spacious ranch kitchen and breakfast room, a formal dining room to seat 30, a drawing room with grand piano and a library/TV room. High ceilings, antique furnishings and a sense of history make Paauhau an old-fashioned, romantic retreat. English, Spanish, French, German spoken here.

Rates: Master Suite $200; Yellow Room $100; Kona Cottage $140; Mauka Cottage $110; Hilo Cottage $140; Waimea Cottage $100; $15 extra person

★ *Palms Cliff House Inn*

38-3514 Mamalahoa Highway, Honomu, HI 96728-0189. 808-963-6076; e-mail: palmscliffhouse@aol.com; www.palmscliffhouse.com.

Located 15 minutes north of Hilo town, this secluded Victorian-style estate features eight suites with private baths and lanais, and amenities like private jacuzzis with ocean views, gourmet breakfasts, afternoon tea, yoga and cooking classes. Recognized by *Travel & Leisure* and earning a reputation as one of the best, this is a place to relax and enjoy all the advantages of a well-run B&B.

Rates: $150-$275

★ *Waianuhea*

P.O. Box 185, Honoka'a, HI 96727; 888-775-2577; 808-775-1118; fax 888-296-6302; e-mail: waianuha@starband.net; www.waianuhea.com.

This is a special place, too, offering a more contemporary perspective from a secluded, peaceful *mauka* (mountain) location 2,500 feet above the Hamakua Coast. Waianuhea offers five distinctive guest rooms, each with its own Hawaiian name and individual personality. All are complete with private baths, TV/DVD and CD players and internet access. The bigger accommodations have large soaking tubs and gas or wood stoves. A hot gourmet breakfast is provided daily, or continental breakfast in your room if you prefer. Privacy is their specialty, but your hosts can arrange massage, island tours and other activities to fill your time. A great relaxation room with treatment area and outdoor solar-heated jacuzzi are available in the common area. It's also a nice location for intimate weddings, retreats and exclusive workshops.

Rates: $150-$300

★ *Waipi'o Wayside B&B*

P.O. Box 840, Honoka'a, HI 96727. 800-833-8849; phone/fax 808-775-0275; e-mail wayside@bigisland.net; www.waipiowayside.com.

This is a refurbished 1932-era sugar plantation home, with colorful tropical flowers and plants decorating the grounds. There are five bedrooms, all with private bath: Moon Room with full-size bed and garden view, Plantation Room with double beds, Chinese Room with full-size bed, Bird's Eye Room with queen bed, and Library Room with queen bed and ocean view. Easy access to Waipi'o Valley, Waipi'o Ridge Walk, Kalopa Park, the Hamakua Coast and Waimea town. Member-HIBBA.

Rates: $95-$155; $25 extra person

HOTELS, HOSTELS AND HOMES

Hotel Honoka'a Club

P.O. Box 247, Mamane Street, Honoka'a, HI 96727. 800-808-0678; phone/fax 808-775-0678; e-mail: cathy@hotelhona.com; www.hotelhono.com.

This rambling old wooden building has been a Honoka'a landmark for years, centrally located on the main street of town off Highway 19. Two different types of accommodations are available: backpacker rooms and hotel rooms. The backpacker rooms are inexpensive, basic lodging in dormitory rooms or private rooms with shared baths. Hotel rooms (all nonsmoking) offer cable TV, private bath, queen-size beds and continental breakfast. Corner guest rooms have ocean views.

Rates: Dorm $15, Backpacker $25-$35, Standard $50-$55, Oceanview $60-$70

Waipi'o Lookout Vacation Rentals

P.O. Box 5022, Kukuihaele, HI 96727. 877-924-7464; 808-775-1306; e-mail: waipiohi@interpac.net.

Hale Ono is a one-bedroom country rental on the cliffs overlooking the majestic Waipi'o Valley. Expect gorgeous sweeping coastal vistas, cliffs and cascading waterfalls. Forty acres of pasture with grazing horses complete the view. The rental has a queen bed, living room with full-size futon, a full bathroom, lanai, cable TV and phone; it sleeps up to four. It's a 30-minute walk down to the valley's black-sand beach. The quiet village of Kukuihaele is a short stroll away; larger Honoka'a town is nine miles away and has shopping and dining.

Rates: $85; $15 extra person; $510/week

Waipi'o Ridge Vacation Rentals

P.O. Box 5039, Kukuihaele, HI 96727. 808-775-0603.

This renter has a one-bedroom home, which sleeps 4; it's fully furnished with refrigerator, microwave oven, coffee maker, fans, television, etc. Located near the Waipi'o Valley.

Rates: $75-$85

Hilo

BED AND BREAKFASTS

Bay House

42 Pukihae, Hilo, HI 96720. 808-961-6311; e-mail: bigbayhouse@excite.com; www.bayhousehawaii.com. Reservations through Hawai'i's Best B&Bs, P.O. Box 520, Kamuela, HI 96743. 800-262-9912; 808-885-4550; fax 808-885-0559; e-mail: reservations@bestbnb.com; www.bestbnb.com.

This attractive home overlooks Hilo Bay from a bluff setting. Guests enjoy oceanfront bedrooms with private bayside decks, private baths, TVs, and a sumptuous breakfast with a view and a hot tub. Historic downtown Hilo is a short five-minute walk away; easy access to east Hawai'i attractions and activities. The home is wheelchair accessible. Each room sleeps two. Member-Hawai'i's Best, HIBBA.

Rates: $105-$120

Hale Kai Hawai'i B&B

Honoli'i Pali, Hilo, HI 96720. 808-935-6330; e-mail: stay@halekai hawaii.com; www.halekaihawaii.com.

This custom home perches on a *pali* (cliff) above the ocean two miles from downtown Hilo. Five bedrooms each have ocean views and private baths, king or queen beds and cable TV. Gourmet breakfast is served daily and the house is decorated with the owner's dramatic photography. Easy access to area attractions. Two-night minimum stay.

Rates: $95-$115; $15 extra person

Hilo Oceanfront B&B

1923 Kalanianaole, Hilo, HI 96720. 800-363-9524; 808-934-9004; fax 808-934-7128; e-mail: oceanfrt@gte.net; www.hilooceanfront.com.

This beachside home is located in the Keaukaha area of Hilo four miles from the center of town. The two units have private entrance, bath, king bed, kitchenette, TV/VCR and phone. The Dolphin Studio has a private deck overlooking the beachside ponds. The Whale Suite has air conditioning and a large living room and opens onto a deck with hot tub. Easy access to all east Hawai'i attractions and activities, dining, shopping etc. Member-HIBBA.

Rates: Dolphin Studio $105; Whale Suite $110; $10 extra person

Hilo Seaside Retreat

P.O. Box 10960, 1941 Kalanianaole, Hilo, HI 96721. 800-961-9602; phone/fax 808-961-6178; e-mail: pattio@aloha.net; www.hilo-inns.com.

This is a contemporary three-bedroom home with an adjoining apartment suite on a half-acre of tropical lawns and gardens leading to a private beach and ocean tidal pools; it's located in the Keaukaha area of Hilo just minutes from downtown. The Seaside Suite apartment unit has bedroom, living room, bath and kitchenette with private entrance and sleeps four or five; Master Suite bedroom has private bath, lanai access and ocean view and sleeps two; Lanai Room has lanai access and ocean view and sleeps two. Guests have use of jacuzzi, Japanese furo bath, private beach for swimming and snorkeling, and onsite massage therapy. Enjoy pleasant oceanside environment, listen to the soothing surf, forget the rest of the world for a while. Easy access to all east Hawai'i attractions and activities. Member-HIBBA.

Rates: $103-$135

Holmes' Sweet Home B&B

107 Koula Street, Hilo, HI 96720. 808-961-9089; fax 808-934-0711; e-mail: homswhom@gte.net; www.hilohawaiibandb.com.

This island home has two guest units each with private bath, lanai, entrance and queen beds. There are also a sitting room and dining room to enjoy a fresh island breakfast; quiet private location with sweeping views of Hilo Bay. Member-HIBBA.

Rates: $70-$85; $10 extra person

Maureen's B&B

1896 Kalanianaole, Hilo, HI 96720. 808-935-9018; fax 808-961-5596; e-mail: info@maureenbnb.com; www.maureenbnb.com.

This lodging is the old Saiki family mansion (c. 1932) located in the Keaukaha area of Hilo, opposite James Kealoha Beach Park, four miles from town just past the Mauna Loa Shores condo high-rise. The home is lovely redwood and cedar finished with a huge open-beam cathedral ceiling in the living room. Arched doorways and windows give this home a touch of New England. Dual staircases wind up to open balconies and guest rooms, with quaint antique furniture pieces, bookcases and artwork to make this inviting lodging seem almost like a gallery. Five guest rooms accommodate two singles and four doubles, a total of ten guests. With the beach right across the street, swimming, snorkeling and sunning are steps away. There is also cable TV/VCR. Children under 7 years old are not allowed due to high stairs and balcony areas.

Rates: $50-$100

★ ***Shipman House B&B***

131 Kai'ulani Street, Hilo, HI 96720. 800-627-8447; phone/fax 808-934-8002; e-mail: bighouse@bigisland.com; hilo-hawaii.com. Reservations through Hawai'i's Best B&Bs, P.O. Box 520, Kamuela, HI 96743; 800-262-9912; 808-885-4550; fax 808-885-0559; e-mail: reservations@bestbnb.com; www.bestbnb.com.

The Shipman House is special. This elegant Victorian-style home dates from 1900 and has been home to the Shipman family since 1901. The home is on both the State and National Historic Registers. Now owned by the Shipmans' great-granddaughter's family, it's one of Hilo's most historic B&Bs. The main home features a wide wraparound lanai and three-story rounded tower with conical roof, reason for local children to call the home "the Castle." The home is on 5.5 acres including a magnificent tropical gulch and is landscaped with tropical fruit trees, handsome palms and flowering plants. One guest room in the main house has twin beds; two other upstairs rooms have queens; two guest rooms in the separate 1910 guesthouse have queen beds. All rooms have ceiling fans, private baths, TVs and refrigerators. The historic home is lovingly restored throughout with much original furniture and period pieces, original heirloom china, ceramics and objets d'art. Expanded continental breakfast is served on the lanai. The Shipman House is a living early-20th-century museum where you can experience history first-hand. Stay where Jack London and his wife Charmian stayed for a month while visiting Hilo in 1907. Sit at the same dining table where Queen Liliuokalani, Hawai'i's last monarch, was entertained during Hilo visits in the early 1900s. This is the inn for guests who love an immersion in the local history, culture, charm and authentic hospitality of old Hawai'i. Member-Hawai'i's Best, HIBBA.

Rates: from $149; $25 extra person

Wild Ginger Inn

100 Pu'ueo Street, Hilo, HI 96720. 800-882-1887; 808-935-5556; www.wildgingerinnhilo.com.

This quaint old-fashioned inn dates from 1947 and is easily spotted on a rainy Hilo day by its bright tropical pink exterior. The 27 guest rooms provide essential accommodations with private baths (except for two rooms). Good quality breakfasts feature fresh Hawaiian fruits and bakery-delivered organic multigrain breads, Portuguese sweetbreads and more. Occasional on-site barbecue parties offer a chance to meet fellow travelers, backpackers and families. Two blocks from downtown Hilo dining and shopping.

Rates: $50-$90

HOTELS, HOSTELS AND HOMES

★ Arnott's Lodge

Apapane Road, Hilo, HI 96720. 808-969-7097; e-mail: info@arnottslodge.com; www.arnottslodge.com.

These people go the extra mile to provide backpackers and adventurers with a quality, affordable vacation. The lodge is located in the Keaukaha area of Hilo near the beach parks, offering private and bunk rooms with shared bathrooms, a common kitchen and TV room. Some units have private kitchen and bath. They offer added services such as an around-the-island "Big Island Experience," with stops at important historical and cultural sites and daily hiking excursions including Hawai'i Volcanoes National Park, Mauna Kea Summit, Hilo Waterfalls and Puna as well as custom adventure expeditions. Free shuttle service from Hilo International Airport.

Rates: Bunk room $17; Semi-private room $37-$44; Private room $49; Deluxe room $57; 2BR Suite $120; $15 extra person; tenting per person $9

Country Club Condo Hotel

121 Banyan Drive, Hilo, HI 96720. 808-935-7171.

A no-frills lodging with 130 air-conditioned units with phone and TV. Pool, restaurant, cocktail lounge and meeting room are on premises. Located across the street from Naniloa Country Club golf course, within walking distance of Coconut Island and Liliuokalani Park.

Rates: Standard $65, Deluxe $80; $7 extra person

Dolphin Bay Hotel

333 Iliahi Street, Hilo, HI 96720. 808-935-1466; fax 808-935-1523; e-mail: johnhilo@gte.net; www.dolphinbayhilo.com.

This small 18-unit hotel is located in a quiet old residential area of Hilo, four blocks from the downtown area and three blocks from Hilo Bay. There are few amenities other than fans and TV; no room telephones. Kitchen facilities are included in all units. The rooms are bright, airy, spacious and very clean.

Rates: Standard $66, Superior $76, 1BR Suite $89, 2BR Suite $99; $10 extra person

Hawai'i Naniloa Hotel

93 Banyan Drive, Hilo, HI 96720. 808-969-3333; 800-367-5360; fax 808-969-6622; e-mail: hinan@aloha.net; www.planet-hawaii.com/sand/naniloa.

This 325-room tower has long been a Hilo landmark overlooking Hilo Bay. The spacious rooms are air-conditioned with TV. The hotel features two restaurants, and there is a cocktail lounge and a complete health spa/fitness center and resort pool. There is no beach as the shoreline is rugged lava rock. It is located across from the Naniloa Country Club golf course and in the heart of Banyan Drive hotel row; walking distance to Coconut Island and Liliuokalani Park.

Rates: Standard $100, Partial Oceanview $120, Oceanview $140, Partial Oceanview Suites $120, Oceanview Suites $240; $15 extra person

Hilo Bay Hostel

101 Waianuenue Avenue, Hilo, HI 96720. 808-933-2771; e-mail: hawaiihostel@hawaiihostel.net; www.hawaiihostel.net.

Something new for Hilo, an inexpensive lodging in a convenient location right downtown. Located in what claims to be the oldest surviving wooden structure on the island, the fully restored 1913 hotel provides private and dormitory rooms with ceiling fans, a common area with cable TV, storage lockers, billiards table, high-speed internet access, an outdoor patio garden and a kitchen with free coffee and tea. Island tours can be arranged and it's within walking distance to movies, museums, shopping and restaurants.

Rates: from $18

★ *Hilo Hawaiian Hotel*

71 Banyan Drive, Hilo, HI 96720. 808-935-9361. Reservations: Castle Resorts & Hotels 800-367-5004, fax 808-596-0158, e-mail: terry@castle-group.com, www.castle-group.com.

There's something special about Hilo Hawaiian—quiet, unpretentious but genuinely inviting with a wide, attractive lobby overlooking the bay, and easy strolling distance to the "celebrity" banyan trees, Liliuokalani Gardens and Coconut Island. This is a Hilo classic and favorite gathering place for *kama'aina* (residents) in town for family reunions, weddings, sports events or other special occasions. Time spent in the lounge will guarantee you meet some interesting people. With lovely views of Hilo Bay, Coconut Island and the Hilo waterfront, the 235 spacious, comfortable rooms all have TV with movies on demand, private bath, coffeemaker, standard hotel amenities, room service and maid service. Restaurant, cocktail lounge (with live entertainment and dancing on the weekends), coffee shop, meeting rooms and shops are on-site as well as a swimming pool, massage facility and travel agency. The Naniloa Country Club golf course is across the street. We found the suites to be an exceptional value, particularly for families, including equipped kitchen facilities, living-dining area and two TVs. There is a particular charm (for those of us who live on the "dry side" of the island) in waking up to a gentle rain and having our hot Kona coffee out on the lanai as the sun slowly colors a cloudy Hilo morning.

Rates: Standard $120, Superior $150, Junior Suite $185, 2BR Suite, Oceanview Suite $365; $17 extra person

Hilo Seaside Hotel

126 Banyan Drive, Hilo, HI 96720. Reservations: Sand & Seaside Hotels 800-560-5557, 808-935-0821, fax 808-969-9195, e-mail: info@sand-seaside.com, www.sand-seaside.com.

This 150-room hotel is located just opposite Reeds Bay small boat harbor and the Ice Pond swimming hole but there is no good beach here. The rooms are standard but clean and feature ceiling fans and TV. Restaurant, cocktail lounge and meeting rooms are on premises. It is adjacent to the Naniloa Country Club golf course and walking distance to Liliuokalani Park and Coconut Island.

Rates: Standard $88, Deluxe $110, Kitchenette $110; $15 extra person

Uncle Billy's Hilo Bay Hotel

87 Banyan Drive, Hilo, HI 96720. 800-367-5102; 808-935-0861; fax 808-935-7903; e-mail: resv@unclebilly.com; www.unclebilly.com.

This is a 145-room standard hotel located right on Hilo Bay. The rooms are all air-conditioned with TV. Uncle Billy's restaurant with nightly entertainment, luau and hula show, cocktail lounge, gift shops and lovely tropical gardens are on grounds. There is no beach as the shoreline is rugged lava rock. It is located across from the Naniloa Country Club golf course and walking distance to Coconut Island and Liliuokalani Park.

Rates: Standard $84-$92, Superior $94-$102, Oceanfront $104-$112, Superior/kitchen $99-$122; $10 extra person

Puna District

BED AND BREAKFASTS

Aloha Junction Bed & Breakfast

19-4040 Post Office Lane, Volcano, HI 96789. 888-967-7289; 808-967-7289; www.bbvolcano.com.

Located close to Volcanoes National Park, Aloha Junction offers rooms with private or shared baths, hot tub and fireplace with a great breakfast served every morning.

Rates: $99 private bath, $75 shared bath

Carson's Volcano Cottages B&B

P.O. Box 503, Volcano, HI 96785. 800-845-LAVA; 808-967-7683; fax 808-967-8094; e-mail: carsons@aloha.net; www.carsonscottage.com.

Accommodations at this quiet, secluded location include six individually themed guest rooms: Kahaualea, reminiscent of Princess Kaiulani's Hawai'i during the monarchy; Kobayashi, with exotic Japanese motif; Ka'u with bright tropic colors and collectibles from the '40s and '50s; Ginger, Pakalana and Pakaki with treetop views into the rainforest canopy. There are also three romantic "storybook cottages" and two cozy family cottages. Rates include full breakfast served fireside in the dining room and daily maid service. Easy access to national park activities, golf course, restaurants. Deposit required to confirm reservation.

Rates: $105-$165

Country Goose B&B

P.O. Box 597, Volcano, HI 96785. 800-238-7101; 808-967-7759; fax 808-985-8673; e-mail: cgoose@interpac.net; www.hawaii-bnb.com/congse.html.

This home has 1BR with private bath and entry, king-size bed and double futon quilt. Electric baseboard and electric blankets take the chill out of the crisp Volcano air. Very peaceful and quiet setting. Member-HIBBA.

Rates: $75-$95

Green Goose Lodge

P.O. Box 422, Volcano, HI 96785. 808-985-9050 or 985-7172; e-mail: conard@greengooselodge.com, www.greengooselodge.com.

A B&B & G! This bed-and-breakfast operation bills itself as "a golfer's dream," located overlooking the fairways of Volcano Golf & Country Club. Individual guest quarters feature TVs and electric blankets, in-room coffee and tea service and golf-course views. Common areas have a large wood-burning fireplace, TV/VCR, library, washer and dryer. Gourmet breakfast and "Tea on the Tee" served daily.

Rates: $85-$95

MILITARY RECREATION CENTER

The Big Island is unique among Hawai'i's Neighbor Islands in that it has an official armed forces recreation center. This is the **Kilauea Military Camp** located at Hawai'i Volcanoes National Park. KMC has 55 rental cabins available plus dormitory facilities and the KMC Mess Hall, a military-style cafeteria that serves standard but ample chow. Entertainment and activities are presented in the Lava Lounge. The rustic, well-kept cabins are 1BR, 2BR and 3BR units, fully equipped with fireplace, TV and full bath. Some have kitchen and jacuzzi facilities. The cabins are available only to active-duty regular military personnel, military reserve, national guard or retired personnel or Department of Defense and Foreign Service civilians and their families. The dining hall, like the lodgings, is not open to the general public. Cabin rentals are very reasonable and are based on the rank and grade of the personnel. Reservations are required.

KMC guests enjoy a full range of recreation activities and programs in the national park as well as tours to various scenic attractions around the island. Rental equipment is available, including tennis racquets, bicycles, back packs, sleeping bags for camping and snorkeling gear. KMC also has billiards, ping-pong, video games, mini-golf and a six-lane bowling alley. There are also Hawaiian music and hula, Hawaiian storytelling, lei making and much more. In addition, you'll find the Lava Lounge and a PX. KMC is only about one mile from the national park visitors center and Volcano House Hotel and restaurant. Volcano Country Club Golf Course is just across the highway. KMC also offers a special "Wild Ginger Tour Package," which is a four-day/three-night stay and includes a meal package, lodging, four island tours of popular attractions and airport transportation. Check with the reservations desk for details. For reservations, contact: Reservations Desk, Armed Forces Recreation Center, Kilauea Military Camp/Lodging, Hawai'i Volcanoes National Park, Hawai'i 96718; 808-967-8333; 808-967-833; fax 808-967-8343. From Honolulu, call 808-438-6707; 24-hour headquarters line 808-967-7315; e-mail: reservations@kmc-volcano.com; www.kmc-volcano.com.

When making reservations, you can also arrange a free shuttle pick-up at the Hilo airport, unless you want to rent your own car for the 45-minute trip to the camp. KMC guests must pay the standard national park one-time entry fee of $5 per vehicle or $3 per person (when using the KMC shuttle) upon entering the park.

Current rates are as follows: 1BR $46-$79; 1BR w/jacuzzi $55-$88; 1BR Cottage $49-$82; 1BR Cottage w/jacuzzi $58-$91; 2BR Cottage $58-$98; 2BR Cottage w/kitchen $70-$103; 2BR Cottage w/kitchen/jacuzzi $78-$111; 3BR Cottage w/kitchen/jacuzzi $87-$120; 3BR Apt $71-$104; extra person $10-$13.

Hale Nui B&B

18-7879 Leonaka Road, P.O. Box 127, Mountain View, HI 96771. 808-968-HALE; 808-968-6577; fax 808-968-8900; e-mail: halenui@aol.com; www.bbonline.com/hi/halenui.

Hale Nui is a large comfortable country home located off Highway 11 and just 14 miles south of Hilo in a quiet country atmosphere at 1,500-foot elevation, on the edge of Ola'a Rainforest preserve. Four individually themed guest rooms; continental breakfast buffet served daily in the dining room. It's just minutes to all the attractions and activities of east Hawai'i including Volcanoes National Park, orchid and anthurium farms, botanical gardens, historic Hilo town, shopping and dining. Member-HIBBA.

Rates: $45-$60

Hi'iaka House

Reservations through Hawai'i's Best B&Bs, P.O. Box 520, Kamuela, HI 96743. 800-262-9912; 808-885-4550; fax 808-885-0559; e-mail: reservations@bestbnb.com; www.bestbnb.com.

This is a 1939-era family mountain retreat in Volcano dating from the days when those who were able kept a mountain house to escape to the cooler uplands during warm spells on the coast. Lovely artwork decor in the home, a very comfortable 3BR, one and a half baths, with nicely landscaped grounds. It has a full kitchen, wood stove in living room and a relaxing front porch. Great for families or groups. Two-night minimum stay. Member-Hawai'i's Best.

Rates: $135; $15 extra person

Hydrangea Cottage and Mountain House

Reservations through Hawai'i's Best B&Bs, P.O. Box 520, Kamuela, HI 96743. 800-262-9912; 808-885-4550; fax 808-885-0559; e-mail: reservations@bestbnb.com; www.bestbnb.com.

This country cottage and house are on a three-acre estate in the Volcano forestlands landscaped with pink and blue hydrangeas and a variety of other plants. Units are completely furnished including living room, kitchen and fireplace. The cottage sleeps three and the house has two master suites and one small room. Two-night minimum stay. Member-Hawai'i's Best.

Rates: Cottage $150, Mountain House suites $150, small room $80; $15 extra person

★ The Inn at Volcano

P.O. Box 998, Wright Road, Volcano, HI 96785. 800-937-7786; 808-967-7786; fax 808-967-8660; 800-577-1849; e-mail: reservations@volcano-hawaii.com; www.volcano-hawaii.com.

Part of the Chalet Kilauea Collection of B&Bs, which offers a variety of lodgings in the cool Volcano Village area. The Inn at Volcano is their flagship property and it is a work of art. The luxury-class boutique resort has six distinctive, themed rooms, each with their own intriguing personality. Let your surroundings match your mood with settings such as Out of Africa, Oriental Jade, the Owner's Suite, Continental Lace Suite, Hapu'u Forest Suite or the one-of-a-kind Treehouse Suite. For families or groups wishing for more privacy, there are separate cottages including Ohia Hideaway Cottage, Volcano Country Cottage, Pink Protea Palace, Pele's Plantation House and Hoku Mana House. Relax in the hot tub, enjoy the fireplace and library and wake up to a gourmet breakfast in the art deco dining room. Located at the cool 3,800-foot elevation just minutes from Hawai'i Volcanoes National Park, village store and restaurants. French spoken here.

Rates: $49-$399

Kalani Garden Cottages

19-4245 Road B, P.O. Box 698, Volcano, HI 96785. 808-967-8642; e-mail: diane@volcanogetaway.com; www.volcanogetaway.com.

Enjoy the quiet, cool ambiance of Volcano at a 3,600-foot elevation and the privacy of your own island-style cottage just minutes from Volcanoes National Park. Choose the Teahouse Cottage for a touch of the Orient or Lehua Cottage for the feel of old Hawai'i. Surrounded by lush tropical gardens and rainforest, the cottages have kitchenettes and fireplaces to take the chill out of the cool Volcano nights. Generous island-style breakfast included. Complimentary guided hike with three-night stays. Member-HIBBA.

Rates: $110-$120

Kia'i Kai B&B

HC 3 Box 10064, Kea'au, HI 96749. Phone/fax 808-982-9256; 888-KIAIKAI; e-mail: innkeeper@hawaii-ocean-retreat.com; www.hawaii-ocean-retreat.com.

This modern custom-built home has an octagon common area and large windows to see whales, dolphins and seascape views; it's located at the ocean's edge in Hawaiian Paradise Park off Highway 130 south of Hilo and Kaloli Point. The Hawai'i Loa Cottage (sleeps 4) has two bedrooms with king beds, kitchen, private bath and living area. Makali'i Room has ocean view, queen bed, private entrance and private bath; Holomoku Suite has ocean view, queen bed, private entrance, shared bath. Guests share common areas in and around the home. Full continental breakfast each morning plus afternoon refreshments. Easy access to Volcanoes National Park and all other east Hawai'i attractions and activities. Member-HIBBA.

Rates: $85-$145; $10 extra person

★ Kilauea Lodge B&B

P.O. Box 116, Old Volcano Road, Volcano, HI 96785. 808-967-7366; fax 808-967-7367; e-mail: stay@kilauealodge.com; www.kilauealodge.com.

One of the best accommodations on the island, Kilauea Lodge was once a YWCA camping lodge and dormitory built in 1938. It has since been transformed into a romantic, cozy country inn and restaurant and won wide acclaim for comfort, service, quality and fine dining. Set amid the quiet, cool country air of Volcano Village near Hawai'i Volcanoes National Park, there are 14 attractively decorated guest units with private bathrooms and fireplaces. The restaurant offers a full Continental/international dinner menu nightly. Room rates include full American breakfast.

Rates: Hale Maluna Building rooms w/fireplace $135; The Cottage w/fireplace and porch $145; Hale Aloha Building rooms w/garden view $125; Honeymoon Deluxe room w/fireplace and king bed $145; Tutu's Place $155; 2BR cottage with hot tub $175

Lava Tree Tropic Inn

P.O. Box 6300, Hilo, HI 96720. 877-390-9200; 808-965-7441; fax 808-965-7410; e-mail: information@lavatreetropicinn.com; www.lavatreetropicinn.com.

This is a unique two-story plantation-style inn. It provides several smoke-free comfortable guest rooms. Decor includes bright island-style furnishings and artwork accents from the owner's personal Hawaiiana art collection. Guest clubhouse facilities include a lounge for big-screen TV, a billiard parlor room and large commercial kitchen. Complimentary continental breakfast. Located 25 minutes/20 miles southeast from Hilo Airport past Pahoa town on Highway 132 to Kapoho, just past Lava Tree State Park. Lush tropical garden setting, easy access to area attractions.

Rates: $85-$125

Lokahi Lodge

P.O. Box 998, Volcano, HI 96785. 800-937-7786; 808-985-8647; e-mail: reservations@volcano-hawaii.com; www.volcano-hawaii.com.

This lodge is part of the Chalet Kilauea Collection operation of inns and lodges. This luxury four-room inn combines modern convenience with Volcano country charm. Located one mile from Volcanoes National Park entrance, this plantation-style home has rooms with private bath, cable TV and VCR.

Rates: $129-$149; $15 extra person

Ma'ukele Lodge

P.O. Box 162, Volcano, HI 96785. 888-507-7421; 808-985-7421; e-mail: volcanobb@hotmail.com; www.volcano-bb.com.

This large country home is located at the 4,000-foot elevation level near Kilauea Volcano. The home has a high open-beam living room with two warm, inviting fireplaces and beautiful woodwork throughout. The three large guest bedrooms have private baths and queen

KALANI OCEANSIDE RETREAT

★ **Kalani Oceanside Retreat** offers a wide variety of interesting seminars, healing retreats, yoga, dance and meditation workshops and other mindful things, in addition to quality lodging and meal services. Choose from cottages with private baths and ocean vistas, rooms in cedar lodges, triple dorm rooms or orchard campsites. The facility has gorgeous acres of botanical and fruit orchards and gardens. Amenities include an Olympic-size swimming pool, two jacuzzis, sauna, massage/wellness gazebo, recreational sports courts and covered meeting/activity hall space for groups. There are shared kitchen facilities and both shared/private bath facilities. Located about 25 miles south of Hilo, past Pahoa town on the coast highway/beach road. Rates: Cottage $155; Campsites $20-$30; Lodge room, private bath $35; Lodge room, shared bath $110; $60 extra person. RR2 Box 4500, Pahoa, HI 96778, at Ocean Highway, 137-Pahoa Beach Road. 800-800-6886; 808-965-7828; e-mail: kalani@kalani.com; www.kalani.com.

beds. It's in a rainforest setting of towering *ohia* trees and *hapu'u* ferns with lots of birdlife. Easy access to the national park and area activities.

Rates: $95; $25 extra person; house (sleeps 7) $250

Mountain View B&B

P.O. Box 963, South Kulani Road, Kurtistown, HI 96704. 888-698-9896; 808-968-6868; fax 808-968-7017; e-mail: janechao@bbmtview.com; www.bbmtview.com.

This large modern home is located about 15 miles south of Hilo in the rolling farm and forestlands of the Mountain View village area. The home is on a large lot surrounded by forest and lush greenery. The owner/operators are noted Big Island artists and instructors, Linus and Jane Chao, who have an art studio on the lower level where they conduct art classes. Inquire about special art class/room packages. The living and guest quarters are on the upper level. The Cherry Blossom and Heliconia Rooms have king or queen beds and private bath; the Plumeria Room has two twin beds; and the Lehua Room has a queen and shared bath. There is easy access to shopping, dining and attractions of the East Hawai'i–Hilo area and Hawai'i Volcanoes National Park is just minutes away. Smoke free; Chinese spoken here. Member-HIBBA.

Rates: $55-$65 shared bath; $75-$110 private bath

★ *My Island B&B*

P.O. Box 100, Volcano, HI 96785. 808-967-7216; 808-967-7110; fax 808-967-7719; e-mail: myisland@ilhawaii.net; www.myislandinn.com.

This secluded getaway is located in the pleasant, cool climate of Volcano Village, not far from Hawai'i Volcanoes National Park visitors center. The house is a historic century-old missionary-style home set amid a rambling botanical garden and fern forest jungle. The grounds have a fine collection of exotic plants from around the world. Rooms are neat, comfortable and cozy with various bed arrangements: singles, doubles, triples and families. Color TV and a library of Hawaiiana are available for entertainment. All the mac nuts you can eat. Member-HIBBA.

Rates: $50-$135

Oma's Hapu'u Hideaway

P.O. Box 611, Volcano, HI 96785. 808-985-8959; e-mail: todd@volcanovillage.net; www.volcanovillage.net.

This forest retreat is located in the heart of Volcano Village surrounded by native *ohia*, *koa* and *hapu'u* tree ferns, on Hale Ohia Road, within walking distance of village shops, general store, post office and restaurants. The Hapu'u Hideaway is a cedar A-frame cottage with fully equipped kitchen, phone, living room, fireplace, TV/VCR and a loft master bedroom with queen bed and picture-window views. The two bedrooms downstairs have a queen bed and children's bunk beds; sleeps six. Also on the grounds behind the owner's home is the Maid's Quarters cottage. This nicely decorated unit has a bright cheery look with queen bed. There's a fully equipped kitchen and dining area, living room with fireplace, TV/stereo and a gas fireplace in the bedroom. Overlooks nice semi-tropical gardens. Fifth night free.

Rates: Hapu'u Hideaway $105, Maid's Quarters $95; $15 extra person

★ Volcano B&B

998 Wright Road, Volcano, HI 96785. 800-937-7786; 808-967-7779; fax 800-577-1849; e-mail: reservations@volcano-hawaii.com; www.volcano-hawaii.com.

This B&B is part of the Chalet Kilauea Collection of inns and lodges. The peaceful country home is located in the heart of cool, lush Volcano Village, a mile from the entrance and visitors center of Hawai'i Volcanoes National Park. The house provides six single/double rooms with shared bath. The renovated 1912-vintage three-story home is on a three-quarter-acre landscaped site with fireplace, sun room, reading room, piano, cable TV/VCR and shared kitchen facilities. Access to national park provides year-round hiking, biking, sightseeing and other recreational activities. Near village stores and restaurants.

Rates: $49-$69; $15 extra person

Volcano Country Cottages

P.O. Box 545, Volcano, HI 96785. 800-967-7960; 808-967-7960; fax 808-985-7349; e-mail: aloha@volcanocottages.com; www.volcanocottages.com.

This is one of Volcano Village's oldest family estates, nestled among a stand of large old-growth forest and ferns. Ohelo Berry Cottage is a private studio cottage with kitchenette and sleeps two. Artist's House is a two-bedroom unit with full kitchen and woodstove for cool Volcano nights and sleeps up to eight. Full continental breakfast is provided. Easy access to Volcanoes National Park attractions, fine dining, shopping and activities in the village. Enjoy seclusion and cool Volcano climate. Discounts for extra nights. Member-HIBBA.

Rates: Ohelo Berry Cottage $95, Artist's House $125; $15 extra person

Volcano Inn

P.O. Box 490, Volcano, HI 96785. 800-997-2292; 808-967-7293; fax 808-985-7394; e-mail: volcano@volcanoinn.com; www.volcanoinn.com.

Volcano Inn is actually two separate lodgings, located in the heart of Volcano Village, only a mile from the national park entry. Volcano Inn I is more contemporary, with four guest rooms with private baths, an art gallery, expansive lanai, exercise room and a house full of artworks including the owner's handmade Hawaiian quilts. Volcano Inn II is a lovingly restored 1928 mission-style home, offering three guest rooms and a cottage, each with private bath and decorated with antiques, fine art and other treasures. The common areas hold an elegant library, dining room and lava stone fireplace. Family-style breakfast is served daily, as well as afternoon tea; picnic baskets may be ordered in advance. Member-HIBBA.

Rates: Singles $45-$95, doubles $75-$135; $20 extra person

Volcano Rain Forest Retreat

P.O. Box 957, Volcano, HI 96785. 800-550-8696; 808-985-8696; e-mail: volrain@bigisland.net; www.volcanoretreat.com.

This quiet and secluded sanctuary is surrounded by towering fern forest. Designed to emphasize tranquility, the three attractive cottages feature beautiful furniture and woodwork with a handcrafted feel. Each is equipped with full kitchen, living area with wood stove, sleeping loft and private, oversized bathtub open to the forest. Two-night minimum stay. Member-Hawai'i's Best, HIBBA.

Rates: $155; $15 extra person

Volcano Teapot

P.O. Box 511, Volcano, HI 96785. 808-967-7112. Reservations through Hawai'i's Best B&Bs, P.O. Box 520, Kamuela, HI 96743; 800-262-9912; 808-885-4550; fax 808-885-0559; e-mail: reservations@bestbnb.com; www.bestbnb.com. Also through The Cottages of Volcano, 800-967-7995; e-mail: places@aloha.net; www.alohaweb.com/cottages.

This is a nicely restored turn-of-the-20th-century two-bedroom cottage set on landscaped grounds in Volcano Village. Lovely decorative touches and tea-theme accents are featured throughout. There is a comfy porch and warm wood-burning stove to take the chill out of the crisp Volcano air, and a hot tub pavilion in a romantic garden setting. The cottage sleeps four. Member-Hawai'i's Best.

Rates: $150; $20 extra person

HOTELS, HOSTELS AND HOMES

Hale Ohia Cottages and Hostels

P.O. Box 758, 11-3968 Hale Ohia Road, Volcano, HI 96785. 800-455-3803; 808-967-7986; fax 808-967-8610; e-mail: haleohia@bigisland.com; www.haleohia.com.

This elegant and charming country B&B home (c. 1931) offers various private cottages and suites. Units have kitchens, living rooms and private baths. A large covered deck has table, chairs and barbecue for cookouts. There are well-kept, nicely landscaped grounds and gardens in this exclusive old family estate. Located one mile from national park entrance and visitors center, near hiking trails, picnic areas, golf, volcano observatory, restaurants, etc.

Rates: Suites $95-$120, Cottages $110-$160; $15 extra person

Holoholo Inn

19-4036 Kalani Honua Road, P.O. Box 784, Volcano, HI 96785. 808-967-7950; fax 808-967-8025; e-mail: holoholo@interpac.net; www.enable.org/holoholo.

Located in the heart of Volcano Village near the entry to Volcanoes National Park, this hostel operator provides basic dorm lodging and services for budget backpackers. Amenities include kitchen facilities, TV, heated room, laundry facilities, hot showers and sauna. Located off Highway 11 in Volcano Village, just off Haunani Road on Kalani Honua Road near the old Japanese schoolhouse. Japanese spoken here.

Rates: Dorm room $17 (HI-AYH member $15); Private double room $40

Pineapple Park Hostel

P.O. Box 639, Kurtistown, HI 96760. 877-865-2266; 808-968-8170; e-mail: ppark@aloha.net; www.pineapple-park.com.

Located about 15 miles south of Hilo in the Fern Acres subdivision on Pikake Road, off Highway 11 and Kulani Road. This large frame country home sits amid nicely landscaped grounds, lots of tropical flowers, palm trees, bamboo groves and tree ferns, a real tropical rainforest environment. Rooms are clean, comfortable and spacious with well-kept furnishings and appointments. Some rooms have private bath while others share. Guests enjoy breakfast, barbecue, game room, pool table, TV/VCR, community kitchen, vending machines and laundromat facilities. Discounts for extra nights. They also have inexpensive hostel accommodations for budget/backpacker travelers. German spoken here. Member-HIBBA.

Rates: Private rooms $55-$65, hostel bunks $20

Rainforest Retreat

HCR1 Box 5655, Kea'au, HI 96749. 888-244-8074; 808-961-4410; fax 808-966-6898; e-mail: retreat@bigisland.net; www.rainforestretreat.com.

This private home is surrounded by native *ohia* forest, orchids and horse pastures. A garden studio has private entry and bath, king bed, TV, kitchenette and laundry facilities. Located just off Highway 130 and 20 minutes from Hilo. Member-HIBBA.

Rates: $75-$105; $15 extra person

Ka'u District

BED AND BREAKFASTS

Becky's Paradise B&B

P.O. Box 673, Na'alehu, HI 96772. 800-235-1233; phone/fax 808-929-9690; e-mail: beckys@hi-inns.com; 1bb.com.

This is a 60-year-old plantation home in the southernmost community of the U.S., near green-sand and black-sand beaches, South Point and Volcanoes National Park. Located halfway between Hilo and Kona in the rural Ka'u countryside. All guest rooms have private bath. Full traditional island-style breakfast included. Member-HIBBA.

Rates: from $70; $15 extra person

Bougainvillea B&B

P.O. Box 6045, Ocean View, HI 96737. 800-688-1763; phone/fax 808-929-7089; e-mail: peaceful@interpac.net; www.hi-inns.com/bouga.

This plantation-style home is located on three acres in historic Ka'u, midway between Kona and Hilo. Specializing in "Nights and Breakfasts to Remember," the Bougainvillea offers four romantic guest rooms with private entrance and bath, therapeutic beds and TV/VCR. Pavilion area with barbecue, pool, hot tub, ping-pong, horseshoe pit, exercise equipment and awesome star-gazing. Massage therapies by appointment.

Rates: $70-$75; $15 extra person

Macadamia Meadows Farm B&B

P.O. Box 756, Na'alehu, HI 96772. 888-929-8118; phone/fax 808-929-8097; e-mail: kaleena@aloha.net; www.macadamiameadows.com.

This is a contemporary two-story, open-beamed cedar home on an eight-acre working macadamia nut farm near Waiohinu, off South

Point Road. The Two-Bedroom Suite has the Pauli Room with both a king and queen bed and refrigerator; the adjoining Mala Room has full bed; suite has private bath but rooms can be rented separately. The Mokupuni Room has queen bed, private bath, microwave and refrigerator. The Honeymoon Suite has teak-canopied queen bed, private bath and an antique tub on a private lanai. Guests share a tennis court and swimming pool; nice ocean views and footpaths through the macadamia nut orchards to the meadows; superb nighttime stargazing area. Full continental breakfast provided. Member-HIBBA.

Rates: $65-$135

CONDOS, HOTELS AND HOMES

Colony One at Seamountain at Punalu'u

P.O. Box 70, Pahala, HI 96777. 800-488-8301; 808-928-8301; fax 808-928-8008; e-mail: seamtn@mymailstation.com; www.seamtnhawaii.com.

This condominium has 26 units available in rental programs. It is located at the Seamountain Golf Course behind Punalu'u Beach Park at Ninole Cove in the remote southern Ka'u District. It's five miles from the small town of Pahala, 55 miles to Hilo and 65 miles to Kona. The units are comfortably furnished with full kitchens, laundry, TV and ceiling fans. Guests have access to golf course, tennis, pool, jacuzzi and the nearby beach park. Punalu'u Bay is very nice for swimming, snorkeling and enjoying the beach. This is a very rural quiet area away from the hustle and bustle. Two-night minimum stay.

Rates: Studio $78-$108, 1BR $100-$135, 2BR $133-$174

Ohana House

P.O. Box 6351, Ocean View, HI 96737. 888-999-9139; 808-929-9139.

This private vacation home includes secluded cottages on four acres of forested land on the Big Island's south end at Hawaiian Ocean View Estates subdivision. Near historic South Point and remote green- and black-sand beaches. Quiet, tranquil country atmosphere, generally fine sunny weather at the 4,000-foot elevation level. It's a 40-minute drive from Kona; 90 minutes from Hilo. Licensed massage therapist available. A mindful, semi-rustic getaway for meetings, workshops and healing retreats, using alternative energy in simple surroundings. Two-night minimum stay, third night free.

Rates: $60

Shirakawa Motel

P.O. Box 467, Na'alehu, HI 96772. 808-929-7462.

Advertised as "The Southernmost Motel in the U.S.," this 12-unit country motel offers simple accommodations for relaxation, peace and quiet. It is nestled amid the cool climate of a coffee tree grove and lush vegetation. The Shirakawa family combines the warmth of true old-fashioned Hawaiian hospitality with simple yet modern conveniences; no TV. This is a simple, no-frills getaway for those wanting the solitude of the countryside.

Rates: Standard $35, Kitchenette unit $42, 1BR Suite $50; $10 extra person

Sunterra at Seamountain

P.O. Box 460, Pahala, HI 96777. 800-344-7675; 808-928-6200; fax 808-928-8075; e-mail: seamount@gte.net; www.sunterra.com.

This condominium/hotel has 35 rental units available. Located in the fairly remote Punalu'u area of Ka'u, the development is situated at the Seamountain Golf Course and near the ocean front and Punalu'u Black Sand Beach and Ninole Cove. The nearest town is Pahala, five miles away. Hilo is about 55 miles away, Kona about 65 miles. This is a peaceful rural area, suitable for beach strolling and leisurely golf. All units have full kitchens, TV, laundry facilities, lanai, ceiling fans and standard hotel amenities. Golf clubhouse, cocktail lounge, swimming pool, tennis courts, golf course, barbecue, meeting rooms are on the grounds or nearby. Two-night minimum stay.

Rates: Studio $80-$100, 1BR $100-$125, 2BR $125-$155; $10 extra person

★ ***Volcano House***

P.O. Box 53, Hawai'i Volcanoes National Park, HI 96718. 808-967-7321; fax 808-967-7321.

Historic, unique Volcano House has been rebuilt several times since its establishment 1866, with an extensive refurbishment in 1989. It now features 37 comfortable rooms with private bath and even heat—an unusual feature for hotels in Hawai'i. Volcano House has two gift shops, Uncle George's Lounge for cocktails, Ka Ohelo Dining room (possibly the world's only restaurant perched on the edge of an active volcano) and a lobby fireplace that has burned continuously for more years than anyone can remember. It's sort of a Volcano House tradition and the fire burns day and night to help keep guests comfortable. The wood paneling and cozy decor create a rustic country lodge atmosphere that gives the Volcano House its special charm.

Rates: $95-$185

Rental Agents

BED & BREAKFAST AGENCIES

Following are booking services for bed and breakfasts islandwide that provide a selection of accommodations and price ranges.

All Islands B&B

800-542-0344; 808-263-2342; fax 808-263-0308; e-mail: inquiries@all-islands.com; www.all-islands.com.

Over 700 modest to magnificent accommodations on all islands. Reduced rates for interisland air and car rentals.

Alternative Hawai'i Accommodations

e-mail: admin@alternative-hawaii.com; www.alternative-hawaii.com/accomg.htm.

Bed & Breakfast Hawai'i

P.O. Box 449, Kapa'a, HI 96746. 800-733-1632; 808-822-7771; fax 808-822-2723; e-mail: reservations@bandb-hawaii.com; www.bandb-hawaii.com.

Bed & Breakfast Honolulu

3242 Kaohinani Drive, Honolulu, HI 96817. 800-288-4666; 808-595-7533; fax 808-595-2030; e-mail: rainbow@hawaiibnb.com; www.hawaiibnb.com.

Chalet Kilauea Collection

P.O. Box 998, Volcano, HI 96785. 800-937-7786; 808-967-7786; fax 800-577-1849 or 808-967-8660; e-mail: reservations@volcano-hawaii.com; www.volcano-hawaii.com.

Go Native Hawai'i

800-662-8483; e-mail: reservations@gonativehi.com; www.gonativehi.com.

This booking service handles reservations for several B&Bs around the Big Island and the Hawaiian islands in general.

Hawai'i's Best B&B

P.O. Box 520, Kamuela, HI 96743. 800-262-9912; 808-885-4550; fax 808-885-0559; e-mail: reservations@bestbnb.com; www.bestbnb.com.

This booking service caters exclusively to upscale B&Bs on the Big Island. The island's best lodgings, ranging from the most traditional host-home rooms to private country cottages, have been selected for inclusion in the "Hawai'i's Best" collection. Each home or cottage has been chosen for its distinctive personality, inspired attention to detail, and for the warm hospitality offered by its hosts. Each offers a beautiful setting, tasteful and comfortable accommodations, attentive service and a relaxed atmosphere. Host accommodations are available around the island in Kamuela, Hilo, Volcano, Kona and on the Kohala Coast. Rates from $95-$250, with weekly rates available at most properties.

Hawai'i Island B&B Association (HIBBA)

P.O. Box 1890, Honoka'a, HI 96727. E-mail: hibba@stayhawaii.com; www.stayhawaii.com.

No phone. Their website provides listing of member B&Bs on Big Island only.

Hawai'i Island Bed & Breakfast Inns and Accommodations Index

www.hawaii-inns.com.

This website provides a number of links to bed-and-breakfast operators on the Big Island as well as throughout the Hawaiian islands.

Hawai'i Bed & Breakfast Inns Directory

hi-inns.com.

This online directory lists several Big Island B&Bs along with information on dining specials at local restaurants for B&B guests.

Hawaiian Islands B&B

572 Kailua Road #201, Kailua, HI 96734. 800-258-789; 808-261-7895; fax 808-262-2181; e-mail: hi4rent@aloha.net; www.lanikaibb.com.

CONDOMINIUM AND HOME RENTAL AGENCIES

The following agencies can assist with rentals of condominiums, private estates and vacation residences, in a wide range of prices and locations islandwide.

A Piece of Paradise

P.O. Box 1314, Pahoa, HI 96778-1314. 808-965-1224; e-mail: info@apoparadise.com; www.apoparadise.com.

This booking service has vacation homes in the Puna–Kapoho and Waikoloa areas, as well as Kailua-Kona and Hilo town, ranging from 1BR to 5BR; varied facilities and amenities; units accommodate up to 12 people. Rates from $99.

All Globe Travel

800-688-2254; e-mail: info@vacation2hawaii.com; www.greathawaiivacations.com.

This rental listing service has some 620 properties listed for all areas of the Big Island and includes condos and private homes priced $75-$500.

Always Sunny Condos

P.O. Box 3567, Silverdale, WA 98383. 360-698-7007; 800-479-2173; fax 360-692-9428; e-mail: calnan@konacondos.com; www.konacondos.com.

Aston Hotels & Resorts

2255 Kuhio Avenue, Honolulu, HI 96815. 800-922-7866; in Hawai'i 800-321-2558; fax 808-922-8785; e-mail: astonres@aston-hotels.com; www.aston-hotels.com.

Century 21

75-5759 Kuakini Highway, Suite 200, Kailua-Kona, HI 96740. 800-546-5662; 808-326-2121; fax 808-329-6768; e-mail: vacation@ilhawaii.net; www.islandsrentals.com.

This full-service realty and property management firm provides a wide variety of vacation rental condos from $60-$100 and private homes from $150 on the Big Island's Kona and Kohala coasts. Weekly rates available

Castle Resorts & Hotels

1150 South King Street, Honolulu, HI 96813. 808-591-2235; 800-367-5004; fax 800-477-2329; e-mail: reservations@castleresorts.com; castle resorts.com.

Condo in Hawai'i

c/o Ron Roddick. 604-943-0085; 888-292-3307; fax 604-943-0056; e-mail: konacondo@telus.net; www.condoinhawaii.com.

Elite Properties Unlimited

P.O. Box 5273, 505 Front Street #228, Lahaina, HI 96761. 800-448-9222 U.S. & Canada; 808-665-0561; fax 808-669-2417; e-mail: homes@eliteprop.com; www.eliteprop.com.

Family homes and luxury estates with 3-6 bedrooms to accommodate 4-12 people. Big Island vacation homes available at Kohala Coast/Puako, Mauna Kea Resort, Mauna Lani Resort, Kailua-Kona area, and Kealakekua Bay/Honaunau. Weekly and monthly rentals from $325-$1,900. One-week minimum stay. Maid service, chefs and concierge services available.

Hawai'i Condo Exchange

1817 El Cerrito Place, Los Angeles, CA 90068. 323-436-0300; 800-442-0404; fax 323-436-0331; www.hawaiicondoexchange.com.

Hawai'i Resort Management

P.O. Box 39, Kailua-Kona, HI 96745. 808-329-9393; 800-622-5348 or 888-KONA-HAWAII; fax 808-326-4137; e-mail: islander@konahawaii.com; www.konahawaii.com.

★ Hawai'i's Best B&Bs

P.O. Box 520, Kamuela, HI 96743. 800-262-9912; 808-885-4550; fax 808-885-0559; e-mail: reservations@bestbnb.com; www.bestbnb.com.

This bed-and-breakfast booking service also represents several fully equipped vacation rental homes and cottages in the Puako and Wailea areas of the Kohala Coast. The homes and cottages have oceanfront settings with easy beach access and rent from $85-$165. Facilities and furnishings vary and units sleep up to six people.

Hawai'i Vacation Rentals

7 Puako Beach Drive, Kohala Coast, HI 96743. 808-882-7000; fax 808-882-7607; e-mail: seaside@aloha.net; www.vacationbigisland.com.

This booking service has a variety of condo and home rental units in the Puako Beach area of the Kohala Coast and at Waikoloa Village for $235-$1,200; units accommodate 4-14 people.

Kapoho Tropical Vacation Rentals

Kapoho Beach Lots, RR2 Box 3909, Pahoa, HI 96778. 808-965-8508.

This booking service has three fully furnished beachside homes available for $60-$100; they accommodate up to six people. Access to swimming pool and oceanfront tide pools.

Keauhou Property Management Company

P.O. Box 390220, Kailua-Kona, HI 96739. 808-326-9075; 800-745-KONA; fax 808-326-2055; e-mail: kona@kpmco.com; www.kpmco.com.

Knutson & Associates

75-6082 Ali'i Drive #8, Kailua-Kona, HI 96740. 808-329-6311; 800-800-6202; fax 808-326-2178; e-mail: knutson@aloha.net; www.konahawaii rentals.com.

Kona Hawai'i Vacation Rentals

75-5776 Kuakini Highway #105C, Kailua-Kona, HI 96740. 800-622-5348; 808-329-3333; fax 808-326-4137; e-mail: kona@konahawaii.com; www.konahawaii.com.

This booking service has several condo and private home rentals for $42-$545, accommodating from three to eight people. Three-night minimum stay.

Kona Oceanfront Rental Homes

P.O. Box 35563, Monte Sereno, CA 95030; 800-464-6038; fax 408-243-4029; e-mail: pearne@ix.netcom.com; www.hawaiiholidaybeachhomes.com.

This private home owner has three separate vacation houses available. Two are in the Keauhou area near Kahalu'u Beach Park: Mehina Mele House ($175-$225) sleeps up to five guests, and Sea Breeze House ($250-$400 or $1,610/week) accommodates up to ten. They also offer Dock of the Bay ($250-$400) at Alae Point in Hilo town for up to ten guests. Full facilities and amenities included.

Marc Resorts Hawai'i

2155 Kalakaua Avenue, 7th floor, Honolulu, HI 96815-2351. 808-922-9700; 800-436-1304; fax 800-633-5085; e-mail: marc@aloha.net; www.marcresorts.com.

Maui & All Islands Condominiums

P.O. Box 947, Lynden, WA 98264. 800-663-6962; fax 888-654-MAUI; e-mail: paul@mauiallislands.com; www.mauiallislands.com.

Outrigger Hotels Hawai'i

2375 Kuhio Avenue, Honolulu, HI 96815. 800-OUTRIGGER; fax 800-622-4852; e-mail: reservations@outrigger.com; www.outrigger.com.

Pleasant Hawaiian Holidays

2772 Townsgate Road, Suite B, Westlake Village, CA 91361. 800-672-4587; e-mail: sales@islandsplendor.com; www.islandsplendor.com.

Property Network

75-5799 B-3 Ali'i Drive, Kailua-Kona, HI 96740. 808-329-7977; 800-358-7977; fax 808-329-1200; e-mail: vacation@hawaii-kona.com; www.hawaii-kona.com.

Realty Executives Hawai'i

75-5665 Kuakini Highway, Kailua-Kona, HI 96740. 800-377-3077; 808-325-2828; fax 808-329-1753; e-mail: rentals@rehpm.com; www.rehpm.com.

This rental service has 15 varied home and condo rentals available for $67-$350 in the Kona area, ranging from 1BR to 3BR with varied furnishings and amenities.

Royal Hawai'i Condos

888-722-6284; fax 520-223-3243; e-mail: info@royalhawaii.com; www.royalhawaii.com.

★ South Kohala Management

P.O. Box 384900, Waikoloa, HI 96738. 800-822-4252; 808-883-8500; fax 808-883-9818; e-mail: info@southkohala.com; www.southkohala.com.

One of the best, South Kohala only handles high-end vacation residences ($235-$4,000, average about $1,200) located in the luxurious Kohala Coast resort communities. They are happy to help you choose a home or condo unit to suit your family's particularities and preferences for an ultimate getaway experience. Listings include the Kumulani condominiums at Hapuna, the exclusive homes of The Fairways or Moani Heights at Mauna Kea Resort, and luxury condos of Mauna Lani Terrace, Mauna Lani Point and The Islands at Mauna Lani. They also handle other private homes and villas on the Kona and Kohala coasts. Car rental packages available.

★ Sunquest Vacations

77-6435 Kuakini Highway, Kailua-Kona, HI 96740. 808-329-4000; 800-367-5168; fax 808-329-5480; e-mail: sqvac@sunquest-hawaii.com; www.sunquest-hawaii.com.

Also one of the best, Sunquest handles a wide variety of condo properties islandwide, in sizes to suit all families and all vacation budgets. Quality service provided to visiting guests by phone or via Sunquest's excellent website.

Trading Places International

23807 Aliso Creek Road #100, Laguna Niguel, CA 92677. 949-448-5150; 800-365-1048; fax 949-448-5140; e-mail: info@tradingplaces.com; www.tradingplaces.com.

Triad Management

P.O. Box 4466, Kailua-Kona, HI 96745. 808-329-6402; 800-345-2823; fax 808-326-2401.

West Hawai'i Property Services, Inc.

Keauhou Shopping Village, 78-6831 Ali'i Drive #237, Kailua-Kona, HI 96740. 808-322-6696; 800-799-KONA; fax 808-324-0609; e-mail: whps@ilhawaii.net; www.konarentals.com.

CHAPTER 4

Where to Dine

The Big Island is big on food. Every special occasion is a great opportunity to indulge. And, with its diverse ethnic population, fabulous climate for a wide variety of produce and easy access to bountiful fresh fish and seafood, it has something to offer even the pickiest eater. We invite you to make food a part of your Big Island vacation; expand your boundaries a little and discover a new favorite. We encourage you to leave your prejudices in your suitcases, and get your mind set on trying a few new tastes. We know that memories are made from all five senses, and taste should never be overlooked. Hawai'i as a state and an island is developing excellent chefs and a style of fun, eclectic cuisine that brings together East and West in creative ways, using an amazing palette of local fruits and vegetables, ocean fish and farm-raised seafood, and excellent meats. This is not to say that if you're strictly a meat-and-potatoes kind of person, you're going to be hungry.

Vegetarians too will find plenty to choose from, in eateries from fine hotel dining rooms to corner plate-lunch places islandwide, but to be honest, you're going to have to look a little bit harder. The Big Island is big on meat. However, thanks to Asian influences, vegetable or tofu stir-fry and noodle dishes are common; Italian places offer one or two meatless pastas or pizzas, and it's not at all hard to find fresh salads and fruits. On the plus side, the Big Island is also big on sweets, and if you go a little light on dinner, you can more than make up for it with dessert.

As mentioned, the Big Island has been in the tourist business for a long time. You're going to find whatever you like for breakfast wherever you stay. The larger hotels offer extensive buffet breakfasts for your indulgence and local restaurants serve up eggs and bacon just like home, along with a few more exotic items you might like to try.

Lunch is the best time to experiment and explore a few new tastes. Without making a big financial commitment (i.e., wasting a lot of money if you don't like what you order) you can try a *musubi*, bento or bowl of saimin and take it from there. At dinnertime, your choices are practically limitless-just about any kind of food you and your family prefer in a wide range of settings and styles.

If you go to a luau you'll have a chance to taste more "Hawaiian" food, and you should. Try some poi; eat it with your fingers. Its mild taste is somewhere between starch and yogurt and it is not at all bad. In fact, it makes a great accompaniment to almost anything, and local households serve it with *lomi* salmon, cream and sugar, even hot dogs. Poi is made by boiling taro root and pounding it smooth with specially carved stone poi pounders. It is probably the most important food in Hawaiian culture, but likely more for nutritional qualities than taste.

For a more familiar, sit-down, semi-fancy dinner, try the good-quality American or European-style restaurants islandwide. The Kohala Coast resorts in particular pride themselves in presenting fresh-caught local fish in a variety of preparations, quality steak (some from the island's Parker Ranch), chicken, pork and pasta, accompanied by salads from abundant local produce with house-made, delectable desserts. We'd like to call your attention to the appetizer, or *pupu* menu, which you'll find almost everywhere, offering smaller portions of house specialties that can make a fun meal when everybody orders something different.

A word about service. This is a laid-back place. Restaurant service, like the rest of the Big Island lifestyle, can be easygoing and leisurely. In some Big Island restaurants, particularly those with a faithful regular clientele, you may have to wait a bit. While this can be understandably annoying, we invite you to raise your patience threshold a notch, enjoy the atmosphere and relax. With apologies in advance, we promise that in almost every case a smile and a tolerant-to-friendly attitude will win you a lot better service than a demanding demeanor.

For simplicity, the restaurant listings do not include McDonald's, Burger King, Jack in the Box, Kentucky Fried Chicken, Taco Bell, Dairy Queen, Pizza Hut or similar fast-food outlets or 7-Eleven and other convenience stores located around the Big Island. At the end of the chapter are some of the Big Island's popular commercial *luau* offerings and "dinner experiences" on shipboard and an upcountry ranch.

Restaurant listings are first organized geographically as you proceed around the island from Kona to the Kohala and Hamakua coasts, Hilo, Puna and Ka'u. Under each geographic section, restaurants are further broken down into price categories: *Inexpensive* (up to $10 per person prior to adding alcoholic beverages, tax and gratuity), *Moderate*

SWEET STUFF

Hawai'i-made ice creams and sorbets are out of this world. For a change of pace try island flavors like guava, mango, Kona coffee, *lilikoi* or, even more unique, lychee, green tea, *haupia, kalolo* and *adzuki* bean. There's Hawaiian vintage chocolate well-worth seeking out, all kinds of macadamia nut delectables, tropical fruit cheesecakes and pies. And then, there are local treats you need to experience: *malasada* (a fresh, warm donut pastry, plain or filled with wonderful things), *manapua* (a stuffed sweet bun), mochi, shave ice, *haupia* (an old-fashioned coconut pudding), Portuguese sweetbread and much more. There are exquisite local bakeries in unlikely corners whose empty racks after the lunch hour testify to their reputation.

($10-$30 per person) and *Expensive* (over $30). Primary culinary styles are indicated after each name. Due to changes in menus, management, supplies or other factors, restaurant prices are obviously subject to change at any time. If you are a senior citizen, be sure to ask about a senior citizen discount as more restaurants are extending such a courtesy. Nearly every restaurant offers a *keiki* (children's) menu.

Those restaurants marked with a ★ indicate an exceptional value in quality of food and service, decor and ambiance, unique and unusual cuisine, overall dining experience or a combination of these factors, and not just cost alone. Stars were awarded based on personal experience as well as reputation established by this and other travel references; however, we'd like to remind you that any rating system is subjective. Restaurants go through changes in menu, staff and circumstance, and even the best have a bad night once in a while. Please use these suggestions only as they are intended: a guideline for your own exploration and discovery of the Big Island's smorgasbord of unforgettable tastes.

Our recommendations for best family-dining establishments are indicated with a girl with a hat. While many restaurants offer *keiki* menus, we feel these recommended restaurants have great food, good value (although some are fine-dining establishments and will not be inexpensive) and wonderful atmosphere. If there's no *keiki* menu, most restaurants are happy to down-size standard portions and reduce the cost.

As we've said often, avoid disappointment by calling ahead for specific hours and days of service as some change their hours seasonally based on a variety of factors. Finally, as you travel around the Big Island, you may come across an eatery not listed in this book. It may be new, or one we've missed, and we'd love to hear about it.

Ethnic Foods

The cultural diversity of the Hawaiian islands benefits visitors and residents alike. As immigrants arrived, they brought with them many varied foods from their native lands; some may be familiar while others are new and interesting. little background on some ethnic foods may tempt you to try a few new foods as a part of your dining adventure on the Big Island.

CHINESE FOODS

Bean threads: thin, clear noodles made from mung beans
Char siu: roasted pork with spices
Chow mein: thin noodles prepared with veggies and meat in various combinations, also cake-noodles style
Crack seed: preserved fruits and seeds, some are sweet, others are sour
Egg/Spring/Summer roll: deep-fried or fresh pastry roll with various veggie, meat or shrimp fillings
Kung pao chicken: deep-fried or sauteed spicy chicken pieces
Long rice: clear noodles cooked with chicken and vegetables
Mongolian beef: thinly sliced charbroiled beefsteak
Peking duck: charbroiled duck with *char siu* flavoring
Pot stickers: semisoft pan-fried filled dumplings
Sweet-and-sour sauce: sugar-and-vinegar-based sauce with tomato sauce, salt and garlic flavorings
Szechuan sauce: hot chili–flavored sauce used extensively in beef, chicken, pork, seafood dishes
Wonton: crispy deep-fried dumpling with meat or veggie fillings; also soft style cooked in soups or noodle dishes

FILIPINO FOODS

Adobo: chicken or pork cooked with vinegar and spices
Cascaron: a donut made with rice flour and rolled in sugar
Chicken papaya: chicken soup with green papaya and seasonings
Dinadaraan: blend of prepared pork blood and meats
Halo halo: a tropical fruit sundae that is a blend of milk, sugar, fruits and ice
Lumpia: fried pastry filled with vegetables and meats
Pancit: noodles with vegetables or meat
Pinacbet: stir-fry of bitter melon, okra, pork and various seasonings
Pork and peas: traditional entree of pork, peas, flavorings in a tomato paste base
Sari sari: soup entree of pork, veggies and flavorings

HAWAIIAN FOODS

Haupia: a sweet custard made of coconut milk

Kalua pig: roast pig cooked in an underground *imu* oven, very flavorful

Kulolo: a steamed pudding using coconut milk and grated taro root

Laulau: pieces of pork or chicken, flavored with butterfish, topped with luau (taro) leaves, wrapped in ti leaves, then steamed

Lomi lomi salmon: diced and salted salmon with tomatoes and green onions

Long rice: clear noodles made from mung beans, cooked with squid or chicken broth

Opihi: saltwater limpets eaten raw and considered a delicacy

Poi: pureed taro corms, best eaten fresh

Poke: raw fish that has been spiced. A variety of fish are used and are often mixed with seaweed; for example, ahi *poke* is raw tuna while *tako poke* is marinated octopus

JAPANESE FOODS

Chicken katsu: deep-fried, breaded chicken pieces served with *katsu* sauce

Donburi: chicken, pork or fish entree with veggies and special soy sauce served over steaming rice and topped with egg

Kamaboko: fish cake of white fish and starch steamed together

Miso soup: soup of fermented soy beans

Mochi: a rich sweet dessert made from cooked rice, pounded into a soft dough

Okazuya: this is a style of serving where you select dishes from a buffet line; the food represents a variety of ethnic cuisines

Sashimi: very fresh firm raw fish, usually yellowfin tuna (*ahi*), sliced thin and dipped in wasabi-*shoyu* sauce

Shabu shabu: thinly sliced beef with veggies, noodles and *ponzu* sauce

Shoyu: soy sauce, same thing

Soba/saimin: thin noodles served with/without broth; cold soba served as salad with vegetables

Sukiyaki: thinly sliced beef with veggies, noodles and tofu in a broth

Sushi: white rice rolls or cakes with various seafood, seaweed and veggie fillings

Tempura: deep-fried shrimp, fish, seafood and veggies dipped in a light flour batter

Teriyaki: flavorful, savory soy sauce and ginger marinade for beef, chicken, pork and seafood

Tonkatsu: pork cutlet grilled golden brown, served with *tonkatsu* sauce

Udon: noodles served with soup broth, green onions, fish cake slices, optional meat

Wasabi: very spicy green horseradish root used to dip sushi into

KOREAN FOODS

Kalbi ribs: flavored similarly to teriyaki, but with chili pepper, sesame oil and green onions

Kim chee: spicy pickled cabbage flavored with ginger and garlic

Mandoo: fried dumplings with meat and vegetable fillings

Mandoo kook, Bi bim kook, yook kae jang: soups served with *mandoo* dumplings, noodles, vegetables, variety of meats

Meat or fish jun: fried or broiled beef or fish with teriyaki-type sauce

Spicy barbecue beef, chicken or pork: broiled soy sauce–flavored beef, chicken or pork laced with spicy hot chili

LOCAL FAVORITES

Bento: a box lunch might include tempura shrimp, veggies, scoop of noodles, sushi roll or rice

Loco moco: traditionally a bowl of rice, topped with a hamburger pattie, fried egg, and gravy. Now there's Spam *moco*, salmon *moco*, teri chicken and even veggie mocos

Musubi: a kind of sandwich made with rice and Spam or tuna, pressed in a mold and wrapped with *nori* (seaweed)

Ogo: A generic term for the edible seaweed used as an essential ingredient for many seafood dishes

Plate lunches: a traditional favorite might include teriyaki beef or chicken, hamburger with gravy, roast pork, fried fish or any of several other entrees, always served with rice and often a scoop of macaroni salad

Saimin: noodles served in broth with fish cake, veggies

Shave ice: ground ice—mainlanders know it as snowcones, except the ice is more finely shaved—topped with flavored syrups such as strawberry, pineapple, guava, vanilla, mango, root beer, *lilikoi*.

PORTUGUESE FOODS

Malasadas: a kind of doughnut, light, deep-fried and rolled in sugar, sometimes filled

Sweetbread: a dense yeast bread, sometimes flavored with taro or fruit

PUERTO RICAN FOODS

Pasteles: an exterior of grated green banana that is filled with pork and vegetables

THAI/VIETNAMESE FOOD

Fried noodles/fried rice: crispy/soft fried noodles with meat entree and soft rice with meat and vegetables

Green curry: choice of meat entree with peas, string beans, coconut milk and sweet basil

Mein noodles: egg noodle soup with shrimp, seafood or other entree

Musaman curry: curry with onion, peanuts, carrots and potatoes in coconut milk

Pad Thai: Thai-style pan-fried noodles with choice of meat entree or veggies garnished with sprouts

Pho noodle soup: noodle soup with beefsteak, meatball, chicken or combination with veggies

Red curry: choice of meat entree with bamboo shoots in coconut milk and sweet basil

Rice noodle soup: rice stick noodles with shrimp, pork, fish cake, squid or other seafood

Satay sticks: broiled chicken, pork or beef on skewer sticks, served as a side dish

Vermicelli cold noodles: thin, clear noodles combined with meat or seafood entree and veggies

Yellow curry: chicken with coconut milk and potatoes

A FEW WORDS ABOUT FISH

Whether you are dining out or buying fresh fish at the market, Hawaiian fish names can be confusing. Among the more common fish caught commercially and that you'll see at the market and on restaurant menus are *ahi* (yellowfin tuna) which is most-preferred for *sashimi*, mahimahi (dolphin fish not the mammal) served in many different preparations almost everywhere, and several species of marlin. Other popular table fish include *ono* (wahoo), *opakapaka* (pink snapper) and *onaga* (red snapper) which provide delicate white flaky meat. Here is some background on what you might find on your dinner plate.

A'ama: a small black crab that scurries over rocks at the beach. A delicacy required for a Hawaiian *luau*

Ahi: yellowfin (Allison tuna) is caught in deep waters and weighs 60 to 280 pounds; pinkish red meat is firm yet flaky and popular for sashimi.

Aku: a bluefin tuna that has a stronger taste than ahi.

Albacore: a smaller version of the ahi, averages 40 to 50 pounds and is lighter in both texture and color; also called *koshibi*.

A'u: the broadbill swordfish, or marlin; a dense and sometimes dry fish.

Ehu: orange snapper.

Hapu: Hawaiian sea bass.

Ika: Hawaiian squid

Kamakamaka: island catfish, very tasty but a little difficult to find.

Lehi: a silver-mouth member of the snapper family, with a stronger flavor than *onaga* or *opakapaka* and a texture resembling *mahimahi*.

Mahimahi: called the dolphin fish, but has no relation to Flipper or his friends; caught while trolling and weighs between 10 to 65 pounds; excellent white meat that is moist and light and very good sauteed; a seasonal fish that commands a high price when fresh. **Beware**: While excellent fresh, mahimahi is often served in restaurants having arrived from the Philippines frozen, making it far less pleasing. A clue as to whether it's fresh or frozen may be the price tag. If it runs less than $10 to $15 it is probably the frozen variety. Fresh mahimahi will run more.

Onaga: caught in holes that are 1,000 feet or deeper, this red snapper has an attractive hot-pink exterior with tender, juicy white meat inside.

Ono: also known as *wahoo*; a member of the barracuda family, its white meat is firm and more steaklike. *Ono* means delicious in Hawaiian.

'Opae: shrimp

Opakapaka: pink snapper; meat is very light and flaky with a delicate flavor.

Papio: a baby *ulua* caught in shallow waters.

Uku: grey snapper, light, firm and white meat with a texture that varies with size.

Ulua: also known as pompano, this fish is firm and flaky with steaklike, textured white meat.

Dining Best Bets

Barbecue Billy Bob's Park & Pork in Kona

Chinese Royal Jade Garden in Kona; Leung's Chop Suey House in Hilo

Food Court Waiakea Center food court in Hilo; Kings' Shops in Waikoloa Beach Resort

French La Bourgogne in Kona

German/Continental Edelweiss in Waimea

Greek Cassandra's in Kona

Hawai'i Local Style Ocean View Inn, Sam Choy's Restaurant or Manago Hotel in Kona; Ken's Pancake House in Hilo; Cafe 100 in Hilo (and many other places); Kamuela Deli in Waimea

Hawai'i Regional Cuisine Oodles of Noodles (among others) in Kona; Aloha Angel Cafe in Kainaliu, Kona; Merriman's or Daniel Thiebaut in Waimea; Bamboo in Hawi, North Kohala; at least one in each of the Kohala Coast resorts

Italian Paolo's Bistro in Pahoa; Pescatore in Hilo; Michaelangelo's in Kona

Japanese Nihon Cultural Center in Hilo
Japanese/Fusion (new and interesting) Restaurant Kaikodo in Hilo
Kids Choice Denny's in Kona; Ken's Pancake House in Hilo; Paniolo Country Inn in Waimea; Kohala Ohana Grill in Hawi, North Kohala
Malasadas Tex Drive In in Honoka'a
Mexican Reuben's in Hilo and Kona; Tako Taco in Waimea
Mochi Two Ladies Kitchen in Hilo
New and Interesting/Peruvian Hawaiian Jungle in Hilo
Polynesian, Authentic Ahkovi's Kitchen Co. in Hilo
Pizza Kona Brewing in Kona
Pupus Seafood Bar in Kawaihae
Romantic Evening Donatoni's at Hilton Waikoloa Village
Romantic Evening with Ocean View CanoeHouse at Mauna Lani Bay Hotel
Romantic Evening with Volcano Kilauea Lodge in Volcano
Saimin Restaurant Osaka, Nori's Saimin and many others in Hilo
Seafood Seaside Restaurant in Hilo, and too many others to name!
Steaks on a Budget Outback Steakhouse in Kona
Steaks and Ribs on a Budget Koa House Grill in Waimea
Steaks Not on a Budget The Grill at Fairmont Orchid
Sunday Brunch Mauna Kea Beach Hotel on the Kohala Coast
Sushi Nihon Cultural Center in Hilo; Wasabi's in Kona
Sweetbread Punalu'u Bakery in Punalu'u
Thai Naung Mai in Hilo; Thai Thai in Volcano; Bangkok House in Kona
Vegetarian (restaurants with vegetarian specialties) Aioli's or Maha's Cafe in Waimea; The Vista in Kona; Hale Samoa, Kona Village Resort; Ken's Pancake House in Hilo
Top Restaurants The very best consistently excellent restaurants are concentrated in the Kohala Coast resorts. Fine food, exquisitely prepared, professionally presented and served in artful settings, surrounded by an atmosphere of gracious hospitality—these are all standard. Naturally, quality comes with a price. Meals at the following "first-tier" restaurants can run upwards of $100 per person. But generally a gourmet meal at any of these fine restaurants will be a memorable part of your Big Island vacation, and we encourage you to indulge. As a rule, most fine dining rooms here have gone the route of casual dress in

You might want to explore the web, not just for individual restaurant websites, but for informal forums among visitors and residents, discussing their experiences in Big Island restaurants and attractions. One of the good ones we've found is www.konaweb.com.

recent years; however, please keep in mind that dinner jackets for gentlemen may be required. Ask when you call for reservations (strongly recommended)—and *bon appetit*!

The Batik (Mauna Kea Beach Hotel); Brown's Beach House (Fairmont Orchid); CanoeHouse (Mauna Lani Bay Hotel); Donatoni's (Hilton Waikoloa Village); Hale Samoa (Kona Village Resort); Pahu I'a (Four Seasons)

Top Restaurants in a More Casual Atmosphere There is a somewhat more nebulous "second tier" of Big Island restaurants that have earned a reputation for excellence. They may be a degree less expensive, and still offer consistently fine food and service in a quality, sometimes very unique, atmosphere. *Kona District:* Edward's at Kanaloa; Huggo's; Oodles of Noodles. *Kohala Coast:* Coast Grille (Hapuna Beach Prince Hotel); The Gallery (Mauna Lani Resort); The Grill (Fairmont Orchid); Hale Moana (Kona Village Resort); Hawai'i Calls; Kamuela Provision Company (Hilton Waikoloa Village); Roy's Waikoloa Bar & Grill; Kings' Shops (Waikoloa Beach Resort). *North Kohala District*: Bamboo. *Waimea:* Daniel Thiebaut; Edelweiss; Koa House Grill; Merriman's. *Hilo:* Harrington's; Seaside Restaurant. *Puna District:* Kilauea Lodge; Paolo's Bistro

Kona District

Inexpensive-priced Dining

Aki's Café *(Japanese)*
75-5699 Ali'i Drive, just opposite Hulihe'e Palace in the Kailua Bay Shopping Plaza; 808-329-0090.

Hours: 9 a.m. to 9 p.m. *Sampling:* The menu features a little bit of everything including a variety of lunch fare such as burgers, sandwiches, fish and chips, light meals, snacks, etc., and dinner selections like steak, chicken teriyaki, fish *misoyaki*, sushi and other Japanese specials. *Comments:* There is open-air dining with tables outside overlooking Kailua Bay.

Bad Ass Coffee Co. *(Coffee Shop/Espresso Bar/Sandwiches/Snacks)*
Waterfront Row, 75-5770 Ali'i Drive, Kailua-Kona, 808-326-4637; other locations: Kailua Bay Inn Shopping Plaza, 75-5699 Ali'i Drive, Kailua-Kona; Keauhou Shopping Village, 78-6831 Ali'i Drive, Kailua-Kona; on Highway 11 ten miles south of Kailua-Kona in Kainaliu.

Hours: 8 a.m. to 5 p.m. *Sampling:* This small coffee bar, with locations throughout Kona, features snacks, ice cream, sandwiches and pastries along with a variety of freshly brewed Kona coffee.

★ ***Basil's Pizzaria & Ristorante*** *(Italian)*
75-5707 Ali'i Drive, right across from Hulihe'e Palace, Kailua-Kona; 808-326-7836.

Hours: 11 a.m. to 11 p.m. *Sampling:* The all-Italian menu offers pizza, pasta, seafood, eggplant parmigiana, chicken cacciatore, chicken marsala, sausage and peppers, individual gourmet pizzas, New York–style pizzas, sandwiches, soups, salads and more. *Comments:* Nice atmosphere, open-air views across Ali'i Drive to Kailua Harbor. Good food, good service. Beer and wine are served.

★ ***Bianelli's*** *(Italian)*

75-240 Nani Kailua Road, Kailua-Kona; 808-329-7062.

Hours: Monday through Friday 11 a.m. to 10 p.m.; Saturday 4 p.m. to 10 p.m. Closed Sunday. *Sampling:* This Italian eatery offers New York hand-tossed or Chicago deep dish–style pizza plus a variety of freshly made pastas daily including lasagna, spaghetti, manicotti and eggplant pasta; they also have calzones, Philly steak subs and other sandwiches.

★ ***Buns in the Sun*** *(Sandwiches/Snacks)*

Lanihau Center, 75-5595 Palani Road, Kailua-Kona; 808-326-2774.

Hours: Monday through Friday 5 a.m. to 4 p.m.; Saturday and Sunday 5 a.m. to 3 p.m. *Sampling:* Expect a full range of fresh baked pastries, breads, rolls, desserts and gourmet sandwiches. Ask about specials including the spicy breakfast sandwich, Kona cheesesteak or Bird of Paradise (sliced turkey, bacon and Swiss cheese on grilled sourdough bread). *Comments:* This small bakery/deli/coffee shop is bright, clean and very popular with residents and visitors alike.

Bong Brothers Coffee Company *(Coffee/Sandwiches/Snacks)*

84-5227 Mamalahoa Highway, between mile markers 106 and 105, Honaunau; 808-328-9289; fax 808-328-8112.

Hours: 9:30 a.m. to 6 p.m. *Sampling:* Kona coffee, fresh fruits and vegetarian food to go.

Coffee Shack *(Sandwiches/Pizza)*

83-5799 Mamalahoa Highway, between mile markers 108 and 109, south of Captain Cook; 808-328-9555.

Hours: 7 a.m. to 5 p.m. *Sampling:* A nice stop on the way south, Coffee Shack has eggs for breakfast, plus a delicious menu of deli sandwiches, salads and fresh-made soups, plus individual gourmet pizzas and a nice selection of cakes and pies, muffins, cinnamon rolls and other desserts.

Cruisin Coffee Kona *(Coffee Shop/Espresso Bar)*

75-5702 Kuakini Highway, Kailua-Kona; 808-326-9555.

Hours: Open 24 hours. *Sampling:* This coffee house features a variety of espresso, Italian sodas, milkshakes, pastries and snacks. They feature Kona coffee and Seattle's Best coffees.

Cuz'uns *(Sandwiches/Snacks)*
75-5744 Ali'i Drive, oceanfront in the Kona Inn Shopping Village, Kailua-Kona; 808-326-4920.

Hours: 9 a.m. to 9 p.m. *Sampling:* This small deli snack bar features fresh deli sandwiches, pizza, salads, snacks and beverages. Great smoothies include flavors like mango, guava and pina colada, along with a spirulina energy smoothie and high-protein sports smoothie. Or try Hawaiian-made ice creams, frozen yogurts and sorbets.

Dara's Thai Cuisine *(Thai)*
74-5476 Kaiwi Street, one street north of Palani Road, Kailua-Kona; 808-329-0795.

Hours: 11 a.m. to 9 p.m. *Sampling:* Over 130 items on their exotic menu, featuring complete, reasonably priced lunch and dinner selections of appetizers, soups, salads, hot entrees, noodles and rice dishes. *Comments:* Beer and wine served.

Daylight Donuts & Deli *(Sandwiches/Snacks)*
Keauhou Shopping Center, 78-6831 Ali'i Drive, Keauhou; 808-324-1833.

Hours: 6 a.m. to 4 p.m. *Sampling:* This is the only donut shop in Kona, providing a variety of fresh-made-daily donuts, *malasadas* and specialty pastries. They also have fresh deli items like breakfast rolls, deli sandwiches for lunch, salads and hot and cold beverages.

★ **Denny's** *(American)*
Crossroads Shopping Center, 75-1027 Henry Street, Kailua-Kona; 808-334-1313.

Hours: Open 24 hours. *Sampling:* This is the Big Island's first Denny's, and you'll find pretty much the same menu as the numerous mainland outlets. If you're looking for basic comfort-type food, egg dishes, burgers and fries, steaks, chicken, spaghetti and so forth, this is the place.

Don's Chinese Kitchen *(Chinese)*
Kona Coast Shopping Center, 74-5588 Palani Road, Kailua-Kona; 808-329-3770.

Hours: 10 a.m. to 9 p.m. Closed Sunday. *Sampling:* This small lunch counter specializes in a variety of Chinese plate-lunch fare and take-out plus *manapua* (steamed meat-filled buns). *Comments:* This is a popular spot with the shopping center crowds; sidewalk table seating available.

★ **Drysdale's Two** *(Steaks/Burgers)*
Keauhou Shopping Center, 78-6831 Ali'i Drive, Kailua-Kona; 808-322-0070.

Hours: 11 a.m. to 11:30 p.m., bar closes at 1 a.m. *Sampling:* A great *pupu* menu, plus heavier fare, including prime rib, steak and fresh island fish. *Comments:* An energetic, fun sports bar and island eatery featuring two large-screen TVs for sports events. Indoor-outdoor table seating and a large bar space.

★ ***Durty Jake's*** *(Sandwiches/Snacks/American)*
Coconut Grove Marketplace, 75-5819 Ali'i Drive, Kailua-Kona; 808-329-7366.

Hours: 7 a.m. to 10 p.m., bar may be open later. *Sampling:* This indoor/outdoor bar-cafe offers a breakfast menu of waffles, specialty egg dishes, bagels, fresh pastries and other morning items. For lunch and dinner, try their juicy burgers, fresh fish, salads, soups, sandwiches, pasta and other specials plus bar beverages.

★ ***Harbor House*** *(American/Seafood)*
74-425 Kealakehe Parkway, located in Gentry Marina, Honokohau Harbor, Kailua-Kona; 808-326-4166.

Hours: Monday through Saturday 11 a.m. to 7 p.m.; Sunday 11 a.m. to 5:30 p.m. *Sampling:* The menu offers fish or calamari and chips, burgers, clam chowder, a variety of hot and cold sandwiches (including grilled surimi crab salad) and local favorites. *Comments:* This is an old-fashioned bar and grill right on the marina at Honokohau. We enjoy this large, airy dining room with its great views of the busy activities of the boat harbor, along with a cold 18-oz. "schooner" of beer.

★ ***Holuakoa Cafe Espresso Bar*** *(Coffee Shop/Espresso Bar/Sandwiches/ Snacks)*
76-5901 Mamalahoa Highway, right in Holualoa Village, five miles above Kailua-Kona; 808-322-2233.

Hours: 6:30 a.m. to 3 p.m. Closed Sunday. *Sampling:* This small snack bar offers fresh Kona coffee and local pastries, plus for lunch sandwiches, salad and soup of the day.

Hong Kong Chop Suey *(Chinese)*
Kealakekua Ranch Center, Highway 11, Kealakekua; 808-323-3373.

Hours: 9:30 a.m. to 8:30 p.m. Closed Tuesday. *Sampling:* This simple but clean Chinese kitchen serves up delicious Hong Kong–style food. Many daily plate-lunch and dinner dishes feature chicken, pork, beef and vegetarian choices. House specials include pepper shrimp or calamari, Hong Kong–style crispy duck, and shrimp with black bean sauce. *Comments:* You'll find good Chinese food at reasonable prices here. Take-out is available as well as catering.

★ ***Island Lava Java*** *(Sandwiches/Snacks/Coffee Shop/Espresso Bar)*
Ali'i Sunset Plaza, 75-5799 Ali'i Drive, Kailua-Kona; 808-327-2161.

Hours: 6 a.m. to 10 p.m. *Sampling:* This bakery and bistro espresso bar features fine coffees and teas, fresh-baked croissants, muffins, scones, pastries, cakes, fresh sandwiches, snack items and more.

Jill's Country Kitchen *(Sandwiches/Snacks)*
Kona Bali Kai Condo, 76-6246 Ali'i Drive, Kailua-Kona; 808-329-6010.

Hours: 7 a.m. to 7 p.m. Closed Sunday. *Sampling:* This small operation serves up sandwiches, burritos, daily specials and a variety of snack items along with a range of bakery goods and products.

King Yee Lau *(Chinese)*
Ali'i Sunset Plaza, 75-5799 Ali'i Drive #A6, Kailua-Kona; 808-329-7100.

Hours: Lunch 11 a.m. to 2 p.m., dinner 5 p.m. to 9 p.m. *Sampling:* Their extensive menu lists 100 varied items including soups, chicken and duck, beef and pork, seafood, egg-veggie-tofu, noodles and rice dishes, Mandarin cuisine, served family style: chef's shrimp with pineapple, and kung pao with fried noodle. House specialties include a Peking duck dinner. They also offer an all-you-can-eat buffet lunch.

Kona Cakes & Coffee *(Sandwiches/Snacks)*
74-5588 Pawai Place, Building A, Kailua Kona; 808-329-6679.

Hours: 9 a.m. to 2 p.m. Closed Sunday and Monday. *Sampling:* A bakery with a lot to choose from, including cakes for all occasions, baklava, muffins, tortes and tarts and mochi specialties. They also offer a "Munchie Menu" of sandwiches, bagels, salads and vegetarian specials.

★ ***Mac Pie Factory*** *(Bakery/Snacks)*
74-5035 Queen Ka'ahumanu Highway, Kailua-Kona; 808-329-7437; 888-622-7437; www.macpie.com.

Hours: 9 a.m. to 6 p.m. Closed Sunday. *Sampling:* OK, this is not actually a restaurant, but the Mac Pie is one of those irresistible things about the Big Island that almost guarantees you'll be back. The shop also has espressos and lattes by the Hawaiian Coffee & Tea Company, smoothies and sweet treats from Kona confections.

★ ***Manago Hotel*** *(Hawai'i Local Style/American)*
Highway 11, ten miles south of Kailua-Kona at Captain Cook; 808-323-2642; www.managohotel.com.

Hours: Tuesday through Sunday for breakfast 7 a.m. to 9 a.m., lunch 11 a.m. to 2 p.m., dinner 5 p.m. to 7:30 p.m. Closed Monday. *Sampling:* There's no menu; the day's selections are on a board on the wall, but popular items include fried fish, teriyaki and their famous special pork chops. *Comments:* Worth the drive for the good home cooking and Japanese-American specialties, enjoyed by local folks and visitors alike. Call ahead for box picnic lunches to pick up on the way to the Volcanoes National Park.

Manna Korean Bbq *(Korean)*

Crossroads Shopping Center, 75-1027 Henry Street, Kailua-Kona; 808-334-0880.

Hours: 10 a.m. to 8:30 p.m. Closed Sunday. *Sampling & Comments:* This is a clean, bright lunch counter operation with a menu board plus steam table of fresh selections. The menu features generous servings of excellent Korean cuisine including *kalbi*, BBQ beef and chicken, chicken *katsu*, fish jun, spicy pork, *man doo*, several soup and noodle dishes and other specials, including "the #1 chicken in Kona." Manna plates let you choose the entree and choice of four veggies and two scoops of rice. It's a lot to eat for $7-$8.

★ ***Ocean View Inn*** *(Hawai'i Local Style/American)*

75-5683 Ali'i Drive, in the heart of Kailua-Kona just down from Kailua Pier (an easy stroll from Royal Kona Resort or King Kamehameha's Kona Beach Hotel); 808-329-9998.

Hours: Breakfast 6:30 a.m. to 11 a.m., lunch 11 a.m. to 2:45 p.m., dinner 5:15 p.m. to 9 p.m. Closed Monday. *Sampling:* A landmark Kona eatery for many years, Ocean View Inn has an amazing, extensive, eclectic menu offering almost anything you can think of for breakfast, lunch or dinner. Chinese, American, Hawaiian and local-style food is served up in interesting combinations and plentiful portions. *Comments:* It's not new and it's not fancy, but the food is good, the view is unbeatable and the service is generally personable. If you sit by the window, you can people-watch and enjoy the ocean breeze. Feel free to ask questions or request a smaller serving for a taste of something new. Go early for dinner as it gets crowded rapidly. Also bar and take-out food.

Orchid Thai Cuisine *(Thai)*

74-5563 Kaiwi Street, Kailua-Kona; 808-327-9437.

Hours: Monday through Friday 11 a.m. to 9 p.m.; Saturday 11:30 a.m. to 9 p.m. Closed Sunday. *Sampling:* A variety of mild-to-hot spicy Thai cuisine for lunch and dinner, featuring appetizers such as Thai spring rolls and stuffed chicken wings, green papaya, calamari or shrimp salad, Thai soups and entrees like red, green or yellow curry with beef or chicken, cashew chicken, BBQ hen, *pad* tofu, *pad woon sen*, *pad* Thai, and an assortment of noodle and rice dishes. Many of the entrees come with your choice of fish, seafood, chicken, beef and pork.

Paparoni's *(Italian)*

82-6127 Mamalahoa Highway, Captain Cook; 808-323-2661.

Hours: 11 a.m. to 9 p.m. *Sampling:* Deli sandwiches, soups and salads, or heartier fare such as a lasagna or chicken parmesan dinner with salad and garlic bread. *Comments:* A hard-to-miss, friendly stop for great pizza, pasta and more. Daily specials, take-out and pizza by the slice.

Peacock House Restaurant *(Chinese)*

81-6587 Mamalahoa Highway in Kealakekua, across from Kamigaki Market; 808-323-2366.

Hours: 10 a.m. to 8 p.m. Closed Sunday. *Sampling:* The menu is Cantonese-Chinese cuisine with dim sum. House specialties include spicy pork ribs, prawns and scallops.

Pot Belli Deli *(Plate Lunches/Sandwiches/Snacks)*

74-5543 Kaiwi Road, Kailua-Kona; 808-329-9454.

Hours: 6 a.m. to 4 p.m. *Sampling:* This full deli serves sandwiches, salads, plate lunches, and other deli items. *Comments:* The booths and tables are jammed in tightly, making for crowded conditions. It is located in the industrial area and caters to the people working there and is very busy during lunch. Take-out available.

Quinn's Restaurant *(Seafood)*

75-5655A Palani Road, Kailua-Kona; 808-329-3822.

Hours: 11 a.m. to 1 a.m. *Sampling:* This comfortable eatery and neighborhood pub offers great burgers, sandwiches and sides, plus a nice dinner menu featuring steaks, fresh island fish and seafood. *Comments:* They offer casual late-night dining on the lanai, one of the few Kona dining spots serving late-night dinner.

★ ***Reuben's Mexican Food II*** *(Mexican)*

75-5711 Kuakini Highway, Kailua-Kona; 808-329-4686.

Hours: Monday through Saturday 11 a.m. to 9 p.m.; Sunday 5 p.m. to 9 p.m. *Sampling:* The menu features generous servings of good quality crab enchiladas, chicken *flautas*, *chiles rellenos*, chimichangas and much more—from mild to spicy hot (if you like it really hot, just ask). Beer, wine and cocktails and margaritas by the pitcher or the glass. *Comments:* A fun eatery for Mexican food lovers. Our visit happened on a night when the whole family was entertaining the room with songs and dances, but we don't suppose this is a scheduled event. Take-out available.

★ ***Rocky's Pizza & Deli*** *(Italian)*

Keauhou Shopping Center, 78-6831 Ali'i Drive, Kailua-Kona; 808-322-3223.

Hours: 11 a.m. to 9 p.m. *Sampling:* The popular menu features excellent pizza (whole or by the slice) with choice of four sizes and 32 toppings. House special pizzas include the Hawaiian, Italian White Pie, Mexican Pizza, "Meatsa" Pizza, Veggie, and Rocky's Combo. They also claim to be home of "Kona's Largest Pizza," a 26-inch party pie for $25.99. There are a variety of calzones, pasta such as spaghetti, lasagna, ravioli, manicotti and eggplant parmesan. And rounding out the menu are BBQ ribs, a variety of sandwiches, salads and sides (ask about their hot wings).

★ ***Royal Jade Garden*** *(Chinese)*
Lanihau Center, 75-5595 Palani Road, Kailua-Kona; 808-326-7288.

Hours: 10:30 a.m. to 9 p.m. *Sampling:* This neat family-run restaurant offers a full line of delicious Chinese food. The varied cuisine features regional hot and spicy dishes and house specialties include Hong Kong honey-garlic shrimp and Mongolian beef. *Comments:* The food is generally good quality and of ample quantity, served in clean, bright and comfortable surroundings. Take-out, too.

Senor Billy's Y Granmas *(Mexican)*
Highway 11, Captain Cook; 808-323-2012.

Hours: 10 a.m. to 8 p.m. Closed Sunday. *Sampling:* Excellent and varied Mexican food including tacos, burritos, enchiladas, local-style plate lunches, sandwiches and more. *Comments:* Easy-to-find location right off the highway.

Seven Senses *(Coffee Shop)*
79-7941 Mamalahoa Highway, Keauhou-Kona; 808-324-4414; e-mail: pvnlog@aol.com.

Hours: 8 a.m. to 6 p.m. *Sampling:* 100 percent Kona coffee, espresso and homemade scone and other goodies, reasonably priced.

★ ***Sibu Cafe*** *(Indonesian)*
Kona Banyan Court, 75-5695E Ali'i Drive, Kailua-Kona; 808-329-1112.

Hours: Lunch 11:30 a.m. to 2:30 p.m., dinner 5 p.m. to 9 p.m. *Sampling:* A unique menu featuring intriguing Indonesian dishes such as chicken and beef satay, curry and other special exotics. A variety of imported beers is featured. *Comments:* If you like it hot, ask for the extra-spicy version of their Southeast Asian cuisine. Noted by mainland and local magazines as one of the most interesting, moderately priced places to eat on the island. Inside and lanai-courtyard dining. No reservations, no credit cards.

Sunset Grille *(Sandwiches/Snacks)*
Ali'i Sunset Plaza, 75-5799 Ali'i Drive, Kailua-Kona; 808-329-4668.

Hours: 10:30 a.m. to 5:30 p.m. Closed Sunday. *Sampling:* Made-to-order sandwiches like reuben, New Yorker, Broadway, veggie, etc., with fresh sliced turkey, roast beef, corned beef, salami, salmon and more.

Tacos El Unico *(Mexican)*
Kona Marketplace shopping center, just off Ali'i Drive, Kailua-Kona; 808-326-4033.

Hours: 10:30 a.m. to 9:30 p.m. *Sampling:* Chef-owner Jose y Lupe and his family offer good quality, authentic Mexican specialties. Choose from *carne asada*, burritos of chicken, beef, *lengua* or *cabeza*, *tripas* and *tortas* of *chorizo*, *carne asada*, *lengua* and chicken. *Comments:* Tacos El Unico means "the only one," and while this little sidewalk cafe–type eatery is not the only Mexican restaurant in Kona, it's certainly getting a lot of attention among aficionados. The menu is still growing, as is the popularity of this pleasant, unique eatery.

Taeng-on Thai Cafe *(Thai)*
Kona Inn Shopping Village, 75-5744 Ali'i Drive, Kailua-Kona; 808-329-1994.

Hours: Lunch 11 a.m. to 2:30 p.m., dinner 5 p.m. to 9:30 p.m. Closed Sunday. *Sampling:* The extensive menu is authentic Thai with selections like red or yellow curry, Thai noodles, Thai dumpling soup, sweet and sour veggies, spicy fried rice and many more, with choice of mild, medium or Thai hot seasoning. *Comments:* This airy upstairs dining room has tropical decor combined with touches of Thailand.

Teru's Ii Restaurant & Bar *(Hawai'i Local Style)*
74-5555 Kaiwi Street, old industrial area of Kailua-Kona; 808-326-7700.

Hours: Monday through Saturday for breakfast and lunch 7 a.m. to 2 p.m., dinner 5 p.m. to 9 p.m.; Sunday 8 a.m. to 1 p.m. *Sampling:* This local-style cafe offers a varied menu including selections like teriyaki chicken and steak, beef stew, liver and onions, fried fish, pork chops, chili and rice, a wide variety of hot and cold sandwiches, soups and salads, plus a number of daily specials. *Comments:* Nothing fancy about this blue-collar eatery but the food is good and reasonable in cost.

★ ***Teshima's Restaurant*** *(Japanese/American)*
79-7251 Mamalahoa Highway, Kealakekua, seven miles south of Kailua-Kona; 808-22-9140.

Hours: Breakfast and lunch 6:30 a.m. to 1:45 p.m., dinner 5 p.m. to 10 p.m. *Sampling:* Specialties are Japanese-American cuisine and local favorites and the menu has something for everyone. *Comments:* This neat, clean family restaurant is popular and features friendly old-fashioned service by the Teshima family. If you want to see what a country Hawaiian cafe is like, this is the place.

★ ***Thai Rin Restaurant*** *(Thai)*
Ali'i Sunset Plaza, 75-5799 Ali'i Drive, Kailua-Kona; 808-329-2929.

Hours: Monday through Saturday for lunch 11 a.m. to 2:30 p.m., dinner 5 p.m. to 9 p.m.; Sunday 5 p.m. to 9 p.m. *Sampling:* This restaurant turns out great versions of trendy hot and spicy Thai cuisine. The menu features over two dozen items including traditional Thai crispy and fried noodles, chicken satay, five different kinds of curry, spicy soups, Thai garlic shrimp or squid and much more.

★ ***Tropics Cafe*** *(Hawai'i Local Style/American)*
Royal Kona Resort, 75-5852 Ali'i Drive, Kailua-Kona; 808-329-3111; www.royalkona.com.

Hours: 6:30 a.m. to 9:30 p.m. *Sampling:* Chef Frank's menu features Hawaiian-style specials and American cuisine including sandwiches and burgers, varied seafood salads (a specialty), omelets and local favorites like saimin noodles, fish and chips, stir-fried beef and chicken, chow mein, fried noodles and more. Breakfast is served a la carte or buffet style. Chef Frank is famous for his generous buffet dinners on holidays or other special occasions. *Comments:* Enjoy the food while overlooking views of Kailua Bay and the village from this edge-of-the-water location.

★ ***Wasabi's*** *(Japanese)*
Coconut Grove Marketplace, 75-5815 Ali'i Drive, Kailua-Kona; 808-326-2352.

Hours: 10 a.m. to 9 p.m.; Friday through Saturday 10 a.m. to 10 p.m. *Sampling:* Traditional Japanese diner specializing in bento box lunches for take-out. The varied menu includes *yakisoba*, tempura udon, *katsu* chicken, exotic freshwater eel, teriyaki and chow fun. Their specialty is creative sushi, and they offer a wide variety of various rolls including California roll, shrimp tempura roll, dragon roll and crazy roll. *Comments:* This small but busy operation is located toward the backside of the Marketplace and is worth seeking out; there's even room for larger parties. Good fresh food, quick service.

Moderate-priced Dining

★ ***Aloha Angel Cafe*** *(Hawai'i Local Style/International)*
In the old Aloha Theater Building on Highway 11, Kainaliu; 808-322-3383.

Hours: Breakfast 8 a.m. to 11 a.m., lunch 11 a.m. to 3 p.m., dinner 5 p.m. to 9 p.m. *Sampling:* Daily specialties are fresh-baked pastries and cookies, sandwiches, charbroiled burgers, organic salads and fresh local fish. Beer and wine are served along with fresh juices, Kona espresso and herb teas. Vegetarians have plenty of options. Chef Donna Stickel's years of experience bring a fresh taste to the place, with a delicious dinner menu featuring elegant dishes like bleu cheese–stuffed filet mignon, New Zealand lamb chops, and pork loin with wild rice and diced cranberries. *Comments:* This delightful, funky old building is a treat to visit, and it's even better to stay and eat in. There's a take-out counter in the 1920s theater lobby, but seating winds three-quarters around the building on a rustic, wooden lanai with great views of the countryside. Go early and allow time for an indulgent dessert like Kona lime pie or mac nut turtle bar, then enjoy a selected film at the theater, half-price with your dinner receipt.

Ba-le French Sandwich & Bakery *(Sandwiches/Vietnamese)*
Kona Coast Shopping Center, 74-5588 Palani Road #103, Kailua-Kona; 808-327-1212.

Hours: Monday through Saturday 10 a.m. to 9 p.m.; Sunday 11 a.m. to 7 p.m. *Sampling:* A Vietnamese restaurant with a selection of deli sandwiches and house-baked French bread and croissants. The varied menu includes a variety of hot entrees, rice noodle and other Asian salads, egg drop soup and summer rolls, stir fry, *pho* (Vietnamese noodle soup), "French" deli sandwiches and a selection of interesting desserts like homemade taro or mango tapioca. Several vegetarian options. *Comments:* Eat in or carry out.

★ **Bangkok House** *(Thai)*
King Kamehameha Mall, 75-5626 Kuakini Highway, Kailua-Kona; 808-329-7764.

Hours: Monday through Friday for lunch 11 a.m. to 3 p.m., dinner nightly 5 p.m. to 9 p.m. *Sampling:* This Thai cuisine restaurant offers a variety of the popular, spicy, hot food of southeast Asia. The extensive menu features 100 selections including beef, chicken, seafood and vegetarian specials. Items like spring rolls, *pad* Thai noodles, beef *panang* curry, sizzling chicken Thai-style and fried rice are excellent. *Comments:* Take-out and delivery available.

★ **Billy Bob's Park & Pork** *(American)*
81-6372 Mamalahoa Highway, just south of 111-mile marker, Captain Cook; 808-323-3371.

Hours: 5 p.m. to 9 p.m. Closed Wednesday. *Samplings:* Possibly the Big Island's only barbecue specialist, Billy Bob's barbecues pork or beef ribs, shredded pork or beef or chicken, and serves your choice with sides like cole slaw, chuckwagon beans, chili, cornbread with honey butter or campfire spuds. There's also a house special Caesar salad, veggie enchiladas, fresh catch and a plate called "hog fries" with cheese, sour cream, salsa, olives and jalapenos. *Comments:* This is a place for people who know how to eat. It's a fun, lively restaurant, worth the trip, with live music every Saturday night. Child's plate available.

★ **Bubba Gump Shrimp Co.** *(Seafood)*
Waterfront Row, 75-5776 Ali'i Drive, Kailua-Kona; 808-331-8442.

Hours: Breakfast 7 a.m. to 10:30 a.m., lunch and dinner 11 a.m. to 10 p.m.; Friday through Saturday till 11 p.m. *Samplings:* The breakfast menu is traditional. But the lunch–dinner menu is heavy on shrimp dishes such as New Orleans barbecue shrimp and sausage, drunken shrimp, dumb luck coconut shrimp, plus other

seafood choices like fish and chips, Bourbon Street mahimahi, Dixie-style baby back ribs and fresh Northwest salmon. There's also a variety of appetizers, salads, sandwiches, burgers and desserts. *Comments:* This seafood eatery is part of a national chain that has outlets in California, Florida, New Orleans, etc. The decor is funky boat dock, shrimp-fishers shack and beach flotsam and jetsam.

★ ***Cassandra's*** *(Greek)*
Kona Plaza Arcade, 75-5669 Ali'i Drive, Kailua-Kona; 808-326-2840; www.cassandraskona.com.

Hours: 11 a.m. to 9 p.m. *Sampling:* For lunch, they offer a good selection of burgers, pizzas, fish and chips and gyros. For dinner, step out of bounds and choose from tempting appetizers like spanakopita, *santorini* shrimp cocktail, *kafteri*, hummus and many more. Then indulge in *moussaka* (eggplant and beef in bechamel sauce), *dolmades* (beef-stuffed grape leaves with *avgolemono* sauce) or *sountzoukia* (spiced meatballs in Cassandra's favorite tomato sauce) along with fresh catch, seafood specialties, lamb, pork and chicken dishes. *Comments:* This inside/outside cafe is the Big Island's first and foremost Greek restaurant and presents a fine menu of authentic gourmet selections accented with island touches. Occasionally, Cassandra treats her customers to belly dancing on the weekends.

Hama-yu at Kona Japanese Restaurant *(Japanese)*
In the Kopiko Plaza below the Lanihau Center, Palani Road, Kailua-Kona; 808-326-7799.

Hours: Lunch 11:30 a.m. to 2 p.m., dinner 5:30 p.m. to 9 p.m. *Sampling:* Traditional dishes include teriyaki beef, pork *tonkatsu*, broiled fish, shrimp, *donburi*, noodles and more.

Hang Loose *(Seafood/Hawai'i Local Style)*
Kona Inn Shopping Village, 75-5744 Ali'i Drive, Kailua-Kona; 808-331-1155.

Hours: 11 a.m. to 9:30 p.m. *Sampling:* The menu highlights seafood and fresh catch (*ono*, ahi, swordfish, spearfish and mahimahi may be available) prepared singularly or in combination platters, Oriental-style, in salads or creative pasta dishes. *Comments:* Hang Loose occupies a great open-air building overlooking Kailua Bay—great views to complement the food.

Happi Yu Japanese Steak House *(Steaks)*
75-5770 Ali'i Drive, in the Waterfront Row complex across from St. Michael's Church, Kailua-Kona; 808-326-5653.

Hours: 5:30 p.m. to 9 p.m. *Sampling:* This Japanese-style *teppanyaki* steak house is next door to Yu Sushi, a companion operation. The menu features varied grill selections including chicken, teriyaki steak, filet mignon, fresh island fish, lobster, shrimp and scallop. *Comments:* Place your order and be entertained by the chef as he slices, dices, chops, tosses and sizzles your meal at the table.

★ ***Hard Rock Cafe Kona*** *(American)*
Coconut Grove Marketplace, 75-5815 Ali'i Drive, Kailua-Kona; 808-329-8866.

Hours: 11 a.m. to 11 p.m. *Sampling:* The restaurant's decor, ambiance and menu of American cuisine, burgers and daily specials is much like the other Hard Rocks in this international chain. *Comments:* The Hard Rock Cafe Kona is in a shopping/dining complex and occupies a two-level building with nice views overlooking Kailua Bay. The lower level has the Hard Rock logo shop while the open-air restaurant is located upstairs.

★ ***Huggo's on the Rocks*** *(American/Seafood)*
75-5828 Kahakai Road, Kailua-Kona; 808-329-1493; www.huggos.com.

Hours: Monday through Friday 11:30 a.m. to 2:30 p.m., dinner 5:30 p.m. to 10pm; Saturday and Sunday 5:30 p.m. to 10 p.m. *Sampling:* Enjoy your favorite beverages along with lunch and dinner. Order from their bar menu of *pupus*, seafood specials, pizza and sandwiches or from Huggo's regular lunch and dinner menus. *Comments:* This is a beach hut bar addition to the well-known and popular Huggo's main beachside restaurant and is located right next door at water's edge.

★ ***Jameson's by the Sea*** *(Continental-International/Seafood)*
77-6452 Ali'i Drive next to Magic Sands Beach, Kailua-Kona; 808-329-3195.

Hours: Monday through Friday for lunch 11:30 a.m. to 2:30 p.m., dinner nightly 5 p.m. to 9 p.m. *Samplings:* The menu highlights fresh fish and also features varied American-Continental selections such as pasta, beef, veal, lamb, chicken and fresh island fish. Specialties include veal piccata, filet mignon, lobster, calamari and rack of lamb. *Comments:* A *kama'aina* (resident) favorite, the oceanfront setting at Magic Sands Beach makes for a romantic atmosphere to enjoy an excellent meal. Smooth, soothing Hawaiian background music, white tablecloths, candlelight, fine service and cheerful bright surroundings add a gracious touch. Beautiful sunsets complimentary with dinner.

Kama'aina Terrace *(Hawai'i-Pacific Regional Cuisine/International)*
Ohana Keauhou Beach Resort, 78-6740 Ali'i Drive, Keauhou-Kona; 808-322-3441.

Hours: Monday through Saturday for breakfast and lunch 6:30 a.m. to 10:30 a.m., dinner 5:30 p.m. to 9 p.m.; Sunday 6:30 a.m. to 1 p.m., 5:30 p.m. to 9 p.m. *Sampling:* The menu here focuses on local-style Hawaiian-Pacific favorites with international accents. Selections range from steaks to hibachi chicken, fresh island fish and seafood and traditional selections in a breakfast buffet. *Comments:* This is a nice open-air dining room with a relaxing ambiance, located near the pool and oceanfront hotel terrace extending over the tidepools.

★ ***Keei Café*** *(Continental-International)*
Highway 11, half-mile south of Kainaliu; 808-328-8451.

Hours: Tuesday through Saturday 5 p.m. to 9 p.m. Closed Sunday and Monday. *Sampling:* The menu is a mix of Continental and international fare that changes frequently. The varying menu may include appetizers like black bean soup, eggplant rolls and green papaya salad, entrees such as tofu or chicken fajitas, fettuccine primavera with tofu or chicken, and Hawaiian seafood in a variety of preparations including red Thai curry, pan-seared, or grilled on a bed of baby lettuce with peanut miso dressing.

★ ***Kimo's Family Buffet*** *(Hawai'i-Pacific Regional Cuisine/Local Style)*
Uncle Billy's Kona Bay Hotel, 75-5739 Ali'i Drive, Kailua-Kona; 808-329-1393.

Hours: Breakfast 7 a.m. to 11 a.m., dinner 5:30 p.m. to 9 p.m. *Samplings:* The menu changes nightly but usually offers beef, chicken, seafood and other local favorites. *Comments:* One of the last bargains in Kona, this open-air dining room sits just above busy Ali'i Drive in the heart of town. It has sort of a 1940s South Seas atmosphere and a buffet-only menu heavy in local-style Hawai'i cuisine. There is often evening entertainment and a hula show included. Reservations suggested for dinner.

★ ***Kona Beach Restaurant*** *(Hawai'i-Pacific Regional Cuisine/International)*
King Kamehameha's Kona Beach Hotel, 75-5660 Palani Road, Kailua-Kona; 808-329-2911.

Hours: Breakfast buffet 6:30 a.m. to 10:30 a.m., lunch 11 a.m. to 2 p.m., dinner 5:30 p.m. to 9 p.m. *Sampling:* The menu features specialties such as Pacific broiled salmon, *kiawe*-smoked prime rib, herbal breast of chicken, Cajun prawns with pasta and more. They also offer an interesting variety of buffet dinners every night of the week: Monday's Hawaiian specialties, Tuesday's Crab and Tempura, Wednesday's Chinese Food, Thursday's Italian Cuisine, and Friday and Saturday's Prime Rib and Seafood, along with the "King Kam's" famous Sunday champagne brunch. *Comments:* Their attractive dining room has old-fashioned whaling-ship decor. There are big picture windows providing unbeatable views for each table, of Kailua Wharf, Ahu'ena Heiau and Kamakahonu Beach. Delightful setting with live piano music, attractive wood paneling and fish tanks to amuse the kids. Good service and they take good care of youngsters, providing extra goodies. Reservations suggested.

★ ***Kona Brewing Co.*** *(Italian/Pizza)*
North Kona Town Center, 75-5629 Kuakini Highway, Kailua-Kona; 808-334-2739; www.konabrewingco.com.

Hours: 11 a.m. to 9 p.m.; Friday and Saturday till 10 p.m. *Sampling:* Their fresh-made brews are worth trying just for their names, but are also good quality: Pacific Golden Ale, Longboard Lager, Fire Rock Pale Ale, Lilikoi Wheat Ale, Duke's Draft Blonde Ale, Lavaman Red Ale, Castaway IPA and Black Sand Porter. The brew pub menu features a fascinating variety of delicious pizza such as BBQ Chicken, Kona Garden, Kona Wild Mushroom, Puna Pie, Captain Cook, Hawaiian Luau and more. The menu also has sandwiches, salads, bar snack foods and more. *Comments:* This is Kona's original brew pub, where they make hand-crafted ales and lagers. Survivors of the microbrewery craze of recent years, Kona Brewing Company remains a popular, fun and satisfying place to eat and drink. The bar closes an hour after dinner.

Kona Galley *(Seafood/American/Hawai'i Local Style)*
Seaside Mall, 75-5663 Ali'i Drive, across from King Kamehameha's Kona Beach Hotel and Kailua Pier, Kailua-Kona; 808-329-5550.

Hours: 11 a.m. to 9:30 p.m. *Sampling:* The menu offers fresh catch of the day, seafood, pasta, pizza, chicken, sandwiches and local favorites. *Comments:* There are open-air harbor views of Kailua Bay and lovely sunsets from its upstairs location. Reservations suggested.

★ ***Kona Inn Restaurant*** *(Seafood)*
Kona Inn Shopping Village, 75-5744 Ali'i Drive, Kailua-Kona; 808-329-4455.

Hours: 11:30 a.m. to 10 p.m. *Sampling:* The menu features fresh island fish, seafood, prime rib, steak and local favorites. *Comments:* There is a pleasant casualness in this open-air veranda restaurant that is the original dining room of the old Kona Inn Hotel. The ceiling fans add to the tropical ambiance and informality. This is one of our favorite places to take visitors, with its beautiful view of Kona Bay and amicable, consistent service. Dinner reservations suggested.

Lasko's Restaurant and Nightclub *(American/International)*
Pottery Terrace complex, 75-5995A Kuakini Highway, Kailua-Kona; 808-331-2558.

Hours: Monday through Friday 11 a.m. to 2 a.m.; Saturday and Sunday 2 p.m. to 2 a.m. *Sampling:* A tasteful menu, well prepared and presented with a variety of choices from elegant to home-style. *Comments:* Comfortable bar is open after-hours.

Lulu's *(American)*
75-5819 Ali'i Drive, Kailua-Kona; 808-329-6766; www.luluskona.com.

Hours: 11 a.m. to 10 p.m.; dancing and libations till 2 a.m. *Sampling:* Boasting "red carpet service at shag rug prices," Lulu's offers a colorful, eclectic menu with a little bit of everything for lunch, dinner and *pupus*. Choose from pepper-smoked turkey wings, Cajun cornmeal fried *opo* shrimp, Tiajuana mahi tacos with chipotle aioli, Fisherman's Bucket, or something from "Big Sweaty's Barbecue Pit," slow-smoked on *kiawe* and guava wood, in small, medium and "sumo" portions.

★ ***Michaelangelo's Italian and Seafood Restaurant*** *(Italian/Seafood)*
75-5770 Ali'i Drive, Waterfront Row, across from St. Michael's Church, Kailua-Kona; 808-329-4436.

Hours: 11 a.m. to 10 p.m. *Sampling:* The menu features varied Italian fare. Appetizers include crusted mozzarella planks, Marietta escargot in garlic butter, fried calamari and Palermo clam chowder plus a house and Caesar salad. Traditional hearty Italian dishes include spaghetti bolognese, house-made lasagna, chicken cacciatora, chicken or eggplant parmigiana. There is a nice selection of vegetarian pasta dishes like fettuccine alfredo or primavera, pink penne rigatoni or manicotti *formaggio*, and tempting seafood pastas such as "lava-fire" calamari, macadamia nut sea scallops, cioppino, garlic lobster and Trilogy of Fresh Fish. A dessert tray rounds out the menu. *Comments:* Located on the upper level of the complex, this room has a lovely, open-veranda view of the ocean. Dancing until 10 p.m.

Ocean Seafood Chinese Restaurant *(Seafood/Chinese)*
King Kamehameha Mall, 75-5626 Kuakini Highway, Kailua-Kona; 808-329-3055.

Hours: 10:30 a.m. to 9 p.m. *Sampling:* The menu features lobster, crab, fresh scallops, shrimp, oysters and traditional Cantonese cuisine like beef, pork, chicken, duck and noodles, plus a generous all-you-can-eat buffet at lunch and dinnertime.

★ ***Oodles of Noodles*** *(Hawai'i Regional Cuisine/International)*
Crossroads Shopping Center, 75-1027 Henry Street, Kailua-Kona; 808-329-9222.

Hours: 8 a.m. to 9 p.m. *Sampling:* Specializing in "cross-cultural" noodles in a variety of creative ethnic and fusion preparations, Chef Amy Ferguson Ohta serves what she sells: oodles and oodles of various noodles. The menu reminds us of a Dr. Seuss book. There are rice noodles, cake noodles, udon and soba, somen and saimin and nice raviola. (Sorry, Chef.) The flavorful noodle dishes feature fresh local produce, meats, fish and seafood, well prepared and attractively presented. *Comments:* Chef Ohta's many years of professional culinary experience ranged from France to Houston before she established herself as a founding mother of Hawai'i Regional Cuisine from her post at the five-star Hotel Hana Maui. Now Kona is lucky to have her and her small dining room tucked in a corner of Crossroads Shopping Center. With Oodles, she takes HRC to the next level, bringing together Vietnamese, Thai, Italian, Japanese and American cookery in a fun, delicious way.

★ ***Outback Steakhouse*** *(Steaks)*

Coconut Grove Marketplace, Ali'i Drive, Kailua-Kona; 808-326-2555.

Hours: 4:30 p.m. to 10 p.m. *Sampling:* Big Island version of the popular chain restaurant, featuring their famous steaks, *pupus* like the popular Bloomin' Onion, Shrimp on the Barbie, plus Jackeroo Chops, Botany Bay Fish of the Day and Toowoomba Pasta, side orders, desserts and much more in the signature Australian-style dining room.

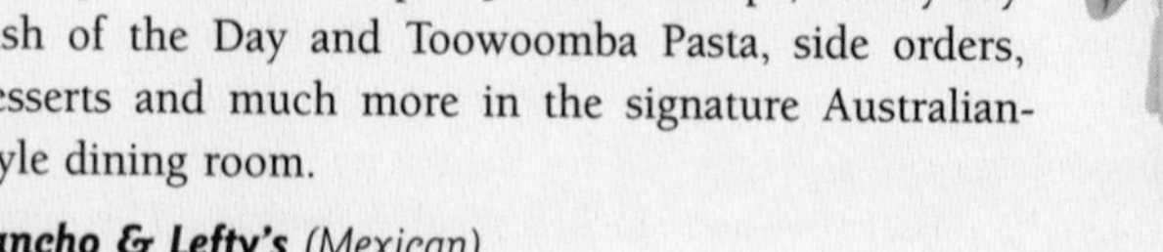

Pancho & Lefty's *(Mexican)*

75-5719 Ali'i Drive, across from Kona Inn Shopping Village in the Kona Plaza Condos, upstairs overlooking Ali'i Drive; 808-326-2171.

Hours: 8 a.m. to 10 p.m. *Sampling:* The menu features the usual Mexican fare such as tacos, burritos, enchiladas, chimichangas, tamales, tostadas and varied *pupus*. *Comments:* Very informal.

Restaurant Yokohama *(Japanese)*

Sunset Ali'i Plaza, 75-5799 Ali'i Drive, Kailua-Kona; 808-329-9661.

Hours: Monday through Friday for lunch 11 a.m. to 2 p.m., dinner 5:30 p.m. to 9 p.m.; Saturday and Sunday 5:30 p.m. to 9 p.m. *Sampling:* This Japanese-style restaurant features teriyaki chicken and beef, *tonkatsu*, tempura, *misoyaki* pork, *sukiyaki*, *shabu shabu*, sushi, sashimi, noodles and fresh island fish. Bento lunch take-out available.

★ ***Rooster's the Restaurant*** *(American)*

75-5699 Ali'i Drive, across from the seawall in the Kailua Bay Inn shopping plaza, Kailua-Kona; 808-327-9453.

Hours: 8 a.m. to 9 p.m. *Sampling:* Rooster's is an interesting, friendly kind of place, open for breakfast, lunch and dinner, with mostly American-style egg dishes, sandwiches and burgers during the day for busy people on the go. Dinnertime brings out the tablecloths and more leisurely service, along with upper-end entrees such as live lobster, baby back ribs, fresh catch and filet mignon with crab imperial, all served with house salad and "shnizzle bread" (garlic and cheese).

★ ***Royal Thai Cafe*** *(Thai)*
Keauhou Shopping Center, 78-6831 Ali'i Drive, Keauhou-Kona; 808-322-8424.

Hours: 10 a.m. to 10 p.m. *Sampling:* The menu is strictly classic Thai cuisine ranging from *pad* Thai noodles and jasmine rice to exotic and spicy red, green and yellow curries, to seafood, chicken, beef and pork specialties and chef's special pineapple fried rice. Diners can choose the degree of spiciness from hot to medium to mild. *Comments:* This small cafe is very clean with an attractive traditional Thai decor. Ample parking.

★ ***Sam Choy's Restaurant*** *(Hawai'i-Pacific Regional Cuisine/Local Style)*
73-5576 Kauhola Bay 1, in the Kaloko Industrial Park near the airport, Kailua-Kona; 808-329-9222.

Hours: Monday through Saturday 6 a.m. to 2 p.m.; Sunday 7 a.m. to 2 p.m. *Sampling:* Sam's excellent cuisine is simple Hawaiian-style comfort food with his own creative and innovative additions. The lunch menu features such things as Kaloko steak with grilled onions, *poke* (cut fresh fish marinated with a variety of Hawaiian ingredients) served uncooked or fried, veggie stir fry, Kaloko noodle mania, teriyaki beef and chicken, beef stew and chicken salad. *Comments:* This small, out-of-the-way place in an unassuming building is one of Kona's most popular restaurants. Chef, cookbook author and TV personality Sam Choy is a well-known Hawai'i celebrity, with two restaurants in Honolulu, one on Maui and one in Tokyo, taking his "original Kona cuisine" far beyond the Big Island. It's tricky to locate but worth the trouble: turn into the Kaloko Industrial Area just north of Kailua-Kona, south of the airport. Look for the Kauhola Street sign to locate the building; it's one road before the road leading up to the Costco discount store. Too bad for us, Sam's not open for dinner at present, but this is still a great stop for lunch (particularly if you have time for a nap afterwards).

★ ***Tres Hombres*** *(Mexican)*
75-5864 Walua Road, at the intersection of Ali'i Drive and Walua Road, across from the Royal Kona Resort, Kailua-Kona; 808-329-2173.

Hours: 11:30 a.m. to 9 p.m. *Sampling:* The menu has tasty Mexican selections like tacos, enchiladas, quesadillas, fajitas and burritos. Other entrees include fresh island fish, chicken and more, plus a nice *pupu* menu. *Comments:* We enjoy visiting this great old building with its long row of open windows overlooking Kona town, and the food is good, too.

★ ***The Vista*** *(Hawai'i-Pacific Regional Cuisine/International)*
Kona Country Club, 78-7000 Ali'i Drive, Kailua-Kona; 808-322-3700.

Hours: Breakfast and lunch year-round 8 a.m. to 3 p.m.; open for dinner November-April, Wednesday-Saturday 5:30 p.m. to 9 p.m. *Sampling:* Chef Dennis De La Cruz, born and raised on the Big Island, knows exactly where to find the best of his favorite ingredients, particularly fish. His menus vary, but sparkle with use of coconut, pineapple, daikon, wasabi, lemongrass and ginger. His sauces are all vegetable-based to improve flavor for vegetarians and meat-eaters alike. A recent sampling featured taro-crusted ahi, Asian shrimp cocktail with sweet chili sauce and whole Keahole Kampachi. Jill's Country Kitchen provides specialty cheesecakes for dessert. *Comments:* After 30 years as a Kona landmark, the Vista must be doing something right. Golfers already know they serve generous all-day breakfast and tasty lunches year-round, but the real treat is their seasonal dinner. Full-service bar, amazing ocean views and friendly service.

Yasu's Kona Sushi *(Japanese)*

Ali'i Sunset Plaza, 75-5799 Ali'i Drive, Kailua-Kona; 808-326-1696.

Hours: Monday, Wednesday, Friday and Saturday noon to 1:30 p.m.; dinner nightly 5 p.m. to 10 p.m. *Sampling:* The menu here is authentic Japanese sushi including *nigiri*, *unagi* eel, squid, fish, veggie California-style and chef's special "Kona Wave" with scallop and spicy *tobiko*.

Expensive-priced Dining

Beachcomber's *(Steaks/Seafood)*

75-5770 Ali'i Drive, Kailua-Kona; 808-329-2451.

Hours: 5 p.m. to 9 p.m. *Sampling:* Select from appetizers such as seared pepper ahi with Cajun spices and lemon-vodka sauce, clam chowder, their signature Caesar or Chart House salad bar, then indulge in cuts of beef like the 22 oz. "Callihan Cut," or fresh catch such as MaiTai Mahi with dark rum butter sauce. If you can't decide, have it all with a combination plate and add hot chocolate lava cake for dessert (order before dinner). *Comments:* An elegant menu and a great location on the *makai* (ocean) side of Ali'i Drive. Paradise Lounge upstairs.

★ ***Edward's at Kanaloa*** *(Continental-International)*

Kanaloa at Kona Condominium, 78-261 Manukai Street, Keauhou; 808-324-1434.

Hours: 8 a.m. to 9 p.m. *Sampling:* European-trained Chef Walter Mares takes pride in his creative preparations and innovative style. A recent menu featured appetizers of soft shell crab in a pommery mustard sauce, baked oysters with spinach and artichoke and grilled quail. Dinner entrees are again uncommon, such as mussels provencal, *coq au vin*, cornish game hen and seafood orzo pesto. An excellent wine list is available by the glass or bottle. The lunch menu is equally intriguing, with interesting dishes such as a barbecue-salmon salad with field greens, bleu cheese, walnuts, dried apricots and raspberry vinaigrette, a portobello mushroom sandwich with goat cheese or low-fat ostrich burger. *Comments:* Edward's has long been considered one of Kona's most romantic restaurants, with a killer view of the ocean that adds to the already-excellent food. Smokers are accommodated at the bar. Not easy to find, but worth the trouble. Call for directions and reservations.

★ ***Huggo's*** *(Seafood/Continental-International)*
75-5828 Kahakai Road, Kailua-Kona; 808-329-1493; www.huggos.com.

Hours: Sunday through Thursday 11 a.m. to 9 p.m.; Friday and Saturday 11 a.m. to 10 p.m. *Sampling:* The menu features a variety of appetizers like island sashimi, seared ahi, Kona *poke* and *kalua* chicken quesadilla plus varied soups and salads. Among the creative entrees are shrimp scampi provencal, seafood linguine, fresh Kona catch, New York steak, black Angus prime rib, sweet chili chicken, wild mushroom pasta and others. Cocktails and beverages at the bar. *Comments:* A Kona tradition and favorite of *kama'aina* (residents) for over 35 years, this delightful open-air oceanside restaurant is just next door to the Royal Kona Resort and sits over the water's edge, affording beautiful views of Kailua Bay and romantic sunsets. A great oceanfront location on Kailua Bay, beautiful sunsets, pleasant ambiance and generally great food.

★ ***La Bourgogne French Restaurant*** *(French)*
Kuakini Plaza South Center, 77-6400 Nalani, off Kuakini Highway #11, just three miles south of Kailua-Kona; 808-329-6711; e-mail: burgundy@hawaii.rr.com.

Hours: 6 p.m. to 10 p.m. Closed Sunday. *Sampling:* Owner and chef Ron Gallaher is a classically trained French cook who prides himself in offering food with "soul and character." A recent menu tempted us with such intriguing presentations as foie gras and sea scallops in a roasted apple raspberry reduction, house-made lobster bisque, osso buco, filet *de chevreuil*, venison with pomegranate glaze, fresh catch, Maine lobster and 100 percent organic Angus beef. Luscious desserts like chocolate grand marnier souffle, baked caramel apple with cinnamon ice cream and cherries jubilee climax your meal. *Comments:* La Bourgogne is one of Kona's best-kept secrets, highly rated by this and other travel guides. Reservations suggested.

Martini Yacht Club *(Seafood)*
75-5820 Ali'i Drive, Kailua-Kona; 808-329-8200.

Hours: Monday through Friday for lunch 10:30 a.m. to 4 p.m., dinner nightly 5:30 p.m. to 9:30 p.m. *Sampling:* Chef/proprietor Stephan Schoembs offers Kona a sophisticated alternative. Begin dinner with escargot, seafood chowder or frogs legs, the club's signature ceviche martini, classic Caesar or mozzarella salad. Then enjoy fish fresh from Kona waters in creative preparations such as grilled *ono* with bok choy and Okinawa spinach, pan-roasted *opah* with asparagus and roasted apricots, lobster, sea scallops with "forbidden rice," and beef, chicken and lamb specialties. *Comments:* Nice shipwreck atmosphere overlooks Ali'i Drive and the bay.

Kohala Coast

SOUTH KOHALA DISTRICT

Inexpensive-priced Dining

Boat Landing Pavilion *(Sandwiches/Snacks)*
Hilton Waikoloa Village, 425 Waikoloa Beach Drive, Waikoloa; 808-886-1234.

Hours: 6 a.m. to 11 p.m. *Sampling:* The food court features on-the-go breakfasts, sandwiches, salads, pizza and many children's favorites. There is also a sushi bar for fresh-made California roll, tempura shrimp roll and more plus a full-service bar. *Comments:* This Hilton dining option is especially for families with youngsters looking for a quick snack, lunch or dinner. It's located at the atrium of the resort's Ocean Tower in front of the Palm Terrace Restaurant.

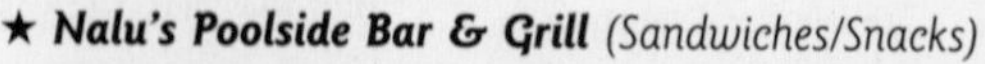

★ ***Nalu's Poolside Bar & Grill*** *(Sandwiches/Snacks)*
Waikoloa Beach Marriott, 69-275 Waikoloa Beach Drive, Kohala Coast; 808-886-6789.

Hours: 10 a.m. until sunset. *Sampling:* This poolside bar and grill has a light fare menu. Salads include Caesar, sea breeze fruit salad, Indonesian chicken salad and seafood Cobb salad. Sandwiches range from turkey to tuna salad, mahi burger to crab salad; desserts, too. Tropical beverages round out the menu.

Pop's Café *(Sandwiches/Snacks/Pizza)*
68-1845 Waikoloa Road, Waikoloa; 808-883-3712.

Hours: 6:30 a.m. to 9 p.m. *Sampling:* The diner-style menu offers hot breakfasts, burgers, plate lunches, pizzas and daily specials. *Comments:* Located in a shaded kiosk by the fountain at Waikoloa Highlands Center, Pop's is a quick, convenient choice for breakfast, lunch or dinner. There are several outdoor tables, or you can get take-out for a picnic as you tour the island. Deliveries available within Waikoloa Village.

Senor Nachos *(Mexican)*
Kings' Shops at Waikoloa Beach Resort food court, Kohala Coast; 808-886-5400.

Hours: 9:30 a.m. to 9:30 p.m. *Sampling:* This fast-food lunch counter operation serves up a variety of good Mexican fare including tacos, burritos, quesadillas and chimichangas with choice of beef, chicken, pork, or vegetarian styles plus Mexican salad and more.

3 Frogs Cafe *(Sandwiches/Snacks)*
Hapuna Beach State Park, Kohala Coast; 808-882-0459.

Hours: 10 a.m. to 5 p.m. *Sampling:* 3 Frogs features hot dogs and burgers, fish tacos, salads and sandwiches, coffee and cold soft drinks—plus shave ice and smoothies. *Comments:* A great place for lunch, just up from the beach. Reasonably priced. Try their Hawaiian salad of romaine lettuce with pineapple and mango, chicken, toasted mac nuts and coconut, only $7.25.

Moderate-priced Dining

Anthony's Restaurant & Beat Club *(Italian/Irish Pub)*
68-1845 Waikoloa Road, Waikoloa; 808-883-9609.

Hours: 11:30 a.m. to 2 a.m. *Sampling:* Lunch and dinner menus feature good burgers, salads like the generous chicken tostada, English-style fish and chips, steaks, chicken, fresh catch, quality *soup du jour* and a selection of excellent pastas and pizzas. Vegetarians, it's worth the drive for their pasta with artichoke, feta cheese and roasted red pepper cream sauce. *Comments:* Located in the Waikoloa Highlands Center, Anthony's is a neighborhood pub with a bistro atmosphere, good food and friendly service. (Plus, it's the only place we've found with Guinness on tap.) After dinner, the dance floor opens for DJ-driven hip-hop music or live bands, including the proprietor's own, Johnny Shot, of the rock-and-roll persuasion.

Arnie's *(American)*
Hapuna Beach Prince Hotel at Mauna Kea Resort, 62-100 Kauna'oa Drive, Waikoloa; 808-880-3192.

Hours: 11 a.m. to 4:30 p.m. *Sampling:* The menu features truly great cheeseburgers with seasoned waffle-cut fries, a variety of sandwiches, fresh catch, Japanese-style golden curry, ahi sashimi, big salads like their seafood Cobb, daily specials and desserts. Try their enormous bowl of saimin (noodle soup with garnishes). *Comments:* A large, bright clubhouse with small bar overlooking the stellar Hapuna Golf Course, Arnie's is a great spot for a leisurely lunch. *Keiki* menu available.

Beach Bar *(Sandwiches/Snacks)*
Hapuna Beach Prince Hotel at Mauna Kea Resort, 62-100 Kauna'oa Drive, Waikoloa; 808-880-3192.

Hours: 11 a.m. to 4:30 p.m. *Sampling:* Amicably set next to the hotel's attractive, whale-shaped swimming pool, the Beach Bar serves up snacks, sandwiches and salads for lunch and afternoon munchies, plus your favorite libations. *Comments: Keiki* menu available. A short walk up from Hapuna Beach State Park, open air with tropical breezes and ocean views.

Beach Tree Bar & Grill *(American)*
Four Seasons Resort Hualalai, 100 Kaupulehu Drive, Kaupulehu-Kona; 808-325-3000.

Hours: 11 a.m. to 8:30 p.m. *Sampling:* The menu features a variety of light California-style American fare and special selections, plus fresh-baked breads and an extensive salad bar. The Beach Tree also offers two theme buffet evenings: "Asian Persuasion" on Monday and "Surf, Sand & Stars Barbecue" on Saturday. *Comments:* This oceanside dining spot creates a relaxing and informal atmosphere for lunch, cocktails, and casual evening dining. Contemporary island entertainment nightly.

Big Island Steak House *(Steaks)*
250 Waikoloa Beach Drive, Suite C1, Waikoloa; 808-886-8805; fax 808-886-0455.

Hours: 5 p.m. to 10 p.m. *Sampling:* The menu features steaks, of course, plus fresh Big Island produce, local fish and seafood in a variety of preparations. Start off with *pupus* like Black & Blue ahi sashimi, spinach and artichoke dip or prawn cocktail, then select from their steak menu, or choose rotisserie-roasted luau chicken, coconut prawns or Thai pasta with stir-fry vegetables and your choice of chicken, tenderloin or prawns. Top it off with Kona coffee macadamia nut pie or a Big Island banana split for two. *Comments:* Located in the King's Shops at Waikoloa Resort, this large, interesting dining room has decor reflecting the romantic Polynesian image of 1950s movies, with nostalgic travel posters and collections of bric-a-brac from Hawai'i's early days of tourism. Upstairs, the Merry Wahine Bar provides entertainment and tropical libations.

Blue Dolphin Restaurant *(Burgers/Seafood)*
61-3616 Kawaihae Harbor Road, Highway 270, one mile from the intersection of Routes 270 and 19, on the mauka side of the road across from the harbor; 808-882-7771.

Hours: Friday and Saturday 5:30 p.m. to 11:30 p.m. *Sampling:* The menu, of course, emphasizes fresh fish, and their signature burgers, along with "world famous" teriyaki beef strips, plate lunches, pastas, salads and desserts. Kids' menu developed from years as a drive-in, with simple items like "Noodles & Nothing" to please pickier eaters. *Comments:* This little place has evolved from a drive-up carry-out window into a full-fare, open-air dining and music hall. They serve up great island food and live entertainment on the weekends by the Big Island's notable musicians.

★ ***Cafe Pesto-Kawaihae*** *(Italian/Hawai'i Regional Cuisine)*
Kawaihae Shopping Center, Kawaihae; 808-882-1071; www.cafepesto.com.

Hours: 11 a.m. to 9 p.m.; Friday and Saturday till 10 p.m. *Sampling:* Although this busy restaurant is best known for its island-style gourmet pizzas, they also offer a wide variety of excellent and creative soups and salads, pasta and risottos, hot sandwiches, calzones and house-made desserts. Appetizers include crostini, focaccia, Pacific crab cakes and salmon pizzette. Dinner entrees include selections like smoked chicken linguini, fresh island fish, Asian-style fettuccine, wok-fired shrimp and scallops, mango-glazed chicken and many more specials. They have an excellent kids' menu.

★ ***Grand Palace*** *(Chinese)*
Kings' Shops at Waikoloa Beach Resort, 250 Waikoloa Beach Drive; 808-886-6668.

Hours: 11 a.m. to 9:30 p.m. *Sampling:* The menu is perhaps the Big Island's most extensive offering of Chinese cuisine, listing 151 separate items of primarily Cantonese selections. There are some varied Chinese exotics thrown in for good measure: five-spiced octopus, cold jellyfish, shark's fin soup, squid with pepper salt, and scalded shrimp with dipping sauce. More familiar traditionals for the less-adventurous include chow mein, fried rice, spring rolls, Peking duck and a wide selection of beef, pork, chicken, seafood and vegetable dishes. *Comments:* The Grand Palace features a bright, clean dining room with formal table settings, fine Chinese artwork decor and white tablecloths. Carry-out orders and prix-fixe menus for one to five people are available.

Hama Yu Japanese Restaurant *(Japanese)*
Kings' Shops at Waikoloa Beach Resort, 250 Waikoloa Beach Drive; 808-886-6333.

Hours: Lunch 11:30 a.m. to 2 p.m., dinner 5:30 p.m. to 9 p.m. *Sampling:* The traditional Japanese menu offers such favorites as teriyaki beef, pork *tonkatsu*, shrimp or vegetable tempura, broiled fish, shrimp, *donburi*, noodles and more. A small sushi bar serves a good selection of made-to-order sushi rolls. *Comments:* This small restaurant features bright contemporary Japanese decor.

Hang Ten *(Sandwiches/Snacks)*
Hilton Waikoloa Village, 425 Waikoloa Beach Drive, Waikoloa; 808-886-1234.

Hours: 10:30 a.m. to 4:30 p.m. *Sampling:* This restaurant offers lunch only with a menu of sandwiches, burgers, hot dogs, chili, salads, smoothies and desserts. *Comments:* This casual open-air deck eatery sits next to the famed dolphin lagoons where diners can watch the dolphins frolic and play. The bar serves up exotic drinks.

★ ***Hau Tree Restaurant & Gazebo Bar*** *(Sandwiches/Snacks)*
Mauna Kea Beach Hotel, 62-100 Mauna Kea Beach Drive, Kohala Coast; 808-882-5810.

Hours: 11 a.m. to 3 p.m. *Sampling:* It's hard for anything to taste bad with a view this good. Right off the sand at Kauna'oa Bay, the Hau Tree is about the island's best beachside lunch spot. Fresh fruit, salads, sandwiches and other light lunch fare is served at beach umbrella tables, along with ice cream treats like the old-fashioned Ovaltine Froth. *Comments:* Right next door is the Gazebo Bar, home of the best Big Island barstool for enjoying a libation at sunset; beer and wine, soft drinks and cocktails, cool blended tropicals along with "virgin" smoothies. The Hau Tree is also the setting for the resort's Saturday-night Clambake seafood buffet, which is the best seafood feast on the Big Island, featuring crab claws, Keahole-Maine lobsters, shrimp, sashimi, a make-your-own ice cream sundae bar and a whole lot more (including meats and vegetables for the less-seafood-inclined), plus live island entertainment. Reservations suggested for the Clambake.

Honu Bar *(Pupus/Desserts)*
Mauna Lani Bay Hotel, 68-1400 Mauna Lani Drive, Kohala Coast; 808-885-6622.

Hours: 5:30 p.m. to 9 p.m. *Sampling:* The Honu Bar serves a wide selection of after-dinner drinks, coffees, lattes and espresso along with remarkable desserts such as crepes suzette, spumoni *bombe* and tiramisu. A heavy *pupu* or light supper menu features Big Island sashimi, seafood antipasto, and oven-baked focaccia flatbreads with sausage, grilled portobello mushrooms or seafood. *Comments:* This sophisticated cocktail lounge affords a private-club atmosphere just off Mauna Lani's atrium lobby. Nightly live entertainment features jazz on weekends; game room with pool tables, chess and backgammon tables.

★ ***Kawaihae Harbor Grill*** *(Seafood)*
Across from the Kawaihae Wharf on Highway 270 in Kawaihae; 808-882-1368.

Hours: Lunch 11:30 a.m. to 1:30 p.m., dinner 5:30 p.m. to 9:30 p.m. *Sampling:* The restaurant is serious about quality fresh fish, but they also have good burgers, a lot of different local-style *pupus* (order several and share), salads, sandwiches and tempting dinner entrees like steamed clams, Thai seafood curry, Asian baby back ribs, Maine lobster, Alaskan king crab and *kiawe*-smoked prime rib, plus daily specials and take-out. *Comments:* This small country-style restaurant has a great setting in the renovated old Chock Hoo general store, built in the early 1900s. It's warmly decorated in a bright, simple style with colorful Big Island paraphernalia. Next door is its sister restaurant, the popular Seafood Bar.

19th Hole *(Sandwiches/Snacks/American)*

Mauna Kea Beach Hotel, 62-100 Mauna Kea Beach Drive, Kohala Coast; 808-882-5810.

Hours: 11 a.m. to 4:30 p.m. *Sampling:* An indoor-outdoor restaurant right off the first tee at Mauna Kea Golf Course, the 19th Hole offers relaxing country club privacy and a menu of lunch dishes and libations you don't have to be a golfer to enjoy. Thick sandwiches, good burgers and hot dogs, house-made soups and desserts, generous salads and the signature 19th Hole Noodles are served up by the personable waitstaff, making for a satisfying midday break. *Comments: Keiki* menu available. After lunch, take a look around the pro shop for your new designer golf togs.

Ocean Grill *(Sandwiches/Snacks/American)*

Mauna Lani Bay Hotel, 68-1400 Mauna Lani Drive, Kohala Coast; 808-885-6622; www.maunalani.com.

Hours: 7 a.m. to 9 p.m. *Sampling:* The menu offers snacks and light fare of sandwiches, seafood specials, salads and more. *Comments:* This oceanside cafe provides a bright, breezy location between the hotel pool and the beach. A great spot for sunset libations and tropical cocktails anytime.

★ ***Orchid Cafe*** *(American)*

Hilton Waikoloa Village, 425 Waikoloa Beach Drive, Waikoloa; 808-886-1234.

Hours: 6:30 a.m. to 3:30 p.m. Soda fountain 11 a.m. to 5 p.m. *Sampling:* The breakfast menu is quite traditional while lunch features specials like soups, salads, a variety of sandwiches, tortilla wraps, pizza and Japanese specialties. Soda fountain has snacks, beverages and ice cream treats. *Comments:* This hotel coffee shop has a pleasant poolside setting with parasol-covered tables sur-

rounded by coconut trees. Kids will enjoy the colorful, raucous parrots and macaws, who squawk and talk a language all their own.

★ ***Seafood Bar*** *(Seafood)*

Across from Kawaihae Wharf on Highway 270 in Kawaihae; 808-880-9393.

Hours: 2:30 p.m. to 10:30 p.m.; Friday and Saturday till 11 p.m. *Sampling:* The menu changes daily, featuring ample *pupu* selections such as oysters Rockefeller, coconut shrimp and nightly pizza specials, plus island *poke* burgers, steamed clams and various West Coast oysters. *Comments:* The Seafood Bar is run by the same people who made Kawaihae Harbor Grill such a treat. Specializing in heavy *pupus* (appetizers) and cocktails, the place is rapidly growing in popularity with visitors and local folks alike. They don't take reservations, and it can get busy in the evenings with hotel workers stopping by for their *pau hana* (after work) beverage of choice.

Sharky's *(American)*

Waikoloa Highlands Center, Waikoloa Village; 808-883-0020.

Hours: Monday through Saturday 11:30 a.m. to 2 a.m.; Sunday 5 p.m. to 2 a.m. *Sampling:* Sharky's offers a full American standard menu with some local flair and an active sports bar attitude. Not family dining.

Tres Hombres Beach Grill *(Mexican)*

Kawaihae Shopping Center, Kawaihae; 808-882-1031.

Hours: Sunday through Thursday 11:30 a.m. to 9 p.m.; Friday and Saturday 11:30 a.m. to 10 p.m. *Sampling:* An essentially Mexican menu also offers fresh island fish, seafood and other entrees in a colorful island atmosphere highlighted by surfing memorabilia. The Mexican food (tacos, enchiladas, quesadillas, fajitas, tostadas and burritos) is good in quality and quantity and the *pupu* menu is outstanding (nachos grande is a meal and a half). *Comments:* Choose a seat in the comfortable dining room with windows overlooking the harbor, on the outside lanai or at the surfboard-tables in the bar (with an interesting selection of tequilas).

Village Steak House *(Steaks)*

In the Waikoloa Village Golf Course clubhouse building, off Laie Street, Waikoloa; 808-883-9644.

Hours: 11 a.m. to 9 p.m. *Sampling:* For dinner, select from chef's soup *du jour*, spinach or Caesar salad, and interesting entrees like pork chops with pineapple and Maui onion, roast chicken with Ka'u orange sauce, fresh catch, nightly specials and house-made desserts. During a recent visit, we particularly enjoyed the curry coconut prawns with mango chutney from an excellent table overlooking the course and Mauna Kea beyond. *Comments:* There are two restaurants here: an open-air lunch room and bar catering to golfers and the *pau hana* (after work) beverage crowd, and a more-formal dining room with white tablecloths, fresh flowers and tall glass walls overlooking the golf course.

Waikoloa Beach Grill *(American)*

1022 Keana Place in the Waikoloa Beach Golf Course Clubhouse at Waikoloa Resort; 808-886-6131.

Hours: Breakfast and lunch 7 a.m. to 4:30 p.m., dinner 5:30 p.m. to 10 p.m. *Sampling:* The menu features a variety of appetizers, salads and sandwiches for lunch and steaks, chicken and seafood for dinner entrees. The menu also has a nice selection of wines. *Comments:* There is attractive contemporary decor and fairway views lend a nice accent.

Expensive-priced Dining

★ ***The Batik*** *(Continental-International)*

Mauna Kea Beach Hotel, 62-100 Mauna Kea Beach Drive, Kohala Coast; 808-882-7222.

Hours: 6 p.m. to 9 p.m., varying seasonally *Sampling:* The menu shifts from time to time, but emphasis remains on creative Euro-Asian cuisine, East Indian and Thai curries, island fish, seafood and local meats, along with specialty garden-fresh produce and such decadent desserts as the longstanding favorite grand marnier souffle (order before dinner). *Keiki* menu available. *Comments:* This is the hotel's signature fine dining room that, over the last three decades, has earned acclaim as one of Hawai'i's very best. The room is grand, with high ceilings and vast glass walls overlooking a trellised garden walk with ocean beyond. There's Indonesian-inspired elegance, along with traditional brass charger plates, whimsical terra cotta animal accents, and upper-tier seating designed to resemble an emperor's *hoodah.* Please make reservations and allow enough time to experience The Batik to the fullest—a three- or four-course dinner with a recommended wine from their extensive list and perhaps coffee and brandy on the moonlit terrace. The ambiance, service and overall dining experience are superb. The dress code is evening resort attire, with jackets suggested, but not required, for gentlemen.

Bay Terrace *(American)*

Mauna Lani Bay Hotel, 68-1400 Mauna Lani Drive, Kohala Coast; 808-885-6622; www.maunalani.com

Hours: 6:30 p.m. to 9:30 p.m. *Sampling:* This open-air garden terrace restaurant provides delightful dining *al fresco*. The a la carte dinner menu features American-style selections of beef, fresh island fish, seafood, chicken, lamb, and many specialties. *Comments:* Reservations recommended.

★ ***Brown's Beach House*** *(Hawai'i-Pacific Regional Cuisine)*
Fairmont Orchid Hawai'i, 1 North Kaniku Drive, Kohala Coast; 808-885-2000.

Hours: Closed for major renovations until December 2003. Please call ahead. *Sampling:* The menu is inspired by Brown's ocean setting and emphasizes creative Hawaiian and "East meets West" cuisine with various other interesting regional accents. Signature specialties include crab-crusted sauteed *opakapaka*, wok-seared Kona lobster with lobster wonton ravioli and Kobe-style ribeye steaks, plus equally creative and diverse appetizers, salads and desserts. Chef's daily specials include "Spa Cuisine" selections, lower in fat and cholesterol. *Comments:* This open-air oceanfront restaurant is named after the Brown *ohana* (family), whose members such as Francis H. I'i Brown and Kenneth Brown contributed much to the resort's cultural vision. Its atmosphere is intended to be reminiscent of their traditional vacation retreat at Kalahuipua'a, where guests were welcomed with generous Hawaiian hospitality, and it has become a popular dining option for visitor and local residents alike. Live island-style entertainment. Reservations recommended. A major renovation in fall 2003 promises to add even more seating and enhanced menu offerings.

★ ***CanoeHouse*** *(Hawai'i Regional Cuisine/International)*
Mauna Lani Bay Hotel, 68-1400 Mauna Lani Drive, Kohala Coast; 808-885-6622; www.maunalani.com.

Hours: 11 a.m. to 9 p.m. *Sampling:* The dinner menu features exotic *pupus* such as sashimi and *poke*, Chinese wontons, and eggplant curry. Entrees include fresh seared mahimahi, pesto seared scallops, hibachi salmon, grilled marinated *ono*, New Zealand lamb chops, and Thai seafood curry. *Comments:* OK, this is personal. We love the CanoeHouse. It's expensive, the service can be sometimes less than shiny and the food excellence is more consistent at The Batik. But, in all fairness to the other fine restaurants along the Kohala Coast, nobody comes close to CanoeHouse's breathtaking location down by the ocean, where everything tastes better and you could hardly have a bad time if you tried. The dining room is a lovely, indoor/outdoor space and the chef specializes in Pacific Rim cuisine with only the best local seafood, meat and market produce. The food is wonderfully diverse; the service is genuinely warm-to-superb and the contemporary Hawaiian music is a relaxing and romantic accompaniment to the sounds of surf. Reservations recommended. Request an outside table if it's not windy.

★ ***Coast Grille*** *(Hawai'i-Pacific Regional Cuisine)*
Hapuna Beach Prince Hotel, 62-100 Kauna'oa Drive, Kohala Coast; 808-880-3192.

Hours: 6:30 p.m. to 9:30 p.m. *Sampling:* Executive Chef Piet Wigman's menu presents a wide selection of fresh island fish and seafood plus prime cuts of lamb, veal and beef in a variety of preparations. Emphasis here is on Hawai'i Regional Cuisine, featuring the freshest local ingredients in an eclectic meld of "East-meets-West" flavor sensations, exquisitely prepared and served by professional waitstaff. A recent dinner menu tempted us with Coast Grille Sampler of seared ahi foie gras sandwich, tempura lobster sushi roll and oven-roasted scallops, a pan-seared *opah* with fingerling potatoes and cardomom sauce, and pork tenderloin with smoked apple chutney and corn pudding. There is an extensive wine list and a selection of irresistible house-made desserts as well. *Keiki* menu available. One of Coast Grille's most unique features is the international oyster bar, where the chef will open choice local and imported oysters and present them on the half shell just for you. *Comments:* The hotel's signature award-winning restaurant, this spacious, domed dining room overlooks the north end of Hapuna Beach and the whale-shaped hotel swimming pool. All food selections are exquisitely prepared and presented. Reservations recommended.

★ ***Donatoni's*** *(Italian)*
Hilton Waikoloa Village, 425 Waikoloa Beach Drive, Waikoloa; 808-886-1234.

Hours: 6 p.m. to 10 p.m. *Sampling:* The intriguing menu features fine northern Italian cuisine and offers an extensive selection of Italian antipasti, gourmet pastas and pizzas, entrees of veal, seafood, chicken and more, plus cappuccino and international coffees. But let's talk about dessert. Among other things, Pastry Chef David Brown presents lemon mascarpone cheesecake with *lilikoi* sauce (decorated with a marzipan mouse) and the carnival mask of Venice in white chocolate on a layer of flourless chocolate cake with frangelico sauce and fresh fruit. *Comments:* Donatoni's is something special. About the most romantic restaurant on the island, its Italian palazzo design offers *al fresco* seating along the waterway and four individual dining rooms indoors, accompanied by Italian musicians. Donatoni's has our stamp of approval for both fine food and service, and that in itself is an accomplishment. Popular among local residents as well as visitors, the lovely contemporary classic decor provides a lush, pleasant ambiance for special occasions. Reservations suggested.

★ ***The Gallery Restaurant and Knickers Bar*** *(Continental-International)*
Golf Course Clubhouse, Mauna Lani Resort, 68-1400 Mauna Lani Drive, Kohala Coast; 808-885-7777; www.maunalani.com.

Hours: Lunch 11 a.m. to 3 p.m.; bar menu till 5 p.m.; dinner 5:30 p.m. to 9 p.m. *Sampling:* The dinner menu features varied Continental selections plus steak, fresh island fish, seafood and pasta selections. The Gallery's Caesar salad wins our stamp of approval, and that's something special. *Comments:* This award-winning dining room is located adjacent to the resort's golf course clubhouse, and provides an casual-elegant dining option for lunch and dinner. The comfortable bar and dining room have lovely views of the Francis I'i Brown Golf Course, lots of open windows and a warm, private-club feel. The Gallery's food is consistently superb and service attentive. Reservations recommended.

★ ***The Grill*** *(Continental-International/Steaks)*
Fairmont Orchid Hawai'i, 1 North Kaniku Drive, Kohala Coast; 808-885-2000

Hours: 6 p.m. to 9:30 p.m. *Sampling:* This upscale dining room has the atmosphere of a plush manor house club room and offers creative Continental/international cuisine. Emphasis here is on dry-aged, corn-fed prime beef, rubbed with Hawaiian sea salt, extra virgin olive oil and a house blend of organic fresh herbs and roasted garlic. Other menu samplings might include appetizers such as lobster and scallop pot pie, *panko*-crusted crabcake and New Zealand clams; soups and salads include asparagus bisque, Maui onion soup, and Caesar salad; entrees include roasted loin of lamb, veal medallion and crab dumpling, marinated Hawaiian snapper, rosemary and thyme-crusted swordfish steak, and grilled prawns. Top dinner off with some incredible dessert choices. *Comments:* Service, presentation and quality are superb. Live dinner music featured. Reservations suggested.

Hakone Steakhouse*Sushi Bar *(Steaks/Japanese)*
Hapuna Beach Prince Hotel, 62-100 Kauna'oa Drive, Kohala Coast; 808-880-3192.

Hours: 6 p.m. to 9 p.m. *Sampling:* This excellent restaurant features a great combination of island-raised Kobe-style beef, steaks and chops grilled to order, along with one of the Big Island's best sushi bars. Traditional Japanese cuisine such as *shabu shabu* and complete sukiyaki dinners are also on the intriguing menu, as is *nabemono* Kahua Ranch beef with Chinese cabbage, enoki and shiitake mushrooms, chrysanthemum leaves, tofu, spinach, onions and noodles. *Comments:* The atmosphere is tranquil and relaxed, with contemporary furnishings and Japanese accents in decor. *Keiki* menu available. Reservations recommended.

★ ***Hale Moana*** *(Continental-International/Hawai'i Regional Cuisine)*
Kona Village Resort, Kaupulehu-Kona; 808-325-5555.

Hours: Breakfast 7:15 a.m. to 9:45 a.m., lunch 12:30 p.m. to 2 p.m., dinner 6 p.m. to 9 p.m. *Sampling:* Their legendary buffet lunch is a magnificent spread of salads, hot and cold entrees, grill items and delectable desserts. On Saturdays, ask about their Paniolo Lunch buffet, which includes a tasty BBQ lunch buffet and a complimentary cruise on the resort's glass-bottom boat. Hale Moana's dinner menus change nightly, but the chef's emphasis remains on fish from local waters and island market produce presented with aloha in a sophisticated tropical ambience. Freshest catch of the day is offered in your choice of preparations from broiled with herb butter or pineapple salsa, sauteed with lime-beurre blanc, capers or macadamia nuts, or baked in white wine. But there's more. A recent five-course menu sampling was rather remarkable: chilled lobster and soba noodles or fresh island fruits in a papaya shell, miso soup with tofu, *opakapaka* and chives, Caesar salad or stuffed avocado with crab meat remoulade; *then* a choice of osso buco, grilled chicken, Moana seafood platter, or a trio of ostrich, buffalo and beef medallions with mushroom–port wine sauce, and a selection of desserts to die for. *Comments:* Hale Moana is the pleasant and airy main dining room for this very special South Seas-style resort with its trademark individual thatched *hale* (houses). Tall glass walls overlook the beach for poetically beautiful sunset dinners, and an adjacent outdoor garden area is open daily for an elegant lunch. Reservations required.

★ ***Hale Samoa*** *(Continental-International/Hawai'i Regional Cuisine)*
Kona Village Resort, Kaupulehu-Kona; 808-325-5555.

Hours: 6 p.m. to 9 p.m. *Sampling:* The menu is surprisingly international, what we might call the best of Hawai'i Regional Cuisine that embraces the rest of the world. Selections vary nightly, but always include freshest catch of the day prepared to your liking and chef's special vegetarian selection. A recent example of Hale Samoa's creative, eclectic dinner menus tempted us with a Duet of Dim Sum or coconut-crusted soft shell crab, clear abalone broth with bok choy or cream of roasted Maui onion soup, house-cured gravlax with organic greens or salad Samoa with Kona mango dressing. For the entrees, crab-stuffed giant prawns with purple sweet potato, Hawaiian spiny lobster tail, rib steak Kaupulehu, rack of lamb and much more. *Comments:* The resort's special style and spirit is re-affirmed in Hale Samoa. This warm, intimate dining room features an interesting Samoan motif complete with decorative crafts and an outrigger canoe suspended from the ceiling. Attentive service in a romantic South Seas atmosphere is the tradition here. The sunsets are gorgeous. Reservations are a must.

★ ***Hawai'i Calls*** *(Hawai'i-Pacific Regional Cuisine)*
Waikoloa Beach Marriott, An Outrigger Resort, 69-275 Waikoloa Beach Drive, Kohala Coast; 808-886-6789.

Hours: Breakfast and lunch 6 a.m. to 2 p.m., dinner 5:30 p.m. to 9:30 p.m. *Sampling:* The menu is a combination of Hawaiian ingredients teamed with classic Mediterranean recipes, flavors and cookery, sort of a Mediterranean-infused Hawaiian cuisine. Seafood entrees include *moi* fish "thread fin," Kohala Coast *laulau*, Keahole lobster and prawn brochettes; other entrees include New York steak, tournedos of beef Oscar, lamb chop *trois poivre*, pork Manila and some innovative appetizers, salads, soups and desserts. The lunch menu has some Asian-Pacific inspired entrees like ahi piccata, Malaysian beef kebabs, Asian pork and chicken stir fry plus sandwiches, soups and salads. The restaurant serves a traditional breakfast menu with an extensive buffet table as well. *Comments:* This beautiful restaurant is the hotel's signature dining room and evokes the nostalgia of the romantic era of 1930s travel to Hawai'i with matching decor and artwork. The casual dining room is open-air.

Hualalai Club Grille *(American/Hawai'i Regional Cuisine)*
Four Seasons Resort Hualalai, 100 Kaupulehu Drive, Kaupulehu-Kona; 808-325-5000.

Hours: 11 a.m. to 9 p.m. *Sampling:* Overlooking the Hualalai Golf Course, the Grille serves up what the resort refers to as Pacific Club cuisine. Selection includes salads, sandwiches, brick-oven pizzas, grill items and chef's specialties. Try their signature *pupu*, the Makalapua Onion.

★ ***Imari*** *(Japanese)*
Hilton Waikoloa Village, 425 Waikoloa Beach Drive, Waikoloa; 808-886-1234.

Hours: 6 p.m. to 10 p.m. *Sampling:* The menu is traditional Japanese with sushi and sashimi, among a number of appetizers followed by varied specials of tempura, sukiyaki, *shabu shabu*, teriyaki and other creative offerings. For those wanting a little more flair, *teppanyaki* chefs prepare your selections of chicken, steak, shrimp and all manner of Asian vegetables right before your eyes. *Comments:* A visit to this distinctive Japanese restaurant allows you to step into the quiet serenity of old Japan. An authentically designed Zen meditation garden, koi ponds, splashing waterfalls, shoji doors, and a background of gentle Japanese music put you into a tranquil state of mind for an exotic meal. Reservations suggested, casual dress.

★ ***Kamuela Provision Company*** *(Hawai'i Regional Cuisine)*
Hilton Waikoloa Village, 425 Waikoloa Beach Drive, Waikoloa; 808-886-1234.

Hours: 5:30 p.m. to 10:30 p.m. *Sampling:* The menu is very creative featuring Pacific Fusion–style appetizers like macadamia nut shrimp with mango chutney and charred volcano-spiced ahi and a variety of soups and salads. Contemporary entrees include creative preparations of pork tenderloin, lamb chops, somen noodles and fresh seafood, *hukilau* pie, fresh island fish and seafood selections, and certified black Angus beef steaks, ribeyes and filets. They also feature a special Big Island Luau Dinner, a personalized family luau just for you. Exotic desserts, tropical ice creams, sorbets and coffees complete the menu and a complete list of Old and New World wines is available for tasting in the wine bar. *Comments:* This is a beautiful open-air restaurant situated on a bluff overlooking the Kohala Coast surf and shoreline. Greenery, artwork and ceiling fans provide a pleasant, relaxing ambiance to the multileveled rooms.

★ ***Kirin Restaurant*** *(Chinese)*
Hilton Waikoloa Village, 425 Waikoloa Beach Drive, Waikoloa; 808-886-1234.

Hours: Lunch 11:30 a.m. to 2:30 p.m., dinner 5:30 p.m. to 11 p.m. *Sampling:* This is a stylish authentic Chinese restaurant offering the classic cooking styles of China's four major regions: Hunan, Szechuan, Peking and Canton. The extensive menu has over a hundred fascinating selections. Among the more exotic are such items as five-spiced beef, jelly fish, "eight treasures" tofu soup, Yangtze black cod, Szechuan smoked duck, General Tsao's chicken, *wu xi* ribs, *ma po* tofu, various noodle and fried rice dishes, plus the popular dim sum for lunch. *Comments:* The attractive room has classic Chinese decor accents and is located above Donatoni's Italian Restaurant overlooking the boat canal and gardens of the resort. Reservations suggested.

★ ***Orchid Court*** *(American)*
Fairmont Orchid Hawai'i, 1 North Kaniku Drive, Kohala Coast; 808-325-8000.

Hours: Breakfast 7 a.m. to 10 a.m., dinner 5:30 p.m. to 9 p.m. *Sampling:* The menu features American favorites and "comfort food" cuisine, with generous sandwiches, half-pound burgers, Upcountry pasta, *paniolo* beef stew, grilled Pacific salmon and daily specials, along with the chef's "Spa Cuisine," lower in fat and cholesterol. The Orchid Court also serves a la carte and buffet breakfast daily. *Comments:* Their casual open-air terrace dining room offers indoor or outdoor seating among the picturesque garden courtyards.

★ ***Pahu I'a Restaurant*** *(Hawai'i Regional Cuisine)*
Four Seasons Resort Hualalai, 100 Kaupulehu Drive, Kaupulehu-Kona; 808-325-5000.

Hours: Breakfast 7 a.m. to 11:30 a.m., dinner 5:30 p.m. to 10 p.m. *Sampling:* Pahu I'a features the skilled combination of fine Western and Asian cuisine with local Hawaiian accents (coined Contemporary Pacific cuisine), celebrating the freshest island ingredients in simple, elegant preparations. *Comments:* This is the resort's signature dining room, which earned the AAA five-diamond award in 2001. Those familiar with the Four Seasons level of service and quality know what to expect; those who don't may wish to experience what is considered top of the line. The dramatic beachfront setting creates its own ambience, and terraced indoor-outdoor seating maximizes the breathtaking views. Evening resort wear, reservations required.

★ ***Palm Terrace*** *(Buffet)*
Hilton Waikoloa Village, 425 Waikoloa Beach Drive, Waikoloa; 808-886-1234.

Hours: Breakfast 6 a.m. to 11 a.m., dinner 5 p.m. to 9:30 p.m. *Sampling:* This dining room specializes in buffet dining for breakfast and dinner, with the main attraction the varied international buffets for dinner. It is an attractive pastel peach-pink colored room with lots of greenery and lovely waterfalls and pools with swans drifting by. The varied buffet menus change daily and feature Paniolo Barbecue (Tuesday through Friday), Orient Express (Wednesday), An Evening in the Tropics (Monday through Thursday), an All American Prime Rib Buffet (Sunday), and a Specialty Buffet (Saturday). There is also an a la carte menu.

★ ***Pavilion at Manta Ray Point*** *(American/International/Hawai'i Regional Cuisine)*
Mauna Kea Beach Hotel, 62-100 Mauna Kea Beach Drive, Kohala Coast; 808-882-5810.

Hours: Breakfast 6:30 a.m. to 11 a.m., dinner 6:30 p.m. to 9 p.m. *Sampling:* This beautiful, spacious restaurant is the Mauna Kea's original dining room, serving breakfast and dinner indoors or out, along with spectacular ocean views. For breakfast, choose from the well-provisioned, tempting buffet or menu selections. For dinner, the chef offers Big Island beef, fish and chicken dishes as well as lighter options of pizzas and pastas and splendid desserts from the pastry kitchen. A complete wine list, by the bottle or the glass, complements the gourmet fare in appropriate style. *Keiki* menu available. *Comments:* Pleasant live dinner music by local legend Berne Hal-Mann lends a sophisticated yet relaxed manner to the evening. After dark, stroll down to Manta Ray Point and watch the giant, graceful manta rays careen and seem to dance for their supper. Reservations for dinner recommended.

★ ***Roy's Waikoloa Bar & Grill*** *(Hawai'i-Pacific Regional Cuisine)*
Kings' Shops at Waikoloa Beach Resort, 250 Waikoloa Beach Drive; 808-886-4321.

Hours: Open seasonally for lunch (check ahead for hours), dinner nightly 5 p.m. to 10 p.m. *Sampling:* The emphasis is on combining fresh local products with equally fresh, creative cookery methods. The menu features such items as mac nut-crusted mahimahi, sesame-seared *opakapaka*, lemongrass *shutome* and blackened ahi, Mongolian lamb, garlic herb chicken and many other dishes. *Comments:* This is local Hawai'i celebrity chef Roy Yamaguchi's Big Island outlet in his now international chain of Roy's restaurants. The style here is similar to the trendy local regional cuisine and culinary approach of his other restaurants.

★ ***The Terrace*** *(Sunday Brunch Buffet)*
Mauna Kea Beach Hotel, 62-100 Mauna Kea Beach Drive, Kohala Coast; 808-882-5810.

Hours: Sunday 10 a.m. to 2 p.m. *Sampling:* Chef's specials vary weekly, but there are always selections of sashimi, crab claws and shrimp on the cold table, as well as a bountiful salad bar and fresh fruits. The "hot" line features made-to-order omelets and Belgian waffles, prime rib, fresh catch and other entrees, along with chef's soup *du jour* and a bread table offering muffins, pastries, artisan breads and rolls from the pastry kitchen. If that's not enough, stop at the tempura station for crisp-fried vegetables, or the sushi station for made-to-order specialties. The dessert table requires total abandonment of self-control. One of our favorite places to bring visitors, we recently enjoyed the full array, stuffing our *opu* (tummies) with ahi and *ono* sashimi, fernshoot and marinated mushroom salads, lobster bisque, black-olive bread and butter, whole Waimea strawberries, a loaded omelet that was a work of art, and a taste of everything else including a chocolate cake so dense we could hardly lift the fork. *Comments:* This is the home of Mauna Kea's traditionally excellent Sunday brunch buffet. Come hungry and indulge in a leisurely meal of your very favorite things while you enjoy the open-air ocean view and live island music to feast by. Reservations suggested. $38 adults, $19 children.

NORTH KOHALA DISTRICT

Inexpensive-priced Dining

Hawi Bakery
Akoni Pule Highway, Hawi town

Hours: Monday through Friday 6 a.m to 8 p.m.; Saturday 8 a.m. to 8 p.m.; Sunday 9 a.m. to 8 p.m. *Sampling:* This brand-new welcome addition to the North Kohala district offers daily breads, along with fresh-baked muffins and bagels, homemade soups, salads, sandwiches and pizza with fresh-squeezed juices.

★ ***Hula La's Mexican Kitchen & Salsa Factory*** *(Mexican)*

P.O. Box 190585, off Highway 270, Hawi; 808-889-5668; 866-HULA-LAS; e-mail: hulalas@hotmail.com.

Hours: 10 a.m. to 9 p.m. *Sampling:* A carry-out counter with a few tables, the Mexican menu offers fun-sounding burritos like Auntie Bertha's Beans, Pele's Pollo (chicken), and Kamehameha Combo "Fit for a King." Or, try Humu Humu Nuku Nuku Acapulco Salsa or Kick Butt Kilauea Salsa (sold by the pound, too) with your nachos, meat or veggie quesadilla or fresh fish tacos with a tall Kohala Ginger Lemonade Crush. On the weekends 9 a.m. to 11 a.m., your eggs come with Portuguese sausage, Pololu pork or fresh fish, a warm tortilla, Spanish rice and beans. *Comments:* A hole in the wall in Hawi town, Hula La's may be one of North Kohala's best-kept secrets. Check out their selection of logo shirts and souvenirs.

J&R's Place *(Sandwiches/Snacks)*

One block west of intersection of Highways 250 and 270, Kapa'au town; 808-889-5500.

Hours: 10 a.m. to 7 p.m.; Friday and Saturday till 8 p.m.; Sunday 10 a.m. to 3 p.m. *Sampling:* This small-town country cafe features Italian food, pizza, sandwiches, snacks, and plate lunches. *Comments:* Simple decor, reasonable prices.

★ ***Jen's Kohala Cafe*** *(Sandwiches/Snacks)*

Main Street, Highway 270, right across from the King Kamehameha Statue and the old courthouse, Kapa'au; 808-889-0099.

Hours: 10 a.m. to 5 p.m. *Sampling:* This is a snack shop/cafe/ice cream parlor featuring sandwiches, salads, daily lunch specials and other snacks and goodies. As a special treat, Jen's occasionally offers Thai cuisine by a guest chef at dinnertime.

Kohala Coffee Mill *(Coffee Shop/Espresso Bar)*

One block west of intersection of Highways 250 and 270, Hawi town; 808-889-5577.

Hours: Monday through Friday 6:30 a.m. to 6 p.m.; Saturday and Sunday 7 a.m. to 5:30 p.m. *Sampling:* This coffee shop serves up fresh-brewed Kona coffee, espressos, cappuccinos and other coffees and beverages along with special snacks and ice cream. *Comments:* They also have gift bags of various Kona plantation coffees, whole beans or fresh-ground, along with Hawai'i-made jams and jellies, sauces and other food items.

★ ***Kohala Ohana Grill*** *(Hawai'i Local Style)*

Hawi Road, Hawi town

Hours: Wednesday through Friday for breakfast 6 a.m. to 11 a.m., lunch 11 a.m. to 2 p.m., dinner 5:30 to 8:30 p.m.; Saturday 8 a.m. to 2 p.m. *Sampling:* This family-run restaurant serves up good quality homestyle food in generous portions for the *kama'aina* appetite, and visitors too. Enjoy saimin, *loco moco*, beef stew, Korean chicken and much more in a friendly atmosphere.

Moderate-priced Dining

Aunty's Place *(German/International)*
Above Akoni Pule Highway, across the street from Bamboo, in Hawi town; 808-889-0899.

Hours: 11 a.m. to 10 p.m. *Sampling:* The menu features German foods like imported bratwurst, pork schnitzel, sauerkraut (available by the quart) and other house specialties, with a good selection of local-style dishes like chicken *katsu*, *kalua* pig, *shoyu* chicken, sweet and sour pork and daily specials. They also offer daily fresh catch, Gerda's famous fish and chips and her homemade "soups-from-scratch," like creamy potato with turkey and Hungarian goulash. Her small bar at the restaurants's entry serves cocktails, wines, and 20 brands of domestic and imported beers (including Erdinger and 6 other Germans). On Sundays, check out her prime rib dinner. The three-dollar *keiki* menu is very reasonable and includes four dinner selections and chocolate pudding for dessert. *Comments:* This unassuming little place offers a refreshing change of pace for local and visiting diners in a comfortable homey dining room owned and operated by chef Gerda Medeiros. With all this, Aunty's is a hidden treasure that won't stay hidden for long. Smokers accommodated out on the lanai.

★ ***Bamboo*** *(Hawai'i-Pacific Regional Cuisine)*
Main Street, near the intersection of Highways 250 and 270 in Hawi town; 808-889-5555; fax 808-889-6152; e-mail: bamrest@interpac.net; www.thebamboorestaurant.com.

Hours: Monday through Saturday for lunch 11:30 a.m. to 2 p.m., dinner 6 p.m. to *pau* (closing); Sunday brunch 10:30 a.m. to 2 p.m. *Sampling:* Their menu is actually three in one. *Mauka* (mountain) features steaks, barbecued ribs, beef tenderloin with coffee brandy cream sauce and a Kohala cordon bleu. *Makai* (ocean) offers fish catch served in various styles like Hawai'i Thai, Margaritaville, macadamia nut-crusted or crispy polenta. And, there's "Da Local Style" with Pacific stir-fried noodles or *kalua* pork and cabbage, to name a few. A *keiki* menu is available, as are fresh-made soups and generous salads, daily dessert specials and a hearty *pupu* selection. Fresh fruit smoothies, tropical margaritas and full bar serv-

Hidden in an alleyway in Hawi is **The Landing**, advertised as a *kawa* bar, soothing garden, treasure shop and Thursday night supper club. *Kawa* is a Hawaiian herb with relaxing properties, once used by *kahuna* in rituals and ceremonies. Presently finding its own niche in health-food stores and left-of-center cafés state-wide, *kawa* tea has a mild taste and no more discernible side effects than any soothing herbal tonic. Open Monday-Wednesday 11 a.m. to 5 p.m., Thursday 2 p.m. to 10 p.m., Friday 11 a.m. to 5 p.m., Sunday 12 p.m. to 5 p.m. Closed Saturday. This tiny, funky hole in the wall is located behind Bamboo restaurant. 808-889-1000.

ice. Sundays are special with weekly brunch. *Comments:* This is it, the funky, old-fashioned island-style restaurant with great food and authentic aloha that you hoped would be here. The building was an old hotel for sugar cane workers originally built by the Harada family between 1911 and 1915. In 1926, the Takata Store took over the property and ran it as a mercantile shop until 1991, with the motto "everyone should leave the building smiling!" Everyone does. Bamboo keeps its atmosphere alive with colorful artwork and genuine Fred Savage menus from the Matson Cruise Lines of the 1950s. They call their food "Fresh Island style," borrowing from the best of the best of Hawai'i Regional Cuisine, well-prepared and presented. Some weekends present good local bands and entertainers.

Waimea Town

Inexpensive-priced Dining

Don's Pake Kitchen *(Chinese)*
Highway 19 in the old Fukushima Store building, just east (Honoka'a side) of Waimea; 808-885-2025.

Hours: 10 a.m. to 8:30 p.m. *Sampling:* This smallish Chinese kitchen serves up a varied menu of freshly prepared Cantonese specialties. House specials are *char siu* and roast duck. *Comments:* Look for the old-fashioned gas pump in front.

Great Wall Chop Suey *(Chinese)*
Waimea Center (where McDonald's is), Waimea; 808-885-7252.

Hours: 11 a.m. to 8:30 p.m. *Sampling:* A recent menu featured interesting selections such as seaweed tofu soup or abalone soup, *kung pao* shrimp, eggplant Szechuan style, roast duck, mahi with sweet-sour sauce and spicy chicken cake noodle, along with more than a few chop sueys, chow meins and several versions of fried rice. The no-meat menu includes *mu shu*, almond tofu and curry vegetables. *Comments:* Billing themselves as the place for "healthy Chinese food—low calories," Great Wall has presented a wide variety of Cantonese-style cuisine, excellent in quality and quantity, for years. Take-out available.

★ ***Hawaiian Style Cafe*** *(Sandwiches/Plate Lunches)*
Kawaihae Road, Waimea; 808-885-4295.

Hours: Monday through Friday 6 a.m. to 1 p.m.; Sunday 7:30 a.m. to 12 p.m. Dinner on Wednesday, Thursday, Friday and Saturday only, 4 p.m. to 8 p.m. *Sampling:* Everybody loves Hawaiian Style Cafe for breakfast. Big portions, bottomless cups of coffee and fine friendly service in a pleasant neighborhood environment make a great start to your day. They are also open for lunch and dinner, with a varied menu featuring local-style plate-lunch favorites including teriyaki, fried fish, chicken, burgers, sandwiches and more. *Comments:* Not fancy, just a good inexpensive meal. Eat at the counter or carry-out.

★ ***Maha's Cafe*** *(Hawai'i Regional Cuisine/Sandwiches/Snacks)*
1 Waimea Center, Kamuela; 808-885-0693.

Hours: 8 a.m. to 4 p.m. Closed Tuesday and Wednesday. *Sampling:* Vegetarians, there is plenty for you here. From her tiny, efficient kitchen, Maha produces remarkable breakfast dishes such as poi pancakes, home-style banana bread, papaya coffee cake and Maha's granola parfait with fruit, nuts and yogurt. For lunch, try Waipi'o Ways (based on the Waianae Diet) with broiled fresh fish, taro and sweet potato over a bed of mixed greens, Maha Had a Little Lamb Sandwich, the double-decked Lalamilo veggie sandwich or whopping Kohala Harvest salad of market vegetables and Ahualoa feta cheese with sweet cornbread. *Comments:* Maha's is located in Waimea's first frame home, the historic Spencer House, built in 1852. Now converted into a pleasantly meandering cluster of dining rooms, this hidden treasure is proudly run by Ms. Harriet Ann Namakaokalani Schutte, "Maha" to her friends and customers.

Morelli's Pizza *(Pizza/Sandwiches/Snacks)*
Waimea Center, Waimea; 808-885-8557, delivery 808-885-8664.

Hours: Monday through Saturday 11 a.m. to 8 p.m.; Sunday till 7 p.m. *Sampling:* A great little place for pizza, whole or by the slice, with a wealth of fresh toppings including a loaded vegetarian combo. Morelli's also features oven-baked sandwiches, salads and cakes for dessert. *Comments:* Delivery available in the Waimea area.

★ ***Paniolo Country Inn*** *(Hawai'i Local Style/American)*
65-1214 Lindsey Road, next door to Waimea Country Lodge, in the heart of Waimea; 808-885-4377.

Hours: 7 a.m. to 8:45 p.m. *Sampling:* The menu features a variety of burgers and sandwiches, BBQ ribs, chicken, pasta, Mexican food and pizza. We've enjoyed the individual pizzas and half-sandwich and soup of the day combos. Beer and wine is available; coffee is always fresh. *Comments:* This comfortable family cafe has a real country ambience and ranch-style decor, with wide booths and open windows. There is an interesting collection of branding irons from Big Island ranches decorating the walls and a large, beautiful aquarium with Hawaiian reef fish to fascinate the *keiki*. Smokers accommodated in a separate dining room. Good food, reasonable prices, friendly service make this a good choice for a casual meal, but it does tend to get busy on the weekends, so bring your patience.

★ ***Tako Taco*** *(Mexican)*
65-1271 Kawaihae Road, Waimea; 808-887-1717.

Hours: 12 p.m. to 8 p.m. Closed Sunday. *Sampling:* The menu mains are burritos, tacos, salads and daily specials. *Comments:* This small lunch counter on the west edge of town serves up a variety of fast fresh Mexican food to eat here or take out. Both indoor and outdoor seating available.

Waimea Coffee & Co. *(Sandwiches/Snacks)*
Parker Square, Highway 19, Waimea; 808-885-4472.

Hours: Monday through Friday 7 a.m. to 5 p.m.; Saturday 8 a.m. to 4 p.m. *Sampling:* This small coffee shop offers light fare such as pastries, croissants, bagels, light lunches, sandwiches, soups, salads, desserts and daily specials. They specialize in over 20 varieties of arabica coffee from around the world. Daily beverages include a coffee of the day, espresso, cappuccino, chocolate drinks, fresh juices and more.

★ ***Yong's Kal-bi*** *(Korean)*
Waimea Center, 65-1158 Mamalahoa Highway, Waimea; 808-885-8440.

Hours: 9:30 a.m. to 9 p.m. Closed Sunday. *Sampling:* This small family restaurant features local and Asian foods with an emphasis on Korean cuisine. The menu lists *kalbi* ribs, barbecue beef, Korean chicken, chicken *katsu*, *mandoo* (Korean wonton), fish and more. *Comments:* The food is very good with ample portions served plate-lunch style. Clean, attractive location, simple decor; eat here or take out.

★ ***Zappa's Pizza*** *(Italian)*
65-1210 Kawaihae Road, Waimea; 808-885-1511.

Hours: Monday through Saturday for breakfast and lunch 6:30 a.m. to 1:30 p.m., dinner 4:30 p.m. to 7:30 p.m. Closed Tuesday and Saturday nights. *Sampling:* This small eatery is in an old quonset hut building that doubles as the Waimea Country Store and gas station, next door to Edelweiss restaurant on Kawaihae Road on Waimea's west side. Tucked away in the back is a remarkable little kitchen that cooks up some of the best pizza on the island, featuring a thin, crispy crust and fresh toppings with more than one vegetarian special, can be ordered hot to go or finish cooking at home. Other good things available, too, such as freshmade Caesar salad, sandwiches, burgers and pasta selections.

Moderate-priced Dining

★ ***Aioli's Restaurant*** *(Continental-International)*

Opelo Plaza, 65-1227 Opelu Road, just off Kawaihae Road, west side of Waimea; 808-885-6325.

Hours: 11 a.m. to 9 p.m. *Sampling:* The menu features Hawai'i-raised meats, fresh fish and market produce and is changed by the chef every three weeks, always offering something special for vegetarians. A recent dinner sampling included Aioli's "weed salad" (organic spicy greens), creamy garlic soup and intriguing entrees like herb-crusted black Angus beef, Frenched rack of lamb, roasted pepper and onion lasagna florentine, and fan fillet of ostrich with black raspberry sauce. Homemade breads, cookies and dessert specials round out the menu. They have a breakfast menu of traditional fare and a lunch menu of sandwiches, soups, salads and daily specials. *Comments:* This small country-style cafe has earned acclaim in recent years for excellent food and fine service in an interesting atmosphere. They do not sell alcoholic beverages on-site, but customers are invited to bring their own wines at no corkage fee. Kamuela Liquor Store, just down the street, can suggest wine pairings for Aioli's menus. Their hours are subject to change; best to call ahead.

★ ***Edelweiss*** *(Continental-International)*

Highway 19, Kawaihae Road, Waimea; 808-885-6800.

Hours: Tuesday through Saturday for lunch 11:30 a.m. to 1:30 p.m., dinner from 5 p.m. till *pau* (closing). Closed the month of September. *Sampling:* Master Chef Hans-Peter Hager's extensive menu features varied Continental-international cuisine with European accents, and is unlike anything you'll find elsewhere on the island. The well-trained waitstaff begins service with a recitation of intriguing daily specials (if there was a quiz afterward you would not name them all). His regular menu features hot and cold appetizers such as melon prosciutto, *croute aux champignons* and escargots, varied house-made soups of the day and fresh salads. Entrees include roast pork and sauerkraut, weiner schnitzel, roast duck bigarade, rack of lamb, veal cutlet portofino, filet mignon and chef's own pasta *al fresco*. A little lighter for lunch, the Edelweiss bratwurst and sauerkraut is a highlight, along with sandwich selections, soup, salad and daily hot plate specials. Ask for smaller portions for *keiki*, or chef can make plain pasta, burgers, grilled cheese and simpler fare. *Comments:* This delightful chalet-like village inn seems right at home in the cool, upcountry climate of Waimea town, where it has been a landmark for over 20 years. The unassuming building flanked by ironwood trees opens into a cozy, bright dining room, charmingly arrayed with white tablecloths, fresh flowers and original paintings of the green countryside. Reservations suggested.

★ ***Koa House Grill*** *(Steaks/Hawai'i-Pacific Regional Cuisine)*
65-1144 Mamalahoa Highway, next door to Waimea Center, Waimea; 808-885-2088.

Hours: Lunch 11:30 a.m. to 2:30 p.m., dinner 5:30 p.m. to 9 p.m. *Sampling:* The Koa House Grill's extensive menu features Hawai'i Regional Cuisine-creative entrees like *lilikoi* barbecue spare ribs that make a mountain on your plate, shrimp scampi, rosemary lamb chops, and, of course, island-raised beef. Although meats are featured here, vegetarians will find plenty to choose from, like the generous pastas and one of the best salad bars around, with a large selection of fresh local ingredients and house-made dressings. Very important: Save room for dessert (like Chocolate Decadence or the Jack Daniels cookie). *Comments:* This is the most recent incarnation of the landmark Cattleman's Steakhouse where *paniolo* (cowboys) used to tie their horses up to the hitching post and have a few *pau hana* (after work) brews. Now a bright, inviting dining room with rich *koa* wood paneling, lots of windows open to the Waimea countryside and excellent island-inspired food, Koa House Grill is a delight. A separate bar-room (with local ranch brands seared into the wall) accommodates smokers, and features live island entertainment on the weekends. *Pupu* menu available all day.

Parker Ranch Grill *(Steaks)*
In the Parker Ranch Center off Mamalahoa Highway, Waimea; 808-887-2624.

Hours: Lunch 11:30 a.m. to 4 p.m., dinner 5 p.m. to 9 p.m. *Sampling:* For lunch, try homemade Portuguese bean soup or Tami's spinach salad, tall sandwiches like crab and avocado club, burgers or a selection of hot entrees. For dinner, they offer a "mauka—makai" (from the mountains to the sea) menu with steaks, of course, from an 8 oz. prime rib to a 20 oz. "Big Bronco" T-bone, along with coconut shrimp and calamari steak, pastas and several vegetarian dishes. Fine desserts, cappuccino, latte or espresso, full bar service. *Comments:* This traditional Waimea restaurant has also been through several "past lives" since it was known as the Broiler.

The Parker Ranch Store is right next door. Still a pleasant, ranch-house dining room, with extensive use of natural wood and stone, and original paintings of Waimea countryside, the Grill is very much as we remembered it. Hearty *pupu* menu all day.

Expensive-priced Dining

★ ***Daniel Thiebaut*** *(International/Hawai'i-Pacific Regional Cuisine)*
65-1259 Kawaihae Road, Waimea; 808-887-2200; www.danielthiebaut.com.

Hours: 5:30 p.m. to 9 p.m. *Sampling:* Located in the historic old Chock-In Store in Waimea town, Thiebaut's is challenging the better restaurants with finely prepared, elaborately presented lunch and dinner dishes. Market-fresh salads with house-made dressings; local-style *pupu* plates include *lomi* salmon, spring rolls and crabcake; for dinner try bacon-wrapped tenderloin, crab-crusted mahi or select from nightly special entrees. Creative desserts such as Waimea strawberry *mille feuille* or peppered strawberries in red wine sauce with coconut ice cream. *Comments:* The quaint dining area winds around and through various restored rooms, with decor reminiscent of the restaurant's previous life as a mercantile store. The small, cozy bar is a fine place to wait for your table and enjoy one of the imported draft beers on tap, good wines or your favorite libation. We've enjoyed an early dinner in the bar, making a meal out of several of Chef Daniel's tempting appetizers. Complimentary shuttle service from Kohala Coast resorts.

★ ***Merriman's*** *(Hawai'i-Pacific Regional Cuisine)*
Opelo Plaza, 65-1227 Opelo Road, just off the Kawaihae Road, Kamuela; 808-885-6822.

Hours: Lunch 11:30 a.m. to 1:30 p.m., dinner 5:30 p.m. to 9 p.m. *Sampling:* This menu features island-raised beef, fresh island fish, cioppino, steaks, veal, Kahua Ranch lamb, chicken and daily specials. An interesting selection of appetizers, soups, salads, house-baked breads and specialty desserts rounds out a fine menu. *Comments:* This restaurant has won wide acclaim for fine dining specializing in fresh Big Island products expertly prepared. Chef Peter Merriman has established a reputation for excellence and has received wide recognition for his contributions to the Hawai'i Regional Cuisine movement. Reservations suggested.

Hamakua Coast

Inexpensive-priced Dining

Baker Tom's *(Baked Goods/Plate Lunch)*
Highway 19, a few miles north of Hilo (across the road from Pinkie's bright storefront), Papaikou; 808-964-8444.

Hours: 5:30 a.m. to 6:30 p.m. *Sampling:* Baker Tom's is a bakery and food stand tempting passersby with goodies such as creative cheesecakes, fresh hot *malasadas* (local doughnuts), and decadent cinnamon rolls. *Comments:* The place is decorated with images from chef/owner Tom Wall's home state, Alaska, and fish specials feature, of course, salmon.

CC Jon's Snack in Shoppe *(Sandwiches/Snacks)*
Honoka'a; 808-775-0414.

Hours: Monday through Friday 6:30 a.m. to 4 p.m.; Saturday til 3 p.m. Closed Sunday. *Sampling:* There is a wide range of local and international foods, short-order items, and snacks available in this small deli-café.

★ ***Country Store & Snack Shop*** *(Sandwiches/Snacks)*
45-3321 Mamane Street, Honoka'a; 808-775-0672.

Hours: 9 a.m. to 9 p.m. *Sampling:* The snack shop specializes in great local-style Portuguese bean soup, homemade chili and rice, sandwiches, snacks and beverages. *Comments:* This small-town main street operation combines a country gift shop with a diner/snack shop. The gift shop has a nice collection of antiques and collectibles, vintage Hawaiiana, Beanie Babies and more.

Earl's Drive In *(Drive In)*
Located in the landmark Paauilo Store on Highway 19, Paauilo.

Hours: Monday through Friday 8:30 a.m. to 7 p.m.; Saturday 8:30 a.m. to 6 p.m.; Sunday 8:30 a.m. to 12:30 p.m. *Sampling:* The menu features local-style fast foods and snacks including sandwiches, teri beef and chicken plates, saimin, chili and rice, and more. *Comments:* There are a couple of tables on the veranda of this old plantation store where you can relax and enjoy the genuine country atmosphere of the place.

Herb's Place *(American/Hawai'i Local Style)*
Main Street, Honoka'a; 808-775-7236.

Hours: Breakfast and lunch 6:30 a.m. to 2 p.m., dinner 5 p.m. to 9 p.m. *Sampling:* The menu features steak and seafood, chicken, and other local favorites with a salad bar. *Comments:* Located in heart of Honoka'a town in an unassuming storefront on the main street.

Jolene's Kau Kau Korner *(American/Hawai'i Local Style)*
Located at the intersection of Lehua and Mamane streets, Honoka'a; 808-775-9498.

Hours: Monday through Saturday 10 a.m. to 8 p.m. Closed Sunday. *Sampling:* They have a varied menu of mahimahi, shrimp tempura, seafood platter, beef teriyaki, New York steak, captain's plate, chicken *katsu*, plus burgers, sandwiches, salads and desserts. *Comments:* Jolene's is a nicely renovated old shop space, made clean and bright with attractive, simple decor and curtains on the windows.

★ ***Tex Drive In & Restaurant*** *(Hawai'i Local Style/American)*
45-690 Pakalana, just off Highway 19 above Honoka'a; 808-775-0598.

Hours: 6:30 a.m. to 8:30 p.m. *Sampling:* The menu is long and features mostly local-style dishes, but their burgers are good and there's a variety of other foods to choose from. If nothing else, Tex's is a must-stop to try their fresh hot *malasadas* (doughnuts). *Comments:* Listed elsewhere in the guide as a drive-in, Tex's has also grown into a pretty good sit-down restaurant in recent years. There is a large indoor-outdoor dining area and souvenir shop, sometimes entertainment on the weekends, and sometimes interesting cultural events in the parking lot (including an annual psychic fair.) Second location recently opened in Pahala.

Hilo

Inexpensive-priced Dining

★ ***Ahokovi's Kitchen*** *(Authentic Polynesian Cuisine/ Hawai'i Local Style)*
1348-A Kilauea Avenue, Hilo; 800-961-4481.

Hours: Monday through Saturday 8 a.m. to 5 p.m. Closed Sunday. *Sampling:* This small lunch counter operation features authentic Polynesian food and specializes in take-out only. There is a daily menu board but staples include a Polynesian mix plate of cornbeef *lu* or lamb *lu* and beef, chicken chop suey or baked chicken. The regular plate lunch has entree choices of cornbeef *lu*, lamb *lu*, fresh cornbeef and cabbage, lamb curry, New Zealand sausage, *palosami*, and beef or chicken chop suey. All plates served with salad and starch of the day—rice, taro, *ulu* (breadfruit), green banana, sweet potato, *tavioka* root or *ufi* (yam). Side orders include squid, fish in coconut milk and special desserts. *Comments:* This is very good and authentic South Pacific–style Tongan-Samoan cuisine.

Arirang Lunch Korean Bar-B-Q *(Korean)*
165 East Kawili Street, across from Hawai'i Community College campus, Hilo; 808-969-7151.

Hours: Monday through Saturday 10 a.m. to 7:30 p.m. Closed Sunday. *Sampling:* The menu features Korean barbecue, plate lunches, spicy soups and special burgers. The best items are *bulgogi* (charbroiled lean beef), *kalbi* ribs, *yukejang* spicy soup, and *bulgogi* kimchee burger (hot!).

Ayuthaya Thai Restaurant *(Thai)*
804 Kilauea Avenue, Hilo; 808-933-2424.

Hours: Monday through Friday for lunch 10:30 a.m. to 3 p.m., dinner nightly 5 p.m. to 9 p.m. *Sampling:* This very small eatery is a popular spot for the hot and spicy Thai cuisine. The menu has an extensive listing of over 60 authentic Thai dishes including such items as golden calamari, royal chicken soup, green papaya salad, Thai curries (red, yellow or green), spicy basil chicken, ong choy beef or chicken, several seafood selections plus noodles, rice, salads, soups and veggie choices. House specialties are the *musaman* curry and something called "Ayuthaya Evil Beef," possibly worth tasting just for the name; it's available spiced mild, medium or hot. *Comments:* Carry-out available.

Bear's Coffee *(Sandwiches/Snacks/Coffee)*
106 Keawe Street, downtown Hilo; 808-935-0708.

Hours: Monday through Friday 7 a.m. to 5 p.m.; Saturday 8 a.m. to 5 p.m. Closed Sunday. *Sampling:* Best known for its selection of international coffees, espresso and fresh pastries, the menu also features a variety of salads, sandwiches, individual pizza, and other light lunch specials. *Comments:* This small cafe is a Hilo favorite, perfect for perching under the awning on a rainy morning to people-watch.

★ ***Canoes Café*** *(Sandwiches/Snacks)*
308 Kamehameha Avenue, in the S. Hata Building, downtown Hilo; 808-935-4070.

Hours: Monday through Saturday 8:30 a.m. to 4:30 p.m.; Sunday 9 a.m. to 8 p.m. *Sampling:* This popular deli occupies the ground-floor Atrium Court area of a restored Hilo landmark building and features gourmet fresh-made sandwiches, soups, salads, pastries, desserts, espresso coffees and local specials like somen salad, daily stew, Chinese chicken salad and others. *Comments:* The Atrium Court provides a pleasant atmosphere with tables for a relaxing coffee break or lunch. They also serve a special themed dinner the first and second Saturday evenings of each month; call for reservations and details.

★ ***Don's Grill*** *(American)*
485 Hinano Street, Hilo; 808-935-9099.

Hours: Tuesday through Thursday 10:30 a.m. to 9 p.m.; Friday till 10 p.m.; Saturday and Sunday 10 a.m. to 9 p.m. Closed Monday. *Sampling:* The menu features beef, chicken, pork chops, fish, sandwiches, burgers, soups and salads, daily specials and many local favorites. The house specialty is an excellent rotisseried chicken. *Comments:* This pleasant family restaurant has proven to be one of Hilo's consistently best inexpensive dining-out options. Should you have to wait in line awhile, it's well worth it. Clean facilities, fast courteous service, generally great food and very reasonable prices.

★ ***Dotty's Coffee Shop*** *(Filipino)*

Prince Kuhio Plaza, 111 East Puainako, Hilo; 808-959-6477.

Hours: Monday through Friday 7 a.m. to 9 p.m.; Saturday 7 p.m. to 8 p.m.; Sunday 7 a.m. to 7 p.m. *Sampling:* The daily dinner menu offers family favorites and several daily specials including one or two Filipino dishes. Homemade cornbread, banana muffins and fruit cream pies are delicious! *Comments:* Generally good food at reasonable prices.

Empire Café *(Filipino)*

29 Haili Street, downtown Hilo; 808-935-1721.

Hours: Monday through Saturday 8 a.m. to 3 p.m. Closed Sunday. *Sampling:* The menu features standard breakfast items and lunch/dinner selections such as Salisbury steak, teriyaki beef, chicken or beef broccoli, Asian curry and Filipino specials like chicken and pork *adobo*, *sari sari* pork soup, *sari sari* with shrimp, *dinadaraan* (exotic blend of prepared pork blood and meats), *pinacbet* (stir-fry bitter melon, okra, pork and seasonings), pork with peas, and chicken papaya. There are also short-order selections like sandwiches, tacos, enchiladas, fried saimin, fried rice, *loco moco*, and various daily specials. *Comments:* This hole-in-the-wall diner is across the street from the Palace Theater and just up the street from the bayfront Kamehameha Avenue. It's not a fancy place and has several tables packed tightly together plus lunch counter service.

Freddy's Restaurant *(Hawai'i Local Style)*

454 Manono at Pi'ilani Street, opposite the Civic Auditorium, Hilo; 808-935-1108.

Hours: The fast-food side is open daily 6:30 a.m. to 9 p.m. The dining room is open daily for breakfast and lunch 6:30 a.m. to 2 p.m., and dinner 5 p.m. to 9 p.m. *Sampling:* The menu features such items as teriyaki beef and chicken, beef and noodles, beef stew, island fish, plate lunches, burgers, sandwiches plus daily specials. Their general store/deli next door offers a variety of fresh-made deli-style sandwiches and other goodies. There is sit-down a la carte dining on one side of the restaurant and plate lunch/fast food dining on the other.

Happy Valley Seafood *(Chinese)*

Hilo Shopping Center, 1263 Kilauea Avenue, Hilo; 808-933-1083.

Hours: Monday through Saturday 10 a.m. to 9 p.m.; Sunday 4 p.m. to 9 p.m. *Sampling:* This clean, bright dining room features a Chinese menu listing some 150 items, not counting a daily hot buffet table of specials. There is plenty of standard Chinese fare along with quite a few unusual selections like cold jellyfish, West Lake soup, sizzling rice soup, Mongolian chicken, capital pork ribs, *mu shu* pork, spinach with garlic sauce, several shrimp, scallop, prawn, lobster, squid, abalone and fresh fish dishes, chop suey, chow mein and other noodle dishes, plus set dinner menus. *Comments:* Good varied Chinese food at reasonable prices in clean surroundings.

Hiro's Place *(Hawai'i Local Style/Japanese)*
KTA Supermarket Center, 50 East Puainako, Hilo; 808-959-6665.

Hours: 6 a.m. to 5 p.m. *Sampling:* This is a local fast-food operation serving up Oriental-American specialties including teriyaki beef, chicken, fish, plate lunches, sandwiches, sushi rice, noodles, bentos and more. *Comments:* Tables on walkway; eat here or take out.

Honu's Nest *(Japanese)*
270 Kamehameha Avenue on the bayfront, Hilo; 808-935-9321.

Hours: 7 a.m. to 4 p.m. *Sampling:* This small cafe has a variety of tasty Japanese specials and local favorites. The menu features items like sesame chicken, spicy chicken, *katsu* chicken, fresh island fish, tofu steak, sauteed squid, teri chicken, ahi tuna, several types of tempura and *donburi*, a variety of sandwiches, curries, soups, salads, summer rolls and more. *Comments:* Excellent innovative cuisine. There are a half-dozen tables to dine in or meals are boxed to take out.

★ ***Island Infusion*** *(Hawai'i-Pacific Regional/Local Style/International)*
Waiakea Center food court, next to Wal-Mart and Office Max on Kanoelehua Avenue, Hilo; 808-933-9555.

Hours: 10 a.m. to 9 p.m. *Sampling:* One of the most intriguing eateries to come along in a while, this attractive little food counter serves up a variety of innovative island-style dishes at surprisingly reasonable prices. Check out their panini sandwiches made with poi focaccia, interesting boboli pizzas, Waikiki wraps like the Ama Ebi (shrimp and sausage with wild greens, tomatoes and mozzarella). Hot plates include *laulau*, rotisserie chicken, highly touted barbecue pork and beef ribs and more (some sold by the pound). Vegetarians will find plenty of satisfying options, as will dessert lovers like us. *Comments:* Chef Mark Mattos states his aim is to offer "creative island cuisine infused with the flavors of Hawai'i embraced with the spirit of aloha," and while that may be an ambitious statement, this place earns our stamp of approval, and that's something special. Eat in or carry out; lunch delivery available in Hilo.

★ ***Jimmy's Drive In*** *(Hawai'i Local Style/American)*
362 Kinoole Street, Hilo; 808-935-5571.

Hours: Monday through Saturday 8 a.m. to 9:30 p.m. *Sampling:* The menu offers a variety of food favorites including Hawaiian, Japanese, Korean and American dishes. *Comments:* This local-style coffee shop is more of a diner than a drive-in, with sit-down service in booths and tables in a wide, brightly lit dining room. The decor and ambiance are simple, and the food is good local fare with large portions served family style. We like to order different things and share.

Kalbi Express *(Korean)*
Waiakea Center food court, 315 Makaala Street, Hilo; 808-935-7997.

Hours: 10 a.m. to 9 p.m. *Sampling:* This popular local lunch counter serves up excellent Korean cuisine including *kalbi* ribs, BBQ beef, chicken and pork, spicy squid, meat and fish jun, fried *man doo*, *bi bim bap* and combination plates for a taste of everything. *Comments:* Carry-outs and all-size catering menu available at very reasonable rates.

Kay's Lunch Center *(Korean)*
684 Kilauea Avenue, Hilo; 808-969-1776.

Hours: Despite its name, Kay's is open for breakfast and lunch 6 a.m. to 2 p.m. (Saturday and Sunday from 5 a.m.) and 5 p.m. to *pau* (closing). Closed Monday. *Sampling:* This is a real local-style restaurant featuring Korean cuisine including BBQ beef, short ribs, and the original crispy Korean chicken. Homemade cream cheese pies for dessert are special. *Comments:* This sit-down dining spot also provides plate/box lunches to take out. Servings are generous and reasonably priced. The decor and ambiance here are simple, nothing fancy, nothing glitzy.

★ ***Ken's Pancake House*** *(American/International/Hawai'i Local Style)*
1730 Kamehameha Avenue, at the intersection of Kamehameha Avenue and Banyan Drive near Hilo's hotel row; 808-935-8711.

Hours: Open 24 hours a day. *Sampling:* Ken's is one of our favorite places to eat breakfast, 24 hours a day, but the enormous menu of this '50s-style diner offers a taste of absolutely everything for lunch and dinner, too. Try plate-size mac nut, banana or coconut pancakes, or the "Kilauea," stacked with bacon, ham and eggs. Or, consider an omelet from the long list (including snowcrab and shrimp), four different kinds of eggs benedict, waffles, sweet bread French toast and eggs-your-way with just about anything you can think of. For lunch or dinner, Ken's has killer chili, big sandwiches, burgers, local-style stews, various saimin and wonton *min*, and a list of *loco moco* including "Sumo Moco" (6 scoops rice, Spam, hamburger or mahi, and 3 eggs with gravy or chili). They also have a variety of American diner-style plates including beef, chicken and turkey, pork liver and onions, fish, seafood and spaghetti. They have a good *keiki* menu and, in spite of the heavy-sounding specials, are kind to vegetarians or dieters, offering Egg Beaters, meatless bacon and sausage, tempeh and hearty entrees like veggie *moco*, chili, vegetarian benedict and omelets, sandwiches, salads and homemade desserts including shakes, sundaes and ice cream floats. *Comments:* Check out the celebrity photos at the cash register. Carry-out available.

Kope Kope *(Sandwiches/Snacks)*
Hilo Shopping Center, 1261 Kilauea Avenue, Hilo; 808-933-1221.

Hours: Monday through Friday 6:30 a.m. to 6 p.m.; Saturday till 3 p.m. Closed Sunday. *Sampling:* This bright, attractive coffee shop is a good place to stop for coffee, snacks and desserts. The menu has a wide variety of fresh island and Kona coffees, espresso, cappuccinos and lattes as well as international coffees, teas, sodas and other specialty beverages. There is also a lunch, supper and snack menu of light fare such as soups, sandwiches, fresh-baked bread and croissants, muffins, desserts and more.

Koreana Restaurant *(Korean)*
Waiakea Square Shopping Center, 200 Kanoelehua Avenue, Hilo; 808-961-4983.

Hours: Lunch 10:30 a.m. to 2:30 p.m., dinner 5 p.m. to 10 p.m. *Sampling:* This small restaurant offers a full menu of Korean cuisine including *kalbi* ribs, Korean spicy chicken, BBQ beef, and more. *Comments:* Korean food tends toward the hot spicy side and those with that preference will enjoy trying these dishes.

Kow's Restaurant *(Chinese)*
87 West Kawailani Street, Hilo; 808-959-3766.

Hours: Sunday through Thursday 10 a.m. to 9 p.m.; Friday and Saturday till 10 p.m. Closed Monday. *Sampling:* Featuring Cantonese-style food, Kow's serves up a wide range of delectable items such as beef broccoli, chicken and Chinese peas, sweet and sour shrimp, cake noodles and more. *Comments:* Everything is good.

Kuhio Grille *(Hawai'i Local Style)*
Located at the back of the Prince Kuhio Plaza on Kanoelehua Avenue, Hilo; 808-959-2336.

Hours: Monday through Friday 5 a.m. to 8 p.m.; Saturday and Sunday 5 a.m. to 2 p.m. *Sampling:* This small eatery features a local-style menu of short orders, plate lunch items and light meals. Menu items include corned beef hash, teriyaki beef, chili, homemade biscuits, burgers, sandwiches and daily plate lunch specials and bento take-out. *Comments:* Good food at reasonable prices.

L & L Drive In *(Hawai'i Local Style/American/Chinese)*
315 Makaala Street, at Mamo Street, across from Hawai'i-Tribune Herald newspaper building, Hilo, 808-934-0888, fax 808-935-5048; Waiakea Center food court, 315 Makaala Street off Kanoelehua Avenue, next to Wal-Mart and Office Max, Hilo, 808-935-3888.

Hours: 10 a.m. to 9 p.m. *Sampling:* L & L says they have the "best plate lunch in Hawai'i," and their broad menu covers all the bases

Text continued on page 256.

DRIVE-INS AND PLATE-LUNCH SHOPS

Local-style "fast food" drive-ins and plate-lunch shops generally offer similar fare for breakfast, lunch and dinner: egg and pancake items for breakfast, sandwiches, burgers, saimin, and a variety of local-style beef, pork, chicken and fish dishes with rice for lunch and dinner. The emphasis is on quantity and fast service. Generally, you can count on a good meal for a reasonable price. You'll run across two terms: plate lunch and bento. A plate lunch is simply a lunch meal you eat with a fork (or chopsticks) as opposed to a sandwich or burger you eat with your hands. On the plate is one or two scoops of rice, a side dish like macaroni salad, and one or two hot items such as fried chicken, beef stew, chili, teriyaki steak or Spam (Hawai'i is the country's largest consumer of Spam). A bento is a smaller version of the plate lunch, sold to-go in a bento box, a segmented plastic tray, and may have more Asian items like egg roll, stir fry or egg foo yung. You should also know what a *musubi* is because it sounds awful but tastes great: Take a slice of Spam, fry it in teriyaki sauce, then press between two layers of cooked rice and wrap with *nori* (seaweed)—it's a funky kind of sandwich that's great when you're on the run. Another Big Island favorite is *loco moco,* two scoops rice with a hamburger patty and fried egg on top, slathered with brown gravy. Since it originated at Cafe 100 in Hilo a few years ago, *loco moco* has become an island standard on lunch menus around the island. Of the following little eateries islandwide, half are in Hilo and each has a personality, style and specialty all its own.

Blane's Drive In, just off Kanoelehua Avenue (Volcano Highway) in the industrial area, is the original location of this popular eatery. Check out the "menu hotline" for daily specials. 150 Wiwoole Street, Hilo; 808-935-2259, 808-935-4488 (menu hotline). Second location: 217 Waianuenue Avenue above the post office, Hilo; 808-969-9494, 808-969-6677 (menu hotline).

★ **Cafe 100** has been a Hilo institution for many years, named in honor of the highly decorated 100th Infantry Division of Japanese Americans in WWII. A vast menu offers hot meals along with soda fountain treats to take out or eat at picnic tables. You might catch local vintage car clubs here on the weekends. Open daily except Sunday 6:45 a.m. to 8:30 p.m. 969 Kilauea Avenue, Hilo, across from Kapiolani School; 808-935-8683.

Cap's #1 Drive In Highway 11, Captain Cook, Kona; 808-323-3229.

Earl's Drive In is open Monday through Friday 8:30 a.m. to 7 p.m., Saturday 8:30 a.m. to 6 p.m., Sunday 8:30 a.m. to noon. Highway 19 in Paauilo, Hamakua Coast.

Hilo Lunch Shop is one of the best and most popular. 421 Kalanikoa, Hilo; 808-935-8273.

K's Drive In is a half-block below St. Joseph's School. 194 Hualalai Street, Hilo; 808-935-5573.

★ **Kamuela Deli** has two outlets: Waimea Center, Highway 19, Waimea, 808-885-4147; Kona Coast Center, 74-5588 Palani Road, Kailua-Kona, 808-334-0017.

Kandi's Drive In is near the intersection of Kilauea Avenue and Kawailani Street. 56 West Kawailani Street, Hilo; 808-959-8461.

Karen's Lunch Shop 31 Haili Street, Hilo; 808-935-0323.

Kawamoto Lunch Shop is one of the best in town. 784 Kilauea Avenue, Hilo; 808-935-8209.

Koji's Bento Korner 52 Ponahawai Street, Hilo; 808-935-1417.

Kona Mix Plate has an amazingly big menu for a small place: plate lunches, sandwiches, burgers, soups and sides. Kopiko Plaza, below Lanihau Center, Palani Road, Kailua-Kona; 808-329-8104.

Sato's Lunch Shop 750 Kinoole Street, Hilo; 808-961-3000.

Sandy's Drive In has a good old-fashioned breakfast, lunch and dinner featuring burgers and sandwiches, plate lunches and local favorites. And there's always room for Jell-O. Open daily 7 a.m. to 8 p.m. On Highway 11 at Kainaliu, Kona, about 5 miles south of Kailua-Kona; 808-322-2161.

★ **Tex Drive In** is a must-stop for their fresh hot *malasadas* (local doughnuts). Tex has a large indoor-outdoor dining area, restrooms and souvenir shop-and is just about the only stop on the road between Waimea and Hilo. 45-690 Pakalana, just off Highway 19 above Honoka'a; 808-775-0598.

3 Frogs Cafe is a great reasonably priced place for lunch, just up from the beach. 3 Frogs features hot dogs and burgers, fish tacos, salads and sandwiches, coffee and cold soft drinks—plus shave ice and smoothies. Try their Hawaiian salad of romaine lettuce with pineapple and mango, chicken, toasted mac nuts and coconut, only $7.25. Open daily 10 a.m. to 5 p.m. Hapuna Beach Park, Kohala Coast; 808-882-0459.

Verna's Drive In Off Highway 130, Kea'au, across from Kea'au School; 808-966-9288.

Verna's Too Drive In Highway 11, Mountain View; 808-968-8774.

Verna's III Drive In At the intersection of Kamehameha and Kanoelehua avenues, Hilo; 808-935-2776.

Verna's IV Drive In Corner of Hanama Place and Kuakini, 75-5702 Kuakini Highway; 808-334-0449.

Verna's V Drive In At the end of Highway 137 south of Pahoa, where the lava flows covered the highway, Kalapana; 808-965-8234.

Y's Lunch Shop 263 Keawe Street, Hilo; 808-935-3119.

from local favorites like *loco moco* and teriyaki to Chinese combination plates, burgers and hot dogs, chili, saimin, a seafood platter and even prime rib. *Comments:* Small, medium and large party pans available with advance order.

★ Leung's Chop Suey House *(Chinese)*

530 East Lanikaula Street at the intersection of Kanoelehua Avenue, Hilo; 808-935-4066.

Hours: 9 a.m. to 8:30 p.m. Closed Tuesday. *Sampling:* A range of Cantonese a la carte dishes and a buffet counter to select your own plate lunch/dinner are available. Cake noodles are a must! *Comments:* This small eat-in/take-out Chinese kitchen is popular with folks working in the nearby industrial area of Hilo. Good quality food at good prices in a not-too-fancy place.

Ling's Chop Suey House *(Chinese)*

Puainako Town Center, 2100 Kanoelehua, Hilo; 808-981-1689.

Hours: 10 a.m. to 9 p.m. *Sampling:* This Chinese eatery serves up a number of Cantonese-style dishes including beef, pork, chicken, seafood and more. Special items range from cake noodles to crispy chicken with oyster or lemon sauce, to saimin, wonton *min* and much more. They feature a daily lunch buffet of steam table specials where you create your own plate from several choices.

Low International Food *(Hawai'i Local Style/International)*

222 Kilauea at Ponohawai Street, Hilo; 808-969-6652.

Hours: 9 a.m. to 8 p.m. Closed Wednesday. *Sampling:* Operated by the Low family for many years, this popular Hilo diner has a varied menu of Chinese, Korean and local-style plate lunches, sandwiches and specials. Chicken *tonkatsu*, teriyaki beef, and burgers are popular items here. They also bake a line of unusual and delicious-sounding homemade breads such as sweet potato, taro, pumpkin, passion fruit, mango, coconut, banana, guava and "rainbow." *Comments:* You can eat in—several tables are available on the lanai area—or take out.

Maui Tacos *(Mexican)*

Prince Kuhio Plaza, 111 East Puainako Street, Hilo; 808-959-0359; www.mauitacos.com.

Hours: 10 a.m. to 7 p.m.; Friday and Saturday till 9 p.m. *Sampling:* Mexican fast food items with a fresh flair called "Mauitude," this small eatery in the mall offers interesting chicken, fish, beef and veggie burritos and other fare, reasonably priced. Try a "Lahaina" with two cheeses, guacamole and chicken or steak, or a "Ho'okipa" with fresh island fish and black beans.

Miyo's *(Japanese)*

Waiakea Villas shops complex, 400 Hualani Street, Hilo; 808-935-2273.

Hours: Lunch 11 a.m. to 2 p.m., dinner 5:30 p.m. to 8:30 p.m. Closed Sunday. *Sampling:* This inexpensive family-style restaurant features excellent Japanese cuisine. Sample selections include sashimi, sesame chicken, *tonkatsu*, tempura, teriyaki beef, fish, noodles, and *donburi* soups. *Comments:* The upstairs location makes for nice views, overlooking lovely Waiakea Fish Pond and Wailoa Park.

★ ***Naung Mai Thai Kitchen*** *(Thai)*
86 Kilauea Avenue, tucked behind Garden Exchange, Hilo; 808-934-7540.

Hours: Monday, Tuesday, Thursday, Friday for lunch 11 a.m. to 2 p.m., dinner Monday through Saturday 5 p.m. to 8:30 p.m. Closed Sunday. *Sampling:* The interesting, 50-item menu features red, green or yellow *musaman* curry, chicken *rama*, eggplant with Thai basil, spicy basil chicken, garlic shrimp, *pad* Thai and a selection of various other chicken, beef, pork and seafood dishes, prepared mild-to-hot at your request. The eclectic Thai soups are here, as well as salads and *pupus*, plus daily lunch bargains and dinner specials including quality fresh fish. *Comments:* Everybody's talking about Naung Mai. Called a treasure by its enthusiastic operators, this small cafe has been in business (in Pahoa and Hilo) for over 13 years, earning acclaim from customers for authentic Thai cuisine that's "the best we ever had." The small dining room has an open kitchen area and a few tables. Carry-outs available. Excellent Thai food at reasonable prices (the most expensive item on the menu is steamed salmon at $13.95).

New China Restaurant *(Chinese)*
510 Kilauea Avenue, next to Hawai'i Hardware Company, Hilo; 808-961-5677.

Hours: 10 a.m. to 9 p.m. Closed Monday. *Sampling:* The menu features Cantonese- and Hong Kong–style cuisine with a wide selection of beef, pork, chicken, duck, seafood and noodle dishes. They feature some interesting sizzling platters with fresh seafood and a house special stuffed tofu with pork hash. Consider the more unusual items like abalone soup, squid with green pepper and black beans, and lots more to tempt your exotic palate. Try the potstickers or very reasonable lunch buffet at only $6.95. *Comments:* You'll find good food at reasonable prices here. This is a very clean, bright restaurant with simple, pleasant decor.

★ ***New Saigon Vietnamese Restaurant*** *(Vietnamese)*
421 Kalanikoa Street, Hilo; 808-934-9490.

Hours: Sunday through Friday 10 a.m. to 9 p.m. *Sampling:* This small, clean and bright eatery serves up an interesting variety of authentic Vietnamese cuisine. The extensive menu lists appetizers like spring and summer rolls, green papaya shrimp salad and Vietnamese crepes. *Pho* noodle soup is a specialty with several varieties like round beef steak, beef meatball and chicken. There is also mein soup, rice noodle soup and beef stew noodle soup. There are several cold vermicelli noodle dishes like noodles and charbroiled pork and veggies, shrimp and veggies, and spiced beef noodle soup. Rice plates include grilled pork chop and veggies, charbroiled shrimp and veggies, beef stew rice plates and more. They also have several types of fried rice and fried noodles plus special set Chinese five-course meals. *Comments:* Good Southeast Asian cuisine not readily available elsewhere on the Big Island.

New Star Restaurant *(Chinese)*
172 Kilaeua Avenue, Hilo; 808-934-8874.

Hours: 10 a.m. to 9 p.m. Closed Tuesday. *Sampling:* New Star's specialties include seafood dishes such as *kung pao* shrimp with cashew, live lobster or crab and "Lover's Shrimp." The hearty lunch buffet offers a wide range of selections at a very reasonable price. *Comments:* Good quality, reasonably priced Chinese food prepared by chefs with over 40 years of experience. Banquet facilities available for larger gatherings.

★ ***Nori's Saimin*** *(Japanese)*
688 Kinoole Street, across from the Hilo Lanes bowling alley, Hilo; 808-935-9133.

Hours: Sunday 10:30 a.m. to 9:30 p.m.; Monday 10:30 a.m. to 3 p.m.; Tuesday through Friday for lunch 10:30 a.m. to 3 p.m., dinner 4 p.m. to 12 a.m. (Friday and Saturday till 1 a.m.) *Sampling:* This Japanese-American noodle shop promotes itself as having the best saimin in town and is a huge hit, especially with folks from other islands. They also have bento box lunches as well as killer chocolate mochi, a rich, gooey, sweet rice dessert, and they're the only place in the state to get green saimin (call first to make sure it's available). *Comments:* The varied hours are a little confusing, but they're worth figuring out.

Ocean Sushi Deli *(Japanese)*
239 Keawe Street, downtown Hilo; 808-961-6625.

Hours: Monday through Saturday for lunch 10 a.m. to 2 p.m., dinner Saturday 4:30 p.m. to 9 p.m. Closed Sunday. *Sampling:* This small but clean diner has a wide variety of freshly made sushi and daily specials. They specialize in sushi and you can choose from a varied list including *nigiri*, *hosomaki*, jumbo *maki*, and sushi boxes and family platters. They also have seafood *poke*, sashimi, and ready-to-cook meals including *yosenabe*, sukiyaki, *shabu shabu* and *gyoza*. *Comments:* Very good authentic Japanese cuisine for reasonable prices. This place earned our stamp of approval and that's something special.

O'Keefe & Sons Bread Bakers *(Baked Goods/Sandwiches/Snacks)*
374 Kinoole Street, Hilo; 808-934-9334; fax 808-961-5800.

Hours: Monday through Friday 6 a.m. to 5 p.m.; Saturday 6 a.m. to 3 p.m. Closed Sunday. *Sampling:* A highly rated bakery featuring at least 25 different varieties of breads throughout the month, along with pastries, scones, focaccia and more. Fresh homemade sandwiches and other good things.

Panda Express *(Chinese)*
Prince Kuhio Plaza, 111 East Puainako, Hilo; 808-959-1277.

Hours: Monday through Friday 10 a.m. to 9 p.m.; Saturday 9:30 a.m. to 7 p.m.; Sunday 9:30 a.m. to 6 p.m. *Sampling:* This national chain outlet features Mandarin-style Chinese cuisine with a menu of varied buffet selections. Specials include lemon chicken, Szechuan tofu, Szechuan shredded pork, beef and green peppers, spicy chicken and more.

★ ***Restaurant Osaka*** *(Japanese)*
762 Kanoelehua Avenue, Hilo; 808-961-6699.

Hours: Monday and Wednesday 5:30 a.m. to 9 p.m.; Tuesday 11 a.m. to 9 p.m.; Thursday and Friday 5:30 a.m. to 10 p.m.; Saturday 7 a.m. to 10 p.m.; Sunday 7 a.m. to 9 p.m. *Sampling:* This restaurant-lounge combination has a good variety of Japanese-American food, and is a favorite stop of neighbor-islanders for their different kinds of saimin. Complete meals Japanese or American style include beef, pork, chicken, and seafood as well as sandwiches.

★ ***Reuben's Mexican Food*** *(Mexican)*
336 Kamehameha Avenue on the bayfront in old downtown Hilo; 808-961-2552.

Hours: Monday through Saturday 11 a.m. to 9 p.m. Closed Sunday. *Sampling:* They serve warm chips and homemade salsa to start, then offer a good selection of Mexican fare: a variety of enchiladas (try the crab), chicken *flautas*, *chiles rellenos*, chimichangas and *burros* (not donkeys, but the biggest burritos you ever want to eat). *Comments:* Reuben's is one of our all-time favorite places in Hilo. There is nothing like a long, rainy evening spent engrossed in conversation and spicy cheese enchiladas with a couple of Dos Equis. This family-run restaurant is a big, open room made festive with colorful serapes on the tables and an amazing collection of sombreros and hand-painted murals on the block walls. Carry-outs available. Good in quality, variety, and quantity. A full bar with Mexican beers and several margaritas by the pitcher or glass.

Royal Siam *(Thai)*
70 Mamo Street, downtown Hilo; 808-961-6100.

Hours: Monday through Saturday for lunch 11 a.m. to 2 p.m., dinner 5 p.m. to 9 p.m.; Sunday 5 p.m. to 9 p.m. *Sampling:* The menu features over 50 items including chicken, seafood, beef, pork and veggie dishes and wonderful Thai curries, a selection of appetizers and house special Buddha Rama. Food can be ordered either mild, medium or spicy hot. *Comments:* Popular place. Take-out available.

Ryan's Restaurant Okazu-Ya *(Japanese/Hawai'i Local Style)*
399 East Kawili Street, Hilo; 808-933-1335.

Hours: Monday through Saturday 5:30 a.m. to 2 p.m.; Sunday 7 a.m. to 2 p.m. *Sampling:* This small local lunch counter has a menu of Asian and American dishes. They offer a traditional breakfast menu, and for lunch they have a variety of local favorite plates such as chopped steak island-style, beef stew, pork tofu, *shoyu* roast pork, teriyaki beef, chicken *katsu*, pork *tonkatsu*, fried fish, *loco moco*, bento box lunches, sandwiches, burgers, saimin noodles and more. *Comments:* They have one small dining sideroom with a handful of tables. Pleasant, clean and generally good food.

Sum Leung Chinese Kitchen *(Chinese)*
KTA Supermarket Center, 50 East Puainako Street, Hilo; 808-959-6025.

Hours: Monday through Friday 9 a.m. to 6:30 p.m.; Friday till 7:30 p.m., Saturday till 6 p.m. Closed Sunday. *Sampling:* A full range of Chinese plate lunches, noodles, and varied Chinese specialties. Take-out available.

Sunlight Café *(Hawai'i Local Style/American)*
Hilo Shopping Center, 1263 Kilauea Avenue, Hilo; 808-934-8833.

Hours: Monday through Friday 7 a.m. to 8 p.m.; Saturday 8 a.m. to 7 p.m.; Sunday 8 a.m. to 2 p.m. *Sampling:* This small shopping center diner offers a menu of standard breakfast, lunch and dinner selections. The menu is a mixture of American-Oriental and local-style favorites, offering selections like steak, teriyaki chicken and beef, pork chops, tropical lemon chicken, *shoyu* mahimahi and roast chicken, plus soups, salads, burgers and sandwiches.

★ ***Tsunami Grill & Tempura*** *(Japanese)*
250 Keawe Street, Hilo; 808-961-6789.

Hours: Monday through Saturday for lunch 10:30 a.m. to 2:30 p.m., dinner 4:30 p.m. to 9 p.m. Closed Sunday. *Sampling:* Tsunami has a menu of special bento box take-out meals, skewer and tempura plates, several types of *donburi*, udon and soba noodles, *kushikatsu*, Japanese curry, seafood and much more. *Comments:* This is a very popular place. Reservations are suggested.

★ ***Two Ladies Kitchen*** *(Japanese)*
274 Kilauea Avenue, Hilo; 808-961-4766.

Hours: Wednesday through Saturday 11 a.m. to 6 p.m. Closed Sunday through Tuesday. *Sampling:* Mochi is a sweet Japanese treat, made by pounding rice into a soft, smooth dough, which can be shaped, flavored and filled with a variety of fruits, sweet *adzuki* beans and other goodies and daily surprises. Their varied menu of take-out items also includes delectable pie crust *manju* (a small tart filled with sweet bean paste and other things) and fresh-made apple pies, pumpkin pies and biscuits. Their far-and-away winner is strawberry mochi, one whole fresh strawberry covered by sweet bean paste and wrapped in soft mochi. It's a unique and delightful taste sensation that you must try. *Comments:* We can't go to Hilo without stopping at Two Ladies. This is not a café or restaurant but rather a Japanese-style bakery shop that makes quite possibly the best mochi on the planet. The small, unassuming storefront is easy to miss, so watch for it on the right-hand (*mauka*) side of Kilauea Avenue as you head out of town (free parking along the curb). Behind the screen door is an amazing kitchen from which comes handmade delicacies in a wide array of shapes and colors.

★ **What's Shakin'** *(Sandwiches/Snacks)*

27-999 Old Mamalahoa Highway, four-mile scenic route, Pepeekeo; 808-964-3080.

Hours: 10 a.m. to 5:30 p.m. *Sampling:* Acclaimed by local folks and national magazines, What's Shakin' is famous for fresh fruit smoothies like their signature Papaya Paradise. They also offer island juices, fruit snacks, sandwiches, daily specials and desserts. *Comments:* This country-style snack bar is located two miles north of the famous Hawai'i Tropical Botanical Gardens on old Highway 19. Carry out or enjoy your meal on the lanai or picnic tables under the shade of the banana patch.

Yammy Korean BBQ *(Korean)*

Prince Kuhio Plaza, Kanoelehua Avenue, Hilo; 808-959-9977.

Hours: Monday through Friday 10 a.m. to 9 p.m.; Saturday till 7 p.m.; Sunday till 6 p.m. *Sampling:* This small diner serves up a variety of Korean specials like *kalbi* ribs, spicy Korean chicken, BBQ beef and several daily specials.

Yichiba Noodle House *(Chinese/Japanese)*

Waiakea Center food court, 315 Makaala Street, Hilo; 808-935-6880.

Hours: Monday through Saturday 9 a.m. to 9 p.m.; Sunday till 8 p.m. *Sampling:* A wide variety of Asian-inspired noodle dishes for lunch and dinner, plus party trays and local-style favorites like teriyaki chicken, beef curry, miso and wonton soup, and tempura. Choose from fried noodles, crispy noodles, chow fun, udon or ramen with chicken, beef, shrimp, *char siu*, veggies or tofu.

Moderate-priced Dining

★ ***Cafe Pesto*** *(Italian/Hawai'i-Pacific Regional Cuisine)*

308 Kamehameha Avenue, in the S. Hata Building, downtown Hilo; 808-969-6640; www.cafepesto.com.

Hours: Sunday through Thursday 11 a.m. to 9 p.m.; Friday and Saturday 11 a.m. to 10 p.m. *Sampling:* The menu emphasizes Asian–Pacific Rim cuisine, with a variety of creative pastas, appetizers, salads and sandwiches and the house special wood-fired pizzas scented with native *ohia* and guava hardwoods with a variety of creative toppings and ingredients, like eggplant pizza and chile-grill pizza. Interesting regional dishes include grilled beef filet and jumbo shrimp, wok-fired shrimp and scallops, mango-glazed chicken and house special tenderloin with shrimp tempura. Seasonal fresh island fish such as ahi, *opakapaka*, *ono* and mahimahi are served in a variety of preparations. A nice variety of pastas, risottos and calzones round out the menu. *Comments:* With locations in Hilo and Kawaihae, Cafe Pesto has earned acclaim for good quality fresh food and service on both sides of the island. There is bright contemporary decor in the old-fashioned high-ceiling room with open kitchen area. They have a great kids' menu.

Dotty's II *(American/Hawai'i Local Style)*

Hilo Seaside Hotel, 136 Banyan Way, off Banyan Drive, Hilo; 808-935-0821.

Hours: Breakfast 7 a.m. to 10:30 a.m., dinner 5 p.m. to 8 p.m. *Sampling:* Already famous for Dotty's Coffee Shop, this restaurant's present operators have revitalized a longstanding Hilo eatery. Fresh catch, Kohala beef and Kauai shrimp are featured menu items, along with an excellent sirloin steak and Dotty's well-known homemade desserts. *Comments:* The hotel and restaurant are just across the street from the Reed's Bay "ice pond," a popular spring-fed swimming hole for local kids that flows directly into the ocean.

★ ***Hawaiian Jungle*** *(Mexican/South American)*

110 Kalakaua Street, next to Kalakaua Park, downtown Hilo; 808-934-0700.

Hours: Sunday through Thursday 11 a.m. to 9 p.m.; Friday and Saturday till 10 p.m. *Sampling:* House specialities include crab enchiladas, *chiles rellenos*, cheese, chicken or tofu tamales, tropical smoothies and daily Peruvian specials. *Comments:* This place, with an unlikely menu for Hilo, is getting a lot of attention from *kama'aina* (residents) and visitors for unique Mexican and Peruvian food, well-presented in an interesting atmosphere. Live music (and sometimes a belly dancer) Friday through Sunday adds to the fun.

★ ***Nani Mau Garden Restaurant*** *(American/International/Hawai'i Local Style)*

421 Makalika Street, just south of town off Volcano Highway, Hilo; 808-959-3500.

Hours: Lunch daily 11 a.m. to 2 p.m.; Friday and Saturday 5 p.m. to 10 p.m.; Sunday brunch 10 a.m. to 2 p.m. *Sampling:* The dinner menu features various appetizers and local-style regional specials such as hibachi steak and chicken, *paniolo* pork chops and fresh island fish and several garden special entree plates. Lunch is buffet-style local specials and a la carte dinner is served in the Orchid Pavilion. The Sunday brunch features breakfast and luncheon specials including Hawaiian, Chinese, Japanese and other regional dishes. *Comments:* This eatery is part of Nani Mau Gardens, a lush collection of tropical, botanical and flower gardens just outside of Hilo town.

★ ***Nihon Cultural Center*** *(Japanese)*
123 Lihiwai Street, just opposite the Liliuokalani Gardens and Banyan Drive hotels, Hilo; 808-969-1133.

Hours: Lunch 11 a.m. to 1:30 p.m., dinner 5 p.m. to 8 p.m. Closed Sunday. *Sampling:* The menu offers a full range of Japanese cuisine including beef, pork, chicken, fish and seafood, plus noodle dishes and our favorite, red miso soup. Nihon has won our friend Keoki's stamp of approval for its sushi bar, and he's tried almost every one on the menu so that's something special. The sushi chef's special include *poke* roll, mac nut roll and *lomi* salmon roll, but there are many more to choose from (sushi bar closed on Tuesday). *Comments:* The attractive building is Japanese-style architecture, beautifully set overlooking Hilo Bay. The interiors are decorated with elegant Japanese art; diners are greeted with traditional Japanese music and waitresses are costumed in Oriental *hapi* coats. Good Japanese food in authentic surroundings with gracious service.

★ ***Pescatore*** *(Italian)*
On the corner of Keawe and Haili streets, downtown Hilo; 808-969-9090.

Hours: Saturday and Sunday for breakfast and lunch 7:30 a.m. to 2 p.m., dinner nightly 5:30 p.m. to 9 p.m. (Friday and Saturday till 10 p.m.). *Sampling:* The restaurant features genuine Italian cuisine. Tasty soups, salads and appetizers complement creative seafood, chicken, veal, vegetarian and pasta dishes. Melt-in-your-mouth bread and scrumptious desserts begin and end a filling lunch or dinner. *Comments:* Warm woodwork decor, great food and pleasant service make this small eatery a real dining-out discovery. Reservations suggested.

Queen's Court *(American/Hawai'i Local Style/International)*
Hilo Hawaiian Hotel, 71 Banyan Drive, Hilo; 808-935-9361.

Hours: Monday through Saturday for lunch 11 a.m. to 1:15 p.m., dinner 5:30 p.m. to 9 p.m.; Sunday 10:30 a.m. to 1:30 p.m. *Sampling:* The weekly a la carte menu features varied Continental, American and local-style items. Weekend buffets on Friday, Saturday and Sunday feature seafood and Hawaiian cuisine and are very popular with local folks and visitors. *Comments:* This is one of Hilo's nicest dining rooms with lovely views of Hilo Bay and Coconut Island. Live musical entertainment with dinner. Reservations suggested.

Restaurant Miwa *(Japanese)*

Hilo Shopping Center, Kekuanaoa and Kilauea avenues, Hilo; 808-961-4454.

Hours: Monday through Saturday 5 p.m. to 10 p.m.; Sunday 5 p.m. to 9 p.m. *Sampling:* They offer a menu of varied Japanese/American cuisine. Items include sushi, teriyaki chicken and steak, island fish, udon noodles, etc. *Comments:* Reservations suggested.

★ ***Seaside Restaurant*** *(Seafood)*

1790 Kalanianaole Street, Keaukaha area of Hilo; 808-935-8825; www.seasiderestaurant.com.

Hours: Tuesday, Thursday and Sunday 5 p.m. to 8:30 p.m.; Friday and Saturday till 9 p.m. Closed Monday and Wednesday. *Sampling:* Local mullet, rainbow trout, *aholehole*, *menpachi*, tilapia and other fresh fish selections make up the menu in a variety of creative preparations. They also have fresh imported salmon, steak and chicken for non-seafooders, and more. Food presentation is beautiful, service is genuine and the desserts are to die for. *Comments:* This place earns our stamp of approval and that's something special. One of the most unique restaurants islandwide, the Seaside has been operated by the Nakagawa family for over 70 years and is a Hilo institution. It's located in the middle of Keaukaha's fish ponds area, where seafood can't get any fresher; they raise their own in the surrounding ponds. Reservations accepted for groups of four or more only, and it does get crowded because this is a great place for families and groups. Great food and warm, friendly local-style service have made this is one of the Big Island's best for many years.

Ting Hao Naniloa Restaurant *(Chinese)*

Hawai'i Naniloa Hotel lower lobby, 97 Banyan Drive, Hilo; 808-935-8888.

Hours: Lunch 11 a.m. to 2 p.m., dinner 5 p.m. to 9 p.m. Closed Tuesday. *Sampling:* The menu features Mandarin cuisine, exotic spicy Szechuan and Hunan specialties, non-spicy gourmet fare from Taiwan, Beijing and other regions of China. Selections include soups, appetizers, pork, beef, chicken, duck, seafood and vegetarian dishes plus noodles, fried rice, spring rolls and potstickers. Seafood specials include scallops and veggies, oyster with tofu, lobster with black bean sauce and many more. *Comments:* This small dining room has hotel courtyard and Hilo Bay views, and offers standard Chinese cooking.

Uncle Billy's *(Seafood)*

Uncle Billy's Hilo Bay Hotel, 87 Banyan Drive, Hilo; 808-935-0361.

Hours: Breakfast 7:30 a.m. to 10 a.m., dinner 5:30 p.m. to 9 p.m. *Sampling:* An extensive menu features steak and fresh island seafood. *Comments:* The attraction here is casual dining in a Polynesian atmosphere with island decor. Nightly Hawaiian hula show from 6 p.m. and Hawaiian dinner music 7:30 p.m. to 9 p.m.

Expensive-priced Dining

★ ***Harrington's*** *(American/Hawai'i-Pacific Regional Cuisine)*
135 Kalanianaole Avenue, Hilo; 808-961-4966.

Hours: Lunch 11 a.m. to 3:30 p.m., dinner 5:30 p.m. to 9:30 p.m. *Sampling:* The menu highlights fresh island fish and seafood in interesting preparations such as escargot *en casserole*, seafood Caesar salad, Thai scampi and seafood brochette or linguine. Also steak, duck and other specials. Desserts are simply rich and wonderful, like their house bread pudding with butter rum cream sauce. *Comments:* Located right on the water, opposite Banyan Drive. The restaurant features relaxed dining in a great, scenic location, with lots of windows open to the "ice pond" and Reed's Bay. Reservations suggested.

★ ***Restaurant Kaikodo*** *(Japanese)*
60 Kiawe Street, Hilo; 808-961-2558.

Hours: Monday through Saturday for lunch 11 a.m. to 2:30 p.m., dinner 5 p.m. to 9:30 p.m.; Sunday for brunch 10:30 a.m. to 2 p.m., dinner 5 p.m. to 9:30 p.m. *Comments:* This restaurant located in the historic Toyama building (constructed by the Masonic Order in 1908) promises to be something new and very special for traditional old Hilo town. A high-end contemporary Japanese and "East meets West" fusion-style cuisine is presented in several elegant private dining rooms tastefully decorated with Chinese and Japanese antiques and artworks.

Sandalwood Room *(American/Continental-International)*
Hawai'i Naniloa Hotel, 93 Banyan Drive, Hilo; 808-969-3333.

Hours: Breakfast and lunch 6:30 a.m. to 2 p.m., dinner 5:30 p.m. to 9 p.m. *Sampling:* The menu features American and Continental selections. Specialties include seafood, steak, local favorites and a Hawaiian plate. *Comments:* Dining is in a tropical garden setting overlooking Hilo Bay. Reservations suggested for dinner.

Puna District

Inexpensive-priced Dining

Black Rock Café *(American)*
Pahoa Village Center, 15-2870 Main Government Road, Pahoa; 808-965-1177.

Hours: Monday through Saturday 7 a.m. to 9 p.m.; Sunday 7 a.m. to 8 p.m. *Sampling:* This family-style cafe has a varied menu with several different cuisines and dishes but is basically American. They feature a bunch of burgers and sandwiches plus several hot and cold submarines. There are mixed appetizers like mozzarella sticks, cheddar cheese poppers, popcorn chicken, Santa Fe chicken egg roll and several salads. Entrees include teriyaki steak, New York strip, filet mignon, *kalbi* ribs, chicken *katsu*, seafood platters, fresh catch, an oriental combo platter, baby back pork ribs, *kiawe*-smoked beef ribs, and several pasta dishes plus pizza.

★ ***Charley's Bar & Grill*** *(American)*
Kea'au Town Center, Kea'au; 808-966-7589.

Hours: Sunday through Wednesday 11 a.m. to 11 p.m.; Thursday through Saturday 11 a.m. to 2 a.m. *Sampling:* The menu is mostly American with a few local-style favorites for variety. There are a variety of hot and cold sandwiches, burgers, shrimp scampi, pasta, pizza, fajitas, New York steak, soups and salads. *Comments:* This pleasant family eatery is located in a busy small-town shopping center. It combines a bar and grill operation with inside or outdoor sidewalk seating. Nice clean atmosphere, pleasant service, generally good food.

Hiro's Snack Shop *(Sandwiches/Snacks)*
Kea'au Town Center, Kea'au; 808-966-6313.

Hours: Monday through Friday 7 a.m. to 6 p.m.; Saturday 6 a.m. to 5 p.m.; Sunday 7 a.m. to 2 p.m. *Sampling:* This small lunch counter operation features varied local favorites including plate-lunch choices like chicken *katsu*, Korean chicken, teri beef and chicken, fish and chips, fried ahi, ahi tempura, mixed plates, *loco moco*, sandwiches, burgers and bentos plus several daily specials.

Kea'au Chop Suey House *(Chinese)*
Kea'au Town Center, Kea'au; 808-966-7573.

Hours: Monday through Saturday 9 a.m. to 7:30 p.m. *Sampling:* This Chinese restaurant specializes in Cantonese cuisine and the menu features 60 items. Among the selections are saimin noodles, seaweed soup, beef chow mein, Mongolian beef, lemon chicken, roast duck, hot and spicy chicken, egg foo yong, *mu shu* pork, pork chop suey, and a variety of appetizers. *Comments:* Take-out available.

Koa Shop Kaffee Restaurant *(Hawai'i Local Style)*
Just past the 12-mile marker, Mountain View; 808-968-1129.

Hours: Breakfast 7 a.m. to 9:45 a.m., lunch 10 a.m. to 4:30 p.m., dinner 4:30 p.m. to 7:30 p.m. Closed Tuesday. *Sampling:* Generous breakfasts, plate lunches, burgers and daily specials like teriyaki beef, mahimahi, shrimp, *kalbi* and *katsu*. *Comments:* Next door is Dan De

Luz's Woods, with an amazing selection of carvings and gift items from Hawaiian and exotic woods.

★ ***Lava Rock Cafe*** *(American)*
Old Volcano Road, behind Kilauea General Store, Volcano Village; 808-967-8526.

Hours: Sunday 7:30 a.m. to 4 p.m.; Monday 7:30 a.m. to 5 p.m.; Tuesday through Saturday 7:30 a.m. to 9 p.m. *Sampling:* The menu is varied, featuring American breakfast dishes, plate lunches like chili, teriyaki beef and chicken, grilled mahimahi, chow fun noodles, and "Stir-Crazy" stir-fry beef, chicken or veggies. There are also a bunch of burgers, varied sandwiches, fajitas, lasagna, soups and salads. For dinner, choose from steaks, shrimp, fresh catch and other house specialties. Prime Rib Special Saturday night. *Comments:* This popular cafe opened in a renovated area at the back of the general store, and is bright and attractive with interesting woodwork throughout, and table or booth seating. Live local music several nights a week.

Luquin's Mexican Restaurant *(Mexican)*
Highway 130, on the main street in Pahoa; 808-965-9990.

Hours: 7 a.m. to 9 p.m. *Sampling:* The menu features a variety of Mexican dishes like tacos, burritos, enchiladas, *botanas* (appetizers), soups, salads and American specialties such as burgers and sandwiches. The bar serves tropical fruit margaritas by the pitcher, small or large. *Comments:* This place will appeal to the adventurous diner who likes Mexican food. The decor is Mexican and tempers the rough exterior of the old wooden building in which it's located. It's also home to Pahoa Orchid Inn, the only hotel in Pahoa.

Pahoa Chop Suey House *(Chinese)*
Just off the main highway, across from the 7-11 store, in Pahoa; 808-965-9533.

Hours: 10 a.m. to 8 p.m. *Sampling:* This Chinese eatery offers Cantonese-style cuisine. The full menu features seafood, pork, beef, chicken and duck dishes, fried rice, cake noodle and a variety of chop suey. *Comments:* Set dinners for 2-4 people are also available.

★ ***Sawasdee Thai Cuisine*** *(Thai)*
15-2955 Main Government Road, in the middle of the old row buildings lining main street, Pahoa 808-965-8186.

Hours: 12 p.m. to 8:30 p.m. *Sampling:* This small unimposing cafe specializes in authentic Thai cuisine. The menu lists some 40 selections including appetizers like spring and summer rolls, *satay gai* chicken skewers and deep-fried tofu. Salads include green papaya, spicy veggie, fresh seafood, calamari, and noodle salad. Soups range from hot and sour mushroom or seafood to simmered coconut milk.

Noodle dishes include *pad* Thai fried rice noodles, chow mein and *pad woon sen* bean thread noodles, among others. There are several interesting curries including yellow, green, red and "Muslim-style." Entree choices include tofu, veggies, squid, shrimp, fish, chicken or pork prepared in your choice of creative Thai cookery style such as sauteed garlic and pepper, with stir-fried string beans and curry sauce, steamed mixed veggies, eggplant stir fry and Thai basil, or Evil Jungle Prince (which is a blend of two curry flavors in a thick basil garlic coconut milk).

Moderate-priced Dining

★ ***The Godmother*** *(Italian)*
15-2969 Pahoa Road, along the old main street row of town buildings at the south end, Pahoa; 808-965-0055.

Hours: Dinner 3:30 p.m. to 9 p.m. *Sampling:* Face it, we all love island cooking, but this is something special: mouth-watering, authentic Italian food like calamari piccata with white wine, lemon butter and capers, house-made ravioli, parmigiana, lasagna, fettuccine, piccata, marsala, scampi and many other offerings you can't refuse. *Comments:* This is the unmistakable black-and-white-striped building in Pahoa town with a bright, clean, simple decor and great Italian house music.

★ ***Kilauea Lodge Restaurant*** *(Continental-International)*
Highway 11, Volcano Village; 808-967-7366; www.kilauealodge.com.

Hours: 5:30 p.m. to 9 p.m. *Sampling:* Kilauea Lodge doesn't have to be this good. Without a lot of competition, Chef Albert Jeyte tempts his guests with inspired cuisine that reflects his German heritage. The menu changes daily, but a recent sampling featured creative entrees like Kilauea pasta, chicken milanese, five-pepper steak, medallions of venison, lamb provencal and seafood Mauna Kea. *Hasenpfeffer* and duck *a l'orange* are some of the house specials. A selection of fine desserts and international coffees complete the evening. *Comments:* This cozy dining room is part of the Kilauea Lodge Bed and Breakfast operation. Fine service in an attractive setting with a cheery dining room fireplace and relaxed country lodge atmosphere.

★ ***Paolo's Bistro*** *(Italian)*
333 Pahoa Road, along the old main street row of town buildings, Pahoa; 808-965-7033.

Hours: Tuesday through Sunday 5:30 p.m. to 9:30 p.m. *Sampling:* The dinner menu changes daily and features authentic Italian-Tuscan cuisine. Start with seared ahi *alla mediterrania* or gnocchi, then enjoy a selection of pastas such as fresh ravioli *bandiero*, *puttanesca* with black olives, anchovies and capers, pesto or seafood capellini, the house special cioppino or Paolo's "speciale del giorno." There is also espresso, cappuccino, special coffees and desserts (Paolo makes tiramisu and you gotta love him for that). *Comments:* This small restaurant has just a dozen tables and bright simple decor, nothing elegant.

★ ***Thai Thai Restaurant*** *(Thai)*
19-4084 Old Volcano Road, Volcano Village; 808-967-7969; e-mail: value@aloha.net.

Hours: 5 p.m. to 9 p.m. *Sampling:* The menu has appetizers like *pad* Thai rice noodles, Thai spring rolls, deep-fried tofu and chicken satay. Soups include *tom yum* spicy sour soup, *tom kha* soup with coconut milk and Thai herbs, noodle soup and rice soup. Traditional curries include red, green, yellow, *penang* and *musaman*, all with choice of shrimp, chicken, beef or pork and served either hot, medium or mild. There are also stir-fry dishes like ong choy, Chinese broccoli, mixed veggies, shrimp with garlic and pepper, cashew chicken, and chicken with ginger. Salads include papaya salad, long rice salad, and pork, beef or chicken with lemongrass. *Comments:* This restaurant is in the middle of old Volcano Village and has a clean, bright, cheery appearance with contemporary decor and Thai artwork as decorative touches.

Ka'u District

Inexpensive-priced Dining

Desert Rose *(Bakery/American/Sandwiches/Snacks)*
Pohue Plaza, Ocean View; 808-939-7673.

Hours: 7 a.m. to 7 p.m.; Friday through Sunday till 8 p.m. *Sampling:* A bakery and restaurant in one, Desert Rose says "life is short, eat dessert first." Menu offerings include a variety of sandwiches on homemade breads, fresh-baked pastries and cookies daily, good burgers and plate-lunch specialties with made-from-scratch soups, salsas and salad dressings. For dinner, select from American family-style chicken, beef and fresh fish entrees, along with the full lunch menu. Fridays are prime rib nights. Beer and wine are served.

Na'alehu Coffee Shop *(American)*
Across the street from the Na'alehu Shopping Center in the middle of the "southernmost community in the USA"; 808-929-7238.

Hours: Monday through Saturday 8 a.m. to 8 p.m. Closed Sunday. *Sampling:* This country coffee shop serves up American-style food including steaks, seafood, fresh island fish, chicken and salads. Sandwiches are featured for lunch.

★ ***Na'alehu Fruit Stand*** *(Sandwiches/Snacks)*
Main Street, Highway 11, Na'alehu town; 808-929-9009.

Hours: Monday through Thursday 8 a.m. to 7 p.m.; Friday and Saturday till 8 p.m.; Sunday till 6 p.m. *Sampling:* This snack shop features a variety of sandwiches, pizza, fresh-baked pastries, macadamia nut treats, and fresh-squeezed juices.

Ocean View Pizzaria *(Italian)*
Ocean View Town Center, Highway 11, Hawaiian Ocean View Estates, Ocean View; 808-929-9677.

Hours: Sunday through Thursday 11 a.m. to 7 p.m.; Friday and Saturday till 8 p.m. *Sampling:* This small eatery features pizza, pizza sandwiches, sub sandwiches, hot and cold mixed sandwiches, soups, salads, fresh-baked goods and more.

Tex Drive II *(Hawai'i Local Style/American)*
Highway 11, Pahala town; 808-775-0598.

Hours: 6:30 a.m. to 8:30 p.m. *Sampling:* A sequel to the long-standing favorite in Honoka'a, Tex's boasts a menu of mostly local-style dishes, plate lunches and snacks, but their burgers are good and there's a variety of other foods to choose from. If nothing else, Tex's is a must-stop for their fresh hot Portuguese *malasadas* (doughnuts).

★ ***Volcano Country Club Restaurant*** *(Hawai'i Local Style/American)*
Just off Highway 11 on Pi'i Mauna Road, Volcano Country Club Golf Course, at the 30-mile marker from Hilo, across from Kilauea Military Camp, Hawai'i Volcanoes National Park; 808-967-8228; www.volcanogolfandrestaurant.com.

Hours: Monday through Friday 8 a.m. to 2 p.m.; Saturday and Sunday 7 a.m. to 2 p.m. *Sampling:* The menu features a variety of sandwiches, burgers and local-style favorites like saimin, chili and rice, stir-fry veggies, Hawaiian stew, *loco moco*, chow mein, *kalua* pork, oxtail soup (only on Sundays), teri beef and chicken, garlic chicken, and Portuguese bean soup. *Comments:* This rustic dining room is located in the golf course clubhouse. Nice pleasant atmosphere, friendly service and generally good food.

Moderate-priced Dining

★ ***Ka Ohelo Room*** *(Continental-International)*
Volcano House Hotel, Hawai'i Volcanoes National Park; 808-967-7321.

Hours: Breakfast 7 a.m. to 10:30 a.m., lunch 11 a.m. to 2 p.m., dinner 5:30 p.m. to 8:30 p.m. *Sampling:* The menu features prime rib, steaks, Cornish hen, pork medallions, fresh island fish, several types of pasta and a variety of soups, salads and appetizers. The daily buffet lunch is popular with visitors and features a variety of hot entrees, salads and more. *Comments:* The dining room overlooks majestic Kilauea Caldera and its steaming vents. The rustic country lodge atmosphere makes for a nice ambiance, and dining on the edge of the volcano adds a special charm to the generally good cuisine and pleasant service.

Luaus

Several of the Kona and Kohala hotels present a weekly luau for their guests, which is open to the public. Prices vary and commonly include a buffet dinner and hula performance; alcoholic beverages, tax and gratuity are additional. *Keiki* prices are usually available. The buffet will feature traditional luau food such as poi (the Hawaiian staple made of taro root), *lomi* salmon (fresh fish salad with diced tomato and green onion), pork roasted in an underground *imu* (oven) and *laulau* (fish and beef steamed in spinach-like taro leaf), along with more familiar foods like steak, chicken, fresh catch, a variety of salads and desserts. After dinner, sit back and enjoy the show. The performances vary; you may see ancient (*kahiko*) and modern (*auwana*) hula, or colorful and energetic dances from New Zealand, Fiji and Samoa, along with the hip-rattling rhythm of Tahiti, or a breathtaking fire dancer. Almost always, the audience is invited to participate, and if you don't actually send your spouse up onstage, you at least find yourself on your feet, swaying and waving to the Hukilau Song.

We know, we know, you have to do it. But to be perfectly honest, we think the whole luau experience is over-rated. This is not to say that the many fine restaurants and hotels that offer luau don't do a great job—it *is* to say that there are other ways to experience "authentic" Hawaiian food and hula performances, but you have to look a little harder and be a little lucky.

The traditional luau was an ancient celebratory feast, served at *makahiki* (new year) and other special occasions. The menu was likely *imu*-roasted pig, poi, raw fish or *tako* (squid), *opihi* (limpets), *a'ama* crab (small spidery crabs served raw or alive), seaweed, sweet potatoes and some bananas. There was no teriyaki chicken, macaroni salad or

The luau is definitely not a low-calorie dining option. So eat and enjoy, but just in case you are interested, here is the breakdown! *Kalua* pig 1/2 cup, 150 calories; *lomi lomi* salmon 1/2 cup, 87 calories; poi 1 cup, 161 calories (but who could eat that much!); fried rice 1 cup, 200 calories; fish (depending on type served) 150-250 calories; chicken long rice 283 calories; *haupia* 128 calories; coconut cake 200-350 calories; mai tai 302 calories; pina colada 252 calories; fruit punch 140 calories; blue Hawai'i 260 calories; chi chi 190 calories.

dessert table. We don't advocate going back to that kind of a menu, but we do encourage visitors to get out into the community, eat what the local people eat, and attend a hula performance that showcases the artistry and history of the dance culture, not its mylar, commercialized version.

All that being said, the various places that offer luau really are a lot of fun as well as excellent photo-ops. For authenticity of atmosphere, we suggest Kona Village. Go early for a property tour and a chance to see the whole pig unearthed from the *imu*. Ladies receive a

NIGHTCLUB/LOUNGE/BAR ENTERTAINMENT

Consult the local visitors publications and newspapers to see what entertainers or groups are currently playing what clubs. Except for the Kailua-Kona area and a few clubs in Hilo town, the Big Island is not real big on nightlife. It's a quiet place that appreciates things like the sun going down and the sound of surf on the rocks; most restaurants close early (compared to other tourist destinations). But you can find great bars with dancefloors and DJs spinning hip-hop, pop and disco, or live bands rocking the house. Contemporary local bands run the whole musical spectrum, from country-western, rap, the reggae fusion called "Jawaiian," pop, rock-and-roll to traditional steel guitar and ukulele. More than anything else, island style dominates the evening scene. Almost every hotel lounge features the sweet, laid-back guitar and special energy of local singers, and sometimes hula dancers. These performers are consistently excellent.

Kona District Billfish Bar (King Kamehameha's Kona Beach Hotel); Billy Bob's Park & Pork; Hard Rock Cafe; Huggo's on the Rocks (next to Royal Kona Resort); Lulu's; Kalani Kai Bar (Ohana Keauhou Beach Resort); Michaelangelo's; Paradise Lounge (above Beachcomber's); Verandah Lounge (Ohana Keauhou Beach Resort); Windjammer Lounge (Royal Kona Resort)

South Kohala District Anthony's Restaurant & Beat Club (Waikoloa Highlands Center); Blue Dolphin Restaurant; Clipper Lounge (Waikoloa Beach Marriott, An Outrigger Resort); Copper Bar (Mauna Kea Beach Hotel); Honu Bar (Mauna Lani Bay Hotel); Nalu's Bar (Waikoloa Beach Marriott, An Outrigger Resort); Reef Lounge (Hapuna Beach Prince Hotel); The Polo Bar and Paniolo Lounge (Fairmont Orchid Hawai'i)

North Kohala District Bamboo

Waimea Koa House Grille

Hilo Crown Room (Hawai'i Naniloa Hotel); Uncle Billy's (Hilo Bay Hotel); Wai'oli Lounge (Hilo Hawaiian Hotel)

Puna District Lava Rock Café; Lava Lounge (Kilauea Military Camp)

lei *po'o*, head lei, and the menu includes Hawaiian choices along with more familiar options. A colorful hula show follows dinner.

For value, try Royal Kona Resort, on Ali'i Drive in Kona town. There are crafters including coconut tree-climbers, demonstrating their handiwork prior to dinner, artfully set along the oceanfront. There is a good buffet selection of luau and familiar food, and a professional hula show by Tihati Productions, featuring dance and music from various Polynesian islands and a chance to get your picture taken with a bevy of hula girls or shirtless men in *malo*, loincloth.

For hula, consider Mauna Kea Beach Hotel's luau. The after-dinner entertainment is presented by the skilled dancers of Halau Hula o Kaholoku, prestigious winners of Merrie Monarch Festival awards. Their show begins with hula *awana* (ancient) and progresses through hula *kahiko* (contemporary) and Hapa styles, ending with a Royal Court presentation from Old Hawai'i's monarchy days. The food is very good and the oceanside setting is unbeatable.

Whichever you choose—enjoy! And remember that prices are subject to change.

Hilton Waikoloa Village

425 Waikoloa Beach Drive, Kohala Coast; 808-886-1234 ext. 54; www.hiltonwaikokoavillage.com.

The "Legends of the Pacific" luau dinner and hula show takes place at Kamehameha Court on Fridays only at 6 p.m. The bountiful luau buffet, presented in the grand Hilton style, includes traditional foods such as roast pork, poi, island *poke*, sushi, *lomi* salmon, chicken *laulau*, fish, crab, and fresh tropical fruits. More familiar entrees, steamed mahimahi, Parker Ranch ribs, and roasted mango chicken are offered, along with a good selection of fresh salads and desserts like coconut and strawberry *haupia* and warm banana-pineapple cobbler that appeal to the pickiest of eaters and guarantee a full *opu* (tummy). Following dinner is a captivating show of Pacific Rim songs and dances that is one of the most exciting and colorful productions on the Kohala Coast. Reservations required. $65 adults, $32 children 5-12.

★ King Kamehameha's Kona Beach Hotel

75-5660 Palani Road, Kailua-Kona; 808-329-2911; luau reservations 808-326-4969.

This authentic Island Breeze luau is put on each Sunday, Tuesday, Wednesday and Thursday evening from 5:30 p.m. to 8:30 p.m. (You can watch the pig being placed in the *imu* at 10:15 a.m. on luau days.) The luau begins with the arrival of torch bearers via canoe from Ahuena Heiau, King Kamehameha's temple, fronting Kamakahonu Beach and the hotel grounds. Conch shells are sounded as the torch bearers land and light the pathway to the luau grounds. Visitors can then watch the ceremonial removal of the roast pig from the *imu*. The luau that follows is a feast of authentic Hawaiian foods and specialties from Oceania. A Polynesian performance of song and dance follows the luau, including a Samoan fire-knife dance. Reservations required; aloha attire preferred. It's all very colorful, touristy and good fun. $54 adults, $21 children 6-12, free for kids under 5.

★ *Kona Village Resort*

Queen Ka'ahumanu Highway, six miles north of Kona Airport at Kaupulehu; 808-325-5555.

The Kona Village Resort, with its individual thatched *hale* (houses) in the style of the South Seas, presents its *aha'aina* (feast) with an element of authenticity others don't quite match. It has something to do with the magical beachside environment and the faraway sense of place that only Kona Village still provides. Reservations are required to enter the property, and we suggest you arrive by 5:15 p.m. to enjoy a personable tour of this fascinating resort. Ladies are welcomed with fragrant lei *po'o* (head lei) and at 5:30 p.m. the roast pig is removed from its *imu* with some ceremony, followed by cocktails and the luau feast. The endless buffet of Hawaiian and Polynesian foods is probably the most nearly authentic luau spread on the Big Island (unless you happen to be invited to join someone's family). Feel free to ask your servers questions about the food or the luau; most are very friendly and open to conversation (which could have something to do with them being shirtless, at least the males). An exciting performance of Polynesian chant, song and dance is a stirring end to a memorable evening. Reservations are required; aloha attire preferred. Fridays only, 5:15 p.m. tour, 6:30 p.m. *imu* ceremony. Rates: $76.

★ *Mauna Kea Beach Hotel*

62-100 Mauna Kea Beach Drive, Kohala Coast; 808-882-5810.

Mauna Kea Beach Hotel began its luau tradition in the 1960s, when the hotel was new and the coast between it and Kona Village was empty. As a special event for *Time* magazine, the general manager leveled a fancy picnic area along the lava-rock oceanfront, hired the best dancers and musicians on the island, and served up an elaborate spread of the exotic luau food along with the executive chef's more Continental cuisine. Although *Time* never ran the story, that energy began a decades-long tradition which families return to enjoy year after year. Today's luau is just as delicious, the setting every bit as romantic and the hula performance still one of the best you're likely to experience in Hawai'i. Following the dinner feast of both traditional luau foods and familiar delectables, guests are treated to a trip through island history from *kahiko* (ancient) to *auwana* (modern) in

AN EVENING AT KAHUA RANCH

For a completely different Hawai'i dinner experience, visit **Kahua Ranch**, which offers weekly *paniolo* (cowboy) barbecues on the grounds of their 8,500-acre working ranch in upcountry Kohala. Transportation is provided from the Waikoloa area up to 3,200 feet above sea level, where the sunset views are spectacular. After a brief welcome reception and introduction to the ranch, enjoy a hearty chuckwagon barbecue featuring Kahua Ranch meats and produce from the Big Island farming community (including macadamia nut pie). Then the fun begins. In addition to dance music from island entertainers, you'll have a chance to try your hand at roping, horseshoes and other ranch games, have your photo taken with the animals, "talk story" around the campfire and do a little star-gazing with the ranch's telescope. An evening at Kahua Ranch is available Tuesdays and one other day each week, subject to change. Reservations are required. Jeans, sweaters and closed shoes recommended for the cool evening weather. Rates start at $68. P.O. Box 384598, Waikoloa, HI 96738; 808-987-2108, 808-883-8601; eveningatkahua.com.

story, dance and song. The show is choreographed by Nani Lim Yap, whose hula *halau* (troupe) Na Lei O Kaholoku has won distinguished honors at the prestigious annual Merrie Monarch Festival (the world's best). Reservations required; aloha attire preferred. Tuesdays only. $78 adults, $38 children ages 5-12, free for children under 5.

★ *Royal Kona Resort*

Ali'i Drive, Kailua-Kona; 808-329-7700; 800-624-7771 75-5852; www.royalkona.com.

The"Lava—Legends & Legacies Luau" is presented by Tihati Productions four nights weekly in a dramatic, oceanside setting at Royal Kona Resort. The luau includes an aloha shell lei greeting, traditional opening of the *imu* and removal of the roast pig, torchlighting to the sound of the *pu* (conch shell horn), and *pahu* drum. The lavish buffet with authentic Hawaiian foods includes *imu kalua* pork, turkey, chicken, beef and island fish, poi, Hawaiian sweet potatoes, *lomi* salmon, fried rice, large salad bar, dessert selections. Full open bar with mai tais is included. An elaborate Polynesian revue follows dinner, with colorful performances of song and dance from the South Pacific Islands, including the Samoan fire-knife dance, fast-motion Tahitian and several styles of Hawaiian hula. Reservations are suggested; aloha attire preferred. Monday, Wednesday, Friday, Saturday. $55 adults, $23 children 6-12, free for kids 5 and under.

★ *Waikoloa Beach Marriott, Outrigger Resort*

69-275 Waikoloa Beach Drive, Kohala Coast; 808-886-6789.

The Royal Luau begins at sunset along the shore of 'Anaeho'o-malu Bay, with the traditional torch-lighting ceremony, conch shell blowing and removal of the roast pig from the *imu*. The music, dance, food and costumes are reflections of Hawai'i's history in one of the most authentic presentations on the island. More than just entertainment, the cultural program after dinner includes a journey through Polynesia with music and dance from Tahiti, New Zealand and Samoa. Guests enjoy a sumptuous feast of fish and seafood, chicken, *imu kalua* pork, teriyaki steaks, *lomi lomi* salmon, poi, salads and desserts, with full open bar. Wednesday and Sunday only. Rates: $67.

CHAPTER 5

Beaches

Respect the ocean. If we've learned anything about Hawai'i, it's this. We've seen it turn from something like a giant turquoise bathtub into a raging gray monster in a matter of hours. It can take away a beach overnight and wreck homes in the blink of an eye, then soothe your soul with its gentle, lapping waves along the shore. Too many people, engrossed in what they're doing, forget the ocean's power and ferocity. A moment's carelessness can leave a heavy price to pay. Watch, listen, take a friend, trust your instincts and, when in doubt, get out. Do be aware, but don't be afraid. The experience is well worth it.

The Big Island has over 100 beaches, and they come in white, black, grey and green. The beaches tend to be smaller and some are harder to get to than those on Hawai'i's other islands, but visitors and locals agree they are some of the best anywhere. Many of the beaches are more rocky than smooth, and *tabis* (reef shoes) are recommended. This is due to the geologic fact that the Big Island is still relatively young and the rocks along its shorelines haven't eroded into the fine, powdery sand you might expect. As you stroll along different beaches, it's interesting to scoop up a handful of sand and observe its composition for tiny shell fragments, green olivine crystals, coral, black and red lava gravel. Hawai'i is still a growing island, with new beaches being formed every day from volcanic activity while the ocean transforms old coastline. It's an amazing process. Some of the most interesting are "storm beaches," made when high surf crashes against the *pali* (cliffs) and leaves enough sand for a beach up there, far above the ocean.

Although every one of Hawai'i's beaches are by law open to the public, some of the beaches you see on the map are not easily accessible for the average visitor or resident. For more detailed information on the Big Island's beaches, see *Beaches of the Big Island* by John R. K. Clark, published by the University of Hawai'i Press (1985). And, be sure to pick up a copy of the free *Big Island Beach & Activity Guide* (www.beachactivityguide.com) when you arrive.

Beachgoers should also be aware that some of the parks and campgrounds near the beach have become long-term residential locations for local homeless and transient people. This is not necessarily something to fear as much as something to be aware of, with an attitude of "live and let live." However, just like any other vacation destination, do not leave valuables in your car, lock the doors and use common sense. If you feel uncomfortable, trust your instincts and move to another spot.

Hawai'i's residents, wherever you find them, are some of the friendliest, warmest and most compassionate people you'll meet anywhere. Aloha is very real here, and you're likely to experience that directly in some way. And while most people recognize that visitors are a big part of our livelihood, there are some who may look at outsiders as an intrusion on their *aina* (land) whether they own it or not. To put it simply, the Big Island's beach parks are relatively trouble-free, but there's no guarantee even here. We've found it works best to keep a friendly, benign attitude and if confronted by someone who makes us uncomfortable, to walk away. All that being said, don't worry, you're in for some beautiful days at the beach.

THEFT DOES HAPPEN

It is vital that you leave nothing of importance in your car because theft, especially at some of the more remote locations, is high. And be careful of watchful eyes if you stow your valuables in your trunk. There are some unscrupulous folks who may be looking for visitors to do just that. Car-rental companies often advise customers to leave nothing in the car and keep the vehicle unlocked to minimize damage in a break-in. In the unhappy event that you do experience a theft, call the police non-emergency number 808-935-3311 or, in an emergency, 911.

Snorkelers will find good areas to explore near some of the more popular and easy-to-reach beaches around the island. A little bit more of a swim leads to better snorkeling over lava rock outcroppings, rocky coves and small bays where the water is usually fairly calm. Good coral patches and beds grow around these areas, which attract varied fish, sea turtles and other marine life. However, because the Big Island is so young geologically, there are no extensive fringing coral reefs that encircle the island or extend out from the shoreline. As in all ocean areas, snorkelers need to be aware of their direction and distance from the shore, and keep alert to currents, surges and surf action especially near rock outcroppings. And don't forget the sunblock!

Along almost any shoreline, tidepools are fascinating mini-worlds to explore. Wear your *tabis* or sneakers and walk up onto the rocks to find a place where the tide has left water behind. Wait quietly for a few minutes and see what life emerges. You might encounter tiny fish, shrimp and crabs, a floating sea cucumber, spiky black sea urchins (don't touch them), the long strands of a spaghetti worms, snails, mysterious cowrie that open their shells when they think you've passed. We once found a moray eel that lifted its head out of the water to have its picture taken. Do keep an eye on the waves; tides can sneak in quickly and cut off your return access, forcing you into an unplanned swim. We'd also suggest that you not take shells from tidepools since creatures might still be living in them.

Beach Precautions

WATER SAFETY

The Big Island's beaches are for the most part, more rugged than those on the neighboring islands of Maui or O'ahu, for example. As mentioned earlier, its beaches are geological "teenagers" that will need much more time to erode into smooth, level strands of soft sand. The western (Kona-side) coasts of the island have reef systems that afford some protection; however, many beaches are gravelly-to-rocky with surf conditions that can change suddenly. Most of the island's beaches are not serviced by lifeguards and many have few or no facilities, including drinking water. Again, we recommend picking up a free copy of the *Big Island Beach & Activity Guide*.

The more remote beaches (Pololu, Waipi'o, Green Sands, for example) we can only recommend to the seasoned hiker and swimmer. You may see surfers at beaches where we'd suggest you enjoy the view and stay out of the water. Keep in mind that just because there is someone else in the water, it doesn't mean it's safe.

Please, treat the Big Island's wild beaches with respect. Since many have no restroom facilities, try to use the bathroom before you head to the beach. If you must relieve yourself, go well away from the waterline and bury your deposit and any tissue you used. Also, pack out your trash and bring out a little bit that someone else left, too.

Wherever you go to enjoy the beach, do not take undue risks. Others might be visitors just like you, but not as well-informed. Common sense needs to be employed at all beaches.

We don't want to be alarmists, but we'd prefer to report the beaches conservatively. Always, always use good judgment. Here are some basic water safety tips and terms.

OCEAN MENACES

The Big Island's ocean playgrounds are among the most benign in the world. There are, however, a few ocean creatures that you should be aware of. We will attempt to include some basic first-aid tips should you encounter one of these. Since some people might have a resulting allergic reaction, we suggest you contact a local physician or medical center if you have an unplanned encounter with one of them.

Portuguese Man-of-War are sea animals seen only rarely but caution is in order. Most resorts and public beaches will post warning signs to help you avoid them. These small creatures are related to the jellyfish and are adrift in the ocean via the currents and the wind. Sometimes blown on shore by unusual winds, they can cover the beach with their glistening crystal orbs filled with deep blue filament. If they are on the beach, treat them as if they were still in the water—stay away. On rare occasions they will be seen drifting in the ocean during a snorkeling cruise or sea excursion and the cruiseboat staff may change snorkeling destinations if this is the case. The animal has long filaments that can cause painful stings. If you are stung, rinse the affected area with sea water or fresh water to remove any tentacles. If you need to pick out the tentacles, do not use your bare fingers; use gloves, a towel or whatever is available to protect yourself. Vinegar, isopropyl alcohol and human urine, once considered effective remedies, are no longer recommended treatments.

As mentioned above, avoid touching **sea urchins** (*wana*). Their long sharp spines are brittle, and easily break off in your fingers or toes. If you do encounter one, be sure the entire spine is removed. Soaking the wound in vinegar helps to dissolve the spine; for pain, soak the puncture in hot water for 30 to 90 minutes.

A **shorebreak** occurs when the waves break directly on the beach. Small shorebreaks may not be a problem, but waves that are more than a foot or two high may create undertows and hazardous conditions. Conditions are generally more severe in the winter months. Even venturing too close to a shorebreak could be hazardous, as standing on the beachfront you may encounter a stronger, higher wave that could catch you off-guard and sweep you into the water. *Keiki* must be watched carefully even when playing near a shorebreak.

Coral is made up of many tiny living organisms. Coral cuts require thorough disinfecting and can take a long time to heal. If an inflamed wound's redness begins to spread, it suggests an infection and requires medical attention. So stay off the coral—and don't touch it.

Cone shells look harmless enough, are conical and come in colors of brown or black. The snails that inhabit these shells have a defense mechanism that they use to protect themselves—and to kill their prey. Their stinger does have venom so it is suggested that you just enjoy looking at them. Cleaning the wound and soaking it in hot water for 30 to 90 minutes will provide relief if you're stung.

Eels live among the coral or in rock crevices and are generally not aggressive. You may have heard of divers who trained an eel to come out and then take food from their hands, but we don't recommend you try to make an eel your pal. While usually non-aggressive, their jaws are extremely powerful and their teeth are sharp. And any sea animal could mistake an approach or sudden movement as an aggressive act. Just keep a comfortable distance—for you and the eel. Also, never reach into the coral or any other place where you can't see your hands. Your fingers might be mistaken for lunch.

Sharks? Yes, there are many varied types of sharks. However, there are more people injured by coral than sharks in Hawai'i. Resorts post warning signs if a shark is sighted off the coast. If you should see one, don't move quickly. Swim slowly away while you keep an eye on it. Avoid swimming in murky waters near river mouths after it rains. Also, stay out of the water if you have open cuts and remember, urine or other bodily fluids might attract sharks, so be on the safe side and don't urinate in the water.

A **rip current** can often be seen from the shore. This is a fast-moving, river-like current that sometimes can be seen carrying sand or sediment. They are common in reef areas that have open channels to the sea. A rip current can pull an unsuspecting swimmer quickly out to sea. Swimming against a strong rip current may be impossible even for the best swimmers. If you find yourself being pulled offshore, relax, signal for help, and try to swim across, rather than against, the current.

Undertows happen when a rip current runs into incoming surf. This accounts for the feeling that you are being pulled down. They are more common on beaches that have steep slopes.

Kona winds generated by southern-hemisphere storms cause southerly swells that affect leeward shores. This usually happens in the summer and lasts several days, and surf may be higher, particularly in winter months. Although it may appear fun to play in these waves, many minor to moderate injuries are recorded at these times. Resorts will post red warning flags along the beach during times of unsafe surf conditions. Most beaches are affected during this time with water turbidity and poor snorkeling conditions. At a few places, such as Kawaihae, these conditions may create good surfing for a few days.

TIPS

Here are some additional beach safety and etiquette tips:

• "Never turn your back to the ocean" is an old Hawaiian saying. Don't be caught off-guard; waves come in sets, with spells of calm in between.

• Use the buddy system; never swim or snorkel alone.

• If you are unsure of your abilities, use flotation devices attached to your body, such as a life vest or inflatable vest. Never rely on an air mattress or similar device from which you may become separated.

There are remarkable sea turtles in the Big Island's waters, and many people report great experiences swimming with them. The bad news is, they do bite. They are also a protected species and should not be disturbed if you find them sunning on the beach. As with all things, treat them with respect.

• Study the ocean before you enter; look for rocks, shorebreak and rip currents.

• Duck or dive beneath breaking waves before they reach you.

• Never swim against a strong current; swim across it.

• Know your limits.

• Small children should be allowed to play near or in the surf *only* with close supervision and should wear flotation devices—and even then, only under extremely calm conditions.

• When exploring tidepools or reefs, always wear protective footwear and keep an eye on the ocean. Also, protect your hands—don't reach anywhere you can't see.

• When swimming around coral, be careful where you put your hands and feet. Urchin stings can be painful and coral cuts can be dangerous. You can also damage or injure the coral. Coral is living animal which grows very slowly—so don't knock into it or stand on it while snorkeling.

• Respect the yellow and red flag warnings when placed on the developed beaches. They are there to advise you of unsafe conditions.

• After heavy rains, stay out of the ocean until the water clears.

• Avoid swimming in the mouths of rivers or streams or in any areas of murky water.

• Always use fins when boogie boarding.

• Don't feed the fish.

• Keep your distance from pole and net fishermen.

• Remember, it's illegal to do *anything* that causes a dolphin, monk seal, turtle or whale to change its behavior, so do not approach them.

Surface water temperature varies little, with a mean temperature of 73 degrees Fahrenheit in January and 80.2 degrees in August. Minimum and maximum range from 68 to 84 degrees. This is an almost ideal temperature (refreshing, but not cold) for swimming and you'll find most resort pools cooler than the ocean. Of course, if it's windy, it may feel chilly when you get out of the water.

Note: Ulysses Press, Paradise Publications and the authors of this guide have endeavored to provide current and accurate information on the Big Island's beautiful beaches. However, remember that nature is unpredictable and weather, beach and current conditions can change. Enjoy your day at the beach, but utilize good judgment. Ulysses Press, Paradise Publications and the authors of this guide cannot be held responsible for accidents or injuries incurred.

Best Bets

Most Beautiful Beaches 'Anaeho'omalu Beach; Hapuna Beach State Park; Kauna'oa Beach (Mauna Kea Beach)

Safest Playing/Swimming Beaches for *Keiki* *Kailua-Kona:* Kamakahonu ("King Kam") Beach, Old Kona Airport State Recreation Area, Kaloko-Honokohau National Historic Park; *South Kona District*: Kahalu'u Beach Park, Kamakahonu Beach, Old Kona Airport State Recreation Area, Kaloko-Honokohau National Historic Park; *South Kohala:* 'Anaeho'omalu Beach, Hapuna Beach State Park, Spencer Beach Park, Kauna'oa Beach; *Hilo:* Onekahakaha Beach Park, Leleiwi Beach Park, Coconut Island

Shelling/Tidepooling Beaches *Kailua-Kona:* Old Kona Airport State Recreation Area; *Hilo*: Onekahakaha Beach Park; *South Kohala:* Holoholokai Beach Park

Snorkeling Beaches *South Kona:* Napo'opo'o Beach Park (Kealakekua Bay State Historical & Underwater Parks), Honaunau Bay, Ho'okena Beach Park; *Keauhou-Kona*: Kahalu'u Beach Park;

Text continued on page 286.

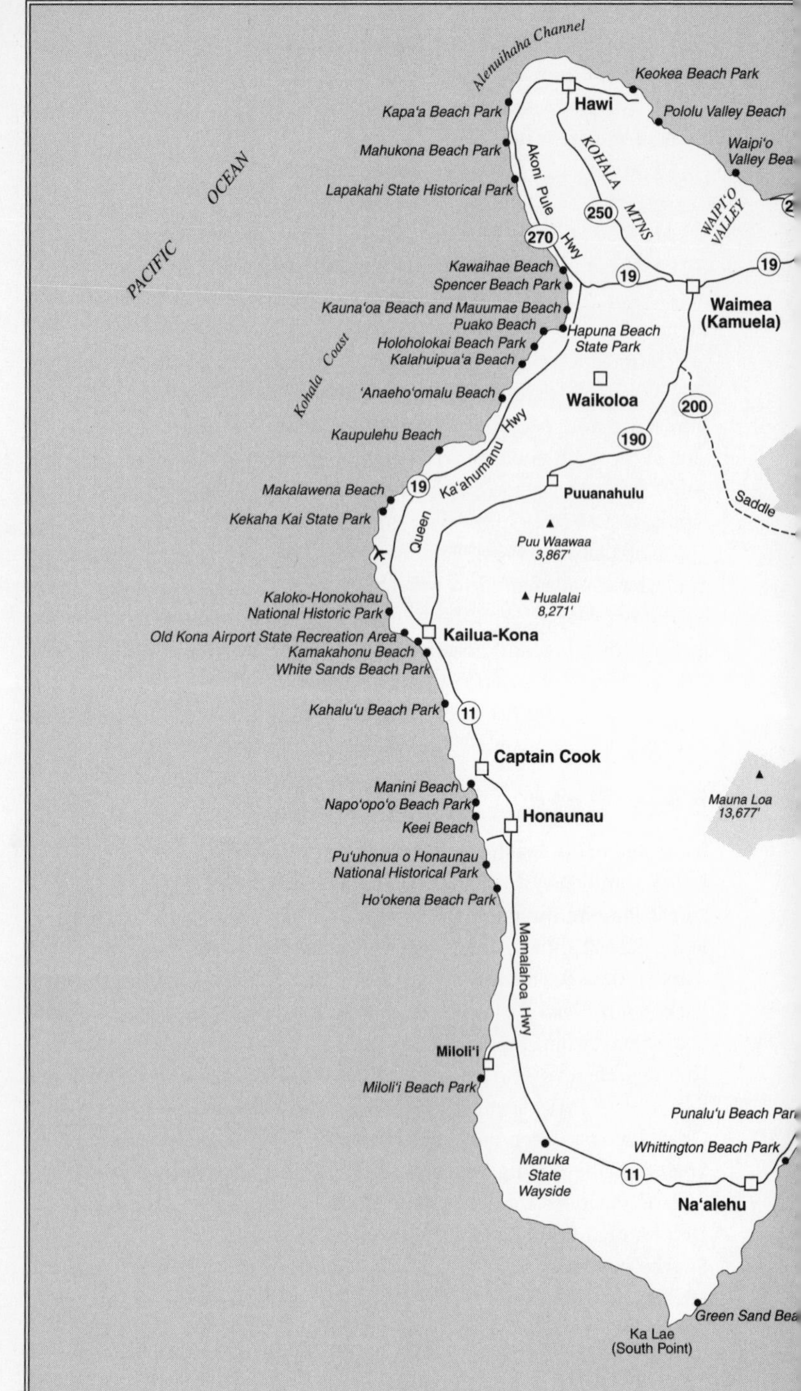
Alenuihaha Channel
PACIFIC OCEAN
Kohala Coast
Hawi
Keokea Beach Park
Pololu Valley Beach
Waipi'o Valley Bea
Kapa'a Beach Park
Mahukona Beach Park
Lapakahi State Historical Park
Akoni Pule Hwy
KOHALA MTNS
WAIPI'O VALLEY
250
270
19
Kawaihae Beach
Spencer Beach Park
Kauna'oa Beach and Mauumae Beach
Puako Beach
Hapuna Beach State Park
Holoholokai Beach Park
Kalahuipua'a Beach
Waimea (Kamuela)
'Anaeho'omalu Beach
Waikoloa
200
190
Kaupulehu Beach
Ka'ahumanu Hwy
Makalawena Beach
Kekaha Kai State Park
Puuanahulu
Saddle
Queen
Puu Waawaa 3,867'
Hualalai 8,271'
Kaloko-Honokohau National Historic Park
Old Kona Airport State Recreation Area
Kailua-Kona
Kamakahonu Beach
White Sands Beach Park
Kahalu'u Beach Park
11
Captain Cook
Manini Beach
Napo'opo'o Beach Park
Keei Beach
Honaunau
Mauna Loa 13,677'
Pu'uhonua o Honaunau National Historical Park
Ho'okena Beach Park
Mamalahoa Hwy
Miloli'i
Miloli'i Beach Park
Punalu'u Beach Par
Whittington Beach Park
Manuka State Wayside
Na'alehu
Green Sand Bea
Ka Lae (South Point)

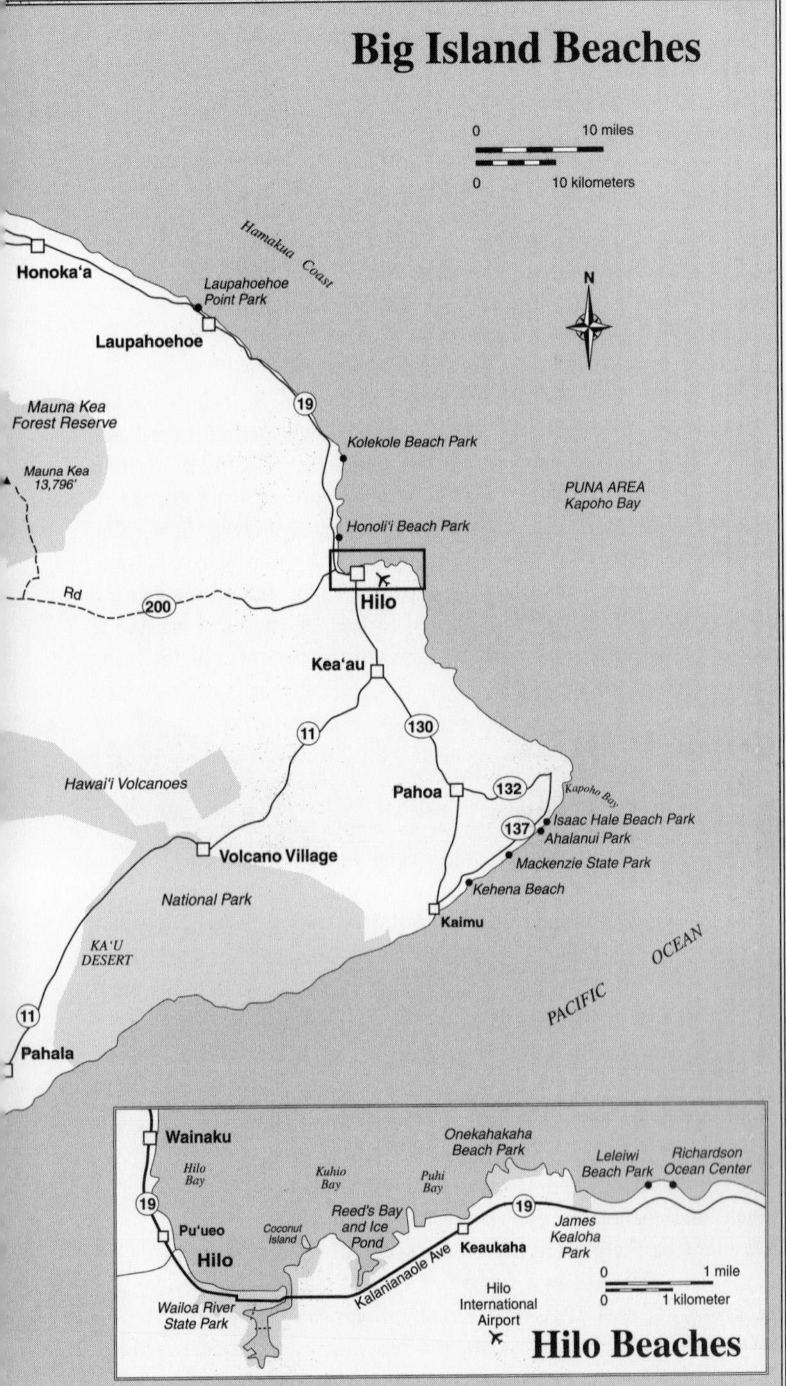
Big Island Beaches
0
10 miles
0
10 kilometers
Hamakua Coast
Honoka'a
Laupahoehoe Point Park
Laupahoehoe
N
Mauna Kea Forest Reserve
19
Kolekole Beach Park
Mauna Kea 13,796'
PUNA AREA
Kapoho Bay
Honoli'i Beach Park
Rd
200
Hilo
Kea'au
11
130
Hawai'i Volcanoes
Pahoa
132
Kapoho Bay
137
Isaac Hale Beach Park
Ahalanui Park
Volcano Village
Mackenzie State Park
Kehena Beach
National Park
Kaimu
KA'U DESERT
OCEAN
PACIFIC
11
Pahala
Wainaku
Onekahakaha Beach Park
Hilo Bay
Kuhio Bay
Puhi Bay
Leleiwi Beach Park
Richardson Ocean Center
19
Reed's Bay and Ice Pond
19
James Kealoha Park
Pu'ueo
Coconut Island
Keaukaha
Hilo
Kalanianaole Ave
0
1 mile
Hilo International Airport
0
1 kilometer
Wailoa River State Park
Hilo Beaches

Kohala Coast: ʻAnaehoʻomalu Beach, Kaunaʻoa Beach; *Hilo:* Leleiwi Beach Park; *Puna District:* Kapoho Bay

Sunbathing Beaches White Sands Beach Park, Kailua-Kona; ʻAnaehoʻomalu Beach, Kohala Coast; Hapuna Beach State Park; Kaunaʻoa Beach (Mauna Kea Beach)

Using This Chapter

The following listings refer to a variety of beaches and beach parks. The **pail and shovel icon** indicates beaches that are recommended for family activities. They are more protected and most likely have lifeguards on duty. Also check for ★, which identify special recommendations.

A close look at the map will reveal many more Big Island beaches than are described here. We like to say there's a beach for everybody, and everything you like to do at the beach. Some go by more than one name, with locations pinpointed only by local word-of-mouth. Some are little more than a pocket of sand between craggy lava walls. Some are intimate little gems you might discover for yourself. Some require a 4WD vehicle and a good pair of shoes, but all are waiting for you to explore. We've attempted to include the more-accessible beaches here, and invite you to share your experiences at those we may have omitted.

Kona District

KAILUA-KONA TOWN

The beaches listed here will have a considerable number of visitors as well as local residents populating the sand and facilities. These beaches are generally quite nice and equipped for all sorts of watersports and activities. Their proximity to the hotels and resorts of Kailua-Kona make them busy places on most good beach days.

★ *Kahaluʻu Beach Park*

This is one of the most popular swimming and snorkeling sites in the Kona area, located next to the Keauhou Beach Hotel, just south of Kailua-Kona. The beach is composed of white sand speckled with black lava pebbles, cobblestones and fragments. Excellent snorkeling and near-shore scuba diving in bay waters protected by a fringing reef, and the area is generally free of strong currents. Outside the reef, surfers can find good waves to ride but the rip currents along the reef edge are extremely strong.

Caution is advised. Park facilities include picnic pavilions, restrooms, showers, water, lifeguard, parking and concession stands.

★ *White Sands Beach Park*

Located on Ali'i Drive four miles south of Kailua-Kona town, also called Laaloa Beach. Facilities include restrooms, showers, lifeguard and small parking lot. A grove of coconut trees provides some shade and lends a touch of beauty to this small beach park. The lovely white sand and small wave action make this a popular swimming and boogieboarding beach for both residents and visitors. Winter storms often wash the white sand into deeper water, only to carry it back later, hence the park's other names of "Disappearing Sands" and "Magic Sands."

★ *Kamakahonu Beach*

This is a small cove of sandy beach immediately next to the Kailua Pier and fronting King Kamehameha's Kona Beach Hotel. Extending onto a peninsula in front of the beach is Ahu'ena Heiau, the temple of King Kamehameha the Great. Kamehameha resided here at Kamakahonu during the last years of his life. The beach is very protected and is excellent for sunbathing and swimming, especially good for young children. No public facilities exist on the beach itself but there are public restrooms on the adjacent pier.

'Alula Beach

The beach is located in a small protected cove just to the south of Honokohau Harbor near Kailua-Kona and is a lovely crescent of white sand speckled with black lava fragments. It is a secluded spot for sunbathing, swimming, snorkeling and near-shore scuba diving. The boat traffic of Honokohau Harbor can be viewed easily from the beach. The shallow sandy bottom makes this a pleasant calm beach especially for youngsters. Public facilities at adjacent boat harbor.

Old Kona Airport State Recreation Area

The area consists of a long beach composed of pebbles, rocks and a few pockets of white sand, with safe sand channels for entering the water. Although the coast here tends to be rocky, there are tidepools to explore all along the coastline. The swimming and snorkeling are generally fair to good here, but best on calmer days. Facilities include a jogging trail, picnic pavilions, restrooms, showers, water and plenty of parking. Next to the beach is the old runway, good for skating or rollerblading. Community ball fields are right next door.

★ *Kaloko-Honokohau National Historic Park*

This 1,160-acre park spans a two-mile stretch of the Kona coast adjacent to and north of Honokohau Small Boat Harbor, north of Kailua-Kona. The park was founded to preserve, protect, interpret and demonstrate native Hawaiian activities and culture and to demonstrate historic land use. Archaeological resources include ancient Hawaiian house platforms, fishing shrines, canoe landings, petroglyph rock carvings, religious temples and fishponds. The tidal wetlands are home to many waterbirds, including the Hawaiian black-necked stilt and Hawaiian coot, both endemic to Hawai'i. The park landscape also includes scenic coastlines, sandy beaches, marine tidal pools and native plants. Located three miles north of Kailua-Kona, three miles south of Keahole Airport. There is an unimproved access road just opposite Kaloko Industrial Park open daily 8 a.m. to 3:30 p.m. There is also access to a hiking trail into the park from Honokohau harbor. This is a hot, dry, windy area of open, rough lava flows. Hikers and visitors should come prepared with sunscreen, hats, hiking shoes and water. No water, but toilets are available at the fishpond and beach. A visitor facility is open daily. No camping or fires are allowed. For further information, contact Kaloko-Honokohau NHP, 73-4786 Kanalani Street #14, Kailua-Kona, HI 96740; 808-329-6881; www.nps.gov/kaho.

Kaupulehu Beach

This fronts the Kona Village and Four Seasons Resort north of Kailua-Kona. The white-sand beach is speckled with black lava fragments and pebbles. Kahuwai Bay is good for swimming and snorkeling, although in some areas you need to walk over rock or coral shelf. There is convenient public access (parking is provided by the resorts), restrooms and showers. According to legend, these waters have healing properties. This is one of those rare places you might see huge sea turtles sunning themselves in the sand.

Kekaha Kai State Park

This beach park is located just a couple of miles north of Kona's Keahole Airport. It is reached off Highway 19 by a narrow, somewhat bumpy road that winds across the lava fields for 1.5 miles. A regular car can make it but drive slowly. The beach is a high sand dune beach with good tidal pools for snorkeling and swimming, but don't go out too far. The park is still being developed and there are only temporary restroom facilities and a few picnic tables plus an unimproved parking lot area. Bring your own water.

Makalawena Beach

More of a surfing spot than a beach, Makalawena is located north of Kekaha Kai State Park, near Opaeula Pond. It can be reached by a moderately rugged hike along the coastal foot trail. The shoreline is made of intricate caves and is backdropped by sand dunes. Lots of shell-collecting and bird-watching opportunities. No facilities or drinking water at the site.

SOUTH KONA DISTRICT

The beaches of South Kona are fairly isolated, mostly used by local residents. None of these listed are near any resorts, major towns or commercial areas.

Ho'okena Beach Park

Three miles south of Pu'uhonua o Honaunau at the end of a narrow, winding and bumpy paved spur road off Highway 11 is Ho'okena. A small coconut grove with several old Hawai'ian homes and beach houses, the park offers restrooms and picnic tables and some shade trees. Reach the beachfront by a very narrow one-lane roadway between old stone walls. The beach is a combination of black-and-white sand and mixed lava debris, giving the sand a gray cast. The bay is generally calm, and swimming, snorkeling and diving are good, but caution is advised during high surf times.

★ *Pu'uhonua o Honaunau National Historical Park*

This is one of the Big Island's most popular attractions. In addition to the visitors center, a reconstructed Hawaiian village and impressive, tiki-guarded *heiau*, the park has restrooms, a picnic area, and some of the best near-shore snorkeling and scuba diving on the island at nearby Honaunau Bay. Swimming and sunbathing is not permitted within the park. The generally rocky shoreline has pockets of sandy beach here and there and the shoreline waters teem with marine life. For further information, call the visitors center at 808-328-2288.

★ *Napo'opo'o Beach Park*

Adjoining the village of Napo'opo'o at Kealakekua Bay, the beach consists of pebbles, cobblestones and boulders with only a very narrow strip of sand at the water's edge. The beach attracts many sunbathers and swimmers and the limited wave action attracts some surfers and boogieboarders. The adjacent Napo'opo'o Beach Park has very limited parking, restrooms and a couple of picnic tables. Also next to the park are the ruins of Hikiau Heiau, an old Hawaiian temple. Snorkelers will revel in the offshore Kealakekua Bay State Historical & Underwater Parks. The area is full of colorful marine life and offers excellent snorkeling and scuba diving. Many of the commercial boat tours from Kailua-Kona include Kealakekua Bay

Note: Because of the Big Island's rugged coastlines, finding whole, intact seashells is an uncommon thing. Some tiny shells, however, may be found mixed in the sand on almost any beach.

as part of their route. At the north end, beyond the towering cliffs and on a flat point of land jutting into the bay, is the Captain James Cook Monument, erected to honor the famous British explorer. A plaque at the water's edge notes the spot where Cook met his fate in a dispute with the Hawaiians in 1779.

Manini Beach

A very small beach in an out-of the way location just south of Napo'o-po'o. Rough water and rocky coast can make swimming a challenge, but offshore diving is decent. Turn toward the coast on Manini Street. At the end of the road, park and take the short walk to the point. No facilities.

Keei Beach

Very shallow water at this quarter-mile-long salt-and-pepper beach allows for safe but limited swimming; good snorkeling due to lots of coral. It's away from the tourist area, with excellent views of Kealakekua Bay, so you'll likely only encounter locals. In Captain Cook take Napo'opo'o Road down to Kealakekua Bay. At the bottom of the hill, go left toward the Pu'uhonua o Honaunau National Historical Park. Take this road a half-mile, turn right onto a lava-bed road and follow this extremely rough road another half-mile to the beach. No facilities.

Miloli'i Beach Park

Another challenging beach to reach, this one is outside of Miloli'i town, about 33 miles south of Kailua-Kona. Turn off onto a very winding, one-lane, macadam road. It's about a half-hour drive to finish the five miles to the beach. Lots of beautiful tidepools here, as well as reefs that create great swimming and snorkeling spots (but be careful if you venture beyond the reefs). No facilities.

Manuka State Wayside

Located 19 miles west of Na'alehu on Mamalahoa Highway, this lovely botanic garden has stunning ocean views at nearly 2,000 feet above sea level. Native and imported trees dot the grassy, rolling terrain. Restrooms and picnic area available. About five miles off Mamalahoa Highway down a 4WD trail, Manuka Bay and Kaulanamauna Cove are secluded areas, supposed sites of ancient ruins and *heiau*. There are no facilities at the shore.

Kohala Coast

SOUTH KOHALA DISTRICT

South Kohala has the best sandy beaches on the island, perfect for swimming and sunbathing. Some, like Hapuna and Spencer parks, are favorites of local residents and visitors alike. Others, like 'Anaeho'omalu and Kauna'oa beaches, front major resort hotels and are mostly used by their guests. However, as with every other beach in Hawai'i, they are available to the public. Access to the beaches is provided by the resorts (look for the blue "wave" signs), but parking can be limited and a free pass may be required. You may have to wait at the entry if beach parking is crowded, or you might want to visit the property to go shopping, check out a tee time or have lunch before you hit the beach (this is a big hint). Once there, please keep in mind that amenities such as chairs, umbrellas and towels are provided for the resort guests who pay considerably for them. Although it may be tempting to take advantage of same, and may not seem fair, remember that the resorts take the responsibility to clean and maintain these beautiful beaches and their facilities for everyone to enjoy, and they earn their money from their paying guests.

★ *'Anaeho'omalu Beach*

This is a beautiful, long, curving, white-sand beach speckled with gravelly grains of black lava, but you might want *tabis* or slippers if you want to walk it. It is a lovely crescent accented with graceful coconut palms and backed by two old fishponds, Ku'uali'i and Kahapapa, which were reserved for Hawaiian royalty in the old days. The beach park fronts the Waikoloa Resort and plenty of free public parking is provided. One of the best places for ocean activities, "A-Bay" offers swimming, snorkeling, scuba diving, windsurfing and board surfing and more. A watersports activities concession on the beach provides equipment rentals and instruction for hotel guests and other visitors, as well as sign-ups for sunset sails, glass-bottom boat cruises and more. The beach park facilities include restrooms, showers and picnic tables plus parking.

Kalahuipua'a Beach

Located at the Mauna Lani Resort, the beach is adjacent to a series of well-maintained old Hawaiian fishponds that are still used for aquaculture purposes. The beach access is through a historic preserve and public park maintained by the Mauna Lani Resort. The best swimming area of the beach is Nanuku Inlet, a wide, shallow, sandy-bottomed cove enclosed by natural lava rock barriers. This part of the lovely white-and-black-sand speckled beach immediately fronts the Mauna Lani Bay Hotel.

★ *Holoholokai Beach Park*

This public-access beach park is located just north of the Fairmont Orchid. The park was developed by the Mauna Lani Resort Company and provides restrooms and showers, parking stalls for over 30 cars and barbecue grills on the beach. The beach is not sandy but composed of white coral rocks and some black lava and debris. There are small pockets of sand here and there. It's a good beach for sunning, tidepool exploring, shelling and snorkeling in the larger tidal pools. Great views of the Kohala Coast. A trail from the parking lot leads to the Puako Petroglyph Fields, which provide an interesting view of old Hawaiian rock carvings and drawings.

Puako Beach

The beach extends along Puako Road in North Kohala south of Hapuna Beach State Park. The shoreline is mostly rocks and pebbles indented by inlets, coves and tidal pools, but sunbathers, swimmers and snorkelers can find some white-sand beach stretches to enter the water. Public access is via the boat ramp at Puako Bay or any of several points along Puako Road, which follows the shoreline homes. Look for the "wave" access signs. Parking may be limited and there are no facilities along these beaches.

Waialea Bay ("Beach 69's")

Finding this popular local beach and surfing spot is a bit of a challenge for the uninitiated, unless the surf's up and you can follow the crowd. Watch for the sign to Puako on the *makai* (ocean) side of Highway 19. Turn in, take the first right onto a narrow unmarked road behind a residential area. Look for parking at 69-mile marker (there may not be a beach-access "wave" sign) and take the short hike across the lava.

★ *Hapuna Beach State Recreation Area*

Hapuna is undoubtedly one of the best—a beautiful, user-friendly beach with ample, convenient facilities. This is the Big Island's largest expanses of fine white sand. It stretches for over a half mile and provides shallow waters that slope gently to deeper offshore waters. Swimming, snorkeling, bodysurfing, windsurfing and near-shore scuba diving are excellent. Shallow, protected coves at the beach's north end provide sandy-bottomed pools that are ideal for little children to splash and play in. The beach facilities are some of the best as well, including private scenic picnic lanai spread along the bluffs, a pavilion for larger groups, restrooms, showers, lifeguards, public phones, great lunch and sweet treats at 3 Frogs snack bar, and plenty of free parking. At the far north end, you will see the grounds of Hapuna Beach Prince Hotel, where nice lunch and libations are served by the swimming pool, just a short walk up from the beach (coverups required).

★ *Kauna'oa Beach*

One of the most photographed beaches on the island, this is the beach that inspired Laurance S. Rockefeller to build his legendary Mauna Kea Beach Hotel in 1965. It is a long, wide crescent of fine white sand that slopes gently into the deeper offshore waters and offers excellent swimming, snorkeling and windsurfing. Surf conditions often permit good bodysurfing and occasional board-surfing; watersports activity gear is available for rent. Mauna Kea Resort provides public access and some parking (go early, or you may have to wait for a pass at the gate). It also maintains convenient public restrooms and showers near the beach. No cooking is permitted, but there is a good lunch restaurant. Once the playground of *ali'i* (Hawaiian royalty), Kauna'oa Beach is still enjoyed by the elite. In 2000 it was named the #1 beach in the nation by "Dr. Beach" (Stephen Leatherman of Florida International University) and is consistently highly rated by readers of *Condé Nast* and *Travel & Leisure.*

Mauumae Beach

Located just off a private estate parcel within the Mauna Kea Resort, Mauumae is a small, secluded beach with no public facilities. To visit, stop at the security shack at Mauna Kea Beach Hotel and request a beach pass for Mauumae. Parking is very limited and access is via an easy trail from the hotel's support area to the beach. (Note: Despite Mauumae's former reputation as a clothing-optional beach, nude swimming or sunbathing is not legal in Hawai'i.)

Spencer Beach Park

The park is located near the port village of Kawaihae and immediately below Pu'ukohola Heiau National Historic Park, a famous temple built by Kamehameha the Great. The beach here is a fine white-sand expanse with a very gentle slope to deeper water. The conditions are excellent for swimming, snorkeling and near-shore scuba diving. The protected nature of the bay affords very calm waters with usually gentle surf. It is a good swimming beach for little children. This popular beach can get crowded, especially on weekends and holidays. Keep an eye on the kids in the parking lot, and do remember to lock the car.

Kawaihae Beach

This is a coral rubble and landfill beach next to the boat harbor that resulted when the harbor was dredged years ago. Many local folks use the area for varied activities such as fishing, canoe paddling, sailing, windsurfing, swimming and picnicking. From the south end of the landfill area is a great view of the nearby Pu'ukohola Heiau, and if conditions are right, this can be a good place to hunt for seashells.

NORTH KOHALA DISTRICT

The beaches of North Kohala tend to be of a more rugged variety, often composed of small pockets of coral pebbles and small rocks with an isolated pocket of sand. Often the beach area is lava rock outcropping.

★ *Lapakahi State Historical Park*

The park is north of Kawaihae Harbor, and although it has no good sandy beaches, it does have a rather remarkable restoration of an ancient Hawaiian village along the rugged coastline. Well worth a stop (especially early in the day before the temperature soars) Lapakahi is one of the Big Island's best-kept secrets. As for beachgoers, there are small pockets of coral pebbles and rocky beaches where swimmers and snorkelers can enter the water. At the point where the park trail follows the shoreline and meets a small peninsula of land, there is a small cove with remarkably clear water that slopes gradually before dropping off sharply. Swimmers and snorkelers should not venture out more than 50 yards into the cove, however, due to strong alongshore currents in the area. There are no facilities right on the shore but restrooms are located near the parking lot area and entrance.

Mahukona Beach Park

Between Kawaihae and Hawi on Highway 270 is the site of an old port of the Hawai'i Consolidated Railway Company, which transported sugar from the Kohala Mill to boats for trans-ocean shipment. Remnants of the old railway port still exist and old train wheels, parts and related rubble attract snorkelers and divers in the bay's clear waters. There is no real sand beach here, only coral rubble and pebbles, but it's a great place for shoreline fishing. Facilities include picnic tables, a pavilion, restrooms, showers, camping area and parking lot, but all facilities are rough and in need of some maintenance work.

Kapa'a Beach Park

Off Highway 11 about 14 miles north of Kawaihae, Kapa'a is a small, picturesque beach park with a great view of Maui. There's a tiny cove ringed by *kiawe* trees, but it has no sand. Better for photo-ops than swimming, the beach is a pleasant stop along your drive through North Kohala. Facilities are limited to restrooms and picnic areas.

Keokea Beach Park

A nice spot for a picnic, with restroom facilities and camping allowed, although this area gets lots of heavy rainfall. There is a small sandy, cliff-rimmed cove, and the lawn is fringed by palm trees. Water tends to be rough and the coastline is rugged. Located about six miles east of Hawi off Highway 270; turn at the sign and follow the winding road for one mile.

Pololu Valley Beach

At the end of Highway 270, past the village of Kapa'au, the beach is reached by a difficult trail down to the valley at the end of the highway. The trail is often treacherous if wet, and caution is advised. The beach is a wide expanse of fine black sand with high dunes at the back shore. While swimmers, bodysurfers and surfers use the beach, there are dangerous rip currents that are real hazards. This is a remote, isolated beach, and extreme caution is advised. The flatlands of the valley were once extensively planted in taro farms but are now abandoned. There are no facilities of any kind on the beach.

Hamakua Coast

The eastern side of the Big Island, the Hamakua Coast, is marked by high *pali* (cliffs), in some places a sheer vertical drop of more than 200 feet. The coastline here is very rough and rugged, with very few places where sandy beaches have had a chance to form. The fact that there is no coral reef extending outward from the coast accounts for the lack of coral sand here. Waipi'o Valley Beach, the one exception listed, is composed of black lava sand eroded from the surrounding lava rock. Like the Hamakua Coast, the North Hilo area has formed few sandy beaches. There are small pockets of black lava rock sand in some areas, but coral sand beaches are non-existent. The generally high coastline *pali* also accounts for a lack of good beaches in the area. However, the area has a special rugged beauty that is captured in places like Laupahoehoe Park.

Waipi'o Valley Beach

This beach is a worthwhile challenge to reach. At the end of Highway 240 is the Waipi'o Valley State Park lookout. Below that, down a hazardous and very steep single lane road carved along the valley wall, is a long black-sand crescent bisected in the middle by the Waipi'o River. There are many large smooth boulders and rubble at the south end. While some swimmers, bodysurfers and surfers ride the often good waves here, the presence of strong rip currents make the beach extremely dangerous for even advanced swimmers. Caution is advised. There are no facilities of any kind on the beach and a 4WD vehicle is required. A better plan may be to contact one of the reputable tour and excursion providers listed elsewhere in this guide.

★ *Laupahoehoe Point Park*

The park is a lava rock peninsula jutting into the ocean at Laupahoehoe. The area is typical of the Hamakua Coast in that there are steep rugged cliffs and hardly any safe sandy beaches. The beach on this sea-level peninsula is mostly coral pebbles and rocks. Strong surf and rip currents prevent most water activities, although some people do swim and surf. The rocky shoreline requires extreme caution. Park facilities include picnic pavilions, restrooms, showers, water, parking, camping sites and a small boat launch. It is a pleasant park at which to picnic and enjoy the scenic beauty of the Hamakua Coast. On a warm day, lots of ironwood trees provide cool shade to enjoy the pastoral Hawaiian scenery. Look for the poignant Tidal Wave Memorial.

Hilo

★ *Kolekole Beach Park*

Despite not having a sandy beach, this is one of the Big Island's loveliest parks. It is fronted by a shoreline of smooth waterworn lava rocks with an adjacent coldwater stream and waterfall. The park grounds and surrounding valley walls are lush and full of tropical vegetation. The stream flows from the beautiful Akaka Falls Park located upstream some four miles. While water activities are somewhat limited, the park is an excellent place for a day outing to picnic, explore and enjoy Hawai'i's tropical outdoors. Park facilities include restrooms, pavilions, water, showers and camping areas. Located just off Highway 19, about 12 miles northwest of Hilo.

Honoli'i Beach Park

Located just north of Hilo off Highway 19, on the old scenic route Mamalahoa Highway, this is a favorite with local teenagers as it is one of the best surfing beaches in the Hilo area. Restrooms and very limited parking along the roadside are available. A good spot for watching local kids catch the waves on a nice day.

★ *Coconut Island*

Although there's no beach here, Coconut Island is a great place to stop and play along Hilo Bay, rain or shine. Park beside the Hilo Hawaiian Hotel and take the footbridge across to the park to enjoy a picnic lunch, try your hand at fishing, explore the tidepools or relax in the grass. Pavilions and restrooms are available.

low inlet here just off Banyan Drive that is a popular swimming hole for local kids. The Ice Pond is a spring-fed stream that flows into Hilo Bay via Reed's Bay small boat harbor. You'll sometimes see families playing there, though more often you'll see carloads of teenagers cruising Banyan Drive. While the water is calm and the spot is scenic, there are better places to play.

★ Onekahakaha Beach Park

Located behind Hilo Airport off Highway 137 just outside of Hilo town, this is a favorite spot for visitors and *kama'aina* as well. The park features a breakwater and retaining walls that create protected sandy-bottom swimming areas. Facilities include lifeguard service, pavilions, picnic tables, camp sites and restrooms.

James Kealoha Park

The park has a smooth lava-rock beach and picnic areas and restrooms. Good swimming, surfing and snorkeling are available here. Located east of Hilo along Kalanianaole Avenue.

★ Leleiwi Beach Park

This park also has a smooth lava rock beach and pavilions, picnic areas and restrooms. Swimming, snorkeling and surfing are good here. Adjacent to the park is the Richardson Ocean Center, a marine education and aquatic display center open to the public; see "Traveling With Children: Entertainment" in Chapter 1 for details on the Richardson Ocean Center.

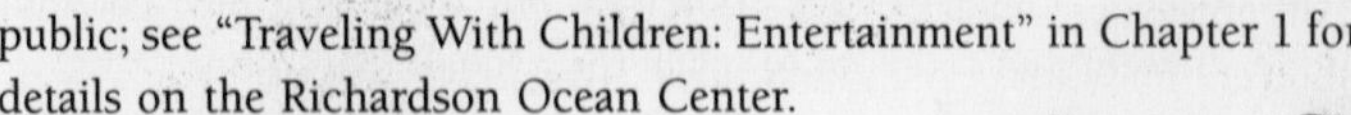

Puna District

The Puna beaches tend to be in fairly isolated areas several miles from the nearest town or commercial districts. The black-sand beaches of Puna have long been among the Big Island's most dramatic attractions (but please don't be tempted to carry away sand as a souvenir). Visitors should keep in mind that the following beaches tend to be crowded and their facilities heavily used.

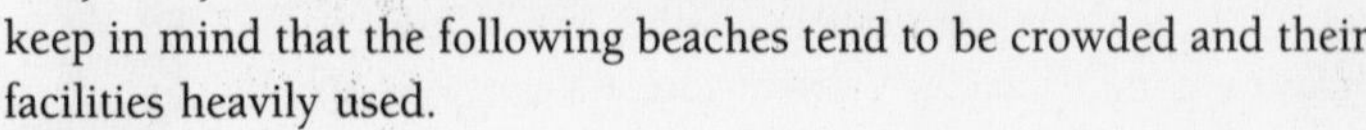

Kapoho Bay

The bay is the backshore area fronting Kapoho Beach Lots and Vacationland Estates subdivisions in the Kapoho area. While there isn't a sandy beach here, there is a beautiful tidal pond and pool area that is great for snorkeling and swimming. The tidal pools host a variety of marine life and small fish. There are no facilities.

Isaac Hale Beach Park

The park is on Cape Kumukahi, along the Puna Coast, and is the site of a busy boat-launching ramp used by commercial fishermen. Other activities of the bay include surfing, bodyboarding and swimming. The beach here is mostly smooth pebbles and cobblestones and not fine sand. There are restrooms and showers available. Behind the beach area in a natural lava rock pool are the Pohoiki Warm Springs, a natural warm-water bath heated by underground geothermal action that is used for bathing and soaking.

Kehena Beach

Located on Pohoiki Road between Cape Kumukahi and Kaimu-Kalapana, the beach is a broad expanse of fine black sand below the Kehena Lookout and parking area. Access is via a steep trail down the cliff face. Kehena Beach is popular with swimmers and bodysurfers. No facilities available.

★ Ahalanui Park

The area's newest beach park, the three-acre Ahalanui Park was established with a federal grant to replace parks lost at Kalapana to the volcanic lava flows of the 1990s. It's located two and a half miles south of the junction of Highways 132 and 137 on the Kapoho coast southeast of Pahoa town. You'll find a half-acre pond/pool fed by thermal freshwater springs for a 95-degree natural hot tub experience. Facilities include lifeguard service and shaded picnic areas, restrooms and outdoor showers but no drinking water. There is no real beach here since it is all lava rock shoreline, but there is a nice coconut grove surrounding the pool to make for a lovely photo-op.

Mackenzie State Recreation Area

Just two miles down Highway 132 from Ahalanui is a whispering pine forest along the ocean coast. Although there is no beach here, soft pine needles, cool breezes and gorgeous views make it a worthwhile stop along the way. There's a picnic area and pit toilets.

Ka'u District

The Ka'u area is most famous for its Green Sand Beach, which is quite remote but accessible via a long, hot hike or commercial ATV excursion. Ka'u is very dry with long stretches of empty countryside. The South Point area from which Green Sand Beach can be reached is an interesting historical site with old Hawaiian canoe landings and ruins in place.

Punalu'u Beach Park

Located near Pahala, this moderately long black-sand beach is backed by low dunes. The bay has a small boat-launching ramp, a freshwater fish pond and shaded picnic areas with palm trees. Generally good for sunbathing and swimming, snorkelers should be cautious about venturing beyond the boat ramp due to a powerful rip current running out to the boat channel. The current converges with an even stronger shore current outside the bay that makes it more hazardous. Stay inside the ramp area and enjoy the varied sea life here. Hawaiian green sea turtles are quite numerous and easily seen as they surface and close in to shore, where they feed on seaweed growing on the rocks and coral. Showers, restrooms and picnic pavilion are available.

Green Sand Beach

Worth the long trip, the beach at Mahana Bay is reached via the end of South Point Road and a very rough four-mile (round trip) coastal road, reached only by a four-wheel-drive vehicle or fairly rugged hike. If you hike, just be sure you take enough water and other necessities because there are no facilities or emergency phone at the beach. The beach is accessed by a steep and hazardous trail down the cliff side, which has loose rocks and cinders that make for slippery footing. Caution is advised. The tinted sand is loaded with green olivine crystals, a component of Hawai'i's lava. Big grains of olivine give the sand a distinctly green color and glassy luster. The beach, at the base of a huge eroding volcanic cinder cone, is exposed to the sea directly and heavy surf and storms create dangerous surf conditions. Swimming and snorkeling are advised on only the calmest of days and extreme caution is in order. A permit to cross Hawaiian Home Lands is required for the trip to Green Sands Beach. For details, contact: Department of Hawaiian Home Lands, 160 Baker Avenue, Hilo, HI 96720; 808-974-4250. They will mail an application to your home, or fax it to your condo or hotel. A return fax is all that's required at this time; no fees. Apparently some confusion in this procedure causes the gates to be padlocked from time to time, but there is room to drive or hike around the problem. Avoid disappointment and call ahead.

Whittington Beach Park

About three miles to the northeast of Na'alehu, Whittington Beach Park is just off Highway 11 on the eastern coast, across from an abandoned sugar mill. A rocky shoreline park with a small black-sand beach, Whittington offers picturesque scenery, picnic tables and pavilions, restrooms and nice tidepools for the kids to explore.

CHAPTER 6

Recreation and Tours

The Big Island is big on fun. Its diverse climate, terrain and geophysical features provide an enormous range and scope of sports and recreation activities from the mountains to the sea. There is something to please everyone, from the laid-back toes-in-the-water set to the adventure-seeking backpacker bent on exploring the most remote areas. This chapter details some of the more popular activities available to visitors. Listings marked with ★ indicate Big Island activities that are particular favorites for fun, value or new and interesting. Please keep in mind that planned activities are a great way to spend time on vacation, and we encourage visitors to try something they wouldn't have the chance to try at home. However, as we've mentioned before, your time is valuable. Leave yourself some breathing room to explore independently, relax and enjoy the laid-back lifestyle at your own pace.

Best Bets

For Golfers A round of championship golf at either the Mauna Kea Golf Course or the Mauna Lani Resort Golf Course, both named among America's Top 12 resort courses.

For Ocean-lovers A snorkeling adventure at Kahalu'u Bay at Keauhou-Kona, Kealakekua Bay State Historical & Underwater

Parks in Kona, 'Anaeho'omalu Bay on the Kohala Coast, or Leleiwi Beach Park in Hilo.

For Ocean-lovers Who Don't Want to Get Wet A submarine cruise or glass-bottom boat cruise along the Kona or Kohala coast, over spectacular coral gardens alive with tropical fish.

For Volcano-watchers A helicopter "flightseeing" tour over Hawai'i Volcanoes National Park and the current eruption at Kilauea.

For Extreme Skiers If conditions permit, a ski run down Mauna Kea's fabulous snow-covered slopes.

For Horse Lovers A look at *paniolo* life on a guided trail ride through cool upcountry ranchlands, or a wagon tour through the peaceful valley of Waipi'o.

For Adventurous Anglers A fishing boat charter to pursue Pacific blue marlin or giant yellowfin tuna in the fabled waters of the Kona Coast.

For Hikers A trek through any of Hawai'i Volcanoes National Park trails to take in the awesome natural beauty and wonders of the volcanoes.

For Something Different An adventure kayak cruise through the Kohala Mountains on the old Kohala Ditch irrigation canal system, or let the whole family explore their artistic nature on a "watercolor safari" to one of the island's picturesque settings (contact Honoka'a artist Janice Gail at Windward Studio; 808-775-0466; e-mail: janice gailart@aol.com).

Activity Booking Services

A word about activity reservations on land and sea. Many timeshare, condominium and new subdivision sales ventures often run their own activity-booking services. These offer considerable discounts on island activities (and sometimes free breakfast or lunch) in exchange for your time on a free tour of the property and a (usually heavy) sales pitch. Be aware who you're talking to when you stop by a kiosk or activity desk, and bear in mind that you can purchase activities at a higher price elsewhere without committing to the property tour. If you're married, both spouses must attend and no-shows are charged full price for their bookings. It's not a bad way to "earn" a good discount, but keep in mind that vacation time is precious, and if you're not really in the market for real estate it might not be the best way to go. On the other hand, these are convenient, one-stop locations to help organize your vacation time with knowledgeable assistants. It's up to you.

Check with your hotel or resort activity desk, or any of the following agencies, to make reservations and arrangements for a full range of ocean sports and activities on the Kona and Kohala coasts. They can help you arrange everything from whale watching, diving and snorkeling cruises, fishing charters, sailboat rentals, surfboard and windsurfing rentals or custom charters just for you. They represent many of the individual cruise, snorkel, and dive operators and fishing charters listed, and reservations can be made directly with the operators or through these agencies. You will notice that the majority of ocean activities take place in the Kona–Kohala area of the island, although Hilo offers a few charter boat opportunities.

Activity Connection This booking service can make reservations for various water sports and ocean-related activities from deep-sea fishing charters to scuba and snorkel cruises. They also connect you with hikes, luau reservations and many other island activities. P.O. Box 3380, Kailua-Kona, HI 96745; 808-329-1038; www.beachactivityguide.com.

Activity Warehouse This booking service can make arrangements with numerous tour operators and activity vendors around the Big Island as well as throughout the Hawaiian islands. 800-923-4004 or Big Island 877-862-4355; Kona, 808-334-1155; Waikoloa 808-883-0100; Hilo 808-935-0400; www.travelhawaii.com.

Activity World This booking service can arrange varied ocean-related cruises, excursions and water sports activities. Waikoloa Beach Resort at the Kings' Shops 808-886-2083; Kohala Coast 808-886-2083; 76-5828 Ali'i Drive, near the Royal Kona Resort, Kailua-Kona, 808-329-7700.

Charter Desk This booking service offers charter deep-sea fishing from a large fleet of professional fishing boats. Watch the daily fish weigh-ins at 11 a.m. and 3 p.m. on the Honokohau Harbor docks from the free public viewing area. Deli, gas station, clothing store and general store also available; restaurant at the harbor. 74-381 Kealakehe Parkway, Honokohau Harbor, Kailua-Kona, HI 96740; 808-329-5735; fax 808-329-5747; 888-KONA4US.

Charter Locker This service specializes in fishing and boat charters, private or shared basis, full or half day. Kealakehe Parkway, Honokohau Harbor, Kailua-Kona, HI 96740; 800-247-1484; 808-326-2553.

Kona Beach Activity Shack This service can arrange a variety of water sports activities, (fishing, boating, cruises) along with rentals of snorkel gear, kayaks, paddle boats and a variety of beach accessories. At the Kona Pier on Ali'i Drive in front of the King Kamehameha Kona Beach Hotel, Kailua-Kona; 808-329-7494.

★ ***Kona Charter Skippers Association, Inc.*** This professional operation provides complete, personalized booking service for Kona's charter fishing fleet, recreational, snorkel-diving cruises and related water sports and activities. 74-857 Iwalani Place, Kailua-Kona, HI 96740; 800-762-7546; 808-329-3600; e-mail: konafish@hawaii.rr.com; www.konabiggamefishing.com.

Kona Marina Sports Activities This service can arrange a variety of ocean sports activities and specializes in deep-sea fishing and dive charters. They can arrange full- or half-day as well as share-parties. Japanese language available. 74-425 Kealakehe Parkway, 3rd floor, Honokohau Harbor, Kailua-Kona, HI 96740; 808-329-1115; fax 808-329-9104; e-mail: uki@ilhawaii.net.

Adventures and Tours

AIR TOURS

Small-plane Flightseeing

See the Big Island from a bird's-eye view on a scenic flight in a small plane. Flights depart from Hilo or Kona airports and generally include the island's most outstanding features and attractions such as volcano activity, waterfalls and valleys, lava deserts, rainforests and dramatic ocean coastlines.

Big Island Air This small airline offers complete Big Island Volcano Tour, Big Island Sunset Tour, Circle Big Island/Volcano Tour, Sunset Volcano Tour and a Super Saver Volcano Tour, plus custom charter flights can be arranged; they fly 9- and 15-passenger aircraft. Rates: Volcano tours $135 per person, Circle-island tours $185 per person. Kailua-Kona, 800-303-8868; 808-329-4868; e-mail: bigisle@ilhawaii.net.

Island Hoppers A different perspective on island air tours, from a fixed-wing aircraft with 360-degree views from each seat. Flights tour the eruption area at Kilauea and along the rugged cliffs of the North Kohala coastline. Free video memento of the flight with music and narration. Hilo International Airport; 808-969-2000; e-mail: info@hawaii-paradise.com.

Mokulele Flight Service This Hawaiian family–owned operator offers airborne photo safaris in high-winged aircraft for unobstructed views of the island's magnificent valleys and waterfalls and the awesome home of Pele at Kilauea. Fully narrated, with two-way communication between passengers and the pilot, guaranteed window seats for all, complimentary video and lots of aloha. Two-hour circle-island air tours begin at $189 per person; 40-minute volcano tours from Hilo start at $69 per person. Kona International Airport, P.O. Box 830, Holualoa, HI 96725; 808-326-7070; www.mokulele.com.

Pacific Wings This commuter airline based in Maui also operates 2.5-hour day flightseeing tours to neighbor islands including a Big Island/Kohala/Kona/Historical Tour and a Big Island Kilauea Volcano Air Excursion taking in the sights of Hawai'i Volcanoes National Park, Hilo and the Hamakua Coast. Tour rates start at $219 per person. 888-575-4546; 808-873-0877; fax 808-873-7920; e-mail: res@pacificwings.com; www.pacificwings.com.

Sporty's Academy Hawai'i This airtour operator provides personalized volcano and scenic coastal flights, twilight flights and circle-island tours. Take in Mauna Kea, Mauna Loa, Kilauea Volcano, Hamakua Coast, Kohala, Waipi'o Valley and more; video of flight included. These deluxe air adventures have 360-degree-view seating via large windows. Departures from both Hilo and Kona airports. Rates: from $89 per person. Locations at Hilo International Airport, or Kona International Airport, Kailua-Kona; 808-935-8799; e-mail: above@aloha.net; www.fly-hawaii.com.

Or, for pilots who prefer to take to the skies on their own, consider **Koa Air Service Hawai'i**. Cessna 150 and 172 airplane rentals available for do-it-yourself photo safaris and island tours. Kona International Airport, Kailua-Kona, HI 96740; 808-326-2288.

Helicopter Tours

One of Hawai'i's best, a helicopter "flightseeing" tour is a thrilling way to experience the volcano up close and personal. Although pricey, you get a lot of Big Island for your buck. In general, tours either cover the beautiful and dramatic Hamakua Coast with its tropical rainforests, hidden valleys and countless waterfalls, or they give you the very best (and safest) vantage point to witness the current lava flow at Kilauea, or both. Costs vary accordingly and tours departing from Hilo can be less expensive (keeping in mind the 1.5-hour drive from Kona or Kohala Coast resorts). Tours range from about $100-$410 per person, depending on length of flight, aircraft and departure location. Most lines require a minimum number of people for their various tours, advance reservations are required and tours always depend upon Mother Nature. Also, no scuba diving within 24 hours prior to your flight.

★ ***Blue Hawaiian Helicopters*** This tour service offers a full range of island air tours to the volcano areas and all major Big Island attractions, featuring Bose electronic noise-canceling headsets and optional digital video system for a personal movie of your flight. Winner of FAA's Certificate of Excellence since 1998. Tours offered include Circle of Fire/Waterfalls (from Hilo); Big Island Spectacular and Kohala Coast Adventure (from Waikoloa). Rates: $165-$410 per person. Ask about the exclusive ECO-Star craft. P.O. Box 384473, Waikoloa Helipad, Waikoloa, HI 96738; 800-786-BLUE, 808-961-5600; and Hilo International Airport, Hilo, HI 96720; www.bluehawaiian.com.

Island Outfitters This is something different—a 25-minute helicopter flight into almost inaccessible Honokane Nui Valley, and a half- or full-day hike along a streamside trail and the old Kohala Ditch. Tours include day packs, water bottles, weather gear and snacks (lunch on the full-day tour). Experienced owner/guide Tom McAuliffe has backpacked every major trail in Hawai'i and is a UH honors grad in geography. Custom tour packages may be arranged to include hiking, diving, photography, star-gazing and volcano treks, mountain biking, kayaking, scuba, hunting, fishing, birding and, yes, just sightseeing. P.O. Box 4441, Hilo, HI 96720; 808-966-7933; 800-840-9974; fax 808-966-6931; e-mail: islehike@aloha.com; www.islandoutfittershawaii.com.

Safari Helicopters This family-owned company has been in business since 1987, with a sturdy reputation for safety and professionalism. Safari's ASTAR birds are state of the art, with two-way radio communication between passengers and pilot, FAA-approved multiple-camera video system, a "Super Mega Window" for superior viewing and New Generation Bose X headsets. They specialize in air tours of the Big Island's volcano country with a special three-video camera system that captures all the scenery of your one-hour Volcano & Waterfalls flight along with the pilot's narration and your conversation. Rates start at $99 per person. Hilo International Airport, Hilo, HI 96720; 808-969-1259; 800-326-3356; e-mail: reservations@safari helicopters.com; www.safariair.com.

★ ***Sunshine Helicopters*** Fly the "Black Beauties" with this 30-year veteran helicopter service, offering custom CD music, "sky-cam" five-camera video system and other comforts. Their tour menu offers 45- to 120-minute flights over lush, unspoiled coastal valleys and the ever-changing drama of the volcano. Rates: $160 Kohala/Hamakua Coast, $175 Formations of Pele–Kilauea Volcano, $390 Big Island Volcano Deluxe. 21-100 Kauna'oa Drive, Hapuna Heliport–Mauna Kea

SOMETHING DIFFERENT

Wa'akaulua, a 50-year-old double-hulled Hawaiian sailing canoe, gives six passengers a seldom-seen perspective of the ocean, along with valued lessons in Hawai'i's history, natural sciences and seafaring. Not a "cruise" (you'll be expected to paddle if the wind is lax) and not a whale-watching photo-op, this is an authentic sail with an experienced master boat builder and sailor, well-versed in ocean culture and the particular beauty of the Big Island shoreline. The canoe lives in Punalu'u, but voyages depart from Hilo, Kona, Puako or Kawaihae, depending on your interest and Mother Nature. 808-938-5717; e-mail: kiko@waakaulua.com; www.waakaulua.com.

Resort, Kohala Coast, HI 96743; 800-622-3144; 808-882-1223; fax 808-882-1100; e-mail: sales@sunshinehelicopters.com; www.sunshinehelicopters.com.

Tropical Helicopters This pilot-owned and -operated air tour company offers various tours of the Big Island including Volcano-Waterfall Adventure, "Feel the Heat" doors-off look at the eruption; and the Hawai'i Experience, from the mountains to the sea. Custom charter flights available. Rates range from $99-$335. Main Terminal Building, Hilo International Airport, Hilo, HI 96720; 808-961-6810; fax 808-969-1632; www.tropicalhelicopters.com.

Volcano Helicopters They offer a full range of sightseeing tours into Hawai'i Volcanoes National Park and surrounding countryside. Hilo International Airport, P.O. Box 626, Volcano, HI 96785; 808-961-3355.

BIKING

The Big Island offers some of the most varied scenery anywhere in the Hawaiian islands. It also has some of the largest expanses and stretches of wide-open uninhabited country in the islands. The geography ranges from desert beaches to tropical rainforests to dry lava deserts. An excellent way to see and experience the changing scenes is by bicycle touring.

Many visitors to the Big Island bring their own bicycles and camping equipment with them and make up their own itinerary. (Check on your hotel's bike policy first. Some do not permit bicycles, skateboards, roller skates or scooters on-property). The Big Island's highway system is generally good-to-excellent in most areas but often the shoulders are unimproved. Bikers need to exercise caution on the open road, especially in narrow winding sections of highway. If you are an adventurous bicyclist, you may want to plan your own tour of the island. Just keep in mind the long distances between towns in some areas like the Ka'u, South Kona, and the Kohala Coast area and plan accordingly for water, food, lodging and other needs. If you want to opt for an organized commercial bicycle tour you might try the following operators.

Biking Resources

For more information on biking and trails on the Big Island, contact the following groups and organizations:

Peoples Advocacy for Trails Hawai'i (PATH) This nonprofit community group advocates the development and improvement of trails around the Big Island for non-motorized multi-use: recreation, fitness and alternative modes of transportation. P.O. Box 62, Kailua-Kona, HI 96745; 808-326-9495; e-mail: path@aloha.net; www.hialoha.com/path.

Big Island Mountain Bike Association There are two tour guide/maps available online for Big Island visitors and bikers, containing trail descriptions, maps and safety information on ten featured trails located around the Big Island. Riders at every level, from beginner to advanced, will discover scenic trails along the coastline, through rainforest, rolling open pasture country and perfect picnic spots. Unique points of interest are included along with trail characteristics rated according to trail type, distance, rider level, elevation changes, riding time and more. Their website has the trail guide online. P.O. Box 6819, Hilo, HI 96720; 808-961-4452; www.interpac.net/~mtbike.

Bike Tours

★ ***Kona Coast Cycling Tours*** This outfitter and operator offers several bike adventures from 4-9 hours. The Kohala Mountain Downhill is 20 miles, 4-5 hours; North Kohala Adventure is a challenging 53 miles, 8-9 hours; scenic/historic Coffee Country Ride is 17 miles, 4-5 hours; Old Mamalahoa Highway is 20 miles, 4-5 hours. A shorter bike trek that might be better for families is Coffee Country Express, a 7.5-mile downhill ride, about 2.5 hours long. Enjoy the changing panorama of the Big Island via the less-traveled and offroad routes of these unique biking adventures. Children must be 2 years old to participate. Rates: $95-$145 per person. 74-5588 Pawai Place, Suite G4, P.O. Box 2627, Kailua-Kona HI 96745; 808-327-1133; fax 808-327-1144; e-mail: bikeinfo@cyclekona.com; www.cyclekona.com.

★ ***Mauna Kea Mountain Bikes Inc.*** This bike outfitter offers private guided tours of rainforest trails, scenic highways and some of the Big Island's best backcountry mountain and ranch areas. Adventures range from 2-4 hours with varied distances, from the easy 2.5-hour Kohala Downhill tour for beginners to increasingly tougher rides along Mana Road or Mud Lane in Waimea Hill Country. The 3.5-hour Mauna Kea Kamikaze ride is a 13-mile bike trek on steep gravel and paved roadways starting from Mauna Kea's summit, 13,796 feet, and zooming downhill with incredible 360-degree views all the way (if you have time to turn your head). All rides include full equipment and bike. They provide a range of mountain and offroad touring bikes and equipment. Rates: $75-$80 Kohala downhill, $55-$65 Mana Road or Mud Lane, $90-$120 Mauna Kea Kamikaze. P.O. Box 44672, Kamuela, HI 96743; 888-MTB-TOUR; 808-883-0130; e-mail: mtbtour@aol.com.

Bike Rentals

Aquatic Perceptions Multi-Sports Tours This multi-sport outfitter provides mountain bike rentals, Volcano downhill runs and Coastal Jungle bike treks and excursions around Hilo Bay, the Hamakua Coast and the Puna Coast areas. Instruction also available. RR3, Box 1450, Paha'a, HI 96778; 808-935-9997; e-mail: kayakscuba@aol.com; www.multi-sport-hawaii.com.

B&L Bike & Sports This shop carries a full line of bikes and equipment and other sporting goods and gear. They also do repairs. Rates: $20-$30 per day. 75-5699 Kopiko Place, Kopiko Plaza, Kailua-Kona, HI 96740; 808-329-3309; 808-329-9718; fax 808-329-7340; e-mail: sports@ilhawaii.net; www.bibikes.com.

C&S Outfitters Friendly, experienced outfitter provides full line of kayak and bike gear and supplies, plus sun protection, souvenirs, snacks and beverages. Open Monday through Saturday 9 a.m. to 5 p.m. Bikes are $30 a day, including helmet and toolkit if needed. C&S suggests bikers bring their own bike shoes and pedals along if they don't want to bring their own bikes. In Waimea at Cook's Corner, intersection of Highway 19 and Kamamalu Street; 808-885-5005; fax 808-885-5683.

Dave's Bike & Triathlon Shop This shop has a variety of mountain bikes and road bikes to rent by the hour, day or week. They also provide service, repairs, accessories and supplies. 75-5669 Ali'i Drive, Kailua-Kona, HI 96740; 808-329-4522; e-mail: davesbic@gte.net; www.davebikes.com.

H P Bike Works They have a full line of bike rentals (daily, weekly, monthly) as well as also equipment sales, rentals and repairs. Rates: $20-$30 per day. 74-5599 Luhia, Kailua-Kona, HI 96740; 808-326-2453.

Hawaiian Pedals Bike Rentals This shop has a wide range of bike rentals available including mountain bikes, performance bikes and tandem touring bikes. They also have a range of tour excursions available. Rates: $9 per day for a seven-day rental. 75-5744 Ali'i Drive, Kona Inn Shopping Center, Kailua-Kona, HI 96740; 808-329-2294.

Hilo Bike Hub This shop specializes in mountain bikes and related equipment and has rentals available; repairs. Ask about their special "Fun Rides." 318 East Kawili Street, Hilo, HI 96720; 808-961-4452; e-mail: hilobke@gte.net; gtesupersite.com/hilobikehub.

Island RV Safari Activities This company carries a full line of bicycle and equipment rentals. 75-5785 Kuakini Highway, Kailua-Kona, HI 96740; 800-406-4555; 808-334-0464; e-mail: info@islandrv.com; www.islandrv.com.

Mauna Kea Mountain Bikes Inc. They have a full line of bike and related equipment rentals. P.O. Box 44672, Kamuela, HI 96743; 888-MTB-TOUR; 808-883-0130; e-mail: mtbtour@aol.com.

Mid Pacific Wheels This shop offers a full line of rental bikes and equipment. 1133C Manono Street, Hilo, HI 96720; 808-935-6211; 808-935-6211.

Bike Trails

There are several bike paths and trails around the Big Island ranging from easy rides to more challenging backcountry, offroad and mountain trails for skilled riders. Regardless of your bike-riding skill level, there's a Big Island bike trail waiting for you to explore. There's everything from a difficult mountain climb or cruise down a volcano to an easy peddle along a mostly smooth coastal trail. While biking the Big Island's bike trails, you'll be able to enjoy the many scenic vistas and unspoiled panoramic views of the island's less traveled offroad back-country trails and paths that you get only from a bike seat.

Kona District **Walua Road** is off Kuakini Highway just a few miles south of downtown Kailua-Kona; just opposite the Kilohana/Komohana housing tract, turn onto Lako Street. The paved trail begins above the Chevron gas station; it's a 6.4-mile round-trip, 45-minute ride through housing subdivisions. The trail crosses residential streets so be aware of local traffic; ride climbs uphill gradually, from 400 feet to 1200 feet elevation. There are nice panoramic ocean views and tropical landscaping all along the way. The ride back is downhill all the way.

Pine Trees trail is just north of town but south of Kona International Airport just off Highway 19 at the Natural Energy Lab of Hawai'i (NELHA) grounds. Turn into NELHA just before airport entrance and go about one mile to the coastline. This is a 6.4-mile round-trip, 1.5-hour ride. The trail begins 50 yards north of the parking lot. The lava trail turns to sandy beach road that winds along the coast for 1.2 miles. The trail ends at the Ho'ona Historical Preserve. From the parking lot, the trail heads south, and where the trail curves, veer right and follow the beach trail for 2 miles. This is an easy ride for beginners; warm and windy but nice coastal panoramas.

North Kohala Coast **Highway 270** between Kawaihae and Hawi town along the North Kohala coastline is about a 10-mile stretch, a beautiful, scenic run of wide, fairly straight and level highway with bike shoulders and good visibility that wins our stamp of approval. Bikers can trek along a portion of the Ironman Triathlon bike route, have lunch in Hawi town and return along the same path, or take the winding mountain road down to Waimea and back to Kawaihae, although some portions of this route are very narrow and weather may be a factor. Although the coastal highway is pretty consistently sunny, the wind can be strong so use caution and don't forget sun-block and plenty of water.

Pohue Road trail is located in the North Kohala District between Hawi town and Mahukona. There are two access points. From the Kohala Mountain Road (Highway 250), turn onto Pohue Road just past the 17-mile marker. Follow the gravel road 50 yards, turn right on the grassy road and go through the gate. From the Akoni Pule Highway (Highway 270, the coastal route north from Kawaihae), look for the access just past the 18-mile marker and turn inland. This country road maintained by the government features varied terrain and wonderful open views of ranchlands and Maui across the sea. Road surfaces vary from rocky cinder to dirt lanes across ranchlands. Riders have a choice of riding uphill or downhill or both. Either way is 5 miles, round-trip 10 miles. It takes a half-hour to ride down, one hour or more to ride up. Wide open panoramic views in generally warm, breezy conditions.

Kohala Mountain Road (Highway 250) runs 20 miles up and over the Kohala Mountains between Waimea and Hawi. This is perhaps the Big Island's most scenic pastoral route and passes through rolling ranch country, green mountains and pastures, herds of grazing cattle and sheep, and beautiful views of the distant Kohala Coast. This is a narrow, winding road and is lined with ironwood trees that serve as a windbreak along the upper reaches where the Kohala winds can be brisk. Caution is advised; moderate in difficulty.

Highway 270 from Kapa'au to the Pololu Valley in North Kohala is a pleasant, easy, 8-mile, one-way ride through old sugar plantation country and lush open coastal hill country. It's a narrow winding road so caution is advised. The area has several old plantation settlements with a distinct rural Hawaiian charm. Along the way, the road passes by the historic Wo On Store and Wo Tong Chinese Society Building dating from 1886, Keokea Beach Park and several churches and other buildings in this historic area. Other roads branch off and meander in this North Kohala area, providing many miles of exploration and discovery for adventurous bikers.

Saddle Road/Mauna Kea Backcountry **Mana Road** is one of the Big Island's most scenic and longer backcountry bike trails and passes around the east and north sides of Mauna Kea, Hawai'i's tallest mountain at 13,769 feet. Take the Saddle Road up the mountain from either the Hilo or Kona side. Take the Mauna Kea Access Road leading to the summit, just opposite a hunter check-in hut. Drive north on this road about 2 miles and turn right (east) on the dirt road leading down and across pasturelands; cross a cattle guard gate. From Waimea, the Mana Road access junction is on Mamalahoa Highway, just across from the Department of Hawaiian Home Lands complex. This upcountry trail links Saddle Road and Waimea. It's a 45-mile trek either way and is an all-day, 6-8-hour ride, taking your time. Elevation changes from 3,000 feet to 6,500 feet. The trek ranges from smooth, level dirt or gravel road through cattle pastures to rough, rugged and rutted trail in dense upland forest. This is also a 4WD vehicle road used by hunters. There are unspoiled vistas of mountain slopes and forest overlooking distant ranchlands. There are stands of magnificent old *koa* trees throughout the upcountry pastures. Don't be surprised to come upon herds of cattle. They'll usually scatter upon seeing people. There are numerous cattle gates to pass through, be sure to close them all. To bike Mana Road one way, arrange to have someone meet you at the other end. You'll need lots of food and water plus cool weather rain gear. On clear days, there are any number of great picnic spots along the Mana Road to just relax and enjoy Mauna Kea's magnificent upcountry. There are a couple of cabins available to campers along the trail; contact State Forestry and Wildlife, 808-974-4221.

Kilohana Trail is accessed via the Saddle Road. Look for the Kilohana Hunter Check-in Station sign between 44- and 45-mile markers on the Saddle Road. Turn onto this gravel road and the trail begins on this northwest side of Mauna Kea. This is a 6.6-mile, one-way ride for experienced riders only, about 1.5 hours each way. The road climbs gradually on gravel then dirt surface, where it gets rough. At 2.2 miles go right at the fork and this takes you to Ahumoa, a cinder cone at 7,042-foot elevation with nice views of surrounding country. The road continues up (you may have to walk part way) for another 3.1 miles to Pu'u La'au and a hunter's cabin surrounded by eucalyptus trees at 7,446-foot elevation. This is a good place to rest, picnic and enjoy the views before heading back down the same route.

Hamakua Coast Highway 240 runs from Honoka'a north to the Waipi'o Valley overlook, a 10-mile, one-way ride through rolling hills and old sugar plantation lands along the Hamakua Coast. The road passes through the old plantation settlements of Kawela, Kapulena and Kukuihaele before reaching the top of Waipi'o Valley. It's a pleasant, easy ride with nice views of the north side of Waipi'o Valley.

Hilo **Kulani Trails** is just south of Hilo off Highway 11. At 4.2 miles south of Hilo, turn right onto Stainback Highway at the sign for Panaewa Rain Forest Zoo. Continue 2.6 miles and turn right at Waiakea Arboretum. Take the first left off the highway and the first set of trails begin. This is a challenging, dense forest ride on single-track trails with lots of slippery conditions, roots, rocks, fallen logs and lots of mud but is otherwise a cool forest ride. There are majestic 100-foot-tall eucalyptus trees all around. Distances and times vary; routes wind throughout the Waiakea Forest Reserve area.

Puna District **Old Puna Trail** runs along the Puna coastline from Hawaiian Paradise Park subdivision north to Haena Beach. Head south from Hilo to the turnoff for Highway 130 at Kea'au. Take Highway 130 about 4.5 miles and turn left on Kaloli Road and go another 4.2 miles to Beach Road. Head left on Beach Road and pick up the trail, which is still under development and somewhat rough and rugged. With improvements it will be a smoother ride. The trail follows the old Puna trail that linked the area with Hilo back in the 1800s. Near Hilo, the trail passes the airport. The ride is through lush tropical forest with fruit trees, flowers and bright foliage; 4WD trails branch off to fishing spots on the coast but these are rough trails to be avoided. You'll see Haena Beach nestled in evergreens and Norfolk pines. It is a 10-mile ride one-way, about 3-4 hours long.

Puna Coast Beach Road is accessed by heading south on Highway 11 from Hilo and, at Kea'au, turning onto Highway 130 for 4.6 miles. At Kaloli Road in Hawaiian Paradise Park subdivision, turn left and go 4.2 miles downslope to Beach Road at the coast and turn right on Beach Road for 1.2 miles. The old Puna trail begins here and runs 10.5 miles one way, an hour ride. It is mostly level on a cinder and dirt road through fields of wild orchids and coastal rainforest. There are great views along this isolated and remote rugged coastal area. The dirt road ends at Kapoho but the coastal road, Highway 137, continues 12 miles to the settlements of Pohoiki, Opihikao and Kalapana areas. This would be advised only if you can arrange a pickup at the Kalapana end. Otherwise it's a long ride back the same route or via Pahoa town and Highway 130.

Ka'u District/Volcanoes National Park **Volcano Trails** are 30 miles south of Hilo and 97 miles south of Kona via Highway 11 at Hawai'i Volcanoes National Park. All paved roads in the park are open to bikers, although some unpaved trails may also be open. Check with park rangers at entrance or visitors center and get a map.

The 11-mile **Crater Rim Drive** circles Kilauea Volcano summit caldera and goes through tropical rain and fern forest, past steaming vents and smoking sulphur banks, craters and cinder cones. There are a number of short walks at places like Devastation Trail and Thurston Lava Tube plus several craters and overlooks. The Chain of Craters Road winds downslope from Crater Rim Drive some 20 miles to the recent eruption sites along the Kalapana Coast, the national park's southern boundary area. The road terminates where the latest lava flows have crossed it. If eruption activity is still ongoing, it's possible to see steam plumes where the lava enters the ocean. Visitors might also be able to see the lava flows at a close distance if rangers feel it safe enough.

Bikers can take Chain of Craters Road but should be warned it gets a lot of traffic and is a long climb back up from the coastal flats. Distances and times for bike trails vary within the national park.

Ainapo Trail is located south of Hawai'i Volcanoes National Park on Highway 11. At 12.2 miles past the park entrance, turn right on an access road marked by a gravel turnout, gate, and Ainapo Trail Road sign. Hang right for about .1 mile. The ride alternates on a dirt and grass track, gradually climbing through pasture, guava tree thickets and rocky outcroppings. There is a gate 1 mile in and in another 3.5 miles the road forks; keep right for 4.4 miles to the Ainapo Trailhead. The famed Ainapo Trail is for hikers only and leads to the summit of Mauna Loa. There is a cabin about a 3.5-hour hike up at the 7,750-foot level. To reserve the cabin, call State Forestry & Wildlife, 808-974-4221. Bikers return the same route. This ride is 9 miles long, 3 hours up to trailhead and 1 hour back down.

BOWLING

The Big Island has locations on both sides of the island in Hilo and Kona. Both are full-service bowling lanes with equipment rentals and snack bars. They're open daily, except major holidays, but check for specific hours as they may vary from time to time.

Hilo Lanes 777 Kinoʻole Street, Hilo; 808-935-0646

Kona Bowl 75-5586 Ololi Road, in the Lanihau Center, Kailua-Kona; 808-326-2695

CAMPING

The Big Island has numerous county, state and national parks in both inland and coastal locations. Some are designed strictly for those with their own tents and camping gear, and some have basic cabins or shelters for overnight or longer rentals. Facilities vary widely.

County of Hawaiʻi Parks

The County of Hawaiʻi maintains 11 parks around the island with designated campgrounds for those with their own tents and camping gear. County parks have no cabins and facilities vary. Some have full restrooms, showers and drinking water; others may have primitive pit latrines and no drinking water. Check ahead on what facilities are available to avoid disappointment. Permits are required for campgrounds and for use of the pavilions. County campsites are on a first-come, first-served basis, with advance reservations required for peak seasons like the winter and summer holidays. Camping permits are issued for one week per park in summer months and two weeks per park in other months. Camping fees at county parks are adults $5 per day, juniors (13-17) $2 per day, children (12 and under) $1 per day. For reservations, permits and complete information regarding any of the County of Hawaiʻi parks, contact: Department of Parks and Recreation, County of Hawaiʻi, 25 Aupuni Street, Hilo, HI 96720. 808-961-8311; in Kona 808-327-3560; e-mail: cohparks@hotmail.com; www.hawaii-county.com. Hours are Monday through Friday 7:45 a.m. through 4:30 p.m.

Campgrounds are found at the following county parks:

Kona District—Hoʻokena Beach Park, Miloliʻi Beach Park

Kohala Coast—Keokea Beach Park, Kapaʻa Beach Park, Mahukona Beach Park, Spencer Beach Park

Hamakua Coast—Laupahoehoe Point Beach Park, Kolekole Beach Park.

Puna District—Isaac Hale Beach Park

Ka'u District—Punalu'u Beach Park, Whittington Beach Park.

State of Hawai'i Parks & Recreation Areas

The State of Hawai'i maintains a system of parks and recreation areas around the Big Island. Three of them presently are designated for use as campgrounds and two have simple lodging facilities. Parks are equipped with developed campgrounds, camping shelters, and basic housekeeping cabins or barracks-type group accommodations. The condition of these facilities is subject to change, depending on weather and the uncertainties of government maintenance and upkeep. (We've heard stories from fine to deplorable.) Check first with the State Parks office. Campers need to be aware that most state camping cabins and facilities will be very rustic accommodations with few amenities short of the basics. There are no entrance, parking, picnicking or camping fees. However, permits are required for camping and lodging in the parks. The maximum length of stay allowable in any park is five nights. Advance reservations are required for any state park cabin or campground. Keys for reserved cabins are available from the park caretaker or Division of State Parks office in Hilo, 75 Aupuni Street. Check-in time is 2 p..m., check-out time is 10 a.m. For complete information on obtaining a camping and lodging permit, contact: Department of Land & Natural Resources, Division of State Parks, Hawai'i District Office, P.O. Box 936, 75 Aupuni Street #204, Hilo, HI 96721-0936. 808-974-6200. The office is open 8 a.m. to 3:30 p.m. Monday through Friday.

Hapuna Beach State Recreation Area Located on Queen Ka'ahumanu Highway 19, 2.3 miles south of Kawaihae on the Kohala Coast, this is one of best stretches of white-sand beach on the island. Picnic pavilions are available. Six simple four-person A-frame cabins/shelters are available and have a table, wooden platforms for sleeping bags, electrical outlets and shared cooking facilities, showers and toilets. Cabins are $20 per night.

Kalopa State Recreation Area Located at 2,000-feet elevation on Kalopa Road, 3 miles upland of Highway 19 about 5 miles south of Honoka'a on the Hamakua Coast, this site has picnic pavilions, campgrounds, group cabins (for up to 32 people total) and a shared recreation/mess hall.

Group cabins (1-8 people) are $55 per night; $5 per night per extra person

MacKenzie State Recreation Area Located on breezy and warm coastal cliffs in an ironwood grove on Kalapana-Kapoho Road, Highway 137, southeast area of the Big Island. Picnic pavilions available; primitive campground, no drinking water.

Mauna Kea State Recreation Area Closed indefinitely.

Hawai'i Volcanoes National Park

The national park maintains three drive-in campgrounds within Volcanoes National Park for campers with their own tents and gear. Each has pavilion shelters with picnic tables and fireplaces but you need to bring your own wood or fuel. Check the discount stores in Hilo or Kona for camping supplies. No permit is needed and there is no charge for camping. Camping is on a first-come, first-served basis. Stays are limited to seven days per campground per year.

The park service also maintains three simple backcountry cabins for hikers but you must register at park headquarters for overnight stays; cabins are first-come, first-served, but they're not heavily used so hikers can usually be accommodated. It is necessary to check on trail conditions and water supplies before undertaking a backcountry hike. The cabins are located in remote, desolate areas, some at high elevations where severe weather can occur, especially during the winter months. Check with park rangers for information.

One campground, **Namakani Paio**, has simple A-frame cabins that can accommodate four people in one double bed and two single bunks. The cabins all share a central restroom and shower facility. Outside each cabin is a picnic table and a barbecue grill. You must provide your own charcoal and cooking utensils. Cabins include bed linens, towels and blankets (picked up at Volcano House, 3 miles away). It's recommended you bring extra blankets or sleeping bags (especially in winter) as the cabins are not heated and temperatures can drop to the mid-50s. Rates: $40 per night, double. Reservations are recommended and can be made through Volcano House, P.O. Box 53, Hawai'i Volcanoes National Park, HI 96718; 808-967-7321; fax 808-967-7321.

For complete information, contact: Superintendent, Hawai'i Volcanoes National Park, Volcano, HI 96718. 808-985-6000; www.nps.gov/havo.

COFFEE FARMS

In November each year, the **Kona Coffee Cultural Festival** celebrates Kona's prized product with picking contests, cupping competition, parades and all kinds of food, music and arts events from Kona's diverse ethnic population. For more information contact Kona Coffee Cultural, P.O. Box 1112, Kailua-Kona, HI 96745; 808-326-7820; www.konacoffeefest.com. They also put together an excellent Kona Coffee Country Driving Tour map and brochure (if you take one sip at every stop you're guaranteed to be wired by the time you get back to your hotel).

Following are a few of Kona's coffee farms that open some portion of their operation to the public. There are others, but we invite you to explore and discover for yourself!

Bay View Farms This coffee farm is just above Pu'uhonua o Honaunau Place of Refuge on Painted Church Road. Free explanatory tours of the farm and processing plant, coffee tasting and a shop. P.O. Box 680, Honaunau, HI 96726; 800-662-5880; 808-328-9658; fax 808-328-8693; e-mail: bayview@aloha.net.

Coffee Shack Located just north of 108-mile marker. Enjoy coffee production displays and tasting room with espresso bar overlooking the Kona coast and Kealakekua Bay. P.O. Box 510, 83-5799 Mamalahoa Highway 11, Captain Cook, HI 96704; 800-800-6267; 808-328-9555; fax 808-328-9461; www.coffeeshack.com.

★ ***Country Samurai Coffee Company*** One of the best, this third-generation coffee plantation is located high upcountry in Keauhou *mauka*, but their retail operation is conveniently located in downtown Kailua-Kona. Country Samurai produces only 100 percent Kona coffee of the better grades: Fancy, Extra Fancy, Peaberry and Kona No. 1. By family tradition, they allow the trees to grow 15 to 20 feet tall, rather than keep them stunted for easy harvest, and age the beans for 1.5-2 years before processing. The result is a fragrant, buoyant coffee that elevates the spirits. Enjoy a cup of freshly brewed Kona coffee, learn about their history and coffee secrets (including how to make the perfect cup of coffee) and shop for *omiyage* (gifts). They pack and ship special orders to the mainland. Guaranteed quality! Kona Square, 75-5669 Ali'i Drive #1104A, Kailua-Kona HI 96740; 888-666-KONA; 808-331-1444; 808-322-0656; e-mail: kunitake@earthlink.net; www.countrysamurai.com.

Ferrari Coffee Hawaiian Mountain Gold Visitors Center The Visitors Center is located on Mamalahoa Highway in the Holualoa area just five miles south of the Palani Road/Highway 190 junction. Look for them across the street from the "pink hotel." Ferrari produces some of the more popular coffee on the island and its friendly center reportedly hosts "Kona's largest doll collection," along with movie star photos and memorabilia. P.O. Box 390486, Kailua-Kona, HI 96739; 800-288-1542; phone/fax 808-324-1542; www.ferraricoffee.com.

Greenwell Farms Visitor tours of historic coffee estate groves and facilities and samples of Kona coffee Monday-Saturday 8 a.m.-4 p.m. 81-6560 Mamalahoa Highway, between 111 and 112 mile markers, P.O. Box 248, Kealakekua, HI 96750; 888-592-5662; 808-323-2275; fax 808-323-2050; www.greenwellfarms.com.

Heavenly Hawaiian Farm/The Other Farm Half a mile up Old Poi Factory Road. Pottery studio and miniature donkeys also on site. Please call ahead for tours. 78-1136 Bishop Road, Holualoa; 800-756-0210; 808-322-7720; fax 808-322-7721; www.heavenlyhawaiian.com.

Holualoa Kona Coffee Co. Tour coffee milling and roasting operation and taste the finished product Monday-Friday 8 a.m.-4 p.m. 77-6261 Mamalahoa Highway in Holualoa, one mile north of 1-mile marker; 800-334-0348; 808-322-9937; www.konalea.com.

Kona Blue Sky Coffee Company This is the family-run Twigg-Smith Estate located on 500 acres on the slopes of Mount Hualalai. They offer 100 percent Kona coffee; tour the visitor center and gift shop at Holualoa. They also have an outlet shop at the Waikoloa Beach Marriott, Kohala Coast. P.O. Box 470, Holualoa, HI 96725; 877-322-1700; 808-322-1700; www.konablueskycoffee.com.

Kona Connoisseur Organic Kona coffee and chocolates. Call ahead for a tour. 79-989 Kealaola Street, Kealakekua; 800-322-1859.

Kona Historical Society's Kona Coffee Living History Farm Located in Captain Cook, this is an excellent opportunity to visit the past and present with coffee farm and mill tours, living-history programs, hands-on demonstrations and a retail shop on-site. Open daily; however, please call ahead for tour reservations. 808-323-2006; fax 808-323-9576; www.konahistorical.org.

Kona Joe Coffee Just below Lanakila Church in Kainaliu. Shop, tastings and tours Monday-Friday 9 a.m.-5 p.m. 877-KONA-JOE; 808-322-2100; fax 808-322-2770; www.konajoe.com.

Kona Mountain Cafe Coffeehouse with snacks and sandwiches. Call ahead for tours of the Kona Mountain Estate Coffee farm. 81-6637 Mamalahoa Highway, Kealakekua; 808-323-2700; fax 808-322-3676; www.konamountaincoffee.com.

A tour guide brochure of interest to Big Island visitors, and bikers in particular, is the **Kona Coffee Country Driving Tour,** published by the County of Hawai'i and the Kona Coffee Cultural Festival. This brochure has a map and comprehensive listing of coffee farms, mills, shops and museums of the Kona Coast. The brochure has information on the history of Kona coffee and the annual cultural festival. There is information on how to get to the coffee farm areas, what to look for along the way, tips on buying and brewing coffee and even a recipe or two. It's a bright, colorful guide to a driving tour of Kona's famed coffee country. 808-326-7820; www.konacoffeefest.com.

Kona Pacific Farmers Cooperative Look for the Pink Donkey to find this 300-farmer co-op building with historical displays, farm tours and farm-direct outlet store. Open Monday-Friday 7 a.m.-4 p.m. Call ahead for tours. 82-5810 Napo'opo'o Road, Captain Cook; 808-328-2411; fax 808-328-2414; www.kpfc.com.

Langenstein Farm Tours of processing plant, coffee (hand-picked to roast) and macadamia nut orchards. Coffee tastings, too. 84-4956 Mamalahoa Highway, Honaunau; 800-621-5365; 808-328-8356; fax 808-328-8981; www.kona-coffee.com.

Royal Kona Coffee Mill & Museum Displays on history of Kona coffee farming, production and culture. Sample some of Kona's best and talk story with friendly folks and resident "coffee cats" in the gift shop. 83-5427 Mamalahoa Highway, Captain Cook, HI 96704; 808-328-2511; fax 808-328-8616; www.royalkonacoffee.com.

Ueshima Coffee (UCC Hawaii) Corp. Roastery and Coffee Bar open daily 9 a.m.-5 p.m. for tours and tastings. Or call ahead for the "Roastmaster Experience" and try your hand at your own private reserve coffee blend. 82-5810 Napo'opo'o Road, Captain Cook; 888-822-5662; 808-328-0604; fax 808-328-5663; www.ucc-hawaii.com.

FISHING

There are few places in the world that can match the Kona Coast for the thrill and excitement of big-game fishing. In August, Kona is the site of the annual Hawaiian International Billfish Tournament, which for the past 30 years or so has attracted participants from around the world. In addition, there are numerous other fishing tournaments held throughout the year.

Kona harbors a large fleet of charter fishing boats that offers a complete range of full- and half-day arrangements (or longer if you like), from budget-minded small charters to top-of-the-line high-tech, high-dollar excursions. Prices vary depending upon the size of the boat and how it is equipped (showers, beds, fully stocked galley). Full-day charters can range from around $275-$450 while half-day charters can range from around $175-$295. These prices are for the entire boat, not a per person rate.

You can private charter the entire boat or share charter with other anglers. Half-day share rates start at about $60-$75 per person. Non-fishing guests can just ride along for $35-$45 per person. Most boats are only licensed to carry six anglers at a time and provide all fishing equipment. Generally you must bring your own food and beverages as these are not included in charter rates. You are not required to have a fishing license.

Because of Hawai'i's generally low charter boat rates in comparison to other areas, the general policy among charter boat associations is that any fish caught belongs to the boat rather than the fisherman. Boat captains and owners sell caught fish on the market to augment their low charter fares. This is the reason for the policy. However, if you want to keep your catch, or part of it, request it from the captain. In the case of good table fish such as mahimahi or ahi tuna, most captains will be more than happy to share the catch with the fishing party to enjoy a fresh fish dinner. For a fee, the chef at your hotel will most likely be happy to prepare your fish for dinner.

And so what can you expect to catch, with a little traditional fishing luck? Kona's waters teem with a variety of Hawaiian game fish. Perhaps most popular is the Pacific blue marlin with an average size of 300-400 pounds, but with "granders" of 1,000 pounds entirely possible. Striped marlin average 50-100 pounds and black marlin average 200 pounds. Sailfish are also common in Kona's waters and average 50 pounds or less. Swordfish are generally more difficult to catch but average 250 pounds when they are landed. The popular yellowfin tuna ranges up to 300 pounds while the dolphin (mahimahi) averages 25 pounds.

If you're familiar with deep-sea fishing and boat chartering, you may contact any of the following boats directly. However, if you are unsure of just what chartering a boat entails, you would be best advised to contact one of the boat-chartering agencies below. Some of these agencies represent several boats and can give you complete information on booking a charter.

Boat-chartering Agencies

Charter Desk Kealakehe Parkway, Honokohau Harbor, Kailua-Kona, HI 96740; 808-329-5735; fax 808-329-5747; 888-KONA4US.

Charter Locker Kealakehe Parkway, Honokohau Harbor, Kailua-Kona, HI 96740; 800-247-1484; 808-326-2553.

Kona Beach Activity Shack Kona Pier on Ali'i Drive in front of the King Kamehameha's Kona Beach Hotel, Kailua-Kona; 808-329-7494.

★ **Kona Charter Skippers Association, Inc.** 74-857 Iwalani Place, Kailua-Kona, HI 96740; 800-762-7546; 808-329-3600; e-mail: konafish@hawaii.rr.com; www.konabiggamefishing.com.

Kona Marina Sports Activities 74-425 Kealakehe Parkway, 3rd floor, Honokohau Harbor, Kailua-Kona, HI 96740; 808-329-1115; fax 808-329-9104; e-mail: uki@ilhawaii.net.

★ **Ocean Sports-Waikoloa** Located on 'Anaeho'omalu Beach in front of the Waikoloa Beach Marriott, An Outrigger Resort, 69-275

Waikoloa Beach Drive, Kohala Coast, HI 96743; 808-886-6666; 800-SAIL234; www.hawaiioceansports.com.

★ **Red Sail Sports** 425 Waikoloa Beach Drive, Hilton Waikoloa Village, Kohala Coast, HI 96743; 877-RED-SAIL; 808-886-2876; fax 808-886-4169; and Hapuna Beach Prince Hotel at Mauna Kea Resort; 808-880-1111; e-mail: redsailsport@yahoo.com; www.redsail.com.

Charter Boats

All charter fishing boats are completely certified and licensed. In addition to being licensed as commercial fishing boats, the captains and boats must be fully certified and licensed by the United States Coast Guard.

Action—35' Blackfin, Capt. Doug Armfield, Kailua-Kona; 808-329-3013; www.sportfishingkona.com

Adobie—30' Topaz, Ron Platt, P.O. Box Y, Kailua-Kona, HI 96745; 808-329-5669

Anxious—31' Bertram, Capt. Neal Issacs, P.O. Box 2765, Kailua-Kona, HI 96745; 808-326-1229

Blue Hawai'i—53' Hatteras, Capt. James Dean, P.O. Box 390387, Kailua-Kona, HI 96739; 808-895-2970, 808-322-3210

Cherry Pit II—26' Blackman, Capt. Jim Cherry, P.O. Box 278, Holualoa, HI 96725; 808-326-7781; e-mail: cherry@kona.net

Enterprise—40' Custom, Capt. Doug Armfield, Kailua-Kona; 877-329-3013; www.sportfishingkona.com

Foxy Lady—42' Uniflite, Capt. Terry and June Dahl, P.O. Box 762, Kailua-Kona, HI 96745; 808-325-5552

Hapa Laka—Capt. Alan Borowski, P.O. Box 2051, Kailua-Kona, HI 96745; 808-322-2229, e-mail: hapalaka@gte.net

Happy Times—41' Sportfisher, Capts. Tom and Chris Armstrong, P.O. Box 9014, Kailua-Kona, HI 96745; 808-325-6171; 808-325-7060; e-mail: tom@fishkona.com; www.fishkona.com

Humdinger—37' Rybovich, Capt. Jeff Fay, P.O. Box 1995, Kailua-Kona, HI 96745; 808-325-3449; boat phone 808-936-3034; fax 808-325-0831; www.humdinger-online.com

Hustler—34' Blackfin, Capt. Glen Hodson, P.O. Box 4976, Kailua-Kona, HI 96745; 808-960-0351; e-mail: hustler@kona.net

Ihu Nui Sportfishing—This is a professional sportfisher, available for full-day charters, P.O. Box 1896, Kailua-Kona, HI 96745; book through the Charter Desk at 808-329-5735, 888-KONA4US

Illusions—39' Topaz, Capt. Tim Hicks, P.O. Box 5061, Kailua-Kona, HI 96745; 808-883-0180; 808-960-7371

Jun Ken Po—42' Bertram, Capt. Bert Byrd, P.O. Box 4841, Kailua-Kona, HI 96745; 808-325-7710

Kalama—28' Albin Flybridge, book through the Charter Locker at 808-326-2553

Kona Rainbow—35' Bertram Sportfisher, Capt. Larry Pries, Kailua-Kona; 808-325-1775; boat phone 808-989-4982

Lady Dee—47' Bertram, 78-6626 Ali'i Drive, Kailua-Kona, HI 96740; 808-322-8026

Layla—31' Innovator, Capt. Bruce Evans, P.O. Box 5567, Kailua-Kona, HI 96745; 808-329-6899; boat phone 808-936-3232; e-mail: layla1@gte.net

Lehuanani—38' Pacifica, Capt. Kenny Llanes; 808-329-3171

Lei Aloha—40' Jersey, Capt. Kenny Llanes, 73-1277 Awakea, Kailua-Kona, HI 96740; 808-326-1387

Mariah—28' Sportfisher, Capt. Jay Lighty; 808-325-1691; boat phone 808-936-3993; www.mariahkona.com

Marlin Grando—38' Bertram, Capt. Dan Gibbons; 808-326-4851; boat phone 808-937-2903; www.marlingrando.com

Marlin Magic—43' Custom, Capt. Marlin Parker, Kaloko, Kona; 808-325-7138

Medusa—38' Ocean Yacht, Capt. Steve Kaiser, P.O. Box 857, Holualoa, HI 96725; 808-329-1328; boat phone 808-936-4383; www.medusasportfishing.com

Notorious—This professional sportfisher offers charter fishing for the entire family, P.O. Box 1018, Kealakekua, HI 96750; 888-584-KONA; 808-322-6407; e-mail: laxe87a@prod.com

Pacific Blue—45' Hatteras, Capt. Bill Casey, 74-4924 Mamalahoa Highway, Holualoa, HI 96725; 808-329-9468; boat phone 808-936-3055; e-mail: kcinkona@aol.com

Pamela—38' Bertram, Capt. Peter Hoogs, 74-857 Iwalani Place, Kailua-Kona, HI 96740; 808-329-1525; 800-762-7546; e-mail: konafish@hawaii.rr.com; www.konabiggamefishing.com

Prime Time—40' Custom, Capts. Tom and Chris Armstrong, P.O. Box 9014, Kailua-Kona, HI 96745; 808-325-6171; e-mail: fishkona@kona.net

Reel Action—30' Sportfisher, Capt. Del Dykes, P.O. Box 5619, Kailua-Kona, HI 96745; 808-325-6811

Reel Pleasure—36' Topaz, Capt. Greg Kaufmann, Kawaihae Harbor, Kohala Coast; 808-882-1413; e-mail: H2Osport@kohaladivers.com

Sea Baby III—35' Sportfisher, Capt. W. Kobayashi, Kalaoa, Kona; 808-325-7727

Sea Dancer—31' Bertram, Capt. Jerry Allen, 77-357 Nohealani Street, Kailua-Kona, HI 96740; 808-322-6630; e-mail: jerry@kona.net

Sea Genie—39' Rybovich, Capt. Gene Vander Hoek, P.O. Box 4126, Kailua-Kona, HI 96745; 808-325-5355; fax 808-325-5366; e-mail: geni@aloha.net; www.seageniesportfishing.com

Sea Wife II—38' Delta, Capt. Tim Cox, P.O. Box 2645, Kailua-Kona, HI 96745; 888-329-1806; 808-329-1806; e-mail: seawife@hawaii.rr.com; www.fishkona.org/html/sea_wife.html

Start Me Up—Capt. Doug Armfield, Kailua-Kona; 808-329-3013; www.sportfishingkona.com

Sundowner—35' Bertram, Capt. Norm Isaacs, P.O. Box 5198, Kailua-Kona, HI 96745; 808-325-0333

Tara Sportfishing—46' and 53' Hatteras boats, P.O. Box 4363, Kailua-Kona, HI 96745; 808-325-5887

Terminator Sports Fishing—46' Post, Capt. Randy Llanes, 73-1071 Ahulani, Kailua-Kona, HI 96740; 808-325-2353; boat phone 808-936-2344

Thrill Seeker—36' Uniflite, Capt. Bob Sylva, Kailua-Kona, HI; 888-823-2232; 808-326-6054; boat phone 808-987-4782; e-mail: konafish@kona.net

Vixen Sportfishing—44' dive/fishing boat, Capt. Rennie Boyd; 808-329-5382; e-mail: rennie@aloha.net; www.vixensportfishing.com

GARDENS

The Big Island is a botanical garden in and of itself, with diverse environments from desert-like rocky shoreline to lush forests where wild gingers and orchids grow along the roadside. State and county parks are free and provide many good examples of Hawaiian flora. Commercial botanical gardens are privately owned and may charge fees or donations, but if plants are your passion, they may be well worth the price. Some gardens focus exclusively on Hawaiian ethnobotany, while others take advantage of the climate to produce beautiful tropical flowers, trees and greenery from around the world. We'd also like to suggest visiting garden shops, florists and flower farms for less-formal lessons in the beautiful things that grow in Hawaii. For example, a stop by Akatsuka Orchids or the other excellent growers in the Volcano area guarantees a glimpse of at least one amazing specimen you haven't seen before. Chat with them about ordering cut flowers or shipping plants to the mainland. The following are among the Big Island's best botanical gardens. Contact them for specific hours and admission rates as these are sometimes seasonal.

★ ***Amy B. H. Greenwell Ethnobotanical Garden*** This traditionally planted 15-acre garden has numerous native Hawaiian plants such as sweet potato, taro, breadfruit, sugar cane, banana and gourd, as well as Hawaiian medicinal plants and more. Learn about early Hawaiian horticulture and farming methods and how old Hawaiians used plants in their early subsistence lifestyle. Open Monday through Friday 8:30 a.m. to 5 p.m., guided tours second Saturday each month at 10 a.m. Admission: $4. Located on Highway 11, at the 110-mile marker about 12 miles south of Kailua-Kona at Captain Cook. It's just a short distance north of the Manago Hotel. P.O. Box 1053, Captain Cook, HI 96704; 808-323-3318; 808-323-3318; fax 808-323-2394; www.bishopmuseum.org/greenwell.

★ ***Hawai'i Tropical Botanical Garden*** This garden is located about 8.5 miles north of Hilo on the scenic four-mile drive on old Highway 19. The gardens are at Onomea Bay and nature trails meander through the rainforest and plantings of palm, heliconia, ginger, bromeliad and more, some 2,000 species in all from around the tropical world. Follow trails as they cross streams and waterfalls and pass along the crashing surf of the ocean. Open daily 9:30 a.m. to 5 p.m. (last admission at 4 p.m.). Museum and gift shop on-site. Admission: $15 adults, $5 children under 16, $35 1-year Family Pass. 27-717 Old Mamalahoa Highway, P.O. Box 80, Papaikou, HI 96781; 808-964-5233; fax 808-964-1338; e-mail: htbg@ilhawaii.net; www.hawaiigarden.com.

Hawaiian Gardens This colorful garden is located on the slopes of Mount Hualalai at 1,400-foot elevation above Kailua-Kona town. The gardens have a variety of tropical plants and trees and are also a full-service tropical garden center. It is marked by towering trees, attractive landscaped grounds and numerous flowering and ornamental plantings. Visitors can stroll the grounds and enjoy the many plants. Check the shop for exotic tropical cut flowers and blooming florals such as orchids, bromeliads and bonsai trees to take home. Enjoy a cup of fresh Kona coffee while browsing the open, garden-setting gift shop. Junction of Highway 190 and Highway 180, 3 miles north of Kailua-Kona; 888-879-2485; 808-329-5702; e-mail: hawngard@gte.net.

★ ***Nani Mau Gardens*** One of Hilo's most popular attractions, 20 acres of beautiful tropical flowers, orchids, anthuriums, native Hawaiian plants, palms, pools, stream and waterfalls plus restaurant, wedding gazebo and gift shop. Stroll the gardens on your own or take a narrated tram ride of the grounds. Daily 8:30 a.m. to 5 p.m. Admission: $10 adults, $5 children 4 to 10, children under 4 free. Located 3 miles south of Hilo Airport on the Volcano Highway; watch for turnoff at Makalika Street and the large floral "Aloha" sign. 421 Makalika Street, Hilo, HI 96720; 808-959-3500; e-mail: garden@nanimau.com; www.nanimau.com.

★ ***World Botanical Gardens*** This garden opened in 1995 and covers some 300 acres. There are numerous species of tropical plants and trees including ornamentals, fruit trees and plants, flowering plants and more. Take a stroll along Rainbow Walk and enjoy the colorful tropical splendor. The Rain Forest Walk follows a trail through the forest and past native and introduced species to the fantastic overlook at the 300-foot cascades of Umauma Falls. Free samples of fruit and juice in season. Open Monday through Saturday 9 a.m. to 5:30 p.m., closed Sunday. Admission: $8 adults, $4 teens, children under 12 free. Located 16 miles north of Hilo at the 16-mile marker on Highway 19. P.O. Box 411, Honomu, HI 96728; 808-964-5330, fax 808-963-5433; e-mail: info@wbgi.com; www.wbgi.com.

GOLF

Heralded as the "golf capitol of Hawai'i," the Big Island hosts some of the finest golf courses in the world. From top-dollar resort courses with $200 green fees and near-perfect golf weather year-round to neighborly (if sometimes rainy) municipal courses upcountry where you might play for $50, we have a golf experience for every player. The Kohala Coast resorts have established high-caliber, full-service golf facilities offering everything a quality club can provide: lessons, equipment rentals, fully stocked pro shops with restaurants and bars-even tournament planning. Advance reservations are recommended, although different resorts have different policies protecting times for their hotel guests, particularly in the morning. You might not be able to reserve too far in advance, and some resorts may not take players who are not their guests. A little homework goes a long way in preventing disappointment. Most offer room and golf packages, and golf vacations can also be arranged through travel providers and golf specialists on the internet. Many courses also offer discounted twilight rates for afternoon play. Green fees usually include a shared cart but, again, ask first. Soft spikes are becoming a requirement on Hawai'i's golf courses, and pro shops can provide them for your shoes at a nominal fee.

If you're looking to just drive a few balls and have some fun, you might want to try **Swing Zone**, located at the corner of Makala and Kuakini Highway just opposite of the Old Kona Airport Park entry. They have a full driving range plus putting and chipping area along with a bunker. 74-5562 Makala Boulevard, Kailua-Kona, HI 96740; 808-329-6909. There is also **Menehune Country Club**, which is an all-grass putting course like mini-golf. They also have outdoor baseball batting cages. Open 8 a.m. to 9 p.m. daily. Driving range rates: 1 token/60 balls $6; Menehune course round $6; baseball batting cages/10 balls $1.

Big Island Country Club This is one of the Big Island's best-kept secrets-an 18-hole country club course with beautiful undulating fairways and well-set greens, designed by Pete and Perry Dye. Cooler temperatures of the upcountry setting make for pleasant play. Call for tee times. Rates: $85 mornings, $55 after 12 p.m. Located about midway between Waimea and Kailua-Kona on Highway 190. P.O. Box 1690, Kailua-Kona, HI 96740; 808-325-5044.

Discovery Harbour Golf and Country Club This is a very nice 18-hole course in the middle of a country residential sub-division in a remote southern coast area of the Big Island. Rates: $30 includes cart. Located in the small town of Waiohinu, Ka'u District. P.O. Box 130, Na'alehu, HI 96772; 808-929-7353.

★ ***Hamakua Country Club*** It's a nine-hole course laid out on very sloping terrain. Lovely views of Honoka'a and the ocean. Entrance is easy to miss, just off the highway and next to the Union 76 gas station. Rates: $15. Located on Highway 19 in Honoka'a on the Hamakua Coast about 40 miles north of Hilo. P.O. Box 751, Honoka'a, HI 96727; 808-775-7244.

★ ***Hapuna Golf Course*** This 18-hole championship links-style course, designed by Arnold Palmer and Ed Seay, is earning a reputation as one of the Big Island's best. Celebrating its tenth birthday this year, Hapuna plays along natural contours from sea level to about 700 feet elevation. There are stunning views of coastline, ocean and surrounding volcanic mountains. Fully stocked pro shop for all your golf attire, equipment and accessories, plus locker rooms, driving range, lessons, clinics, club and shoe rentals and refreshment cart on the course. Arnie's Clubhouse restaurant on premises. Rates: $145, twilight (after 1 p.m.) $105. Located at the Hapuna Beach Prince Hotel, Mauna Kea Resort. 62-100 Kauna'oa Drive, Kohala Coast, HI 96743; 808-880-3000.

★ ***Hilo Municipal Golf Course*** This is a very nicely maintained 18-hole course operated by the County of Hawai'i. It gets a lot of use from local golfing cadres, especially on weekends. During Hilo's rainy periods the fairways can get pretty water-logged. There is a driving range lighted for night use. Rates: $25 weekdays, $30 weekends; 9 holes $8, cart $14.50. 340 Haihai Street, Hilo, HI 96720; 808-959-7711.

Hilton Waikoloa Village Golfers enjoy 36 holes of great golf on two courses: the Beach Course, designed by Robert Trent Jones, Jr., or the Kings Course, designed by Tom Weiskopf and Jay Morrish. There's also an 18-hole Seaside Putting Course. Open to the public, but with preference given to guests. Book well in advance. 425 Waikoloa Beach Drive, Kohala Coast, HI 96743; 808-886-1234.

★ ***Kona Country Club*** This is actually two golf courses in one, reportedly offering a great day of golf with "no strong winds." The 18-hole championship course runs oceanside and in the heart of the Keauhou resort condo area. The Mountain Course 18-hole layout runs upslope, providing spectacular ocean and coastline views. Complete pro shop with rental clubs, carts and instruction available. The Vista Restaurant & Lounge are on premises. Rates: $165 Ocean Course, $135 Mountain Course. Open daily, starting times required. Located six miles south of Kailua-Kona in the Keauhou resort area. 78-7000 Ali'i Drive, Kailua-Kona, HI 96740; 808-322-2595; www.konagolf.com.

Makalei Hawai'i Country Club Located about five miles above Kailua-Kona town on Highway 190 on the cool, breezy forested slopes of Mount Hualalai, with a pristine pastoral setting and spectacular views at 2,000 feet elevation. The 18-hole layout is a par-72 championship length of 7,100 yards. Most of the holes play downslope with undulating fairways and challenging greens. Rates: $110. 72-3890 Mamalahoa Highway, Kailua-Kona, HI 96740; 808-325-6625.

★ ***Mauna Kea Golf Course*** This is the one that started it all. Created by Robert Trent Jones, Sr., in 1965 from barren lava rock and brackish water, Mauna Kea set the bar very high for Hawai'i golf courses. Consistently ranked in *Golf Digest*'s Top 100, this championship golf course continues to win acclaim for its rewarding-yet-challenging play. Lush, mature landscaping enhances panoramic seascapes from almost every hole, and the over-the-ocean shot at the legendary third tee may be the most-photographed in Hawai'i. Friendly, experienced staff at the fully stocked pro shop assist with tee times, lessons, clinics, shoe and club rentals, golfing attire, equipment, gifts and accessories. Driving range, putting green, locker rooms, great food and libations at the 19th Hole Clubhouse, refreshment cart on the course. Soft spikes required. Call in advance for tee times. Rates: $195, twilight (after 1 p.m.) $155. Mauna Kea Resort, 62-100 Mauna Kea Beach Drive, Kohala Coast, HI 96743; 808-882-5400.

★ ***Mauna Lani Resort Golf Course*** The Francis H. I'i Brown Golf Course is a gorgeous and challenging 36-hole layout with two

GOLF AID

If you're unable to book a tee time at the course of your choice or you want to check on rates, a golf booking service may be able to help on obtaining a tee time. Try **Stand-by Golf**. They can assist with guaranteed tee times and discounted rates. They charge a fee for their services. 888-645-2665. **Fins and Fairways Hawai'i** can arrange accommodations at hotels/condos along the Kona and Kohala coasts and book tee times at most of the major resort golf courses. Look for their free publication at concierge desks and tourist kiosks island-wide. It's loaded with information and discount coupons. P.O. Box 9014, Kailua-Kona, HI 96745; 800-367-8014; 808-325-6171; e-mail: golfkona@kona.net; www.golfkona.com.

separate North and South championship courses. There are several breathtaking holes and fairways carved out of raw lava rock that climb across the rugged coastline, providing every level of golfer with an extraordinary day of play. The links surround the Mauna Lani Bay Hotel, the Fairmont Orchid and condo complexes. The course has won wide acclaim from golf groups and the media and provides an incredibly beautiful golfing experience. Call for tee time. Rates: $185, twilight (after 3 p.m.) $75. Mauna Lani Resort. 68-1310 Mauna Lani Drive, Kohala Coast, HI 96743; 808-885-6655.

Naniloa Country Club This is a short nine-hole, par-35 course. There is a pro shop with club and cart rentals available, instruction and driving range. Rates: $25 weekdays, $30 weekends. On hotel row along Hilo Bay. 120 Banyan Drive, Hilo, HI 96720; 808-935-3000.

Sea Mountain Golf Course This is a superb 18-hole championship course located in the peaceful southern coast area of the Big Island. The fairways are nicely landscaped with lots of greenery and flowering plants. The biggest factor are the strong coastal breezes. Rates: $42 weekdays, $45 weekends and holidays. Located in Punalu'u in the Ka'u District. P.O. Box 190, Pahala, HI 96777; 808-928-6222.

★ ***Volcano Golf and Country Club*** This is a lovely and lush 18-hole course set amidst the grandeur of the national park country. There is a pro shop with club and cart rental and the Volcano Country Club Restaurant is on premises. Rates: $50. Call for tee time. Located 1.5 miles west of entrance to Hawai'i Volcanoes National Park on Highway 11, P.O. Box 46, Pi'i Mauna Road, Volcano, HI 96718; 808-967-7331.

★ ***Waikoloa Beach Resort*** Located between the Waikoloa Beach Marriott and the Hilton Waikoloa Village at Waikoloa Resort, Kohala Coast are two highly rated golf courses, the Beach Course and the King's Course, each with a personality all its own and each offering a distinctive style of play. The Beach Course was designed by Robert Trent Jones, Jr., and set amidst the dramatic contrast of black lava flows and the blue Pacific Ocean. The King's Course is a par-72 championship layout, created out of barren lava desert by Tom Weiskopf and Jay Morrish, who were influenced by the famous open, windswept links of Scotland. The course features some of the most intimidating bunkers and sand traps of any Big Island course. The challenges to golfers come from Mother Nature—the strong Waikoloa winds, lava rock formations, sand traps, bunkers and an occasional water hazard. Not an easy round, but an accomplishment even for the best golfers. Full-service pro shop, lessons, rentals and Beach Grill restaurant. Rates: $165, twilight (after 2 p.m.) $75. 1020 Keana Place, Waikoloa, HI 96738; 808-886-7888; 877-WAIKOLOA; www.waikoloagolf.com.

★ ***Waikoloa Village Golf Club*** Robert Trent Jones, Jr., artfully designed this 6,791-yard, par-72 golf course to challenge the serious golfer and please the beginner as well. Reasonable green fees and consistent weather make it an exceptional value. Full-service pro shop, lessons, driving range, restaurant and lounge on-site. Call for tee times. Rates: $80, after 12 p.m. $55. Located in the cool and breezy uplands between Highways 19 and 190. P.O. Box 383910, 68-1792 Melia Street, Waikoloa Village, HI 96738; 808-883-9621.

Waimea Country Club The 6,661-yard, par-72 layout is spread through former ranch pasturelands and takes in the natural undulating and rolling hill terrain. Stands of forest and pastures border the fairways along with strategic water hazards and sand traps. It can get breezy and foggy out in the fairways at times when low cloud fronts move through. Pro shop and snack bar on-site. Rates: $65 morning, after 12:30 p.m. $50. Located about two miles east of Kamuela on the Mamalahoa Highway in the heart of Parker Ranch country. P.O. Box 2155, Kamuela, HI 96743; 808-885-8053.

HEALTH AND FITNESS CENTERS (*See also* Spas)

To keep up with the demand for exercise equipment by visitors, almost every resort and hotel now offers fitness centers with work-out rooms. The larger facilities will also have classes in Yoga, aerobics, cycling or spinning-along with saunas, locker rooms and a full menu of spa therapies and salon services. If your hotel, condo or B&B doesn't have one and you want to keep up with your workout regimen, you might try any of the following health and fitness centers. They welcome the public on a walk-in basis. They generally charge an hourly use fee for the equipment, spa, pool, saunas and other equipment.

Gold's Gym 5 a.m. to 10 p.m. Monday through Friday, 7 a.m. to 7 p.m. Saturday and Sunday. Rates: $15 trial day. 74-5583 Luhia, Kailua-Kona; 808-334-1977.

Hawai'i Naniloa Resort Spa 6 a.m. to 9 p.m. Monday through Friday, 10 a.m. to 6 p.m. Saturday and Sunday. Rates: $10 per day. Hawai'i Naniloa Hotel, 93 Banyan Drive, Hilo; 808-969-3333.

Orchid Isle Fitness 4:45 a.m. to 9 p.m. Monday through Friday, 8 a.m. to 3 p.m. Saturday, 8 a.m. to 12 p.m. Sunday. 29 Shipman Street, Suite 104, Hilo; 808-961-0003.

Pacific Coast Fitness Open long hours to suit busy people: 4 a.m. to 9 p.m. Monday through Thursday, 4 a.m. to 8 p.m. Friday, 7:30 a.m. to 9 p.m. Saturday. Rates: $8 per day. 65-1298A Kawaihae Road, next to Kamuela Inn, Waimea; 808-885-6270.

Spencer Health & Fitness Center 5 a.m. to 9 p.m. Monday through Friday, 5 a.m. to 3 p.m. Saturday. Rates: $10 per day, $25 per week. 197 Keawe Street, Hilo; 808-969-1511.

The Club in Kona 5 a.m. to 10 p.m. Monday through Friday, 7 a.m. to 7 p.m. Saturday and Sunday. Rates: $15 per day. Kona Sports Center, 75-5699 Kopiko Street, Kailua-Kona; 808-326-2582.

HIKING

Guided Tours/Outfitters

There are some commercial guided hiking tour operators and outfitters who lead various nature and wilderness hikes, cultural and historical walks and other excursions and outings into Big Island wilderness areas, national and state parks, and other areas of interest. Hikers might want to check with any of the following:

Arnott's Lodge These people go the extra mile to provide backpackers and adventurers with a quality, affordable vacations. The lodge is located in the Keaukaha area of Hilo near the beach parks. They offer added services such as an around-the-island "Big Island Experience" with stops at important historical and cultural sites, and daily hiking excursions including Hawai'i Volcanoes National Park, Mauna Kea Summit, South Point, Hilo Waterfalls, and Puna on the Rift Zone as well as custom adventure expeditions. Free shuttle service from Hilo International Airport. Apapane Road, Hilo, HI 96720; 808-969-7097, fax 808-961-9638; e-mail: info@arnottslodge.com; www.arnottslodge.com.

★ ***Hawai'i Forest & Trail*** This outfitter offers some of the Big Island's best soft-adventure guided nature hikes to unique island forest ecosystems. Hikers are led to remote locales by a naturalist-guide on easy to moderately difficult hikes through the primeval forest, complete with geologic wonders, incredible views and native Hawaiian flora and fauna. There are half- and full-day adventures for both children and adults. Half-day adventures include Valley Waterfall Adventure, Kahua Cloud Forest Adventure, Kohala Mule Trail Adventure and Kaupulehu Cave Adventure. Full-day adventures include Rainforest Discovery Adventure, Volcanoes Adventure, Hakalau National Wildlife Refuge Birding Adventure and Rainforest and Dry Forest Birding Adventure. Half-day adventures begin at $89 for adults, $79 for children; full-day adventures being at $139 for adults, $99 for children. Excellent guides provide all necessary equipment, service and guided narration on background culture, history, natural history and more. The Valley Waterfall and the Mule Trail Adventure in North Kohala are especially fun and adventurous and highly recommended. Reservations are essential. Hikes are fully equipped and serviced with morning coffee, snacks, lunch, beverages/water and daypacks, sweatshirts, ponchos and binoculars. Hiking time varies from

2-4 hours over moderate terrain; groups limited to 10 hikers; hikers provide their own hiking/walking footwear; hotel pick-ups included. Open 7 a.m. to 5 p.m. daily. 74-5035B Queen Ka'ahumanu Highway, Kailua-Kona, HI 96740; 808-331-8505; 800-464-1993; fax 808-331-8704; e-mail: hitrail@aloha.net; www.hawaii-forest.com.

★ ***Hawai'i Volcano GeoVentures*** This is one of the island's best soft-adventure, eco-tourism outfitters for tours and guided hikes in the Big Island's unique volcano environment. They offer personalized tours and guided hikes in Hawai'i Volcanoes National Park, beginning with stunning, panoramic views of the Kilauea summit crater. On drives and hikes through the national park, guests will see dramatic features of a stark volcanic desert, smell sulfur gas escaping from fissures, taste Hawaiian *ohelo* berries growing wild at the crater, hear native birds in their natural rainforest environment, and feel steam rising from cracks in the ground. Guests can also peer into lava tree molds, search for Pele's tears and hair, explore an underground lava tube and, if conditions permit, witness molten fiery lava explode into the Pacific Ocean, creating billowing clouds of steam. The hikes also provide informative natural history on the volcanic eruptions, insight into Hawai'i's unique cultural heritage and background on the flora and fauna of the national park. Janet Babb, the guide, is an avid geologist and educator skilled at explaining the science of volcanoes and the natural history of Hawai'i's environment. Hawai'i Volcano GeoVentures offers a range of guided geological adventures from personalized custom hikes for individuals to families and larger groups. P.O. Box 816, Volcano, HI 96785; phone/fax 808-985-9901; e-mail: geoventures@aloha.net; www.planet-hawaii.com/hea/volcano.

Hawaiian Walkways This hiking outfitter offers a variety of half- and full-day hikes over the Big Island's mountains and valleys and along its shorelines. Spectacular mountain and coastline vistas, secluded beaches, upland meadows, lush tropical rainforest, hidden pools and streams, fishponds and ancient Hawaiian petroglyphs or rock carvings are some of the features of these hiking tours. Hikes include half-day Waipi'o Rim Trail, $95; half-day Kona Cloud Forest, $95; full-day Kilauea Volcano, $175 for the first adult (over 12) and $110 for each additional. Exclusive hiking excursions and other customized adventures by arrangement. 800-457-7759; 808-775-0372; e-mail: hiwalk@aloha.net; www.hawaiianwalkways.com.

Hiking Resources

The **Kona Hiking Club** is an informal group that takes monthly day hikes to the Big Island's less accessible and private beaches, forests and backcountry areas. Most of these hikes are not difficult or long and require minimal gear or hiking experience. The group encourages family hiking outings. The club generally takes hikes on the first Saturday and third Thursday of each month. Membership is open to everyone. There are no dues or fees and visitors are welcome to participate. This is a good way to get to know some local folks and enjoy a Hawaiian outdoors experience. Watch the local Big Island newspapers community news files for hike announcements.

For maps and information on hiking the national park, contact: Superintendent, Hawai'i Volcanoes National Park, Volcano, HI 96718; 808-985-6000.

For information and maps relating to state forest reserve lands, contact: Forestry & Wildlife Division, Department of Land and Natural Resources, Island of Hawai'i, 75 Aupuni Street, Hilo, HI 96720; 808-974-4221.

For information on state parks, contact: Division of State Parks, Hawai'i District Office, Dept. of Land and Natural Resources, P.O. Box 936, Hilo, HI 96720; 808-974-6200.

For information on county beach parks, contact: Department of Parks and Recreation, County of Hawai'i, 25 Aupuni Street, Hilo, HI 96720; 808-961-8311.

Other good sources of hiking information are *Hawai'i Trails* by Kathy Morey, Wilderness Press (1992), *Hiking Hawaii—The Big Island* by Robert Smith, HOA Publications (1990), and *Hawaiian Hiking Trails* by Craig Chisholm, Fernglen Press (1994).

Hiking Trails

The Big Island has a wide range of hiking trails through the varied ecosystems, terrain and climates of coastal beach, valley jungle, mountain rainforest, lava desert, and alpine mountain summit. Trails are located in state forest reserves and parks, county parks, national park areas and remote coastal regions. Visitors can hike on their own, take a guided hiking adventure or walk with one of the operators or outfitters listed in the previous section.

Kona District **Kealakekua Bay and Captain Cook Monument** are reached by a moderately difficult hiking trail leading off from Highway 11 near Captain Cook town. This is a 2.5-mile, 3-hour round trip. To locate the trail, turn off Highway 11 at Napo'opo'o Road to Kealakekua Bay. Just 100 yards from the turnoff is a dirt-gravel trail directly across from three big royal palm trees and running downslope between fence rows. Park along the road. This is the old wagon road leading to the former Ka'awaloa settlement on the bay. The trail varies from steep to level, rough rocky/loose gravel to solid footing.

The first several hundred yards of trail are under shade trees along the fence rows but the trail soon opens to the warm sun and lava fields, so take hat, sunscreen and water. As the road nears the bay, it passes through old stone foundations of the former village. The trail ends at the bay. There is a tall cement monument to Captain James Cook and a smaller plaque marking the spot where he was killed by Hawaiians in a skirmish in 1779.

Snorkel and dive cruise boats filled with tourists anchor in Kealakekua Bay daily to swim and frolic in the waters of the Kealakekua Bay Underwater Marine Reserve, with its varied and colorful marinelife. The hike back up is quite steep and tiring, so allow some extra time.

Kaloko-Honokohau National Historic Park Trail is a coastal trail still under development. The distances vary from 1-2 miles and 1-2 hours hiking time. It is three miles north of Kailua-Kona, opposite Kaloko Industrial Area on a rough access road and adjacent to Honokohau Boat Harbor. Hikers can access the park trail from the Honokohau Harbor side. Turn right from Kealakehe Parkway leading to the harbor and follow the road to the end. The trail to the park starts opposite of the large rock berm. There are 1100 acres that span two miles along the coast, encompassing several old Hawaiian settlements. Archaeological sites include house foundations, fishing shrines, canoe landings, and petroglyph rock carvings. There are tidal pools and wetlands that serve as a preserve for migrant water birds and marine life. There are nice sandy beach areas and much plant life native to this coastal ecosystem. Restrooms at Kaloko fishponds; no facilities otherwise. Take water, sun gear and snacks.

Kohala Coast **Puako Petroglyph Fields Trail** is located next to Holoholokai Beach Park, fronting the Fairmont Orchid Hawai'i. The trailhead is marked by a sign next to the parking lot and is .5 mile one way, 20 minutes, passing through dry forest and brush areas before coming to open lava fields and the petroglyph rock carvings. The carvings are various Hawaiian depictions of men, canoes, animals, designs and more. This can be a very warm walk so take sunscreen, hat and water.

Ala Loa Trail (the King's Trail) and **Ala Kahakai Shoreline Trail** are part of an old Hawaiian trail system that was believed to have connected the coastal settlements in ancient times and even encircled the island. Parts of the trail system are still accessible for varying distances. One easy access point is on Waikoloa Beach Drive just before the Kings' Shops Center. The rocky trail passes through the golf courses and petroglyph fields. The same trail can also be accessed at Mauna Lani Resort near the golf course clubhouse and several places along the resort coastline. The trail follows lava flows near the rugged coast. Some parts of the trails are paved with smooth, waterworn rocks to make walking easier but much of it is on very rough lava rock surfaces in hot, dry conditions, so prepare accordingly with good footwear, sunscreen, hat and water.

Kiholo Bay is located about six miles south of Waikoloa Beach Resort on Highway 19. There are private housing developments around this bay and a private access road. However, the public can access the beach area and beautiful aquamarine lagoons and ponds via a moderate hiking trail from the highway. The trail is about a mile or so long, leading through open lava fields with some *kiawe* trees. There are no public facilities at Kiholo Bay but good swimming and snorkeling. Parking is along the highway. Watch for cars parked near the trailhead, which is about a mile north of a traffic turnoff and overlook for Kiholo Bay.

Waimea/Kamuela **White Road** is one of the Big Island's most scenic hiking trails and one of its best-kept secrets. Leaving Waimea town for the Hamakua Coast, look for White Road on the left, turn in and follow the road to its end and park along the right shoulder. The easy hiking trail leads through pastures and bamboo forest to the "bowl" at the top of Waipi'o Valley and an amazing scenic overlook. This trail is becoming more popular and you may encounter fellow hikers and their dogs out for some exercise.

Hamakua Coast **Akaka Falls State Park** is a special place. The half-mile loop trail takes about 30 minutes, but allow time to enjoy this veritable Garden of Eden setting. Located 11 miles north of Hilo, turn off Highway 19 at Honomu to Highway 220 and go through the small country town and upslope about 3.5 miles. The road terminates at the park. This is a moderately difficult walk only because there are some steep but short sections to climb. The trail meanders through lush tropical rainforest of *hapu* ferns, red and white ginger, banana trees, birds-of-paradise, plumeria, and giant philodendrons. Handrails aid in areas where the paved trail is quite steep and tends to be slippery when wet. Crossing the first bridge, if you've taken the right-hand route from the trailhead, you'll pass under a towering stand of giant bamboo. Further along, at the point where the trail makes a sharp left turn, is a small lookout for Kahuna Falls, a tumbling cascade which rolls down the north side of the canyon. Follow the trail on up the ridge to the main attraction, the beautiful 420-foot Akaka Falls, which plummets down a sheer cliffside in veiled mists to Kolekole Stream below. There is a rain shelter at this lookout. It's just a nice place to pause and soak in all the tropical beauty and lushness of Hawai'i. Continue on the trail back to the parking lot.

Waipi'o Valley is on the Hamakua Coast just about 50 miles north of Hilo. Take Highway 19 to Honoka'a, about 40 miles, then Highway 240 north 9 miles to Kukuihaele and the Waipi'o Valley State Park Lookout. Leave your car in the parking lot. It's a picture-postcard view from the lookout of the north wall of the valley; the beach and a great expanse of the valley are visible. The **Waipi'o Valley Trail** is actually a .75-mile paved, narrow and extremely steep 4WD road leading to the valley floor. At the valley floor, the road turns right for another .75 mile on a narrow dirt (if wet, muddy and rutted) lane to the mouth of the valley and Wailoa Stream. The beach here is good for picnics and relaxing but most of it lies on the other side of Wailoa Stream. There is a waterfall trailing off the south wall near the beach area. Back at the junction, the road leads left into the valley. This road follows the stream and leads toward several falls including Hi'ilawe Falls and others. However, the topside streams are tapped for irrigation by landowners above and thus sometimes there is little water for the waterfalls. Since much of Waipi'o Valley is privately owned, it's best to stick to the main road. This road has several stream crossings and passes by many taro patches. You may see resident taro farmers working in their fields. The valley is a wondrously lush green environment. There is wild guava and even papaya and bananas growing along the way. However far you wander, remember that you still have to return to the junction at the base of the valley cliff road and it's still .75 mile up and out of the valley.

Waipi'o and Waimanu Valley Trail (Muliwai) leads north out of Waipi'o Valley. This is a difficult 2- to 3-day wilderness backpacking trip for experienced hikers only and advisable only during the drier May-to-October period due to the several flood-prone streams that must be crossed. The trail is an 18-mile round trip from Waipi'o Valley to Waimanu Valley. The trail is accessed at the north end of Waipi'o Valley beach after fording Wailoa Stream. The trail is 100 yards from the beach in a forest at the base of the north wall cliff. This is a switchback "Z" trail up the 1,200-foot cliff and reaches the high coastal plateau between the two valleys. The trail crosses some 14 gulches and streams along this rugged coastline, passing through dense coastal rainforest. The trail can be heavily overgrown in places and can be muddy, rocky and slippery as well. There is a trail shelter suitable for picnicking and camping about two-thirds of the way to Waimanu. Be on the lookout for horses and pig-hunters who frequent the area. After an equally steep descent into Waimanu Valley, turn right toward the beach, ford the stream and locate a suitable camping spot on or near the beach. You need a camping permit from the State Forestry and Wildlife office. Any stream water used must be purified and/or boiled first.

Kalopa State Park in the Hamakua Forest Reserve is 42 miles north of Hilo on Highway 19, turning left at the Kalopa State Park sign just past the 39-mile marker. This state park has a 100-acre block of native Hawaiian rainforest that is kept preserved in its natural state as much as possible, i.e., limiting incursions of alien species, pigs, and other destructive animals. There are several enjoyable hiking trails throughout. The **Kalopa Native Forest Nature Trail** is an easy .7-mile loop

A WORD OF CAUTION

The national park is an awesome place full of wonders to explore. But it is also a place of hazard and danger for the uninformed and careless. Anybody can get lost, and we hate hearing about otherwise "happy campers" having to spend the night alone in the woods, or worse. When hiking the national park, or anywhere on the Big Island, for that matter, be sure to take the following very important (and very simple) precautions:

- Take a buddy.
- Stay on the trail.
- Let someone know where you are going, how long you expect to be gone and where your starting point is. Check in with rangers if appropriate.
- Take more water than you think you will need, food, sunscreen, hat, simple first-aid items and any medication you need on a regular basis.
- Pack a poncho or large plastic trash bag for some protection in case you get caught in the rain.
- Take your cell phone and some way to signal rescuers in the air-a mirror, bright-colored tape, etc.
- In the unlikely and unfortunate event that you should have trouble, rescue teams advise you **stay put** so they can find you. Once you know you're lost, don't keep walking.

trail, 1-hour-long walk, through a true Hawaiian rainforest. Trails are well marked, as are a number of tree and plant species. Pick up a trail guide at the trailhead near the parking lot. The nature trail is just opposite the cabins and leads into dark forest under towering *ohia* trees. The forest here also has large tree ferns, *kolea*, *kopiko*, *olomea*, *pilo*, ground ferns and much more. The **Kalopa Gulch Rim Loop** is a 2.8-mile, 2-hour-long walk, suitable for all hikers. Pick up a trail guide at the parking lot display. This walk is through a 1930s reforestation project that was planted to conserve land and soil that had been badly overgrazed and misused. Fast-growing non-native species were introduced, including blue gum, paper bark, silk oak, ironwood and swamp mahogany. This large standing forest is still thriving and a native Hawaiian forest is beginning to re-establish itself. The area has various trails linking to the main loop trail and is a pleasant walk in the woods.

Puna District **Kaumana Trail** is a .5-mile, 1-hour hike and connects with the Saddle Road at two points, 17.4 and 19.8 miles from Hilo. The trail is a remnant portion of the old Pu'u O'o–Kaumana Trail, which was used as an access route between Hilo and the saddle area between Mauna Kea and Mauna Loa. It extends along the 1855 lava flow from about 5,200 feet down to 4,800 feet. Vegetation on the lava flow is scrubby *ohia* and tree fern. Common native birds are readily sighted along the trail. It is suited for short nature hikes. Hikers can be dropped off at one end and picked up at the other.

Lava Tree State Park is an easy .8-mile loop trail, 30-minute walk, located about 25 miles from Hilo. Take Highway 11 south from Hilo, turn left at Kea'au to Highway 130 south to Pahoa and then left onto Highway 132 about 3 miles to the park entrance. A 1790 lava flow from Kilauea Volcano covered the present site, which was a forest of *ohia lehua* trees. The lava destroyed the *ohia* trees and left a number of tree-shaped lava shells as the rapidly flowing lava drained away. The resulting "stumps" are almost like abstract sculptures in lava rock but are completely natural. They provide some truly unusual and strange formations. The *ohia lehua* trees with puffy red or red/orange blossoms have made a comeback in the park. There are other ornamental trees, shrubs and flowering plants as well, including heliconia or lobster claw ginger, torch ginger, colorful crotons, bracken fern, tree ferns and others. This is an enjoyable, level stroll through a tropical botanical garden. The park has restrooms and picnic shelters but can have lots of mosquitoes as well; bug repellent is advised.

Hawai'i Volcanoes National Park Hawai'i Volcanoes National Park has some of the Big Island's best hiking trails, from short and easy walks to intermediate hikes, to long and challenging overnight and multiday backcountry treks. Hikers are best advised to contact the Superintendent, Hawai'i Volcanoes National Park, HI 96718, 808-985-6000, or stop at the park's Kilauea Visitor Center for a map and details on hiking the park. Hikers are required to register and obtain permits for backcountry overnight hikes.

Some national park trails require you to sign in and out. Do not, under any circumstances, venture out onto lava flows and fields by yourself, and do stick to marked trails. Old lava flows are marked by deep holes and crevasses that are extremely hazardous to hikers. The hardened crust of lava can be deceiving. What looks like a firm rigid shell can be a thin weak cover to a large hole or crevasse and people can fall in and get lost. You could be badly injured or even lost in a remote area with little chance of rescue. Also, do not attempt to hike across lava fields at night. Trails are extremely difficult to follow in the dark and the potential danger and hazards are great. Hike only in daylight hours when the chances of disorientation and confusion are diminished. Don't take chances with your health and safety and those of your family. Listen to the rangers. Near the eruption site, conditions can change suddenly and frequently. Fumes can be dangerous to pregnant women and people with heart or respiratory conditions and other ailments. Pay attention, be smart and enjoy the most awe-inspiring natural show in Hawai'i. The following are some of the park's most popular hikes.

Kilauea Iki is a moderate 4-mile, 2- to 3-hour loop hike. Begin from Crater Rim Trail or Crater Rim Drive east of Kilauea Crater. Trail begins in young rainforest on the rim of the crater and leads down a 400-foot descent into Kilauea Iki Crater and across the lava floor. Watch footing on descent as some areas are loose gravel and rock and can be slippery. The trail across the crater floor has stone cairns marking the way. There are steaming vents and cracks in the floor. Look for Pele's hair (the Hawaiian volcano fire goddess) along the way, long slivers of olivine crystals from the lava that collect in the recesses of the jumbled rocks. The views all around are imposing; the immense cinder cone of Pu'u Pua'i, which erupted in 1959, created the crater lava flow and the sheer vertical cliffs that surround you as you walk across the steaming crater floor. The trail switchbacks up the opposite crater wall and leads back to the forest.

Devastation Trail is an easy, level, 1-mile, 30-minute walk on an asphalt-paved trail across the edge of Pu'u Pua'i cinder cone, formed by the 1959 eruption of Kilauea Iki. The trail links the parking lots of Kilauea Iki Overlook and Devastation Trailhead. The trail can be walked as a round trip or one way if a pickup is arranged at the other end. The trail follows along the edge of the *ohia* and tree fern forest, where it meets the open, barren cinder cone. The eruption destroyed much of the nearby forest that was downwind and was covered with cinders and pumice. The forest is now making a regrowth comeback. The area covered by the cinders and pumice is still stark, with numerous dead trees sticking up from the dark barren surroundings providing a surreal contrast.

Thurston Lava Tube is a .3-mile, 20-minute loop trail. This is one of the park's more fascinating walks. Begin at the parking lot on Crater Rim Drive about two miles from Kilauea Visitor Center. The trail is paved asphalt and has a couple of steep sections but there are steps and handrails. It's often damp and rainy here and the trail can be slippery, so use caution. The trail passes through a dense *ohia* and tree fern forest descending into the lava tube. The tube is like a tunnel, 1,494 feet long, up to 22 feet wide and 20 feet high in places. Some areas are considerably lower and you must watch your head so you don't meet a rock. The tube is lighted but a flashlight would help as well. There are water puddles in the tube due to the natural percolation of rainwater from above and it can be quite cool and damp. The lava tube was created over 400 years ago when a flow formed an outer crust while the interior kept flowing. Once the lava drained away, the resulting lava tube remained intact. This is an enjoyable short hike providing a close-up glimpse of the Hawaiian *ohia* and tree fern forest and a unique geological attraction.

Halema'uma'u Trail is a moderate, 3-mile one-way or 7-mile loop trail, 3-6 hours, to Halema'uma'u Crater in the Kilauea Caldera. The trail begins behind the Volcano House Hotel. The trail descends 500 feet through forest into Kilauea Caldera and crosses the floor to the Halema'uma'u Crater Overlook. The wind is usually brisk across the caldera and the sulfur gas smell is strong, making breathing difficult at times. Those with breathing difficulties or related problems should not attempt the hike. There are panoramic vistas of the caldera, steaming vents and cracks, old lava flows and close-up views into still-steaming Halema'uma'u Crater. Those hiking one way can meet their pickup in the Halema'uma'u parking lot. Those doing the round-trip hike back to Volcano House Hotel can pick up the Byron Ledge Trail, which loops across the caldera and up to the Byron Ledge ridge then back to the Volcano House Hotel.

Crater Rim Trail is a challenging 11-mile, day-long trek on varying terrain from forest trails to open, hot and windy lava rock trails. This is for experienced hikers only. The trail passes through a wide variety of geological and biological environments, circling the summit of Kilauea Caldera. The trail passes the Hawaiian Volcano Observatory and Jaggar Museum, Halema'uma'u Crater, near Devastation Trailhead and past Thurston Lava Tube. On this full-day hike, you will see a cross-section of the entire summit area, including its *ohia* and tree fern forests, dry open scrubland and desert, open lava fields and recent flow areas. Bring water and food, and be prepared for rain along the way. Sulfur gas fumes will be strong in the downwind southeast rift zone and Halema'uma'u areas.

Pu'u Loa Petroglyphs Trail is a 1.5-mile round-trip, 1- to 2-hour, moderate walk over level to rolling lava fields. The trail is smooth with some rough, rocky sections. The trail is some 20 miles southeast of Kilauea Visitor Center off the Chain of Craters Road, near the coastal flatlands and a few miles from the end of the highway, which is closed due to lava flows. The trail leads to fields of smooth *pahoehoe* lava mounds on which the petroglyphs are carved. There are many different types of petroglyphs in varying shapes, sizes and designs. Petroglyphs are fragile so don't step on or damage these artworks in any way. This is an open, very breezy lava field with no shade trees. It can get very hot, and this area is downwind of the eruption site just up the coast so volcanic sulfur fumes can be intense.

Mauna Iki/Footprints Trail is a moderate to difficult 8.8-mile, 5- to 6-hour hike through the rocky, cinder trails of the Ka'u Desert. The trail begins off Highway 11 about 9 miles southwest of Kilauea Visitor

Center. The trail links the Hilina Pali Road and Highway 11 and bisects the Ka'u Desert Trail. The trail allows hikers to cut hiking distances to certain points of interest in the Ka'u Desert and Hilina Pali areas. Extensions are possible for overnight camping treks via Ka'u Desert Trail, Hilina Pali Trail and Halape Trail; camping permits from park visitors center required for these treks. The first .8 mile of the trail is an easy hike on sandy or cinder trails to the "Footprints" exhibit. The footprints, preserved under glass cases, are supposedly those of Hawaiian warriors who had gathered in the area in 1790 to battle with the forces of Kamehameha the Great for control of the island. The gathered warriors were overcome by fumes and volcanic dust from an eruption at Halema'uma'u Crater to the east. Their footprints were left hardened in the ash and the army dispersed. The trail beyond the exhibit passes through the upper sections of the Ka'u Desert and unique desert ecosystem plants and volcanic formations. This is an area of extreme temperatures, sun and high winds; caution is advised and take hat, sunscreen, water and food.

Kipuka Puaulu (Bird Park) begins off Highway 11 on the Mauna Loa Strip Road about 2.5 miles west of the entrance to Hawai'i Volcanoes National Park. Kipuka Puaulu is about 1.5 miles in on the Strip Road. This is an easy 1-mile loop trail, through a special ecological preserve area and is one of the national park's most enjoyable walks. The *kipuka* is an "island" of native forest and rare plants surrounded by fairly recent lava flows that have isolated this forest glen from the rest of the nearby forest lands. The trail meanders through dense old-growth forest and open meadowlands. There is some gentle slope and climb but overall is an easy hike. The area is alive with native Hawaiian birdlife fluttering among the trees. Best to visit early mornings or late afternoons. This is a very tranquil, pleasantly cool and breezy place to enjoy the pleasures of one of Hawai'i's unique deep forest trails. Picnic tables and restrooms available.

Mauna Loa Summit Trail is at the end of Mauna Loa Strip Road (6,662-foot level) off Highway 11 2.5 miles west of the entrance to Hawai'i Volcanoes National Park. This is a challenging 36.6-mile, 4-day round-trip hike for experienced hikers only. It takes two days to climb the south rim of Mokuaweoweo Caldera at 13,250 feet. Hikers spend the first night in Red Hill Cabin (10,035 feet) and proceed to the summit shelter on the second day. It takes an additional half day to hike around the caldera to the true summit at 13,677 feet. Hikers are subjected to high winds, altitude sickness, snow and cold temperatures. A shorter but equally difficult 13-mile, 2-day round-trip hike begins at the Mauna Loa Weather Observatory at the 11,000-foot level on the north side, accessed via the Saddle Road. Before taking this trail, hikers are advised to spend the night in their cars at the end

A WALK IN THE PARK

Banyan Drive and **Liliuokalani Park** is a half-mile walk, 1 hour or longer, depending on how long you pause to enjoy the stops along the way. This walk begins in Hilo near the Seaside Hotel and follows the loop around the Waiakea Peninsula along hotel row to Liliuokalani Park. Banyan Drive is lined with giant banyan trees, hence its name. Each was planted by a visiting celebrity of the mid-20th-century. Each tree carries a sign at its base with the name of the person who planted it and the date planted. VIPs who planted the famous trees include Babe Ruth, Amelia Earhart, President Franklin D. Roosevelt, Lincoln Ellsworth (famed Arctic explorer), author Fannie Hurst and several other lesser notables. There is even a tree planted by some obscure U.S. senator named Richard Nixon. The trees make a virtual tree tunnel along Banyan Drive as it loops past the hotels and restaurants to Liliuokalani Park. The Japanese park is on the shores of Hilo Bay and is one of Hawai'i's loveliest cultural parks—and it is free.

of the road near the observatory since no accommodations are available and to acclimate their bodies to Mauna Loa's elevation. Good hikers can do the trail in one day, but it's better to spend the night at Mauna Loa. A backcountry camping permit is required for either trip; check with Kilauea Visitor Center rangers.

Ka'u District Ka Lae (South Point) and **Green Sand Beach** is a moderate 6-mile round-trip, 2-hour, coastal trail hike through open grassy areas following jeep trails. The area is reached via South Point Road, which branches off Highway 11 about 6 miles west of Na'alehu town. South Point Road is a narrow asphalt lane winding down 12 miles through open pasture country. It passes by the Kamao'a Wind Farm, a wind-powered electricity-generating facility using huge windmill-like turbines. The winds at Ka Lae (South Point) are usually brisk and continuous. Ka Lae is believed to be where the first Hawaiians landed, around 400 A.D., in their early migrations across the Pacific. There are old canoe mooring holes in the rocks and the ruins of a fishermen's *heiau*. Fishermen still use the area to moor their boats but they hoist them up and down the high cliffs to the calm water below. The road turns east through the remnants of a World War II communications station, terminating at a small boat-launching harbor about a mile or so east. This is the beginning of the coastal trailhead. It's 3 miles to Green Sand Beach through open rolling grasslands along the coast. Mahana Bay, where the beach is located, is marked by a high cliff promontory rising along the coast and is visible from a distance. A hazardous trail leads down to the beach. Rough waters and currents make it unsafe for water activities but it's a nice place to just picnic and relax. You can easily see why it's called Green Sand Beach due to the presence of green olivine crystals in the sand. There are no trees or shade along this entire warm, breezy coastline so take hat, sunscreen, water and food. Permits are required to access Green Sand Beach across the private property of Hawaiian Home Lands; 4WD vehicle access may be restricted; there is no charge for the permit, which can be faxed to your hotel or condo. For permit, contact the Department of Hawaiian Home Lands, 160 Baker Avenue, Hilo, HI 96720, 808-974-4250.

Manuka Nature Trail is a moderate 2.25-mile, 2-hour walk and is at the southwest tip of the Big Island's Ka'u District, very near the South Kona District. Located at Manuka State Wayside off Highway 11 just west of the 81-mile marker, or 81 miles from Hilo, roughly 40 miles from Kailua-Kona. This is a nice botanical garden park with varied species of ornamental trees and shrubs and wide grassy areas. There is a picnic pavilion and restrooms. The nature trail is a loop walk that climbs into a forest of native *ohia lehua*, tree ferns and *pukiawe* plus *kukui*, guava and other introduced plants and trees. This is a hike through an upland dry forest ecosystem. You'll also see and hear a lot of birdlife in this habitat.

HORSEBACK RIDING

For the would-be *paniolo* and *paniola* there are stables and trail-ride operators with a variety of ways to experience Hawai'i on horseback. Guided trail rides provide a unique opportunity to get close to the Big Island's rolling green hill country, with its fascinating landscapes, scenic ranch and mountain ranges. Prices vary but start at about $50-$75 per person for a basic 1.5- to 2-hour trail ride; longer rides of 5 hours are up to $145 per person. Wagon/carriage rides of 1.5 hours start at about $40 per person and some include transportation to the stables and refreshments. Age restrictions (very young children not allowed) and rider weight restrictions also apply, so ask first and avoid disappointment. Donkeys and mules give great trail-riding adventures too!

★ ***DaHana Ranch*** DaHana Ranch is home to the 1994 International World Cup champion roughriders. This operator specializes in open-range rides on American Quarterhorses, *paniolo*-style in the uplands of Waimea ranch country. They take first-time to experienced riders and encourage family adventures that include children as young as three; 1.5- and 2.5-hour rides daily. P.O. Box 1293, Kamuela,

HI 96743, 7.5 miles east of Waimea town on Old Mamalahoa Highway; 808-885-0057; e-mail: dahana@gte.net; www.dahanaranch.com.

Donkey Tales of Hawai'i This is a fun, year-round activity for kids 6 to 12 years old. Kapapala Ranch in Ka'u conducts summer and holiday camping and excursion adventures for kids, using very gentle and tame donkeys for trail rides on day trips or up to a rustic bunkhouse camp out near the 4,000-foot elevation on Mauna Loa's foothills. Donkeys available for special events, parties, riding lessons, and more. P.O. Box 1768, Kea'au, HI 96749; 808-968-6585; www.kapapala.com.

Giddy-Up Go Trail Rides This outfitter/operator offers trail-ride excursions in the upland forest and ranchlands of the Hamakua Coast region. They'll also take good care of kids. P.O. Box 34, Papa'aloa, HI 96780; 808-962-6840.

★ Hawai'i Forest & Trail One of the best and most popular, this excellent outfitter/operator has a special Kohala Mule Trail Adventure down into North Kohala's beautiful Pololu Valley. Ride a switchback trail down to the valley, past the crashing surf, then follow a 2.5-mile loop trail through forest and across streams and back to a black-sand beach. Rides are 3 hours, departing from Mule Station atop Pololu Valley near the end of Highway 270. Rates: $89 adults, $69 children. 74-5035B Queen Ka'ahumanu Highway, Kailua-Kona, HI 96740; 800-464-1993; 808-331-8505; fax 808-331-8704; e-mail: info@hawaii-forest.com; www.hawaii-forest.com.

King's Trail Rides O' Kona They offer horseback trail rides exploring the backcountry lands of 20,000-acre Kealakekua Ranch and Kona Coast trail rides to beaches for a picnic lunch and a swim. Monday through Saturday 8:15 a.m. to 12:15 p.m. Kealakekua, Kona; 808-323-2388.

Kapapala Trails This outfitter/operator has various adventure activities available on Kapapala Ranch on the slopes of Mauna Loa Mountain. The 30,000-acre working cattle ranch is in the southern Ka'u District. There are horseback ranch rides. With an emphasis on ecotourism and respect for the environment, custom overnight camping trips can be arranged, as well rental cottages at reasonable rates. Guests are encouraged to spend time on the ranch alongside the *paniolo* to share the lifestyle and gain hands-on experience. P.O. Box 1768, Kea'au, HI 96749; 808-968-6585; e-mail: info@kapapala.com.

Kohala Na'alapa Trail Rides This operator offers open-range trail rides at scenic Kahua Ranch in the Kohala Mountains; ride through historic Kahua Ranch, a 12,000-acre working cattle ranch with panoramic views of Mauna Kea, Hualalai and the Kohala Coast. Custom picnic rides available. Riders must be at least 8 years old and not more than 230 pounds. Weather permitting, tours depart from Kohala Ranch Mountain Security Station daily at 8:30 a.m. and 1 p.m. Rates:

$78.13 morning, $57.30 afternoon. P.O. Box 992, Kamuela, HI 96743; 808-889-0022; e-mail: naalapa@ilhawaii.net; www.naalapastables.com.

★ ***Paniolo Riding Adventures*** This operator offers trail rides on an 11,000-acre working ranch in the scenic Kohala Mountain country. Skilled, knowledgeable guides lead riders on trained horses through lush pasturelands with scenic vistas of the Kona and Kohala coastlines. They also offer mule rides using special Australian stock saddles. There is a standard 2.5-hour trail ride or a 4-hour picnic adventure ride with gourmet lunch included. P.O. Box 363, Kohala Mountain Road, Honoka'a, HI 96727; 808-889-5354; fax 808-880-9101.

Waipi'o Na'alapa Trail Rides Leisurely paced 2.5-hour trail ride through the lush beauty of the famous Waipi'o Valley on the Hamakua Coast, taking in waterfalls, jungle trails, freshwater steams, taro patches and breathtaking views. Riders must be at least 8 years old and not more than 230 pounds. Tours depart Monday through Saturday from Waipi'o Valley Artworks in Kukuihaele town at 9 a.m. and 12:30 p.m. Closed Sunday. Rates: $78.13. P.O. Box 992, Kamuela, HI 96743; 808-775-0419.

★ ***Waipi'o on Horseback and Taro Farm*** This outfitter takes riders down into the beautiful scenic Waipi'o Valley. Explore trails through the lush rainforest jungles, see Hawaiian taro patches on a working old-fashioned taro farm, waterfalls, streams and black-sand beach. P.O. Box 183, Honoka'a, HI 96727; 808-775-7291.

Waipi'o Ridge Stables They provide a 2.5-hour "Valley of the Kings" ride and a 5-hour "Hidden Waterfalls" ride in the Waipi'o Valley. Rates: $145 for a 5-hour ride including lunch, $75 for a 2.5-hour ride with snacks. Located at Kukuihaele near the Waipi'o Valley overlook; 808-775-1007; www.topofwaipio.com.

HUNTING

Outdoors and hunting enthusiasts will enjoy the challenge of an outing to the fields and slopes of Mauna Kea or other island hunting grounds. Hawaiian big game like wild boar, Mouflon sheep and mountain goat, or wild game birds like turkey, quail, pheasant, chukar or francolin partridge are available in season. Hunting the Big Island provides special thrills, action and unique outdoor experiences. Hunting seasons may vary annually. The following hunting guide services and outfitters can make all the arrangements.

Ginger Flower Charters Fishing and hunting guide Kenny Llanes specializes in wild boar hunting on the Big Island's remote mountain and forest slopes. In addition, bird hunting for wild turkey, pheasant, quail, chukar and francolin is available November through January. Archery hunts are available for sheep and goat in season. 73-1277 Awakea, Kailua-Kona, HI 96740; 808-325-7600.

WAGON RIDES

★ **Kohala Carriages Ltd.** operates comfortable, cushioned wagon rides along the scenic North Kohala coast. A pair of gentle giant Belgian draft horses pull the wagon through the green pastureland of Parker Ranch. Five tours daily Tuesday through Saturday 10 a.m. to 2 p.m. Rates: $15 adults, $12 seniors and children. Other tour locations and special events on request. Old Halaula Mill Road, Kapa'au; also at Parker Ranch Shopping Center in Waimea; 808-889-5955; 808-885-5881. **Waipi'o Valley Wagon Tours** takes you "back in time" from the Last Chance Store in Kukuihaele town, down into unspoiled Waipi'o Valley. From there, you climb aboard an old-fashioned mule-drawn wagon, whose storyteller/drivers share Waipi'o's culture and history as you take in lush tropical foliage, cultivated taro patches, the mythic Hi'ilawe waterfall and much more. Cushioned seats, Amish springs and shock absorbers make for a comfortable ride through a quieter, less-complicated place. This is a tour for people with imagination and respect for authenticity. Weather permitting, 1.5-hour tours depart Monday through Saturday 9:30 a.m., 11:30 a.m., 1:30 p.m., 3:30 p.m. Rates: $40 adults, $20 children, kids under 3 free. P.O. Box 1340, Honoka'a, HI 96727; 808-775-9518; e-mail: wagonaloha@hotmail.com; www.waipiovalleywagontour.com.

Glenn Kokubun This outfitter has various hunting tours available in the upland mountain areas, open grasslands and forest areas for all game. 15-1922 Naupaka, Kea'au, HI 96749; 808-982-7349.

Hawai'i Hunting Tours Guide Eugene Ramos specializes in custom hunts for sheep, wild boar, goat and game birds on private hunting grounds on the slopes of Mauna Kea, Mauna Loa and Hualalai. Scenic 4WD tours through majestic backcountry are also available. P.O. Box 58, Paauilo, Hamakua, HI 96776; 808-776-1666.

Kealia Ranch This outfitter offers guided hunts and excursions for all game in the upland ranchlands and forest areas of the South Kona region above Honaunau and Kealakekua Bay. Kealia Ranch c/o Post Office, Honaunau, HI 96726; 808-328-2662.

KAYAKING (*See also* Sea Excursions; Snorkeling)

Adventures in Paradise This complete kayak and snorkeling outfitter provides equipment plus morning and afternoon tours of historic, beautiful Kealakekua Bay. Rates: $25 per person for equipment, $45 per person for tours. Located south of Kona between mile markers 111 and 110, 81-6367 Mamalahoa Highway, Kealakekua; 808-323-3005; 866-824-2337; www.bigislandkayak.com.

★ ***Aloha Kayak Co.*** Guided kayak excursions and adventures. Locations at old Honalo town and in the Kona Inn Shopping Village, Ali'i Drive, Kailua-Kona, 808-331-8558; 79-7428 Mamalahoa Highway, Honalo, HI 96750; 877-322-1444, 808-322-2868, fax 808-322-1444; e-mail: alohakayak@yahoo.com; www.alohakayak.com.

★ ***C&S Outfitters*** Kayak rentals include paddles, back rests, life vests, gear bag, leash and car rack (damage-free, for use on any type of car). Friendly, experienced outfitter provides full line of kayak gear and supplies, plus sun protection, souvenirs, snacks and beverages. Open Monday through Saturday 9 a.m. to 5 p.m. Rates for kayaks: Half-day (12 p.m. to 5 p.m.) $25 single/$35 tandem, full-day $30 single/$45 tandem, weekly $120 single/$160 tandem. In Waimea at Cook's Corner, intersection of Highway 19 and Kamamalu Street; 808-885-5005; fax 808-885-5683.

Clear Blue Kona This is something different: a see-through kayak. Float along on your own "window" into the undersea world of tropical fish, coral reefs, sea turtles and spinner dolphins. A truly unique experience. Rates: 2-hour tour $52 includes snacks, 4-hour tour $89 includes lunch. 808-322-2868; www.clearbluehawaii.com.

Hawai'i Pack & Paddle Tours This operator provides kayak, hiking and camping tours along the Kona Coast and customized two- to five-day kayak outings around the Big Island. 87-3187 Holomoku Road H, Captain Cook, HI 96704; 808-326-2388.

Kayaks to Go They specialize in kayak rentals; they'll help you plan your kayak excursion along the Kona Coast. Kayak rental rates: $25-$40 per day. On Ali'i Drive in Kailua-Kona, next to Huggo's Restaurant and Snorkel Bob's; 808-326-4699.

★ ***Kealakekua Bay Kayak Rentals*** They offer a full line of ocean kayak rentals, including the Dagger Kayak, 4" wider and 11" longer for a more stable ride; guided tours are available. Also snorkel equipment, boogieboard and other rentals. On Highway 11 in Kealakekua, right next to McDonald's at 112-mile marker; 808-323-3329; www.konakayaks.com.

★ ***Kohala Mountain Kayak Cruise*** "Flumin Da Ditch" is one of the Big Island's best adventures and a unique kayaking excursion that you won't find anywhere else. It's a three-mile, three-hour cruise by inflatable kayak through the old Kohala Ditch, a concrete waterway built in 1905 to irrigate the sugar plantations of the North Kohala District. Escorted groups of kayakers float down scenic waterways, tunnels and flumes of the original ditch, through rainforest and mountain pastures with breathtaking panoramic views. The original 22.5-mile-long irrigation ditch was a major engineering feat in its time, spanning the rugged gorges and valleys to reach the old Kohala Sugar Plantation for 70 years until its demise in 1975. "Flumin Da Ditch" is an attempt to bring eco-tourism activities to North Kohala and help restore the ditch and highlight the unique cultural history of the area. Snacks and hot/cold drinks are included at the end of the cruise, and kayakers can visit a secluded rainforest waterfall and swimming hole for a dip. Morning and afternoon departures. Cruises start with a van ride from Kapa'au town to the ditch site. Rates: $85 adults, $65 children 5 to 18. Headquarters for this popular activity is Kapa'au town, at the intersection of Akoni Pule Highway and Hawi Road/Kohala Mountain Highway, behind the Nakahara Store Building; P.O. Box 190573, Hawi, HI 96719; 877-449-6922; 808-889-6922; fax 808-889-6944; e-mail: res@flumindaditch.com; www.kohalakayaks.com.

Kona Boys Homegrown Adventures This operator has a variety of kayaking tours and excursions available, including half- and full-day sea treks and overnight tours; kayak and snorkel equipment rentals and instruction also available. Staffed by lifelong watermen and women, the Kona Boys share their enjoyment of the ocean, along with a sense of respect, gratitude and "fluidity." Mamalahoa Highway, Kailua-Kona; 808-328-1234 or 808-322-3600; www.konaboys.com.

Ocean Safari's Kayaks This operator offers varied ocean kayaking tours, excursions, equipment rentals and instruction. Rent your own, or join in Ocean Safari's 3.5-hour Keauhou Sea Cave Tour, a 2-hour Dolphin Quest Tour or 4-hour Whale Watch. Tours include snacks, drinks, snorkel gear and fun. Tour Rates: $59-$75 adults, children under 12 half-price. Kayak Rentals $25 single, $40 double. P.O. Box 515, Kailua-Kona, HI 96745; 808-326-4699; fax 808-322-3653; e-mail: kayakhi@gte.net; www.oceansafariskayaks.com.

Planet Ocean Watersports This operator and outfitter rents a full line of watersports equipment including kayaks. They also offer scuba and snorkeling dive cruises plus guided kayak tours. Kayak tours: $40-$50 per person; kayak rentals: single $25-$35 per day, double $30-$40 per day. 100 Kamehameha Avenue, Hilo, HI 96720; 808-935-7277; www.hawaiidive.com.

LAND TOURS

The Big Island earned its reputation among the other Hawaiian islands. It's big, bigger than the other islands put together. There's a lot of open space here, and a wide variety of scenic places to visit and enjoy. We're of the opinion that one of the Big Island's best pleasures is driving, exercising the American custom of taking a ride. With basically only one road (two in some places) around the island, relatively light traffic, reliable weather and beautiful country to watch roll by, the island cruise is a delight. We highly recommend you take a look at the "Driving" section of Chapter 1 and make your own adventure.

Tours however, have their own charms and benefits, particularly for some of the more remote or harder to find places beyond the reach of rental cars. In addition to regular land tours of the island, this section lists some unique tours to places like Waipi'o Valley and the summit of Mauna Kea. These operators provide special insight on their respective attractions and areas of the Big Island and make sure you see what you came to see.

ATV Outfitters Hawai'i This outfitter/operator offers ATV riding adventures through private ranchlands and coastal areas of the North Kohala District of the Big Island. Take in mountain and sea coast trails, visit historic sites, and ride along beautiful seacliffs and old plantation roads. Explore and discover from sea to mountain. All equipment including gloves, goggles, and a helmet is provided. One-and-a-half-hour guided tours daily, 9 a.m., 12 p.m. and 2 p.m. Ask about their Ocean Seacliff, Rainforest and Waterfall Adventures. Riders must be at least 16 years old. Reservations recommended, and long pants and closed shoes are required. Rates: $90 per person. Sakamoto Store Building, Kapa'au, North Kohala, HI 96755; 808-889-6000; www.outfittershawaii.com.

★ ***HMV Tours*** This tour operation is owned by the same folks who operate the Kohala Mountain Kayak Cruise. HMV Tours use a 4WD military-type Hummer vehicle to explore the deep jungle and rainforest of Kohala Mountain. Take an adventure-filled ride into the real offroad backcountry of the Big Island mountain forest. Tours go twice daily. Located at the intersection of Akoni Pule Highway and Hawi Road in Hawi, North Kohala; P.O. Box 190573, Hawi, HI 96719; 877-449-6922; 808-889-6922; fax 808-889-6944; e-mail: res@hmvtours.com; www.hmvtours.com.

Operating out of two Kohala Coast locations at Kawaihae and Puako, **Hawaiian Adventure Tours** specializes in land and sea eco-adventures, professionally guided and outfitted for maximum guest experience. 3.5-hour tours depart at 8:30 a.m., with free transportation to Waikoloa hotels. Rates: $59 adults, $35 children under 12. 808-882-4678; www.hawaiianadventuretours.com.

Kukui ATV & Adventures This operator provides 2.5-hour guided adventures aboard automatic, easy-to-handle all-terrain vehicles. Old sugarcane backroads lead through beautiful country with mountain streams, waterfalls and pools, eucalyptus groves and wild gardens of ginger and tropical plants. Rest stop with snacks and beverages included. Tours depart daily from Waipi'o Valley Artworks in Kukuihaele town at 9:30 a.m. and 1 p.m. Riders must be at least 16 years old, 100-300 pounds. Rates: $100 per person. P.O. Box 6368, Kamuela, HI 96743; 808-775-1701.

★ ***Mauna Kea Summit Adventures*** This operator specializes in evening-sunset and star-gazing tours via 4WD vehicle to the summit of 13,796-foot Mauna Kea and the telescope observatory complex. Pickups in Kona (Lanihau Center) and Kohala (Waikoloa Kings' Shops) are provided for the daily tour departure at 3 p.m., returning about 10:30 p.m.; parkas and hot drinks included. Rates: $144. P.O. Box 9027, Kailua-Kona, HI 96745; 888-322-2366; 808-322-2366; fax 808-322-6507; e-mail: kaymaunakeasummit@msn.com; www.maunakea.com.

★ ***Polynesian Adventure Tours*** This operator specializes in deluxe "Grand Circle Island Tour," a complete 260-mile, ten-hour drive around the island. All the major sites and attractions are included. Daily departures from Kona and Kohala Coast hotels in spacious, deluxe "big window" mini-coaches or mini-buses are 6:45 a.m. to 8:30 a.m., with return at 6 p.m. to 6:30 p.m. They also offer a special "Hawai'i Volcano Adventure" from Hilo area hotels departing at 9 a.m. and returning between 5-6 p.m. daily. The tours take in the major attractions of the Big Island and Volcanoes National Park. Rates: Grand Circle Island Tour (from Kona or Kohala Coast) $70.83 adults, $57.29 children under 12; Hawai'i Volcano Adventure (from Hilo) $50 adults, $39.58 children under 12. 73-4818 Kanalani Street, Kailua-Kona, HI 96740; 800-622-3011; 808-329-8008; fax 808-531-1357; e-mail: sales@polyad.com; www.polyad.com.

★ ***Robert's Hawai'i Inc.*** They offer mini-coach/motorcoach full-day "Grand Circle Island Tour" from Kona and Kohala Coast hotels, stopping at all the Big Island's major attractions and a "Volcano Special Tour" taking in the highlights of Hawai'i Volcanoes National Park. Rates: Circle Island Tour adults $55, children under 12 $48; Volcano Special Tour adults $52, children under 12 $36. Hilo International Airport, Hilo, HI 96720; P.O. Box 579, Kailua-Kona, HI 96740; 800-831-5541; 808-966-5983; 808-329-1688; www.roberts-hawaii.com.

★ ***Waipi'o Valley Shuttle & Tours*** These experienced guides specialize in comprehensive 4WD tours of the lush Waipi'o Valley and its history, culture and sense of place. Tours available Monday through Saturday at 9 a.m., 11 a.m., 1 p.m. and 3 p.m. (no 9 a.m. tour on Monday). Rates: $40 adults, $20 children under 12. P.O. Box 5128, Kukuihaele, HI 96727; 808-775-7121.

★ ***Waipi'o Valley Wagon Tours*** This operator takes guests on 1.5-hour adventure explorations in an old-fashioned mule-drawn wagon along the roadways and back lanes and across streams of the beautiful Waipi'o Valley on the Hamakua Coast. Fully narrated historical and cultural tour takes in majestic waterfalls, meandering streams, taro patches still being cultivated, lush tropical jungle rainforest and more. Cushioned seats and stable suspension provide a smooth and comfortable ride. The one-and-a-half-hour tours depart several times daily. Departures from the Last Chance Store in Kukuihaele just before Waipi'o Valley, with two tours daily, weather permitting. Rates: $40 adults, $20 children, free kids under 3. Honoka'a; 808-775-9518.

MOTORCYCLE AND MOPED ADVENTURES

Adventure-seeking visitors can rent motorized wheels to explore the backroads and byways of the Big Island. Operators rent everything from humble mopeds to Harley Hogs. It's recommended you have a motorcycle driver's license from your state of residence. Typical rates for motorcycles: Small Harley Sportster $90-$120 day; medium Heritage $100-$145 day; large Road King $140-$175 day. Motorscooters for two riders are $45 day; mopeds for one rider are $25 day. Check for the latest full-day and weekly rates, which are generally more inexpensive. Motorcycles, motorscooters and mopeds can be rented from the following outfitters/operators.

★ ***DJ's Rentals*** This outfitter rents a variety of two-wheeled machines. Big Road King Harleys rent for $140-$175 per day; Harley Heritage medium bikes for $100-$145 per day; small Harley Sportster bikes for $90-$120 per day. Motorscooters for two riders are $45 day; mopeds for one rider are $25 day. Across from the King Kamehameha Hotel and Kona Pier, 75-5663 Palani Road, Kailua-Kona, HI 96740; 800-993-HOGS; 808-329-1700; e-mail: rent@harleys.com; www.harleys.com.

★ ***Island RV/Safari Activities Rentals*** Motorscooter and moped rentals. 75-5785 Kuakini Highway, Kailua-Kona, and booth at Coconut Grove Marketplace, Ali'i Drive; 800-406-4555; 808-334-0464; e-mail: info@islandrv.com; www.islandrv.com.

★ ***Kona Harley Davidson*** This motorcycle dealer has a full range of Harley Davidson and Kawasaki motorcycles for rent. 74-5615 Luhia, Suite E, Kailua-Kona, HI 96740; 808-326-9887; e-mail kona hd@kona.net; www.konaharleydavidson.com.

T & K Motorcycles Inc. This Harley-Davidson dealer has a wide range of motorcycles for rent. 471 Kalanianaole Street, Hilo, HI 96720; 808-969-4991.

MUSEUMS

Big Island museums are small and personable. In the last 200 years, the island has radically changed-from a subsistence farming and fishing society to a diverse and growing American tourist destination. An hour or so invested in exploring one captures the colorful culture and history of a truly unique and special place. Each location has its own story to tell-from restored Hawaiian villages and *heiau*, to the last palace of the monarchy and missionary homes of the 1800s; from histories of the sugar cane plantations, which dominated life in east Hawai'i, and the coffee farms of Kona on the west side, and the *paniolo* culture on the huge ranches of Waimea. These museums introduce you to the diverse ethnic groups that immigrated here to work those industries, and details how their heritage, language and even food contribute to the Big Island's multicultural island style. There's a museum dedicated to tsunami, one perched on the edge of a volcanic crater and even one dedicated to space exploration.

Ellison S. Onizuka Space Center Located at the Kona International Airport, this memorial museum of space flight and astronaut lore is dedicated to Hawai'i's own son, Astronaut Ellison S. Onizuka, who was lost aboard the 1986 space shuttle disaster at Cape Canaveral. Colonel Onizuka was born and raised in Kona and grew up on his family's coffee farm. The museum features memorabilia from his career in space exploration and includes various hands-on exhibits and a piece of "moon rock" donated by NASA. Open daily 8:30 a.m. to 4:30 p.m. Admission: $3 adults, $1 children under 12. P.O. Box 833, Kailua-Kona, HI 96745; 808-329-3441.

★ ***Hulihe'e Palace Museum*** This attractive and imposing beachside structure was built in 1838 and used as a summer residence by the ruling Hawaiian monarchs. The palace is maintained by the Daughters of Hawai'i as a historical showcase of Hawaiian heritage and culture. The palace has some beautiful antique Hawaiian furniture, original bedroom furnishings, and antique handmade Hawaiian quilts and other memorabilia from the days of Hawaiian royalty. Open Monday through Friday 9 a.m. to 4 p.m., Saturday and Sunday 6 a.m. to 4 p.m. Admission: $4 per person. 75-5718 Ali'i Drive, Kailua-Kona, HI 96740; 808-329-1877.

Kamuela Museum This privately operated museum has a large collection of ancient Hawaiian weapons, World War II artifacts, furniture of Hawaiian royalty, and other art objects and antiques on display. Open daily 9 a.m. to 4 p.m. Admission: $5 adults, $2 children under 12. At the intersection of Highways 19 and 250 (Kohala Mountain Road) just west of Waimea town. 808-885-4724.

Kona Historical Society Museum Housed in the historic Greenwell Store, one half-mile south of Kealakekua town on Highway 11, this old stone country store maintains an extensive collection of historic manuscripts, photographs, maps and artifacts. It also houses displays and exhibits of early Kona ranching, coffee farming, related commercial activities and general lifestyle of the Big Island's Kona District. The museum is part of the old Greenwell Ranch. KHS also operates the **D. Uchida Farm** as a "Living History Farm." This is a seven-acre working coffee and macadamia nut farm. The farm's educational tours and programs help bring the history of Kona's coffee farming community alive through the use of historic buildings, authentic landscapes, artifacts, costumed interpreters and guides, live animals, working machinery and equipment and producing orchards and fields. Coffee farm tours are $20 per person; tours held Tuesday and Thursday only, 8:30 a.m. and 10:30 a.m. Museum hours are 9 a.m. to 3 p.m. weekdays; closed holidays. P.O. Box 398, Captain Cook, HI 96704; 808-323-3222; 808-323-2005.

Laupahoehoe Train Museum The museum preserves the Hamakua Coast's railroad heritage with historic displays and exhibits and welcomes visitors 9 a.m. to 4:30 p.m. Monday through Saturday and 10 a.m. to 2 p.m. Sunday. They're in progress on restoring some old train rolling stock and related displays. The museum serves as an official visitors center for the Hilo-Hamakua Heritage Coast Trail. Look for the brown Heritage Coast sign. Located in Laupahoehoe town at the intersection of the main street and Highway 19. P.O. Box 358, Laupahoehoe, HI 96764; 808-962-6300; fax 808-962-2221; e-mail: ltmhawaii@aol.com.

★ ***Lyman Museum & Mission House*** This is an early New England–style missionary home built in 1839 for Hilo missionaries Rev. David and Sarah Lyman. Next door to the original Lyman House is the modern museum building that holds a unique collection of memorabilia of early Hilo and Big Island lifestyles. Displays cover the pre-Western, old Hawaiian days, the missionary and Hawaiian monarchy era of the 1800s, and the vast changes brought by the 20th century. There are many cultural artifacts representing the various ethnic peoples, including Portuguese, Chinese, Japanese, Korean and Filipino, who immigrated to Hawai'i over the generations and made this their home. Tours offered daily, except Sunday, at 10 and 11 a.m. and 1, 2 and 3 p.m. Open daily 9:30 a.m. to 4:30 p.m. Admission: $7 adults, $5 seniors, $3 children 6 to 17, children under 6 free, $21 families. 276 Haili Street, Hilo, HI 96720; 808-935-5021; e-mail info@lyman museum.org; www.lymanmuseum.org.

Mauna Kea Visitors Center The Visitors Center, accessible by cars without four-wheel drive, has displays and a variety of programs about Mauna Kea and astronomy. Star-gazing lectures and hands-on telescope programs are conducted every evening from 6 to 10 p.m., weather permitting, using an 11-inch Celestron telescope. Mauna Kea summit day tours are conducted on Saturday and Sunday only at 1 p.m. These day tours depart from the visitors center in a vehicle convoy to the 13,796-foot mountain summit and the Mauna Kea Science Complex of observatories; 4WD vehicle required for summit tours. Families are encouraged to visit; however, participants must be at least 16 years old and in good health with no cardiac or breathing problems; pregnant women are not allowed. Visitors should dress for freezing conditions (30-40 degrees) and take adequate food and hot drinks as no services are available on the mountain. For weather updates and snow and road conditions on Mauna Kea, call 808-969-5582. Visitors Center open daily, 9 a.m. to 10 p.m. Located at the 9,200-foot elevation level (6.5 miles up the Mauna Kea Summit Road) off the Saddle Road between Hilo and Waimea/Kohala, Highway 200 (about 1 hour from Waimea or Kohala Coast). 808-961-2180.

★ ***Pacific Tsunami Museum*** This is one of the island's most unique and fascinating museums. It's located in the old First Hawaiian Bank along downtown Hilo's bayfront Kamehameha Avenue. Check the museum website for information and developments on current programs and displays. The museum serves as a repository of information and research for scholars on global tsunami and tidal wave phenomena and as an educational museum for the public. Museum displays and exhibits preserve the social and cultural history of the local community and serve as a living memorial to those who lost their lives in past tsunami in Hawai'i. Guided tours, movies of tsunami events, and interactive computer terminals are available, and there is a museum gift shop. Open Monday through Saturday 10 a.m. to 4 p.m. Admission: $5 per person. 130 Kamehameha Avenue, P.O. Box 806, Hilo, HI 96721; 808-935-0926; fax 808-935-0842; www.tsunami.org.

★ ***Parker Ranch Visitor Center*** The center is located in the Parker Ranch Shopping Center on Highway 19 in the heart of Waimea town. Here visitors can discover the fascinating history and operations of Parker Ranch and the Hawaiian *paniolo* lifestyle still in existence today. A large-screen video presentation highlights day-to-day ranching activities of the 100 or so ranch hands and cowboys employed by Parker Ranch. Enjoy browsing through the museum, which depicts the six generations of the Parker family through 150 years of ranching history. Open daily except Sunday, 9 a.m. to 4 p.m. Admission: $6.50 adults, $5.50 seniors, $5 children 4 to 11. P.O. Box 458, Kamuela, HI 96743; 808-885-7655; www.parkerranch.com.

Parker Ranch Historic Homes Another Parker Ranch Visitor Center attraction is the historic Parker Ranch home complex one mile west of Waimea on Highway 190. Here visitors can tour through Mana, the quaint New England–style house built by John Palmer Parker I in 1847. The interior is made entirely of native Hawaiian *koa* wood. Pu'u-opelu, built in 1862, is the main ranch residence, featuring an outstanding 8,000-square-foot art gallery with an impressive collection of original paintings plus many other *objets d'art* and antiques. The art collection was owned by the previous owner of Parker Ranch, Richard Smart. Pu'uopelu is open daily except Sunday, 9 a.m. to 5 p.m. Admission: $8.50 adults, $7.50 seniors, $6 children 4 to 11. 808-885-5433.

★ ***Thomas A. Jaggar Museum*** One of the Big Island's best, this museum and working science observatory is about 3 miles from the park entrance and main visitors center. Visitors, along with vulcanologists on 24/7 duty, watch multiple seismograph readings from the island's four active and dormant volcanoes, as well as the 20-year old eruption at Kilauea. You can even create your own earthquake at one exhibit. There is an awesome view of Halema'uma'u Crater, where the emptiness marked by steaming vents makes you marvel at what the forces of nature have created. Educational displays explain the formation of volcanoes and related geology with samples of many different kinds of lava rock, olivine crystals, "Pele's hair" and other products of eruptions. As interesting in a completely different way are the interpretive displays of Hawaiian mythology and religious culture created around the volcano. Admission included with national park admission ($10 per vehicle). P.O. Box 52, Hawai'i Volcanoes National Park, HI 96718-0052; 808-985-6000.

SCUBA DIVING (*See also* Sea Excursions; Snorkeling)

Dive Makai Charter Personalized diving cruises and personal service are the emphasis of this dive operator. Complete dive packages and equipment rentals are available. The basic 2-tank boat dive is $95 per person, departing Kailua Pier at 7:15 a.m., returning 1 p.m. 808-329-2025; www.divemakai.com.

★ ***Fair Wind*** Two Snorkel/Scuba Cruises and two Orca Rafting Adventures aboard *Fair Wind II*, a 60-foot catamaran with 100-passenger capacity, depart daily from Keauhou Bay pier. Cruises include snorkel gear and instruction, floats and water toys, with Snuba and custom videos as options. For snorkelers and scuba divers, the Luncheon Cruise, 9 a.m. to 1:30 p.m., includes continental breakfast and burgers for lunch. The Afternoon Cruise, 2 p.m. to 5:30 p.m., includes soft drinks and snacks. Raft Adventures are on *Orca*, a 28-foot hard-bottom power raft for excursions along the Kona Coast for close-up views of the sea caves, lava tubes and other formations of the rugged coastal area. Four-hour Morning Adventure, 8:30 a.m. to 12:30 p.m., and three-hour Afternoon Adventure, 1 p.m. to 4 p.m., include snorkel gear, instruction, snacks and soft drinks. Snorkel rates: Luncheon

Cruise $87 adults, $50 children 4 to 12; Afternoon Cruise $55 adults, $35 children 4 to 12. Children 3 and under free. Scuba rates: $122-$164 per person. Rafting Adventure rates: Morning $73 adults, $60 children 6 to 12; Afternoon $55 adults, $45 children 6 to 12. Children must be at least 6 to go on the raft. 78-7130 Kaleiopapa Street, Keauhou Bay, Kona, HI 96740; 800-677-9461; 808-322-2788; e-mail: snorkel@fair-wind.com; www.fair-wind.com.

★ ***Jack's Diving Locker*** This dive operator offers special scuba diving charters, night dives, instruction and certification, and complete diving equipment sales and rentals. Dive rates begin at $90 per person for 2-tank day dives, $95 per person for night dives. 75-5819 Ali'i Drive, Coconut Grove Marketplace, Kailua-Kona, HI 96740; 808-329-7585; 800-345-4807; e-mail: divejdl@gte.net.

★ ***Kona Aggressor II*** This is part of the international Aggressor Fleet of high-quality dive boat operations with sites in Micronesia, Tahiti and Fiji. The Kona dive operation features one-week trips with unlimited diving. Guests live aboard an 80-foot luxurious full-service diving yacht. There are private state rooms with bath, a 24-hour open galley, an onboard photo processing lab, and a sundeck. This is the ultimate in diving luxury. The boat accommodates up to 12 divers. The *Kona Aggressor* is a Handicapped Scuba Association–approved barrier-free vessel. Occasional special dive programs are also coordinated with Jean-Michel Cousteau Expeditions, which are led by famed international diver Jean-Michel himself. The Kona cruise includes all meals and bar beverages. Custom dive charters are available at special rates. Cruises depart Kailua Pier each Saturday. Rates range from $1,795-$1,895 per person for a week of cruising and diving. Reservations are suggested 30 days in advance. Live/Dive Pacific Inc., 74-5588 Pawai Place, Building F, Kailua-Kona, HI 96740; 800-344-5662; 808-329-8182; fax 808-329-2628; e-mail: livedive@compuserve.com; www.pacifiicagressors.com.

Aloha Dive Company This pro dive operator accesses some of the outermost dive sites of the Big Island; explore fabulous lava tubes and coral reef formations, see a myriad of marine species; blue water dives and night dives a specialty; top-of-line equipment. One-tank dives begin at $65. P.O. Box 4454, Kailua-Kona, HI 96745; 800-708-KONA; phone/fax 808-325-5560; www.alohadive.com.

East Hawai'i Divers This NAUI-certified outfitter specializes in custom tours and certification classes, scuba tours, snorkel tours, introductory dives and offers a full range of equipment rentals. Scuba tours begin at $45 person, snorkel tours at $30 person, introductory dives at $60. P.O. Box 2001, Pahoa, HI 96778; 808-965-7840.

★ ***Eco-Adventures*** This operator has a comprehensive range of services including daily boat dives, special night dives and manta ray

ASSORTED WATERSPORTS

Aloha Jet Ski is Kona's only jet ski company, renting Kawasaki equipment that handles up to three passengers at a time. Instruction and safety gear provided; must be 18 years old to rent and drive. Open daily 10 a.m. to 4 p.m. Rates: $75 for one hour, $50 for a half-hour. Located at Kailua Pier; 808-329-2SKI; e-mail: jetski@kona.net; www.alohajetskirentals.com. **Torpedo Tours** is something new: a battery-powered "torpedo" tows snorkelers or scuba divers along at 2 mph to get you where you want to be in the sea. Take off from the beach or boat on daily adventures scheduled for 9 a.m. and 2 p.m. from four locations. Rates: $46-$90 beach tours, $99-$129 boat tours. Instruction and specialty and private charters available. 808-938-0405; e-mail: torpedo@kona.net; www.torpedotours.com. The calmer waters of the Kailua Bay area are favorable for the exhilarating flights of parasailers. ★ **UFO Parasail of Kailua-Kona** provides adventure parasailing excursions high above the Kona Coast with departures from Kailua Pier. Take off from and land on a large powerboat that pulls the parasail through the sky for one or two passengers together. Exhilarating ride, panoramic views of the Kona Coast and something called optional "simulated free-fall" offered at no extra charge. Rates: "Atmospheric" travel $47 for 7 minutes at 400 feet, "Stratospheric travel" $57 for 10 minutes at 800 feet. P.O. Box 5438, Kailua-Kona, HI 96745; 808-325-5UFO; 808-325-5836; 800-FLY-4UFO; fax 808-331-2440; www.ufoparasail.com.

dives, introductory dives, scuba certification instruction, snorkeling and cruising plus kayaking, hiking, biking and other activities. Standard one-tank beach dives begin at $65; two-tank boat trips begin at $102; other guided dives and excursions available. King Kamehameha's Kona Beach Hotel, 75-5660 Palani Road, Kailua-Kona, HI 96740; 800-949-3483; 808-329-7116; fax 808-329-7091; www.ecodive.com.

Get Wet Kona This outfitter provides a range of boat charters, dive and snorkeling tours and complete dive equipment rentals. Kona Village Inn Shopping Center, 75-5744 Ali'i Drive, Kailua-Kona, HI 96740; 808-329-0046.

Honu Sports Dive equipment rentals, one- and two-tank morning dives, torpedo propulsion vehicles, night dives, instruction and scuba-kayak adventures. Rates: $79-$139 charters including equipment, snacks and cold drinks; torpedo $40 additional. Located on Ali'i Drive in downtown Kailua-Kona; 808-938-9795.

Kohala Divers Ltd. This shop offers a full range of professional diving services, equipment sales and rentals, and dive charters along the Kohala Coast. Open daily 8 a.m. to 6 p.m. Basic 2-tank, half-day boat dive is $99. Kawaihae Shopping Center, Kawaihae, HI 96743; 808-882-7774; www.kohaladivers.com.

★ ***Kona Coast Divers*** They offer diving charters and a full range of sales/service/rentals on professional diving equipment plus dive certification classes. Basic 2-tank half-day dives are $80 per person, departing 8 a.m. and returning 1 p.m. Night manta ray dives are $65-$99, also good for snorkelers. Children allowed if certified. Multidive discounts available. Open daily 7 a.m. to 6 p.m. 75-5614 Palani Road, Kailua-Kona, HI 96740; 800-KOA-DIVE; 808-329-8802; e-mail: divekona@ilhawaii.net; www.konacoastdivers.com.

Kona Honu Divers Complete menu of one-, two- and even three-tank day and night dives, instruction, gear rentals, seasonal whale watching, snuba, kayaking and snorkel adventures. Scuba specialty courses offered in Nitrox, night and deep diving, underwater photography and videography and more. Rates: $64.95-$164.95 for boat dives, $55 whale or dolphin cruise, $129.95-$474.95 instruction courses. Honokohau Small Boat Harbor, Kailua-Kona; 808-324-4668.

Manta Ray Dives of Hawai'i This operator features the 14-passenger glass-bottom dive boat, *Rainbow Diver II* and offers multidive packages and PADI certifications. Night-time dives for manta rays are a specialty but since the rays are somewhat unreliable, check ahead as to availability and best times. 800-982-6747; 808-325-1687; e-mail: rainbow@rainbowdiver.com; www.rainbowdiver.com.

★ ***Mauna Kea Divers*** Conveniently located near Kohala Coast resorts at Kawaihae Harbor, near the Blue Dolphin restaurant. Complete diving packages, underwater tours, charters and equipment rentals are available. Also offers PADI scuba certification, seasonal whale watching, personalized private charters and full-service dive shop. 63-3616 Kawaihae Road, Kawaihae, HI 96743-9721; 808-883-9298; www.maunakeadivers.com.

★ ***Nautilus Dive Center Inc.*** This shop features complete sales/service/rentals of professional diving equipment. They also provide PADI dive instruction and have a five-day certification program. Scuba charters along the East Hawai'i coast are available. Open Monday through Saturday 9 a.m. to 4 p.m. 382 Kamehameha Avenue, Hilo, HI 96720; 808-935-6939.

Ocean Eco Tours Full menu of beach and boat dives, instruction and certification, equipment rentals and private charters. Rates: $85 shore dive, $95 boat dive, $125 intro dive. Honokohau Small Boat Harbor; 808-324-7873; www.oceanecotours.com.

Pacific Rim Divers This operator has daily charters for up to six divers, plus they offer manta ray dives, introductory dives and full PADI certifications. Basic 2-tank daytime boat dives are $89, departing Honokohau Harbor at 8 a.m., returning at 1 p.m. P.O. Box 4602, Kailua-Kona, HI 96745; 808-334-1750; www.pacificrimdivers.com.

★ ***Planet Ocean Watersports*** This operator offers island-wide scuba dives to some of best locations; full PADI instruction and certification; full-service watersports, kayak and equipment rentals. They offer fully equipped and guided beach and shore dives. Rates are $40-$75 per person. 100 Kamehameha Avenue, Hilo, HI 96720; 808-935-7277; e-mail: scuba@hilo.net; www.hawaiidive.com.

★ ***Sandwich Isle Divers*** One of Kona's most reputable operators (and really nice people), this shop provides small charters, up to six passengers, with a fun, personable Big Island ocean experience. Daily scuba, snorkel and fishing cruises along the Kona Coast customized to your age group, interest and level of expertise for optimal pleasure in seeing lava tubes, coral reefs and tropical fish. Snorkel, scuba and boogieboard rentals, air fills, repairs and instruction, too. Open 8 a.m. to 8 p.m. daily. Basic 2-tank day dives are $80 ($95 with all gear included), departing Honokohau Harbor at 9 a.m., returning at 1:30 p.m.; 2-tank twilight dives $94/$110; 1-tank night dives $65/$75 per person. 75-5729 Ali'i Drive, Kona Marketplace, Kailua-Kona, HI 96740; 888-743-3483; 808-329-9188; fax 808-326-5652; e-mail: sandive@aloha.net; www.sandwichisledivers.com.

Sea Paradise Scuba This shop offers a full range of morning, afternoon and night dives as well as beginner dives and snorkeling outings on dive cruises. A complete line of equipment rentals is available. Cruises depart from Keauhou Bay dock. 78-7128 Kaleiopapa Road, Kailua-Kona, HI 96740; 800-322-5662; 808-322-2500.

SEA EXCURSIONS, SAILING, CRUISES (*See also* Scuba Diving; Snorkeling; Whale Watching)

The Big Island is big on boats. A playground for all kinds of water sports, it offers everything from deep-sea fishing charters to sunset cocktail sails, glass-bottom boat excursions, rubber raft adventures, scuba, snuba and snorkel cruises, Hawaiian sailing canoe voyages, and even a submarine dive. Most are concentrated in the Kailua-Kona area, or at the Kohala Coast resorts.

What's the difference between a pleasure cruise and a snorkel cruise? Not much! Thanks to the Big Island's fine fleet of activity craft, most boats can offer a visiting family as much, or as little, adventure and participation as they choose. Generally, basic recreational sightseeing or snorkel cruises sail along the Kona Coast, taking in historic sites such as Kealakekua Bay State Historical & Underwater Parks and the Captain Cook Monument, and the Pu'uhonua o Honaunau National Historic Park at Honaunau. Cruises are usually half-day in length, with morning departures. Snorkel equipment and towels are normally included along with refreshments—from light snacks to full lunch with open bar. Prices vary accordingly, and it's a good policy to ask what's included. Whale-watching adventures are seasonal from about December to March, when humpbacks occupy the warm Hawaiian waters to bear their young. Some whale species can be spotted year-round, along with worlds of colorful tropical fish, sea turtles and dolphins. If your idea of an idyllic day on the ocean is relaxing on the sun deck while the kids snorkel and Uncle Harry hooks a sportfish, you can do that. Many of the listings here are cross-referenced under more than one category, and if you don't see what you're looking for, we invite you to ask the reservationists, who we've found to be knowledgeable and friendly.

★ ***Aloha Adventure Cruises*** The 65-foot *Coral See* is a 149-passenger luxury glass-bottom yacht and does two daily Kona Coast Dolphin Eco-Adventure cruises; seasonal whale-watching cruises. Local historians narrate each cruise, detailing the culture, history and background of the Kona area. Enjoy the splendid coastal views from the covered top deck and gaze below through the glass-bottom windows to see a myriad of marine life, from turtles, dolphins and manta rays to colorful tropical reef fish. The Kona Coast Dolphin Eco-Adventure cruise departs daily at 9:30 a.m. and 12 noon. There is also a Sunset Cocktail Cruise (includes two cocktails per adult) several evenings each week at 5:15 p.m. Cruises depart from Kailua-Kona pier; tour office across from Pier below Galley Restaurant. Rates for Eco-Adventure and Sunset cruises are adults $44, children 11 to 16 years $24, youngsters free. 75-5663 Palani Road, Kailua-Kona, HI 96740; 808-331-2992.

Big Island Water Sports Offering something for ocean-lovers of all ages, Big Island Water Sports provides a full range of snorkel, kayak, snuba, scuba, seasonal whale watching and private charters. Tours include equipment, instruction and underwater guide. Underwater cameras and digital video available. P.O. Box 9020, Kailua-Kona, HI 96745; 808-324-1650; fax 808-324-4719; e-mail: fun@bigislandwatersports.com; www.bigislandwatersports.com.

Capt. Bean's Dinner Cruise A longstanding Kona tradition, this sunset dinner cruise aboard Capt. Bean's Polynesian-style double-hulled catamaran departs Kailua Pier daily at around 5 p.m. (varies with sunset). Cruise along the famous Kona Coast to live island music and entertainment, with open bar and all-you-can-eat buffet and beverages. Adults 21 and over only. Call for reservations and transportation pick-up at area hotels and condos. Rates from Kailua-Keauhou hotels $55 per person, from Kohala Coast hotels $63-$66 per person. Aloha

ATLANTIS SUBMARINES

If you're a scuba diver or snorkeler, do that. If you're not, we recommend a voyage with **Atlantis Submarines**. This air-conditioned submersible craft goes down 150 feet to introduce you to a galaxy of tropical fish, marine life and coral, and possibly a shark or barracuda, as close as you can get without getting wet. Departing from King Kamehameha's Kona Beach Hotel pier, a cutter takes you out to the *Atlantis* mooring, where it's an easy transfer down into the submarine. Passengers sit on two long rows facing multiple windows, and the ride is smooth and easy, not queasy. Fish identification cards are mounted along the windows and a knowledgeable narrator tells you everything you need to know. If you've taken Atlantis Sub trips before, we say you haven't done it in Hawai'i. Daily cruises depart 10 a.m., 11:30 a.m. and 1 p.m. from Kailua Pier. Adults $84, children under 12 $42 for morning cruises; $69 adults, $39 children for afternoon. 75-5660 Ali'i Drive, Kailua-Kona, HI 96740; 808-329-6626; fax 808-329-1153; www.goatlantis.com.

attire is preferred. 73-4800 Kanalani Street, Suite 200, Kailua-Kona, HI 96740; 808-329-2955; www.robertshawaii.com.

★ ***Captain Zodiac*** Daily expeditions in motorized inflatable rubber white-water rafts along the Kona Coast. Explore sea caves and old Hawaiian village sites, and snorkel in Kealakekua Bay marine reserve on a four-hour cruise. Snorkel equipment and tropical snacks included. Two cruises daily at 8:15 a.m. and 1 p.m. Rates: $78 adults, $63 children under 12. 74-425 Kealakehe Parkway, Honokohau Harbor, Kailua-Kona, HI 96740; 800-422-7824; 808-329-3199; fax 329-7590; e-mail: seakona@interpac.net; www.captainzodiac.com.

★ ***Dolphin Discoveries*** This operator does small-group (6 people max) whale and dolphin watching tours plus snorkeling excursions with a 26-foot Nautica raft vessel; snorkel gear is provided. Tours by dedicated marine mammal naturalists focus on respect for and education about whales and dolphins and Hawaii's underwater world. Explorations of Kona Coast lava tubes, sea caves and beautiful coral reefs along Kealakekua Bay and Honaunau Bay are unforgettable. Morning cruise 8:30 a.m. to 12:30 p.m. includes refreshments; afternoon cruise 12:30 p.m. to 3:30 p.m. Departures from Keauhou Bay, just south of Kailua-Kona. Morning cruise adults $78, children under age 12 $59; afternoon cruise adults and children $59. 77-116 Queen Kalama, Kailua-Kona, HI 96740; 808-322-8000; e-mail: dolphindiscoveries@aloha.net; www.dolphindiscoveries.com

Dolphin Journeys Captain Nancy guides half-day or full-day excursions to encounter dolphins and ocean scenery along the Kona coast. Her unique approach to the experience also includes week-long dolphin seminars several times each year. Custom journeys welcomed. 75-5822 Pelekila Place, Kailua-Kona, HI 96740; 808-329-3030; e-mail: new@aloha.net, www.dolphinjourneys.com.

Dream Cruises A "barefoot fun cruise," sailing along the Kona coastline for swimming, snorkeling or relaxing on the sundeck while the kids enjoy a water trampoline, kick boards, "water noodles" and other toys. Continental breakfast, deli lunch and soft drinks are included with no-host bar on board. Daily sails 9 a.m. to 1 p.m. Rates: $74.95 adults, $39.95 children 4 to 12. Dream Cruises also offers the Island Grill dinner cruise nightly 5:30 p.m. to 7:30 p.m. with a fresh gourmet menu, welcome mai tai, live entertainment and no-host bar aboard the trimaran *Kona Dream*. Rates: $49.95 adults, $32.95 children 4 to 12. 808-326-6000; 800-400-7300; fax 808-592-5214; e-mail: aloha@dream-cruise.com; www.dream-cruises.com.

Hawai'i Sailing Company Inc. This operator offers a variety of sailings and cruises including half-day and weekly cruises, picnic sails, whale watching and snorkeling. Departures from Honokohau Harbor. 44-2050 Kaapahu Road, Pa'auilo, HI 96776; 808-776-1505.

Honu Sail Charters Half-day, full-day and sunset sails out of Honokohau Small Boat Harbor. 808-896-HONU.

In to Spirit, Inc. Two-hour marine mammal ocean adventures departing daily from Honokohau Harbor just north of Kailua-Kona. The vessel *Lilikoi* accommodates up to 16 "fun-filled" passengers on a search for seasonal humpback whales, Hawaiian spinner, spotted and bottlenose dolphins, pilot whales, sea turtles and their neighbors. Certified marine mammal naturalist provides narration; light snacks/ beverages provided. Rates: 8 a.m. to 12 p.m. adults $69, children $42; Afternoon whale watching 1 p.m. to 4 p.m. (seasonal) adults $45, children $35. 808-936-1470; www.dolphinshawaii.com.

★ ***Kailua Bay Charter Co.*** *Marian*, a 36-foot glass-bottom tour boat, accommodates 32 passengers on hour-long cruises around Kailua Bay to observe the underwater coral reefs and marine life. Cruises go slow over the reefs so you can see things. Expert guided narration highlights what you see. Daily cruises at 10 a.m., 11 a.m. and 1 p.m., or by demand, and depart from Kailua Pier. Rates: adults $25, children 7 to 12 $10, youngsters free. P.O. Box 112, Holualoa, HI 96725; 808-324-1749; fax 808-324-0413; e-mail: info@konaglassbottom boat.com; www.glassbottomboat.com.

Kale Kai Half-day and full-day sailing charters plus two- to three-hour champagne sunset sails aboard a 42-foot Morgan racing sloop. Six-person maximum. Honokohau Small Boat Harbor, slip J48, P.O. Box 1084, Kailua-Kona, HI 96745; 808-960-3367.

Kona Dream This cruise operator provides affordable private charters for dolphin and whale watching experiences and snorkeling excursions along the Kona Coast. The Dolphin Eco-Adventure Cruise is daily at 1:30 p.m. to 4 p.m. and includes cruising along the Kona Coast to sight dolphins, seasonal whales, and other marine life. The Lanikila Snorkel Cruise is twice daily at 9 a.m. and 1 p.m. The snorkel cruise includes light snacks, beverages and snorkel gear. Dolphin Eco-Adventure adults $37, children under 12 $25; snorkel cruise adults $70, children under 12 $40. 75-5744 Ali'i Drive, Kailua-Kona, HI 96740; 808-326-6000.

Maile Charters One of the most familiar boats in Kawaihae, this long-standing operator with 20 years of sailing experience offers a variety of special adventure cruises aboard the 50-foot Gulfstar *Maile*, including overnight and interisland outings, whale watching, snorkeling and scuba diving explorations along the Kohala Coast, ecology tours, fishing, sunset sails and private custom cruises from half a day to five days including food and soft drinks. With advance notice, *Maile*'s experienced crew is happy to cater to your individual dining and alcoholic beverage requests (additional costs may apply). Rates: $575 half day for 6 passengers ($39 each additional), $950 full day for 6 ($52 additional), $2,700-$3,700 three-day cruise, $4,500-$5,500 five-day cruise. P.O. Box 44335, Kamuela, HI 96743; 800-726-SAIL; 808-326-5174; fax 808-882-7689; e-mail: sailing@adventuresailing.com; www.adventuresailing.com.

★ ***Ocean Sports-Waikoloa*** Specialists in making the most of anybody's ocean experience with champagne sunset sails, guaranteed (seasonal) whale watching with marine naturalist, scuba lessons, one- and two-tank dives, snorkel/picnic sails, exclusive deep-sea fishing charters, and awesome glass-bottom boat cruises over coral gardens. Beach toys, equipment rentals and instruction available. Picnic/Snorkel Sail $79 adults, $39 children; Kayak Adventure $85 adults, $42 children; Whale watching $59 adults, $39 children; Glass-bottom Boat $19 adults, $9 children; Champagne Sunset Sail $69 adults, $39 chil-

BOAT RENTALS

Captain Cruise Boat Rental rents "mini yachts," pontoon boats fully outfitted with ice chest, propane BBQ, CD player, cellphone, maps, fishing and snorkel gear for up to six people. No license or experience necessary to enjoy the feel of your own boat in Kona's friendly waters. Rates $49 per hour, $180 half day, $350 full day. In Kailua-Kona; 808-329-4977. With **Kona Boat Rentals** you take your own boat out to sightsee, fish or snorkel without a license or a crowd. Fishing and snorkel gear, maps and more. 808-326-9155; 800-311-9189.

dren; Scuba $59-$139. Private charters welcomed. Located on 'Anaeho'omalu Beach in front of the Waikoloa Beach Marriott, 69-275 Waikoloa Beach Drive, Kohala Coast, HI 96743; 808-886-6666; 800-SAIL234; www.hawaiioceansports.com.

★ ***Red Sail Sports*** Everything from luxury catamaran cruises aboard the 50-foot *Noa Noa* to deluxe snorkel and scuba sails aboard the 38-foot Delta dive boat *Lani Kai*. Sunset cocktail sails, seasonal whale watching and a complete line of water sports equipment and toy rentals—plus bicycle adventures and watersport/hotel packages. Transportation provided from nearby hotels. Snorkel Cruise $68-$75 adults, $34-$37.50 children; Sunset Sail $53-$59 adults, $26.50-$29.50 children; Whale Watch $59 adults, $29.50 children; Scuba $39-$159. 425 Waikoloa Beach Drive, Hilton Waikoloa Village, Kohala Coast, HI 96743; 877-RED-SAIL; 808-886-2876; fax 808-886-4169; and Hapuna Beach Prince Hotel at Mauna Kea Resort, 808-880-1111; e-mail: redsailsport@yahoo.com; www.redsail.com.

SKIING

To the surprise of many, visitors can enjoy some fabulous seasonal snow skiing on the Big Island, the only place in Hawai'i where it is possible. It's strictly a seasonal activity, and at best is sporadic and unpredictable given the erratic nature of snowfall on Mauna Kea the past few winters. However, from approximately November through March (sometimes as late as May), the nearly 14,000-foot summit of Mauna Kea can be covered with snow. When conditions are just right, skiers can enjoy some incredible downhill runs on the treeless slopes. The experience is one of a kind, but not without its negatives. The run is rocky and deceptive; weather conditions on the mountain change suddenly and there are no ski lifts, lodge, restrooms, medical help, emergency phone or any facilities whatsoever on the summit. A 4WD vehicle is almost always required.

On the bright side, however, there is one ski tour operator specializing in Mauna Kea ski tours. **Ski Guides Hawai'i** offers complete package tours to Mauna Kea on snow days, including 4WD transportation, ski rental, equipment and lunch. P.O. Box 1954, Kamuela, HI 96743; 808-885-4188.

SNORKELING

Body Glove Cruises This 55-foot trimaran offers daily morning and afternoon Snorkel-Dolphin Sails along the Kona Coast to Pawai Bay. Departures from Kailua Pier at 9 a.m. and 2 p.m. Continental breakfast, deli lunch and premium bar included in the morning sail (4.5 hours); snacks and premium bar in the afternoon (3 hours). Snorkel adventures include exploration of caves and sea arches to meet

Hawai'i's rich marine life, dolphins, manta rays and turtles. Snorkel gear and instruction, towels, flotation and water toys (including a 15-foot water slide) included. Upgrade to Scuba Diving available morning and afternoon. Transportation available from nearby hotels ($20 adults, $16 children from Kohala Coast resorts). Rates: Morning $84 adults, $46 children 6 to 12; Afternoon $52 adults, $32 children 6 to 12; Seasonal whale watching $48 adults, $29 children 6 to 12. Children 5 and under free. Upgrade to Scuba, $40-$60 per person. P.O. Box 4523, Kailua-Kona, HI 96745; 800-551-8911; 808-326-7122; fax 808-326-7123; e-mail: bcruises@gte.net; www.bodyglovehawaii.com.

★ ***Kamanu*** This is a beautiful 36-foot catamaran offering two daily snorkeling cruises along the Kona Coast. Each 3.25-hour cruise includes 1.5 hours of snorkeling time plus all gear, instruction, drinks and a light tropical lunch. Good for beginning snorkelers, novices or experts. Hand-feed colorful fish at Pawai Bay. Cruises depart daily from Honokohau Harbor at 9 a.m. and 1:30 p.m. Rates: $65 adults, $45 children under 12. P.O. Box 2021, 74-425 Kealakehe Parkway #16, Kailua-Kona, HI 96745; 800-348-3091; 808-329-2021; fax 808-329-7590; e-mail: info@kamanu.com; www.kamanu.com.

Pacific Passion This operator runs the 40-foot *Pacific Passion* fast pleasure craft, combining a snorkel and kayak boat tour accommodating up to 26 passengers. Cruise to pristine snorkel and kayak shores, coves, reefs and secluded beaches along the Kona Coast. Various cruise tours available. Morning snorkel/kayak cruise, 9 a.m. to 1 p.m., $79 adults, $49 children; afternoon seasonal whale-watching cruise (call for times) $57 adults, $36 children; afternoon seasonal snorkel/kayak cruise, 1:30 to 4:30 p.m., $57 adults, $36 children. Private charters available. 75-5629 Kuakini Highway, Suite R651,

WATERSPORTS RENTALS

Miller's Snorkel & Surf rents all types of watersports and beach equipment including masks, snorkels, fins, flotation vests, beach chairs, boogieboards, viewing boards, picnic coolers, umbrellas and surfboards by the day or the week. Open daily 8 a.m. to 5 p.m. 76-6246 Ali'i Drive #102, three miles south of Kailua-Kona at the Kona Bali Kai Condo; 808-326-1771; fax 808-326-1772. Just about anything you'd ever want to get wet is available from local legend **Snorkel Bob's**. This outfitter offers complete snorkeling equipment rentals including mask, fins, sterilized snorkel, underwater cameras and boogieboards. Rates start at $2.50 for smaller items; $15 for snorkel gear, $9-$46 for cameras. 75-5831 Kahakai Road, Kailua-Kona, HI 96740; 808-329-0770; www.snorkelbobs.com.

Kailua-Kona, HI 96740; 877-KONASUN; 808-325-0766; e-mail: info@pacificpassion.com; www.pacificpassion.com.

★ ***Sea Quest Rafting Adventure*** This operator offers snorkeling cruises with inflatable boats taking in the remote areas between Keauhou Bay and Honaunau. The cruises take in sea caves, lava tubes, Captain Cook's Monument at Kealakekua Bay and the Pu'uhonua o Honaunau National Historic Park at Honaunau, with diving time allowed. Cruises include morning (8 a.m. to noon.) or afternoon (1 to 4 p.m.) adventures; rates include snacks, beverages and snorkel gear. P.O. Box 390292, Kailua-Kona, HI 96739; 888-SEA-CAVE; 808-329-7238; e-mail: equest@kona.net; www.seaquestrafting.com.

Aquatic Perceptions Multi-Sports Tours This outfitter provides kayaking and snorkeling tours with guided excursions around Hilo Bay, the Hamakua Coast and the Puna Coast areas. Instruction and full range of equipment rentals also available. RR3, Box 1450, Pahoa, HI 96778; 808-935-9997; e-mail: kayakscuba@aol.com; www.multi-sport-hawaii.com.

SNUBA (*See also* Scuba Diving; Sea Excursions; Snorkeling)

Snuba provides a way for the novice to experience the sensation of diving without restrictive equipment or lengthy instruction. Air supply is contained on a floatation device, with a 25-foot air hose and regulator that allows the diver to go on guided underwater tours. Snuba Beach Dives daily at 9 a.m., 11 a.m., 1 p.m. and 3 p.m.; Boat Snuba Dives 9 a.m. to 1:30 p.m. Beach Dives $69 adults, $34.50 children; Boat Dives $132 adults, $95 children. P.O. Box 9020, Kailua-Kona, HI 96745; 808-326-7446; www.snubabigisland.com.

SPAS AND HEALTH RETREATS

For a soulful experience of a physical nature, consider a relaxing day of soothing massage and body therapies in tranquil, mindful environments. The Big Island is home to some truly excellent spas, most concentrated in the Kohala Coast resorts. Spa therapies include some Hawaiian options like traditional *lomi lomi* massage, heated stone relaxation, tropical aromatherapy, or exotic body wraps and scrubs using Hawaiian herbs, aloe, ti leaf, sea salt or seaweed, even poi and Kona coffee. The facilities are generally excellent and some offer beautiful, private outdoor massage locations near the ocean or a wooded waterfall. Policies change, and although the spas are designed for resort guests, they are usually open to the public for a nominal day charge.

Whether you're staying in one of these luxury properties or not, we invite you to experience a "day of beauty" as a very special indulgence during your stay. As always, please call in advance and avoid disappointment.

Kohala Sports Club & Spa This 25,000-square-foot facility has everything from whirlpools, weight rooms, aerobics, yoga, tai chi, sauna and steam baths to a full-service beauty salon and a delightful variety of massage, body treatments and other spa therapies. Hilton Waikoloa Village, Kohala Coast; 808-886-2828, www.kohalaspa.com.

Spa Without Walls The Spa Without Walls, one of the best healing facilities on the island, has undergone an extensive renovation and enhancements to its extensive menu of massage and body therapies and salon treatments. Featuring a variety of private, outdoor settings that incorporate Hawai'i's therapeutic natural environment and ancient healing arts, Spa Without Walls also employs unique practices such as "art as healer" classes, "power walks" through lava trails, ayurvedic elemental treatments and the "BodyTalk System" of self-healing and synchronization, along with more familiar options such as yoga and meditation sessions, and soothing aromatherapies with local products. Fairmont Orchid, Kohala Coast; 808-887-7540.

Mauna Lani Spa Mauna Lani Spa offers spa treatments in a quaint indoor/outdoor setting designed to resemble a Hawaiian village, with nine individual thatched *hale* (huts). Features include a lava-sauna, healing herb and fragrance garden, a selection of massage styles, body therapies, yoga, meditation, consultations and more. Admission to the spa is $25, or complimentary with a scheduled spa treatment. Mauna Lani Resort, Kohala Coast; 808-881-7922.

Hualalai Sports Club & Spa This is one of the best on the island, presenting state-of-the-art exercise equipment, expert fitness classes from yoga to kickboxing, an eight-court tennis club (four lighted), open-air gym, 25-meter lap pool, basketball and volleyball courts, saunas and steam rooms, and nine individual *hale* for an eclectic range of massage therapies and body treatments. There's also a 24-foot climbing wall, with special Junior Climb for kids 8 to 14. Four Seasons Resort Hualalai, Kaupulehu-Kona; 808-325-8440.

If a luxury day spa is not in your budget, don't worry-there are numerous licensed massage therapists in almost every neighborhood. We refer you to your hotel or condo concierge desk or the Yellow Pages. Please note that "adult" massage service is not at all common here, so you can call advertised massage services with confidence.

You might also contact the following:

Big Island Academy of Massage 201 Kino'ole Street, Hilo; 808-935-1405.

Hawaiian Islands School of Body Therapy 81-6587 Mamalahoa Highway, Captain Cook; 808-323-3800; e-mail: massages@gte.net; www.hawaiianmassageschool.com.

On a slightly different level, the Big Island has earned a new nickname in recent years: the "Healing Island." This is not only due to the increasing variety of alternative healing therapies available, but to some very sound, state-of-the-art Western medicine as well. Because of the diverse ethnic population, as well as the mid-Pacific geographic location, the Big Island can bring together Eastern and Western practices in a nearly perfect climate for healing work of many different kinds. The **North Hawai'i Community Hospital** in Waimea incorporates not only Eastern practices such as acupuncture and massage into its everyday operation, but alternative therapies like "healing touch" energy work and specially designed architecture, natural lighting and custom-written house music. 808-885-4444; www.planet-hawaii.com/nhch.

In line with that, groups such as **Five Mountain Medical** work to promote the island as a special healing destination, encouraging health professionals not only to visit but to work and research here in the unique environment. Many doctors have already begun projects that bridge the gap between high-tech machines and low-tech cultural healing practices. 808-887-1280; www.fivemtn.org.

SURFING, WINDSURFING, KITE SURFING

The Big Island is not world-famous for surfing like the North Shore of Oahu, or for aerial windsurfing like Maui. Easygoing tradewinds and gentler ocean conditions prevail most of the year, although in winter months the western shores might see the 10- to 15-foot sets surfers wait for all year long. On all Big Island beaches, generally speaking, conditions are favorable year-round for boogieboarding, body surfing, sailing and windsurfing-depending on the mood of Mother Nature. The Kona and Kohala areas have more availability of facilities and rentals for these activities, as well as more consistent sunshine, but keep an eye on the weather and don't rule out the Hilo side and its share of great beaches, too.

Big Island Kite Surfing A fun challenge, perfect for the Big Island's uncrowded waters and consistent weather conditions. You stand on a small surfboard with straps and the wind pulls you across the water, thanks to a large kite high overhead. We have not tried this, but it's wild to watch. Instruction, equipment rentals and purchase available. 808-960-2785; e-mail: wndridr@hotmail.com.

Hawai'i Life Guard Surf Instructors This operator features trained and certified professional life guards who provide safe surfing instruction for beginner or advanced. Lessons are usually held in the Kona area. 808-324-0442; cell 808-938-3583; e-mail: tuberider@rocketmail.com.

Ocean Eco Tours Surfing lessons for groups or individuals at Kona's #1 surf school as well as equipment rentals. Rates: $85-$225 surf lessons. Honokohau Small Boat Harbor; 808-324-7873; www.oceanecotours.com.

Ocean Safari's Kayaks This operator has group or private surfing lessons and board rentals. Surf lessons: $65 group, $85 private. P.O. Box 515, Kailua-Kona, HI 96745; 808-326-4699; fax 808-322-3653; e-mail: kayakhi@gte.net; www.oceansafariskayaks.com.

Surfin Safari's Surfing lessons and surf adventures with Hawai'i lifeguard certified instructors. Waves may be subject to Mother Nature. Rates: $75 4-hour safari, $110 6-hour surf camp (includes snacks). 808-326-4699; www.surfinsafaris.com.

SWIMMING POOLS

The County of Hawai'i maintains seven free public swimming pools around the island. These facilities are generally excellent and include full programs of swimming and aquatics instruction, adult lap swimming, and open recreational swimming hours daily and weekly. For specific daily and weekly schedules of activities contact the individual pools listed.

Kona District Kona Community Aquatic Center, Old Kona Airport Park complex, 808-327-3500; and Kona Swimming Pool, Konawaena High School, Kealakekua, 808-323-3252

Kohala Coast Kohala Swimming Pool, Kamehameha Park in Kapa'au; 808-889-6933

Hamakua Coast Honoka'a Swimming Pool, Honoka'a High School, 808-775-0650; and Laupahoehoe Swimming Pool, Laupahoehoe High School, 808-962-6993

Hilo Kawamoto Swim Stadium, at Ho'olulu Stadium Complex, 808-961-8698; and NAS Swimming Pool, which stands for Naval Air Station, is a remnant of Hilo's World War II military airfield, at the old Hilo Airport Terminal, 808-961-8697

Puna District Puna Pahoa Swimming Pool, Pahoa; 808-965-2700

Ka'u District Pahala Swimming Pool, Ka'u High School, Pahala; 808-928-8177

TENNIS

Public Courts

The County of Hawai'i maintains a number of tennis courts at county parks and locations around the island. Some are lighted for evening use and are basically on a first-come, first-served basis.

For a map detailing public tennis court locations around the island contact the Department of Parks and Recreation, County of Hawai'i, 25 Aupuni Street, Hilo, HI 96720; 808-961-8311.

The following is a listing of the public tennis court facilities around the island.

Kona District *Greenwell Park* in Captain Cook; *Higashihara Park* in Keauhou; *Kailua Park* at Old Kona Airport; *Kailua Playground* on Kuakini Highway near town.

Kohala Coast *Kamehameha Park* in Kapa'au town; *Waimea Park* in Waimea-Kamuela town.

Hamakua Coast *Honoka'a Park* in Honoka'a town; *Papa'aloa Park* in Papa'aloa Village.

Hilo *Edith Kanakaole Tennis Stadium* has 3 indoor lighted courts and 5 outdoor courts. Reservations suggested. Rates: $2 per hour for indoor courts 9 a.m. to 4 p.m., $4 per hour 4 p.m. to 10 p.m. Corner of Pi'ilani and Kalanikoa streets; 808-961-8720. There are also *Ainaola Park*, *Hakalau Park*, *Lincoln Park*, *Lokahi Park*, *Malama Park*, *Mohouli Park* and *Panaewa Park* (most of these are right in the Hilo town area).

Puna District *Kurtistown Park* on the highway in Kurtistown; *Shipman Park* at junction of Volcano and Pahoa highways in Kea'au town.

Ka'u District *Na'alehu Park* on the highway through Na'alehu town; *Pahala School Grounds* at the school in Pahala Village.

Private Tennis Courts Open to the Public

While tennis is currently not enjoying the same boom as golf, this is good news for the recreational player who wants to take advantage of Hawai'i's great weather to play a few sets. Court times are generally easy to book and relatively inexpensive. The following are mostly hotel/resort private courts that are open to the public on a user-fee basis. Many offer a game-matching service, locker rooms and rentals, but may have a dress code, so please ask first.

Fairmont Orchid Hawai'i The Tennis Pavilion has ten hard-surface courts, seven lighted for night play, a stadium court, and full-service pro shop. Daily clinics, instruction, ball machine rental. Rates: $12.50 per day, unlimited play. 1 North Kaniku Drive, Kohala Coast; 808-885-2000.

Hilton Waikoloa Village Kohala Tennis Shop features eight plexi-cushion courts and a tournament stadium. Full-service pro shop, equipment rentals and sales, ball machine and instruction available. Rates: $30 per person all day. 425 Waikoloa Beach Drive, Kohala Coast; 808-886-1234.

King Kamehameha's Kona Beach Hotel Operated by Bondallian Tennis, the hotel property has four hard-surface courts with two lighted for night play. Full-service pro shop, instruction, rentals and sales available. Open Monday through Saturday 8 a.m. to 5 p.m., Sunday 8 a.m. to 12 noon. Courts lighted until 9 p.m. with pre-paid reservation. Rates: $5 per person for one hour, $10 per person all day. 75-5660 Palani Road, Kailua-Kona; 808-334-9889.

Mauna Kea Tennis Shop One of the largest tennis facilities in the state, with 11 plexi-pave tennis courts stretched along breathtaking oceanfront property. Quality pro shop arranges court times, matching, lessons and clinics, ball machine, video lessons, racquet stringing and rentals. Great line of tennis attire, accessories and gear. Air-conditioned locker rooms, shaded refreshment lanai. Rates: $12.50 per person per day, unlimited play. Mauna Kea Resort, 62-100 Mauna Kea Beach Drive, Kohala Coast; 808-882-5420.

Mauna Lani Bay Hotel & Bungalows Mauna Lani offers two separate tennis facilities: the Tennis Garden with ten hard-surface courts, and the Racquet Club with six hard-surface courts (three lighted for night play) and a stadium court. Full-service pro shop, instruction, rental equipment and sales on-site. Rates: $20 per hour court fee. 68-1400 Mauna Lani Drive, Kohala Coast; 808-885-6622.

Ohana Keauhou Beach Resort They have six hard-surface courts, two lighted for night play; pro shop available. Open 7:30 a.m. to 5 p.m. Courts lighted until 10 p.m. with advance reservations. Rates: $5 per person for one hour, $10 per person all day. 78-6740 Ali'i Drive, Keauhou-Kona, HI 96740; 808-322-7987.

Waikoloa Beach Marriott, An Outrigger Resort The Tennis Club has six hard-surface courts, full-service pro shop, private and group instruction available, equipment rentals and sales. Rates: $10 per day, unlimited play. 69-275 Waikoloa Beach Drive, Kohala Coast; 808-886-6789.

Royal Kona Resort The Tennis Club has four hard-surface courts, three lighted for night play; pro shop available. Rates: $10 for one person all day, $15 for two people all day. 75-5852 Ali'i Drive, Kailua-Kona; 808-329-3111.

THEATERS

Movie Theaters

There are a number of movie theaters around the island that show first-run movies on a regular daily schedule. Theaters in Hilo and Kailua-Kona are modern, stadium-style facilities with multiple screens and snack bars. Aloha Theatre in Kainaliu, Kahilu Theatre in Waimea and the People's Theater in Honoka'a show movies on weekends. Check local newspapers for times and titles.

Akebono Theater Pahoa Town, Puna District; 808-965-9943

Aloha Theatre Not just for movies, this restored classic offers live performances on occasion and the added benefit of a great restaurant, the Aloha Angel Café. 79-7384 Mamalahoa Highway, Kainaliu town; 808-322-2323

Honoka'a Peoples Theater Honoka'a Town, Hamakua Coast; 808-775-0000

Kahilu Theatre Parker Ranch Center, Waimea town; 808-887-6368

Keauhou Cinemas Keauhou Shopping Center, Keauhou, Kona; 808-324-7200

Kress Cinemas 174 Kamehameha Avenue, downtown Hilo; 808-961-3456

Na'alehu Theatre Na'alehu, South Kona; 808-929-9133

Prince Kuhio Theaters Prince Kuhio Shopping Plaza, Hilo; 808-959-4595

Stage Productions/Performances

For information on stage productions, hula performances, band, choral and orchestra concerts and other shows, contact any of the following community theaters for details. A community production, especially as part of one of the cultural festivals, can make a great memory for your Big Island vacation. Please call for schedule and ticket information.

Hilo Community Players 141 Kalakaua, Hilo; 808-935-9155

Kahilu Theatre The Big Island's best facility for live performances, Kahilu was established by the late Richard Smart of the Parker Ranch *ohana* (family) to bring elements of culture to the Waimea community, and create an avenue for his own off-Broadway talents. A full season of varied international concerts and dance performances is presented, along with youth theater workshops, "circus camp," first-run movies and annual appearances by Hawai'i's celebrated Cazimero Brothers and the Honolulu Symphony. Parker Ranch Center, P.O. Box 549, Kamuela, HI 96743; 808-885-6868; www.kahilutheatre.org

Kona Association for the Performing Arts Company Kainaliu town; 808-322-9924

University of Hawai'i-Hilo Theater 200 West Kawili Street, Hilo, HI 96720; 808-974-7310

Waimea Community Theater Uilani Plaza in Waimea town; 808-885-5818; www.waimeacommunitytheatre.org.

WALKING TOURS

★ ***Downtown Hilo Walking Tours*** Free guided walking tours are conducted the third Saturday of each month and are 1-2 hours long. Tours begin at the museum and include sites like Kalakaua Park (originally conceived as a civic center by King Kalakaua), Niolopa, the old and new library buildings, the old federal building, Lyman Museum and others. As an alternative, call the museum or stop by and pick up a free map to do the walking tour on your own. Sponsored by Lyman Museum and the American Association of University Women. For reservations contact Lyman Museum, 276 Haili Street, Hilo, HI 96720; 808-935-5021.

★ ***Kona Historical Tours*** The Kona Historical Society Museum conducts two guided walking tours in the Kona area. There is a walking tour of historic Kailua Village and a walking tour of the Uchida Coffee Farm. Both provide insight into the colorful history and culture of early-day Kona and the coffee farming community. The 1.5-hour Kailua Village tour is Tuesday through Saturday mornings at 9:30 a.m. and per person cost is $10. A special Friday afternoon tour at 1:30 p.m. is $14 per person and includes a visit to the Hulihee Palace. The 1.5-hour Uchida Coffee Farm tour is Tuesday and Thursday only at 8:30 a.m. and 10:30 a.m. and is $20 per person. Tours depart from the Kona Historical Society Museum on Highway 11 near Kealakekua. The Society also conducts special tours by appointment for groups, including a Captain Cook at Kealakekua Bay and Keauhou Archaeological Tour. Call for details and reservations. P.O. Box 398, 81-6551 Mamalahoa Highway, Captain Cook, HI 96704; 808-323-2005.

WHALE WATCHING (*See also* Sea Excursions; Snorkeling)

If you visit between November and May, you have to go whale watching. Although you can see whales from the shore as they breach and splash in the water, there is nothing like being out at sea with them. Just so you know, hundreds of humpback whales travel to Hawai'i's warm waters annually from Alaska to give birth to their young, mate and return. Poor mamas. They swim all that way with nothing to eat, give birth, feed the young hundreds of gallons of milk a day, *then* as mother nature's little joke, they go into heat! There's a whole lot of whale activity going on, and it's incredible to watch.

From the boat, you spot a distant spout, a plume of sea spray that is the whale's breath, and as you get closer you see different-sized spouts for mothers and babies. You may see males competing for female attention by slapping the water with their fins or tails, bobbing their massive heads out of the water, or leaping completely airborne with a gigantic crashing splash. Most boats have knowledgeable guides on board to explain what you're watching and answer questions. Some have an underwater microphone they lower to eavesdrop on the whales' unusual song. Most offer refreshments and a photo service.

The humpback is a protected species and boats of any kind are prohibited from moving towards a whale any closer than 100 feet. There are no "swim with the whales" programs or any closer encounters, and anyone who sells you one is breaking the law. Reputable whale watching operations are respectful of the ocean and these major mammals and take care to pass that on to their passengers.

There are many good companies. Ask your concierge. One of the best is Ocean Sports (see "Sea Excursions"), operating out of the Waikoloa Beach Marriott on the Kohala Coast. They offer seasonal whale-watching cruises aboard *Alala*, a sleek, beautiful catamaran with fully air-conditioned cabin and lots of deck space including the "trampoline." The crew includes a marine biologist who tailors the presentation to suit the audience and guarantees you'll leave the boat with more knowledge than you brought on board. Red Sail Sports is another excellent provider; see "Sea Excursions" earlier in this chapter.

Once again, we warn you about photos (and the crew will back us up). The chance of your getting the supreme shot of a whale flying over the ocean is remote. The chance of your getting a roll full of splashes after the fact is very good. We'd encourage you to buy a postcard, leave the camera, and enjoy the view.

Living Ocean Adventures This operator uses a 31-foot Bertram fishing boat equipped to handle just six whale watchers. The standard cruise is a three-hour quest to sight humpbacks, sperm, false killer, melon-headed and pilot whales plus four species of dolphins that frequent the Kona Coast. Daily cruises 8 a.m. to 11:30 a.m. Rates: $55 adults, $40 children under 12; entire boat for 6 people $285. Exclusive charters available. P.O. Box 1622, Kailua-Kona, HI 96745; 808-325-5556.

★ ***Whale Watching Adventures*** A 25-year veteran Kona marine biologist and whale researcher, Captain Dan McSweeney guarantees a whale sighting aboard the 40-foot *Lady Ann*, a 42-passenger U.S. Coast Guard–approved vessel, fully equipped with underwater window and hydrophone for seeing and hearing Hawai'i's various species of whales year-round. Three-hour cruises depart at 7:30 a.m. and 12 p.m. from Honokohau Harbor just north of Kailua-Kona, and include snacks and cold drinks. Captain Dan has been in Kona since 1969 and earned a reputation as an expert, contributing to the Wild Whale Research Foundation through his business. Ask about the "Whale Adoption" program when you make a reservation. Rates are adults $54.50, children under 12 $34.50. P.O. Box 139, Holualoa, HI 96725; 800-WHALES-6; 808-322-0028; e-mail: knoawhales@netscape.net; www.ilovewhales.com.

Suggested Reading

With thanks to Basically Books in Hilo (www.basicallybooks.com) for their assistance and suggestions.

FOR CHILDREN

A Is for Aloha, Stephanie Feeney
Discover Hawai'i series, Katherine Orr
Goodnight Gecko, Gill McBarnet
Hawai'i Is a Rainbow, Stephanie Feeney
How Maui Slowed the Sun, Suelyn Ching Tune
Kapono and the Honu, Edie Bikle
Keiki's First Books series, Wren/Maile
Ki'i and Li'i: A Story from the Stones, Jeremiah Gruenberg
Spooky Stuffs, Eric Knudsen
The Stowaway Fairy series, Mary Koski
Talking Story with Nona Beamer, Nona Beamer
Three Little Hawaiian Pigs, Donivee Martin Laird
Tutu and the Ulu Tree, Tutu and the Ti Plant, Sandra Goforth and Christine Pratt
Ula Li'i and the Magic Shark, Donivee Martin Laird

FOR ADULTS

Hawaii, James Michener (historical fiction). If you only have time to read one book, really this is it. And/or watch the 1966 film starring Julie Andrews, Max Von Sydow and Richard Harris.

History

A Concise History of the Hawaiian Islands, Dr. Phil Barnes
Hawaiian Antiquities, David Malo
Hawaiian Sovereignty: Do the Facts Matter?, Thurston Twigg-Smith
Hawaii's Story by Hawaii's Queen, Queen Liliuokalani
Leper Priest of Moloka'i, Richard Stewart
Memories of the Old Plantation, Frank Hustace
Shaping Hawai'i: The Voices of Women, Joyce C. Lebra
Shoal of Time, Gavan Daws
Six Months in the Sandwich Islands, Isabella L. Bird

Trivia & Humor

Fax to da Max, Pidgin to da Max series, Peppo

Language

Learn Hawaiian at Home, Kahikahealani Wright (book and cassette tapes)
New Pocket Hawaiian Dictionary, Mary Kawena Pukui
Pocket Place Names of Hawaii, Mary Kawena Pukui

Mythology and Folklore

Hawai'i Island Legends, Mary Kawena Pukui
Hawaiian Goddesses II, Linda Ching
Hawaiian Legends of Tricksters, Vivian L. Thompson
Hawaiian Legends of Volcanoes, William D. Westervelt
Hilo Legends, Francis Reed
Hina, the Goddess, Dietrich Varez
Water of Kane and other Legends, Mary Kawena Pukui

Reference

Atlas of Hawaii, 3rd Edition, University of Hawai'i Press

Spirituality/Hawaiian Culture

Change We Must, Nana Veary
Chicken Soup from the Soul of Hawai'i: Stories of Aloha to Create Paradise Wherever You Are, HCI, 2003
Nana I Ke Kumu (Look to the Source) I and II, Mary Kawena Pukui, E.W. Haertig, MD and Catherine A Lee
Secrets & Mysteries of Hawaii, Pila

Island Adventuring, Special Interests and Sports

Beaches of the Big Island and *Hawaii's Best Beaches*, John Clark
Camping Hawaii, Richard McMahon,
Fishing Hawai'i Style, Volumes 1-3, Jim Rizutto
Hawai'i Trails: Walks, Strolls and Treks on the Big Island, Kathy Morey
Hawaiian Reefs: A Natural History Guide, Ron Russo
Hiking Hawaii, the Big Island, Robert Smith
Petroglyphs of Hawaii, Likelike R. McBride
Pocket Guide to Hawaii's Beautiful Birds and *Pocket Guide to Hawaii's Trees and Shrubs*, Douglas Pratt
Pocket Guide to Underwater Paradise, John Hoover
Roadside Geology of Hawai'i, Richard W. Hazlett
Six Islands on Two Wheels, Tom Koch
Stars Over Hawaii, E.H. Bryan, Jr.
An Underwater Guide to Hawai'i, Ann Fielding and Ed Robinson

Fiction

May we humbly recommend a little book of short stories by an author with a familiar name:

Potluck: Stories That Taste Like Hawai'i, Catherine Bridges Tarleton (Goodale Publishing, Honolulu, 2001) available at www.my-desk.com/potluck

Index

Lodging Index

Dining Index

Dining Index by Cuisine

Chinese

Coffee

Continental-International

Drive-ins

Filipino

French

German

Greek

Hawai'i Local Style

Hawai'i-Pacific Regional Cuisine

Hawai'i Regional Cuisine

Indonesian

International

Irish

Italian

Japanese

Paradise Family Guides

Ideal for families traveling with kids of any age—toddlers to teenagers—Paradise Family Guides offer a blend of travel information unlike any other guides to the Hawaiian islands. With vacation ideas and tropical adventures that are sure to satisfy both action-hungry youngsters and relaxation-seeking parents, these guides meet the specific needs of each and every family member.

Hidden Guides

Adventure travel or a relaxing vacation?—"Hidden" guidebooks are the only travel books in the business to provide detailed information on both. Aimed at environmentally aware travelers, our motto is "Where Vacations Meet Adventures." These books combine details on unique hotels, restaurants and sightseeing with information on camping, sports and hiking for the outdoor enthusiast.

The New Key Guides

Based on the concept of ecotourism, The New Key Guides are dedicated to the preservation of Central America's rare and endangered species, architecture and archaeology. Filled with helpful tips, they give travelers everything they need to know about these exotic destinations.

Ulysses Press books are available at bookstores everywhere. If any of the following titles are unavailable at your local bookstore, ask the bookseller to order them.

You can also order books directly from Ulysses Press
P.O. Box 3440, Berkeley, CA 94703
800-377-2542 or 510-601-8301
fax: 510-601-8307
www.ulyssespress.com
e-mail: ulysses@ulyssespress.com

PARADISE FAMILY GUIDES

____ Paradise Family Guides: Kaua'i, $16.95
____ Paradise Family Guides: Maui, $16.95
____ Paradise Family Guides: Big Island of Hawai'i, $16.95

HIDDEN GUIDEBOOKS

____ Hidden Arizona, $16.95
____ Hidden Bahamas, $14.95
____ Hidden Baja, $14.95
____ Hidden Belize, $15.95
____ Hidden Big Island of Hawaii, $13.95
____ Hidden Boston & Cape Cod, $14.95
____ Hidden British Columbia, $18.95
____ Hidden Cancún & the Yucatán, $16.95
____ Hidden Carolinas, $17.95
____ Hidden Coast of California, $18.95
____ Hidden Colorado, $15.95
____ Hidden Disneyland, $13.95
____ Hidden Florida, $18.95
____ Hidden Florida Keys & Everglades, $13.95
____ Hidden Georgia, $16.95
____ Hidden Guatemala, $16.95
____ Hidden Hawaii, $18.95
____ Hidden Idaho, $14.95
____ Hidden Kauai, $13.95
____ Hidden Maui, $13.95
____ Hidden Montana, $15.95
____ Hidden New England, $18.95
____ Hidden New Mexico, $15.95
____ Hidden Oahu, $13.95
____ Hidden Oregon, $15.95
____ Hidden Pacific Northwest, $18.95
____ Hidden Salt Lake City, $14.95
____ Hidden San Francisco & Northern California, $18.95
____ Hidden Southern California, $18.95
____ Hidden Southwest, $19.95
____ Hidden Tahiti, $17.95
____ Hidden Tennessee, $16.95
____ Hidden Utah, $16.95
____ Hidden Walt Disney World, $13.95
____ Hidden Washington, $15.95
____ Hidden Wine Country, $13.95
____ Hidden Wyoming, $15.95

NEW KEY GUIDES

____ The New Key to Costa Rica, $18.95

Mark the book(s) you're ordering and enter the total cost here ➡ ☐

California residents add 8.25% sales tax here ➡ ☐

Shipping, check box for preferred method and enter cost here ➡ ☐

☐ Book Rate (free) ☐ Priority Mail/UPS Ground (call for rates)
☐ UPS Overnight or 2-Day Air (call for rates)

Billing, enter total amt. due here and check payment method ➡ ☐

☐ CHECK ☐ MONEY ORDER

☐ VISA/MASTERCARD________________________ EXP. DATE ________

NAME________________________ PHONE ____________

ADDRESS________________________________

CITY ____________________ STATE________ ZIP__________

MONEY-BACK GUARANTEE ON DIRECT ORDERS PLACED THROUGH ULYSSES PRESS.

About the Author

CATHERINE BRIDGES TARLETON, originally from Virginia, has been a Big Island *kama'aina* since 1989. She is author of *Potluck: Stories That Taste Like Hawai'i*; her shorter works have appeared in *Honolulu Magazine*, *Aloha*, *North Hawaii News* and Bamboo Ridge's *The Best of Honolulu Fiction*. Tarleton graduated from the College of William and Mary and first fell in love with Hawai'i on Kaua'i in 1979. After ten years back on the mainland, she and husband Dwight decided to emigrate to Hawaii permanently. They now live in Waikoloa along with a family of trilingual blue-and-gold macaws who speak a few words of English, Hawaiian and Klingon.